앞서가는 학생들의 일등 비법 봉인 해제!

KB030647

비법 담은 중학 영문법

3

Level

woongjin compass

비법 담은 중학 영문법 Level 3

지은이 한길연, 이나영, 박영은
펴낸이 최회영
기획편집 이윤선
감수 정은화, 김주희, 오승희, 이수진, 이지애, 정은숙
영문교열 David Charlton
디자인 디자인플러스
펴낸곳 (주)웅진컴퍼스
등록번호 제22-2943호
등록일자 2006년 6월 16일
주소 서울특별시 서초구 강남대로39길 15-10 한라비발디스튜디오193 3층
전화 (02)3471-0096
홈페이지 http://www.wjcompass.com
ISBN 978-89-6697-919-6

13 12 11 10 9 8 7 6
28 27 26 25 24

Photo Credits
All photos © Shutterstock, Inc.

Printed in Korea

ⓒ 2016 (주)웅진컴퍼스
· 이 책의 내용에 대한 일체의 무단복제, 전재 및 발췌는 법률로 금지되어 있습니다.
· 파본은 교환해 드립니다.

비법 담은 중학 영문법

비법 담은 중학 영문법 Level 3 교과서 활용 진도표

최신개정교육과정 12종 중학 3학년 교과서와 본 교재의 문법 연계표입니다.

교과서 단원	두산3 (김성곤)	본교재	두산3 (이병민)	본교재	천재3 (이재영)	본교재
1	• 관계사 what • 현재완료진행 • to부정사의 부사적 용법 • to부정사의 형용사적 용법	• Ch10의 P3 • Ch1의 P2~4 • Ch3의 P5~6 • Ch3의 P3~4	• 의문사 + to부정사 • 현재완료진행 • to부정사의 부사적 용법	• Ch3의 P1 • Ch1의 P8 • Ch3의 P5~6	• 명령문, and ~ • It … for + 목적격 + to부정사	• Ch9의 P7 • Ch3의 P2
2	• 부정사의 부정 • 관계대명사의 계속적 용법 • 접속사 as	• Ch3의 P7 • Ch10의 P6 • Ch8의 P1	• 간접의문문 • It … for + 목적격 + to부정사	• Ch9의 P5 • Ch3의 P7	• not only … but also ~ • 관계부사 where, when	• Ch9의 P6 • Ch10의 P7
3	• 동명사 (주어 역할) • suggest + that + 주어 + 동사원형 • do를 이용한 강조구문	• Ch4의 P1 • Ch2의 P5 • Ch13의 P1	• 관계부사 where • 부사구 + 동사 + 주어	• Ch10의 P7 • Ch13의 P3	• 가정법 과거 • should have + p.p.	• Ch11의 P1 • Ch2의 P8
4	• somebody, something + 형용사 • 관계부사 where, when	• Ch7의 P5 (중1의 Ch11의 P1) • Ch10의 P7~8	• 명사절을 이끄는 접속사 if • so that ~ (목적)	• Ch9의 P4~5 • Ch9의 P3	• It seems that ~ (= It seems to ~) • so that ~ (목적)	• Ch3의 P8 • Ch9의 P3
5	• It … that ~ 강조구문 • 사역동사 make • should (not) have + p.p.	• Ch13의 P2 • Ch3의 P10 • Ch2의 P8	• 복합관계부사 whenever • 시간의 접속사 while	• Ch10의 P10 • Ch9의 P1	• too … to부정사 • 명사절(의문사 + S + V)	• Ch3의 P12 • Ch9의 P5
6	• 의문문 + to부정사 • 원급 비교 (as ~ as)	• Ch3의 P1 • Ch8의 P4	• 가정법 과거 • 현재분사의 한정용법	• Ch11의 P1 • Ch5의 P2	• as if 가정법 과거 • 시간의 접속사 while	• Ch11의 P4 • Ch9의 P1
7	• 현재분사의 한정적 용법 • 관계대명사 계속적 용법	• Ch5의 P1 • Ch10의 P6	• let + 목적어 + 동사원형 • 비교급을 이용한 최상급 표현	• Ch3의 P10 • Ch8의 P3	• 양보의 접속사 although • used to + 동사원형	• Ch9의 P2 • Ch2의 P7
8	• must have + p.p. • 과거완료	• Ch2의 P8 • Ch1의 P6	• 과거완료 • 양보의 접속사 although	• Ch1의 P6 • Ch9의 P2	• so … that ~ (결과) • It … that ~ 강조구문	• Ch9의 P3 • Ch13의 P2
9	• help + 목적어 + 동사원형 • 수의 일치 (many, one of ~)	• Ch3의 P10 • Ch12의 P1	• not only … but also ~ • 분사구문	• Ch9의 P6 • Ch5의 P4~8	• with + 목적어 + 현재분사/형용사 • 분사의 한정적 용법	• Ch5의 P8 • Ch5의 P2
10	• 최상급의 표현 (비교급 than any other) • 현재분사의 한정적 용법 • 가정법 과거	• Ch8의 P3 • Ch5의 P2 • Ch11의 P1	• 가정법 과거완료 • 분사구문 동시동작 (with + 목적어 + p.p.)	• Ch11의 P2 • Ch5의 P8	• 관계대명사 계속적 용법 • 명사절을 이끄는 접속사 if와 whether	• Ch10의 P6 • Ch9의 P4

교과서 단원	천재3 (김진완)	본교재	천재3 (정사열)	본교재	시사3 (신정현)	본교재
1	• so ~ that • 명사절을 이끄는 접속사 If	• Ch9의 P3 • Ch9의 P4	• have/get + 목적어 + p.p • 분사구문	• Ch3의 P10 • Ch5의 P4~8	• 간접의문문 • to부정사의 명사적 용법	• Ch9의 P5 • Ch3의 P1~2
2	• It ... to부정사 • 현재완료진행	• Ch3의 P2 • Ch1의 P8	• should have + p.p • 소유격 관계대명사	• Ch2의 P8	• 원급 비교 (as ~ as) • 전치사 + 관계대명사	• Ch8의 P4 • Ch10의 P5
3	• 조동사의 수동태 • It ... that ~ 강조구문	• Ch6의 P2 • Ch13의 P2	• the + 비교급, the + 비교급 • 관계대명사 what	• Ch8의 P3 • Ch10의 P3	• 관계부사 why • It is said that ...	• Ch10의 P7 • Ch6의 P9
4	• 간접의문문 • should have + p.p.	• Ch9의 P5 • Ch2의 P8	• seem to ~ • 독립분사구문	• Ch3의 P8 • Ch5의 P8	• 관계대명사 what • not always (부분부정)	• Ch10의 P3 • Ch13의 P6
5	• It seems that ~ (= It seems to ~) • 과거완료시제	• Ch3의 P8 • Ch1의 P6	• 의문사 + to부정사 • 과거완료	• Ch3의 P1 • Ch1의 P6	• 비교 표현 수식어 • It ... for + 목적격 + to부정사	• Ch13의 P6 • Ch3의 P7
6	• 관계부사 where, when • used to + 동사원형	• Ch10의 P7 • Ch2의 P7	• do를 이용한 강조구문 • It ... that ~ 강조구문	• Ch13의 P1 • Ch13의 P2	• 시간의 접속사 while • ask + 목적어 + to부정사	• Ch9의 P1 • Ch3의 P9
7	• 양보의 접속사 though • 관계대명사 what	• Ch9의 P2 • Ch10의 P3	• 관계대명사 계속적 용법 • 가정법 과거	• Ch10의 P6 • Ch11의 P1	• 관계대명사 계속적 용법 • 명사를 수식하는 현재분사/과거분사	• Ch10의 P6 • Ch5의 P1~2
8	• 가정법 과거 • the + 비교급, the + 비교급	• Ch11의 P1 • Ch8의 P3	• 관계부사 when, where • 도치	• Ch10의 P7 • Ch13의 P3~5	• 분사구문 • It ... that ~ 강조구문	• Ch5의 P4~8 • Ch13의 P2
9	• 분사구문	• Ch5의 P4~8	• both ~ and ... • so that ~ (목적)	• Ch9의 P6 • Ch9의 P3	• 과거완료 • 의문사 + to부정사	• Ch1의 P6 • Ch3의 P1
10	• 관계대명사 계속적 용법 • 조동사 + have + p.p.	• Ch10의 P6 • Ch2의 P8	• 간접화법 • 직접화법	• Ch12의 P4~6	• 가정법 과거 • so that ~ (목적)	• Ch11의 P1 • Ch9의 P3

최신개정교육과정 12종 중학 3학년 교과서와 본 교재의 문법 연계표입니다.

교과서 단원	시사3 (박준언)	본교재	비상3 (이석재)	본교재	지학3 (양현권)	본교재
1	• 의문사 + to부정사 • 가정법 과거완료	• Ch3의 P1 • Ch11의 P2	• It … for + 목적격 + to 부정사 • 이유의 접속사 because	• Ch3의 P7 • Ch9의 P1	• 진리(현재시제) • to부정사의 명사적 용법	• Ch1의 P1 • Ch1의 P1
2	• what + 주어 + be동사 + like • That's because (원인) • That's why (결과)	• Ch9의 P5 • Ch9의 P1	• 관계대명사 계속적 용법 • 현재완료진행	• Ch10의 P6 • Ch1의 P8	• seem to ~ • too … to부정사	• Ch3의 P8 • Ch3의 P12
3	• 간접화법 • I wish + 가정법 과거	• Ch12의 P4~6 • Ch11의 P3	• 관계부사 when, where • so that ~ (목적)	• Ch10의 P7~8 • Ch9의 P3	• 목적격 관계대명사 that • 비교급에 의한 최상급 표현	• Ch3의 P12 • Ch8의 P6
4	• It … for + 목적격 + to부정사 • 관계대명사 which, that, whom	• Ch3의 P7 • Ch10의 P1~3	• 과거완료 • It … that ~ 강조구문	• Ch1의 P6 • Ch13의 P2	• It … that ~ (가주어, 진주어) • 가정법 과거	• Ch13의 P2 • Ch11의 P1
5	• 현재완료진행 • 감정을 나타내는 분사	• Ch1의 P8 • Ch5의 P3	• 소유격 관계대명사 • 등위접속사 and, or	• Ch10의 P1 • Ch9의 P6	• 동사 + 목적어(동명사) • 동사 + 부사 + 목적어	• Ch4의 P2
6	• 분사구문 • whenever	• Ch5의 P4~8 • Ch10의 P10	• 분사구문 • 명사절을 이끄는 접속사 if와 whether	• Ch5의 P4~8 • Ch9의 P4	• ask + 목적어 + to부정사 • used to + 동사원형	• Ch3의 P9 • Ch2의 P7
7	• ~ enough to부정사 • 명사절을 이끄는 접속사 whether	• Ch3의 P12 • Ch9의 P4	• 시제 일치 • It seems to ~	• Ch2의 P2 • Ch3의 P8	• because of • 분사구문	• Ch2의 P7 • Ch5의 P4~8
8	• enable + 목적어 + to부정사 • one, another, the other • some, others	• Ch3의 P9 • Ch7의 P3	• 관계대명사 what • 접속사 as	• Ch10의 P3 • Ch9의 P1	• 명사를 수식하는 과거분사 • 평서문의 간접화법	• Ch5의 P1~2 • Ch12의 P4
9	• 현재완료 수동태 • not only … but also ~	• Ch6의 P5 • Ch9의 P3	• 가정법 과거 • 접속부사 however	• Ch11의 P1 • Ch9의 P8	• 명사를 수식하는 현재분사 • 관계대명사 계속적 용법	• Ch5의 P1~2 • Ch10의 P6
10	• 과거완료 • cannot help -ing	• Ch1의 P6 • Ch4의 P8	• 명사를 수식하는 분사 • 양보의 접속사	• Ch5의 P1~2 • Ch9의 P2	• 관계부사 when • 명사절(의문사 + S + V)	• Ch10의 P7 • Ch9의 P4
11	• 접속사 if • 접속부사 however, therefore	• Ch9의 P2 • Ch9의 P8				

교과서 단원	미래엔3 (배두본)	본교재	금성3 (민찬규)	본교재	교학3 (권오량)	본교재
1	• 간접의문문 • the + 비교급, the + 비교급	• Ch9의 P5 • Ch8의 P5	• so … that ~ • 현재분사의 한정적 용법	• Ch9의 P3 • Ch5의 P2	• 명사절을 이끄는 접속사 if • 조동사의 수동태	• Ch9의 P4 • Ch6의 P2
2	• 과거완료 • too … to부정사	• Ch1의 P6 • Ch3의 P12	• It … that ~ 강조구문 • It … for + 목적격 + to부정사	• Ch11의 P4 • Ch3의 P7	• should have+p.p. • 명사 + 과거분사/현재분사 • It … for + 목적격 + to부정사	• Ch2의 P8 • Ch5 • Ch3의 P7
3	• 관계대명사 what • 양보의 접속사 although	• Ch10의 P3 • Ch9의 P2	• 관계대명사 what • 비교급 강조어구 much	• Ch10의 P3 • Ch8의 P2	• 평서문의 화법 전환 • 관계부사 • 감탄문	• Ch12의 P4 • Ch10의 P7 (중1의 Ch8의 P4)
4	• 명사를 수식하는 현재분사 • 동격	• Ch5의 P1~2 • Ch10의 P2	• 분사구문(단순, 완료형) • to부정사의 부사적 용법	• Ch5의 P6 • Ch3의 P5~6	• 관계대명사의 계속적 용법 • 과거완료 수동태 • may have + p.p.	• Ch10의 P6 • Ch6의 P5 • Ch2의 P8
5	• 현재완료진행 • It seems that ~	• Ch1의 P8 • Ch3의 P8	• 관계부사 • 가정법과거	• Ch10의 P7 • Ch11의 P1	• It … that ~ 강조구문 • 이유의 접속사 since • so that ~ (목적)	• Ch13의 P2 • Ch9의 P1 • Ch9의 P3
6	• 관계대명사 계속적 용법 • used to + 동사원형	• Ch10의 P6 • Ch2의 P7	• 동격절을 이끄는 접속사 that • 접속사 as	• Ch9의 P4, Ch10의 P2 • Ch9의 P1	• 수동태 • 현재완료진행 • 분사구문	• Ch6 • Ch1의 P8 • Ch5의 P4~8
7	• 관계부사 when • It … that ~ (가주어, 진주어)	• Ch10의 P7 • Ch13의 P2	• 조동사 + have + p.p. • as if 가정법 과거	• Ch2의 P8 • Ch11의 P4	• not only … but also ~ • 분사구문 • 가정법 과거	• Ch9의 P6 • Ch5 • Ch11의 P1
8	• 분사구문 • … enough to부정사	• Ch5의 P4~8 • Ch3의 P12	• 복합관계사 • 평서문의 화법 전환	• Ch10의 P9~10 • Ch12의 P4	• So + 동사 + 주어 • as if 가정법 과거	• Ch13의 P5 • Ch11의 P4
9	• so that ~ (결과) • 동사 + 목적어(동명사)	• Ch9의 P3 • Ch4의 P2	• 양보의 접속사 • 가목적어, 진목적어 구문	• Ch9의 P2 • Ch3의 P2	• 동격절을 이끄는 접속사 that • 복합관계부사	• Ch9의 P4 • Ch10의 P10
10	• 가정법 과거완료 • as if 가정법 구문	• Ch1의 P6 • Ch11의 P4	• without + 가정법 과거완료 • 간접의문문	• Ch11의 P5 • Ch9의 P5	• 가정법 • 사역동사 + 목적어 + p.p. • 부대상황 with	• Ch11 • Ch3의 P10 • Ch5의 P8

이 책의 구성과 특징

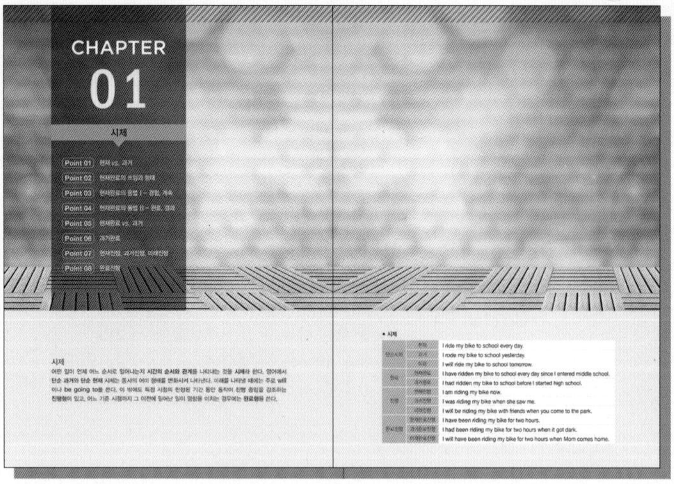

챕터별 목차

✔ 학년별 핵심문법만 적정 단위로 쪼개어 쉽게 정리
✔ 한눈에 파악하는 학습 목표, 배울 내용 확인
✔ 중요한 문법 개념, 용어 간단 정리

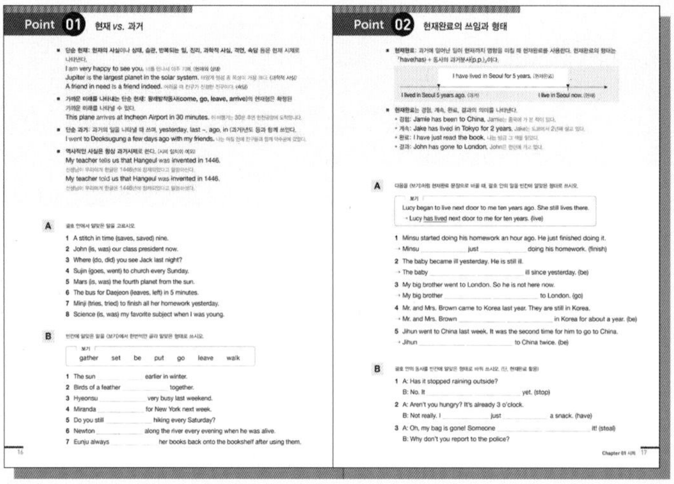

Grammar Point

1. (개념 이해) Grammar Point

✔ **쉽고 정확한 핵심 문법 설명**
✔ 최신 교과서 구문을 반영한 실용적인 예문

2. (개념 확인) Grammar Check-up

✔ 문제 개념 확인을 위한 check-up 문제
✔ 문항 난이도 A → B → C로 점진적 발전: 자신감도 쑥쑥!
✔ 문법 확장 학습: 앞에서 배운 핵심문법을 해당 차시 문법과 연계/누적 확인해 보는 확인 문제까지 수록

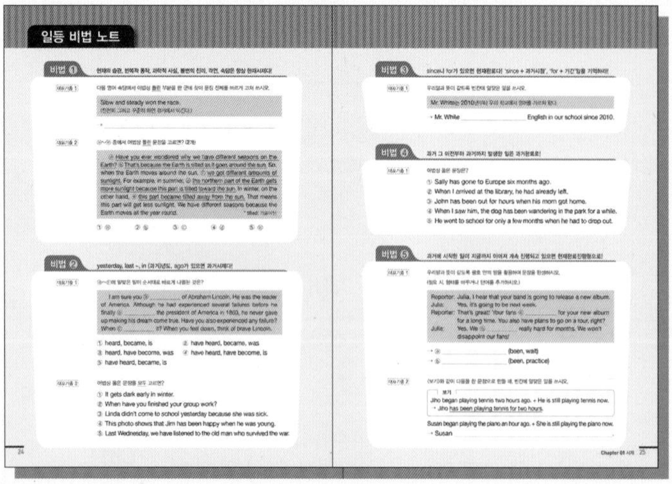

일등 비법 노트

3. (개념 적용) 일등 비법 노트

✔ **꼭 나오는 출제 포인트를 정확히 짚어주는 비법 노트**

4. (실전 맛보기) **학교시험 대표기출 맛보기**

✔ 내신 **대표기출 문제를 풀어보며** 배운 **비법 실전 적용!**
✔ 오답을 피하고 정답을 맞히는 문제 해결력 급상승!

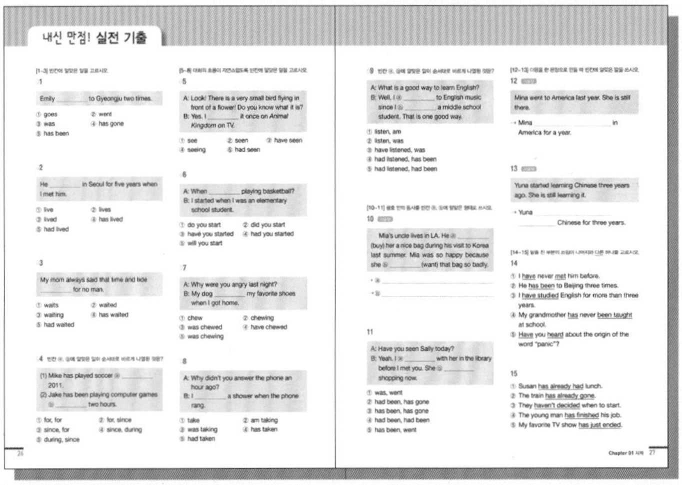

내신만점! 실전 기출

5. 실력 점검 학교시험 기출문제 재구성

✔ 전국 중학교 최근 7개년 기출을 분석 · 반영

✔ **최다빈출 문항** 위주 엄선 수록.

✔ 점점 중요성이 커지는 **서술형 평가 문항** 회당 30%~40% 이상 수록

✔ 변별력을 위해 출제되는 **고난도 문항까지 완벽 대비**

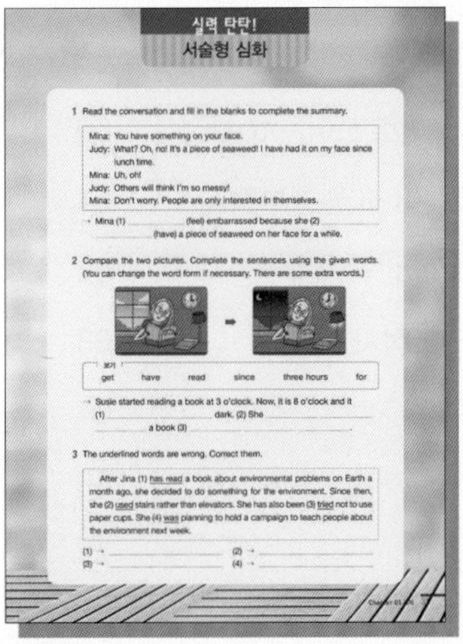

실력탄탄! 서술형 심화

6. 고난도 서술형 완성 서술형 심화

✔ **다양한 표, 그림, 그래프, 포스터 등을 이용한 서술형 문제**

✔ 대화문, 짧은 글과 결합된 **고난도 통합 서술형** 문제

✔ 출제 빈도가 높은 영어 발문이 들어간 서술형 문항까지 자신 있게 대비

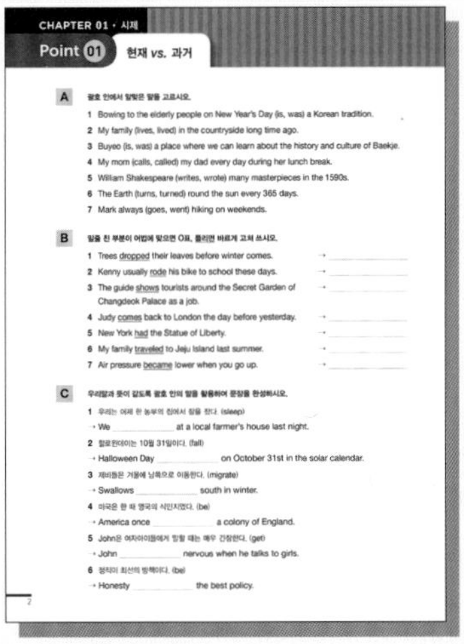

완전학습을 위한 Workbook

7. 체계적인 복습 Workbook

✔ 문법 연계성을 고려해 실제 시험에서 함께 출제되는 Point끼리 한데 묶어 구성한 워크북!

친절한 정답 및 해설

✔ 학생들의 자기주도학습을 돕는 친절한 정답 및 해설

목차

Chapter 01 시제

Chapter 02 조동사

Chapter 03 to부정사

Chapter 04 동명사

Chapter 05 분사

Chapter 06 수동태

Chapter 07 대명사

Chapter 08 비교

목차

Chapter 09 접속사

Chapter 10 관계사

Chapter 11 가정법

Chapter 12 일치와 화법

Chapter 13 특수 구문

CHAPTER 01

시제

- Point 01 현재 *vs.* 과거
- Point 02 현재완료의 쓰임과 형태
- Point 03 현재완료의 용법 Ⅰ – 경험, 계속
- Point 04 현재완료의 용법 Ⅱ – 완료, 결과
- Point 05 현재완료 *vs.* 과거
- Point 06 과거완료
- Point 07 현재진행, 과거진행, 미래진행
- Point 08 완료진행

시제

어떤 일이 언제 어느 순서로 일어나는지 **시간의 순서와 관계**를 나타내는 것을 **시제**라 한다. 영어에서 **단순 과거**와 **단순 현재** 시제는 동사의 어미 형태를 변화시켜 나타낸다. 미래를 나타낼 때에는 주로 will이나 be going to를 쓴다. 이 밖에도 특정 시점의 한정된 기간 동안 동작이 진행 중임을 강조하는 **진행형**이 있고, 어느 기준 시점까지 그 이전에 일어난 일이 영향을 미치는 경우에는 **완료형**을 쓴다.

• 시제

단순시제	현재	I **ride** my bike to school every day.
	과거	I **rode** my bike to school yesterday.
	미래	I **will ride** my bike to school tomorrow.
완료	현재완료	I **have ridden** my bike to school every day since I entered middle school.
	과거완료	I **had ridden** my bike to school before I started high school.
진행	현재진행	I **am riding** my bike now.
	과거진행	I **was riding** my bike when she saw me.
	미래진행	I **will be riding** my bike with friends when you come to the park.
완료진행	현재완료진행	I **have been riding** my bike for two hours.
	과거완료진행	I **had been riding** my bike for two hours when it got dark.
	미래완료진행	I **will have been riding** my bike for two hours when Mom comes home.

Point 01 현재 *vs.* 과거

- **단순 현재: 현재의 사실이나 상태, 습관, 반복되는 일, 진리, 과학적 사실, 격언, 속담** 등은 현재 시제로 나타낸다.
  I am very happy to see you. 너를 만나서 아주 기뻐. (현재의 상태)
  Jupiter is the largest planet in the solar system. 태양계 행성 중 목성이 가장 크다. (과학적 사실)
  A friend in need is a friend indeed. 어려울 때 친구가 진정한 친구이다. (속담)
- **가까운 미래를 나타내는 단순 현재: 왕래발착동사(come, go, leave, arrive)**의 현재형은 확정된 가까운 미래를 나타낼 수 있다.
  This plane arrives at Incheon Airport in 30 minutes. 이 비행기는 30분 후면 인천공항에 도착합니다.
- **단순 과거:** 과거의 일을 나타낼 때 쓰며, yesterday, last ~, ago, in (과거)년도 등과 함께 쓰인다.
  I went to Deoksugung a few days ago with my friends. 나는 며칠 전에 친구들과 함께 덕수궁에 갔었다.
- **역사적인 사실은 항상 과거시제로** 쓴다. (시제 일치의 예외)
  My teacher tells us that Hangeul was invented in 1446.
  선생님이 우리에게 한글은 1446년에 창제되었다고 말씀하신다.
  My teacher told us that Hangeul was invented in 1446.
  선생님이 우리에게 한글은 1446년에 창제되었다고 말씀하셨다.

A

괄호 안에서 알맞은 말을 고르시오.

1 A stitch in time (saves, saved) nine.
2 John (is, was) our class president now.
3 Where (do, did) you see Jack last night?
4 Sujin (goes, went) to church every Sunday.
5 Mars (is, was) the fourth planet from the sun.
6 The bus for Daejeon (leaves, left) in 5 minutes.
7 Minji (tries, tried) to finish all her homework yesterday.
8 Science (is, was) my favorite subject when I was young.

B

빈칸에 알맞은 말을 〈보기〉에서 한번씩만 골라 알맞은 형태로 쓰시오.

보기						
gather	set	be	put	go	leave	walk

1 The sun ______________ earlier in winter.
2 Birds of a feather ______________ together.
3 Hyeonsu ______________ very busy last weekend.
4 Miranda ______________ for New York next week.
5 Do you still ______________ hiking every Saturday?
6 Newton ______________ along the river every evening when he was alive.
7 Eunju always ______________ her books back onto the bookshelf after using them.

Point 02 현재완료의 쓰임과 형태

■ **현재완료**: 과거에 일어난 일이 현재까지 영향을 미칠 때 현재완료를 사용한다. 현재완료의 형태는 「have(has) + 동사의 과거분사(p.p.)」이다.

I have lived in Seoul for 5 years. (현재완료)

I lived in Seoul 5 years ago. (과거) → I live in Seoul now. (현재)

■ **현재완료**는 경험, 계속, 완료, 결과의 의미를 나타낸다.

- 경험: Jamie has been to China. Jamie는 중국에 가 본 적이 있다.
- 계속: Jake has lived in Tokyo for 2 years. Jake는 도쿄에서 2년째 살고 있다.
- 완료: I have just read the book. 나는 방금 그 책을 읽었다.
- 결과: John has gone to London. John은 런던에 가고 없다.

A 다음을 〈보기〉처럼 현재완료 문장으로 바꿀 때, 괄호 안의 말을 빈칸에 알맞은 형태로 쓰시오.

> 보기
> Lucy began to live next door to me ten years ago. She still lives there.
> → Lucy has lived next door to me for ten years. (live)

1 Minsu started doing his homework an hour ago. He just finished doing it.
→ Minsu ______________ just ______________ doing his homework. (finish)

2 The baby became ill yesterday. He is still ill.
→ The baby ______________ ______________ ill since yesterday. (be)

3 My big brother went to London. So he is not here now.
→ My big brother ______________ ______________ to London. (go)

4 Mr. and Mrs. Brown came to Korea last year. They are still in Korea.
→ Mr. and Mrs. Brown ______________ ______________ in Korea for about a year. (be)

5 Jihun went to China last week. It was the second time for him to go to China.
→ Jihun ______________ ______________ to China twice. (be)

B 괄호 안의 동사를 빈칸에 알맞은 형태로 바꿔 쓰시오. (단, 현재완료 활용)

1 A: Has it stopped raining outside?
B: No. It ______________ ______________ yet. (stop)

2 A: Aren't you hungry? It's already 3 o'clock.
B: Not really. I ______________ just ______________ a snack. (have)

3 A: Oh, my bag is gone! Someone ______________ ______________ it! (steal)
B: Why don't you report to the police?

Point 03 현재완료의 용법 Ⅰ – 경험, 계속

- **경험을 나타내는 현재완료**: '~한 적이 있다'라는 의미로, 현재까지의 경험을 나타낸다.
  주로 ever, never, before, once 등이 함께 온다.
  Have you ever read *The Little Prince*? '어린 왕자'를 읽어 본 적이 있니?
- **계속을 나타내는 현재완료**: '지금까지 계속 ~해 왔다'라는 의미로, 과거 어느 시점부터 현재까지 동작이나 상태가 계속되고 있음을 나타낸다. 주로 'for(~동안) + 기간'이나 'since(~이래로) + 기준시점이 되는 과거' 등과 함께 쓰인다.
  We have practiced singing for a month. 우리는 한 달 동안 경연대회를 위해 노래연습을 해 왔다.
  My brother has been sick since yesterday. 내 동생은 어제부터 아팠다.

A 괄호 안의 말을 활용하여 문장을 완성하시오. (단, 현재완료형으로 쓸 것)

1 Some people say that they ______________ UFOs. (see)
2 Mandy ______________ taekwondo for a year. (learn)
3 Susie and I ______________ good friends since childhood. (be)
4 Minho ______________ English for more than 6 years. (study)
5 I ______________ any comments on the Internet. (never, leave)
6 ______________ you ______________ the game 'League of Legends'? (try)
7 We ______________ in this house since my brother was born. (live)

B 우리말과 뜻이 같도록 괄호 안의 말을 활용하여 문장을 완성하시오. (단, 현재완료형 활용)

1 3일동안 계속 눈이 왔다. (snow)
→ It ______________ ______________ for three days.

2 Mr. Brown은 한국에 2010년부터 살고 있다. (live)
→ Mr. Brown ______________ ______________ in Korea since 2010.

3 나는 전에 그 영화배우를 직접 만난 적이 있다. (meet)
→ I ______________ ______________ that actor in person before.

4 Susan은 그 가수를 작년부터 좋아했다. (like)
→ Susan ______________ ______________ that singer since last year.

5 나는 2년 전부터 개를 기르고 있다. (have)
→ I ______________ ______________ a dog since two years ago.

6 너는 우주 공간에 대해 궁금해 본 적 있니? (wonder)
→ ______________ you ______________ about outer space?

7 너는 얼마나 오랫동안 피아노 연습을 해 왔니? (practice)
→ How long ______________ you ever ______________ the piano?

Point 04 현재완료의 용법 II – 완료, 결과

- **완료를 나타내는 현재완료**: '막 ~했다'라는 의미로, 과거에 시작된 어떤 동작이 막 완료되었음을 나타낸다. already, just, yet, now 등이 함께 온다.
  My father has just washed his car. 아버지께서는 막 세차를 끝내셨다.
  cf. just now(방금 전에)는 과거 시제에 쓰인다.

- **결과를 나타내는 현재완료**: '~해서 그 결과 ~되었다'라는 의미로, 과거 사건이 현재에 영향을 미치고 있음을 나타낸다.
  Rebecca has lost her wallet. Rebecca는 그녀의 지갑을 잃어버렸다.
  (= Rebecca lost her wallet, so she doesn't have it now.)
  Minji has gone to New York with her friend. 민지는 친구와 함께 뉴욕에 갔다. (그래서 지금 여기 없다.) (결과)
  cf. I have been to Jeju-do. 나는 제주도에 가본 적이 있다. (경험)

A 다음 두 문장을 한 문장으로 만들 때, 빈칸에 알맞은 말을 쓰시오.

1 Jina went to England. She is still there.
→ Jina ______ ______ to England.

2 Sarah bought a nice dress. She still has it.
→ Sarah ______ ______ a nice dress.

3 Mina left for Busan three hours ago. She is not here.
→ Mina ______ ______ for Busan.

4 Mom started cleaning the living room a while ago. She just finished it.
→ Mom ______ just ______ cleaning the living room.

5 Mira went to the subway station 30 minutes ago. She just arrived there.
→ Mira ______ just ______ at the subway station.

B 괄호 안의 단어와 현재완료를 사용하여 대화를 완성하시오. (필요하면 축약형 사용 가능)

1 A: Would you like to have some more?
B: No, thanks. I ______ ______ enough. (have)

2 A: Is Mr. Brown in town now?
B: No. He ______ ______ ______ Busan. (go)

3 A: ______ you ______ your homework yet? (finish)
B: Not yet. I am taking a break now.

4 A: Let's take a look at the map to find South Africa.
B: I ______ ______ ______ it on the map. (already, find)

5 A: Are you coming to Hanna's party?
B: I don't know. I ______ ______ an invitation from her yet. (not, receive)

Point 05 현재완료 *vs.* 과거

- **현재완료**는 과거에 일어난 일이 현재까지 영향을 미치고 있음을 의미하는 반면에, **과거시제**는 과거에 이미 끝난 일이며, 현재와의 연관성을 내포하지 않는다.
  South Africa produced half of the world's gold last year.
  남아공은 작년에 전 세계 금의 절반을 생산했다. (작년에 일어난 사건이며 현재와는 연관성 없음: 과거)
  South Africa has produced half of the world's gold for a decade.
  남아공은 10년간 전세계 금의 절반을 생산해 왔다. (10년 전부터 지금까지 계속되고 있음: 현재완료)

- **yesterday, ago, last ~, in + (과거)년도 등 명백한 과거 시점을 나타내는 시간부사는 현재완료와 함께 쓰이지 않는다.** 또한 정확한 때를 묻는 **when**(언제)으로 시작하는 질문도 완료형과 함께 쓰지 않는다.
  I have found my lost dog. 나는 잃어버렸던 강아지를 찾았어.
  I ~~have lost~~ my lost dog **yesterday**. (X) / I lost my dog **yesterday**. (O)
  cf. 반면에 since, for 등은 현재완료(계속)와 함께 쓰인다.

A 밑줄 친 부분이 어법에 맞으면 O표, 틀리면 바르게 고쳐 쓰시오.

1 Where <u>have you been</u> last night? → ____________
2 When <u>have you found</u> your lost wallet? → ____________
3 We <u>have celebrated</u> our anniversary last week. → ____________
4 The patient <u>has recovered</u> a lot since yesterday. → ____________
5 She <u>taught</u> middle school science for two years. → ____________
6 Ireland <u>has gained</u> independence from England in 1921. → ____________
7 Thanksgiving Day <u>was celebrated</u> for more than 400 years. → ____________

B 괄호 안의 단어를 활용하여 대화를 완성하시오. (단, 시제에 주의할 것)

1 A: Have you heard from Mike since last summer?
  B: Yes. He __________ me a month ago. (call)
2 A: Why don't you call John to tell him that the meeting is canceled?
  B: I can't because I __________ __________ his phone number. (lose)
3 A: I am so hungry. I __________ __________ anything since this morning. (eat)
  B: Oh, that's too bad. You must be starving now.

C 시제에 유의하여, 괄호 안의 동사를 빈칸에 알맞은 형태로 바꿔 쓰시오.

1 Mina __________ to Thailand last weekend. (go)
2 Someone __________ __________ the desk already. We don't have to move it now. (move)
3 They __________ to build a well in Uganda in 1999. (begin)
4 What __________ __________ __________ as volunteer work so far? (do)

Point 06 과거완료

- **과거완료**: 과거완료는 두 과거 시점을 연관지어 표현할 때 쓴다. 특정한 과거 시점보다 더 이전에 일어난 과거를 대과거라고 한다. 즉, 과거완료 형태는 (1) 대과거에 어떤 일이 일어났거나, (2) 대과거의 일이 과거의 어느 특정 시점까지 이어져서 경험, 계속, 완료, 결과를 나타낼 때 쓴다. 형태는 **「had + 동사의 과거분사(p.p.)」**이다.

I didn't go to the cafeteria because I had already eaten something.
나는 이미 뭔가를 먹어서 식당에 가지 않았다.
Before I started writing the report, I had finished the research.
보고서 작성을 시작하기 전에 나는 조사를 마쳤다.

A 괄호 안에서 알맞은 말을 고르시오.

1 Nothing was left when we sat down because they (ate, had eaten) everything already.
2 When I arrived at the station, the subway (left, had left) a few minutes before.
3 The TV show (ended, had ended) by the time we finished dinner.
4 He (never thought, had never thought) about the question before he did the experiment.

B 괄호 안의 동사를 과거완료(had + p.p.)로 바꾸어 문장을 완성하시오.

1 The price was higher than I ____________ ____________ it to be. (expect)
2 He lost the bike that his uncle ____________ ____________ for him. (buy)
3 He was very proud of last year's project as he ____________ ____________ all the work by himself. (do)
4 We ____________ ____________ almost 10 kilometers before Mr. Park picked us up in his car. (walk)

C 우리말과 뜻이 같도록 괄호 안의 말을 활용하여 문장을 완성하시오.

1 그는 그녀의 전화번호를 잃어버린 것이 유감스러웠다. (lose)
→ He felt sorry that he ____________ ____________ her phone number.

2 그는 엄마에게 받은 용돈을 다 썼다. (receive)
→ He spent all the allowance that he ____________ ____________ from his mom.

3 네가 여기에 왔을 때, 나는 너를 한 시간 째 기다리고 있었다. (wait)
→ By the time you came here, I ____________ ____________ for you for an hour.

4 내가 집에 도착했을 때, 엄마는 벌써 가버리고 없었다. (go)
→ When I got home, mom ____________ already ____________ out.

Point 07 현재진행, 과거진행, 미래진행

- **진행형**은 기준 시점에 진행되고 있는 일을 나타낸다. **현재진행**은 **「be동사의 현재형 + ~ing」**으로, **과거진행**은 **「be동사의 과거형 + ~ing」**, **미래진행**은 **「will be + ~ing」**의 형태로 쓴다.
  I am looking for a bag online. 나는 온라인으로 가방을 찾아보고 있어. (현재진행)
  He was trying on a pair of jeans. 그는 청바지 한 벌을 입어보고 있었다. (과거진행)
  I will be studying when you come back. 네가 돌아올 때는 나는 공부를 하고 있을 거야. (미래진행)
- **왕래발착동사(come, go, leave, arrive)**의 **현재진행형**으로 확정된 가까운 미래의 일을 나타낸다. 이 때 tomorrow, next week 등의 가까운 미래를 나타내는 시간 표현과 대개 함께 쓰인다.
  They are leaving this country next month. 그들은 다음 달에 이 나라를 떠날 것이다.
- **소유, 상태, 감각, 인지 등을 나타내는 동사는 진행형으로 쓰지 않는다.**

진행형으로 쓰지 않는 동사	소유, 상태 동사	have (가지고 있다), belong, own, possess, resemble, exist
	감각, 인지 동사	see, hear, feel, taste, smell, know, believe, think(~라고 생각하다), like, love, hate 등

Do you think modern technology has benefited humans?
너는 현대기술이 인류에게 혜택을 주었다고 생각하니?
Are you thinking modern technology has benefited humans? (X)

cf. 단, 상태, 감각 등을 나타내는 동사도 위와 다른 뜻으로 동작을 나타내거나 주어의 의지가 강한 일시적인 동작, 상태임을 강조할 때에는 진행형으로 쓸 수 있다.
I am thinking of giving up my part-time job. (think: ~을 생각하다, 고려하다)
나는 아르바이트를 그만둘지 고려하고 있다.
People are having lunch on a boat. 사람들이 배 안에서 점심을 먹고 있다. (have: 먹다)

A 괄호 안에서 알맞은 말을 고르시오.

1 What (are, were) you doing when he visited you?
2 I (feel, am feeling) that we are being treated unfairly.
3 He (is, will be) giving a speech when you arrive there.
4 They (have, are having) a simple device to clean water.
5 She (is, was) sitting on a bench when she saw him running away.
6 We (know, are knowing) that some scientists have invented things to help poor countries.
7 It's true that more than 6000 people (are, were) dying every day from drinking dirty water.

B 밑줄 친 부분이 어법에 맞으면 O표, 틀리면 바르게 고쳐 쓰시오.

1 They <u>were having</u> a nice big house then. → ______
2 What <u>are you thinking</u> of Korean culture? → ______
3 She <u>is wearing</u> a T-shirt and blue jeans now. → ______
4 We <u>are having</u> dinner at this time tomorrow. → ______
5 The train for Cheonan <u>is leaving</u> on track two in 5 minutes. → ______

Point 08 완료진행

- **현재완료진행**은 과거 어느 시점에서부터 현재까지 어떤 동작이 계속 진행되고 있음을 강조할 때 쓴다. 형태는 「**have/has been + ~ing**」이다.
  Irish people have been celebrating St. Patrick's Day for more than 1000 years.
  아일랜드 사람들은 천년 이상 St. Patrick's Day를 기념해 오고 있다.
- **과거완료진행**은 과거 이전부터 시작된 동작이 기준시점이 되는 과거 시점까지 계속 진행되고 있었음을 강조할 때 쓴다. 형태는 「**had been + ~ing**」이다.
  I had been playing a computer game before my mom entered my room.
  나는 엄마가 내 방에 들어오시기 전까지 컴퓨터 게임을 하고 있었다.

A 다음을 읽고 괄호 안에서 알맞은 말을 고르시오.

> David started reading the book, *Pride and Prejudice* about three hours ago, and he's still reading it. Now he just finished reading page 100.

1 David (has read, has been reading) the book for about three hours.
2 David (has read, has been reading) 100 pages so far.

B 다음 두 문장을 한 문장으로 만들 때, 빈칸에 알맞은 말을 쓰시오.

1 It is raining now. It began to rain this morning.
→ It ____________ ____________ ____________ since this morning.

2 I started studying math three hours ago. I am still doing it.
→ I ____________ ____________ ____________ math for three hours.

3 My cousin came to our house last week. She still stays at our house.
→ My cousin ____________ ____________ ____________ at our house for a week.

4 John was playing soccer. The teacher told him to come into the classroom.
→ John ____________ ____________ ____________ soccer before the teacher told him to come into the classroom.

C 우리말과 뜻이 같도록 괄호 안의 말을 활용하여 완료진행형 문장을 완성하시오.

1 Mike는 한 시간째 수영을 하고 있다. (swim)
→ Mike ____________ ____________ ____________ for an hour.

2 그녀가 오기 전에, 나는 이미 저녁을 먹고 있었다. (eat)
→ Before she came, I ____________ ____________ ____________ dinner.

3 너는 지금까지 얼마나 오랫동안 TV를 보고 있었니? (watch)
→ How long ____________ ____________ ____________ ____________ TV so far?

4 Jessie는 9시부터 계속 사무실에서 일하고 있다. (work)
→ Jessie ____________ ____________ ____________ in her office since 9 o'clock.

일등 비법 노트

비법 ① 현재의 습관, 반복적 동작, 과학적 사실, 불변의 진리, 격언, 속담은 항상 현재시제다!

대표기출 1 다음 영어 속담에서 어법상 틀린 부분을 한 군데 찾아 문장 전체를 바르게 고쳐 쓰시오.

Slow and steady won the race.
(천천히 그리고 꾸준히 하면 경기에서 이긴다.)

→ ______________________________

대표기출 2 ⓐ~ⓔ 중에서 어법상 틀린 문장을 고르면? (2개)

ⓐ Have you ever wondered why we have different seasons on the Earth? ⓑ That's because the Earth is tilted as it goes around the sun. So, when the Earth moves around the sun, ⓒ we got different amounts of sunlight. For example, in summer, ⓓ the northern part of the Earth gets more sunlight because this part is tilted toward the sun. In winter, on the other hand, ⓔ this part became tilted away from the sun. That means this part will get less sunlight. We have different seasons because the Earth moves all the year round.

* tilted: 기울어진

① ⓐ ② ⓑ ③ ⓒ ④ ⓓ ⑤ ⓔ

비법 ② yesterday, last ~, in (과거)년도, ago가 있으면 과거시제다! when은 완료시제와 함께 쓰지 못한다!

대표기출 1 ⓐ~ⓒ에 알맞은 말이 순서대로 바르게 나열된 것은?

I am sure you ⓐ __________ of Abraham Lincoln. He was the leader of America. Although he had experienced several failures before he finally ⓑ __________ the president of America in 1860, he never gave up making his dream come true. Have you also experienced any failure? When ⓒ __________ it? When you feel down, think of brave Lincoln.

① heard, became, is
② have heard, became, was
③ heard, have become, was
④ have heard, have become, is
⑤ have heard, became, is

대표기출 2 어법상 옳은 문장을 모두 고르면?

① It gets dark early in winter.
② When have you finished your group work?
③ Linda didn't come to school yesterday because she was sick.
④ This photo shows that Jim has been happy when he was young.
⑤ Last Wednesday, we have listened to the old man who survived the war.

비법 ③ since나 for가 있으면 현재완료다! 'since + 과거시점', 'for + 기간'임을 기억하라!

대표기출 1 우리말과 뜻이 같도록 빈칸에 알맞은 말을 쓰시오.

Mr. White는 2010년부터 우리 학교에서 영어를 가르쳐 왔다.

→ Mr. White ________________ English in our school since 2010.

비법 ④ 과거 그 이전부터 과거까지 발생한 일은 과거완료로!

대표기출 1 어법상 옳은 문장은?

① Sally has gone to Europe six months ago.
② When I arrived at the library, he had already left.
③ John has been out for hours when his mom got home.
④ When I saw him, the dog has been wandering in the park for a while.
⑤ He went to school for only a few months when he had to drop out.

비법 ⑤ 과거에 시작한 일이 지금까지 이어져 계속 진행되고 있으면 현재완료진행형으로!

대표기출 1 우리말과 뜻이 같도록 괄호 안의 말을 활용하여 문장을 완성하시오.
(필요 시, 형태를 바꾸거나 단어를 추가하시오.)

Reporter: Julia, I hear that your band is going to release a new album.
Julia: Yes, it's going to be next week.
Reporter: That's great! Your fans ⓐ __________ for your new album for a long time. You also have plans to go on a tour, right?
Julia: Yes. We ⓑ __________ really hard for months. We won't disappoint our fans!

→ ⓐ ________________ (been, wait)
→ ⓑ ________________ (been, practice)

대표기출 2 〈보기〉와 같이 다음을 한 문장으로 만들 때, 빈칸에 알맞은 말을 쓰시오.

보기
Jiho began playing tennis two hours ago. + He is still playing tennis now.
→ Jiho has been playing tennis for two hours.

Susan began playing the piano an hour ago. + She is still playing the piano now.
→ Susan ________________________________.

내신 만점! 실전 기출

[1~3] 빈칸에 알맞은 말을 고르시오.

01

Emily __________ to Gyeongju two times.

① goes ② went
③ was ④ has gone
⑤ has been

02

He __________ in Seoul for five years when I met him.

① live ② lives
③ lived ④ has lived
⑤ had lived

03

My mom always said that time and tide __________ for no man.

① waits ② waited
③ waiting ④ has waited
⑤ had waited

04 빈칸 ⓐ, ⓑ에 알맞은 말이 순서대로 바르게 나열된 것은?

(1) Mike has played soccer ⓐ __________ 2011.
(2) Jake has been playing computer games ⓑ __________ two hours.

① for, for ② for, since
③ since, for ④ since, during
⑤ during, since

[5~8] 대화의 흐름이 자연스럽도록 빈칸에 알맞은 말을 고르시오.

05

A: Look! There is a very small bird flying in front of a flower! Do you know what it is?
B: Yes. I __________ it once on *Animal Kingdom* on TV.

① see ② seen ③ have seen
④ seeing ⑤ had seen

06

A: When __________ playing basketball?
B: I started when I was an elementary school student.

① do you start ② did you start
③ have you started ④ had you started
⑤ will you start

07

A: Why were you angry last night?
B: My dog __________ my favorite shoes when I got home.

① chew ② chewing
③ was chewed ④ have chewed
⑤ was chewing

08

A: Why didn't you answer the phone an hour ago?
B: I __________ a shower when the phone rang.

① take ② am taking
③ was taking ④ has taken
⑤ had taken

09 빈칸 ⓐ, ⓑ에 알맞은 말이 순서대로 바르게 나열된 것은?

A: What is a good way to learn English?
B: Well, I ⓐ __________ to English music since I ⓑ __________ a middle school student. That is one good way.

① listen, am
② listen, was
③ have listened, was
④ had listened, has been
⑤ had listened, had been

[10~11] 괄호 안의 동사를 빈칸 ⓐ, ⓑ에 알맞은 형태로 쓰시오.

10 서술형

Mia's uncle lives in LA. He ⓐ __________ (buy) her a nice bag during his visit to Korea last summer. Mia was so happy because she ⓑ __________ (want) that bag so badly.

→ ⓐ ______________________________

→ ⓑ ______________________________

11

A: Have you seen Sally today?
B: Yeah. I ⓐ __________ with her in the library before I met you. She ⓑ __________ shopping now.

① was, went
② had been, has gone
③ has been, has gone
④ had been, had been
⑤ has been, went

[12~13] 다음을 한 문장으로 만들 때 빈칸에 알맞은 말을 쓰시오.

12 서술형

Mina went to America last year. She is still there.

→ Mina __________ __________ in America for a year.

13 서술형

Yuna started learning Chinese three years ago. She is still learning it.

→ Yuna __________ __________ __________ Chinese for three years.

[14~15] 밑줄 친 부분의 쓰임이 나머지와 다른 하나를 고르시오.

14

① I <u>have</u> never <u>met</u> him before.
② He <u>has been</u> to Beijing three times.
③ I <u>have studied</u> English for more than three years.
④ My grandmother <u>has</u> never <u>been taught</u> at school.
⑤ <u>Have</u> you <u>heard</u> about the origin of the word "panic"?

15

① Susan <u>has already had</u> lunch.
② The train <u>has already gone</u>.
③ They <u>haven't decided</u> when to start.
④ The young man <u>has finished</u> his job.
⑤ My favorite TV show <u>has just ended</u>.

16 짝지어진 대화가 어색한 것은?

① A: How long have you been watching TV?
B: For about an hour or so.
② A: What time do you usually go to bed?
B: I go to bed at 10.
③ A: Where were you last night?
B: I have been in my room reading a book.
④ A: When did you start taking a cooking class?
B: Last month. I really like it.
⑤ A: Shall we go watch a movie tonight?
B: I'd love to, but I haven't finished my homework yet.

최다빈출

17 어법상 옳은 문장은?

① The phone rang, but she couldn't hear it.
② Susie is shocked when she heard the news.
③ Mr. Park has been teaching English in 2000.
④ I have lived in Busan before I moved to Seoul.
⑤ Jessie always got up at six and goes jogging.

18 어법상 어색한 것은?

① Have you been to Africa?
② He has never tried bungee jumping.
③ My team has won the game yesterday.
④ It's been a long time since we last met.
⑤ Did you know that Mark had won the writing contest?

19 밑줄 친 부분의 쓰임이 나머지와 다른 하나는?

① I am leaving for Daejeon tonight.
② Jina is coming home this weekend.
③ This plane is arriving in LA in 30 minutes.
④ We are preparing dinner in the kitchen now.
⑤ They are visiting Seoul National Museum tomorrow.

[20~21] 괄호 안의 말을 활용하여 우리말과 뜻이 같도록 문장을 완성하시오.

20 서술형

우리가 정거장에 도착했을 때 그 버스는 이미 떠났다. (leave)

→ When we reached the stop, the bus ____________ already ____________.

고난도

21 서술형

너는 '높이 나는 새가 더 멀리 본다.'라는 말을 들어본 적이 있니? (hear, see)

→ ____________ you ____________ the saying, 'A bird flying high ____________ further'?

22 서술형

다음을 한 문장으로 다시 쓸 때 빈칸에 알맞은 말을 쓰시오.

It began to snow three days ago, and it is still snowing in New York.

→ It ________________________________ for three days in New York.

23 어법상 틀린 문장을 모두 고르면?

ⓐ I have bought a nice jacket yesterday.
ⓑ She has gone to Paris several times on business.
ⓒ When you called me, I was watching a documentary.
ⓓ Mount Kilimanjaro was covered with snow all year round.
ⓔ Sumi has been practicing tennis for more than two hours.

① ⓐ, ⓒ, ⓔ ② ⓑ, ⓓ, ⓔ ③ ⓑ, ⓒ, ⓔ
④ ⓐ, ⓑ, ⓓ ⑤ ⓐ, ⓑ, ⓔ

[24~26] 어법상 어색한 부분을 찾아 바르게 고쳐 쓰시오.

24 서술형

엄마가 집에 돌아오실 때쯤이면, 나는 숙제를 마칠 것이다.
→ By the time my mom comes back home, I have finished doing my homework.

________________ → ________________

25 서술형

죽기 전에 그는 많은 시와 희곡을 썼다.
→ He has written many poems and plays before he died.

________________ → ________________

26 서술형

Jenny는 그녀의 엄마와 아주 많이 닮았다.
→ Jenny is really resembling her mother.

________________ → ________________

[26~27] 다음을 읽고 물음에 답하시오.

Jinsu: Are you okay?
Minji: (A) I have been sick for a week, and I still feel a little bit weak.
Jinsu: Oh, my! What was wrong?
Minji: I got wet in the rain last weekend, and (B) I had a bad cold since then.
Jinsu: (C) Have you been taking medicine?
Minji: Yes, I have. (D) A doctor prescribed some for me. It really helps.
Jinsu: You should go home early and rest.
Minji: (E) I have some research to do first, but I think that's a good idea.

신유형

27 위 글을 잘못 이해한 학생은?

① 수진: 민지가 지난 주말부터 지금까지 계속 아프구나.
② 민호: 민지는 아직도 좀 기운이 없어.
③ 찬수: 민지는 지난 주에 비에 젖어서 그때부터 심한 감기에 걸려 있구나.
④ 민영: 민지는 의사에게서 받은 처방약을 지금은 먹지 않고 있어.
⑤ 주호: 민지는 아직 조사할 게 좀 남았지만 일찍 집에 갈 거 같아.

고난도

28 위 글의 (A)~(E) 중 어법상 틀린 것은?

① (A) ② (B) ③ (C)
④ (D) ⑤ (E)

29 빈칸 ⓐ~ⓒ에 알맞은 말이 순서대로 바르게 나열된 것은?

A: Hi, Bill. How was your trip to Las Vegas?
B: It was great. My friends and I ⓐ (drove, has driven) through the desert to the Hoover Dam.
A: Wow! How long did that take?
B: It usually takes about 7 hours. But we visited several places on the way, so it took more than that.
A: Hmmm. How many times ⓑ (were you, have you been) there?
B: That was my first time. I ⓒ (has never been, had never been) there before.

① drove, were you, had never been
② has driven, were you, had never been
③ has driven, were you, has never been
④ drove, have you been, had never been
⑤ has driven, have you been, had never been

고난도

30 서술형

다음 대화에서 어법상 틀린 부분을 찾아 그 번호를 쓰고 바르게 고쳐 쓰시오. (2개)

A: (1) What brought you here?
B: (2) I had a sore throat.
A: (3) How long did you have it?
B: (4) It has been three days. Since last Monday.
A: You seem to have a cold. (5) I will prescribe some medicine for you.

→ 틀린 번호: ________

________ → ________

→ 틀린 번호: ________

________ → ________

실력 탄탄!
서술형 심화

1 Read the conversation and fill in the blanks to complete the summary.

Mina: You have something on your face.
Judy: What? Oh, no! It's a piece of seaweed! I have had it on my face since lunch time.
Mina: Uh, oh!
Judy: Others will think I'm so messy!
Mina: Don't worry. People are only interested in themselves.

→ Mina (1) ____________ (feel) embarrassed because she (2) ____________ ____________ (have) a piece of seaweed on her face for a while.

2 Compare the two pictures. Complete the sentences using the given words. (You can change the word form if necessary. There are some extra words.)

➡

보기

get　　have　　read　　since　　three hours　　for

→ Susie started reading a book at 3 o'clock. Now, it is 8 o'clock and it (1) ____________ ____________ dark. (2) She ____________ ____________ ____________ a book (3) ____________ ____________ ____________.

3 The underlined words are wrong. Correct them.

After Jina (1) <u>has read</u> a book about environmental problems on Earth a month ago, she decided to do something for the environment. Since then, she (2) <u>used</u> stairs rather than elevators. She has also been (3) <u>tried</u> not to use paper cups. She (4) <u>was</u> planning to hold a campaign to teach people about the environment next week.

(1) → ____________　　(2) → ____________
(3) → ____________　　(4) → ____________

CHAPTER 02

조동사

Point 01 can, be able to

Point 02 may

Point 03 will

Point 04 must, have to

Point 05 should, ought to

Point 06 had better, would rather

Point 07 used to, would

Point 08 조동사 + have + p.p.

조동사

조동사는 동사와 함께 써서 **동사에 가능, 추측, 허락, 의무 등의 의미를 더해 주는 역할**을 한다. 조동사 뒤에는 동사원형이 오고, 대개 조동사끼리는 나란히 쓰이지 않는다. 또한 「조동사 + have + p.p」의 형태로 지난 일에 대한 추측, 의심, 후회, 유감 등을 나타낼 수 있다.

• **조동사 + have + p.p.**

must have p.p. (~이었음이 틀림 없다)	He **must have overslept**! 그는 늦잠을 잔 게 틀림 없어!
should have p.p. (~했어야만 했다)	I **should have told** you about it. 나는 너에게 그 일에 대해 얘기했어야만 했다.
may have p.p. (~이었을지도 모른다)	She **may have lost** her cellphone. 그녀는 휴대 전화를 잃어버렸을지도 모른다.
cannot have p.p. (~이었을 리 없다)	He **cannot have sold** the house. 그가 그 집을 팔았을 리가 없다.

• 조동사의 여러 가지 쓰임

의미		예문
능력 (~할 수 있다)		I **can** speak French. 나는 프랑스어를 말할 수 있다.
허락 (~해도 된다)		You **may** go home after you finish it. 너는 그 일을 마치면 집에 가도 된다.
추측	(~임에 틀림없다)	He **must** be rich. 그는 부유한 게 틀림없어.
	(~일지도 모른다)	She **may** show up. 그녀가 나타날지도 모른다.
	(~일리가 없다)	He **cannot** be sick. 그는 아플 리가 없다.
미래, 의지 (~할 것이다)		I **will** do the homework tonight. 나는 오늘 밤에 그 숙제를 할 것이다.
필요, 의무 (~해야 한다)		You **must[have to]** wear your name card. 너는 이름표를 착용해야만 한다.
충고, 권유 (~해야 한다)		You **should[ought to]** respect the old. 나이 든 분들을 공경해야만 한다.
경고 (~하는 게 좋겠다)		You **had better** tell him the truth. 너는 그에게 진실을 말하는 게 좋겠다.
과거의 습관 (~하곤 했다)		They **used to[would]** hang out together. 그들은 예전에는 함께 어울려 놀곤 했었다.

Point 01 can, be able to

■ **조동사 can**은 가능, 허락, 요청, 부정적 추측의 의미를 나타낸다.

능력/가능	~할 수 있다 (= be able to)	I can solve the problem. 나는 그 문제를 해결할 수 있다. (= I'm able to solve the problem.) ※ 가능의 can이 미래 의미로 쓰일 때는 will be able to를 쓴다.
허락	~해도 좋다 (= may)	Can I sit here with you? 제가 여기 당신과 앉아도 될까요? (= May I sit here with you?)
요청	~해 주시겠어요?	Can[Could] you let me know by tomorrow? 내일까지 제게 알려주시겠습니까? ※ 요청할 때 「Could ~?」를 쓰면 「Can ~?」보다 더 정중한 표현이 된다.
강한 부정의 추측	~일 리가 없다	That cannot be possible. 그것은 가능할 리가 없다.

■ **can의 부정문**은 「주어 + cannot[can't] + 동사원형」이고, **의문문**은 「Can + 주어 + 동사원형 ~?」의 형태로 쓴다.

He couldn't sleep well last night. 그는 어젯밤 잘 자지 못했다.

※ cannot help + 동사원형-ing: ~하지 않을 수 없다.

I was so tired. I couldn't help taking a nap. 나는 너무 피곤했다. 낮잠을 자지 않을 수 없었다.

A

괄호 안에서 알맞은 말을 고르시오.

1 He could (win, won) the race finally.
2 I cannot (stand, standing) his rude attitude any longer.
3 He wasn't able (answer, to answer) the question.
4 I couldn't help (fall, falling) asleep because I was so sleepy.
5 She will (can, be able to) speak Chinese fluently in a year.

B

밑줄 친 부분과 바꿔 쓸 수 있는 표현을 <보기>에서 골라 쓰시오.

보기
may   was able to   is able to

1 You <u>can</u> go home when you finish the test. → ____________
2 He <u>can</u> speak five different languages. → ____________
3 She <u>could</u> run fastest in her school. → ____________

C

밑줄 친 부분에 유의하여 문장 전체를 우리말로 해석하시오.

1 <u>Can</u> I get some information about it? → ____________
2 The rumor <u>cannot</u> be true. → ____________
3 I <u>couldn't</u> help crying because of the sad ending. → ____________
4 <u>Could</u> you help me with this luggage? → ____________

Point 02 may

■ **조동사 may**는 허락과 추측의 의미를 나타낸다.

허락, 요청	~해도 좋다 (= can)	You may use my computer. 너는 내 컴퓨터를 사용해도 좋다. May I come in? 제가 들어가도 되나요?
불확실한 추측	~일지도 모른다	He may change his mind later. 그는 나중에 마음을 바꿀지도 모른다. Jane might come to the party tonight. Jane은 오늘 밤 파티에 올지도 모른다.

※ 추측의 정도

He **is** tired. > He **must be** tired. > He **may be** tired. > He **might be** tired. > He **could be** tired.

■ **may의 부정문**은 「주어 + may not + 동사원형 ~」, 의문문은 「May + 주어 + 동사원형 ~?」으로 쓴다.
You may not use this room without permission. 허가 없이 이 방을 사용해서는 안됩니다.

■ **may as well + 동사원형**: '(~하지 않을 이유가 없으니) ~하는 것이 좋겠다, 낫다'라는 뜻이다.
They may as well **do** the work together. 그들은 일을 함께 하는 편이 낫다.

A

우리말과 뜻이 같도록 괄호 안에서 알맞은 말을 고르시오.

1 그녀는 혼자 있을지도 모른다.
→ She (should, might) be alone.

2 Peter는 나보다 영어를 잘 할지도 모른다.
→ Peter (must, may) speak English better than I do.

3 당신은 책 전체를 복사해서는 안 된다.
→ You (may, may not) copy the whole book.

4 그는 그 일을 아이들 스스로 하도록 두는 게 낫다.
→ He (may, may as well) let the children do the work by themselves.

B

어법상 틀린 곳을 찾아 밑줄 긋고 바르게 고쳐 쓰시오.

1 He may be never able to see her again. → ____________
2 Mr. White may is in his office. → ____________
3 They might changed their opinion about the matter. → ____________
4 He may as well telling us now. We'll find out sooner or later. → ____________

C

우리말과 뜻이 같도록 괄호 안의 말을 바르게 배열하여 문장을 완성하시오.

1 주목을 해주시겠습니까? (I, attention, may, have, your)
→ ____________________________

2 그녀가 말한 것은 사실일지도 모른다. (might, true, be, she, said, what)
→ ____________________________

3 12시 이후에 언제든 와도 좋다. (may, you, visit, after, twelve, any time)
→ ____________________________

Point 03 will

■ **will**은 '~할 것이다'는 뜻으로 미래의 일, 의지, 요청을 나타낸다.

미래의 일	~일 것이다, ~할 것이다 (= be going to)	I will stay home and finish my homework. 나는 집에 머물면서 숙제를 할 것이다.
의지	~하려고 한다	Jake will not leave here. Jake는 여기를 떠나지 않으려고 한다.
요청, 부탁	~해 주시겠어요?	Will[Would] you help me with these bags? 이 가방들을 드는 것을 도와주시겠어요?

■ 「**would like to['d like to] + 동사원형**」은 '~을 하고 싶다'라는 뜻의 정중한 표현이다.
I'd like to thank you for supporting us. 우리를 지지해준 것에 대해 당신께 감사 드리고 싶어요.

cf. **would like['d like] + 명사**: '~을 원한다'는 표현이다.
I would like something cold. (= I'd like to drink something cold.)
나는 차가운 무언가를 원해요.

A 우리말과 뜻이 같도록 괄호 안에서 알맞은 말을 고르시오.

1 우리는 변화를 따라야만 할 것이다. → We (will, might) have to keep up with the change.
2 세 시간 정도 걸릴 것이다. → It will (take, to take) about three hours.
3 너는 분명 외투가 필요하게 될 거야. → You (may, will) surely need a jacket.
4 내 부탁을 좀 들어주시겠어요? → (Would, May) you do me a favor?
5 나는 5분 정도 늦을지도 모른다. → I (may, will) be late about 5 minutes.

B 우리말과 뜻이 같도록 괄호 안의 말을 바르게 배열하여 문장을 완성하시오.

1 그 곳까지는 세 시간 정도 걸릴 것이다. (it, will, about, three, take, hours)
→ ______________________ to get there.

2 7시에 두 명을 위한 테이블을 예약하고 싶습니다. (I, book, a table, for, two, would, like, to, at 7)
→ ______________________.

3 저를 위해 문을 좀 열어주시겠어요? (you, will, the door, open, me, for)
→ ______________________?

C 대화의 흐름이 자연스럽도록 빈칸에 알맞은 말을 쓰시오.

1 A: What would you like to eat for dinner? (저녁으로 무엇을 드시고 싶으세요?)
B: I ________ ________ ________ ________
a hamburger for dinner. (저는 저녁으로 햄버거를 먹고 싶어요.)

2 A: Would you like some chicken or beef? (닭고기나 소고기를 드시겠어요?)
B: I ________ ________ chicken, please. (닭고기를 원합니다.)

Point 04 must, have to

■ **must**는 필요나 의무, 또는 강한 추측을 나타낸다.

필요, 의무	~해야 한다 (= have to)	We must help the people in need. 우리는 도움이 필요한 사람들을 도와야 한다.
강한 추측	~임에 틀림없다	He must be tired after a long journey. 긴 여행 후에 그는 피곤한 것이 틀림없다.

■ **have to**는 must처럼 '~해야 한다'라는 강한 의무를 나타낸다. have to는 다른 조동사와 달리 주어의 인칭과 수, 시제에 따라 형태를 바꿔 쓴다.
She has to wear the uniform at school. 그녀는 학교에서 교복을 입어야만 한다.
We had to wake up early this morning. 우리는 오늘 아침에 일찍 일어나야만 했다.

※ must는 과거, 미래형이 없기에, 과거는 'had to (~해야 했다)'를, 미래는 'will have to (~해야만 할 것이다)'를 써서 나타낸다.
You may use my computer, but you'll have to bring it back to me before 8.
네가 내 컴퓨터를 써도 좋지만, 8시까지는 돌려줘야만 한다.

■ **must의 부정**: 의미상 다음 두 가지로 나타낼 수 있다.
(1) 강한 금지를 나타낼 때: **must not**(~해서는 안 된다)를 쓴다.
You must not violate the rules. 당신은 규칙을 어겨서는 안 된다.
(2) 강한 추측을 나타낼 때: **cannot**(~일 리가 없다)으로 부정의 뜻을 나타낸다.
He must be sick. 그는 아픈 게 틀림 없다. → He cannot be sick. 그는 아플 리가 없다.

■ **have to의 부정**: **don't have to**로 '~할 필요가 없다'라는 뜻이고, **'need not + 동사원형'** 또는 **'don't need to + 동사원형'**으로 바꿔 쓸 수 있다.
You don't have to wait for me. 너는 나를 기다릴 필요는 없어.
= You need not (= don't need to) wait for me.

A 괄호 안에서 알맞은 말을 고르시오.

1 He (must, have) tell us the truth.
2 They (must, have) to walk many hours to get there.
3 The rumor about him (must, has) be true.

B 괄호안에 있는 우리말과 뜻이 같도록 문장 전체를 다시 쓰시오.

1 You don't have to enter this area. (너는 이 곳에 들어와서는 안 된다.)
→ ______________________________.

2 I must not wake up early tomorrow. (나는 내일 일찍 일어날 필요가 없다.)
→ ______________________________.

C 우리말과 뜻이 같도록 괄호 안의 말을 바르게 배열하여 문장을 완성하시오.

1 그는 그의 엄마에게 거짓말을 해서는 안 된다. (must, lie, not, to, mom, his, he)
→ ______________________________.

2 그는 그의 감정을 숨길 필요가 없었다. (didn't, hide, have to, feelings, his, he)
→ ______________________________.

Point 05 should, ought to

- **should**: '~해야 한다'의 의미로 의무, 당위의 뜻을 나타내며 ought to로 바꿔 쓸 수 있다.
  You should rest to get better. 너는 낫기 위해서 휴식을 취해야만 한다.
  = You ought to rest to get better.

> **PLUS Tip**
> *cf.* **must *vs.* should**: 우리말로는 모두 '~해야만 한다'이지만, 의미와 쓰임에서 차이가 있다. 즉, must는 강제성이 있어 꼭 해야만 하는 의무사항을 나타내어 '반드시 ~해야만 한다'라는 뜻이고, should는 법에 저촉되지는 않지만 도덕적 의무 등으로 양심상 '~해야 한다'라는 비교적 약한 의무감을 부여하거나 충고할 때 쓴다.

- **should**의 **부정형**은 **should not**, **ought to**의 부정형은 **ought not to**로 쓴다.
  You should not talk loudly in the library. 너는 도서관에서 크게 이야기해서는 안 된다.
  We ought not to look down on poor people. 우리는 가난한 사람들을 업신여겨서는 안 된다.
- **주장, 명령, 충고, 제안, 요구, 필요** 등을 나타내는 동사나 형용사가 주절에 쓰였을 때, 종속절에 「should + 동사원형」으로 쓴다. 이 때의 should는 생략 가능하다.

insist, advise, propose, order, demand, require, ask 등의 동사	that + 주어 + (should) + 동사원형
necessary, essential, important, urgent 등의 형용사	

He insisted that we (should) join the project. 그는 우리가 프로젝트에 합류해야 한다고 주장했다.
It is necessary that they (should) be careful. 그들은 조심할 필요가 있다.
cf. 단, 종속절의 의미가 당위적 충고의 의미가 아닐 때에는 시제에 맞게 사용하면 된다.
The message suggests that he likes you. 그가 너를 좋아한다는 사실을 그 메시지가 암시한다.

A 괄호 안에서 알맞은 말을 고르시오.

1 We should (wear, to wear) a uniform on the day of presentation.
2 You ought (follow, to follow) your teacher's advice.
3 I don't know what I (should do, do should).

B 우리말과 뜻이 같도록 괄호 안의 말을 바르게 배열하여 문장을 완성하시오.

1 그는 우리가 팀에 합류해야 한다고 제안했다. (suggested, he, we, join, the team, that)
→ ______________________________.

2 학생들이 공부를 열심히 하는 것은 필수적이다. (essential, it, is, students, hard, study, that)
→ ______________________________.

C 빈칸에 알맞은 말을 〈보기〉에서 찾아 쓰시오.

보기		
ought to think twice	should not believe	ought not to fight

1 You ____________________ before you spend money.
2 You ____________________ with your classmates.
3 You ____________________ everything you read on the Internet.

Point 06 had better, would rather

- **had better + 동사원형**: '~하는 편이 좋겠다'라는 뜻으로 충고와 제안을 나타낸다. 축약형은 「**'d better**」, 부정형은 「**had better not**」을 쓴다.
  You had better hurry up to catch the train. 기차를 타기 위해 서두르는 편이 좋겠다.
  We had better not eat more. 우리는 더 먹지 않는 게 좋겠다.

  ※ had better는 공손한 표현이 아니고 의미상 '충고대로 따르지 않으면 결과가 좋지 않을 것이다'라는 경고, 위협까지도 내포하므로 주의해서 사용해야 한다.

- **would rather**: '차라리 ~하겠다'의 뜻이며 축약형은 「**'d rather**」, 부정형은 「**would rather not**」이다. 「**would rather *A* than *B***」는 'B 하느니 차라리 A 하겠다'의 뜻이다.
  I would rather stay home than go outside tonight. 오늘 밤 외출하기보다는 차라리 집에 머무르겠다.
  I would rather not listen to his advice anymore. 나는 그의 충고를 더 이상 듣지 않겠다.

A

괄호 안에서 알맞은 말을 고르시오.

1 I would (rather, better) ask him to help me.
2 The child (had, would) better not go to bed late.
3 You had better (replace, to replace) the broken window right away.
4 You (had better not, not had better) skip breakfast.
5 We (would rather not, would not rather) go hiking tomorrow.

B

우리말과 뜻이 같도록 괄호 안의 말을 바르게 배열하여 문장을 완성하시오.

1 그는 마감 기한을 맞추기 위해 서두르는 편이 낫겠다. (hurry up, he, had better)
→ ______________________ to meet the deadline.

2 너는 그가 화나지 않도록 다시 늦지 않는 편이 좋겠다. (you, 'd better, be, not, late, again)
→ ______________________ not to make him upset.

3 이것을 먹느니 차라리 아무 것도 먹지 않겠다. (rather, not, anything, eat, I, would)
→ ______________________ than eat this.

4 나는 집에 있느니 차라리 산책을 하겠다. (would rather, than, stay, at home, take a walk, I)
→ ______________________.

C

〈보기〉에서 알맞은 말을 골라 had better 또는 had better not이 포함된 문장을 완성하시오.

보기		
be	give up	exercise

1 You ______________________ regularly to be healthier.
2 You ______________________ late for school again.
3 We ______________________ this great chance.

Point 07 used to, would

■ **used to *vs.* would**: 과거의 반복적 습관, 반복적인 동작을 나타낼 때는 used to 와 would 둘 다 쓸 수 있지만, 과거의 상태를 나타낼 때는 used to만 쓸 수 있다.

과거의 습관	~하곤 했다	He used to take us to the baseball stadium. = He would take us to the baseball stadium. 그는 우리를 야구장에 데려가곤 했다.
과거의 상태	~이었다/있었다	A tall building used to be here. (과거에는) 여기 높은 빌딩이 있었다.

cf. **be used to + 동명사**: ~에 익숙하다
He is used to eating **alone.** 그는 혼자 먹는 것에 익숙하다.

cf. **be used to + 동사원형**: ~하는 데에 사용되다
The room is used to keep **our clothes.** 그 방은 우리의 옷을 두는 데에 사용된다.

A 우리말과 뜻이 같도록 괄호 안에서 알맞은 말을 고르시오.

1 모퉁이에는 작은 서점이 하나 있었다. (지금은 없다.)
→ There (used to, used) be a small bookstore at the corner.

2 우리는 매주 그 공원에 가곤 했다.
→ We (would, would rather) go to the park every week.

3 나는 어릴 때 손톱을 물어 뜯곤 했다.
→ I used to (biting, bite) my nails when I was young.

4 우리 집 근처에 작은 개울이 있었다. (지금은 없다.)
→ There used to (be, being) a small stream around my house.

B 우리말과 뜻이 같도록 괄호 안의 말을 바르게 배열하여 문장을 완성하시오.

1 이곳에는 큰 나무가 있었다. (used, to, there, be, a, tree, big)
→ ______________________________ here.

2 우리는 밖에서 많은 시간을 보내곤 했었다. (used to, we, spend, outside, a lot of, time)
→ ______________________________.

3 그는 크리스마스 때마다 우리에게 선물을 주곤 했다. (would, he, give, presents, some, us,)
→ ______________________________ every Christmas.

C 빈칸에 알맞은 말을 〈보기〉에서 찾아 쓰시오.

보기		
live	cooking	measure

1 I used to ______________ in Busan when I was young.

2 Scales are used to ______________ the weight of things.

3 She is used to ______________ for her family.

Point 08 조동사 + have + p.p.

■ **조동사 + have + 과거분사(p.p.)**: 과거의 사실에 대한 추측, 후회, 의심 등을 나타낸다.

must have p.p.	~이었음에 틀림없다. (과거 사실에 대한 강한 추측)	He must have been handsome when he was young. = It is certain that he was handsome when he was young. 그는 어릴 때 잘생겼음이 틀림 없다.
should have p.p.	~했어야 했다. (그런데 못했다) (과거 사실에 대한 후회)	I should have learned to play some musical instruments when I was younger. = I am sorry that I didn't learn to play some musical instruments when I was younger. 나는 더 어릴 때 악기 연주하는 것을 좀 배웠어야 했다.
may have p.p.	~했을지도 모른다. (과거 사실에 대한 약한 추측)	She may have gone home. = It is possible that she went home. 그녀는 집에 갔을지도 모른다.
cannot have p.p.	~이었을 리가 없다. (과거 사실에 대한 강한 의심)	She can't have done that alone. = It is impossible that she did that alone. 그녀가 그것을 혼자 했을 리 없다.

A

우리말과 뜻이 같도록 괄호 안에서 알맞은 말을 고르시오.

1 나는 역에 좀더 일찍 왔어야 했다. → I (should come, should have come) to the station earlier.

2 그녀가 화가 났을지도 모른다. → She (may have been, should have been) angry.

3 그들은 싸웠음이 틀림없다. → They (may fight, must have fought).

4 그가 내게 그런 말을 했을 리 없다. → He (can't have said, must not say) that to me.

B

우리말과 뜻이 같도록 괄호 안의 말을 바르게 배열하여 문장을 완성하시오.

1 우리는 전에 만난 적이 있었을지도 모른다. (have, met, may, we, before)

→ ______________________________.

2 그는 그 약속을 잊었음이 틀림없다. (he, have, must, forgotten, appointment, the)

→ ______________________________.

3 당신은 그가 알아차리기 전에 진실을 말했어야 했다. (should, told, have, him, the, truth, you)

→ ______________________________ before he found it out.

4 그가 그런 큰 실수를 했을 리가 없다. (cannot, have, such, made, a, big, mistake, he)

→ ______________________________.

C

우리말과 일치하도록 괄호 안의 단어를 활용하여 영작하시오.

1 나는 그에게 소리를 지르지 말았어야 했다. (yell)

→ I ____________________ at him.

2 그는 그가 한 약속을 잊었을지도 모른다. (forget)

→ He ____________________ the promise he made.

일등 비법 노트

비법 ① 조동사 뒤에는 반드시 동사원형이 온다!

대표기출 1

다음 ⓐ~ⓔ 중 어법상 옳은 것은 모두 몇 개인가?

Kijeong Sohn was the first Korean marathon winner at the Olympic Games. He couldn't ⓐ wear the Korean national flag in the Berlin Olympics in 1936 because Korea ⓑ was a colony of Japan at that time. Instead, he had to ⓒ wearing the Japanese national flag. After that, he trained many Korean athletes. Yunbok Seo, one of the athletes trained by Sohn, was able to ⓓ win the Boston Marathon in 1947. What he accomplished should ⓔ be not forgotten in our history.

① 1개　② 2개　③ 3개　④ 4개　⑤ 5개

비법 ② 불필요를 나타내는 「need not = don't need to = don't have to」를 기억하라!

대표기출 1

밑줄 친 부분과 바꾸어 쓸 수 있는 말은?

You need not help us if you don't want to.

① should not
② could not
③ don't have to
④ would rather not
⑤ might not

비법 ③ will must (X) → will have to! will can (X) → will be able to로!

대표기출 1

괄호 안의 지시대로 문장을 바꿔 쓰시오.

You must finish the work. (미래 시제로)

→ ______________________________

대표기출 2

다음 우리말을 영어로 옮긴 문장에서 어법상 틀린 곳을 찾아 고쳐 쓰시오.

나는 내년에 새로운 핸드폰을 살 수 있도록 용돈을 모으고 있다.
I am saving my allowance so that I will can buy a new cellphone next year.

→ ______________________________

비법 4 had better과 would rather의 부정형은 had better not, would rather not이다!

대표기출 1 우리말과 뜻이 같도록 괄호 안의 말을 바르게 배열하여 문장을 완성하시오.

너는 패스트푸드를 먹지 않는 게 좋겠다.
(you, better, fast food, had, eat, not)

→ ______________________________

대표기출 2 다음 문장을 부정문으로 만들려고 할 때, not의 위치로 적절한 곳은?

I ① would ② rather ③ watch ④ a horror movie ⑤.

비법 5 「조동사 + have + p.p.」는 과거에 관한 것이다!
must have p.p.: ~이었음에 틀림없다 / should have p.p.: ~했어야 했는데(후회) /
can't have + p.p.: ~이었을 리가 없다 / may have + p.p.: ~했을지도 모른다

대표기출 1 대화의 빈칸에 알맞은 말은?

A: I failed the test.
B: Really? Didn't you study hard?
A: No, I didn't. I ______________ harder.

① may have studied
② cannot have studied
③ should have studied
④ must have studied
⑤ shouldn't have studied

대표기출 2 두 문장의 뜻이 같도록 빈칸에 알맞은 말을 고르면?

It is certain that she was sick yesterday.
→ She ______________ yesterday.

① may have been sick
② cannot have been sick
③ should have been sick
④ must have been sick
⑤ shouldn't have been sick

내신 만점! 실전 기출

01 밑줄 친 부분과 바꿔 쓸 수 있는 말은?

You can leave after you finish this work.

① will ② may
③ should ④ had better
⑤ are able to

02 밑줄 친 부분과 바꿔 쓸 수 있는 것은?

A: May I help you?
B: Yes. I would like to buy a toy for my little brother.

① can ② may
③ should ④ used to
⑤ want to

03 우리말과 뜻이 같도록 빈칸에 알맞은 말을 모두 고르면?

너는 그에게 진실을 말할 필요가 없다.
→ You ________ tell him the truth.

① should not ② must not
③ need not ④ ought not to
⑤ don't have to

04 밑줄 친 may의 의미가 나머지 넷과 다른 하나는?

① One book may change your life.
② I may be about 10 minutes late.
③ Some people may say it's an easy job.
④ You may use mine anytime you want.
⑤ The bus may be delayed due to traffic.

05 다음 중 어법상 어색한 문장은?

① He will not believe anything I say.
② I won't make the same mistake again.
③ She don't have to wake up early today.
④ They will have to make a decision in the near future.
⑤ The customers will be able to buy the new product next month.

06 서술형

괄호 안의 말을 활용하여 빈칸에 알맞은 말을 써서 대화를 완성하시오. (should, stay up)

A: I was late for school again because I got up late.
B: You ________ ________ ________ ________ late at night!

07 서술형

두 문장의 뜻이 같도록 괄호 안의 말을 활용하여 문장을 다시 쓰시오.

He was able to speak Japanese.

→ ______________________________ (can)

[8~9] 두 문장의 뜻이 같도록 빈칸에 알맞은 말을 고르시오.

08

There was a school around here, but it doesn't exist anymore.
= There ____________ be a school here.

① may ② could
③ should ④ used to
⑤ would rather

09

You __________ me about it. = I am sorry that you didn't ask me about it.

① may have asked
② can't have asked
③ must have asked
④ would have asked
⑤ should have asked

[10~11] 우리말과 뜻이 같도록 빈칸에 알맞은 말을 고르시오.

10

그는 내 메일을 확인했음이 틀림 없다. → He __________ my email.

① may have checked
② should have checked
③ cannot have checked
④ must have checked
⑤ shouldn't have checked

11

나는 그 샌드위치를 먹느니 그냥 굶겠다. → I __________ skip a meal than eat that sandwich.

① have to
② used to
③ ought to
④ cannot help
⑤ would rather

최다빈출

12 밑줄 친 부분의 쓰임이 〈보기〉와 같은 것은?

보기
Can I use this chair?

① He could read a book when he was 5.
② Can you pass me the salt?
③ Gloria can speak four different languages.
④ You can use mine if you don't have yours.
⑤ He cannot help smiling after hearing the news.

13 밑줄 친 부분의 쓰임이 나머지와 다른 하나는?

① We must give the money back.
② He must work hard to pass the test.
③ Students must not cheat on the test.
④ He must be tired after such a long walk.
⑤ You must not touch any works of art in the museum.

14 다음 우리말을 영어로 바르게 옮긴 것은?

그녀가 내게 거짓말을 했을 리 없다.

① She could have told a lie to me.
② She cannot have told a lie to me.
③ She may have told a lie to me.
④ She must not have told a lie to me.
⑤ She should not have told a lie to me.

[15~16] 괄호 안의 말을 활용하여 우리말을 영어로 옮길 때 빈칸에 알맞은 말을 쓰시오.

15 서술형

나는 그 숙제를 더 일찍 마쳤어야 했다. (finish)

→ I ________________ the homework earlier.

16 서술형

그가 그녀에게 그 사실을 말했을지도 모른다.
(may, tell)

→ He ______________________ her the truth.

[17~18] 빈칸에 알맞은 말을 고르시오.

17

A: Have you done your homework?
B: No, but can I watch this program and do it later?
A: No, you __________ turn it off right away.

① may ② used to
③ will not ④ had better
⑤ had to

18

A: What's wrong with you?
B: I am too sleepy. I __________ to bed so late.
A: What time did you go to bed?
B: Around 3 in the morning.

① must have gone ② cannot have gone
③ should have gone ④ shouldn't have gone
⑤ may have gone

19 서술형

어법상 틀린 부분을 찾아 바르게 고쳐 쓰시오.

I started to learn Chinese recently. After Chinese class, I try to write down new words as many times as I can. I think I will can remember them better if I do that.

________________ → ________________

20 서술형

괄호 안의 말을 바르게 배열하여 빈칸 ⓐ에 알맞은 말을 쓰시오.

A: Roy, I heard you've been to India before. Can you give me some tips about their culture?
B: Of course. Well, ⓐ ________________.
It's bad manners if you do that there.
A: Oh, I didn't know about it. Thanks for the tip.

(had better, you, not, eat, with, left hand, your)

→ ________________________________

____

최다빈출

21 다음 중 어법상 틀린 문장은?

① He should have gotten up early.
② I must leave now or I will be late.
③ They cannot have forgotten about it.
④ She may have fallen asleep on the train.
⑤ He's stuck in traffic. He should have took the subway.

22 빈칸에 공통으로 알맞은 말은?

- He ________ be very upset to say that.
- You ________ show your respect to them.
- John ________ have missed the train. Otherwise, he would be here by now.

① should ② have to ③ need to
④ must ⑤ would

최다빈출

23 짝지어진 대화가 어색한 것은?

① A: Do we have to leave now?
B: No, you don't have to.
② A: Wasn't there a two-story house over there?
B: There used to be, but it's not there anymore.
③ A: I was late for class this morning.
B: You should have gotten up earlier.
④ A: Can you help me with this?
B: Sorry, but I cannot have helped you.
⑤ A: There's a sandwich in the refrigerator. Why don't you eat it?
B: I would rather eat nothing than eat that.

24 서술형

두 문장의 뜻이 같도록 괄호 안의 말을 활용하여 문장을 다시 쓰시오.

It is impossible that her computer got broken again. (cannot)

→ Her computer ________________________________
________________________________.

고난도

25 밑줄 친 부분이 어법상 틀린 것은?

A lot of tourists come to Korea these days. You ⓐ may meet them any moment especially in Seoul. Many of them ⓑ are Chinese. They visit many of our tourist attractions, buy Korean products and eat Korean food. They contribute to our economy by spending a lot of money. We ⓒ should have tried to make good impressions on them. That way, they ⓓ can visit again in the future. I suggest we ⓔ be nice to tourists all the time.

① ⓐ ② ⓑ ③ ⓒ
④ ⓓ ⑤ ⓔ

신유형

26 다음 문장에서 틀린 곳을 바르게 고친 학생은?

It was essential that he asked for their help.

① 유나: asked는 asking으로 바꿔야 한다.
② 민수: asked는 asks로 바꿔야 한다.
③ 민호: asked는 ask로 바꿔야 한다.
④ 수지: asked는 should have asked로 바꿔야 한다.
⑤ 한나: 틀린 곳이 없다.

고난도

27 서술형

괄호 안의 말을 활용하여 10단어로 이루어진 영어 문장을 영작하시오. (필요하면 단어를 추가하거나 형태를 바꾸시오.)

그녀는 Mike가 매 주 토요일마다 요양원에 방문해야 한다고 제안했다.
(a nursing home, suggest, on Saturdays, visit)

→ ______________________________

____

28 서술형

대화의 흐름이 자연스럽도록 밑줄 친 우리말을 영작하시오.

A: Who is the fastest student in your school?
B: <u>(예전에는) 민호가 제일 빠른 학생이었지.</u>
But now Sangho is the fastest student.

→ ______________________________

____

29 서술형

뒷 문장의 내용과 자연스럽게 이어지도록 밑줄 친 부분을 어법에 맞게 고쳐 쓰시오.

I think Changsoo <u>must read</u> the book already. He knows the whole story.

→ ______________________________

고난도

30 Choose ALL the incorrect ones.

Tom was going to meet his friend Mike at 8 o'clock this morning, but he ⓐ <u>shouldn't</u> make it. He got up late because he ⓑ <u>can't</u> fall asleep until late last night. He drank too much coke in the evening, and it kept him awake. He thinks Mike ⓒ <u>must</u> be very angry at him. Tom thinks that he should ⓓ <u>call</u> Mike to apologize. Then, Mike ⓔ <u>can</u> be able to forgive him.

① ⓐ, ⓑ, ⓔ
② ⓐ, ⓒ, ⓓ
③ ⓐ, ⓒ, ⓔ
④ ⓑ, ⓒ, ⓔ
⑤ ⓑ, ⓓ, ⓔ

실력 탄탄!
서술형 심화

1 A와 B의 표현을 활용하여 주어진 대화를 완성하시오. (단, 한 번씩만 사용 가능)

<A>	<B>
should have p.p. cannot have p.p. must have p.p.	listen study hard be sick

(1) A: Mom, bring me a towel. I got wet.
B: Oh, Tom. Didn't you bring your umbrella? I told you to take it.
A: No, I didn't. I ____________ ____________ ____________ to you.

(2) A: Why didn't Jack come to the party yesterday?
B: I heard that Jack was sick in bed yesterday.
A: He ____________ ____________ ____________ sick. I saw him in the theater yesterday.

(3) A: Did you hear the news that Paul got a perfect score on math test?
B: Really? He ____________ ____________ ____________ ____________. As far as I know, he is not that good at math.
A: I think you're right. I remember he didn't get a good score last time.

2 다음은 학생들이 각자 후회되는 일을 적은 메모이다. 표의 내용과 일치하도록 (1)~(3)의 문장을 완성하고, (4)번에는 본인이 후회하는 일을 한가지 골라 영작하시오. (단, (4)에는 주어진 내용을 그대로 쓸 수 없음)

Name	Jenny	Tom	Harry	Julie	I
Something to regret	read more books	learn to play the piano	make more friends	be nicer to her sisters	?

보기
Jenny thinks that she should have read more books.

(1) Tom thinks that he ______________________________.

(2) Harry thinks that he ______________________________.

(3) Julie thinks that she ______________________________.

(4) I think that I ______________________________.

CHAPTER 03

to부정사

to부정사

「to + 동사원형」의 형태로 문장 안에서 명사, 형용사, 또는 부사의 역할을 한다. 주어의 인칭과 수에 따라 형태가 정(定)해지는 것이 아니고(不), 항상 「to + 동사원형」 형태로 쓴다고 하여 to부정사(不定詞)라고 부른다.

- **to부정사의 다양한 용법 & to부정사의 의미상의 주어**

명사적 용법	My dream is to be a singer. (보어 역할)
	I don't know **where to go**. (목적어 역할)
형용사적 용법	I need **someone to help** me. (명사 수식)
부사적 용법	I am **glad** to see you again. (감정의 원인)
	He **grew up** to be an English teacher. (결과)
	She **must be rich** to buy such an expensive ring. (판단의 근거)
to부정사의 의미상의 주어	It is hard **for me** to get an A on the math test. (for + 목적격)
	It is nice **of you** to say so. (of + 목적격)

Point 01 to부정사의 명사적 용법 I
– 주어, 목적어, 보어 역할 / 「의문사 + to부정사」

■ **to부정사**는 문장에서 **주어**나 **목적어**, 또는 **보어**로 쓰인다.
To have a true friend is important. 진정한 친구를 갖는 것은 중요하다. (주어 역할)
She wants to buy a new bag. 그녀는 새 가방 사는 것을 원한다. (목적어 역할)
My dream is to be a pilot. 내 꿈은 파일럿이 되는 것이다. (보어 역할)

■ **의문사 + to부정사**: 명사(주로 동사의 목적어) 역할을 한다. (단, 'why + to부정사'는 없음)

· who + to부정사: 누구를(에게) ~할지	· what + to부정사: 무엇을 ~할지
· when + to부정사: 언제 ~할지	· how + to부정사: 어떻게 ~할지, ~하는 방법
· where + to부정사: 어디에서 ~할지	· which + to부정사: 어느 것을 ~할지

■ **「의문사 + to부정사」**는 **「의문사 + 주어 + should + 동사원형」**으로 바꿔 쓸 수 있다.
I don't know how to make a snowman. 나는 눈사람 만드는 방법을 모른다.
→ I don't know how I should make a snowman.

A 밑줄 친 to부정사가 문장에서 주어, 목적어, 보어 중 어떤 역할을 하는지 고르시오.

1 Mary's dream is <u>to become</u> a doctor. (주어, 목적어, 보어)
2 My best friend likes <u>to watch</u> movies. (주어, 목적어, 보어)
3 <u>To take</u> care of my baby sister is not easy. (주어, 목적어, 보어)
4 The teacher advised his students <u>to study</u> hard. (주어, 목적어, 보어)

B 괄호 안에서 알맞은 말을 고르시오.

1 I can't decide (what, who) to eat.
2 Please tell me (why, when) to call you.
3 The traffic sign told us (where, which) to go.
4 I don't know (which, how) to solve the problem.

C 우리말과 뜻이 같도록 괄호 안의 말을 바르게 배열하여 문장을 완성하시오.

1 나의 취미는 만화책을 만드는 것이다. (to, comic, make, books)
→ My hobby is ______________________________.

2 외국어를 배우는 것은 쉽지 않다. (foreign, to, a, learn, language)
→ ______________________________ is not easy.

3 나의 소망은 세계에서 유명한 가수가 되는 것이다. (world-famous, become, to, a, singer)
→ My wish is ______________________________.

Point 02 to부정사의 명사적 용법 II – to부정사와 가주어/가목적어 it

■ 주어나 목적어로 쓰인 to부정사구가 너무 길면, 대개 **가주어 it** 또는 **가목적어 it**을 대신 쓰고 **진짜 주어/목적어인 to부정사구를 뒤로** 보낸다.

(1) 가주어 it

To know yourself well is important. 너 자신을 잘 아는 것은 중요하다.
주어 동사 보어

It is important to know yourself well.
가주어 진주어

(2) 가목적어 it

I found to speak Chinese fluently difficult. 나는 중국어로 유창하게 말하는 것이 어렵다는 것을 알았다.

I found it difficult to speak Chinese fluently.
가목적어 진목적어

A 괄호 안에서 알맞은 말을 고르시오.

1 (That, It) is difficult to make kimchi.

2 It is dangerous (to drive, drive) too fast.

3 It is impossible (tell, to tell) you the secret.

4 I found (it, that) easy to answer the question.

B 두 문장의 뜻이 같도록 주어진 말로 시작하여 문장을 다시 쓰시오.

1 To find your talent is necessary.

→ It ______________________________.

2 To have a true friend is important.

→ It ______________________________.

3 To go to Paris during the vacation is fantastic.

→ It ______________________________.

C 우리말과 뜻이 같도록 괄호 안의 말을 바르게 배열하여 문장을 완성하시오.

1 그녀의 계획은 세계를 배낭여행 하는 것이다. (to, backpacking, go, around the world)

→ Her plan is ______________________________.

2 나는 책을 많이 읽는 것이 중요하다고 생각한다. (it, to, is, many books, read, important)

→ I think ______________________________.

3 그들은 어떻게 그 수학문제들을 풀어야 하는 지 모른다. (solve, to, how, the math problems)

→ They don't know ______________________________.

Point 03 to부정사의 형용사적 용법 I - 명사 수식

- **to부정사**는 앞에 나온 명사, 대명사를 꾸며 주는 형용사 역할을 할 수 있다. 이 때, '~할,' '~하는'이라고 해석한다.
  It's time to go to school. 학교에 갈 시간이다.

- to부정사의 수식을 받는 **명사가 전치사의 목적어인 경우 「명사 + to부정사 + 전치사」**의 형태로 나타낸다.
  You write with a pen. → I bought a pen to write with. 나는 쓸 펜을 하나 샀다.

  You sit on a chair. → She needs a chair to sit on. 그녀는 앉을 의자가 필요하다.

- **-thing, -one, -body로 끝나는 대명사**: 형용사와 to부정사가 동시에 꾸며줄 때, **「-thing/-one/-body + (+ 형용사) + to부정사」**의 어순으로 쓴다.
  I want something (cold) to drink. 나는 마실 (차가운) 무언가를 원한다.

A

괄호 안에서 알맞은 말을 고르시오.

1 She has many friends (to play, to play with).

2 There are no chairs (to sit, to sit on).

3 My teacher gave us a lot of homework (to do, to do with).

4 I have (something to give, to give something) you.

B

〈보기〉에서 알맞은 말을 골라 빈칸에 알맞은 형태로 쓰시오.

보기			
take care of	talk with	ask	wash

1 It is time ________ ________ your hands.

2 She needs a friend ________ ________ ________.

3 He has a question ________ ________ his teacher.

4 The woman has two babies ________ ________ ________ ________.

C

우리말과 뜻이 같도록 괄호 안의 말을 바르게 배열하여 문장을 완성하시오.

1 시험 공부를 할 시간이다. (is, to, time, study, it)
→ ________________________________ for the exam.

2 나는 너에게 말할 비밀이 몇 가지가 있다. (to, tell, secrets)
→ I have some ________________________________ you.

3 연필 좀 빌려줄래? (to, a, write, pencil, with)
→ Could you lend me ________________________________?

Point 04 to부정사의 형용사적 용법 II – be동사 + to부정사

■ 「**be동사 + to부정사**」 형태로 '예정, 의무, 가능, 의도, 운명'의 다양한 의미로 주어를 보충 설명할 수 있다. 부정형은 「**be동사 + not + to부정사**」이다.

(1) **예정**: ~할 예정이다 (= will, be going to)
The movie is to start soon. 영화는 곧 시작할 것이다.

(2) **의무**: ~해야 한다 (= must, have to)
We are to follow the law. 우리는 법을 따라야 한다.

(3) **가능**: ~할 수 있다 (= can, be able to)
Nothing was to be seen in the park. 공원에서 아무것도 볼 수 없었다.

(4) **의도**: ~할 작정이다 (= will, intend to)
Study hard if you are to pass the exam. 시험에 통과할 작정이라면 열심히 공부해라.

(5) **운명**: ~할 운명이다 (= be destined to)
The soldier was to die in the World War II. 그 군인은 2차 세계대전에서 죽을 운명이었다.
He was never to see her again. 그는 그녀를 다시는 만나지 못할 운명이었다.

A 밑줄 친 to부정사의 쓰임을 〈보기〉에서 찾아 쓰시오.

보기				
ⓐ 예정	ⓑ 의무	ⓒ 가능	ⓓ 의도	ⓔ 운명

1 You are to clean your bedroom. → ________
2 Not a star was to be seen in the sky. → ________
3 The boxer was never to be a champion. → ________
4 He is to arrive at Seoul Station at 1 o'clock. → ________
5 If you are to enter a good university, you have to study hard. → ________

B 두 문장의 뜻이 같도록 「be동사 + to부정사」 구문을 활용하여 문장을 완성하시오.

1 I am going to ride my bike after school.
→ I ________ ________ ________ my bike after school.

2 They were destined to fall in love with each other.
→ They ________ ________ ________ in love with each other.

3 We must submit the final report by Friday.
→ We ________ ________ ________ the final report by Friday.

C 우리말과 뜻이 같도록 「be + to부정사」 구문과 괄호 안의 말을 활용하여 문장을 완성하시오.

1 회의는 이번 수요일에 열릴 예정이다. (held)
→ The meeting ________ ________ ________ ________ this Wednesday.

2 우주 비행사들은 30년 후에 지구로 돌아올 운명이다. (come back)
→ The astronauts ________ ________ ________ ________ to Earth in 30 years.

Point 05 to부정사의 부사적 용법 I - 목적

- **to부정사가 부사처럼** 쓰여 '~하기 위해서, ~하러'라는 뜻으로 목적을 나타낼 수 있다.
  이 때 「**in order to + 동사원형**」 또는 「**so as to + 동사원형**」 구문으로 바꿔 써서
  목적의 뜻을 더 분명히 나타낼 수도 있다.
  He saves money to buy a new car. 그는 새 차를 사기 위해 저축한다.
  → He saves money in order to buy a new car.
  → He saves money so as to buy a new car.

- **부정형(~하지 않기 위해)**: to부정사 앞에 not을 붙인다. 「**in order not to + 동사원형**」
  또는 「**so as not to + 동사원형**」으로 바꿔 쓸 수 있다.
  She ran hard not to miss the train. 그녀는 기차를 놓치지 않기 위해 열심히 뛰었다.
  → She ran hard in order not to miss the train.
  → She ran hard so as not to miss the train.

A 괄호 안에서 알맞은 말을 고르시오.

1 He sleeps enough (to stay, staying) healthy.
2 Ann bought a ticket (to see, not to see) a movie.
3 I got up early (not to be, to be not) late for school.
4 She saved money (to buy, buying) a new cell phone.
5 David went to China (so to learn as, so as to learn) Chinese.

B 세 문장의 뜻이 같도록 밑줄 친 부분에 유의하여 빈칸에 알맞은 말을 쓰시오.

1 She studied hard not to fail the exam.
→ She studied hard in ______________________.
→ She studied hard so ______________________.

2 I called the restaurant to make a reservation.
→ I called the restaurant in ______________________.
→ I called the restaurant so ______________________.

C 우리말과 뜻이 같도록 괄호 안의 말을 바르게 배열하여 문장을 완성하시오.

1 나는 과일을 사기 위해 식료품점에 갈 것이다. (to, some, fruits, buy)
→ I'll go to the grocery store ______________________.

2 Terry는 시험에 떨어지지 않기 위해 열심히 공부한다. (not, fail, to)
→ Terry studies hard ______________________ the exam.

3 그녀는 비밀번호를 잊지 않기 위해 적었다. (not, to, order, in, forget)
→ She wrote the password ______________________.

Point 06 to부정사의 부사적 용법 II – 감정의 원인, 결과, 판단의 근거

- to부정사가 부사처럼 쓰여 **감정의 원인**, **결과**, 또는 **판단의 근거**를 나타낸다.
- **감정의 원인**: 감정을 나타내는 형용사 뒤에 to부정사가 오면, '~해서, ~하니'의 뜻이다.

형용사 glad, happy, pleased, sad 등 (~해서 기쁘다/행복하다/슬프다)	+	to부정사

I am glad to see you again. 나는 너를 다시 만나서 매우 기쁘다.

- **결과**: 대개 live, grow up, wake up 등의 동사 뒤에 to부정사가 오면, '~해서 결국 …하다/되다'의 뜻이다.

동사 live, grow up, wake up 등 (~해서 결국 …되다)	+	to부정사

My grandfather lived to be 100 years old. 나의 할아버지께서는 100세까지 사셨다.

※ to부정사 앞에 only가 있으면 결과를 나타내고, '결국 ~했다'라는 뜻이다.

Ben studied very hard only to fail the test. Ben은 열심히 공부했지만 결국 시험에 통과하지 못했다.

- **판단의 근거**: 대개 'must be + 형용사' 뒤에 to부정사가 오면 '~하다니'의 뜻을 가지는 경우이다.
Ben must be smart to act like that. Ben이 그렇게 행동하다니 그는 똑똑한 게 틀림없다.

A 밑줄 친 to부정사의 쓰임을 고르시오.

1 She must be foolish <u>to say</u> that. (목적, 감정의 원인, 결과, 판단의 근거)

2 They are happy <u>to see</u> each other again. (목적, 감정의 원인, 결과, 판단의 근거)

3 The man woke up <u>to find</u> himself in a strange place. (목적, 감정의 원인, 결과, 판단의 근거)

B 〈보기〉와 같이 to부정사를 활용하여 다음을 한 문장으로 만드시오.

> 보기
> I was disappointed. I got a C in math. → I was disappointed <u>to get a C in math</u>.

1 The boy must be honest. He told the truth.

→ The boy must be honest ______________________.

2 My aunt went to South Africa. She helped the poor children there.

→ My aunt went to South Africa ______________________.

C 우리말과 뜻이 같도록 괄호 안의 말을 활용하여 문장을 완성하시오.

1 Tom은 금메달을 타서 매우 기뻤다. (win, very, to, happy)

→ Tom was ______________________ a gold medal.

2 Sally는 커서 비행기 승무원이 되었다. (grew, to, up, be)

→ Sally ______________________ a flight attendant.

Point 07 to부정사의 의미상의 주어, to부정사의 부정

- **to부정사의 의미상의 주어**는 to부정사의 동작을 행하는 주체이다.
  (1) to부정사 앞에 「**for + 목적격**」: 대부분의 to부정사에 사용한다.
  It is easy for her to understand the story. 그녀가 그 이야기를 이해하는 것은 쉽다.
  (2) to부정사 앞에 「**of + 목적격**」: to부정사 앞에 사람의 성격이나 주관적 평가를 나타내는 형용사 (nice, kind, smart, wise, silly, polite, rude, honest, thoughtful 등)가 있을 때 쓴다.
  It is nice of him to offer his seat to an elderly lady. 그의 자리를 노인에게 양보하다니 착하다.
- to부정사의 의미상 주어의 생략: ① 의미상의 주어가 문장의 주어나 목적어와 같은 경우, 또는 ② 의미상의 주어가 일반적인 사람들(예: for people, for them, for us 등)일 때, 또는 ③ 문맥상 to부정사의 의미상의 주어가 명백할 때 생략할 수 있다.
  ① I want to become a famous movie star. (문장의 주어 = to부정사의 의미상 주어)
  ① I want you to become a famous movie star. (문장의 목적어 = to부정사의 의미상 주어)
  ② It is bad (for people) to talk behind someone's back. (사람들이) 뒤에서 욕을 하는 것은 나쁘다.
- **to부정사의 부정**은 to부정사 앞에 not 또는 never를 붙인다.
  I decided not to talk about his faults any further. 나는 더 이상 그의 잘못에 대해 말하지 않기로 결심했다.
- **대부정사**: 동일한 동사구가 앞에 이미 나왔을 때, 뒤에 오는 to부정사의 동사를 생략하고 to만 쓸 수 있다.
  You can go home if you want to (go home).

A 괄호 안에서 알맞은 말을 고르시오.

1 This is the bus (of, for) us to take.
2 I opened the window (of, for) fresh air to come in.
3 It is kind (of, for) her to help the senior citizen get a seat.
4 It is very important (of, for) him to have an interview.
5 It is very thoughtful (of, for) them to plan a surprise party for their teacher.

B 밑줄 친 부분을 어법에 맞게 바르게 고쳐 쓰시오.

1 He ran fast <u>to not miss the train</u>. → ______________
2 He <u>decided to attend not the meeting</u>. → ______________
3 It is <u>impossible of me</u> to get up early. → ______________

C 우리말과 뜻이 같도록 괄호 안의 말을 바르게 배열하여 문장을 완성하시오.

1 거짓말을 하는 것은 옳지 않다. (us, for, tell a lie, to)
→ It is wrong ______________________.
2 깊은 바다에서 수영을 하는 것은 위험하다. (in, swim, to, the deep sea)
→ It is dangerous ______________________.

Point 08 to부정사의 시제

- 「**seem** + **to부정사**」: '~인 것 같다'라는 뜻이다. 「**It seems that** + **주어** + **동사** ~.」로 바꿔 쓸 수 있다.
  The tall boy seems to like you. 그 키가 큰 남자는 너를 좋아하는 것 같다.
  → It seems that the tall boy likes you.
- **to부정사의 시제**
  (1) **단순부정사 「to + 동사원형」**: to부정사의 시제가 주절의 시제와 같을 때 쓴다.

It seems **that** the old man is rich. → The old man **seems** to be rich. 그 노인은 부자인 것 같다.	**It** seemed **that** the old man was rich. → The old man **seemed** to be rich. 그 노인은 부자인 것 같았다.

  (2) **완료부정사 「to + have + p.p.」**: to부정사의 시제가 주절의 시제보다 앞설 때 쓴다.
  The boy seems to have argued with his sister. 그 소년은 그의 여동생과 말다툼을 했던 것 같다.
  → It seems that the boy argued with his sister.
  The boy seemed to have argued with his sister. 그 소년은 그의 여동생과 말다툼을 했었던 것 같았다.
  → It seemed that the boy had argued with his sister.

A 두 문장의 뜻이 같도록 문장을 완성하시오.

1 It seems that the woman is an actress.
→ The woman seems to ______________ an actress.

2 Michael seemed to have been a painter.
→ It seemed that Michael ______________ ______________ a painter.

3 They seem to know each other quite well.
→ It seems that ______________ ______________ each other quite well.

4 She seems to have seen something in the kitchen.
→ It seems that ____.

B 우리말과 뜻이 같도록 괄호 안의 말을 바르게 배열하여 문장을 완성하시오.

1 그는 집들이에서 재미있었던 것 같다. (seems, have, to, fun, had)
→ He ______________________________________ at the house warming party.

2 그녀는 콘서트를 즐겼던 것 같다. (have, to, enjoyed, seems)
→ She ____ the concert.

3 그녀는 매운 음식을 좋아하는 것 같았다. (seemed, like, spicy, to, food)
→ She ____.

Point 09 목적어, 목적격 보어로 쓰이는 to부정사

■ 「**동사 + to부정사(목적어)**」: 다음의 동사들은 **목적어로 to부정사를 취한다.**

동사 want, wish, hope, expect, plan, agree, mean, choose, decide, would like, learn, promise 등	+	to부정사

I hope to enter Seoul National University. 나는 서울대학교에 입학하기를 희망한다.
They planned to go on a field trip this weekend. 그들은 이번 주말에 현장 학습 가는 것을 계획했다.

■ 「**동사 + 목적어 + to부정사**」: want, ask, tell, expect 등이 사용된 5형식 문장에서 목적어와 목적격 보어가 능동 관계일 때, **목적격 보어로 to부정사(구)가 온다.**

동사 want, ask, tell, allow, expect, order, advise, encourage 등	+	목적어	+	to부정사
(~에게 …하도록 원하다/부탁하다/말하다/허락하다/기대하다/명령하다/조언하다/용기를 북돋우다)				

My mom **always** tells me to make my bed. 엄마는 항상 내게 침대를 정리하라고 말씀하신다.
The doctor advised her to exercise every day. 그 의사는 그녀에게 매일 운동할 것을 조언했다.

A 밑줄 친 부분을 어법에 맞게 바르게 고쳐 쓰시오.

1 She wishes studying abroad. → ____________
2 He told me take some vitamins. → ____________
3 I would like you meet my sister. → ____________
4 People expect the team win the game. → ____________
5 My mom allowed me play a computer game for an hour. → ____________

B 괄호 안에서 알맞은 말을 고르시오.

1 My teacher advised me (to study, studied) harder.
2 They want (to buy, buying) new furniture for the living room.
3 We decided (to visit, visited) a nursing home this weekend.
4 He asked me (to take, taking) care of his puppy for a week.
5 Teddy learned (riding, to ride) a horse during the summer vacation.

C 우리말과 뜻이 같도록 괄호 안의 말을 바르게 배열하여 문장을 완성하시오.

1 나의 부모님께서는 시골에서 살기를 원하신다. (to, want, live)
→ My parents ____________________ in the country.

2 그는 그의 아들이 컴퓨터 게임을 하도록 허락했다. (his, allowed, son, play, to)
→ He ____________________ computer games.

3 나의 어머니께서는 내가 6시까지 집에 오기를 기대하신다. (home, me, expects, come, to)
→ My mom ____________________ by 6 p.m.

Point 10 사역동사 + 목적어 + 원형부정사

- **원형부정사**: to가 없이 동사원형만 쓰는 부정사를 원형부정사라 한다.
- **사역동사 make, have, let** 등은 목적격 보어로 원형부정사를 쓴다.

사역동사 make, have, let 등	+	목적어	+	동사원형

(~에게 …을 시키다/~하게 하다/허락하다)

The red light made people stop crossing the street. 빨간 불은 사람들이 길 건너는 것을 멈추게 했다.
She had her son finish his homework. 그녀는 그녀의 아들이 숙제를 마치도록 했다.
Let me check the password. 내가 비밀번호를 확인할게.

- **help**는 목적격 보어로 **to**부정사와 원형부정사 둘 다 올 수 있다.
  He helped me (to) find the building. 그는 내가 그 건물을 찾도록 도와주었다.
- **get**은 사역동사의 의미를 갖지만 목적격 보어로 **to**부정사가 온다.
  He got her to clean the house. 그는 그녀에게 집을 청소하게 했다.

※ **목적어와 목적격 보어가 수동 관계**일 때: 사역동사라도 목적격 보어로 과거분사를 쓴다.
I had my radio fixed. 나는 내 라디오를 수리했다.

A

밑줄 친 부분을 어법에 맞게 고쳐 쓰시오.

1 Let me helping you. → ____________
2 The sad news made me to cry. → ____________
3 I had him to dance on the stage. → ____________
4 Jessica got him pick her up at noon. → ____________
5 Anna had her laptop computer fixing. → ____________
6 Tom helped me moving the furniture. → ____________
7 He let me to go to an amusement park with my friends. → ____________

B

우리말과 뜻이 같도록 괄호 안의 말을 바르게 배열하여 문장을 완성하시오.

1 Ron이 제게 곧 전화하도록 해주세요. (Ron, have, call, back, me)
→ Please ______________________ soon.

2 그는 웨이터에게 물 한잔을 가지고 오도록 시켰다. (had, bring, the waiter)
→ He ______________________ a glass of water.

3 나는 내 여동생에게 그녀의 책상을 치우도록 했다. (got, to, my sister, clean)
→ I ______________________ her desk.

4 그 연사는 우리들에게 미래에 대해 생각하도록 했다. (us, made, think about)
→ The speaker ______________________ our future.

5 그녀는 그녀의 어린 아들이 신발 신는 것을 도와주었다. (little, her, put on, son, helped)
→ She ______________________ his shoes.

Point 11 지각동사 + 목적어 + 원형부정사

■ 5형식 문장에서 **지각동사**의 목적격 보어로 원형부정사가 온다.

지각동사 see, look at, watch, hear, listen to, smell, feel, notice 등	+	목적어	+	동사원형 / 현재분사

(~가 …하는 것을 보다/듣다/냄새 맡다/느끼다/알아차리다)

I saw the baby cry. 나는 아기가 우는 것을 보았다.

※ **지각동사 + 목적어 + 현재분사(-ing)**: 동작이 진행 중임을 강조하기 위해, 지각동사의 목적격 보어로 현재분사를 쓴다.

cf. I saw the baby crying. 나는 아기가 울고 있는 것을 보았다. (진행의 의미를 강조)
He heard someone call[calling] his name. 그는 누군가 그의 이름을 부르는 것을 들었다.

※ **지각동사의 목적어와 목적격 보어가 수동 관계일 때**: 목적격 보어로 과거분사를 쓴다.
I heard my name called. 나는 내 이름이 불리는 것을 들었다.

A 괄호 안에서 알맞은 말을 고르시오.

1 I saw him (dance, danced) in the rain.
2 I noticed him (run, to run) in the election.
3 We heard them (to shout, shouting) for joy.
4 She watched me (make, to make) a snowman.
5 I felt something (to touch, touching) my back.
6 He looked at the man (repairing, repaired) the roof.
7 They listen to the singer (sing, to sing) pop songs.
8 The class president made the students (be, to be) quiet.
9 Sally saw the boys (to play, playing) soccer in the playground.
10 My brother helped me (finishing, to finish) the science homework.

B 우리말과 뜻이 같도록 밑줄 친 부분을 어법에 맞게 고쳐 쓰시오.

1 나는 무언가 타는 냄새를 맡았다.
= I could smell something <u>burned</u>. → ______________

2 나는 누군가 나를 노려보는 것을 느꼈다.
= I felt someone <u>to stare</u> at me. → ______________

3 그녀는 밤에 고양이가 우는 것을 들었다.
= She heard the kitten <u>to cry</u> at night. → ______________

4 나는 그가 교실을 떠나는 것을 알아차리지 못했다.
= I didn't notice him <u>left</u> the classroom. → ______________

Point 12 자주 쓰이는 to부정사 구문

■ 「too + 형용사/부사 + to부정사」는 '너무 ~해서 ~할 수 없는, ~하기에는 너무 ~한'이라는 뜻이며 「so + 형용사/부사 that + 주어 + can't」로 바꿔 쓸 수 있다.

The male athlete is too slow to break the record. 그 남자 선수는 너무 느려서 기록을 깰 수 없다.
→ The male athlete is so slow that he can't break the record.

■ 「형용사/부사 + enough + to부정사」는 '~할 정도로 충분히 ~한'이라는 뜻이며, 「so + 형용사/부사 that + 주어 + can」으로 바꿔 쓸 수 있다.

He is strong enough to carry the books. 그는 책을 들 수 있을 정도로 충분히 힘이 세다.
→ He is so strong that he can carry the books.

A 괄호 안의 말을 바르게 배열하여 문장을 완성하시오.

1 The hot chocolate is ______________________. (too, drink, to, hot)
2 The ruler is ______________________ the length of this wall. (enough, measure, long, to)
3 She is ______________________ the phone right away. (to, too, busy, answer)
4 The weather is ______________________ shorts these days. (cold, to, too, wear)

B 두 문장의 뜻이 같도록 문장을 완성하시오.

1 Jenny was smart enough to pass the test.
→ Jenny was so ________ ________ ________ ________ pass the test.
2 He is strong enough to move the desk.
→ He is so ________ ________ ________ ________ move the desk.
3 The new student is too shy to make friends easily.
→ The new student is so ________ ________ ________ ________ make friends easily.
4 The backpack is too small to hold all my textbooks.
→ The backpack is so ______________________________.

C 우리말과 뜻이 같도록 괄호 안의 말을 바르게 배열하여 문장을 완성하시오.

1 날씨가 캠핑을 가기에는 너무 춥다. (go, too, to, cold)
→ The weather is ______________________ camping.
2 Ben은 경주에서 이기기에 충분히 빠르다. (enough, fast, to, win)
→ Ben is ______________________ the race.
3 그 시계는 내 용돈으로 구입하기에는 너무 비싸다. (expensive, to, too, buy)
→ The watch is ______________________ with my pocket money.

일등 비법 노트

비법 1 to부정사의 의미상 주어는, 사람의 성품 관련 형용사가 오면 「of + 목적격」, 나머지는 「for + 목적격」이다!

대표기출 1 밑줄 친 부분이 어법상 옳은 문장은?

① It is very kind for you to help me.
② It was hard of him to solve the problem.
③ It was silly of me to believe what you said.
④ It was difficult of me to understand the movie in English.
⑤ It was careless for you to cross the road without looking around.

비법 2 지각동사와 사역동사는 목적격 보어로 동사원형을 취한다! (단, 목적어와 목적격 보어가 능동 관계일 때!)

대표기출 1 빈칸에 to를 쓸 수 없는 것은?

① She felt the floor ________ shake.
② He wants me ________ visit his house.
③ I expect him ________ make cookies.
④ My parents wish me ________ study hard.
⑤ She got her students ________ clean their classroom.

비법 3 to부정사의 부정은 「not/never + to + 동사원형」이다!

대표기출 1 우리말과 일치하도록 괄호 안의 말을 활용하여 빈칸에 알맞은 말을 쓰시오. (pretend, see)

Koreans sometimes feel uncomfortable when westerners kiss each other. When they do, Koreans sometimes look another way and ____________________. (그들을 보지 않는 척 한다.)

→ ____________________

대표기출 2 주어진 단어를 활용하여 우리말을 영어로 옮겨 쓰시오. (필요하면 어형을 바꾸거나 단어를 추가하시오.)

선생님께서는 우리에게 수업 시간에 휴대폰을 사용하지 말라고 말씀하셨다.
(in class, use, tell, the teacher, cell phones)

→ ____________________

비법 4 주로 원하고(want), 바라고(hope, wish, expect), 계획하는(plan) 동사들의 목적어로 to부정사가 온다!

대표기출 1 대화의 흐름이 자연스럽도록 밑줄 친 단어를 재배열하여 ⓐ에 알맞은 문장을 완성하시오. (필요하면 어형을 바꾸고, 단어를 추가하시오.)

A: May I help you?
B: Yes, please. I bought this shirt here. ⓐ ____________
(I, want, refund, it) Here is the receipt.

→ ____________

대표기출 2 다음 질문에 대한 자신의 답을 완전한 문장으로 쓰시오.

Q: What are you planning to do this weekend?

→ My own answer: ____________

비법 5 형용사적 용법의 to부정사 뒤에 전치사가 필요한지 여부는 앞의 명사를 to부정사 뒤에 놓아 본다! – 동사와 명사 사이에 전치사가 필요하면 「명사 + to부정사 + 전치사」이다!

대표기출 1 우리말과 뜻이 같도록 영작할 때 빈칸에 알맞은 말을 쓰시오.

나는 같이 놀 친구가 필요해.

→ I need a ______ ______ ______ ______.

비법 6 「의문사 + to부정사 = 의문사 + 주어 + should + 동사원형」이다!

대표기출 1 어법상 어색한 문장을 모두 고르면?

ⓐ Children are not easy to take care.
ⓑ He drove carefully only to get a ticket.
ⓒ I make it a rule to have an apple every morning.
ⓓ I suddenly forgot how to get to my house from school.
ⓔ He doesn't know what he would say when his friends feel sad.

① ⓐ, ⓒ ② ⓑ, ⓓ ③ ⓒ, ⓓ ④ ⓐ, ⓔ ⑤ ⓒ, ⓔ

대표기출 2 두 문장의 뜻이 같도록 빈칸에 알맞은 말을 쓰시오.

They learned how they should use the machine.

→ They learned ______ ______ ______ the machine.

내신 만점! 실전 기출

01 빈칸에 알맞지 않은 것은?

She __________ him study English after school.

① let ② saw ③ had
④ told ⑤ made

02 빈칸에 알맞은 것을 모두 고르면? (2개)

I saw him __________ a gold medal in the English Speech Contest.

① win ② wins ③ to win
④ win to ⑤ winning

03 서술형

우리말과 뜻이 같도록 괄호 안의 말을 활용하여 빈칸에 알맞은 말을 쓰시오.

그녀는 버스에 탄 첫 탑승자가 되어 기뻤다. (become)

→ She was happy __________________ the first passenger to get on the bus.

04 빈칸에 알맞은 말은?

One piece of paper is not enough for me __________ all my wishes on.

① write ② writing ③ to write
④ writing on ⑤ to write with

05 서술형

두 문장의 뜻이 같도록 빈칸에 알맞은 말을 써서 문장을 완성하시오.

I wish to learn how I should play the flute.

→ I wish to learn __________ __________ __________ __________ __________.

06 빈칸에 알맞은 말이 순서대로 바르게 나열된 것은?

- She wants ⓐ __________ to Paris during the winter vacation.
- Tony's mom allowed him ⓑ __________ computer games.

① travel, to play ② to travel, play
③ to travel, to play ④ traveling, to play
⑤ to travel, playing

07 서술형

다음 문장을 주어진 말로 시작하여 다시 쓰시오.

It seems that Mrs. Wilson hates her children's bad habits.

→ Mrs. Wilson seems ____________________ ____________________.

08 어법상 틀린 문장은?

① I found it dangerous drive fast.
② It is important to have a dream.
③ It is not easy to fix the computer.
④ It is hard to answer the question.
⑤ It is impossible for me to finish it by noon.

09 서술형

우리말과 뜻이 같도록 괄호 안의 말을 활용하여 문장을 완성하시오. (필요하면 형태를 바꿔 쓸 수 있음)

그 챔피언은 스스로를 자랑스러워하는 듯 보인다. (be proud of oneself)

→ (1) The champion seems to ____________________.

→ (2) The champion seems that ____________________.

10 두 문장의 뜻이 같도록 빈칸에 알맞은 말은?

> It seems that he is one of my neighbors.
> → He ________ one of my neighbors.

① seemed to ② seems that
③ seems to be ④ seems being
⑤ seems to have been

11 to부정사의 쓰임이 ⓐ와 같은 것은?

> In the 1960s, many Korean nurses and miners went to Germany ⓐ <u>to work</u>.

① She always wants <u>to play</u> badminton.
② Give me a racket <u>to play</u> badminton with.
③ She says that she plays badminton <u>to have fun</u>.
④ It is not so easy <u>to win</u> the badminton match.
⑤ There were many things <u>to buy</u> in the supermarket.

12 짝지어진 두 문장의 의미가 <u>다른</u> 것은?

① She didn't know where to go.
→ She didn't know where she should go.
② Please tell me when to submit the paper.
→ Please tell me when I should submit the paper.
③ I told Tom what to prepare for the party.
→ I told Tom what he should prepare for the party.
④ Can you show me how to use this machine?
→ Can you show me how I should use this machine?
⑤ He taught me how to solve the math problem.
→ I taught him how he should solve the math problem.

13 서술형

괄호 안의 말을 재배열하여 대화를 완성하시오.

> (1) A: What's up?
> B: Keep quiet. I ________ my backpack. (someone, grab, felt)

→ ________________________

> (2) A: When do you feel sad?
> B: I feel sad when I ________ at me. (angry, my, get, mom, see)

→ ________________________

14 서술형

「so ~ that …」 구문을 활용하여 밑줄 친 ⓐ를 완전한 영어 문장으로 다시 쓰시오.

> A: What's wrong with Sally?
> B: ⓐ <u>Her parents are too poor to pay her school tuition.</u>

→ ________________________
____

최다빈출

15 어법상 옳은 문장은?

① It is generous of him to say so.
② It was silly for me to fail the exam.
③ It's nice for her to help other people.
④ It's hard of me to get up early in the morning.
⑤ It is dangerous of them to go out late at night.

16 서술형

「의문사 + to부정사」 구문을 활용하여 ⓐ를 영작하시오.

> Tomorrow is my mom's birthday. So I want to buy a birthday gift for her with my older sister. ⓐ 나는 언니를 언제 만날 지 모른다.

→ I don't know ________________________________.

17 빈칸에 알맞은 말이 〈보기〉와 같은 것을 모두 고르면?

> 보기
> His question is very difficult ______ me to answer.

> ⓐ It is nice ________ her to teach me math.
> ⓑ It is not easy ________ him to cook.
> ⓒ It is difficult ________ me to speak in English.
> ⓓ This chicken soup is too hot ________ me to eat.
> ⓔ It is rude ________ them to talk back to their teacher.

① ⓐ, ⓑ ② ⓐ, ⓓ ③ ⓑ, ⓔ
④ ⓑ, ⓒ, ⓓ ⑤ ⓑ, ⓓ, ⓔ

18 어법상 틀린 문장을 모두 고르면? (2개)

① He wants to be famous.
② I decided to study harder.
③ She agreed starting after lunch.
④ I'd like you think about your future.
⑤ They expect to see the speaker again one day.

19 서술형

우리말과 일치하도록 괄호 안의 말을 활용하여 영작하시오.
(단, 필요한 단어를 하나 추가하시오.)

> 그녀는 그에게 함께 먹자고 부탁했다.
> (him, eat, together, she, asked)

→ ________________________________

20 문장의 의미가 나머지 넷과 다른 하나는?

① It was too cold to swim in the river.
② I was very cold, so I could swim in the river.
③ It was so cold that I couldn't swim in the river.
④ It was very cold, so I couldn't swim in the river.
⑤ Because it was too cold, I couldn't swim in the river.

최다빈출 고난도

21 빈칸 어디에도 들어갈 수 없는 하나는?

> (1) She called me to ask ____________ spaghetti.
> (2) I'm done. Please tell me ____________ the school.
> (3) I'm sorry to hear your bad news. I don't know ____________ to you.
> (4) Can you give me a hand? I really don't know ____________ this problem.

① what to say
② how to solve
③ how to make
④ when to leave
⑤ where to meet

[22~24] 밑줄 친 ⓐ와 쓰임이 같은 것을 고르시오.

22

The best way to know yourself is ⓐ to find out what you are good at. It may help you understand yourself better and find a suitable job.

① I need something to drink.
② His hobby is to take photographs.
③ She studied hard to pass the exam.
④ He went to France to see the Eiffel Tower.
⑤ You should know yourself to find the right job.

23

My family went camping except my sister. She had to prepare a group project, so she didn't have time ⓐ to join us. I hope she will go with us next time.

① They want to have hamburgers.
② I'm very glad to see you again.
③ To play computer games is exciting.
④ I need a magazine to read on the airplane.
⑤ He went to China to see the Great Wall of China.

24

The windmill generated electricity by using the wind. She was amazed ⓐ to see that it worked quite well. She clapped her hands with joy.

* windmill: 풍차

① I expect him to come early.
② She gave me a jacket to wear.
③ He was glad to be back in school.
④ My dream is to become an English teacher.
⑤ It is difficult to learn a foreign language.

25 서술형

표의 내용과 일치하도록 문장을 완성하시오.

오전	오후
feed the dog	take care of my brother

(1) Q1: What did your mom have you do in the morning?

A1: My mom ______________________
______________________.

(2) Q2: What did your mom ask you to do in the afternoon?

A2: My mom ______________________
______________________.

26 빈칸 ⓐ에 알맞은 의문사와 같은 것이 들어가는 문장은?

Do you have a special plan of ⓐ ________ to go on summer vacation? If you don't, why don't you visit England? You can go and see Tower Bridge, Buckingham Palace, and London Eye.

① A: I don't know ________ to use this machine.
B: Let's read the manual.
② A: Mom is angry. I don't know ________ to tell her.
B: You'd better say sorry to her.
③ A: I'm going to meet James this afternoon. Let's go together.
B: Ok. Please tell me where and ________ to meet him.
④ A: You have a nice jacket. Can you tell me ________ to buy one?
B: I bought it at Lily's Closet.
⑤ A: I need to do a survey with two students.
B: Really? Did you deicide ________ to ask the survey questions?

27 서술형

다음을 「so ~that」 구문을 활용하여 완전한 영어 문장으로 다시 쓰시오.

(1) She was too busy to attend the meeting.

→ ______________________

(2) He is diligent enough to get up early every morning.

→ ______________________

고난도

28 서술형

다음 조건에 맞춰 ⓐ를 영어로 바꿔 쓰시오.

조건

1. 괄호 안의 단어를 모두 사용할 것
2. 필요한 단어를 추가할 것
3. 「It ~ to + 동사원형」 가주어 · 진주어 구문을 사용할 것

W: What does Kevin have to do to become a good singer?

M: ⓐ 연습을 가능한 한 많이 하는 것이 그에게 중요해. (practice, important, as, much, him, for)

→ It ______________________.

고난도

29 서술형

밑줄 친 부분이 어법에 맞으면 O, 맞지 않으면 바르게 고쳐 쓰시오.

(1) It is very nice for you to help me.
(2) It is natural of him to help the poor.
(3) It was careless of you to lose the wallet.
(4) It is possible of her to be the class president.
(5) It is so generous of you to offer us this opportunity.
(6) My teacher told us not to make noise during the class.

(1) → ______________________
(2) → ______________________
(3) → ______________________
(4) → ______________________
(5) → ______________________
(6) → ______________________

고난도

30 다음 ⓐ~ⓓ 중 같은 용법으로 쓰인 것끼리 짝지어진 것은?

The Wright Brothers invented the first aircraft. They were very excited ⓐ to see it fly in the sky. People came ⓑ to see their first aircraft. It flew for 12 seconds only. Most people laughed at them, but they decided ⓒ to study more and make a better one. They gained the mechanical skills and read many books ⓓ to succeed.

① ⓐ, ⓒ ② ⓑ, ⓓ ③ ⓒ, ⓓ
④ ⓐ, ⓑ, ⓒ ⑤ ⓐ, ⓑ, ⓒ, ⓓ

실력 탄탄!
서술형 심화

1 그림을 보고, 대화의 흐름이 자연스럽도록 괄호 안의 말을 활용하여 빈칸에 알맞은 말을 쓰시오.

(1)

(2)

(3)

(1) A: What did Nick's mom ask Nick to do?
B: His mom ______________________________. (wash, the dishes)

(2) B: Can you tell me ______________________________ from here?
(how, the bank, get)
G: Sure. You can take bus Number 752.

(3) B: How was the English test?
G: It was ______________________________ the questions.
(difficult, me, answer)

2 Complete the sentence using all the words in brackets. Use infinitives with its own subject. You may add words or change the form if necessary.

> G: I'm thinking of moving out of the house. My roommate makes too much noise late at night. It's really ⓐ __________ a lot of noise.
> B: That's too bad. Did you try to talk to her about the problem?
> G: Of course I did, but nothing has changed.
> B: It's ⓑ __________ making noise.
> G: I know. Probably, it is not ⓒ __________ late at night.
> B: I hope you will find a better place.

→ ⓐ ______________________________ (inconsiderate, make, she)
→ ⓑ ______________________________ (foolish, keep, she)
→ ⓒ ______________________________ (easy, be quiet, she)

CHAPTER 04

동명사

- Point 01 동명사의 역할 I – 주어, 보어
- Point 02 동명사의 역할 II – 목적어
- Point 03 동명사의 의미상의 주어, 동명사의 부정
- Point 04 동명사의 시제와 태
- Point 05 동명사 *vs.* to부정사 I
- Point 06 동명사 *vs.* to부정사 II
- Point 07 동명사 *vs.* 현재분사
- Point 08 자주 쓰이는 동명사 표현

동명사

「동사원형 –ing」의 형태로, 동사의 성질을 가진 채로 문장 안에서 명사처럼 주어, 보어, 목적어의 역할을 한다. 동명사가 목적어의 역할을 할 때, 동사에 따라 동명사만을 목적어로 취하는 경우가 있다. 반면에 to부정사만을 목적어로 취하는 동사도 있으므로 주의해야 한다.

cf. 현재분사도 동명사처럼 「동사원형-ing」의 형태이지만, 현재분사는 문장에서 형용사 역할을 한다.

• 동명사의 역할

주어 역할	**Getting** success doesn't mean just making a lot of money. 성공하는 것은 그저 돈을 많이 번다는 것은 아니다.
보어 역할	His goal is **climbing** to the top of the mountain. 그의 목표는 산 정상에 오르는 것이다.
목적어 역할	Sally really **liked shopping** at Dongdaemun Market. (동사의 목적어) Sally는 동대문시장에서 쇼핑하는 것을 좋아한다.
	Mina is good **at finding** information on the Internet. (전치사의 목적어) 미나는 인터넷상에서 정보를 찾는 것을 매우 잘한다.

Point 01 동명사의 역할 I – 주어, 보어

- **동명사**는 「**동사원형-ing**」의 형태로 문장에서 명사처럼 **주어**, **보어**, **목적어** 역할을 한다.
- 주어나 보어로 쓰인 동명사는 to부정사와 바꿔 쓸 수 있다. 주어로 쓰인 동명사는 **단수 취급**한다.

Reading one book a week is my goal. 일주일에 한 권씩 책을 읽는 것이 나의 목표이다. (주어)
(= To read)

My volunteer work is helping handicapped people. 나의 봉사 활동은 장애우를 돕는 것이다. (보어)
(= to help)

A 괄호 안에서 알맞은 말을 고르시오.

1 Keeping secrets (is, are) very important.

2 (Draw, Drawing) cartoons is her favorite hobby.

3 (Being, Be) a good friend means being a good listener.

4 Guiding tourists around famous places (is, are) her job.

5 Their job is (correcting, correct) wrong information about Korea.

B 두 문장의 뜻이 같도록 빈칸에 알맞은 말을 쓰시오. (단, 동명사를 활용할 것)

1 My goal is to win the English speech contest this year.
→ My goal is ______________ the English speech contest this year.

2 To keep a diary in English is not easy, but it is helpful.
→ ______________ a diary in English is not easy, but it is helpful.

3 A good way to practice English is to watch English movies.
→ A good way to practice English is ______________ English movies.

C 빈칸에 적절한 말을 〈보기〉에서 골라 알맞은 형태로 쓰시오. (단, 한 단어로 쓰시오.)

보기				
get	climb	live	solve	watch

1 ______________ a movie is a good way of relaxing.

2 My hobby is ______________ crossword puzzles.

3 His regular weekend activity is ______________ a mountain.

4 ______________ in the countryside helped him get healthy.

5 The first step to being diligent is ______________ up early in the morning.

Point 02 동명사의 역할 II – 목적어

■ **동사의 목적어로 쓰이는 동명사**: 동사 **mind, enjoy, give up, avoid, finish, escape, practice, stop, consider** 등은 목적어로 동명사가 온다.

mind, enjoy, give up, avoid, finish, escape, practice, stop, consider 등 ☞ m.e.g.a.f.e.p.s.con (메가펩스콘)으로 암기하라!	+	동사원형-ing

He really enjoys **building** things with blocks. 그는 블록으로 무언가 만드는 것을 정말로 좋아한다.

■ **전치사의 목적어로 쓰이는 동명사**: 전치사의 목적어로 동사(구)가 올 때에는 **동명사(동사원형-ing)** 형태로 온다.

John is really good at **fixing** things. John은 정말로 물건 고치는 것을 잘한다.

Jiho is interested in **representing** Korea. 지호는 한국을 대표하는 것에 관심이 있다.

PLUS Tip

(1) **동명사 vs. to부정사**: to부정사도 문장에서 명사 역할을 하지만, 전치사의 목적어로는 쓸 수 없다.
John is really good at ~~to fix~~ things. (x)

(2) **to부정사를 만드는 to *vs.* 전치사 to**: 문장에서 '~에(게), ~으로'라는 뜻으로 쓰이면 전치사 to이고, 'to + 동사원형' 형태로 와서 명사, 형용사, 부사 역할을 하면 to부정사의 to이다.
She likes to help others. 그녀는 다른 사람들을 도와 주는 것을 좋아한다. (목적어로 쓰인 to부정사)
She gives toys to children. 그녀는 아이들에게 장난감을 준다. (전치사 to: ~에게)
She goes to the library after school. 그녀는 방과 후에 도서관으로 간다. (전치사 to: ~로)

A 괄호 안에서 알맞은 말을 고르시오.

1 Do you mind (open, opening) the window?
2 Hojun enjoys (working, to work) on his blog.
3 Thank you for (inviting, to invite) me to the party.
4 Peary never gave up (go, going) to the North Pole.

B 밑줄 친 부분이 어법에 맞으면 O표, 틀리면 바르게 고쳐 쓰시오.

1 She is good at designing web pages. → ______________
2 She tried to avoid to meet him today. → ______________
3 Bill is thinking of make a robot. → ______________

C 우리말과 뜻이 같도록 괄호 안의 말을 활용하여 문장을 완성하시오.

1 그녀는 수업에 늦을까 봐 걱정했다. (be late)
→ She was afraid of ____________ ____________ for the class.

2 Junho는 언어를 배우는 것에 관심이 있다. (learn)
→ Junho is interested in ____________ languages.

3 어머니께서는 내가 숙제를 끝낸 후에 나가도록 허락해 주셨다. (do)
→ Mom allowed me to go out after I finished ____________ my homework.

Point 03 동명사의 의미상의 주어, 동명사의 부정

■ **동명사의 의미상의 주어**: 대개 **동명사 앞에 소유격이나 목적격**을 써서 나타낸다.
Do you mind if I open the window? (open의 행위자가 I) 제가 창문을 좀 열어도 될까요?

Do you mind my[me] opening the window? (문장의 주어 you ≠ 동명사의 행위자인 my/me)

■ **동명사의 의미상의 주어를 생략하는 경우**: 동명사의 행위자가 문장의 주어, 목적어와 같거나 또는 일반적인 사람인 경우에는 의미상의 주어는 따로 명시하지 않고 생략한다.
Do you mind opening the window? 창문을 좀 열어 주시겠어요? (문장의 주어 you = 동명사의 행위자)
Thank you for telling me the truth. 진실을 말해주셔서 고맙습니다. (문장의 목적어 you = 동명사의 행위자)
Getting up late is a bad habit. 늦게 일어나는 것은 나쁜 습관이다. (일반적인 사람들 = 동명사의 행위자)

■ **동명사의 부정**: **동명사 앞에 not, 또는 never**를 쓴다.
Mom was angry at me for not coming back home earlier.
엄마는 내가 더 일찍 집에 돌아오지 않아서 화가 나셨다.

A 괄호 안의 말을 빈칸에 알맞은 형태로 쓰시오.

1 Do you mind ________ taking a picture of you? (I)
2 He was interested in ________ joining the club. (they)
3 I am worried about ________ being disappointed. (she)
4 She was pleased with ________ helping her clean the house. (he)

B 두 문장의 뜻이 같도록 〈보기〉와 같이 빈칸에 알맞은 말을 쓰시오.

> 보기
> She dreamed that she would go back to her hometown.
> → She dreamed about going back to her hometown.

1 I am sorry that I didn't come on time.
→ I am sorry for ________ ________ on time.
2 Do you mind if I turn down the volume?
→ Do you mind ________ ________ down the volume?
3 I am sure that he will not clean his car tomorrow.
→ I am sure of ________ ________ ________ his car tomorrow.

C 우리말과 뜻이 같도록 괄호 안의 말을 바르게 배열하여 문장을 완성하시오.

1 나는 그 때 그녀가 아팠던 것을 알아채지 못했다. (be)
→ I wasn't aware of ________ ________ sick at that time.
2 그녀는 자신이 좋아하는 TV 프로그램을 놓치지 않게 되어서 기뻤다. (miss)
→ She was happy about ________ ________ her favorite TV show.

Point 04 동명사의 시제와 태

■ 동명사의 시제 표현

(1) 문장의 본동사와 동일한 시제일 때: 「동사원형-ing」

I don't mind sharing the table. 테이블을 함께 써도 괜찮습니다.

= I don't mind that I share the table.

(2) 문장의 본동사보다 한 시제 앞설 때: 「having + p.p.」

John is proud of having got an A in math. John은 수학 과목에서 A를 받은 것을 자랑스러워 한다.

= John is proud that he got an A in math.

■ 동명사의 수동태

(1) 문장의 본동사와 같은 시제이고 수동태일 때: 「being + p.p.」

He doesn't like being treated as a little kid. 그는 어린아이로 취급 받는 것을 좋아하지 않는다.

(2) 문장의 본동사보다 한 시제 앞서고 수동태일 때: 「having + been + p.p.」

She felt honored by having been elected as the school president.

그녀는 학생회장으로 선출된 것을 영광으로 여겼다.

A 두 문장의 뜻이 같도록 밑줄 친 부분에 유의하여 〈보기〉와 같이 빈칸에 알맞은 말을 쓰시오.

보기

I am sure that I am ready for the test. → I am sure of being ready for the test.

1 I am proud that I am the winner of the contest.
→ I am proud of ________ the winner of the contest.

2 She is sorry that she lost my book.
→ She is sorry for ________ ________ my book.

3 He was happy that his suggestion was accepted.
→ He was happy about his suggestion ________ ________.

4 He insists that he was treated unfairly.
→ He insists on his ________ ________ ________ unfairly.

5 Mina feels sorry that her success was not known to her friends.
→ Mina feels sorry for her success ________ ________ ________ ________ to her friends.

B 우리말과 뜻이 같도록 괄호 안의 말을 바르게 배열하여 문장을 완성하시오.

1 그는 그녀가 가수일거라고 확신했다. (being, her)
→ He was sure of ____________________ a singer.

2 아버지께서는 내가 자신감을 잃어 버릴까 봐 걱정하신다. (confidence, losing, me)
→ Father is worried about ____________________.

3 어머니께서는 내가 경기를 포기해서 실망하셨다. (up, having, my, given, the competition)
→ Mom is disappointed by ____________________.

Point 05 동명사 *vs.* to부정사 I

■ **동명사만을 목적어로 취하는 동사**

mind, enjoy, give up, avoid, finish, escape, practice, stop, consider 등	+	동명사

I *finished* writing the essay. 나는 그 과제물 쓰는 것을 끝마쳤다.

■ **to부정사만을 목적어로 취하는 동사**

want, expect, hope, wish, decide, plan, promise, refuse 등	+	to부정사

We all *hope* to achieve success in the future. 우리는 모두 미래에 성공을 성취하기를 바란다.

A

괄호 안에서 알맞은 말을 고르시오.

1 Father promised (stopping, to stop) smoking.

2 He decided (saving, to save) money for the trip.

3 She didn't mind (waiting, to wait) for more time.

4 They planned (going, to go) hiking this weekend.

5 Jason has practiced (playing, to play) soccer for more than two years.

6 Susan stopped (talking, to talk) over the phone to hear the sound from outside.

B

밑줄 친 부분이 어법에 맞으면 O표, 틀리면 바르게 고쳐 쓰시오.

1 Yumi never gave up <u>pursuing</u> her dream. → ____________

2 Junho hoped <u>visiting</u> his cousin in China. → ____________

3 Jane considers <u>becoming</u> a nurse in the future. → ____________

4 She didn't really enjoy <u>to listen</u> to the rock music. → ____________

C

빈칸에 알맞은 말을 〈보기〉에서 골라 알맞은 형태로 쓰시오.

보기			
run	start	accept	finish

1 그는 나의 제안을 받아들이기를 거부했다

→ He refused ________________ my suggestion.

2 그는 달리기를 매일 연습한다.

→ He practices ________________ every day.

3 Jake는 자신의 사업을 시작하기를 원하고 있다.

→ Jake wants ________________ his own business.

4 그는 내가 곧 숙제를 끝낼 것으로 기대하고 있다.

→ He expects me ________________ my homework soon.

Point 06 동명사 *vs.* to부정사 II

■ 동명사와 to부정사 둘 다 목적어로 취하는 동사들이 있다.

(1) **의미상 차이가 없는 경우**: 동사 **start, begin, like, love, hate, continue** 등은 별다른 **의미 차이 없이 to부정사와 동명사를 모두 목적어로** 취한다.

She hates fighting with her friends. 그녀는 친구들과 싸우는 것을 매우 싫어한다.
= She hates to fight with her friends.

(2) **의미상 차이가 있는 경우**: to부정사와 동명사를 모두 목적어로 취하지만 **의미가 달라지는 동사들**은 다음과 같다.

remember + 동명사(-ing)	(과거) ~했던 것을 기억하다	remember + to부정사	(미래) ~할 것을 기억하다
forget + 동명사(-ing)	(과거) ~했던 것을 잊다	forget + to부정사	(미래) ~할 것을 잊다
try + 동명사(-ing)	(시도) 시험 삼아 ~해 보다	try + to부정사	(노력) ~하려고 애쓰다
regret + 동명사(-ing)	(과거) ~했던 것을 후회하다	regret + to부정사	(미래) ~하게 되어 유감이다

She forgot to turn off the light. 그녀는 불을 끄는 것을 잊었다. (→ 불을 끄지 않았음)
She forgot turning off the light. 그녀는 불을 끈 사실을 잊었다. (→ 불을 껐음)

※ **쓰임 자체가 다른 경우**: stop의 목적어로는 동명사만 온다. stop 뒤에 to부정사가 올 수는 있지만, 이 때의 to부정사는 목적어(~을/를)가 아니라 '~하기 위해'라는 뜻의 부사적 용법으로 쓰인 것이다.

He stopped taking pictures of the children. 그는 그 아이들의 사진을 찍는 것을 멈췄다.
He stopped to take pictures of the children. 그는 그 아이들의 사진을 찍기 위해 멈췄다.

A 괄호 안에서 알맞은 말을 고르시오.

1 (a) He regrets (not keeping, not to keep) his promise.
(b) I regret (saying, to say) that you are not chosen for our team.

2 (a) She tried (opening, to open) the bottle cap, but she couldn't.
(b) She tried (adding, to add) some sugar into the kimchi stew.

3 (a) Please remember (buying, to buy) some ice cream on the way home.
(b) He didn't remember (telling, to tell) me that he would take me to the zoo.

4 (a) Sangho stopped (picking, to pick) up trash in the hallway.
(b) She stopped (drinking, to drink) coffee in the late afternoon for a good night sleep.

5 (a) I forgot (bringing, to bring) my science book to school, so I shared a book with my friend.
(b) Mom forgot (leaving, to leave) her wallet in her car and looked for it in the house.

B 우리말과 뜻이 같도록 괄호 안의 말을 바르게 배열하여 문장을 완성하시오.

1 그는 주말에 등반하는 것을 매우 좋아한다. (climbing, loves)
→ He ______________________________ the mountain on weekends.

2 그들은 어두워질 때까지 축구연습을 계속했다. (soccer, playing, continued)
→ They ______________________________ until it got dark.

Point 07 동명사 *vs.* 현재분사

- 동명사와 현재분사는 둘 다 형태는 「동사원형-ing」이다. 하지만, **동명사**는 명사처럼 문장에서 **주어, 보어, 목적어의 역할**을 하고, **현재분사**는 **형용사처럼 명사를 수식**하거나 **보어**로 쓰인다.
  Getting **nervous in front of a camera is natural.** 카메라 앞에서 긴장하는 것은 당연한 것이다. (주어: 동명사)
  His dream was climbing **Mt. Everest.** 그의 꿈은 에베레스트 산을 등정하는 것이었다. (보어: 동명사)
  Jina enjoyed giving **a speech to the students.** 지나는 학생들에게 연설하는 것을 즐겼다. (목적어: 동명사)
  Look at the girl smiling **at you.** 너를 보고 미소 짓고 있는 소녀를 봐라. (명사 수식: 현재 분사)
  The girl was smiling **at him.** 그 소녀는 그를 향해 미소 짓고 있었다. (보어: 현재분사)
  ☞ 보어로 쓰인 '동사원형-ing'는 '~하고 있는'으로 해석되면 현재분사이고, '~하기(하는 것)'으로 해석되면 동명사이다.

- 동명사와 현재분사가 명사 앞에 오는 경우: **동명사**는 명사의 **용도나 목적**을 보여주고, **현재분사**는 **상태**를 나타낸다.
  This will be the dancing room for the party.
  여기가 파티의 무도실이 될 것이다. (방의 용도를 설명: 동명사)
  The dancing girl on the stage is my sister.
  무대에서 춤추고 있는 소녀가 내 여동생이다. (소녀의 상태를 설명: 현재분사)

A

밑줄 친 부분이 동명사인지 현재분사인지 구분하시오.

1 People are <u>smiling</u> at the camera. (동명사, 현재분사)
2 His volunteer work is <u>cleaning</u> the park. (동명사, 현재분사)
3 Mina is <u>reading</u> a book in her room now. (동명사, 현재분사)
4 Smoking is allowed only in the <u>smoking</u> room. (동명사, 현재분사)
5 She is really good at <u>arranging</u> flowers in vases. (동명사, 현재분사)
6 Would you tell me how to use this <u>copying</u> machine? (동명사, 현재분사)
7 <u>Living</u> on Mars might come true in the near future. (동명사, 현재분사)

B

밑줄 친 부분에 유의하여 다음 문장을 우리말로 해석하시오.

1 He is called the <u>walking</u> dictionary.
→ ______________________________.

2 The old man is holding a <u>walking</u> stick.
→ ______________________________.

3 I really enjoyed <u>listening</u> to the music of your show.
→ ______________________________.

4 He finally succeeded in <u>climbing</u> to the top of the mountain.
→ ______________________________.

5 The boy <u>wearing</u> headphones in the picture is my brother.
→ ______________________________.

6 Something must be <u>burning</u>! I can see smoke <u>coming</u> out of the room!
→ ______________________________.

Point 08 자주 쓰이는 동명사 표현

■ 자주 쓰이는 동명사 표현은 다음과 같다.

look forward to -ing	~할 것을 고대하다	go -ing	~하러 가다
How[What] about -ing?	~하는 게 어때?	spend *A* (on) -ing	~하는 데 A를 쓰다
be used to -ing	~하는 데에 익숙하다	be busy -ing	~하느라 바쁘다
can't help -ing	~하지 않을 수 없다	have trouble -ing	~하는데 어려움을 겪다
keep[stop] *A* from -ing	A를 ~못하게 하다	feel like -ing	~하고 싶다
there is no -ing	~은 불가능하다	on -ing	~하자마자
It is no use -ing	~해도 소용없다	be worth -ing	~할 가치가 있다

I'm looking forward to seeing you. 너를 만나기를 고대하고 있어.

PLUS Tip

cf.「be used to -ing」 *vs.*「used to + 동사원형」 *vs.*「be used to + 동사원형」

(1) be used to ~ing: ~하는 데에 익숙하다.
Mina is used to taking care of children. 미나는 아이들 돌보는 데에 익숙하다.

(2) used to + 동사원형: ~하곤 했다, 예전에는 ~이었다. (과거의 습관이나 상태)
There used to be a very tall tree here. 전에 여기에 매우 큰 나무가 하나 있었다. (지금은 없다.)

(3) be used to + 동사원형: ~하는 데에 사용되다. (수동태와 to부정사의 부사적 용법이 결합된 구문)
The trees were used to build houses. 그 나무들은 집 짓는 데에 사용되었다.

A 괄호 안에서 알맞은 말을 고르시오.

1 I don't feel like (to go, going) out today.
2 Going (to shop, shopping) makes her happy.
3 She has been busy (to do, doing) her group work this week.
4 Many people spend their money (to help, helping) children in Africa.

B 밑줄 친 부분이 어법에 맞으면 O표, 틀리면 바르게 고쳐 쓰시오.

1 Challenging your limit is worth trying. → ____________
2 How about study in the library for the exam? → ____________
3 They couldn't help to laugh at the funny sight. → ____________
4 She had trouble to find information on the Internet. → ____________

C 우리말과 뜻이 같도록 괄호 안의 단어를 활용하여 문장을 완성하시오.

1 엎질러진 우유를 두고 울어 봐야 소용없다. (이미 엎질러진 물이다.) (cry)
→ It ________ ________ ________ ________ over spilt milk.

2 그들은 놀이공원에 가는 것을 고대하고 있다. (go)
→ They are ________ ________ ________ ________ to the amusement park.

일등 비법 노트

비법 ①

mind, enjoy, give up, avoid, finish, escape, practice, stop, consider
→ m.e.g.a.f.e.p.s.con(메가팹스콘) + -ing!

대표기출 1

밑줄 친 ⓐ~ⓔ중 어법상 어색한 문장끼리 짝지어진 것은?

Reporter: How did you start your own brand?
Tina: ⓐ I like making things such as accessories and hairpins, so I often make things and give them to my friends. One day, ⓑ one of my friends told me to make more and sell them. I thought it was a good idea because ⓒ I really enjoy to make things. It started like that.
Reporter: So, how was your business going at that time?
Tina: ⓓ Making a brand wasn't that easy, and I had really difficult times. But ⓔ I am happy that I didn't give up to start my own business.

① ⓐ, ⓓ ② ⓑ, ⓔ ③ ⓒ, ⓔ ④ ⓑ, ⓓ ⑤ ⓓ, ⓔ

대표기출 2

밑줄 친 ⓐ~ ⓔ에서 어법상 틀린 것을 3개 골라 바르게 고쳐 쓰시오.

Jina: Mom, I want to give up ⓐ to play the piano.
Mom: Oh! Why? I thought you really liked it.
Jina: Yes, but I think I am not that talented. There are many other children ⓑ playing better than I am.
Mom: You will also get better and better if you don't stop ⓒ to practice.
Jina: But I am not sure ....
Mom: Shall I listen to your playing after I finish ⓓ to prepare dinner?
Jina: Will you? Then, you can tell me what ⓔ to decide honestly.

________________ → ________________
________________ → ________________
________________ → ________________

비법 ②

「look forward to」의 to 뒤에는 동사원형이 아니라 동명사가 온다!

대표기출 1

대화를 읽고 질문에 답하시오.
(주어진 He is를 포함하여 총 12단어로 된 완전한 문장으로 답할 것)

Hojin: I am going to visit my uncle in America this summer. I can't wait!
Minji: Wow! That's great! I can see you are so excited!

Q: What is Hojin looking forward to?
A: He is ________________________________.

비법 ③ 전치사 뒤에는 동명사(-ing)!

대표기출 1

빈칸 ⓐ~ⓒ에 알맞은 말이 순서대로 바르게 나열된 것은?

Sally is good at ⓐ __________ things. She made a cushion for Mandy, and she really liked it. So, Mandy told Sally that she wanted ⓑ __________ how to make cushions. Sally said she would teach her. Now they spend an hour ⓒ __________ cushions together on Fridays.

① make, to learn, to make
② making, to learn, to make
③ making, to learn, making
④ to make, learn, making
⑤ make, learn, to make

대표기출 2

대화의 내용과 일치하도록 주어진 질문에 완전한 문장으로 답하시오.
(단, 대화문에서 나온 8개의 단어만을 사용하여 답하시오.)

Mom: Your Spelling Bee is tomorrow, right?
Tom: Yes. I am really nervous now.
Mom: Why? You memorize a lot of words every day.
Tom: I am afraid I might forget how to spell words in the contest.
Mom: Don't worry! You'll do really well.

Q: What is Tom worried about?
A: He is afraid of ________________________________.

비법 ④ 문장의 주어, 보어, 목적어로 쓰인 것은 동명사! 명사를 꾸며주는 것은 현재분사!

대표기출 1

밑줄 친 말의 쓰임이 〈보기〉와 다른 것을 모두 고르면? (2개)

보기
Getting up early in the morning is a good habit.

① Mina was in her room listening to music.
② Eating hamburgers too often can make you fat.
③ It has been snowing for three days in New York.
④ Sleeping on a cold floor can make your back stiff.
⑤ Watching English movies can help you improve your English ability.

대표기출 2

우리말과 뜻이 같도록 총 5단어로 이루어진 영어 문장을 영작하시오.
(단, 괄호 안의 말과 동명사를 활용할 것)

쇼핑하러 가는 것은 나를 피곤하게 만든다. (shopping, make, tired)

→ ________________________________

내신 만점! 실전 기출

[1~3] 빈칸에 알맞은 말을 고르시오.

01

_________ regularly is a healthy habit.

① Eat ② Eats
③ Eating ④ Be eating
⑤ With eating

02

She enjoys _________ a diary in English.

① to keep ② keeping
③ kept ④ to keeping
⑤ keep

03

Mina was interested in _________ Italian cooking.

① learn ② learns
③ learning ④ learned
⑤ to learning

[4~5] 빈칸에 알맞지 않은 것을 고르시오.

04

We were all surprised at _________ giving up the competition.

① he ② his
③ her ④ them
⑤ their

05

She _________ searching for information on the Internet.

① began ② started
③ stopped ④ decided
⑤ kept

[6~8] 우리말과 뜻이 같도록 빈칸에 알맞은 말을 고르시오.

06

그녀는 불을 끄는 것을 잊어버렸다.
→ She forgot _________ off the light.

① turned ② turning
③ turn ④ to turn
⑤ turns

07

그는 집에 가는 길에 세탁소에서 옷을 가져가야 하는 것을 기억하고 있었다.
→ He remembered _________ up his clothes from the laundry.

① picked ② picking
③ pick ④ to pick
⑤ picks

08

그들은 숙제를 제 시간에 끝내기 위해 노력했다.
→ They tried _________ their homework on time.

① finish ② finishing
③ finished ④ to finish
⑤ to finishing

[9~10] 괄호 안의 말을 빈칸에 알맞은 형태로 바꿔 쓰시오.

09 서술형

인도 사람들은 왼손을 사용하는 것을 더럽다고 생각한다. (use)

→ Indians consider __________ the left hand dirty.

10 서술형

나의 개는 나와 산책하는 것을 고대하고 있다. (take)

→ My dog is __________ __________ __________ __________ a walk with me.

[11~12] 밑줄 친 부분의 쓰임이 나머지와 다른 것을 고르시오.

11

① Visiting Jeju Island with you was very fun.
② Lots of fish are dying because of pollution.
③ He is interested in saving the environment.
④ His goal is going forward one step at a time.
⑤ She regretted telling her secret to Jenny yesterday.

12

① That sleeping baby in the cradle is so cute!
② There were some people in the waiting room.
③ The dancing girls in his picture all look beautiful.
④ Swamps are good places to live for many living creatures.
⑤ The leaning tower of Pisa is a famous tourist attraction in Italy.

13 어법상 옳은 문장은?

① Mothers never stop loving their children.
② They decided saving money to buy a new car.
③ Develop a good habit takes a lot of time and effort.
④ She didn't mind to leave her bag in the waiting room.
⑤ Don't forget buying some ice cream when you come back.

14 어법상 어색한 문장은?

① How about taking a break for a minute?
② Global warming is a result of increasing CO_2.
③ Some people wanted to take pictures of themselves.
④ The quiz show host started asking questions of the participants.
⑤ Remember calling me right after you wake up tomorrow morning.

[15~17] 두 문장의 뜻이 같도록 빈칸에 알맞은 말을 쓰시오.

15 서술형

Captain Jack is worried that he might not find the treasure.

→ Captain Jack is worried about __________ __________ the treasure.

16 서술형

I am sorry that I missed the first part of the movie.

→ I am sorry for __________ __________ the first part of the movie.

17 서술형

> He is surprised that his bike was stolen.

→ He is surprised at his bike ___________ ___________ ___________.

18 빈칸 ⓐ~ⓑ에 알맞은 말이 순서대로 바르게 나열된 것은?

> • On ⓐ _________ home, Peter turned on his computer to check the email from Sally.
> • My mom is used to ⓑ _________ up early in the morning.

① return, get
② returns, gets
③ returning, got
④ returning, getting
⑤ returned, getting

19 내용의 흐름상 빈칸 ⓐ~ⓒ에 알맞은 말이 순서대로 바르게 짝지어진 것은?

> My name is Mike. I love playing computer games. I am also very good at ⓐ _________ them, too. So, I want ⓑ _________ a progamer in the future. Today, I entered a computer game competition, and I came in second place. I was so pleased and couldn't help ⓒ _________.

① to play, to become, crying
② to play, becoming, to cry
③ playing, to become, to cry
④ playing, becoming, to cry
⑤ playing, to become, crying

20 대화의 흐름이 자연스럽도록 빈칸에 알맞은 말은?

> A: Dad, I don't like you buying me dolls any more.
> B: Oh! Why not?
> A: I am a teenager. I don't like _________ like a little kid any more.

① to treat
② treating
③ being treated
④ treated
⑤ having treated

21 대화의 흐름이 자연스럽도록 빈칸에 알맞은 말을 모두 고르면?

> A: Did you send your book report via e-mail? I didn't receive it yet.
> B: I'm sorry. ___________________.

① I forgot sending the e-mail.
② I forgot to send the e-mail.
③ I had trouble sending the e-mail.
④ I was very busy sending the e-mail.
⑤ I'm looking forward to sending the e-mail.

[22~23] 어법상 어색한 부분을 찾아 바르게 고쳐 쓰시오.

22 서술형

> 사서는 아이들이 도서관에서 떠들지 못하도록 했다.
> → The librarian kept children in making noise in the library.

___________ → ___________

23 서술형

> Mike는 아빠와 함께 주말에 낚시 가는 것을 매우 좋아한다.
> → Mike likes going to fish on weekends with his father.

________________ → ________________

24 ⓐ~ⓔ의 어법에 대한 설명 중 옳은 것은?

> Jenny is going to give a presentation about the environment tomorrow. She is planning ⓐ to talk about ways of ⓑ help the environment. She is interested in ⓒ saving the planet. She remembers ⓓ to watch a documentary about sea animals dying because of an oil spill the other day. She thinks that ⓔ to show the video clip in her presentation will be very helpful.

① ⓐ는 어법상 어색한 부분이 있다.
② ⓑ는 to help로 바꾸어야 한다.
③ ⓒ는 save로 바꾸어 써야 한다.
④ ⓓ는 어법상 어색한 부분이 없다.
⑤ ⓔ는 showing으로도 쓸 수 있다.

25 서술형

괄호 안의 말을 활용하여 ⓐ를 영어로 옮길 때 빈칸에 알맞은 말을 쓰시오.

> A: You look upset. What's wrong?
> B: ⓐ 나는 매일 똑같은 교복을 입는 것이 싫증이 나.
> (get tired of, wear)

→ I am ________ ________ ________ ________ the same uniform every day.

[26~27] 다음을 읽고 물음에 답하시오.

> Jisu: ⓐ Thank you for inviting me to this concert. ⓑ I have been looking forward to see it for a long time!
> Minho: Really? I am happy to hear that.
> Jisu: ⓒ I spent almost an hour to buy tickets but I couldn't get any.
> Minho: I know. ⓓ I also had trouble getting tickets myself at first. These guys are really popular!
> Jisu: They really are! Can we go a little closer to the stage? ⓔ The tall guys in front of us keep block my sight.
> Minho: ⓕ It seems that there is no getting any closer to the stage because there are so many people.
> Jisu: Oh! What a pity!

신유형

26 위 대화문의 내용을 잘못 이해한 학생은?

① 민지: 민호가 지수를 콘서트에 데리고 갔구나.
② 수지: 지수는 오랫동안 이 콘서트를 기다려 왔어.
③ 찬호: 지수는 표를 구하려고 했지만 사지 못했어.
④ 희진: 지수의 자리에서 무대가 아주 잘 보여.
⑤ 진수: 사람들이 많아서 두 사람이 무대 쪽으로 더 가까이 가는 것은 불가능해.

최다빈출

27 위 글의 ⓐ~ⓕ 중 어법상 틀린 문장을 모두 고르면?

① ⓐ, ⓒ, ⓔ
② ⓑ, ⓓ, ⓕ
③ ⓐ, ⓓ, ⓔ
④ ⓑ, ⓔ, ⓕ
⑤ ⓑ, ⓒ, ⓔ

28 어법상 옳은 문장을 모두 고르면?

ⓐ John will finish building a robot soon.
ⓑ He never gave up to look for his lost dog.
ⓒ His not obeying the rules can get him into trouble.
ⓓ Please stop to talk as the movie is going to start now.
ⓔ They have been practicing singing for more than a month.
ⓕ Jerry was ashamed of he making a mistake in the competition.

① 1개 ② 2개 ③ 3개 ④ 4개 ⑤ 5개

29 서술형

우리말과 일치하도록 괄호 안의 말을 바르게 배열하여 문장을 완성하시오. (단, 필요하면 주어진 단어의 형태를 변화시킬 것)

자신이 어떻게 보이는지에 신경을 쓰는 것이 학생들에게 너무 큰 관심거리가 되어서는 안 된다.
(care, about, look, how, they)

→ ________ ________ ________ ________ ________ should not be a big interest for children.

30 서술형

다음 글의 ⓐ~ⓔ 중 어법상 올바르면 O표, 틀리면 바르게 고쳐 쓰시오.

Do you like to watch movies? Then how about ⓐ becoming movie reviewers? You can enjoy ⓑ watch many movies and still earn money for a living! Their job is ⓒ watching movies and writing reviews about them. Then people who feel like ⓓ to see a movie will read their reviews and decide to watch it or not. It will take a lot of effort, but isn't it worth ⓔ to try?

(1) ⓐ becoming → ________
(2) ⓑ watch → ________
(3) ⓒ watching → ________
(4) ⓓ to see → ________
(5) ⓔ to try → ________

실력 탄탄!
서술형 심화

1 수진이가 작성한 다음 메모의 내용과 일치하도록 빈칸에 알맞은 말을 쓰시오.

	해야 할 일	실행 여부
(1)	arrange books on the bookshelf	X
(2)	help little brother with his homework	O
(3)	play badminton with her friend	X

(1) Sujin forgot ________ ________ books on the bookshelf.
(2) Sujin spent some time ________ her little brother with his homework.
(3) The cold weather stopped Sujin ________ ________ badminton with her friend.

2 그림을 보고 괄호 안의 말을 활용하여, 수업 시간의 규칙에 관한 문장을 완성하시오.

(1)

(raise your hand)

(2)

(use a cell phone)

(3)

(talk with your friends)

Class Rules
1. Please remember ________ ________ ________ ________ if you have a question.
2. ________ ________ ________ ________ is not allowed.
3. Avoid ________ ________ ________ ________.

3 Correct the underlined words.

Jane is the eldest daughter of five children in her family, so she is used to ⓐ take care of children. When her little sisters and brothers were very young, she used to ⓑ feeding them milk when they kept ⓒ to cry. Also, she never avoids ⓓ to help her mother with house chores. She always tries ⓔ helping her mom when her mom is busy.

ⓐ → ________ ⓑ → ________ ⓒ → ________
ⓓ → ________ ⓔ → ________

CHAPTER 05

분사

분사

동사의 형태를 변화시켜 형용사처럼 쓰는 것을 분사라고 한다. 또한 진행형, 수동태, 완료형 문장을 만들 때에도 분사를 쓴다. 분사에는 현재분사와 과거분사가 있는데, 현재분사는 「동사원형-ing」 형태로 능동, 진행의 의미를 나타내고, 과거분사는 대개 「동사원형-ed」의 형태로 수동, 완료의 의미를 나타낸다.

• **현재분사 *vs.* 과거분사**

	현재분사	과거분사
형태	동사원형-ing	동사원형-(e)d 또는 불규칙한 형태
의미	능동(~하는), 진행(~하고 있는)	수동(~된), 완료(~한)
예문	We heard the **surprising** news last night. They're **playing** soccer in the rain.	We were **surprised** by the news. We've **known** her since high school.

Point 01 분사의 종류: 현재분사 *vs.* 과거분사

- **분사**에는 현재분사와 과거분사가 있다.
- **현재분사**: **'동사원형-ing'**의 형태로 **능동(~하는)**과 **진행(~하고 있는)**의 뜻을 나타낸다.
  능동의 의미로 명사를 수식하거나, 또는 진행형 문장을 만들 때 쓴다.
  The singing boy is my younger brother. 노래하고 있는 그 소년이 나의 남동생이다. (명사 수식)
  They are looking at the posters on the wall. 그들은 벽에 붙은 포스터를 보고 있다. (진행)
- **과거분사**: 대개 **'동사원형-ed'**의 형태로 **수동 (~된, ~당한)**과 **완료 (~한, ~해 온)**의 뜻을 나타낸다.
  수동의 의미로 명사를 수식하거나, 수동태 또는 완료형 문장을 만들 때 쓴다.
  We found the broken window. 우리는 깨진 창문을 발견했다. (명사 수식)
  His book will be published next year. 그의 책은 내년에 출간될 것이다. (수동태)
  I have already seen those movies many times. 나는 그 영화들을 이미 여러 번 보았다. (완료)

A

괄호 안에서 알맞은 말을 고르시오.

1 The price of gold is (rising, risen) these days.
2 Our lives are (filling, filled) with a lot of things to do.
3 The watches (making, made) in Switzerland are popular.
4 This program is being (using, used) in many businesses.
5 They have been (playing, played) games for two hours.
6 The magazine is (publishing, published) in fifteen countries.
7 She is going to be (sentencing, sentenced) in the court today.
8 The children got an e-mail (writing, written) in English.
9 Be careful not to wake up the (sleeping, slept) dog.
10 Our house is (surrounding, surrounded) by beautiful mountains.
11 We have been (waiting, waited) here for almost an hour.
12 The old lady was (shocking, shocked) at the scene before her eyes.

B

밑줄 친 부분이 어법에 맞으면 O표, 틀리면 바르게 고쳐 쓰시오.

1 I think my wallet was stealing. → ____________
2 The dishes were broken by Tom. → ____________
3 Her parents were pleasing with the result. → ____________
4 Look at the beautiful girl written a letter. → ____________
5 I am reading a comic book write in English. → ____________
6 I know the girl sitting on the bench over there. → ____________

Point 02 분사의 역할

- **형용사처럼, 명사를 수식 (한정적 용법)**: 분사 한 단어가 명사를 수식할 때에는 명사의 앞에서, 분사가 다른 단어와 함께 쓰여 명사를 수식할 때에는 명사의 뒤에서 꾸며준다.
  I heard the surprising news about him. 나는 그에 대한 놀라운 소식을 들었다. (명사 앞에서 수식)
  I received an e-mail written in English. 나는 영어로 쓰인 이메일을 받았다. (명사 뒤에서 수식)
- **형용사처럼, 보어 역할 (서술적 용법)**: 분사가 주어나 목적어를 보충 설명해 주는 보어 역할을 할 수 있다.
  She looked excited when she heard the news. 그녀는 소식을 들었을 때 신이 나 보였다. (주격 보어)
  I found the book very interesting. 나는 그 책이 매우 재미있다는 것을 알았다. (목적격 보어)
- 진행형이나 완료형, 수동태 문장을 만들 때 분사를 쓴다. ☞ Point 1 (p. 92) 예문 참고

A 우리말과 뜻이 같도록 괄호 안에서 알맞은 말을 고르시오.

1 Lucy는 누군가 그녀를 바라보고 있는 것을 느꼈다.
→ Lucy felt someone (looking, looked) at her.

2 아버지께서는 새 차보다 중고차를 선호하신다.
→ My father prefers a (used, using) car to a new car.

3 나는 할머니께서 뜨개질 하시는 것을 여러 번 보았다.
→ I saw my grandmother (knitting, knitted) many times.

4 그는 파리에서 찍은 사진들을 내게 보여주었다.
→ He showed me some photos (taking, taken) in Paris.

5 그 시계는 스위스에서 생산되었다.
→ The watch was (produced, producing) in Switzerland.

6 그 사람은 매우 작은 소리로 이야기하고 있었다.
→ The man was (speaking, spoken) in a small voice.

7 그 제품들은 전 세계 100여 개 국에서 팔린다.
→ The products are (selling, sold) in over one hundred countries in the world.

B 우리말과 뜻이 같도록 괄호 안의 말을 바르게 배열하여 문장을 완성하시오.

1 나는 이 작가에 의해 집필된 공상 과학 소설들을 좋아한다. (novels, this, written, author, by)
→ I like the science fiction ______________________________.

2 너는 우리 선생님으로부터 그 놀라운 소식을 들었니? (shocking, from, the, our, teacher, news)
→ Did you hear ______________________________?

3 그 레스토랑은 항상 많은 방문객들로 붐빈다. (always, with, crowded, visitors, many)
→ The restaurant is ______________________________.

Point 03 감정을 나타내는 분사

■ 분사가 직접 수식하거나 보충 설명하는 명사가 감정을 유발하는 원인일 경우에는 **현재분사(동사원형-ing)**를 쓰고, 감정을 느끼는 주체일 경우에는 **과거분사(동사원형-ed)**를 쓴다.

현재분사 (~한 감정을 느끼게 하는)	과거분사 (~한 감정을 느끼게 되는)
amazing 놀라운	amazed 놀란
confusing 혼란스럽게 하는	confused 혼란스러운
depressing 우울하게 하는	depressed 우울한
fascinating 매혹적인	fascinated 매료된
frightening 깜짝 놀라게 하는	frightened 깜짝 놀란
disappointing 실망시키는	disappointed 실망한
moving 감동적인	moved 감동한
satisfying 만족스러운	satisfied 만족해하는

His speech for the graduates was amazing. 졸업생들을 위한 그의 강연은 놀라웠다. (현재분사)
Many graduates were amazed by his speech. 많은 졸업생들은 그의 강연에 놀랐다. (과거분사)

A

〈보기〉와 같이 문장을 다시 쓸 때 빈칸에 알맞은 분사를 쓰시오.

보기
The result disappointed many people.
→ The result was disappointing.
→ Many people were disappointed.

1 The story about the old man moved all of us.
→ The story about the old man was ____________.
→ All of us were ____________ by the story about the old man.

2 The teacher's directions confused me.
→ The teacher's directions were ____________.
→ I was ____________ by the teacher's directions.

3 The soccer match excited all the audience.
→ All the audience was ____________ about the soccer match.
→ The soccer match was ____________ to all the audience.

B

괄호 안의 말을 빈칸에 알맞은 형태로 쓰시오.

1 I think she has a ____________ voice. (fascinate)
2 She was ____________ and not sure what to do. (confuse)
3 People were ____________ by the beautiful story. (touch)
4 Most of the audience were ____________ with the play. (bore)
5 I have to tell you some ____________ news. (disappoint)
6 Everyone in the room was ____________ by the loud noise. (frighten)

Point 04 분사구문을 만드는 법

- **분사구문이란**: 분사를 이용하여 부사절(「접속사 + 주어 + 동사」)을 부사구로 줄여 쓴 구문을 말한다.
- **분사구문을 만드는 법**

① 부사절의 접속사를 생략한다. (뜻을 명확하게 강조하고 싶을 경우, 남겨 둘 수도 있다.)
② 주절의 주어와 부사절의 주어가 같으면 부사절의 주어를 생략하고, 다르면 남긴다.
③ 부사절의 동사를 현재분사 형태로 바꾼다.

~~As~~ ~~she~~ was exhausted, Julie decided to go home early.
① ② ③

→ (Being) exhausted, Julie decided to go home early. Julie는 기진맥진해서 집에 일찍 가기로 결정했다.

※ 단, 부사절의 시제가 주절의 시제보다 이전인 경우, 부사절의 동사를 「having + p.p.」 형태로 쓴다.
After he had finished his homework, he went to bed.
→ Having finished his homework, he went to bed. 숙제를 마친 후에, 그는 잠자리에 들었다.

※ 분사구문이 Being 또는 Having been으로 시작할 경우, Being 또는 Having been은 생략 가능하다.

※ 분사구문의 부정: 분사 앞에 not이나 never를 쓴다. (☞ p. 98의 Point 7 참고)

A

문장의 뜻이 같도록 분사구문을 사용해 문장을 다시 쓸 때, 빈칸에 알맞은 말을 쓰시오.

1 When you spend money, you have to think twice.
→ When ______________________________, you have to think twice.

2 Because Sally studied hard, she got a scholarship.
→ ______________________________, Sally got a scholarship.

3 As I felt so tired, I didn't go swimming.
→ ______________________________, I didn't go swimming.

4 Since it is not written clearly, the manual is hard to understand.
→ ______________________________, the manual is hard to understand.

5 While he was waiting for the bus, Tim ran into his friend.
→ ______________________________, Tim ran into his friend.

B

두 문장의 뜻이 같도록 빈칸에 알맞은 말을 〈보기〉에서 골라 쓰시오.

보기		
because	because of	after

1 Having had nothing to eat, he decided to cook himself dinner.
→ __________ he had had nothing to eat, he decided to cook himself dinner.

2 Graduating from school, I got a job in this company.
→ __________ I graduated from school, I got a job in this company.

Point 05 분사구문의 의미 – 부대상황, 시간, 이유/원인

- **동시 동작, 연속상황을 나타내는 분사구문**: while, as (~하면서) / 등위접속사 and로 연결할 때도 있다.
  Smiling beautifully, she hugged her baby tightly.
  아름답게 웃으면서, 그녀는 그녀의 아기를 꼬옥 껴안았다.
  (= While she smiled beautifully, she hugged her baby tightly.)
  Raising his hand, the boy stood up. 그 소년은 손을 들며 일어났다.
  (= The boy raised his hand and stood up.)
- **시간을 나타내는 분사구문**: when(~할 때), while(~하는 동안에), after(~한 후에), before(~하기 전에) 등
  Looking at the calendar, he realized it was his mom's birthday.
  달력을 보았을 때, 그는 엄마의 생신인걸 깨달았다.
  (= When he looked at the calendar, he realized it was his mom's birthday.)
- **이유/원인을 나타내는 분사구문**: as, because, since(~하기 때문에)
  Wanting to stay alone, she didn't make an appointment with her friend.
  혼자 있고 싶었기 때문에, 그녀는 그녀의 친구와 약속을 만들지 않았다.
  (= Because she wanted to stay alone, she didn't make an appointment with her friend.)
- '조건(~라면)'이나 '양보(비록 ~일지라도)'의 부사절은 분사구문으로는 거의 바꿔쓰지 않는다.
  Though we live near my grandparents' house, we don't visit them often.
  → Despite living near my grandparents' house, we don't visit them often.
  우리가 조부모님 댁 근처에 살고 있지만, 우리는 그들을 자주 방문하지 않는다.

A 문장의 뜻이 같도록 분사구문을 사용해 문장을 다시 쓸 때, 빈칸에 알맞은 말을 쓰시오.

1 When I visited France, I met my friend Hannah.
→ ______________________, I met my friend Hannah.

2 Because she was sad, she didn't want to meet anyone.
→ ______________________, she didn't want to meet anyone.

3 While I wash the dishes, I always listen to English radio.
→ ______________________, I always listen to English radio.

B 괄호 안의 말을 바르게 배열하여 분사구문이 들어간 문장을 완성하시오.

1 길을 건너면서, 그녀는 그 우체국을 알아차렸다. (crossing, she, the street, post office, noticed, the)
→ ______________________________________.

2 할 일이 많았기 때문에 그는 휴식을 가질 수 없었다. (many, things, to, having, do, he, couldn't)
→ ______________________________ take a break.

3 그 소식을 들었을 때 그는 창백해졌다. (hearing, news, the, he, pale, grew)
→ ______________________________________.

Point 06 분사구문의 시제와 태 – 완료 분사구문, 수동 분사구문

- **완료 분사구문**: 부사절의 시제가 주절의 시제보다 이전인 경우, 「having + 과거분사(p.p.)」의 형태로 분사구문을 만든다.
  As he had read the book before, he didn't want to read it again.
  → Having read the book before, he didn't want to read it again.
  그는 전에 그 책을 읽은 적이 있었기 때문에, 그 책을 다시 읽기를 원하지 않았다.
  Since she lived in England when she was young, her English is good.
  → Having lived in England when she was young, her English is good.
  어릴 때 영국에 살았기 때문에 그녀의 영어는 유창하다.

- **수동 분사구문**: 「Being + 과거분사(p.p.)」와 「Having been + 과거분사(p.p.)」에서 being 또는 having been은 생략하고 과거분사(p.p.)만 남겨둘 수 있다.
  (Being) Elected as the school president, he was very happy.
  학교 회장으로 선출되어서 그는 매우 기뻤다.
  (Having been) Repaired by my Dad, the car worked well.
  나의 아버지에 의해 수리되고 나서, 그 차는 잘 작동했다.

- 분사구문이 Being 또는 Having been으로 시작할 경우, 이를 생략 가능하다.
  (Being) A good leader, she knows how to persuade people.
  좋은 리더이기 때문에, 그녀는 사람들을 어떻게 설득하는지를 안다.
  (Having been) Careful not to make a mistake, he played the song perfectly.
  실수하지 않으려고 주의해왔기 때문에 그는 그 노래를 완벽하게 연주했다.

A

밑줄 친 부분을 분사구문으로 바꿔 쓰시오.

1 Since she had spent all her money, she couldn't buy new clothes.
→ ______________________________, she couldn't buy new clothes.

2 Because he had been impressed by her music, he became her fan.
→ ______________________________, he became her fan.

3 As he had got a good score on the test, Tim could enter a good university.
→ ______________________________, Tim could enter a good university.

4 After he had finished his work, John went out to meet his friends.
→ ______________________________, John went out to meet his friends.

B

우리말과 뜻이 같도록 빈칸에 생략된 being 또는 having been을 써 넣으시오.

1 그는 천재이기 때문에, 항상 만점을 받는다.
→ ______________________ a genius, he always gets a perfect score.

2 그녀는 프랑스에서 자랐기 때문에 프랑스어를 매우 잘할 수 있다.
→ ______________________ raised in France, she can speak French very well.

3 달변가이기 때문에 그의 연설에는 힘이 있다.
→ ______________________ a great speaker, his words have power.

Point 07 주의해야 할 분사구문 I – 분사구문의 부정, 독립분사구문

- **분사구문의 부정**: 분사 앞에 **not**이나 **never**를 쓴다.
  Not knowing what to do next, she asked for his help.
  (= As she didn't know what to do next, she asked for his help.)
  다음에 무엇을 할지 몰라서 그녀는 그의 도움을 요청했다.
  Not having read the magazine, I couldn't tell you about it.
  (= As I hadn't read the magazine, I couldn't tell you about it.)
  내가 그 잡지를 읽지 않았기 때문에, 그것에 대해 네게 이야기 해 줄 수 없었다.

- **「접속사 + 분사구문」**: 분사구문의 의미를 명확히 전달하기 위해 접속사를 남겨두기도 한다.
  After talking to her, I always feel better. 그녀와 이야기를 하고 나면, 나는 항상 기분이 나아진다.
  (= After I talk to her, I always feel better.)

- **주어가 있는 분사구문 (독립분사구문)**: 주절과 종속절의 주어가 서로 다른 경우, 분사구문에서 주어를 생략하지 않는다.
  It being a fine day, we decided to go on a picnic. 날씨가 좋아서 우리는 소풍을 가기로 했다.
  (= As it was a fine day, we decided to go on a picnic.)

A 밑줄 친 부분에서 어법상 틀린 부분을 한 군데 찾아 바르게 고쳐 쓰시오.

1 There being many people, we had to wait for an hour.
→ As there being many people, we had to wait for an hour.
_______________ → _______________

2 Not wanting to hurt his feelings, she didn't tell him the truth.
→ Since she wanted to hurt his feelings, she didn't tell him the truth.
_______________ → _______________

3 Not having seen each other for a few months, they missed each other.
→ Because they had seen each other for a few months, they missed each other.
_______________ → _______________

4 Not knowing how to solve the problem, I asked Mr. Kim for help.
→ Because I don't know how to solve the problem, I asked Mr. Kim for help.
_______________ → _______________

B 다음 문장과 같은 뜻이 되도록 분사구문을 이용하여 바꿔 쓰시오.

1 Because I didn't feel hungry, I skipped my lunch.
→ ______________________________, I skipped my lunch.

2 Because there was no bus so late at night, he had to take a taxi.
→ ______________________________, he had to take a taxi.

3 As he didn't finish the project, Jake can't go to the movies.
→ ______________________________, Jake can't go to the movies.

Point 08 주의해야 할 분사구문 II - 「with + 명사 + 분사」 구문, 비인칭 독립분사구문

■ **「with + 명사 + 분사」 구문**: '~을 한 채로'라는 뜻으로, 부대상황이나 동시 동작을 나타낸다.

with + 명사 + 현재분사	명사와 분사가 능동 관계	She smiled with tears running down her cheek. 그녀는 뺨에 눈물이 흘러내리는 채로 웃었다.
with + 명사 + 과거분사	명사와 분사가 수동 관계	He is standing with his arms folded. 그는 팔짱을 낀 채로 서 있다.

■ **숙어처럼 자주 쓰이는 분사구문**: 분사구문의 주어가 일반인일 때 주어를 굳이 밝히지 않고 생략한다. 이런 관용적인 표현들을, 문법 용어로 '비인칭 독립분사구문'이라 부른다.

Generally speaking 일반적으로 말해서 Frankly speaking 솔직히 말해서 Strictly speaking 엄밀히 말해서 Speaking of ~에 대해 말하자면	Considering ~을 고려하자면 Judging from ~로 판단하건대 Compared with ~와 비교해보면

Speaking of the holiday, have you made any plans yet? 휴가에 대해 말하니 말인데, 어떤 계획이라도 세웠니?
Considering his age, his writing skill is amazing. 그의 나이를 고려하건대, 그의 작문 실력은 대단하다.

A 두 문장의 뜻이 같도록 「with + 명사 + 분사」 구문을 활용하여 문장을 완성하시오.

1 She fell asleep, and the TV was turned on.
→ She fell asleep ________________________.

2 The man was listening to music, and his eyes were closed.
→ The man was listening to music ________________________.

3 The man is deep in thought, and his arms are folded.
→ The man is deep in thought ________________________.

4 He walked in the park, and his dog was following him.
→ He walked in the park ________________________.

5 Jenny explained the situation, and her finger pointed to the chart.
→ Jenny explained the situation ________________________.

B 우리말과 뜻이 같도록 괄호 안의 말을 활용하여 비인칭 독립분사구문을 완성하시오.

1 그의 억양으로 판단하건대 그는 영국 출신이다. (judge)
→ __________ __________ his accent, he is from England.

2 솔직히 말하자면, 나는 기분이 상했다. (frankly)
→ __________ __________, I felt upset.

3 그녀의 언니와 비교하자면 그녀는 매우 친절하다. (compare)
→ __________ __________ her sister, she is very nice.

4 일반적으로 말하면, 남자들은 여자들보다 강하다. (generally)
→ __________ __________, men are stronger than women.

일등 비법 노트

비법 1 감정을 일으키는 주체이면 현재분사! 감정을 받는 대상이면 과거분사!

대표기출 1 빈칸에 알맞은 말이 순서대로 바르게 나열된 것은?

- The lecture was ___________, so many people fell asleep.
- I didn't have any fun things to do, so I was ___________.

① bored, bored ② bore, boring
③ boring, bore ④ bored, boring
⑤ boring, bored

대표기출 2 다음 중 어법상 <u>틀린</u> 문장은?

① Look at the running boy.
② I was surprised by his smart answer.
③ Her shelves are filled with boring books.
④ The result was quite disappointing to us.
⑤ I feel somewhat depressing during rainy season.

비법 2 분사구문 만들기!
① 접속사 생략! ② 주어가 같으면 생략! ③ 동사원형-ing! ④ being은 생략 가능!

대표기출 1 밑줄 친 부분을 분사구문으로 바꿔 쓰시오.

(1) <u>When I entered the room</u>, I found some gifts on my desk.

→ ______________________, I found some gifts on my desk.

(2) <u>As she didn't remember her password</u>, she couldn't log in to her computer.

→ ______________________, she couldn't log in to her computer.

대표기출 2 밑줄 친 부분을 분사구문으로 바꿔 쓸 때, 빈칸에 알맞은 말은?

As we were surprised to hear the news, we all screamed for joy.
→ ____________ to hear the news, we all screamed for joy.

① Being surprising ② Having surprised
③ Surprised ④ Surprising
⑤ To be surprised

비법 3 부사절의 시제가 주절의 시제보다 이전인 경우에 「having + p.p.」임을 기억하라!

대표기출 1

밑줄 친 부분을 접속사 since가 포함된 절로 바꿔 쓰시오.

(1) Having read the book many times, I even memorized some of the lines.

→ ____________________, I even memorized some of the lines.

(2) Having finished her dinner, Molly is going to order her dessert.

→ ____________________, Molly is going to order her dessert.

대표기출 2

밑줄 친 부분에서 어법상 틀린 부분을 찾아 바르게 고쳐 쓰시오.

A: Why didn't you go to see the movie?
B: Seeing the movie already, I didn't want to watch it again.

____________________ → ____________________

비법 4 「with + 명사 + 분사」 구문에서 명사와 분사의 관계가 능동이면 현재분사, 수동이면 과거분사!

대표기출 1

괄호 안의 말을 바르게 배열하여 문장을 완성하시오. (필요하면 단어의 형태를 바꾸시오.)

(1) 한 노인이 그의 개가 그를 따라가는 채로 길을 걷고 있었다.
(with, follow, dog, his, him)

→ An old man was walking along the street ________ ________ ________ ________ ________.

(2) 그는 눈을 감은 채로 잠자코 서 있었다.
(with, eyes, close, his)

→ He stood silent ________ ________ ________ ________.

대표기출 2

우리말과 같도록 빈칸에 알맞은 말은?

그는 팔짱을 낀 채 문 앞에 서 있었다.
→ He was standing at the door ____________________.

① with his arms folding
② with his arms folded
③ with his arms to be folded
④ with his arms are folded
⑤ with his arms were folded

내신 만점! 실전 기출

[1~3] 빈칸에 알맞은 말이 순서대로 바르게 나열된 것은?

01

- Be careful of the ________ glass on the floor.
- Do you know the boy ________ next to Linda?

① break, sit
② broke, sat
③ broken, sitting
④ breaking, to sit
⑤ to break, is sitting

02

- Mr. Johnson sat ________ by his students and told them the stories.
- I saw a couple of cows ________ on the grass.

① surround, lie
② surrounding, lay
③ surrounded, lying
④ to surround, lying
⑤ to be surrounded, to lie

03 서술형

괄호 안의 말을 바르게 배열하여 문장을 완성하시오.

A: Where is your uncle?
B: He's over there. ________ is my uncle. (man, the, a wheelchair, riding)

→ ________________

____

04 서술형

밑줄 친 ⓐ를 어법에 맞게 바르게 고쳐 쓰시오.

A: Do you know that there are scissors ⓐ <u>making</u> for left-handed people?
B: Oh, really? I've never seen any. How different are they?

→ ________________

05 밑줄 친 부분이 어법에 맞지 <u>않는</u> 것은?

① Look at the girl <u>singing</u> on the stage.
② The boy <u>played</u> on the ground is John.
③ The poem <u>written</u> by Sue was very touching.
④ The people <u>invited</u> to the party didn't show up.
⑤ Movies <u>directed</u> by Christopher Nolan are always amazing.

[6~7] 밑줄 친 부분을 분사구문을 활용하여 바르게 바꿔 쓴 문장을 고르시오.

06

<u>As I knew it was my fault</u>, I sincerely apologized.

① Know my fault, I sincerely apologized.
② Known my fault, I sincerely apologized.
③ As my fault, I sincerely apologized.
④ Knowing it was my fault, I sincerely apologized.
⑤ Having known it was my fault, I sincerely apologized.

07

Because life is very short, we have to do what we like to do.

① Life is very short, we have to do what we like to do.
② Being very short, we have to do what we like to do.
③ Life being very short, we have to do what we like to do.
④ Because life very short, we have to do what we like to do.
⑤ Life having been very short, we have to do what we like to do.

08 서술형

다음을 한 문장으로 바꿔 쓸 때 빈칸에 알맞은 말을 쓰시오.

I saw a huge trailer. It was blocking the narrow road to my house.

→ I saw a huge trailer ______________________
______________________________________.

09 서술형

괄호 안의 단어를 활용하고 〈조건〉에 맞추어 영작하시오.

조건
1. very와 with를 이용할 것
2. I로 시작하는 완전한 영어 문장으로 쓸 것

나는 그 소식에 매우 실망했다. (disappoint)

→ ______________________________________
____

[10~11] 두 문장의 뜻이 같도록 빈칸에 알맞은 말을 고르시오.

10

As she listened to music, she forgot what caused her stress.
= __________ to music, she forgot what caused her stress.

① Listened ② Listening
③ Being listened ④ Having listened
⑤ Having been listened

11

As he was raised by his grandmother, he is very close to her.
= __________ raised by his grandmother, he is very close to her.

① Being ② Been
③ Having been ④ Was
⑤ He

최다빈출

[12~13] 어법에 맞지 않는 문장을 고르시오.

12

① My father loves to eat frozen yogurt.
② The songs performed last night were really nice.
③ The boy carried a box is our class president.
④ The mountain covered with snow was really beautiful.
⑤ I was very frightened to see a big dog on my way home.

13

① Not feeling well, he went straight back home.
② Exhausted, she fell asleep right after she came home.
③ Not being rich, she couldn't buy the watch.
④ Admitted what he did was wrong, he said he was sorry.
⑤ While waiting for my turn, I had a chat with other people.

고난도

14 다음을 분사구문이 포함된 문장으로 바르게 바꿔 쓴 것을 모두 고르면?

> Because I was born and raised in a cold city, I am used to the cold.

① Being born and raised in a cold city, I am used to the cold.
② Born and raised in a cold city, I am used to the cold.
③ Was born and raised in a cold city, I am used to the cold.
④ Having been born and raised in a cold city, I am used to the cold.
⑤ Because being born and raised in a cold city, I am used to the cold.

15 빈칸 ⓐ, ⓑ에 알맞은 말이 순서대로 바르게 나열된 것은?

> 딸은 큰 가방을 들고 있는 아빠를 따라 밖으로 나왔다.
> → The daughter went out, ⓐ __________ her dad ⓑ __________ a big bag.

① follow, carry ② following, carrying
③ following, carried ④ followed, carrying
⑤ followed, carried

[16~17] 다음을 분사구문이 포함된 문장으로 바꿔 쓸 때 빈칸에 알맞은 말을 쓰시오.

16 서술형

> While I was walking along the street, I ran into my friend.

→ ______________________________,
I ran into my friend.

17 서술형

> Because I had not brought my wallet, I didn't have money to buy lunch.

→ ______________________________,
I didn't have money to buy lunch.

18 빈칸에 공통으로 알맞은 말은?

> • He was sitting under the tree __________ his cat sleeping near him.
> • I don't think it's good to study __________ the music turned on.
> • The boy was standing __________ his back leaning against the wall.

① on ② at ③ for
④ with ⑤ by

19 서술형

밑줄 친 부분을 괄호 안의 단어를 활용하여 절로 바꿔 쓰시오.

> She having many friends, her school life is not lonely anymore. (Because)

→ ______________________________,
her school life is not lonely anymore.

20 서술형

두 문장의 뜻이 같도록 분사구문을 활용하여 문장을 완성하시오.

> Because I didn't know how to solve the problem, I asked my sister for help.

→ ______________________________,
I asked my sister for help.

21 서술형

괄호 안의 말을 활용하여, 밑줄 친 부분을 부사절로 다시 쓰시오.

> Being sick, she had to stay at home all day. (since)

→ ______________________________,
she had to stay at home all day.

신유형

22 다음을 분사구문이 포함된 문장으로 만들 때, 어법상 틀린 부분을 찾아 바르게 고친 사람은?

> Because Junsu had lost his wallet, we had to buy him lunch.
> → ⓐ Because ⓑ Junsu ⓒ having been lost his wallet, ⓓ we had to buy him lunch.

① 민호: ⓐ Because를 꼭 생략해야 해.
② 지나: ⓑ Junsu를 생략해야 해.
③ 수지: ⓒ having been lost를 losing으로 바꿔야 해.
④ 예나: ⓒ having been lost를 having lost로 바꿔야 해.
⑤ 준호: ⓓ we를 he로 바꿔야 해.

23 밑줄 친 동사를 어법에 맞는 형태로 바꿔 순서대로 나열한 것은?

> A: Jenny, what do you like to do to relax?
> B: Well, I like to listen to music with my eyes close. It is really relax. How about you?
> A: I like to take a bath. It helps me to relieve my stress.

① closing, relax　② closing, relaxing
③ closed, relaxing　④ closed, relaxed
⑤ close, relaxed

24 다음 문장의 분사구문을 부사절로 바꿀 때 빈칸에 알맞은 말을 모두 고르면?

> Being good at speaking English, he could make foreign friends easily.
> → ______________________________,
> he could make foreign friends easily.

① Though he was good at speaking English
② Because he was good at speaking English
③ Although he was good at speaking English
④ Since he was good at speaking English
⑤ Unless he was good at speaking English

25 빈칸 ⓐ, ⓑ에 알맞은 말이 순서대로 바르게 나열된 것은?

> A: Hey. What's bothering you?
> B: I am reading an email ⓐ ________ in English. But I can't understand it perfectly. Some of the words are very ⓑ ________.
> A: Let me have a look. I think I can help you.

① writing, confusing　② writing, confused
③ written, confusing　④ written, confused
⑤ written, confuse

26 밑줄 친 부분을 부사절로 바꿔 쓸 때 빈칸에 알맞은 말은?

> Not having met for ages, we had many things to catch up on.
> → As we ________ for ages, we had many things to catch up on.

① didn't meet ② didn't have met
③ have not met ④ had not met
⑤ couldn't meet

27 밑줄 친 부분이 어법상 틀린 것은?

① He left the room with the radio turned on.
② I was lying on my back with my knees bending.
③ The man was sitting on a sofa with his legs crossed.
④ She told the story with tears rolling down her face.
⑤ Kevin was reading a newspaper with his wife knitting a sweater.

고난도

28 서술형

다음 ⓐ~ⓑ 중에서 어법상 어색한 부분을 한 군데 찾아 바르게 고쳐 쓰시오. (단, 분사구문을 유지/활용할 것)

> ⓐ Surrounded by the sea, my hometown has many beautiful beaches.
> ⓑ There was no one around me, I couldn't ask for help.

→ 기호: ________

____

____

고난도

29 다음 ⓐ~ⓒ에 알맞은 말이 순서대로 바르게 짝지어진 것은?

> Last weekend, my friends and I visited a local hospital to do some volunteer work. In the hospital, I saw a little girl helping patients and ⓐ (smiling, smiled) beautifully to everyone. She looked like a volunteer like us. Soon, we became friends and I heard the ⓑ (surprising, surprised) news about her. She said she used to suffer from cancer and decided to help patients regularly after she had recovered. I was deeply ⓒ (impressed, impressing) with her story.

	ⓐ		ⓑ		ⓒ
①	smiled	—	surprising	—	impressing
②	smiling	—	surprised	—	impressing
③	smiled	—	surprising	—	impressed
④	smiling	—	surprised	—	impressed
⑤	smiling	—	surprising	—	impressed

30 서술형

〈보기〉와 같이, 우리말과 일치하도록 괄호 안의 말과 「with + 명사 + 분사」 구문을 활용하여 문장을 완성하시오.

> 보기
> 그는 불을 켜놓은 채 자고 있었다. (with, turn, on, light)
> → He was sleeping with the light turned on.

그 소녀는 칠판에 눈을 고정시킨 채 수업을 듣고 있었다.
(with, fix, on the board, her eyes)
→ The girl was listening to the lecture ________
________________________________.

실력 탄탄!
서술형 심화

1 그림을 보고 〈보기〉에서 의미상 알맞은 문장을 골라 (1)~(3)에 분사구문이 들어간 문장을 완성하시오.

(1) 

(2) 

(3) 

보기

ⓐ He waved his hand to his friends.
ⓑ I got first prize in the contest.
ⓒ She was holding her baby in her arms.

(1) ______________________________, I was so proud of myself.
(2) Terry got on the train, ______________________________.
(3) ______________________________, Tiffany looked very happy.

2 다음은 Tim, Jenny, John 세 사람이 각자 어제와 오늘 일을 적은 표이다. 표의 내용과 일치하도록 〈보기〉와 같이 분사구문이 포함된 문장을 완성하시오.

	Yesterday	Today
Tim	I finished the English report.	I can hand it in.
Jenny	I lost my luggage.	I have no clothes to wear.
John	I spent all my money.	I can't buy anything.

보기

Tim: Having finished the English report, I can hand it in.

(1) Jenny: ______________________________
(2) John: ______________________________

3 다음은 Sally가 쓴 일기의 일부이다. 밑줄 친 (A)~(E) 중 틀린 곳을 두 군데 찾아 바르게 고쳐 쓰시오.

April 5th

Having done my homework, I was (A) bored. I was tired of studying inside. (B) Being a fine day, I decided to go to the park.

(C) While walking in the park, I ran into Jane. She had been traveling in Europe. (D) Not seen each other for a couple of weeks, we sat on a bench (E) chatting for a long time. She told me some stories about her trip. It sounded so interesting. Now, I really want to go there, too.

__________ → __________   __________ → __________

CHAPTER 06

수동태

수동태

주어와 동사가 어떤 관계인지 나타내는 형식을 태(voice)라고 하고, 능동태와 수동태, 두 가지가 있다. 주어가 동작을 스스로 행하는 경우에는 **능동태**로 표현하고, 주어가 행동을 받거나 당하는 상황이면 **수동태**로 표현한다. 수동태는 기본적으로 「be동사 + 과거분사(p.p.)」로 쓰고, 형식과 시제에 따라 조금씩 달리 표현한다.

• **수동태를 쓰는 경우**

1. 동작을 행한 주체가 누구인지 불분명하거나 굳이 밝힐 필요가 없을 때
   - My cell phone **was stolen** yesterday. (누가 훔쳐갔는지 모름)
   - Rome **was not built** in a day (by people). (by people이 생략됨)
2. 동작을 행한 주체보다 동작을 받는 대상을 더 강조하고 싶을 때
   - My cell phone **was found** in a waste basket. (누가 발견했느냐보다는, 핸드폰이 발견된 것을 강조)

• 수동태의 여러 형태

수동태 문장의 기본 형태	주어 + be동사 + 과거분사(p.p.) + (by + 행위자) David **is loved** by everybody.
조동사가 있는 경우	주어 + 조동사 + be동사 + 과거분사(p.p.) + (by + 행위자) The problem **can be solved** (by us).
진행형	주어 + be동사 + being + 과거분사(p.p.) + (by + 행위자) The birthday cake **is being baked** by my mom.
완료형	주어 + have[has, had] been + 과거분사(p.p.) + (by + 행위자) His cellphone **has been found** (by him) in the library.
목적어로 쓰인 that절의 수동태	It + be동사 + 과거분사(p.p.) + that절 ~. **It is said that** honesty is the best policy. (= Honesty **is said to be** the best policy.)

Point 01 수동태의 의미와 형태

- **능동태 *vs.* 수동태**: 누가 행동을 했는지 **행위자에 초점을 둘 경우**에는 **능동태**로 표현하고, 누가 행위를 받거나 당했는지 **행위의 대상에 초점을 둘 경우**에는 **수동태**로 표현한다.
  Many people around the world admire him. 전 세계의 많은 사람들이 그를 존경한다. (능동태)
  He is admired by many people around the world. 그는 전 세계의 많은 사람들에 의해 존경 받는다. (수동태)
- **수동태 문장의 기본 형태**: 「주어 + be동사 + 과거분사(p.p.) + (by + 행위자)」의 형태로 나타낸다.
  행위자가 일반적인 사람이거나 불분명한 경우, **'by + 행위자'**는 생략한다.
  English is spoken in Canada (by people). 영어가 캐나다에서 (사람들에 의해) 말하여진다.
- **수동태의 부정문은 「주어 + be동사 + not + 과거분사(p.p.)」**로, **수동태의 의문문은 「의문사 + be동사 + 주어 + 과거분사 ~?」**의 형태로 나타낸다.
  The window was not broken by us. 그 창문은 우리에 의해 깨지지 않았다.
  How much money is needed to pay it off? 그것을 지불하기 위해서는 얼마가 필요한가요?
- **목적어를 갖지 않는 자동사**(appear, disappear, happen, occur, become 등), **소유를 나타내는 동사**(have, belong to), **상태를 나타내는 동사**(resemble) 등은 **수동태로 나타낼 수 없다.**

A 괄호 안에서 알맞은 말을 고르시오.

1 His new movie was (released, releasing) yesterday.
2 People say Jenny (resembles, is resembled) her father.
3 Do you know what (happened, was happened) here?
4 Who is going to (prepare, be prepared) for the event?
5 The kids (built, were built) a sand castle on the beach.
6 More than 100 people (injured, were injured) in the accident.
7 She was (preparing, prepared) a surprise party for her mom.
8. His novels (loves, are loved) by many people around the world.

B 다음을 수동태 문장으로 바꿀 때, 빈칸에 알맞은 말을 쓰시오.

1 People criticized him for his bad manners.
→ He __________ __________ for his bad manners.

2 The bad weather delayed the flight.
→ The flight __________ __________ by the bad weather.

3 A famous artist painted his portrait.
→ His portrait __________ __________ __________ a famous artist.

4 Mr. Jones's team developed a new business.
→ A new business __________ __________ __________ Mr. Jones's team.

5 Her beautiful voice attracts everyone in the class.
→ Everyone in the class __________ __________ __________ her beautiful voice.

Point 02 조동사가 있는 문장의 수동태

- **조동사가 포함된 문장의 수동태는 「조동사 + be + 과거분사(p.p.)」의 형태로 쓴다.**

We will keep the secret forever. 우리는 평생 그 비밀을 지킬 것이다.

The secret will be kept by us forever. 그 비밀은 우리에 의해 평생 지켜질 것이다.

- **부정문**은 조동사 다음에 not을 붙여 **「조동사 + not + be + 과거분사(p.p.)」**로 나타낸다.

You must not park bicycles here. 당신은 여기에 자전거를 주차해서는 안됩니다.

Bicycles must not be parked here (by you). 자전거는 여기 주차되어서는 안됩니다.

A 우리말과 뜻이 같도록 괄호 안의 말을 활용하여 문장을 완성하시오.

1 그 어려운 문제는 그에 의해 해결될 수 있다. (can, solve)

→ The difficult question ________ ________ ________ by him.

2 오늘 밤에 어떤 영화가 상영되나요? (will, show)

→ What movie ________ ________ ________ tonight?

3 그 책들은 다음 주까지 반납되어야 한다. (must, return)

→ The books ________ ________ ________ by next week.

4 그 빵은 내일까지 먹어야 한다. (should, eat)

→ The bread ________ ________ ________ by tomorrow.

5 그 비밀은 반드시 지켜져야 한다. (must, keep)

→ The secret ________ ________ ________.

6 아이들은 독립심을 갖도록 가르침 받아야 한다. (have to, teach)

→ Children ________ ________ ________ ________ to be independent.

B 수동태는 능동태로, 능동태는 수동태 문장으로 바꿔 쓰시오.

1 We can finish the work by the end of this month.

→ ________________________ by the end of this month.

2 Everyone should show a ticket at the door.

→ ________________________ at the door.

3 These products will be loved by consumers.

→ ________________________.

4 Free lunch will be provided by the city government.

→ ________________________.

Point 03 구동사가 있는 문장의 수동태

■ **구동사란?** 동사에 부사나 전치사가 이어져 두 개 이상의 단어가 하나의 동사 역할을 하는 것을 구동사라고 한다.

※ 자주 쓰는 구동사 표현

bring up	~를 기르다	look after / take care of	~을 돌보다
call off	~을 취소하다	look down on	~를 얕보다
carry out	~을 수행하다	make fun of	~을 놀리다
deal with	~을 다루다	pay for	~을 지불하다
give up	~을 포기하다	put off	~를 연기하다
hand in	~을 제출하다	put on	~을 입다
laugh at	~을 비웃다	turn down	~(소리를) 낮추다/거절하다

■ **구동사가 있는 능동태 문장을 수동태로 전환할 경우**: 이 구동사를 한 덩어리로 취급한다. 즉, 동사는 「be동사 + p.p.」로 바꾸고 전치사나 부사는 그대로 쓴다.

Mr. Kim's team will carry out the survey. Mr. Kim의 팀이 그 설문 조사를 수행할 것이다.

→ The survey will be carried out by Mr. Kim's team.

그 설문조사는 Mr. Kim의 팀에 의해 수행될 것이다.

His grandparents brought up John. 그의 조부모님이 John을 기르셨다.

→ John was brought up by his grandparents. John은 그의 조부모님에 의해 길러졌다.

A 밑줄 친 부분에 유의하여 각 문장을 수동태로 바꿔 쓰시오.

1 The teacher <u>called off</u> the school trip.

→ ______________________________.

2 They <u>take care of</u> their baby.

→ ______________________________.

3 Sally <u>gave up</u> the good opportunity.

→ ______________________________.

4 Many people in his country <u>look up to</u> him.

→ ______________________________.

5 They should not <u>look down on</u> the weak.

→ ______________________________.

B 우리말과 일치하도록 괄호 안의 말을 바르게 배열하여 문장을 완성하시오.

1 그 문제는 그녀에 의해 다뤄졌다. (her, the problem, dealt, by, with, was)

→ ______________________________

2 아이들은 부모님의 보살핌을 받아야 한다. (kids, should, looked, after, be, their, by, parents)

→ ______________________________

Point 04 진행형의 수동태

- 진행형의 수동태는 「**be + being + 과거분사(p.p.) + (by + 행위자)**」로 나타내며, 부정문은 be동사 뒤에 not을 붙인다.

Mom **is preparing** the food in the kitchen. 어머니께서는 부엌에서 음식을 준비하고 계신다.
→ The food **is being prepared** by mom in the kitchen. 음식은 부엌에서 어머니에 의해 준비 되고 있다.
The kids **were drawing** funny pictures on the wall. 그 아이들은 벽에 재미난 그림들을 그리고 있었다.
→ Funny pictures **were being drawn** on the wall by the kids.
재미난 그림들이 아이들에 의해 벽에 그려지고 있었다.
They **are not cleaning** the room now. 그들은 지금 방을 치우고 있지 않다.
→ The room **is not being cleaned** by them now. 그 방은 그들에 의해 치워지지 않고 있다.

A

괄호 안에서 알맞은 말을 고르시오.

1 The trees (are cutting, are being cut) now.
2 The car (is not being, is being not) fixed by dad.
3 The worker is (cleaning, being cleaned) the window.
4 The wall (was painting, was being painted) by the children.
5 The building was (destroying, being destroyed) by the workers.

B

우리말과 뜻이 같도록 괄호 안의 말을 활용하여 문장을 완성하시오.

1 점심은 Jane에 의해 준비되는 중이다. (prepare)
→ Lunch ______________ ______________ ______________ by Jane.

2 그 야구 경기가 지금 진행되는 중이다. (play)
→ The baseball game ______________ ______________ ______________ now.

3 그 다리는 그 때 칠해지는 중이었다. (paint)
→ The bridge ______________ ______________ ______________ at that time.

C

다음을 수동태 문장으로 바꿔 쓰시오.

1 She was baking the bread when I walked into the kitchen.
→ ______________________________ when I walked into the kitchen.

2 They are using plants to decorate the building.
→ ______________________________ to decorate the building.

3 She was watering the plant in the garden.
→ ____.

Point 05 완료형의 수동태

■ **완료형의 수동태: 현재완료는 「have/has been + 과거분사 + (by + 행위자)」, 과거완료는 「had been + 과거분사 + (by + 행위자)」로 나타내며 부정문은 have/has나 had 뒤에 not을 붙인다.**

I **have completed** the report perfectly. 나는 보고서를 완벽하게 마무리했다.
→ The report has been completed perfectly by me. (현재완료 수동태)
그 보고서는 나에 의해 완벽하게 마무리 되었다.

Someone **had stolen** expensive jewelry. 누군가 비싼 보석을 훔쳤다.
→ Expensive jewelry had been stolen by someone. (과거완료 수동태)
비싼 보석이 누군가에 의해 도둑 맞았다.

Her parents **had not raised** her. 그녀의 부모님은 그녀를 기르지 않았다.
→ She had not been raised by her parents. 그녀는 부모님에 의해 길러지지 않았다. (완료형 수동태의 부정)

A

괄호 안에서 알맞은 말을 고르시오.

1 The party has (held, been held) annually.
2 The students have (help, been helped) by Gloria.
3 The room had already (cleaned, been cleaned) by us.
4 The event has (being, been) prepared by all the students.
5 All the heavy stuff had been (carrying, carried) by Minho.
6 This camera (has been used, is being used) for almost five years.
7 The message from the book (has not been, has been not) forgotten.
8 Too much information has been (exposing, exposed) online recently.

B

능동태는 수동태로, 수동태는 능동태 문장으로 바꿔 쓸 때 빈칸에 알맞은 말을 쓰시오.

1 Jane has organized the files in the drawer.
→ The files in the drawer ____________ ____________ ____________ by Jane.

2 Mr. White has taught us English for two years.
→ English ____________ ____________ ____________ to us by Mr. White for two years.

3 The new software has been developed by his team.
→ His team ____________ ____________ the new software.

4 The volunteers have provided free meals for homeless people.
→ Free meals for homeless people ____________ ____________ ____________ by the volunteers.

5 The composer has composed many popular songs over the years.
→ Many popular songs ____________ ____________ ____________ over the years by the composer.

Point 06 4형식 문장의 수동태

■ **4형식 문장의 수동태**: 능동태 문장에서의 직접목적어와 간접목적어를 각각 주어로 하여 두 가지 수동태를 만들 수 있다.

능동태(4형식 문장)	Sally gave me(간·목) some souvenirs(직·목) from her trip to New York. Sally는 그녀의 뉴욕 여행의 몇 가지 기념품을 내게 주었다.
직접목적어가 주어인 수동태	Some souvenirs were given **to me** by Sally from her trip to New York. 그녀의 뉴욕 여행의 몇 가지 기념품이 Sally에 의해 나에게 주어졌다.
간접목적어가 주어인 수동태	I was given **some souvenirs** by Sally from her trip to New York. 나는 Sally로부터 그녀의 뉴욕여행의 몇 가지 기념품을 받았다.

※ 단, 직접목적어를 주어로 하는 수동태의 경우, 4형식 문장을 3형식 문장으로 바꿀 때처럼, 간접목적어 앞에 to, for, of 중에서 적절한 전치사를 써야 한다.

to를 쓰는 동사	teach, give, sell, send, show, tell, bring
for를 쓰는 동사	make, buy, cook, get, build
of를 쓰는 동사	ask, inquire

■ 다음 동사들은 **직접목적어만 수동태의 주어로** 쓸 수 있다.

make, buy, cook, get, write, pass, sell, find 등

Mom **cooked** me delicious soup. 엄마는 내게 맛있는 수프를 만들어 주셨다.
→ Delicious soup was cooked for me by mom. (O)
→ I was cooked delicious soup by mom. (X)

A 괄호 안에서 알맞은 말을 고르시오.

1 Some lessons were given (to, for) me by Jina.
2 The lost items were found (for, to) Jack by the police.
3 Some presents were bought (for, to) me by my friends.
4 A great chance was offered (for, to) him by the manager.
5 This cookie was (made me, made for me) by my grandmother.

B 다음 능동태 문장을 주어진 단어로 시작하는 수동태 문장으로 바꿔 쓰시오.

1 My sister told me a funny story.
→ A funny story ______________________.
→ I ______________________.

2 Our mom gave us great responsibility.
→ Great responsibility ______________________.
→ We ______________________.

3 A student asked the teacher a very difficult question.
→ A very difficult question ______________________.
→ The teacher ______________________.

Point 07 5형식 문장의 수동태 I

■ **5형식 문장을 수동태로 만들 때**에도 목적어를 주어로 하고 「**be동사 + 과거분사(p.p.)**」 형태를 쓴다. 이 때 **목적격 보어로 쓰인 형용사, 분사, 명사, to부정사는** 「**be동사 + 과거분사(p.p.)**」 뒤에 그대로 이어서 쓴다.

We **called** the puppy Coco. 우리는 강아지를 Coco라고 불렀다.

→ **The puppy** was called Coco **by us.** 그 강아지는 우리에 의해 Coco라고 불렸다.

→ Coco was called the puppy by us. (X) (→ ※ 목적격 보어는 수동태의 주어로 쓸 수 없다.)

The coach **told** her to practice more than three hours a day.
그 코치는 그녀에게 하루에 세 시간 이상씩 연습하라고 말했다.

→ She was told to practice more than three hours a day by the coach.
그녀는 감독에 의해 하루에 세 시간 이상씩 연습하라는 말을 들었다.

A

5형식 문장을 수동태로 바꾼 문장에서, 어법상 틀린 부분을 찾아 바르게 고쳐 쓰시오.

1 He asked me to come with Jane.
→ I was asked come with Jane by him. ________ → ________

2 They named their cat Nabi.
→ Their cat was named to Nabi by them. ________ → ________

3 The doctor asked me to start exercising.
→ I was asked to starting exercising by the doctor. ________ → ________

4 My mother told me to buy some groceries.
→ I was told buying some groceries by my mother. ________ → ________

B

우리말과 뜻이 같도록 괄호 안의 말을 활용하여 문장을 완성하시오.

1 그녀는 우리에 의해 천사라고 불려졌다. (call, an angel)
→ She ________ ________ ________ ________ by us.

2 그의 집은 일꾼들에 의해 하얀색으로 칠해졌다. (paint, white)
→ His house ________ ________ ________ by workers.

3 그는 밖에 나가기 전에 저녁을 먹으라는 이야기를 들었다. (tell, eat)
→ He ________ ________ ________ ________ dinner before going out.

4 나는 그에 의해 중국어를 배우도록 조언 받았다. (advise, learn)
→ I ________ ________ ________ ________ Chinese by him.

5 나는 다음 주까지 숙제를 제출하도록 이야기를 들었다. (tell, hand in)
→ I ________ ________ ________ ________ ________ the homework by next week.

Point 08 5형식 문장의 수동태 II – 지각동사, 사역동사의 수동태

■ **5형식 문장에서** 지각동사나 사역동사가 쓰였을 때, 다음과 같이 수동태로 전환한다.

(1) 목적격 보어가 동사원형인 경우: 동사원형은 to부정사로 바뀐다.

I heard someone call my name. 나는 누군가가 내 이름을 부르는 것을 들었다.
→ Someone was heard to call my name. 누군가 내 이름을 부르는 것이 들려졌다.
Mom made me turn off the TV. 엄마는 내게 TV를 끄게 시켰다.
→ I was made to turn off the TV by Mom. 나는 엄마에 의해 TV를 끄도록 시켜졌다.

(2) 목적격 보어가 현재분사인 경우: 현재분사(-ing) 형태는 그대로 둔다.

I heard someone calling my name.
→ Someone was heard calling my name.

■ **사역동사 let과 have의 수동태:** 사역동사 let은 「be allowed to + 동사원형」의 형태로, 사역동사 have는 「be asked to + 동사원형」의 형태로 수동태를 만든다.

Our teacher let us play outside. 우리 선생님께서 우리가 밖에서 노는 것을 허락하셨다.
→ We were allowed by our teacher to play outside.
I had my brother clean his room. 나는 남동생에게 그의 방을 치우도록 했다.
→ My brother was asked to clean his room.

A 괄호 안에서 알맞은 말을 고르시오.

1 Birds were heard (sing, to sing) in the forest.
2 We were made (helping, to help) him wash his car.
3 I was (allowed, let) to borrow some of her clothes.
4 Some people (seen, were seen) entering his house.

B 우리말과 뜻이 같도록 괄호 안의 말을 활용하여 문장을 완성하시오.

1 야구를 하는 아이들이 창문을 깨는 것이 우리에 의해 목격되었다. (see, break)
→ Children playing baseball ______ ______ ______ ______ the window by us.

2 우리는 엄마에 의해 집안일을 하게 되었다. (made, do)
→ We ______ ______ ______ ______ housework by our mom.

3 선생님은 학생들이 어떤 질문이든 하도록 허락하셨다. (allow, ask)
→ Students ______ ______ ______ ______ any questions by the teacher.

4 그녀가 크게 떠드는 것이 선생님께 들렸다. (hear, make)
→ She ______ ______ ______ ______ a lot of noise by the teacher.

Point 09 주의해야 할 수동태 I – 목적어로 쓰인 that절의 수동태

■ **동사 believe, consider, expect, know, say, suppose, think 등과 같이 목적어로 that절이 오는 경우,** 두 가지 방법으로 수동태 전환이 가능하다.

(1) 「가주어(It) + be동사 + 과거분사(p.p.) + that절」로 바꿀 수 있다.

(2) 「that절의 주어 + be동사 + 과거분사(p.p.) + to동사원형(that절 내의 동사)」로 바꿀 수 있다.

They say that Mr. White is a very reliable person.
그들은 Mr. White이 매우 믿을만한 사람이라고 말한다.
→ [That Mr. White is a very reliable person] is said (by them).
→ (1) It is said [that Mr. White is a very reliable person]. (가주어 it, 진주어 that절)
→ (2) Mr. White is said to be a very reliable person. (주어 Mr. White, 동사구는 to부정사)

목적절인 that절을 수동태의 주어로 하여 문장을 전환할 때는
(1) that절인 주어가 길기 때문에 앞에 가주어 it을 쓰고 진주어인 that절은 뒤로 보낸다.
(2) that절의 주어를 전체 문장의 주어로 삼고 that절의 나머지 동사구는 to부정사로 바꿀 수 있다.

※ **that절의 시제가 주절의 시제보다 앞서면** that절의 동사를 to부정사구로 고칠 때 **「to + have + 과거분사」**를 쓴다.
The reporter says that many people were injured in the accident.
기자는 그 사고로 많은 사람들이 다쳤다고 말한다.
→ Many people are said to have been injured in the accident by the reporter.

A

두 문장의 뜻이 같도록 빈칸에 알맞은 말을 쓰시오.

1 It is said that tomatoes are good for you.
= Tomatoes ________ ________ ________ ________ good for you.

2 It is thought in China that the number 8 is a lucky number.
= The number 8 ________ ________ ________ ________ a lucky number in China.

B

다음을 〈보기〉와 같이 두 개의 수동태 문장으로 바꿔 쓰시오.

보기
People believed that what he said was true.
→ It is believed that what he said was true.
→ What he said was believed to be true.

1 We suppose that his new movie is great.
→ ____________________
→ ____________________

2 People say that eating an apple a day keeps the doctor away.
→ ____________________
→ ____________________

Point 10 주의해야 할 수동태 II – by 이외의 전치사를 쓰는 수동태

■ **수동태의 기본 형태는 「be동사 + 과거분사(p.p.) + by + 행위자」**이다. 하지만, by 대신 다른 전치사를 **써야 하는 경우가 있다.** 특히 자주 쓰이는 표현은 다음과 같다.

■ **by 이외의 전치사를 사용하는 수동태 표현:**

be ashamed of	~을 부끄러워하다	be known for	~로 유명하다
be based on	~에 근거를 두다	be known to	~에게 알려지다
be bored with	~에 지겨워지다	be made from	~로 만들어지다 (재료의 성질 변화)
be covered with	~으로 덮여 있다	be made of	~로 만들어지다 (재료의 모양 변화)
be composed of	~으로 구성되다	be pleased with	~에 기쁘다
be crowded with	~으로 혼잡하다	be satisfied with	~에 만족하다
be disappointed with	~에 실망하다	be shocked at	~에 충격을 받다
be filled with	~으로 가득 차다	be surprised by(at)	~에 놀라다
be interested in	~에 관심이 있다	be tired of	~에 싫증나다
be known as	~로서 알려지다	be worried about	~에 대해 걱정하다

This table was made of wood. 이 탁자는 나무로 만들어졌다.
The cheese was made from the best quality milk. 그 치즈는 최상급 품질의 우유로 만들어졌다.
The whole town was covered with snow. 마을 전체가 눈으로 덮여 있었다.
He is interested in Chinese culture. 그는 중국 문화에 관심이 있다.

A 빈칸에 알맞은 말을 〈보기〉에서 한번씩만 골라 쓰시오.

보기
at of with about in

1 I was surprised ____________ the news.
2 I am not worried ____________ his future at all.
3 She felt ashamed ____________ her repeated mistakes.
4 My mom is not interested ____________ how my school life is.
5 The first day of a bargain sale is usually crowded ____________ people.

B 우리말과 뜻이 같도록 괄호 안의 말을 활용하여 빈칸에 알맞은 말을 쓰시오.

1 그는 회사의 모든 사람들에게 알려져 있다. (know)
→ He is ____________ ____________ everyone in the office.

2 그 영화는 실제 이야기에 근거를 두고 있다. (base)
→ The movie is ____________ ____________ a real-life story.

3 그녀의 운동화는 먼지로 덮여 있었다. (cover)
→ Her sneakers were ____________ ____________ dirt.

4 많은 사람들이 그 소식에 기뻐했다. (please)
→ Many people ____________ ____________ ____________ the news.

일등 비법 노트

비법 ①

4형식을 수동태로 전환할 때, 뒤에 남은 간접목적어 앞에 적절한 전치사를 써라!
(to: 대부분의 동사 앞에! / for: make, buy, cook (→ *for MBC*) / ask: of)

대표기출 1

어법상 <u>어색한</u> 것은?

① English was taught to me by Mr. Kim.
② A delicious meal was cooked to me by her.
③ An important question was asked of the man.
④ A lot of tuition was paid to the school by my parents.
⑤ Some exciting work was given to me by my teacher.

대표기출 2

다음을 두 가지 형태의 수동태 문장으로 바꿀 때 빈칸에 알맞은 말을 쓰시오.

Dad gave us a cute little puppy.

→ We ____________ ____________ a cute little puppy by Dad.
→ A cute little puppy ____________ ____________
____________ ____________ by Dad.

비법 ②

「be p.p. + to부정사」!
(→ 수동태 뒤의 동사는 to부정사 형태로! 단, 지각동사 뒤에는 -ing도 올 수 있다!)

대표기출 1

빈칸에 알맞은 말은?

He was made ___________ the auditorium after class.

① clean
② cleaned
③ cleaning
④ to clean
⑤ to cleaning

대표기출 2

어법상 빈칸에 알맞은 말을 <u>모두</u> 고르면?

The boy ___________ the old man carrying the box.

① was seen
② was seen helped
③ was seen helping
④ was seen to help
⑤ was seen help

비법 ③ that절이 포함된 문장의 수동태는 ①「It is p.p. that절 ~.」 또는 ②「주어 + be p.p. + to부정사 ~.」로 쓴다!

대표기출 1

수동태로 바꿀 때 빈칸에 알맞은 것은?

People think that taking vitamin pills is helpful.
→ It ________ taking vitamin pills is helpful.

① thought ② be thought
③ is thinking ④ is thought to
⑤ is thought that

대표기출 2

〈보기〉와 같이 문장을 바꿔 쓰시오.

보기
People believe what he said is true.
→ What he said is believed to be true.

People think that English is a global language.
→ English ________________________________.

비법 ④ by 이외의 전치사를 쓰는 수동태는 단골 출제된다! 반복 암기하라!

대표기출 1

빈칸에 by를 쓸 수 없는 것은?

① It will be decided ________ us.
② This chair is made ________ wood and metal.
③ The baby was raised ________ her grandmother.
④ The wall is being painted ________ the children.
⑤ This novel was written ________ the same author.

대표기출 2

빈칸에 알맞은 말이 나머지와 다른 하나는?

① I was pleased ________ her compliment.
② I am interested ________ learning Chinese.
③ The ground was covered ________ grass.
④ My parents were satisfied ________ the work.
⑤ The room was crowded ________ children.

내신 만점! 실전 기출

[1~2] 빈칸에 알맞은 말을 고르시오.

01

This machine can __________ by John because he is skillful.

① fix ② fixing ③ to fix
④ be fixed ⑤ being fixed

02

The new school building is being __________ now.

① construct ② constructing
③ to construct ④ constructed
⑤ been constructed

[3~4] 다음을 수동태 문장으로 바꿀 때, 빈칸에 알맞은 것을 고르시오.

03

You must keep the milk in the refrigerator.
→ The milk __________ in the refrigerator.

① must kept be ② must being kept
③ must be kept ④ must be keeping
⑤ must have kept

04

He has composed many great songs for years.
→ Many great songs __________ by him for years.

① are composing ② were composing
③ were composed ④ have been composed
⑤ have being composed

[5~6] 빈칸에 공통으로 알맞은 말을 고르시오.

05

- We were all bored ⓐ __________ the endless speech made by the principal.
- My heart was filled ⓑ __________ joy when I heard the news.

① with ② at ③ of
④ on ⑤ as

06

- Some of the rules are ⓐ __________ written on the board.
- The room was ⓑ __________ painted by two people.

① have ② being ③ been
④ having been ⑤ having being

07 서술형

다음을 수동태 문장으로 바꿀 때 빈칸에 알맞은 말을 쓰시오.

They are preparing a business report now.

→ A business report __________ __________ __________ by them now.

08 서술형

어법에 맞지 않는 부분을 찾아 바르게 고쳐 쓰시오.

For safety, passwords should change every six months.
(안전을 위해 비밀번호는 6개월마다 변경되어야만 한다.)

__________ → __________

09 서술형

〈보기〉와 같이 빈칸에 알맞은 말을 쓰시오.

보기
A: Who made the cookies?
B: The cookies were made by Jane.

A: Who will clean up the auditorium?
B: The auditorium ________ ________ ________ ________ by us.

10 빈칸에 알맞은 말이 나머지 넷과 다른 하나는?

① A secret tip was given ________ them.
② Some papers were passed ________ us.
③ The e-mail was sent ________ me yesterday.
④ Some items were sold ________ us by them.
⑤ A new suitcase was bought ________ me by dad.

11 다음을 수동태 문장으로 바꿀 때 빈칸 ⓐ~ⓑ에 알맞은 말이 순서대로 나열된 것은?

- The coach made him stop playing after the injury.
  → He was made ⓐ ________ playing by coach after the injury.
- My sister let me use her laptop computer.
  → I ⓑ ________ her laptop computer by my sister.

① stop, was let use
② stopping, was allowed to use
③ to stop, was allowed to use
④ stopped, was let use
⑤ having stopped, was allowed using

12 다음을 수동태 문장으로 바꿀 때 빈칸에 알맞은 말은?

The interviewer asked me many difficult questions.
→ Many difficult questions were asked ________ me by the interviewer.

① for ② of ③ to
④ with ⑤ from

13 밑줄 친 부분이 어법상 틀린 것은?

① I was bored with my routine life.
② We are not interested in history.
③ The man was ashamed of his mistake.
④ Sally was known for her nice personality.
⑤ The tourist was amazed to the beautiful scenery.

14 다음을 수동태 문장으로 바꿀 때 빈칸에 알맞은 말은?

It is believed that Koreans are hardworking and diligent.
→ Koreans ________ hardworking and diligent.

① believe be ② believe being
③ believe to be ④ are believed to be
⑤ are believed being

[15~16] 다음을 주어진 단어로 시작하는 수동태 문장으로 고쳐 쓰시오.

15 서술형

Everyone in his class called Jack captain.

→ Jack ________________________________.

16 서술형

His teacher offered him a great opportunity.

→ (1) He ______________________________
______________________________.

→ (2) A great opportunity ______________
______________________________.

17 능동태 문장을 수동태 문장으로 바꾼 것 중 잘못된 것은?

① They have canceled the appointment.
→ The appointment has been canceled by them.
② He asked me to go to the movies with him.
→ I was asked to go to the movies with him.
③ My father bought me these glasses.
→ These glasses were bought for me by my father.
④ They elected him president last week.
→ President was elected by him last week.
⑤ The doctor must treat the patient with the medication.
→ The patient must be treated with the medication by the doctor.

18 서술형

우리말과 일치하도록 괄호 안의 단어를 활용하여 문장을 완성하시오.

지난 주에 새로운 교복의 디자인이 학생들에게 보여졌다. (show)

→ Last week, the design of the new school uniform __________ __________ __________ students.

최다빈출

19 빈칸에 알맞은 말이 나머지와 다른 하나는?

① We were pleased __________ the result.
② His face was filled __________ happiness.
③ He looks satisfied __________ his job.
④ They must be disappointed __________ my behavior.
⑤ We are tired __________ the same dish every day.

20 밑줄 친 문장을 주어로 하는 수동태 문장을 만들 수 없는 것은?

① He showed me the old book.
② We heard him play the violin.
③ Everyone thinks him a genius.
④ He taught me how to solve the equation.
⑤ Her beautiful smile makes everyone happy.

21 서술형

다음을 주어진 단어로 시작하는 수동태 문장으로 바꿔 쓰시오.

People say that Ji-sung Park is one of the best soccer players.

→ (1) Ji-sung Park ______________________
______________________________.

→ (2) It ______________________________
______________________________.

22 밑줄 친 전치사의 쓰임이 올바른 것은?

① A new bag was bought to me by her.
② A question was asked of Jane by a new student.
③ A love letter was given for her by John.
④ A scholarship was offered of him by the university.
⑤ Some delicious cookies are baked to kids by my mom.

23 밑줄 친 부분의 쓰임이 잘못된 것을 모두 고르면?

① We were all surprised at the scene.
② His name is well-known as many people.
③ The desk was covered of a lot of documents.
④ The inside was filled with plants and trees.
⑤ All of them were worried about their exam results.

신유형

24 서술형

주어진 조건에 맞춰 다음을 영작할 때 5번째로 올 단어를 쓰시오.

조건
1. 'the books'를 주어로 문장 맨 처음에 쓰시오.
2. 총 10개의 단어로 이루어진 완전한 영어 문장을 쓰시오.
3. 'possible'이라는 단어를 포함하시오.

그 책들은 가능한 빨리 반납되는 편이 좋겠다.

→ ____________________
____

25 서술형

수동태로 바꿔 쓴 문장에서, 어법상 어색한 곳을 찾아 바르게 고쳐 쓰시오.

The city government is building a dam in the northern part of the region.
→ The dam is building in the northern part of the region by the city government.

__________ → __________

26 어법상 틀린 문장을 모두 고르면?

ⓐ Is the food being made by her?
ⓑ My hair was cut too short.
ⓒ He was elected by chairman by them.
ⓓ They were heard arguing about something.
ⓔ The boys were made being quiet by their mom.

① ⓐ, ⓑ　② ⓑ, ⓒ　③ ⓒ, ⓓ
④ ⓒ, ⓔ　⑤ ⓒ, ⓓ, ⓔ

27 수동태로 전환한 문장이 어법상 틀린 것은?

① He is repairing his bicycle now.
→ His bicycle is being repaired by him now.
② My mother runs a small bakery.
→ A small bakery is run by my mother.
③ People think he works very hard.
→ He is thought to work very hard.
④ We can recycle most waste these days.
→ Most waste can be recycled these days.
⑤ Tiffany will teach us English next year.
→ We will be taught to English by Tiffany next year.

28 밑줄 친 부분이 어법상 틀린 것은?

A: Hey, did you hear the news?
B: What news?
A: It's not good news actually. A fire ⓐ was broken out at the shopping mall near our neighborhood.
B: Really? ⓑ Was anyone killed?
A: No one ⓒ was reported to die.
According to the radio news, firefighters are ⓓ trying to put out the fire, but smoke still ⓔ can be seen.

① ⓐ ② ⓑ ③ ⓒ
④ ⓓ ⑤ ⓔ

신유형

29 서술형

우리말과 뜻이 같도록 〈보기〉에서 알맞은 단어를 골라 문장을 완성하시오. (단, 필요한 단어만 골라 사용하시오.)

조건

is	looked	look	up
down	to	on	by
looking	people	much	many

이순신은 많은 사람들에 의해 존경을 받는다.

→ Commander Lee Sun-shin ______________
______________________________.

고난도

30 다음 ⓐ~ⓒ에 알맞은 말이 순서대로 바르게 짝지어진 것은?

What is the greatest invention of all time? Many people would answer that it is the computer. A computer is a device that can be ⓐ __________ to carry out a set of logical operations automatically. Since a sequence of operations can be varied, the computer can ⓑ __________ more than one kind of problem. So, who invented the computer? It is known that Charles Babbage, an English mechanical engineer, originated the concept of the computer. He is ⓒ __________ "the father of the computer."

	ⓐ		ⓑ		ⓒ
①	programming	—	solved	—	considering
②	programmed	—	solving	—	considering
③	programmed	—	solved	—	considered
④	programming	—	solve	—	considered
⑤	programmed	—	solve	—	considered

실력 탄탄!
서술형 심화

1 다음은 미나네 학급 규칙이다. 밑줄 친 부분이 어법상 틀린 부분을 두 군데 찾아 바르게 고쳐 쓰시오.

< Class Rules >

(1) Food should not be ate during class.
(2) Homework should be done before class.
(3) Only English must be spoken in the class.
(4) Cell phones must be turn off during class.

__________ → __________   __________ → __________

[2~3] 대화를 읽고 물음에 답하시오.

A: Do you have any plans for summer vacation, Chris?
B: Well, I am going to visit Jeju island.
A: Oh. That sounds fun. ⓐ ______________________.
B: Right. I can't wait to go there. I have heard that both the food and the beaches are great.
A: Have you decided where you are going to stay?
B: Not yet. ⓑ ______________________, so I will do that this week.
A: If you want, I can give you some useful information about good hotels there. My sister knows Jeju really well, so I will ask her and get back to you.
B: Oh, Jenny, you're so nice. That would be great. Thanks.

2 주어진 단어를 바르게 배열하여 빈칸 ⓐ, ⓑ에 각각 알맞은 문장을 완성하시오.

<ⓐ>	<ⓑ>
Jeju island, said, is, be, famous, for, to, beautiful, its, beaches	I, asked, was, by, book, to, a, hotel, my mom

→ ⓐ ______________________
→ ⓑ ______________________

3 대화에서 주어진 정보를 이용하여 다음 질문에 답하시오. (단, 아래 조건에 맞춰 대답할 것)

조건
1. 수동태의 문장으로 답하시오. 2. 주어진 단어를 제외하고 11개의 단어를 사용하시오.

Q: What will be given to Chris by Jenny?
A: Some ______________________ to Chris by Jenny.

CHAPTER 07

대명사

- **Point 01** 재귀대명사
- **Point 02** it의 여러 가지 쓰임
- **Point 03** one *vs.* it / others *vs.* the other(s)
- **Point 04** 짝을 이루어 쓰는 표현
- **Point 05** something *vs.* anything
- **Point 06** 전체부정 *vs.* 부분부정

대명사

명사가 와야 할 자리에 대(代)신해서 쓸 수 있는 것들이 대명사(代名詞)이다. 대명사의 종류로는, 인칭대명사(I, my, me, you, ...), 지시대명사(this, that, ...), 의문대명사(who, which, ...) 그리고 정해져 있지 않은(不定) 불특정한 사람이나 사물을 가리킬 때 쓰는 **부정대명사** 등이 있다. 부정대명사 중에서도 짝을 이루어 자주 쓰이는 표현이 있다.

• 짝을 이루어 자주 쓰는 부정대명사 표현

One ~, the other …	(둘 중에) 하나는 ~, 다른 하나는 … I have two pets. **One** is a puppy, and **the other** is a pig.
One ~, another …, the other –	(셋 중에) 하나는 ~, 다른 하나는 …, 나머지 다른 하나는 – I bought three pens. One is red, **another** is blue, and the **other** is yellow.
One ~, the others …	(셋 이상에서) 하나는 ~, 나머지 모두는 … There are ten people in the room. **One** is a doctor, and **the others** are patients.
Some ~, others …	(불특정 다수의 사람/사물 중에서) 몇몇은 ~, 다른 몇몇은 … There're a lot of fruits in the basket. **Some** are oranges, and **others** are apples.
Some ~, the others …	(특정한 수의 사람/사물 중에서) 몇몇은 ~, 나머지는 … There were twelve kids in the room. **Some** were drawing, and **the others** were doing homework.

Point 01 재귀대명사

■ **재귀대명사**: 인칭대명사의 소유격/목적격에 -self 또는 -selves를 붙여 만든다. '~자신, ~자체'라는 뜻이다.

	1인칭	2인칭	3인칭
단수	myself	yourself	himself / herself / itself
복수	ourselves	yourselves	themselves

■ **재귀대명사의 재귀 용법**: 문장의 주어와 목적어의 대상이 같을 때, 목적어로 재귀대명사를 쓴다.
You passed the exam. You must be proud of yourself.
너는 그 시험을 합격했다. 너는 너 자신이 자랑스러울 게 틀림없다.
Tom made a big mistake. He got angry at himself. Tom은 큰 실수를 해서 그 자신에게 화가 났다.

■ **재귀대명사의 강조 용법**: 재귀대명사가 문장의 주어나 목적어를 강조하는 역할을 하기도 한다. 이 때의 재귀대명사는 강조하는 말 바로 뒤, 또는 문장의 맨 끝에 오며, 생략해도 (강조의 의미가 덜할 뿐) 문장은 성립한다.
I baked the cookies myself. 그 쿠키를 내가 직접 구웠다.
= I myself baked the cookies. (주어 강조, I = myself)

■ 자주 쓰이는 「**전치사 + 재귀대명사**」 표현

between ourselves	우리끼리 얘기지만	help oneself to	~을 마음껏 먹다
by oneself	홀로 (= alone)	in itself	본질적으로
enjoy oneself	즐겁게 지내다	make oneself at home	편안히 지내다
for oneself	혼자 힘으로 (= without any help)	of itself	저절로

A 밑줄 친 재귀대명사의 용법을 괄호 안에서 고르시오.

1 His acting itself was great. (재귀, 강조)
2 I thought to myself, "I can do it." (재귀, 강조)
3 Jack himself cleaned the entire house. (재귀, 강조)

B 괄호 안에서 알맞은 말을 고르시오.

1 Socrates once said, "Know (you, yourself)."
2 I quarreled with James. He doesn't talk to (me, myself) any more.
3 My brother (him, himself) bought this gift for me. He usually gets his wife to buy gifts.

C 우리말과 뜻이 같도록 재귀대명사를 활용하여 문장을 완성하시오.

1 그들은 그들만의 힘으로 요리를 하곤 했다.
→ They used to cook ______ ______.

2 그는 혼자 유럽으로 여행을 갔다.
→ He took a trip to Europe ______ ______.

3 그녀는 거울로 그녀 자신을 보고 있다.
→ She is looking at ______ in the mirror.

Point 02 it의 여러 가지 쓰임

- **대명사 it**: '그것'이라는 뜻으로, 앞에 나온 특정한 명사나 구, 절, 문장을 대신해서 쓴다.
  I got a new cell phone yesterday, and I love it. (it = a new cellphone)
  나는 어제 새 핸드폰을 샀는데, 그것이 무척 마음에 든다.

- **비인칭 주어 it**: 시간, 날짜, 날씨, 계절, 온도, 명암, 거리, 무게 등을 나타내는 문장에서 주어로 it을 쓴다. '그것'이라고 해석하지 않는다.
  It was getting dark. 어두워지고 있었다. (명암)

- **가주어 it**: 진주어가 to부정사구, 동명사구, 명사절이고 길이가 길 때, 주어 자리에 가주어 it을 쓰고 진주어를 뒤로 보낼 수 있다.
  To finish the project by herself is impossible. 그녀 혼자서 프로젝트를 끝내는 것은 불가능하다.
  → It(가주어) is impossible *to finish the project by herself*(진주어).

- **가목적어 it**: 진짜 목적어인 to부정사구, 동명사구, 명사절 대신에 가목적어 it을 사용할 수 있다.
  I found it(가목적어) useful *taking notes*(진목적어) to remember things better.
  나는 기억을 더 잘하기 위해 메모를 하는 것이 유용하다는 것을 깨달았다.

- **「It seems[appears] that + 주어 + 동사 ~.」 구문**: ~인 것처럼 보인다, ~인 듯 하다.
  It seems that they have many things in common.
  = They seem to have many things in common. 그들은 많은 공통점이 있는 것처럼 보인다.

A

밑줄 친 it의 쓰임을 생각하며 각 문장을 우리말로 해석하시오.

1 It was not an easy decision.
→ ______________________

2 It is fun to ride bikes together.
→ ______________________

3 It took two hours to complete the homework.
→ ______________________

4 I found it hard to take care of a pet.
→ ______________________

B

우리말과 뜻이 같도록 괄호 안의 말을 바르게 배열하여 문장을 완성하시오.

1 외국어를 배우는 것은 흥미롭다. (interesting, to, it, learn, languages, foreign, is)
→ ______________________.

2 여름에는 비가 많이 내린다. (rains, it, a lot, summer, in, the)
→ ______________________.

3 나는 규칙적으로 운동하는 것이 필요하다는 것을 알았다. (found, I, necessary, to, it, regularly, exercise)
→ ______________________.

Point 03 부정대명사 one *vs.* it / others *vs.* the other(s)

■ **부정대명사 one *vs.* 지시대명사 it**

one	같은 종류의 다른 하나	My watch is broken, so I need to buy a new one. 내 시계가 고장나서 나는 새 것을 살 필요가 있다. (one = 시계 중 정해지지 않은 '하나')
it	앞서 언급한 같은 대상	I have one more eraser. I will lend it to you. 나에게 지우개가 하나 더 있어. 내가 너에게 그것을 빌려줄게. (it = 앞에서 언급한 바로 그 지우개)

cf. another: 또 다른 하나. 또 다른 사람이나 사물을 의미

I don't like this hat. Can you show me another? (another = 다른 모자)

■ **others *vs.* the others**

others	불특정한 다른 사람/사물들	You should be polite to others. 너는 다른 사람들에게 공손해야만 한다.
the others	나머지 모두들	They have five children. Two of them are daughters, and the others are sons. 그들에게는 다섯 명의 아이들이 있다. 그 아이들 중의 두 명은 딸이고, 나머지 (셋) 모두는 아들이다.

■ **the other *vs.* the others**

the other	나머지 하나	I have **two hobbies.** One is to ride a bike, and the other is to play the violin. 나에게는 두 가지 취미가 있다. 하나는 자전거를 타는 것이고, 나머지 하나는 바이올린을 연주하는 것이다.
the others	나머지 모두들	Some of my classmates wanted to play baseball. The others wanted to play soccer. 나의 반 친구들 중 몇 명은 야구를 하고 싶어했다. (나의 반 친구들 중에서) 나머지 모두는 축구 하기를 원했다.

A 괄호 안에서 알맞은 말을 고르시오.

1 She is always nice to (others, the other).

2 I am sorry, but please bring me (another, other).

3 I didn't bring my pen today. Can I borrow (it, one)?

4 I have two cats. One is black, and (another, the other) is white.

B 우리말과 뜻이 같도록 〈보기〉에서 알맞은 말을 골라 문장을 완성하시오.

보기		
others	another	the others

1 이것은 마음에 들지 않아요. 또 다른 것을 보여주실 수 있나요?

→ I don't like this. Could you show me ____________________?

2 다른 사람들에 대해 덜 신경 쓰고, 스스로를 더 신경 쓰도록 하라.

→ You should care less about ____________________ and care more about yourself.

3 제가 나머지 사람들 모두에게 그 소식을 전달할게요.

→ I will tell the news to ____________________.

Point 04 짝을 이루어 쓰는 표현

■ 「**One ~, the other** …」: 하나는 ~, 나머지 하나는 …

There are two people in our group. One is me, and the other is James.

우리 그룹에는 두 명의 멤버가 있다. 한 명은 나이고, 나머지 다른 한 명의 James이다.

■ 「**One ~, the others** …」: 하나는 ~, 나머지 모두는 …

I have four foreign friends. One is from New Zealand, and the others are from the U.S.

나는 네 명의 외국 친구들이 있다. 한 명은 뉴질랜드 출신이고 나머지는 미국 출신이다.

■ 「**One ~, another ~, the other** …」: (셋 중) 하나는 ~, 다른 하나는 ~, 나머지 하나는 …

I have three sisters. One is a doctor, another is a lawyer, and the other is a teacher.

나는 세 명은 언니가 있다. 한 명은 의사, 또 다른 한 명은 변호사, 나머지 한 명은 선생님이다.

■ 「**Some ~, others** …」: 어떤 사람(것)들은 ~, 또 다른 사람(것)들은 …

In my class, some like pizza and others like burgers.

우리 반에서 어떤 사람들은 피자를 좋아하고 또 다른 사람들은 햄버거를 좋아한다.

■ 「**Some ~, the others** …」: 어떤 사람(것)들은 ~, 나머지 다른 사람(것)들은 …

There are many children in the playground. Some are playing soccer, and the others are playing basketball.

운동장에 많은 아이들이 있다. 어떤 아이들은 축구를 하고 있고 나머지 다른 아이들은 모두 농구를 하고 있다.

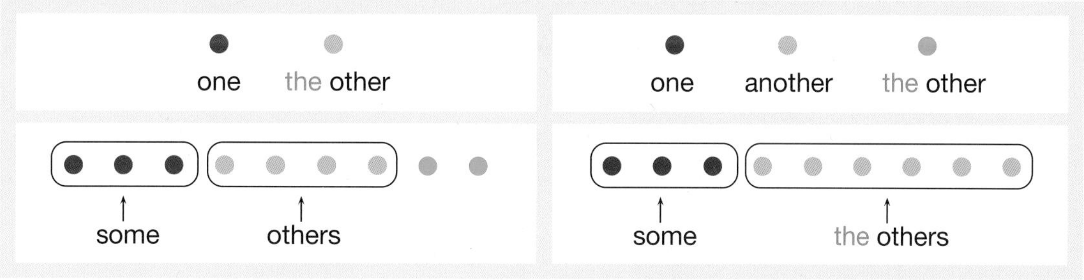

A 〈보기〉에서 빈칸에 알맞은 말을 골라 쓰시오. (단, 중복 사용 가능)

보기					
one	some	another	the other	the others	others

1 I have three caps. ____________ is black, and ____________ are blue.

2 ____________ like going to the sea, and ____________ like going to the mountains.

3 I got two kinds of flowers from him. Some are roses, and ____________ are lilies.

4 My teacher recommended two books to me. One is a novel, and ____________ is an essay.

B 밑줄 친 문장에서 어법상 어색한 부분을 찾아 바르게 고쳐 쓰시오.

1 I have two brothers. <u>One is 20 years old, and another is 18 years old</u>.

____________________ → ____________________

2 Three girls are in the classroom. <u>One is studying, and the other are chatting</u>.

____________________ → ____________________

Point 05 something *vs.* anything

- **-one, -body, -thing**은 some 또는 any와 함께 쓰여 불특정한 사람이나 사물을 가리키며, 항상 단수 취급한다.
- **some**으로 시작하는 부정대명사는 주로 **긍정문과 권유문에 쓰인다.**
  I like to learn something new. 나는 새로운 무언가를 배우는 것을 좋아한다. (긍정문)
  Would you like something cold to drink? 차가운 무언가를 원하시나요? (권유문)
- **any**로 시작하는 부정대명사는 주로 **부정문과 의문문, 조건문**에 쓰인다.
  I haven't eaten anything since this morning. 나는 아침부터 아무것도 먹지 않았다. (부정문)
  Is there anyone here who can help me? 여기 나를 도와줄 수 있는 사람 있나요? (의문문)
  If you need anything, feel free to call me. 무언가 필요하다면 언제든지 제게 연락 주세요. (조건문)

A

빈칸에 알맞은 말을 보기에서 골라 써 넣으시오. (단, 중복 사용 가능)

보기			
something	someone	anything	anyone

1 제가 여기 없는 동안 누군가 전화 했었나요?
→ Did ______________ call me when I was not here?

2 정답을 아는 사람 누구 없나요?
→ Is there ______________ who knows the answer?

3 나는 여기 사무실에서 일하는 누군가를 만나러 왔다.
→ I came to see ______________ who works in the office.

4 나는 네게 어떤 것도 받고 싶지 않다.
→ I don't want to get ______________ from you.

5 나는 추위를 무찌를 무언가 따뜻한 것을 마시고 싶다.
→ I want ______________ hot to drink in order to fight my cold.

6 누군가 복도 창문을 깨뜨렸다.
→ ______________ broke the window in the hallway.

B

밑줄 친 부분을 어법에 맞게 고쳐 문장 전체를 다시 쓰시오.

1 I don't know <u>someone</u> in the city.
→ ____.

2 There isn't <u>something</u> left to eat.
→ ____.

3 You should not worry about <u>something</u>.
→ ____.

4 <u>Anyone</u> in my neighborhood stole my bike last night.
→ ____.

Point 06 전체부정 *vs.* 부분부정

■ **전체부정**: 문장 전체를 부정하는 것으로 '아무(것)도 전혀 ~하지 않다'의 뜻이다.

(1) **nobody[no one]**: '아무도 ~하지 않는다'의 뜻으로 「not + anybody[anyone]」으로 바꿔 쓸 수 있다.
I saw nobody in the classroom. 나는 교실에서 아무도 보지 못했다.
= I didn't see anybody in the classroom.

(2) **nothing**: '아무것도 ~않다'의 뜻으로 「not + anything」으로 바꿔 쓸 수 있다.
She said nothing to me. 그녀는 내게 아무것도 말하지 않았다.
= She didn't say anything to me. 그녀는 내게 아무것도 말하지 않았다.

■ **부분부정**: **every, both, all** 등의 전체를 뜻하는 말이 부정어와 함께 쓰이면 문장 전체가 아닌 〈일부〉만을 부정하는 부분부정이 된다. '반드시(모두, 항상, 둘 다) ~한 것은 아니다'라는 뜻이다.
Not every twin looks the same. (not every + 단수명사 + 단수동사: 누구나 ~한 것은 아니다)
모든 쌍둥이가 똑같이 생긴 것은 아니다.
Not both of my brothers are tall. 내 오빠들이 다 키가 큰 것은 아니다. (둘 다 ~한 것은 아니다)
Not all books are useful. 모든 책들이 유용한 것은 아니다. (모두가 ~한 것은 아니다)

A 우리말과 뜻이 같도록 괄호 안에서 알맞은 말을 골라 문장을 완성하시오.

1 우리 반 아무도 그 소문을 듣지 못했다.
→ (Nobody, Not everybody) in our class heard the news.

2 그들은 어젯밤 아무것도 먹지 않았다.
→ They ate (nothing, not everything) last night.

B 두 문장의 뜻이 같도록 빈칸에 알맞은 말을 쓰시오.

1 I have nothing to tell you.
= I ____________ have ____________ to tell you.

2 I am sorry, but there is no one here by that name.
= I am sorry, but there ____________ ____________ here by that name.

C 두 문장의 뜻이 같도록 괄호 안의 말을 활용하여 문장을 완성하시오.

1 Some of my friends came to the party, but others didn't. (all)
= ____________ ____________ ____________ ____________ came to the party.

2 My elder sister is talkative, but my younger sister isn't. (both)
= ____________ ____________ ____________ ____________ ____________ are talkative.

3 Playing games is fun sometimes, but at other times it isn't. (always)
= Playing games is ____________ ____________ ____________.

4 Some movies are interesting, but others are not. (every)
= ____________ ____________ ____________ is interesting.

일등 비법 노트

비법 1 재귀대명사를 생략할 수 있으면 강조 용법! 생략할 수 없으면 재귀 용법!

대표기출 1

밑줄 친 재귀대명사의 쓰임이 다른 하나는?

① I myself fixed the broken bike.
② Help yourself to the dishes.
③ The boy cleaned the room himself.
④ You will be impressed by the movie itself.
⑤ My sisters themselves will travel around Europe.

대표기출 2

밑줄 친 재귀대명사의 쓰임이 다른 하나는?

① She seems proud of herself.
② Please make yourself at home.
③ My teacher himself wrote this book.
④ I had to do all the work by myself.
⑤ The man thought to himself, "Let's give it a try."

비법 2 뒤에 to부정사나 that절이 있으면 it은 가주어이거나 가목적어이다!

대표기출 1

〈보기〉의 밑줄 친 it과 같은 용법으로 쓰인 것은?

보기
It is practical to learn a foreign language.

① It was dark outside at that time.
② It will take three hours by car.
③ It was a really excellent speech.
④ It seems that I lost my wallet somewhere.
⑤ It is good to spend time together often.

비법 ③ 둘이면 one, the other! 셋이면 one, another, the other이다!

대표기출 1

빈칸에 알맞은 말이 순서대로 나열된 것은?

I have three bags at home. ⓐ __________ is for school, ⓑ __________ is for my academy, and ⓒ __________ is for a trip.

① the other, one, another
② one, another, the other
③ one, the other, another
④ one, another, the others
⑤ one, another, other

대표기출 2

빈칸에 알맞은 말이 순서대로 나열된 것은?

There are two kids at the park. __________ is sitting on the bench, and __________ is running with a ball.

① The other, one
② One, the other
③ One, others
④ One, the others
⑤ One, two

비법 ④ 전체(every, both, all 등)를 부정하면 부분부정! 부분(any)을 부정하면 전체부정!

대표기출 1

다음 중 두 문장의 뜻이 같도록 짝지어진 것이 아닌 것은?

① Not everyone joined the baseball team.
= Some joined the baseball team. Others didn't.
② I don't always listen to him.
= I sometimes listen to him. Other times, I don't.
③ Sally didn't invite any of them.
= Sally invited some of them, not all of them.
④ She doesn't know both of the students.
= She knows one of the students. She doesn't know the other one.
⑤ Not all the applicants had a chance for an interview.
= Some of the applicants had a chance for an interview.

내신 만점! 실전 기출

[1~2] 빈칸에 알맞은 말을 고르시오.

01

A: I've just bought these apples. But they don't look fresh.
B: Oh, I'm sorry. I'll give you some fresh ________.

① it ② one ③ ones
④ other ⑤ them

02

________ people like coffee, and others like tea.

① One ② Another ③ Some
④ Other ⑤ The others

03 밑줄 친 it의 용법이 나머지 넷과 다른 하나는?

① It was nice of you to say so.
② It is surprising that he won the game.
③ It rained cats and dogs last night.
④ It is no use crying over spilled milk.
⑤ It is difficult to understand her accent.

04 밑줄 친 대명사를 생략할 수 있는 것은?

① I solved the problems myself.
② She devoted herself to her family.
③ She burned herself when she made dinner.
④ He said to himself, "You can make it again."
⑤ Please, help yourself. I hope you will like the food.

05 빈칸에 알맞은 것은?

All the other students had to go home early, so I had to clean up the classroom all ________ myself.

① of ② in ③ with
④ by ⑤ at

06 〈보기〉와 밑줄 친 it의 쓰임이 같은 것은?

보기
It is rude of her to say so.

① It needs to be done right away.
② It is getting warmer these days.
③ It was Tom who played the drum.
④ It is my sister's drum, not mine.
⑤ It is good to see all of you here.

07 서술형

두 문장의 뜻이 같도록 빈칸에 알맞은 말을 쓰시오.

James and Minho seem to be very close.

→ ________ ________ that James and Minho are very close.

08 서술형

우리말과 뜻이 같도록 빈칸에 공통으로 알맞은 말을 쓰시오.

Brian은 자기 자신을 자랑스러워 한다. 그 말은 그는 스스로를 매우 사랑한다는 것이다.

→ Brian is proud of ________, which means he really loves ________.

09 밑줄 친 재귀대명사의 용법이 다른 하나는?

① I sometimes talk to myself.
② The movie itself was great.
③ My grandfather himself built this house.
④ You will be impressed by the book itself.
⑤ Even the students themselves don't like the idea.

10 빈칸에 it이 들어갈 수 없는 것은?

① I find ________ important to eat breakfast.
② ________ was getting hotter and more humid.
③ ________ seems that she knows the secret.
④ How long does ________ take to get to Busan by car?
⑤ I thought ________ she would be a doctor.

11 서술형

두 문장의 뜻이 같도록 빈칸에 알맞은 말을 쓰시오.

Helping others in need is rewarding.

→ ________ ________ rewarding helping others in need.

12 빈칸에 공통으로 알맞은 말은? (단, 대소문자는 무시)

- This jacket is too small. Could you show me another ________?
- There are three cameras in my home. ________ is mine, and the others are my brother's.

① some ② one ③ the other
④ another ⑤ each other

13 서술형

빈칸에 공통으로 알맞은 말을 쓰시오.

- I made these cookies for you. Help ________.
- You must take care of ________ first.
- Please, make ________ at home.

→ ________________

최다빈출

14 대화의 흐름이 자연스럽도록 빈칸에 알맞은 말은?

M: Sally, what did you mean that you would be even busier before the vacation?
W: Well, there are two things I have to do before the vacation starts. One is finishing the assignment, and ________ is planning a trip to China.

① another ② the other ③ other
④ one ⑤ others

15 빈칸에 알맞은 말이 순서대로 바르게 나열된 것은?

We have three puppies in my house. ⓐ ________ is a Maltese. ⓑ ________ are Pomeranians. You can't even imagine how cute they are.

① One, Another
② One, Other
③ One, The another
④ One, The other
⑤ One, The others

16 빈칸에 공통으로 알맞은 말은?

- ⓐ __________ is exciting to watch soccer.
- ⓑ __________ will be cold after the rain.
- ⓒ __________ will take less than an hour if we do it together.

① One ② Another
③ That ④ It
⑤ What

17 밑줄 친 부분의 쓰임이 어법상 잘못된 것은?

① Someone left this message for me.
② I will not tell someone about this.
③ She doesn't want anyone to share her room.
④ I don't know anyone else but her in this class.
⑤ I am sure there will be someone who can help me.

18 괄호 안에서 알맞은 말을 고르시오.

A: Jenny, I heard that you are good at languages. How many languages can you speak?
B: I can speak three languages. One is Korean, ⓐ (another, the other) is English, and ⓑ (other, the other) is Chinese.

19 서술형

두 문장의 뜻이 같도록 재귀대명사를 활용하여 문장을 완성하시오.

According to the recent research, the number of people who live alone in Seoul has increased.

→ According to the recent research, the number of people who live __________ __________ in Seoul has increased.

20 서술형

다음 우리말을 영어로 옮길 때 빈칸에 알맞은 말을 쓰시오.

모두가 그 일을 제 시간에 끝내지는 않았다. 어떤 사람들은 그 일을 제 시간에 끝냈고, 나머지 다른 사람들은 그러지 못했다.

→ __________ all of them finished the work on time. __________ people finished the work on time, and __________ __________ didn't.

21 밑줄 친 ⓐ~ⓔ 중에서 비인칭 주어 it은?

ⓐ It is said that Jeju island is a great tourist attraction. ⓑ It has many beautiful beaches. ⓒ It is good to visit Jeju island in any season, but spring might be the best season. ⓓ It is warm in spring, and we can see many beautiful flowers. Visit Jeju island. ⓔ It will be an unforgettable experience.

① ⓐ ② ⓑ ③ ⓒ
④ ⓓ ⑤ ⓔ

22 빈칸에 알맞은 말이 순서대로 바르게 나열된 것은?

- I saw three movies last weekend. One was interesting and ⓐ __________ were boring.
- I have three cousins. One is the same age as me, another is a year younger, and ⓑ __________ is a year older than me.

① others, other
② others, another
③ the other, the other
④ the others, the other
⑤ the others, other

[23~24] 우리말과 뜻이 같도록 빈칸에 알맞은 대명사를 쓰시오.

23 서술형

우리 학급에서 몇몇 학생들은 영어를 좋아하고, 또 다른 몇몇은 수학을 좋아한다.

→ In my class, __________ like English and __________ like mathematics.

24 서술형

강당에는 백 명의 사람들이 있었다. 몇 명은 선생님들이었고 나머지는 학생들이었다.

→ There were 100 people in the auditorium. __________ were teachers and __________ were students.

25 〈보기〉의 밑줄 친 myself와 쓰임이 같은 것은?

보기
I myself prepared the whole dinner for my family.

① She likes to see herself in the mirror.
② You should feel proud of yourself.
③ I'm going to buy a present for myself.
④ James solved the difficult problems himself.
⑤ When I am alone, I sometimes talk to myself.

26 부정을 나타내는 다음 문장 중 그 성격이 다른 하나는?

① Not everyone liked this idea.
② Watching movies is not always fun.
③ Not both of my brothers go to high school.
④ No one in the class could solve the math problem.
⑤ Not all children in that class are active and noisy.

27 밑줄 친 ⓐ~ⓔ 중에서 어법상 틀린 것은?

A: Can I get a discount with my purchase?
B: Sure. There are two kinds of coupons we can offer you. ⓐ One is a 5% discount, and ⓑ the others ⓒ is a $10 discount coupon.
Which ⓓ one would you prefer?
A: I will take the first ⓔ one. Thanks!

① ⓐ ② ⓑ ③ ⓒ
④ ⓓ ⑤ ⓔ

28 서술형

우리말과 뜻이 같도록 괄호 안의 말을 활용하여 완전한 영어 문장을 영작하시오.

A: What do you do in your free time, Julie?
B: I have two things I like to do. One is watching movies, and 나머지 하나는 음악을 듣는 것이야. Both of them help me to relieve my stress.

→ ______________________________
____
______________________ (music, listen, to)

고난도

29 서술형

어법상 어색한 곳을 찾아 바르게 고쳐 쓰시오.

Many people are joining sports clubs these days. Some people join baseball teams and the others join soccer teams.

______________ → ______________

신유형

30 서술형

두 문장의 뜻이 같도록 부정대명사를 사용하여 빈칸에 알맞은 말을 쓰시오.

(1) In our school, Jane got the gold medal, but the rest got nothing.

→ In our school, Jane got the gold medal, but ____________ ____________ got nothing.

(2) In our school, 30% of students like P.E. class, but 50% like music class more.

→ In our school, some students like P.E. class, but ____________ like music class more.

실력 탄탄!
서술형 심화

1 다음은 민호와 지민이네 학급 학생들의 여름방학 계획을 조사한 그래프이다. 그래프의 내용과 일치하도록 적절한 부정대명사를 활용하여 문장을 완성하시오. (각 학급의 학생 수는 20명이다.)

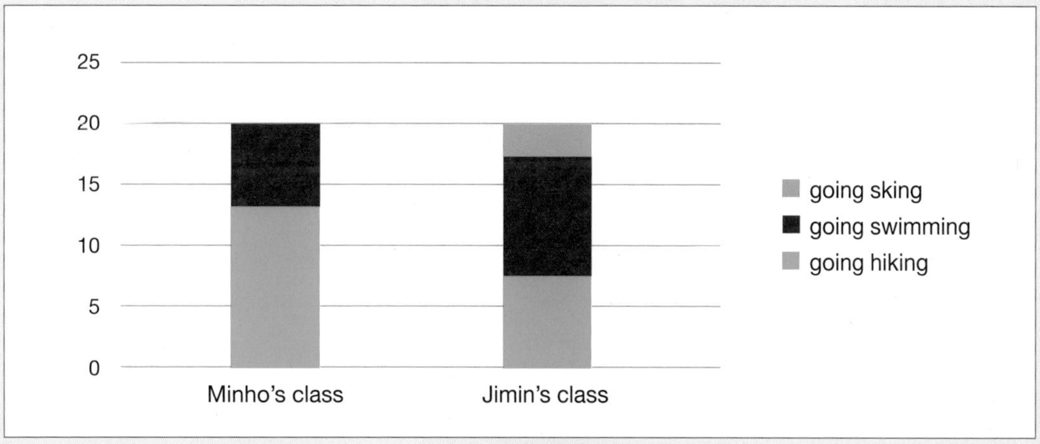

(1) In Minho's class, ______________ will go hiking and ______________ will go swimming during the summer vacation.

(2) In Jimin's class, ______________ will go hiking, ______________ will go swimming, and ______________ will go skiing during the summer vacation.

2 Read the dialogue, and answer the questions.

A: This cap is a bit small for me. Could you show me ⓐ __________?
B: Sure. Try this one.
A: Oh, it looks nice. Okay. I'll take this white shirt, this tie, and this cap.
B: Certainly. ① <u>Do you want me to wrap them up for yourself?</u>
A: ② <u>Only the cap, please. One is a gift.</u> Can you put ⓑ __________ in a shopping bag?
B: Sure. No problem.

(1) Fill in the blanks with the proper word(s) from the Word Box.

Word Box				
another	other	others	the other	the others

ⓐ → ________________ ⓑ → ________________

(2) For ①~②, find and correct the errors among the underlined words.

① ______________ → ______________ ② ______________ → ______________

CHAPTER 08

비교

비교 표현

둘 이상의 사물이나 사람을 비교하여 그 대상의 유사점이나 차이점을 나타내는 표현이다. 형용사/부사의 원래 형태를 그대로 사용해서 비교하는 **원급 비교**와 형용사/부사의 형태를 변화시켜 나타내는 **비교급 비교** 및 **최상급 비교**가 있다.

• 비교 표현

원급 비교	…만큼 ~한/하게	Paul is **two times as fast as** his friends.
비교급 비교	…보다 더 ~한/하게	In Europe, soccer is **much more popular than** baseball.
최상급 비교	가장 ~한/하게	Paul is **the fastest runner on** the team.

Point 01 원급을 이용한 비교: 「as + 형용사/부사 원급 + as」

- **「as + 원급 + as」**는 비교하는 대상의 정도가 같을 때 쓰이며, **'~만큼 ~한/하게'** 라는 뜻이다.
  I am as tall as my older sister. 나는 나의 언니만큼 키가 크다.
  This new bag is as expensive as sneakers. 이 새 가방은 운동화만큼 비싸다.
- **원급 비교의 부정**: 비교하는 두 대상의 정도가 같지 않을 때 **「not + as[so] + 형용사/부사의 원급 + as」**의 형태로 쓰며, **'~만큼 ~하지 않은/않게'** 라는 뜻이다. **'~보다 덜 ~한'**이라는 뜻의 **「less + 원급 + than」** 구문으로 바꾸어 쓸 수 있다.
  James is not as[so] famous as Michael. James는 Michael만큼 유명하지 않다.
  → James is less famous than Michael. James는 Michael보다 덜 유명하다.

A 밑줄 친 부분을 어법에 맞게 고쳐 쓰시오.

1 He can run as <u>fastest</u> as Tim. → ______________
2 She is as <u>prettier</u> as her sister. → ______________
3 Tony jumps as <u>higher</u> as Jessy. → ______________
4 David is not so <u>thinner</u> as Danny. → ______________
5 His shirt is as expensive <u>than</u> mine. → ______________
6 I am not as <u>more diligent</u> as my brother. → ______________
7 My dad makes a cake as <u>better</u> as my mom does. → ______________
8 The woman is as <u>more poor</u> as a church mouse. → ______________
9 My school is not so <u>nearer</u> as the public library. → ______________
10 English is not as <u>the most difficult</u> as world history. → ______________

B 우리말과 뜻이 같도록 「as ~ as」 구문을 사용하여 문장을 완성하시오.

1 그는 Kevin만큼 부유하다.
→ He is ______________ Kevin.

2 과학은 수학만큼 어렵다.
→ Science is ______________ Math.

3 내 가방은 네 것만큼 크지 않다.
→ My bag is ______________ yours.

4 Cindy는 Mandy만큼 배드민턴을 잘 치지 못한다.
→ Cindy does not play badminton ______________ Mandy does.

C 두 문장의 뜻이 같도록 괄호 안의 말을 활용하여 문장을 완성하시오.

1 Sam and Sally are the same height. (tall)
→ Sam is ________ ________ ________ Sally.

2 Los Angeles is warmer than Yellowknife. (warm)
→ Yellowknife is ________ ________ ________ ________
Los Angeles.

Point 02 비교급을 이용한 비교: 「비교급 + than」

- **「비교급 + than」**은 두 가지의 대상을 비교할 때 쓰이며 **'~보다 더 ~한/하게'**라는 의미이다.
  Shame lasts longer than poverty. 수치스러움은 가난보다 더 오래 간다.
  The midterm was more difficult than the final. 중간고사가 기말고사 보다 더 어려웠다.

- **비교급 강조 부사**: 비교급을 강조할 때에는 비교급 앞에 **even, much, still, far, a lot** 등을 붙이며, **'훨씬 더 ~한/하게'**라는 뜻이다.
  I think the girl is much more intelligent than the actor.
  나는 그 소녀가 그 남자 배우보다 훨씬 더 똑똑하다고 생각한다.

  cf. 원급 강조 부사 very: 비교급 앞에는 쓸 수 없다.
  My grandma is very old. (o) 나의 할머니는 연세가 매우 많다.
  My grandma is much older **than** my dad. (o) 나의 할머니는 아빠보다 연세가 훨씬 더 많다.
  My grandma is ~~very~~ older than my dad. (x)

A

괄호 안에서 알맞은 말을 고르시오.

1 I think dogs are (cute, cuter) than cats.
2 She is much (tall, taller) than her mother.
3 He came later (than, to) his classmates did.
4 Their voices were (louder, loudest) than our voices.
5 His backpack is (very, much) heavier than mine.
6 A rattle snake is not so (large, larger) as an anaconda.
7 The sweater is as expensive (as, than) the jumper.
8 She came to the meeting (earlier, more earlier) than I did.
9 My house is (farther, farthest) from school than his house is.

B

우리말과 뜻이 같도록 괄호 안의 말을 바르게 배열하여 문장을 완성하시오.

1 오늘은 어제보다 훨씬 더 따뜻하다. (warmer, much, than)
→ Today is ______________________________ yesterday.

2 Eric의 운동화는 Frank것 보다 더 새것이다. (than, newer)
→ Eric's sneakers are ______________________________ Frank's.

3 흰색 카메라는 검은색보다 더 비싸다. (expensive, more, than)
→ The white camera is ______________________________ the black one.

4 그는 나보다 훨씬 더 많은 돈을 저축한다. (than, more, money, much)
→ He saves ______________________________ I do.

5 우리는 우리 이웃들보다 좀더 일찍 휴가를 떠났다. (earlier, our, neighbors, than, did)
→ We left for vacation ______________________________.

Point 03 최상급을 이용한 비교: 「the + 최상급」

- **「the + 최상급」**은 최상급을 이용한 비교의 표현이다. 최상급 뒤에 **in**, **of**를 써서 비교하는 대상의 범위를 나타낼 수 있으며, **'가장 ~한/하게'** 라는 뜻이다.
  Tony is the smartest boy in school. Tony는 학교에서 가장 똑똑한 소년이다.
  January is the coldest month of the year. 1월은 한 해의 가장 추운 달이다.
- **「one of the + 최상급 + 복수명사」**는 **'가장 ~한 것들 중의 하나'**라는 뜻이다.
  He is one of the funniest students in my class. 그는 우리 반에서 가장 웃기는 학생들 중 한 명이다.
  The rose is one of the most beautiful flowers in the garden. 장미는 정원에서 가장 예쁜 꽃들 중 하나이다.
- **「the + 최상급 + 명사 (+ that) + 주어 + have[has] (+ ever) + p.p.」**는 과거의 한 시점부터 지금까지의 경험을 통틀어 **'~가 가장 ~하다'**는 뜻이다.
  Harry Potter is the best movie that I've ever seen. Harry Potter는 내가 이제껏 본 최고의 영화이다.
  Sally is the cutest girl that I've ever met. Sally는 내가 이제껏 만난 가장 귀여운 소녀이다.

A 괄호 안에서 알맞은 말을 고르시오.

1 Russia is the (larger, largest) country in the world.
2 The black suit is the (good, best) suit in this shop.
3 Henry is one of the best (players, player) on the team.
4 Julie's cell phone is the (newer, newest) one in her class.
5 Economics is the (more, most) difficult subject in my department.
6 Steve is the smartest student I (have ever met, have ever meet).
7 The Grand Canyon is one of (the great, the greatest) natural treasures.
8 The singer's voice is the most beautiful voice that I (heard, have ever heard).
9 *Bulgogi* is (more delicious, the most delicious) dish that I've ever had in Korea.

B 우리말과 뜻이 같도록 괄호 안의 말을 활용하여 문장을 완성하시오.

1 세계에서 가장 높은 산은 무엇이니? (the, mountain, highest)
→ What is ______________________________ in the world?

2 금성은 지구에서 가장 가까운 행성이다. (nearest, the, planet)
→ Venus is ______________________________ to Earth.

3 그는 가장 잘생긴 학생들 중의 한 명이다. (one, students, of, most, the, handsome)
→ He is ______________________________.

4 뉴욕은 내가 방문한 도시들 중 가장 바쁜 곳이다. (that, the, city, busiest, I've, visited, ever)
→ New York is ______________________________.

5 이 학교는 우리나라에서 가장 오래된 학교들 중 하나이다. (the, one, of, schools, oldest)
→ This school is ______________________________ in my country.

Point 04 여러 가지 비교 구문 I
– 배수사 + as + 원급 + as / as + 원급 + as possible

- 「**배수사 + as + 형용사/부사의 원급 + as**」는 '~보다 ~배 ~하다'라는 뜻이다.
  「**배수사 + 비교급 + than**」으로 바꿔 쓸 수 있다.
  This laptop computer is twice as expensive as that cell phone.
  → This laptop computer is twice more expensive than that cell phone.
  이 노트북은 저 핸드폰보다 두 배 더 비싸다.

- 「**as + 원급 + as possible**」은 '가능한 ~한/하게'라는 뜻이고 「**as + 원급 + as + 주어 + can[could]**」로 바꿔 쓸 수 있다.
  Call me back as soon as possible.
  = Call me back as soon as you can. 내게 가능한 빨리 전화해.
  He came home as fast as possible.
  → He came home as fast as he could. 그는 그가 할 수 있는 한 빠르게 집에 왔다.

A 괄호 안에서 알맞은 말을 고르시오.

1 She does volunteer work as often (as, than) she can.
2 The car racer drove the car as (fast, fastest) as he could.
3 He studied for the final exam as hard as (possible, he can).

B 두 문장의 뜻이 같도록 〈보기〉와 같이 문장을 바꿔 쓰시오.

> 보기
> My bag is three times as heavy as his bag.
> → My bag is three times heavier than his bag.

1 This bridge is seven times as long as that bridge.
→ This bridge is ______ ______ ______ ______ that bridge.

2 The encyclopedia is five times as thick as the comic book.
→ The encyclopedia is ______ ______ ______ ______ the comic book.

3 The house with the large garden is twice as expensive as the apartment.
→ The house with the large garden is ______ ______ ______ ______ the apartment.

C 우리말과 뜻이 같도록 괄호 안의 말을 바르게 배열하여 문장을 완성하시오.

1 나는 가능한 빨리 숙제를 끝내기를 희망한다. (as, I, quickly, can, as)
→ I wish to finish my homework ______________________.

2 Minho의 학교 운동장은 Jinsu 학교의 운동장보다 세 배가 더 크다. (as, three, as, times, large)
→ Minho's school playground is ______________________ Jinsu's school playground.

Point 05 여러 가지 비교 구문 II
– 비교급 + and + 비교급 / the 비교급, the 비교급

- 「**비교급 + and + 비교급**」은 '**점점 더 ~한/하게**'라는 뜻이다. 「**more and more + 원급**」도 '**점점 더 ~한/하게**'라는 뜻이다.
  Terry is getting taller and taller. Terry는 점점 더 키가 크고 있다.
  Houses are getting more and more expensive. 그 집들은 점점 더 비싸지고 있다.
- 「**the + 비교급 + 주어 + 동사, the + 비교급 + 주어 + 동사**」는 '**~하면 할수록 더 ~한/하게**' 라는 뜻이다. 의미상 「**As + 주어 + 동사 + 비교급, 주어 + 동사 + 비교급**」으로 바꾸어 쓸 수 있다.
  The harder you study, the better scores you get.
  → As you study harder, you get better scores. 열심히 공부하면 할수록 너는 더 나은 점수를 받는다.

A 괄호 안에서 알맞은 말을 고르시오.

1 As it gets (colder, coldest), you'll sell more jumpers.
2 The little boy is getting (fat and fat, fatter and fatter).
3 (More, The more) you practice, the better results you get.
4 The symptoms are getting (bad and bad, worse and worse).
5 My English test scores are getting (higher and higher, high and higher).

B 우리말과 뜻이 같도록 괄호 안의 말을 활용하여 문장을 완성하시오.

1 잠을 더 자면 잘수록 일어나기가 더 힘들어질 것이다. (the, longer, harder, the)
→ ________ ________ you sleep, ________ ________ it will be to get up.

2 빠르면 빠를수록 더 좋다. (the, the, better, sooner)
→ ________ ________, ________ ________.

3 패스트푸드를 먹으면 먹을수록 너는 더 살이 찔 것이다. (fatter, more, the, fast food, the)
→ ________ ________ ________ ________ you eat, ________ ________ you will get.

4 그는 점점 더 높이 산을 올라가고 있다. (and, higher, higher)
→ He is climbing ________ ________ ________ up the mountain.

C 두 문장의 뜻이 같도록 〈보기〉와 같이 비교급을 활용하여 문장을 다시 쓰시오.

> 보기
> As you save more money, you'll become richer.
> → The more money you save, the richer you will become.

1 As you read more books, you'll get more knowledge.
→ The more books you read, ________________.

2 As the air pollution gets worse, your body will become weaker.
→ The worse the air pollution gets, ________________.

Point 06 여러 가지 비교 구문 III
– 원급과 비교급을 이용한 최상급 표현

■ **원급과 비교급을 이용하여 최상급 의미를 표현**할 수 있다.

No (other) ~ as[so] + 원급 + as …	어떤 ~도 …만큼 ~하지 않은/않게
No (other) ~ 비교급 + than …	어떤 ~도 …보다 ~하지 않은/않게
비교급 + than + any other + 단수명사	다른 어떤 …보다도 더 ~한/하게
비교급 + than + all the other + 복수명사	다른 모든 …보다도 더 ~한/하게

The man is the most famous actor in Korea. 그 남자는 한국에서 가장 유명한 배우이다.
= No (other) actor in Korea is as[so] famous as the man. 한국의 어떤 배우도 그 남자만큼 유명하지 않다.
= No (other) actor in Korea is more famous than the man. 한국의 어떤 배우도 그 남자보다 더 유명하지 않다.
= The man is more famous than any other actor in Korea. 그 남자는 한국에서 다른 어떤 배우보다 더 유명하다.
= The man is more famous than all the other actors in Korea. 그 남자는 한국에서 모든 배우들보다 더 유명하다.

A 주어진 문장과 뜻이 같도록 밑줄 친 부분을 어법에 맞게 고쳐 쓰시오.

1 The teddy bear is the most memorable birthday gift.
(그 곰 인형이 가장 기억에 남는 생일 선물이다.)
(1) No birthday gift is as more memorable as the teddy bear. → ____________
(2) No birthday gift is more memorable as the teddy bear. → ____________
(3) The teddy bear is more memorable than any others birthday gift. → ____________
(4) The teddy bear is more memorable than all others birthday gifts. → ____________

2 The lottery winner is the luckiest person in the world.
(그 로또 당첨자는 세계에서 가장 운이 좋은 사람이다.)
(1) No person is as the luckiest as the lottery winner. → ____________
(2) No person is luckier as the lottery winner. → ____________
(3) The lottery winner is luckier than any other persons. → ____________
(4) The lottery winner is luckiest than other person. → ____________

B 문장의 의미하는 바가 같도록 〈보기〉와 같이 영작하시오.

보기
Mrs. Anderson is the best English teacher in my school.
→ No (other) English teacher in my school is as(so) good as Mrs. Anderson.
→ No (other) English teacher in my school is better than Mrs. Anderson.
→ Mrs. Anderson is better than any other English teacher in my school.
→ Mrs. Anderson is better than all the other English teachers in my school.

1 Mt. Everest is the highest mountain in the world.
→ (1) ________ mountain in the world is ________ ________ ________ Mt. Everest.
→ (2) ________ mountain in the world is ________ ________ Mt. Everest.
→ (3) Mt. Everest is ________ ________ ________ ________ mountain in the world.
→ (4) Mt. Everest is ________ ________ ________ ________ ________ mountains in the world.

일등 비법 노트

비법 ① 비교급을 강조할 때는 very를 쓰지 못한다!

대표기출 1

빈칸에 들어갈 수 없는 것은?

My mom decorated the table __________ more luxuriously than we expected.

① still ② a lot ③ very ④ even ⑤ much

대표기출 2

어법상 틀린 문장은?

① Mark is still younger than Walter.
② Tom is much taller than Brandon.
③ Brandon is very thinner than Patrick.
④ Charlie is a lot smarter than Patrick.
⑤ Abraham is even stronger than Adam.

비법 ② 「비교급 + than + any other + 단수명사」의 변형 표현을 기억하라! = 「비교급 + than + all the other + 복수명사」!

대표기출 1

〈보기〉와 의미하는 바가 다른 것은?

보기
Sarah is more diligent than any other student in my class.

① Sarah is the most diligent student in my class.
② Sarah is as diligent as the other students in my class.
③ No other student in my class is as diligent as Sarah.
④ No other student in my class is more diligent than Sarah.
⑤ Sarah is more diligent than all the other students in my class.

비법 3 「as … as」 사이에는 형용사나 부사의 원급이 온다!

대표기출 1

밑줄 친 부분이 어법상 틀린 것은?

① Scott is as faster as I am.
② He is as smart as his sister.
③ She is as tall as her best friend.
④ His house is as large as her house.
⑤ This phone is as expensive as that one.

비법 4 「최상급 + 명사 + 주어 + have (+ ever) + 과거분사」 표현은 영작 단골 문제!

대표기출 1

우리말과 뜻이 같도록 괄호 안의 말을 활용하여 문장을 완성하시오.

이 흰색 웨딩드레스는 내가 이제껏 본 것 중 가장 아름다운 드레스이다.
(beautiful, see, ever)

→ This white wedding dress is ______________________
______________________________.

비법 5 '점점 더 ~한/하게'의 뜻으로는 「비교급 + and + 비교급」이다!

대표기출 1

밑줄 친 부분이 어법상 틀린 것은?

① It's becoming darker and darker outside.
② The air pollution is getting bad and bad.
③ The weather is getting colder and colder.
④ The fragrance of the perfume got better and better.
⑤ English grammar is becoming more and more difficult to me.

내신 만점! 실전 기출

01 빈칸에 올 수 <u>없는</u> 말은?

She needs ________ than she has.

① much time ② more time
③ far more time ④ a lot more time
⑤ much more time

02 밑줄 친 부분이 어법상 옳은 것은?

① He is <u>as stronger as</u> Tom.
② She can <u>as run fast as</u> you.
③ This chair is <u>as heavy as</u> that one.
④ Yesterday was <u>so not cold as</u> today.
⑤ I want to be <u>popularer than</u> the actor.

03 서술형

다음 우리말을 〈원급 비교〉 표현을 활용하여 영작하시오. (6단어)

그녀는 Jack만큼 유명하다.

→ ________________________

04 우리말과 뜻이 같도록 빈칸에 알맞은 말이 순서대로 나열된 것은?

날씨가 따뜻할수록, 나는 기분이 더 좋아진다.
→ ________ the weather is, ________ I feel.

① warm, good ② warmer, better
③ The warm, the good ④ The warmer, the better
⑤ The warmest, the best

05 서술형

「the + 비교급, the + 비교급」 구문과 괄호 안의 단어를 활용하여 다음 대화문을 완성하시오. (필요하면 형태를 바꾸시오.)

A: I want to lose weight. What should I do?

→ B: __________ (little) you eat, __________ (much) weight you can lose.

06 밑줄 친 부분이 어법상 <u>틀린</u> 것은?

① He feels <u>a lot better</u> today.
② My new bag is <u>very cheaper than</u> my old bag.
③ This diary is <u>much more meaningful than</u> gold.
④ The test was <u>even more difficult than</u> I had expected.
⑤ My mom drives <u>far more carefully than</u> my dad.

07 의미하는 바가 나머지 넷과 <u>다른</u> 하나는?

① Nothing is as beautiful as true love.
② True love is the most beautiful thing.
③ Nothing is more beautiful than true love.
④ True love is one of the most beautiful things.
⑤ True love is more beautiful than any other thing.

08 서술형

괄호 안의 말을 바르게 나열하여 ⓐ를 완전한 문장으로 영작하시오. (필요 시 괄호 안의 단어의 형태를 바꿀 것)

A: Is your mom a good cook?
B: Yes. ⓐ <u>나는 나의 엄마보다 더 요리를 잘하는 사람은 없다고 생각해.</u> (good, than, my, mom no, person, cook)

→ I think ________________________
________________________.

[9~10] 어법상 <u>어색한</u> 것을 <u>모두</u> 고르시오. (2개)

09

① She ran fast and fast in the race.
② The more fantastic it is, the more I enjoy it.
③ He is getting taller and taller as he gets older.
④ The more dangerous it is, the most careful you should be.
⑤ The hotter the weather gets, the more iced tea we drink.

10

① Yuna is the most intelligent girl.
② The movie I saw yesterday was the worse movie.
③ My school uniform is the most comfortable uniform.
④ Gyeongbokgung is the most famous palace in Seoul.
⑤ Internet words are not as regularly as standard language.

11 서술형

다음 세 문장의 뜻이 같도록 빈칸에 알맞은 말을 쓰시오.

Michael has read the most books in his school.

→ (1) Michael has read ________ ________ ________ ________ ________ student in his school.

→ (2) ________ other student in his school has read as ________ ________ ________ Michael has.

[12~13] 〈보기〉와 의미하는 바가 같은 문장을 고르시오.

12

보기
She ran as fast as she could in the race.

① She ran much faster in the race.
② She ran as fast as possible in the race.
③ She ran faster than any other girl.
④ She ran as fast as other girls in the race.
⑤ She ran faster than she could in the race.

13

보기
New York is the most crowded city in the US.

① Every city in the US is as crowded as New York.
② New York is as crowded as other cities in the US.
③ Every city in the US is more crowded than New York.
④ New York is more crowded than any other city in the US.
⑤ New York is not so crowded as other cities in the US.

14 다음 우리말을 영어로 바르게 옮긴 것은?

나무늘보는 내가 본 동물 중에 가장 게으른 동물이다.
* 나무늘보: sloth

① The sloth is the laziest animal.
② The sloth is one of the laziest animals.
③ The sloth is lazier than other animals.
④ The sloth is the laziest animal that I've ever seen.
⑤ The sloth is less lazy than any other animal I've ever seen.

15 서술형

아래 표의 내용과 일치하도록 주어진 구문을 활용하여 질문에 답하시오.

Name	Adam	Eric
Height	172cm	172cm
Weight	67kg	62kg

(1) Q1: Who is taller, Adam or Eric?(as ~ as)
A1: Adam ________________.

(2) Q2: Who is heavier? (비교급)
A2: Adam ________________.

16 다음 우리말을 영어로 바르게 옮긴 것은?

파란색 자는 빨간색 자보다 다섯 배 더 길다.

① The blue ruler is a fifth longer than the red ruler.
② The blue ruler is five times long than the red ruler.
③ The blue ruler is five times longer than the red ruler.
④ The blue ruler is five times longest than the red ruler.
⑤ The blue ruler is five times more longer than the red ruler.

17 서술형

주어진 〈조건〉에 맞춰 우리말을 영작하시오.

조건
1. 단어 fast, the를 사용할 것
2. 해석: 치타는 세상에서 가장 빠른 동물이다.

→ The cheetah is ________ ________ ________ in the world.

18 다음과 같은 뜻의 문장을 모두 고르면?

He and I drink the same amount of milk every day.

① He drinks milk as many as me.
② He drinks as much as my milk.
③ He drinks as much milk as I do.
④ He drinks as many milk as me.
⑤ He drinks milk as much as I do.

19 대화의 흐름이 자연스럽도록 빈칸에 가장 알맞은 말은?

A: What do you think is the most important thing in your life?
B: I think ____________________.

① love is the most important thing
② honesty is as important as love
③ health is more important than wealth
④ friendship is very important in my life
⑤ wisdom is much better than foolishness

20 다음 우리말을 영어로 바르게 옮긴 것은?

이모티콘은 온라인상에서 너의 얼굴 표정을 표현할 수 있는 가장 쉬운 방법이다.

① Emoticons are the easier way to express your facial expressions online.
② Emoticons are easiest the way to express your facial expressions online.
③ Emoticons are the easiest way to express your facial expressions online.
④ Emoticons are one of the easiest ways to express your facial expressions online.
⑤ Emoticons are easy ways to express your facial expressions you've ever used online.

21 서술형

문장 ⓐ를 〈보기〉와 같이 비교급과 than을 활용하여 다시 쓰시오.

보기
Russia is the largest country in the world.
→ Russia is larger than any other country in the world.

ⓐ Michael was the best pitcher in the US.

→ Michael was ____________________ ____________________ in the US.

22 다음을 읽고 (A)를 영어로 바르게 옮긴 것은?

I read a report about a five-year-old genius named Jacob. According to the report, his IQ is 157. (A) <u>그는 수학 선생님만큼 수학 문제를 잘 푼다.</u> He is smart enough to be a member of Mensa. If he joins, he will be its youngest member.

① He solves math problems as well as a math teacher.
② He solves math problems best than a math teacher.
③ He solves math problems as better than a math teacher.
④ He solves math problems less good than a math teacher.
⑤ He does not solve math problems as well as a math teacher.

23 어법상 옳지 <u>않은</u> 것을 <u>모두</u> 고르면?

ⓐ The more you read, the smartest you will be.
ⓑ The colder it is, the easier you can catch a cold.
ⓒ The more you exercise, the healthyer you become.
ⓓ The early you buy, the bigger discount you can get.
ⓔ The longer you play outside, the more tired you will get.

① ⓐ, ⓒ, ⓓ ② ⓐ, ⓒ, ⓔ
③ ⓑ, ⓓ, ⓔ ④ ⓒ, ⓓ, ⓔ
⑤ ⓑ, ⓒ, ⓓ

24 밑줄 친 ⓐ와 바꿔 쓸 수 있는 것은?

Kakao Talk is a free mobile messenger application used on smart phones. It currently offers 13 different languages and has many overseas subscribers. Users can talk to each other at the same time ⓐ <u>much</u> more easily than before.

① so ② lots of ③ very
④ many ⑤ a lot

고난도

25 서술형

우리말과 일치하도록 괄호 안의 단어를 바르게 배열하여 문장을 완성하시오.

나는 Nicole이 춤추는 것보다 어떤 것을 하기를 더 좋아하는지 알고 싶다.
(likes, want, than, dancing, know, I, Nicole, to, do, more, to, what)

→ ______________________________
____

고난도

26 서술형

우리말과 뜻이 같도록 주어진 〈조건〉에 맞게 영작하시오.

조건
1. 「the + 비교급, the + 비교급」을 사용할 것
2. 'I feel'까지 총 11단어로 이루어진 문장으로 영작할 것
3. 다음 어휘를 모두 활용할 것: near, come, nervous, the test date

시험일이 다가올수록, 나는 점점 더 불안해진다.

→ ______________________________
______________________________ I feel.

27 대화의 흐름이 자연스럽도록 빈칸 ⓐ에 알맞은 말은?

A: Did you hear the news?
B: What news?
A: Jordan became the world boxing champion.
B: Really? I am happy for him.
A: Same here. ⓐ ________________

① He practiced as hard as other boxer I knew.
② He practiced harder than other boxers I knew.
③ He practiced hardest of any other boxers I knew.
④ He practiced harder than any other boxer I knew.
⑤ He practiced hardest than any other boxer I knew.

28 서술형

문장 ⓐ~ⓖ에서 어법상 틀린 부분을 찾아 바르게 고쳐 쓰시오. (4개)

ⓐ Tony is as kinder as Sumin.
ⓑ Bell was not here as early as Tim.
ⓒ I have less money than my sister.
ⓓ She wasn't as thin as me in the past.
ⓔ I wonder how I can sing good than him.
ⓕ He does not work so harder as his brother.
ⓖ The teachers in my school teach very better than teachers in other schools.

(1) ____________ → ____________
(2) ____________ → ____________
(3) ____________ → ____________
(4) ____________ → ____________

29 서술형

빈칸 ⓐ에 알맞은 말을 괄호 안의 단어를 바르게 배열하여 영작하시오.

Dear Dad,

I am writing this email to say thank you. I love you very much. ⓐ ____________ You are always generous and kind. Thank you for all you've done for me.

With love,
Joe

→ ________________________________
____

(I, person, think, you, that, are, best, the, the, in, world)

신유형

30 서술형

주어진 두 문장을 〈조건〉에 맞춰 〈보기〉와 같이 한 문장으로 다시 쓰시오.

조건

1. 단어 fast를 쓰시오. (단, 필요하면 단어의 형태를 바꿀 것)
2. 「배수사 + 비교급 + than」 구문을 사용하시오.

보기

- My backpack is $10.
- My brother's backpack is $30.

→ My brother's backpack is three times more expensive than mine.

- The speed limit in the school zone is 30mph.
- The speed limit on the highway is 120mph.

→ The speed limit on the highway is ________ ________ ________ ________ the speed limit in the school zone.

실력 탄탄!
서술형 심화

1 다음 〈조건〉에 맞춰 주어진 우리말을 영작하시오.

조건
1. 「the + 비교급, the + 비교급」 구문을 사용할 것
2. 단어 read, will, become을 사용할 것
3. 총 10단어로 이루어진 완전한 문장으로 영작할 것

더 많은 책을 읽을수록 너는 더욱 지혜로워질 것이다.

→ ______________________________

2 Look at the chart below. Make sentences using all of the given words. You may change the word forms.

(1)

(many, the, than, all, books, other, students)

(2)

(well, no, as, student, as)

(1) James reads __________ __________ __________ __________
__________ __________ __________ in his school.

(2) __________ __________ memorizes English words __________
__________ __________ Ricky does.

3 다음 조건에 맞춰 주어진 우리말을 영작하시오.

조건
1. 비교급 2개를 반드시 문장 안에 포함할 것
2. 「as ~ as」 구문을 사용하여 긍정과 부정을 모두 표현할 것
3. 단어 high, hard를 사용할 것

나의 수학 점수는 너만큼 높지 않아서 나는 너만큼 열심히 공부할 것이다.

→ My math score is __________ __________ __________ __________
yours, so I will __________ __________ __________ __________
you.

CHAPTER 09

접속사

접속사

접속사는 단어와 단어, 구와 구, 또는 절과 절을 **연결해 주는 말**이다. 하는 역할에 따라 **등위접속사**와 **종속접속사**로 구분할 수 있다.

• 접속사의 쓰임

접속사	단어와 단어를 연결	Sally ate bread **and** cheese.
	구와 구를 연결	Hurry up **and** open the door.
	절과 절을 연결	**When** I visited Sam, he was just about to bake some cookies.
		We know **that** he is honest and trustworthy.

• 구(phrase): '주어 + 동사'를 포함하지 않으면서 둘 이상의 단어가 모여 하나의 품사 역할을 하는 것
• 절(clause): '주어 + 동사'를 포함하고 있으며 둘 이상의 단어가 모여 문장의 일부를 이루는 것

• 등위접속사 *vs.* 종속접속사

등위접속사	단어와 단어, 절과 절, 또는 문장과 문장을 〈**대등하게 이어주는 접속사**〉 The car is small **but** convenient. 그 차는 작지만 편리하다.
종속접속사	문법적 역할이 대등하지 않은 〈**종속절을 주절에 연결해 주는 접속사**〉 **① 부사절을 이끄는 접속사** Alice fell asleep **while** she was watching the movie. Alice는 그 영화를 보는 동안 잠이 들고 말았다. **② 명사절을 이끄는 접속사 that** We know **that** you did your best. 네가 최선을 다했다는 것을 우리는 안다.

Point 01 부사절을 이끄는 종속접속사 I – 시간, 이유

- **종속접속사**: 독립적으로 쓰이지 않고 문장의 일부로 쓰이는 절을 종속절이라고 한다. 이러한 **종속절을 주절에 연결해주는 접속사**가 종속접속사이다.
- **문장에서 부사 역할을 하는 절을 이끄는 종속접속사: when**(~할 때), **before**(~하기 전에), **because**(~때문에), **if**(만약 ~라면), **though**(비록 ~일지라도) 등이 있다.
- **시간을 나타내는 종속접속사: when**(~할 때), **while**(~하는 동안), **as**(~하고 있을 때, ~하면서), **before**(~전에), **after**(~후에), **since**(~이래로), **until**(~할 때까지)이 있다.

When I arrived at school, the gate was closed. 내가 학교에 도착했을 때, 문이 닫혀있었다.
I listened to music while I was doing my homework. 나는 숙제를 하는 동안 음악을 들었다.
She saw John as she was walking down the street. 그녀는 길을 걸으며 John을 보았다.
It's been a year since I left the town. 내가 마을을 떠난 이래로 1년이 되었다.

- **이유를 나타내는 종속접속사: because, since, as**가 있고, '~이니까, ~때문에'라는 뜻이다.

※ 이유의 강도: because(~하기 때문에) > since (~하니까) > as (~하므로)

As you are here, let's move the furniture together. 네가 여기 있으니 함께 가구를 옮기자.
Since you are tall, please hang this coat on the wall. 네가 키가 크니까 벽에 이 코트를 걸어줘.
I need to hurry up because I'm late for class. 나는 수업에 늦었기 때문에 서둘러야 해.

※ because 뒤에는 '주어 + 동사', because of 뒤에는 '명사(구)'가 온다.

A

괄호 안에서 알맞은 말을 고르시오.

1 (When, While) I came to school, no one was there yet.
2 (Since, After) the weather is fine, we will go on a picnic.
3 (Until, While) he was out, his best friend, Timmy, called him.
4 (As, Until) the movie was fun, she bought the original novel.
5 (As, Before) she was talking on the phone, she got on a subway.

B

밑줄 친 부분에 유의하여 우리말로 해석하시오.

1 <u>While</u> we're out, take care of your baby brother.
→ ______________________________

2 <u>Since</u> it was rush hour, the traffic was really bad.
→ ______________________________

C

우리말과 뜻이 같도록 문장을 완성하시오.

1 그는 첫 번째 책 출간 이후 베스트셀러 작가가 되었다.
→ He became a bestselling author __________ he released his 1st book.

2 나는 타이타닉 영화가 재미있고 로맨틱해서 세 번이나 보았다.
→ I watched Titanic three times __________ it was so fun and romantic.

Point 02 부사절을 이끄는 종속접속사 II – 조건, 양보, 대조

■ **조건을 나타내는 종속접속사: if**(만일 ~한다면), **unless**(만일 ~하지 않는다면)가 있다.
If it is nice this afternoon, I will go to the park. 만일 오후에 날씨가 좋으면, 나는 공원에 갈 것이다.
Unless it rains hard, I will walk to school. 만일 비가 많이 오지 않으면, 나는 학교에 걸어갈 것이다.
= If it does not rain hard, I will walk to school.

※ 시간, 조건을 나타내는 부사절에서는 현재시제로 미래를 나타낸다.
When I finish the book, I'll lend it to you. 내가 그 책을 다 읽으면, 너에게 빌려줄게.

■ **양보를 나타내는 종속접속사: though**, **even though**, **although**가 있으며 '비록 ~이지만, ~임에도 불구하고'라는 뜻이다.
Although he is poor, he is not sad. 그는 가난함에도 불구하고 슬프지 않다.
Even though she is thin, she is on a diet. 그녀는 말랐음에도 불구하고, 다이어트를 한다.

■ **대조를 나타내는 종속접속사: while**(~하는 반면에)이 있다.
He likes Italian food, while she likes Korean food.
그는 이탈리아 음식을 좋아하는 반면에, 그녀는 한국 음식을 좋아한다.

A 빈칸에 알맞은 말을 〈보기〉에서 골라 쓰시오. (단, 한 번씩만 쓸 것)

보기
if unless although while

1 ____________ you leave now, you can arrive on time.
2 ____________ she is quite old, she still has a very good memory.
3 Tim is very good at English, ____________ his brother is absolutely not.
4 ____________ you sleep enough, you can't concentrate well on your studies.

B 밑줄 친 부분에 유의하여 우리말로 해석하시오.

1 <u>If</u> I miss the school bus, I will ride my bike to school.
→ ________________________________

2 She will be a winner <u>unless</u> she makes any mistakes.
→ ________________________________

3 My parents want me to be a teacher, <u>while</u> I want to be a cook.
→ ________________________________

4 <u>Even though</u> he is only 4 years old, he can write his name neatly.
→ ________________________________

C 우리말과 뜻이 같도록 괄호 안의 말을 바르게 배열하여 문장을 완성하시오.

1 봄인데도 불구하고 밖은 춥다. (is, even though, it, spring)
→ ________________________________, it is still cold outside.

2 어떤 사람들은 야구를 좋아하는 반면, 다른 사람들은 축구를 좋아한다. (others, like, while, soccer)
→ Some people like baseball ________________________________.

Point 03 부사절을 이끄는 종속접속사 III – 결과, 목적

■ 결과를 나타내는 종속접속사

(1) 「so + 형용사/부사 + that + 주어 + can ~」 구문은 '너무 ~해서 …한'의 뜻으로, '…하기에 충분히 ~한'의 뜻인 「형용사/부사 + enough to + 동사원형」 구문으로 바꿔 쓸 수 있다.

Eric is so strong that he can carry the box.
= Eric is strong enough to carry the box. Eric은 매우 힘이 세서 그 상자를 나를 수 있다.

(2) 「so + 형용사/부사 + that + 주어 + can't ~」 구문은 '…하기엔 너무 ~한'의 뜻으로, 「too + 형용사/부사 + to + 동사원형」 '너무 ~해서 …할 수 없는'으로 바꿔 쓸 수 있다.

I am so nervous that I can't make a presentation.
= I am too nervous to make a presentation. 나는 너무 떨려서 발표를 할 수가 없다.
Kelly was so tired that she couldn't keep walking.
= Kelly was too tired to keep walking. Kelly는 너무 피곤해서 계속 걸을 수가 없었다.

■ 목적을 나타내는 종속접속사 so that ~: 「so that + 주어 + 동사」 구문은 '~하기 위해, ~하도록'이라는 뜻으로 목적을 나타낸다. 「in order to + 동사원형」이나 「so as to + 동사원형」 구문으로 바꿔 쓸 수 있다.

I save money so that I can buy a new car.
= I save money in order to buy a new car. 나는 새 차를 사기 위해 저축을 한다.

A 괄호 안에서 알맞은 말을 고르시오.

1 The pants are too big for me (that, to) wear.
2 It was so delicious (that, to) everyone liked it.
3 The soccer player is excellent enough (scoring, to score) a goal.
4 She bought some apples (so that, to) she could make apple pies.
5 He went to the library (so that, in order to) borrow books for his final report.

B 두 문장의 뜻이 같도록 빈칸에 알맞은 말을 쓰시오.

1 His voice is so soft that I cannot understand it.
→ His voice is too ______________________ understand.

2 She was so tired that she couldn't go jogging this morning.
→ She was too ______________________ go jogging this morning.

3 People study English hard so that they can communicate with people around the world.
→ People study English hard in ______________________.

C 우리말과 뜻이 같도록 괄호 안의 말을 활용하여 문장을 완성하시오.

1 Tony는 그 집을 살 수 있을 만큼 부자이다. (enough to)
→ Tony is rich ______________________ the house.

2 그 공이 너무 빨라서 나는 칠 수가 없었다. (so, that)
→ The ball was ______________________ hit it.

Point 04 명사절을 이끄는 종속접속사

- **명사절이란**: 「**접속사 + 주어 + 동사**」 또는 「**의문사 + 주어 + 동사**」가 명사처럼 주어나 보어, 또는 목적어 역할을 하면 **명사절**이라고 부른다.
- **명사절을 이끄는 종속접속사**에는 that, 그리고 if와 whether가 있다.

(1) 명사절을 이끄는 종속접속사 that

「**that + 주어 + 동사**」로 주어, 목적어, 보어 역할을 하며, 목적어절을 이끌 때의 접속사 that은 생략할 수 있다.

- **주어**: That he is smart is obvious. 그가 똑똑하다는 것은 확실하다.
- **목적어**: I believe (that) it will be a White Christmas. 나는 화이트 크리스마스가 될 것을 믿는다.
- **보어**: The important thing is that we have to finish it.
  중요한 것은 우리가 그것을 끝내야 한다는 것이다.

(2) 명사절을 이끄는 종속접속사 if나 whether

「**if[whether] + 주어 + 동사**」는 '~인지 아닌지'라는 의미로 문장에서 주어, 목적어, 보어 역할을 한다. if와 whether는 대개 서로 바꿔 쓸 수 있으나, whether가 if보다 격식체에서 선호된다.

주어	Whether she will meet him or not is uncertain. 그녀가 그를 만날지 안 만날지는 확실하지 않다. ※ 주어로 온 명사절에는 whether만 쓴다. if는 주어절을 이끌 수 없다.
목적어	Let's ask her if[whether] she can make it for us. 그녀가 우리를 위해 그 일을 해줄 수 있나 물어보자. ※ 〈to부정사 앞〉이나 〈전치사 뒤〉에는 whether를 쓰고, if는 쓸 수 없다. I can't decide whether to take the test or not. 그 시험을 치를지 어떨지 결정 못하겠다.
보어	The problem is if[whether] they can come on time. 문제는 그들이 제시간에 올 수 있을지 여부이다.

cf. 접속사 if는 조건을 나타내는 접속사로도 쓰인다. ☞ Chapter 9의 Point 2를 참고

A 괄호 안에서 알맞은 말을 고르시오.

1 (That, Whether) he is rich or not is not important.
2 I don't know (that, whether) he will bring some snacks.
3 (If, That) the boy looks just like his parents is natural.
4 The worst thing is (if, that) all the tickets are sold out.
5 The article tells (if, that) we will have about a 2-week break.

B 우리말과 뜻이 같도록 괄호 안의 말을 바르게 배열하여 문장을 완성하시오.

1 문제는 그 소문이 사실이라는 것이다. (the rumor, true, is, that)
→ The problem is ______________________________.

2 나는 엄마가 집에 있는지 없는지 모르겠다. (if, is, at home, my mom)
→ I don't know ______________________________.

3 그 음식이 좋을지 어떨지가 문제이다. (whether, good, the food, is)
→ ______________________________ or not is the matter.

4 청소년들은 그들의 부모님들이 그들을 이해해주기 바란다. (will, them, their parents, understand, that)
→ Teenagers hope ______________________________.

Point 05 명사절 – 간접의문문

■ **간접의문문**: 의문문이 종속절(명사절)이 되어 다른 문장의 일부로 쓰이는 것을 말한다. 이 때의 종속절은 의문사, 또는 if나 whether로 시작한다.

■ **간접의문문의 형태**

(1) 의문사가 있는 경우: 「의문사 + 주어+ 동사」의 어순으로 쓴다.

ⓐ I don't know. + **What time is it** now? 나는 모른다. 지금 몇 시니?
→ I don't know what time it is now. 나는 지금 몇 시인지 모른다.

ⓑ Show him. + **What did you** buy for him? 그에게 보여줘. 그를 위해 무엇을 샀니?
→ Show him what you bought for him. 그를 위해 무엇을 샀는지 보여줘.

※ 주절의 동사가 think, believe, suppose, imagine, guess 등의 생각, 추측을 나타내는 동사인 경우: 간접의문문의 의문사를 문장 맨 앞으로 보낸다.

ⓒ Do you think? + **Which** is better for me? 너는 생각하니? 나에게 어느 것이 더 낫니?
→ Which do you think is better for me? 나에게 어느 것이 더 낫다고 생각하니?

(2) 의문사가 없는 경우: if나 whether를 써서 「**if[whether] + 주어 + 동사 + (~or not)**」의 어순으로 쓰고, '~인지 아닌지'라고 해석한다.
I wonder. + Will the movie be interesting? 나는 궁금하다. 그 영화가 재미있을까?
→ I wonder if[whether] the movie will be interesting. 나는 그 영화가 재미있을지 없을지 궁금하다.

A

〈보기〉와 같이 두 문장을 한 문장으로 바꿔 쓰시오.

보기
Did you know? + Where did she come from?
→ Did you know where she came from?

1 I wonder. + When is the party?
→ I wonder ________________________________.

2 Nobody knew. + Were the people safe?
→ Nobody knew ________________________________.

3 Do you think? + When did they meet first?
→ ________________________________ they met first?

B

우리말과 뜻이 같도록 괄호 안의 말을 바르게 배열하여 문장을 완성하시오.

1 우체국이 어디에 있는지 말씀해 주실래요? (you, can, me, where, tell, is, the post office)
→ ________________________________

2 그녀는 그가 그녀를 사랑하는지 궁금하다. (she, if, wonders, he, her, loves)
→ ________________________________

3 그는 버스가 언제 도착하는지 물었다. (when, would, the bus, arrive, he, asked)
→ ________________________________

Point 06 상관접속사

■ **상관접속사**: 떨어져 있는 둘 이상의 어구가 짝을 이루어 하나의 접속사 역할을 하는 것을 상관접속사라고 한다.

※ 등위접속사나 상관접속사는 문법적으로 같은 역할을 하는 대등한 관계의 것을 연결한다.
He enjoys cooking and baking. 그는 요리와 제빵을 즐겨 한다.
He enjoys not only cooking but also baking. 그는 요리뿐만 아니라 제빵도 즐겨 한다.

■ **자주 쓰이는 상관접속사 표현**

상관접속사 종류	의미	주어로 올 때 동사의 수 일치
both *A* and *B*	*A*와 *B* 둘 다	동사의 복수형을 취함
not *A* but *B*	*A*가 아닌 *B*	동사의 수는 B에 일치 (= 동사에 가까운 대상에 수 일치!)
either *A* or *B*	*A*나 *B* 둘 중 하나	
neither *A* nor *B*	*A*도 *B*도 아닌	
not only *A* but also *B*	*A*뿐만 아니라 *B*도	
B as well as *A*		

Both Tim and I like playing soccer. Tim과 나는 둘 다 축구 하는 것을 좋아한다.
It is not my pen but his. 그것은 내 펜이 아닌 그의 것이다.
Either Nick or you have to go there. Nick이나 너 둘 중 하나는 거기에 가야 한다.
Neither Sarah nor I am not responsible for that. Sarah도 나도 그것에 책임이 있지 않다.
Not only the children but also their mother likes to watch the TV program.
= Their mother as well as the children likes to watch the TV program.
아이들뿐만 아니라 그들의 엄마도 그 TV프로그램 보는 것을 좋아한다.

A 괄호 안에서 알맞은 말을 고르시오.

1 Neither Jason (or, nor) Becky will pass the exam.
2 Both Mr. Jackson (or, and) Mrs. Jackson like Italian food.
3 Not Ben (and, but) Sarah wants to have a surprise party.
4 Either my mom (or, nor) my dad is going to pick me up.
5 I enjoy watching not only horror movies (but, and) also comedy movies.

B 밑줄 친 부분을 어법에 맞게 고쳐 쓰시오.

1 Both she and he <u>has</u> the same hobby. → ______________
2 Neither Tony nor I <u>likes</u> strawberries. → ______________
3 Not you but Mrs. Smith <u>are</u> a math teacher. → ______________

C 우리말과 뜻이 같도록 빈칸에 알맞은 말을 쓰시오.

1 Tina는 소고기도 돼지고기도 좋아하지 않는다.
→ Tina likes ____________ beef ____________ pork.

2 그녀는 변호사나 경찰 둘 중 하나가 되고 싶어한다.
→ She wants to be ____________ a lawyer ____________ a police officer.

Point 07 「명령문, and/or ...」 구문

- 「명령문 + and ...」: '~해라, 그러면 …할 것이다'라는 뜻이다.
  「If you + 동사의 현재형, you + (조)동사 ~」 구문으로 바꿔 쓸 수 있다.
  Practice hard, and you'll win the game. 열심히 연습해라, 그러면 경기에서 이길 것이다.
  → If you practice hard, you'll win the game.

- 「명령문 + or ...」: '~해라, 그렇지 않으면 …할 것이다'라는 뜻이다.
  「If you don't + 동사원형, you + (조)동사 ~」
  또는 **「Unless you + 동사의 현재형, you + (조)동사 ~」**로 바꿔 쓸 수 있다.
  Hurry up, or you'll be late for school. 서둘러라. 그렇지 않으면, 너는 학교에 늦을 것이다.
  → If you don't hurry up, you'll be late for school.
  → Unless you hurry up, you'll be late for school.

A

접속사를 활용하여 〈보기〉와 같이 바꿔 쓸 때 빈칸에 알맞은 말을 쓰시오.

> 보기
>
> ⓐ Go to the zoo, and your son will love it.
> → If you go to the zoo, your son will love it.
> ⓑ Obey the rule, or you have to pay the fine.
> → If you don't obey the rule, you have to pay the fine.
> → Unless you obey the rule, you have to pay the fine.

1 Take public transportation, and you will save time.
→ ______________________________, you will save time.

2 Submit the report on time, or you will fail the course.
→ ______________________________, you will fail the course.
→ ______________________________, you will fail the course.

3 Run, or you'll be late for the lesson.
→ ______________________________, you'll be late for the lesson.
→ ______________________________, you'll be late for the lesson.

4 Read the directions carefully, and you won't have any trouble.
→ ______________________________, you won't have any trouble.

B

우리말과 뜻이 같도록 괄호 안의 말을 바르게 배열하여 문장을 완성하시오.

1 친절해라, 그러면 사람들이 너를 좋아할 것이다. (people, like, will, you, and)
→ Be nice, ______________________________.

2 열심히 공부해라, 그러면 너의 꿈은 현실이 될 것이다. (true, and, will, come, your dreams)
→ Study hard, ______________________________.

3 조용히 해라, 그렇지 않으면 잠자는 아기가 깰 것이다. (sleeping, or, wake, baby, the, will, up)
→ Be quiet, ______________________________.

Point 08 접속부사

- **접속부사**는 접속사의 뜻을 나타내는 부사로서 절과 절을 연결할 수 없다. 접속부사는 문장에서의 위치가 자유롭고 단독으로도 쓰일 수 있다.
- **자주 쓰이는 상관접속사 표현**

ⓐ 대조	however (그러나), on the other hand (반면에)
ⓑ 결과	therefore (그러므로), as a result (결과적으로)
ⓒ 첨가	in addition (덧붙여, 게다가), besides (게다가), moreover (게다가)
ⓓ 예시	for example (예를 들면), for instance (예를 들면)

ⓐ It was hot. However, I drank hot tea. 날이 더웠다. 그러나 나는 뜨거운 차를 마셨다.
ⓑ It was hot. Therefore, I ate some ice cream. 날이 더웠다. 그래서 나는 아이스크림을 먹었다.
ⓒ It was hot. In addition, the air conditioner was broken. 날이 더웠다. 게다가, 에어컨이 고장 났다.
ⓓ It was hot. Cold drinks, for example, iced water and soft drinks, helped me to cool down. 날이 더웠다. 차가운 음료, 예를 들어 얼음 물, 탄산음료가 나의 더위를 식히는데 도움을 주었다.

A

괄호 안에서 알맞은 말을 고르시오.

1 I don't want to go out to eat. (For example, Besides), I don't have any money.
2 She has a toothache. (Therefore, However), she can't eat well.
3 I like fruits. (For example, On the other hand), apples, and cherries are my favorites.
4 They often fought with each other in the past. (In addition, However), they are good friends now.
5 He didn't follow the traffic rule. (In addition, As a result), he had to pay a fine.

B

빈칸에 알맞은 말을 〈보기〉에서 골라 쓰시오.

보기
Therefore　　However　　Moreover

1 He had a high fever. ______________, he took some medicine.
2 That is mine. ______________, you may use it if you want to.
3 The day was cold. ______________, it was raining.
4 Terra got up late this morning. ______________, she was late for school.
5 Sarah likes to teach her friends. ______________, she doesn't want to be a teacher.

C

우리말과 뜻이 같도록 괄호 안의 말을 바르게 배열하여 문장을 완성하시오.

1 그녀는 예쁘다. 게다가 똑똑하다. (in, she, addition, smart, is,)
→ She is pretty. ______________________________

2 나는 공부를 열심히 하지 않아서 시험을 잘 보지 못했다. (I, therefore, didn't, well, on, do, the test)
→ I didn't study hard. ______________________________

일등 비법 노트

비법 ① 접속사 다음엔 '주어 + 동사'! 전치사 다음엔 '명사(구)'가 온다!

대표기출 1 다음 우리말을 영어로 옮길 때, 어법에 맞는 문장을 모두 고르면?

그는 필리핀이 12월에 따뜻하기 때문에 그곳에 가기로 결심했다.

① He decided to go to the Philippines because its warm weather in December.
② He decided to go to the Philippines because of its warm weather in December.
③ He decided to go to the Philippines because its weather is warm in December.
④ He decided to go to the Philippines because of it is warm weather in December.
⑤ He decided to go to the Philippines because of its weather is warm in December.

비법 ② 시간과 조건의 부사절에선 미래시제 대신 현재시제를 쓴다!

대표기출 1 어법상 옳지 않은 문장은?

① He will go if she comes.
② She will not start if it snows tomorrow.
③ I will attend the party if everybody else does.
④ If you study hard, you will get good grades.
⑤ If it will rain tomorrow, we will postpone the field trip.

비법 ③ 「that + 완전한 절」이면 명사절을 이끄는 접속사 that! 「that + 불완전한 절」이면 형용사절을 이끄는 관계대명사 that!

대표기출 1 밑줄 친 that의 쓰임이 나머지와 다른 하나는?

① That she is very smart is true.
② I have the present that you bought for me.
③ She believes that he will attend the party.
④ He hopes that he can finish his homework on time.
⑤ The problem is that she can't afford to buy the watch.

비법 4 if절이 '만일 ~라면'으로 해석되면 부사절! if절이 '~인지 아닌지'로 해석되면 명사절!

대표기출 1

밑줄 친 if의 쓰임이 다른 하나는?

① Tom asked me if the kimchi was spicy.
② He wasn't sure if the meeting was at 3 or at 4 o'clock.
③ Please let me know if he comes to the library or not.
④ The boy wondered if his dad bought a Frisbee for him.
⑤ You can play badminton with me if you come home early.

비법 5 「not only *A* but also *B*」와 「*B* as well as *A*」는 *B*에 동사를 일치!

대표기출 1

우리말과 일치하도록 밑줄 친 부분을 어법에 맞게 고쳐 쓰시오.

(1) Jisu as well as I go to the same school that she does.
(나뿐만 아니라 지수도 그녀가 다니는 같은 학교에 다닌다.)

→ ______________________________

(1) Not only Cathy but also I likes to travel abroad.
(Cahty뿐만 아니라 나도 해외로 여행가기를 좋아한다.)

→ ______________________________

비법 6 상관접속사는 문법적으로 대등한 품사를 연결한다!

대표기출 1

밑줄 친 부분을 어법에 맞게 고쳐 쓰시오.

(1) Taeho is not only handsome but smartness.

______________ → ______________

(2) He can either visit Nepal or going to Europe.

______________ → ______________

(3) We decided on either watching TV or to listen to the radio.

______________ → ______________

내신 만점! 실전 기출

01 밑줄 친 while의 의미가 나머지와 다른 하나는?

① Please take care of my puppy while I'm away.
② My sister is very good at English, while I'm not.
③ I usually listen to music while I clean the house.
④ He usually eats potato chips while he is watching TV.
⑤ It's not safe to talk on the phone while you're driving a car.

02 어법상 틀린 문장은?

① I wonder that Ann needs my help.
② He'll definitely help you if you want.
③ Do you know if they came to class on time?
④ Julie asked me whether I could come to her house.
⑤ I am very curious if there are other living things out there.

03 〈보기〉의 밑줄 친 while과 의미하는 바가 같은 것은?

보기
While we were hiking, we enjoyed beautiful mountain scenery.

① She is taking a break for a while.
② While Sue likes English, Tom likes science.
③ Please don't listen to music while you are studying.
④ It took quite a while for him to recover from his sickness.
⑤ While he is really good at making things, his brother is hopeless.

04 빈칸에 공통으로 알맞은 접속사는?

ⓐ Some people like juice, __________ others don't.
ⓑ Turn off your electronic devices __________ you are flying on a plane.

① if ② after ③ while
④ since ⑤ until

[5~6] 어법상 어색한 것은?

05

① She both sings and dances.
② They felt both exhausted and sleepy.
③ Both she and her sister lives in San Francisco.
④ Both Sue and Frank can speak Chinese very well.
⑤ Doves are symbols of both peace and freedom.

06

① The table is so heavy that I can't move it.
② He was so tired that he could get up early.
③ The game was so exciting that I couldn't stop playing it.
④ She was so busy that she couldn't come on time.
⑤ The movie is so exciting that the tickets are all sold out.

07 서술형

빈칸에 공통으로 알맞은 접속사를 쓰시오.

ⓐ __________ you know, Julia is the smartest girl in the class.
ⓑ __________ science develops, robots will become a bigger part of our lives.

→ ______________________

최다빈출

08 밑줄 친 that의 쓰임이 나머지 넷과 다른 것은?

① I believe that he is innocent.
② She thinks that he is honest.
③ The truth is that it is just a rumor.
④ The problem is that I can't stop eating sweets.
⑤ I want to invent a machine that is useful for us.

09 빈칸에 however가 들어갈 수 없는 문장은?

① She gave me some advice. ________, I couldn't follow it.
② I think I have a fever. ________, I don't want to take any medicine.
③ White pants look very neat and clean. ________, they get dirty so easily.
④ I had a lot of homework to do. ________, I went shopping with my friends.
⑤ We just finished our group project. ________, we can go out and play soccer.

10 〈보기〉와 의미하는 바가 같은 문장은?

보기
She is too sleepy to read the book.

① She is so sleepy that she reads the book.
② She is so sleepy that she can read the book.
③ She is so sleepy that she can't read the book.
④ She is so sleepy that she could read the book.
⑤ She is so sleepy that she couldn't read the book.

11 어법상 옳은 문장을 모두 고르면? (2개)

① I like not only you but also he.
② Jisu is not only pretty but also warm hearted.
③ Not only Eric but also I are going to attend the meeting.
④ They are learning not only speaking but also write in English.
⑤ Tim is good at not only playing soccer but also playing baseball.

12 〈보기〉의 as와 밑줄 친 부분의 쓰임이 같은 것은?

보기
We were able to see many stars in the sky as it got darker.

① The apple was as sweet as sugar.
② As she is new here, she may need some help.
③ The boy lost his umbrella as his mom said he would.
④ As she grew older, she became known to many people.
⑤ As you know, you'd better put a lot of effort into the project.

13 서술형

빈칸에 공통으로 알맞은 접속사를 쓰시오.

ⓐ He is so little ________ he can't stay home alone.
ⓑ She is so smart ________ she can answer the math questions easily.

→ ________________

14 밑줄 친 ⓐ if와 쓰임이 다른 하나는?

The boy wondered ⓐ if chickens could fly.

① Do you know if he has a girlfriend?
② Could you tell me if I am on the right track?
③ Mrs. Audrey asked me if I had turned in the paper.
④ My mom will get angry if I break my promise.
⑤ He wonders if he should buy a new cell phone.

15 서술형

우리말과 뜻이 같도록 괄호 안의 말을 활용하여 문장을 완성하시오.

학생들은 대개 새 학년이 시작되면 잘 할 지에 대해 걱정한다. (whether, do, well)

→ Students usually wonder ______________ ________ when a new school year begins.

16 〈보기〉의 문장과 같은 의미로 쓰인 것은?

보기
I concentrated on the lecture so hard that I could understand it well.

① I concentrated on the lecture in order to understand it well.
② I concentrated on the lecture too hard to understand it well.
③ I concentrated on the lecture hard enough to understand it well.
④ I concentrated on the lecture hard so that I could understand it well.
⑤ I concentrated on the lecture so hard that I couldn't understand it well.

17 서술형

두 문장의 뜻이 같도록 빈칸에 알맞은 말을 쓰시오.

He went to the library to return the books so that he would not pay the penalty.

= He went to the library to return the books in ____________ ____________ ____________ pay the penalty.

18 서술형

빈칸 ⓐ~ⓓ에 공통으로 알맞은 한 단어를 쓰시오. (단, 대소문자 무시)

ⓐ __________ you like, you can stay in this room.
ⓑ I wonder __________ she can help me to cook Galbi.
ⓒ Do you know __________ Henry won a medal in the contest?
ⓓ I asked my dad __________ he could help with building a model airplane.

→ ______________________________

19 〈보기〉에서 알맞은 말을 찾아 빈칸에 쓰시오. (필요 시 중복 사용 가능)

보기
until before since although unless

ⓐ The meeting lasted __________ 2:00.
ⓑ She waited for him at the bus stop __________ it rained heavily.
ⓒ The students must be in their seats __________ the teacher comes into the class.
ⓓ __________ you woke up late, you'd better hurry up in order not to miss the flight.

20 서술형

우리말과 뜻이 같도록 괄호 안의 말을 바르게 배열하여 문장을 완성하시오.

행복이 멀리 있는 것처럼 느껴질 수 있지만, 그것은 네가 생각하는 것보다 네게 더 가까이에 있을 수 있다.
(happiness, although, may, far, seem, away)

→ ______________________________

______________________________,

it may be closer to you than you think.

21 빈칸에 알맞은 말은?

My grandmother showed me an old picture. In the picture, my grandparents, my dad, and my uncles were standing in front of the house. ________ the house was quite old, they all looked very happy.

① if
② As
③ When
④ However
⑤ Although

22 빈칸에 알맞은 말이 순서대로 바르게 나열된 것은?

Kevin: What's your motto, Sarah?
Sarah: Well. 'Work hard, ________ you can't achieve anything.' How about you?
Kevin: 'Be an early bird, ________ you will get the worms.'
Sarah: Sounds great.

① and, or
② and, and
③ or, or
④ or, and
⑤ so, or

23 서술형

빈칸에 공통으로 알맞은 접속사 한 단어를 쓰시오.

ⓐ ________ it was freezing, he didn't wear socks.
ⓑ ________ the rumor turned out to be false, people still believed it.

→ ______________________________

24 서술형

우리말과 뜻이 같도록 영작하시오.

나는 선인장들이 밤에 산소를 내뿜을 뿐만 아니라 사람들의 숙면에 도움을 준다는 것을 알았다.

→ I knew that cactuses ________ ________ give out oxygen ________ ________ help people sleep well at night.

25 대화의 밑줄 친 ⓐ와 같은 뜻으로 사용된 것은?

Adams: Do you know that Earth's temperature rises every year?
Becky: Yes. Global warming is a serious problem ⓐ since the world is rapidly getting warmer and warmer.
Adams: You're right. So farmers are having a hard time growing vegetables and fruits.

① It's been ten years since she met him.
② I've played the piano since I was five.
③ Today is the coldest day since last month.
④ Since he is free, I can go to see the concert with him.
⑤ It has been three months since the shop opened in this area.

26 서술형

주어진 문장과 뜻이 같도록 괄호 안의 말을 활용하여 문장을 다시 쓰시오.

> She stopped eating junk food in order to stay healthy.

→ ______________________________
______________________________ (so that)

27 빈칸에 알맞은 것은?

> What am I? I have many different colors like red, yellow, and pink. People buy me on special days like on a birthday or Valentine's Day. Also, single men buy me and a ring to propose to their girlfriends. Some people use me not only to make tea __________ aromatherapy oil. Do you know what I am yet? I am a rose!

① to make
② but made
③ but also making
④ but also made
⑤ but also to make

28 서술형

괄호 안의 말을 바르게 배열하여 질문에 알맞은 답을 완성하시오.

> Q: Why are you packing these used clothes?
> A: I am packing them ______________________
> ______________________ in Africa.

→ ______________________________
____

(can, give, that, the, them, poor, to, I, so)

29 서술형

괄호 안의 말을 활용하여 밑줄 친 부분을 영작하시오.
(필요 시 단어를 추가할 것)

> A: Do you know who Mother Teresa was?
> B: Of course. She was known as 'An angel of the poor' ⓐ 그녀는 가난한 사람들을 도와주었기 때문에. (help, the poor)

→ ______________________________
____

고난도

30 서술형

<보기>의 밑줄 친 if와 쓰임이 같은 것을 모두 고르면?

> 보기
> I don't know if I can pass the entrance exam.

> ⓐ If you like it, don't hesitate to buy it.
> ⓑ If it snows a lot, let's make a snowman.
> ⓒ Please tell me if you gave me this present.
> ⓓ They will have dinner if the restaurant is still open.
> ⓔ He wonders if his mom will allow him to sleep over at Jack's house.

① ⓑ, ⓔ
② ⓒ, ⓓ
③ ⓒ, ⓔ
④ ⓐ, ⓑ, ⓒ
⑤ ⓐ, ⓒ, ⓔ

실력 탄탄!
서술형 심화

1 그림을 보고 주어진 〈조건〉에 따라 영작하시오.

(1)

(2)

(1) 조건
1. 다음 어휘를 활용할 것: tall, the roller coaster, enough to
2. 13단어로 이루어진 완전한 영어 문장으로 쓸 것

나는 내가 이 롤러코스터를 탈 수 있는 충분한 키인지 모르겠어.

→ ______________________________

(2) 조건
1. 다음 어휘를 활용할 것: not sure, pass, or not, I'm
2. 10단어로 이루어진 완전한 영어 문장으로 쓸 것

나는 시험에 통과했는지 아닌지 확실하지 않다.

→ ______________________________

2 Mina has several worries. Use the words in the brackets and give advice to her.

(1) Mina: I want to get an A on the English test.
→ ______________ get an A on the English test, ______________ ______________ every day. (you, if, to, prepare and review, want, lessons)

(2) Mina: I don't have enough money to buy a new laptop computer.
→ ______________ carefully, ______________ ______________ a new laptop computer. (you, unless, won't, save, money, you, to buy, enough, have)

(3) Mina: I enjoy eating fast food.
→ ______________ healthy food, you can ______________ ______. (don't, get, if, you, eat, easily, sick)

CHAPTER 10

관계사

- Point 01 관계대명사의 역할, 종류
- Point 02 관계대명사 that
- Point 03 관계대명사 what
- Point 04 관계대명사의 생략
- Point 05 「전치사 + 관계대명사」
- Point 06 관계대명사의 제한적 용법, 계속적 용법
- Point 07 관계부사
- Point 08 관계부사의 생략, 계속적 용법
- Point 09 복합관계대명사
- Point 10 복합관계부사

관계사

관계사는 절 (「주어 + 동사 ~」)을 이끌어 명사를 뒤에서 꾸며주는 말이다. 관계사에는 「접속사 + 대명사」의 역할을 하는 **관계대명사**와 「접속사 + 부사」의 역할을 하는 **관계부사**가 있다.

- **관계대명사와 관계부사**

관계대명사: 「접속사+대명사」의 역할	I watched <u>a thriller movie</u>, <u>and it</u> was very interesting. → I watched <u>a thriller movie</u> [<u>**which[that]** was very interesting</u>]. 나는 매우 재미있는 공포 영화를 보았다.
관계부사: 「접속사+부사(구)」의 역할	New York is <u>the city</u>. We first met <u>in the city</u>. → New York is <u>the city</u> [<u>**where** we first met</u>]. 뉴욕은 우리가 처음 만났던 도시이다.

Point 01 관계대명사의 역할, 종류

- **관계대명사**는 「**접속사 + 대명사**」의 역할을 하며, 관계대명사절은 선행사(앞에 나온 명사)를 수식한다.
  This book is about a girl. And she falls in love with a prince.
  → This book is about a girl [who falls in love with a prince]. 이 책은 왕자와 사랑에 빠지는 소녀에 관한 것이다.

- **관계대명사**는 선행사의 종류에 따라 **who**, **which**, **that** 등으로 쓴다.

선행사	사람	사물/동물	사람/사물/동물
주격	who	which	that
소유격	whose	of which(whose)	whose
목적격	who(m)	which	that

  This is the story of a boy who[that] had a creative idea to help others.
  이것은 다른 사람들을 돕는 창의적인 아이디어를 갖고 있는 한 소년에 대한 이야기이다. (선행사: a boy/사람)
  He used old materials which[that] were from the garbage to make useful things.
  그는 유용한 것들을 만들기 위해 쓰레기에서 온 오래된 물건을 사용했다. (선행사: old materials/사물)

- 관계대명사가 주격일 때, 관계대명사절의 동사는 선행사와 수를 일치시킨다.
  Do you know the boys who are wearing red hats over there?
  너는 저기 저쪽에 있는 빨간 모자를 쓴 소년들을 아니? (동사 are의 주어는 선행사 the boys)
  Tell me about the girl who is waiting for you at the gate now.
  지금 문에서 너를 기다리고 있는 저 소녀에 대해 나에게 말해 보렴. (동사 is의 주어는 선행사 the girl)

A

우리말과 뜻이 같도록 괄호 안에서 알맞은 말을 고르시오.

1 나는 어제 본 역사 시험을 망쳤다.
→ I failed the history test (who, which) I took yesterday.

2 박지성이 내가 가장 존경하는 한국 축구선수이다.
→ Ji-sung Park is the Korean soccer player (which, whom) I admire most.

3 벽이 모두 유리로 되어 있는 그 건물이 바로 그 박물관이다.
→ The building (which, whose) walls are all made of glass is the museum.

B

다음 두 문장을 관계대명사를 이용하여 한 문장으로 만드시오.

1 He found a book. It was titled *Using Energy*.
→ He found a book ____________________.

2 Mary made a new friend. She met her at the park.
→ Mary made a new friend ____________________.

3 The woman is my grandmother. Her hair is grey.
→ The woman ____________________ is my grandmother.

Point 02 관계대명사 that

■ **관계대명사 that의 활용**

(1) 선행사가 〈사람 + 사물〉이나 〈사람 + 동물〉일 때

A girl and her dog that had disappeared have not been found yet.

사라진 소녀와 그녀의 개는 아직 발견되지 않았다. (선행사: a girl and her dog)

(2) 최상급, 서수, the only(유일한), the very(바로 그), the same(같은), all, every, -thing으로 끝나는 부정대명사 등이 선행사에 있을 때 관계대명사 that을 쓴다.

He was the last person that left the room.

그가 그 방을 떠난 마지막 사람이었다. (선행사: the last person)

Tell me everything that you saw about the accident. 그 사고에 관해 네가 본 모든 것을 내게 말해줘.

All that glitters is not gold. 반짝이는 모든 것이 금은 아니다. (선행사: all)

■ **관계대명사 that *vs.* 접속사 that:** 관계대명사 that은 불완전한 문장을 이끌고, 접속사 that은 완전한 문장을 이끈다.

관계대명사 that	Do you know the girl (that is giving a speech now)? 명사 ← that절에 주어가 생략되었음 너는 지금 연설하고 있는 소녀를 아니? (that절이 명사 the girl을 꾸며주는 형용사 역할)
접속사 that	Did you know (that Susan won the speech contest)? that절에 생략된 문장요소 없음 너는 Susan이 웅변대회에서 우승했다는 것을 알았니? (that절이 동사 know의 목적어)

A 밑줄 친 부분이 어법상 바르면 O표, 틀리면 바르게 고쳐 쓰시오.

1 This is all which she wanted. → ____________

2 This is the very bag which I have been looking for. → ____________

3 John was the first runner who crossed the finish line. → ____________

4 Don't forget to bring the boy and his dog that are waiting for you. → ____________

B 우리말과 뜻이 같도록 괄호 안의 말을 바르게 배열하여 문장을 완성하시오.

1 그가 우리에게 말했던 모든 것은 사실로 판명되었다. (he, told, us, everything, that, had)

→ ______________________________ turned out to be true.

2 Tom이 하는 유일한 집안 일은 쓰레기를 밖에 내놓는 것이다. (the only, that, does, chore, Tom)

→ ______________________________ is to take out the garbage.

3 그는 내가 본 가장 키가 큰 소년이다. (He's, I, have ever seen, the tallest, that, boy)

→ ______________________________.

4 네가 본 아무거나 내게 말해 줘. (Tell, anything, me, that, saw, you)

→ ______________________________.

Point 03 관계대명사 what

- **관계대명사 what**: 그 자체가 'the thing(s) that'의 뜻으로, **선행사를 포함**한다.
  따라서, 관계대명사 **what**이 이끄는 절 **앞에는 명사(선행사)가 없다.**
  This blouse is what she bought online last week.
  = This blouse is the thing that she bought online last week.
- **관계대명사 what이 이끄는 절**: 문장에서 명사처럼 주어, 목적어, 보어 역할을 한다.
  관계대명사 what이 이끄는 절이 주어로 쓰이면, 단수로 취급한다는 사실에 유의한다.
  What my brother did today was playing computer games.
  내 동생이 오늘 한 일은 컴퓨터 게임이었다. (주어 역할)
  My mom didn't like what my brother did today.
  엄마는 내 동생이 오늘 한 일을 좋아하지 않았다. (목적어 역할)
  The truth is what I told you. 진실은 내가 너에게 말해 준 것이다. (보어 역할)

A

괄호 안에서 알맞은 말을 고르시오.

1 I couldn't believe (that, what) I saw at that time.

2 This is (that, what) I have done in the morning.

3 The little girl gave the thing (that, what) she had in her pocket to me.

4 (That, What) you can find on the Internet is not always true.

B

우리말과 뜻이 같도록 괄호 안의 단어를 바르게 배열하여 문장을 완성하시오.

1 오늘 우리가 해야 할 것을 말해 주세요. (should, what, do, we)
→ Tell us ______________________________ today.

2 이것이 당신이 찾고 있는 것인가요? (looking, you, for, are, what)
→ Is this ______________________________?

3 내가 지금 하고 싶은 것은 쉬는 것이다. (what, want, do, I, to)
→ ______________________________ now is rest.

4 그녀는 내가 집에 오는 길에 본 것을 듣고 놀랐다. (saw, what, I)
→ She was surprised to hear ______________________________
on my way home.

5 내가 하루 종일 한 것은 내 어린 여동생을 돌보는 것이었다. (what, did, all day long, I)
→ ______________________________ was taking care of my little sister.

6 당신이 우리를 위해 해준 일에 대해 감사 드립니다. (you, have, what, us, done, for)
→ Thank you for ______________________________

Point 04 관계대명사의 생략

- **목적격 관계대명사**는 생략할 수 있다.
  Mr. Smith didn't like the funny story (which) I wrote.
  You are lucky to have friends (whom) you can depend on.
- **「주격관계대명사 + be동사」** 뒤에 분사(또는 형용사)가 올 때, **「주격관계대명사 + be동사」**는 생략할 수 있다. 단, 이런 경우에 관계대명사만 생략할 수는 없다.
  The girl (who is) running into the classroom is Amy. (O) 교실로 뛰어들어오고 있는 소녀가 Amy이다.
  (who만 생략하는 건 안 됨)

A 문장에서 생략할 수 있는 부분을 찾아 동그라미 치시오. (생략할 수 있는 부분이 없으면 문장 옆에 X표 하시오.)

1 The first thing that she did was to look around. ____________
2 Science is the subject which he is interested in. ____________
3 The girl whom he is playing with now is my niece. ____________
4 This is the girl who won first place in the competition. ____________
5 Everyone who was paying attention to the teacher noticed it. ____________

B 문장에서 생략된 것이 있는 곳을 찾아 그 번호를 쓰고, 생략된 말을 쓰시오.

1 I need ① shoes ② I can wear ③ even in the water ④.
→ ____________________________

2 Have you seen ① any movies ② made ③ in India ④?
→ ____________________________

3 The letter ① written ② in English ③ was not easy to read ④.
→ ____________________________

4 The dog ① chasing after ② the cat ③ is my pet, ④ Chuchu.
→ ____________________________

C 우리말과 뜻이 같도록 괄호 안의 말을 바르게 배열하여 문장을 완성하시오.

1 꽃을 들고 있는 남자가 Jake이다. (holding, is, flowers)
→ The man ____________________________ Jake.

2 그녀는 영어로 쓰여진 책을 읽고 있다. (English, in, written)
→ She is reading a book ____________________________.

3 내가 그 곳에서 본 사람은 이 소년이다. (there, I, this, boy, is, saw)
→ The person ____________________________.

4 나는 내가 도서관에서 빌린 책을 가져오는 것을 잊었다. (borrowed, I, had)
→ I forgot to bring the books ____________________ from the library.

Point 05 「전치사 + 관계대명사」

■ **관계대명사가 전치사의 목적어인 경우는** 전치사가 관계대명사 앞으로 올 수 있다.
단, 이 때의 관계대명사는, **목적격이지만 생략할 수 없고, 관계대명사 that으로 바꾸어 쓰지 못한다.**
Hana found the book (which/that) she had been looking for. (which/that: 생략 가능)
= Hana found the book for which she had been looking. (which: 생략 불가)
Hana는 그녀가 찾고 있던 책을 발견했다.

cf. Hana found the book for that she had been looking. (X)

A 괄호 안에서 알맞은 말을 모두 고르시오. (단 필요한 말이 없을 땐, X를 고르시오.)

1 Tom is the boy with (X, who, whom, that) I studied yesterday.

2 That building is the place at (X, which, that) my father is working.

3 This is the candy shop to (X, which, that) Amanda goes every day.

4 I know a nice restaurant (X, which, that) my coworker recommended.

5 The man (X, who, that) is talking with my mom is my uncle.

6 Do you want to see an animal show (X, which, in which, that) tigers are playing?

7 I asked her about the man (X, who, whom, that) she came across on the street.

B 주어진 문장과 뜻이 같도록 빈칸에 알맞은 말을 쓰시오.

1 This is the book. I told you about it.
→ This is the book ____________ I told you about.
→ This is the book ____________ ____________ I told you.

2 Where is the shop? You bought your pants at the store.
→ Where is the shop ____________ you bought your pants ____________?
→ Where is the shop ____________ ____________ you bought your pants?

3 Spain is the country. I want to go to the country some day.
→ Spain is the country ____________ I want to go ____________ someday.
→ Spain is the country ____________ ____________ I want to go someday.

4 Daegu is the city. She has lived in the city for more than 10 years.
→ Daegu is the city ____________ she has lived in for more than 10 years.
→ Daegu is the city ____________ ____________ she has lived for more than 10 years.

5 March 1st is the day. Schools in Korea start a new school year on the day.
→ March 1st is the day ____________ schools in Korea start a new school year ____________.
→ March 1st is the day ____________ ____________ schools in Korea start a new school year.

Point 06 관계대명사의 제한적 용법, 계속적 용법

■ **관계대명사의 용법**

(1) 제한적 용법: 관계대명사절이 선행사를 수식하면서 선행사의 의미를 제한한다.

He has two sons who became singers.

그에게는 '가수가 된 두 아들'이 있다. (→ 가수가 아닌 다른 자녀가 있을 가능성이 있음)

(2) 계속적 용법: 선행사에 추가적인 설명을 덧붙일 때 사용하며, 관계대명사 앞에 쉼표(,)를 쓴다.

이 경우는 **who**와 **which**만 가능하고 that은 쓸 수 없으며, 생략도 할 수 없다.

또한 「**접속사 + 대명사**」로 바꿔 쓸 수 있다.

He has two sons, who became singers.

그에게는 아들이 두 명 있는데, 그들은 가수가 되었다. (who: that으로 바꿔 쓸 수 없음)

= He has two sons, and they became singers. (아들이 두 명밖에 없고, 그 둘 다 가수가 되었음)

My dad took me night fishing, which made me very happy. (which는 이 경우 생략 불가)

■ **계속적 용법으로 쓰인 which**: 앞에 나온 구나 절 전체를 가리킬 수 있다.

<u>He arrived at the station late</u>, <u>which</u> made him miss the train. (앞절 전체를 가리킴)

A 두 문장의 뜻이 같도록 관계대명사를 활용하여 빈칸에 알맞은 말을 쓰시오.

1 She told me her phone number, and I saved it in my cell phone.

→ She told me her phone number, ____________ I saved in my cell phone.

2 She grew up in Seoul, and it is a metropolitan city.

→ She grew up in ____________ a metropolitan city.

3 He brought his friend Jane, and she was from America.

→ He brought ____________ from America.

4 The Eiffel Tower is one of the most popular tourist attractions, and it is in Paris.

→ The Eiffel Tower, ____________, is one of the most popular tourist attractions.

B 밑줄 친 관계대명사의 용법에 유의하여 다음 문장을 우리말로 해석하시오.

1 She had two sons <u>who</u> became soldiers.

→ ____________

2 She had two sons<u>, who</u> became soldiers.

→ ____________

3 The Thames is the river <u>which</u> runs through London.

→ ____________

4 This is London Eye, <u>which</u> is in the center of the capital of England.

→ ____________

5 The word 'narcissism', <u>which</u> came from the Greek myth, means to love yourself too much.

→ ____________

Point 07 관계부사

- **관계부사**는 문장에서 「**접속사 + 부사**」의 **역할**을 하며, 선행사에 따라 달라진다.
  관계부사가 이끄는 절은 앞에 나온 명사(선행사)를 수식하는 형용사절이다.
  This is the house. + Mozart was born in the house. 이 곳이 모차르트가 태어난 집이다.
  → This is the house [where Mozart was born].
  → She showed me the place [where the treasure was hidden]. 그녀는 보물이 숨겨진 곳을 나에게 보여주었다.

- **관계부사**는 「**전치사 + 관계대명사**」로 바꿔 쓸 수 있다.

선행사	전치사 + 관계대명사	관계부사
장소 (the place, the city, the country 등)	at[in, on, to] + which	where
시간 (the day, the week, the time 등)	at[in, on, to] + which	when
이유 (the reason)	for which	why
방법 (the way)	in which	how

  There was a time. + People went from Busan to Seoul on foot at the time.
  → There was a time at which people went from Pusan to Seoul on foot.
  → There was a time when people went from Pusan to Seoul on foot.

- **관계대명사 *vs.* 관계부사**: 관계대명사는 불완전한 절을 이끌고, 관계부사는 완전한 절을 이끈다.
  Europe is the place which she wanted to go to.
  (which가 이끄는 절에서 전치사 to의 목적어인 the place가 생략되었음)
  → Europe is the place to which she wanted to go. 유럽은 그녀가 가고 싶어했던 곳이다.
  → Europe is the place where she wanted to go. (go는 자동사라 목적어가 필요 없음)

A 괄호 안에서 알맞은 말을 고르시오.

1 She told me (which, how) she made her cookies.
2 This is the library (which, where) I used to study in.
3 That is the reason (which, why) he failed the test for.
4 Tomorrow is the day (which, when) my midterm tests end.
5 Seoul is the city (which, where) over one fourth of the Korean population lives.
6 April 5th is the day (which, when) people used to have a holiday to plant trees on.
7 This is the parking lot (which, where) only customers of the restaurant can park their cars.

B 다음 두 문장을 한 문장으로 만들 때 빈칸에 알맞은 말을 쓰시오.

1 That is the reason. + Tom returned home very late for the reason.
→ That is the reason ____________ ____________ Tom returned home very late.
→ That is the reason ____________ Tom returned home very late.

2 Do you still remember the day? + We won the final on the day.
→ Do you still remember the day ____________ ____________ we won the final?
→ Do you still remember the day ____________ we won the final?

Point 08 관계부사/선행사의 생략, 관계부사의 계속적 용법

■ 관계부사 또는 선행사의 생략: 관계부사의 선행사가 **the time, the place, the reason, the way** 등과 같이 일반적인 것일 때 **관계부사나 선행사 둘 중 하나를 생략**할 수 있다.
Do you know (the reason) why he dropped out of school? 너는 그가 왜 학교를 중퇴했는지 아니?
This swimming pool is (the place) where the TV drama was shot.
이 수영장이 TV드라마를 찍은 곳이다.

■ **선행사 the way와 how는 함께 쓰지 않는다**. 반드시 하나를 생략하거나, how 대신 that을 쓴다.
She couldn't figure out the way he solved the problem. 그녀는 그가 문제를 푼 방법을 알아내지 못했다.
→ She couldn't figure out how he solved the problem.
→ She couldn't figure out the way that he solved the problem. (O)

cf. She couldn't figure out the way how he solved the problem. (X)

■ **관계부사의 계속적 용법**: 계속적 용법으로 쓰인 관계부사는 ① 생략할 수 없고, ② 「**접속사 + 부사**」로 바꿔 쓸 수 있다. 단, why와 how는 계속적 용법으로 쓸 수 없다.
She went to England, where she wrote her famous novel. 그녀는 영국으로 갔는데, 거기서 그 소설을 썼다.
→ She went to England, and she wrote her famous novel there.

cf. 계속적 용법으로 쓰인 관계대명사도 생략할 수 없다.
The computer, I bought online, is out of order. (X)

A 주어진 문장의 뜻이 같도록 괄호 안에서 알맞은 말을 고르시오.

1 Did he tell you the way he found the path in the forest?
→ Did he tell you (how, which) he found the path in the forest?
→ Did he tell you the way (that, which) he found the path in the forest?

2 This is our school library, where I usually study after school.
→ This is our school library, and I usually study (where, there) after school.

3 Yesterday was our school's birthday, when we had a big festival.
→ Yesterday was our school's birthday, and we had a big festival (then, when).

B 다음 두 문장을 한 문장으로 만들 때 빈칸에 알맞은 말을 쓰시오.

1 That was the reason. + She was angry at me for the reason.
→ That was ____________ ____________ she was angry at me.

2 He showed the way. I could make a model plane in the way.
→ He showed ____________ I could make a model plane.

3 Do you know the date? + The great king Sejong was born on that date.
→ Do you know ____________ the great king Sejong was born?

4 This restaurant is the place. + You can have Italian food at the restaurant.
→ This restaurant is ____________ you can have Italian food.

Point 09 복합관계대명사

■ 복합관계대명사는 「관계대명사-ever」의 형태로, 명사절 또는 양보의 부사절을 이끈다.

복합관계대명사	명사절		양보의 부사절	
whoever	~하는 누구든지	(= anyone who)	누가 ~할 지라도	(= no matter who)
whomever	~하는 누구든지	(= anyone whom)	누구를 ~할 지라도	(= no matter whom)
whichever	~하는 것은 어느 것이든지	(= anything which)	어느 것을 ~할 지라도	(= no matter which)
whatever	~하는 것은 무엇이든지	(= anything that)	무엇을 ~할 지라도	(= no matter what)

Anyone who comes first will get the prize. 가장 먼저 오는 사람은 누구든지 상을 받을 것이다.
→ Whoever comes first will get the prize. (명사절: 문장의 주어 역할)
Do whatever[anything that] you like. (명사절: 문장의 목적어 역할)
네가 좋아하는 것은 무엇이든 해라.
Whatever[No matter what] I do, my mom always supports me.
내가 무엇을 하더라도, 엄마는 나를 지지해 주신다.
Whoever[No matter who] tries, the door won't open.
누가 시도해 볼지라도, 문은 열리지 않을 것이다.

A 두 문장의 뜻이 같도록 밑줄 친 부분에 유의하여 〈보기〉와 같이 문장을 다시 쓰시오.

보기
No matter what you do, do your best.
→ Whatever you do, do your best.

1 No matter which you choose, I'll give it to you.
→ ______________ you choose, I'll give it to you.

2 Invite anyone whom you meet on the street to the feast.
→ Invite ______________ you meet on the street to the feast.

3 Anyone who wants to get a good grade has to study hard.
→ ______________ wants to get a good grade has to study hard.

B 우리말과 뜻이 같도록 복합관계대명사와 괄호 안의 말을 사용하여 문장을 완성하시오.

1 네가 알고 있는 것은 무엇이든지 나에게 말해라. (know)
→ Tell me ____________ ____________ ____________.

2 무슨 일이 일어나더라도, 나는 너와 함께 갈 것이다. (happen)
→ ____________ ____________, I will go with you.

3 누가 문을 두드리든 간에 문을 열어주지 말아라. (knock)
→ Don't open the door, ____________ ____________ on it.

4 메뉴에서 네가 좋은 것은 어느 것이든지 주문해라. (like)
→ Order ____________ ____________ ____________ from the menu.

Point 10 복합관계부사

■ 복합관계부사는 「관계부사-ever」의 형태로 부사절을 이끈다.

복합관계부사	시간, 장소의 부사절		양보의 부사절	
whenever	~할 때마다	(= at any time when)	언제 ~하더라도	(= no matter when)
wherever	~하는 어디에나	(= at any place where)	어디에서 ~하더라도	(= no matter where)
however	–		아무리 ~해도	(= no matter how)

Call me whenever you need my help. 내 도움이 필요할 때면 언제든지 전화하세요.
(= at any time when)

Superman appears wherever his help is needed. 슈퍼맨은 그의 도움이 필요한 곳은 어디든 나타난다.
(= at any place where)

■ 관계부사가 부사절을 이끌면 「no matter ~」의 의미를 나타낸다.

Wherever you go, try to follow the rules there. 어디에 가든 거기의 규칙을 따르도록 노력해라.
(= No matter where)

However high a mountain is, it is lower than the sky. 산이 아무리 높을지라도, 하늘 아래 있다.
(= No matter how)

Whenever you come, you will be welcome. 네가 언제 오더라도, 너는 환영 받을 것이다.
(= No matter when)

A 괄호 안에서 알맞은 말을 고르시오.

1 He asks (whatever, wherever) questions he has.

2 Paparazzi follow celebrities (wherever, whichever) they go.

3 The little girl hides behind her mom (whenever, whoever) she feels scared.

4 (However, Whatever) hard the question is, there should be a way to solve it.

B 두 문장의 뜻이 같도록 빈칸에 알맞은 말을 〈보기〉에서 골라 쓰시오.

보기		
whenever	wherever	however

1 At any time when he goes jogging, he takes his dog.
→ ______________ he goes jogging, he takes his dog.

2 No matter how upset you are, you should not yell at children.
→ ______________ upset you are, you should not yell at children.

3 No matter where you go, you should respect the local culture.
→ ______________ you go, you should respect the local culture.

C 우리말과 뜻이 같도록 괄호 안의 말과 적절한 복합관계사를 이용하여 문장을 완성하시오.

1 아무리 부자라 할지라도 사람들은 만족하지 못한다. (they, rich, however, are)
→ People never feel satisfied, ______________________________.

2 엄마가 무슨 말을 해도, 그 소년은 귀 기울여 듣지 않았다. (mother, his, said, whatever)
→ ______________________________, the boy didn't listen to her.

일등 비법 노트

비법 1 관계대명사는 선행사가 사람이면 who[that]! 사물이면 which[that]! 관계대명사의 선행사가 없으면? what을 쓴다!

대표기출 1 밑줄 친 부분이 어법상 옳지 않은 것은?

① Will you show me what you bought?
② What she wanted for dinner was spaghetti.
③ I like the clothes that you wore at the party.
④ This is the book what I borrowed from him yesterday.
⑤ Did you find your cell phone which you had lost the other day?

대표기출 2 괄호 안에서 알맞은 말을 고르시오.

A: Are those the pictures that you took?
B: Yes. And these are (which, what) I painted.

→ ________________

비법 2 관계대명사 that 앞에는 전치사나 ',(쉼표)'가 오지 못한다!

대표기출 1 어법상 어색한 문장을 모두 고르면? (2개)

① My cousin bought a bike, which was very expensive.
② Mr. Park has a dog with that he always goes for a walk.
③ There used to be a big tree here, that children liked to climb.
④ Her favorite shop is *All That Sweets*, which is close to her house.
⑤ I have a nice watch, which I received from my friend in Switzerland.

비법 3 관계대명사 뒤에 동사가 바로 올 때는, 선행사에 동사의 수를 일치시켜라!

대표기출 1 밑줄 친 부분이 어법상 옳은 것은?

① What he likes are just playing sports.
② She has a nice voice that moves people.
③ All that she wants are a piece of advice.
④ Give me the thing which are in your hand.
⑤ She saw some children who was hiding behind the bushes.

비법 4 선행사가 이미 정해져 있는 대상일 때는 관계대명사 앞에 ‘, (쉼표)’를 넣어라!

대표기출 1 다음 문장이 의미하는 바를 정확히 설명하는 사람은 누구인가?

David has two daughters, who became singers.

① 선희: David에게는 딸이 두 명 있네.
② 은미: 아니야, David에게는 다른 딸도 있어.
③ 지은: who는 that으로 바꾸어 쓸 수 있겠어.
④ 지훈: daughters는 who가 이끄는 절의 수식을 받는구나.
⑤ 민철: daughters가 선행사니까 who가 아니라 which를 써야 맞는 거야.

비법 5 목적격 관계대명사는 생략 가능! 「주격관계대명사 + be동사」도 생략 가능! 하지만 주격관계대명사만 생략하는 건 불가능!

대표기출 1 다음 중 밑줄 친 부분을 생략할 수 없는 것은?

① This is the bag which John lost yesterday.
② The girl who is dancing on the stage is my niece.
③ A book which is written in English will be given to you.
④ Are you waiting for the girl that is talking with my teacher?
⑤ I bought an old book that I found in a second-hand bookshop.

비법 6 관계사절에서 전치사가 생략되었으면 ‘관계부사(= 전치사 + 관계대명사)’가 온다!

대표기출 1 어법상 틀린 것은?

① That is the chair which she sat on.
② Can you find the pens which I wrote?
③ Do you like the music which he listens to?
④ Here is the house in which he wrote many books.
⑤ May 15th is the day on which the Great King Sejong was born.

내신 만점! 실전 기출

[1~3] 빈칸에 알맞은 말을 고르시오.

01

The astronaut gave some advice to people _________ want to go into space.

① who ② which ③ whom
④ of which ⑤ whose

02

He said to me, "Break a leg", _________ means "Good luck."

① who ② which ③ whom
④ that ⑤ whose

03

There are many words _________ origins are from names of people.

① who ② that ③ what
④ which ⑤ whose

04 우리말과 뜻이 같도록 빈칸 ⓐ에 알맞은 말은?

ⓐ _______________(아무리 어려울지라도), I will not give up.

① It may be however hard
② It may be hard however
③ However hard it may be
④ However hard may it be
⑤ However it may be hard

[5~6] 빈칸에 공통으로 알맞은 말을 고르시오.

05

(1) Do you know _________ 'doggie bag' means?
(2) She told the police officer _________ she saw.

① who ② that ③ what
④ which ⑤ whom

06

(1) There was a giant elephant in the London Zoo _________ was very popular with children.
(2) He said _________ he felt very pleased when he saw me again.

① who ② that ③ what
④ which ⑤ whom

07 서술형

우리말과 뜻이 같도록 괄호 안의 단어를 활용하여 문장을 완성하시오.

그 박물관에서 우리가 볼 모든 화석들을 상상해 봐!
(imagine, the, see, will, fossils, all, that, we)

→ ______________________________
_______________ in the museum!

08 서술형

우리말과 뜻이 같도록 빈칸에 알맞은 말을 쓰시오.

네가 무엇을 하든지 항상 최선을 다해라.

→ _______________ you do, do your best.

09 빈칸에 알맞은 말이 순서대로 바르게 나열된 것은?

- Choose ⓐ __________ color you like.
- ⓑ __________ you come, we will welcome you.

① whichever, Whenever
② whatever, However
③ however, Whenever
④ however, Whichever
⑤ whenever, However

10 밑줄 친 부분의 쓰임이 나머지와 다른 하나는?

① She showed me a backpack that was on sale.
② She said that she prefers waffles to hotdogs.
③ Wear this T-shirt that will make you look fashionable.
④ Would you recommend a book that I can read on the train?
⑤ This is a new model that is very popular among young people.

11 서술형

빈칸 ⓐ, ⓑ에 공통으로 알맞은 말을 쓰시오. (단, 대소문자 무시)

- This is the place ⓐ __________ he found the dog.
- ⓑ __________ can I have my computer repaired?

→ ______________________________

12 다음 문장에서 'who is'가 생략된 곳은?

The boy ① throwing ② a ball ③ is ④ my brother ⑤.

13 서술형

우리말과 뜻이 같도록 괄호 안의 말을 바르게 배열하여 문장을 완성하시오.

나의 삼촌에 의해 보내진 그 책은 정말 재미있었다.
(interesting, sent, my, uncle, was, very, by)

→ The book ______________________________
______________________________.

14 〈보기〉의 밑줄 친 부분과 쓰임이 같은 것은?

보기
I promise that I will do what I can do.

① She asked what 'panic' means.
② What kind of job would you like to have?
③ What I like to do most is to watch movies.
④ He didn't know what he should say at that time.
⑤ I didn't know what to do next to solve the puzzle.

15 서술형

두 문장의 뜻이 같도록 빈칸에 알맞은 말을 쓰시오. 문장을 완성하시오.

The expression 'Pandora's box' comes from the Greek myth, and it tells about gods and goddesses.

→ The expression 'Pandora's box' comes from __________ __________ __________, __________ tells about gods and goddesses.

16 서술형

두 문장의 뜻이 같도록 빈칸에 알맞은 말을 쓰시오.

Do you know how he made the windmill?

→ Do you know ____________ ____________ he made the windmill?

17 빈칸 ⓐ~ⓓ에 알맞은 말이 순서대로 바르게 나열된 것은?

- Is that the hotel ⓐ __________ we will stay tonight?
- That is the reason ⓑ __________ she didn't come early.
- We all remember ⓒ __________ we first won the final match.
- This is the forest through ⓓ __________ people passed to go to the village.

① when, how, when, that
② when, why, when, that
③ where, why, when, which
④ where, why, when, that
⑤ where, how, when, which

18 주어진 조건에 맞춰 다음을 영작하시오.

조건
1. 해석: 이 분은 나의 아버지이신데, 그는 과학을 가르치신다.
2. 다음 단어를 모두 활용: this, science, teach
3. 적절한 관계대명사를 활용

→ ______________________________

____

19 밑줄 친 부분이 어법상 옳은 것은?

① That is the building on which the bank is.
② This is the locker of which I put my school books.
③ He had a passion with which he made the electric car.
④ Germany is the country in which Hamburgers came.
⑤ I gave my brother a toy by which I paid two thousand won.

20 어법상 어색한 것은?

① That was why she couldn't make it in time.
② This is the way how he solved the riddle so easily.
③ I forgot the place where I put my backpack.
④ There was a time when Korea was a Japanese colony.
⑤ Pyramids are places where many tourists want to go.

21 밑줄 친 부분 중 생략할 수 있는 것은?

① I remember when I first met her.
② Do you know the boy with whom John is talking now?
③ Could you recommend a restaurant that you like most?
④ The movie *Avengers*, which children loved to watch, was very fun.
⑤ The word *paparazzi* means annoying photographers who follow stars.

22 밑줄 친 that이 어법상 옳은 것은?

① People could receive <u>that</u> they needed.
② <u>That</u> he saw in the dark was a big wild dog.
③ This is the book <u>that</u> Mandy wanted to borrow from me.
④ Chocolate ice cream is <u>that</u> she wanted to have for dessert.
⑤ Bill had no money, <u>that</u> stopped him from traveling with us this time.

23 우리말을 영어로 옮길 때 어법상 옳지 <u>않은</u> 것은?

> 네덜란드는 땅이 해수면보다 더 낮은 나라이다.

① Netherlands is the country in which the land is below sea level.
② Netherlands is the country where the land is below sea level.
③ Netherlands is the country which the land is below sea level in.
④ Netherlands is the country in that has land below sea level.
⑤ Netherlands is the country whose land is below sea level.

24 서술형

다음 두 문장을 「전치사 + 관계대명사」를 사용하여 한 문장으로 쓰시오.

> Tell me the reason. + You came to class very late for the reason.

→ ______________________________

____

25 서술형

괄호 안의 말을 재배열하여 우리말과 뜻이 같도록 문장을 완성하시오.

> 가을은 잎들의 색깔이 변하는 때이다.
> (color, leaves, when, change)

→ Fall is ______________________________

______________________________.

26 문맥상 빈칸에 알맞은 말을 <u>모두</u> 고르면? (2개)

> Do you know why tears come out when we yawn? That's because we open our mouth big when we yawn. It touches the place ______________, and tears come out of our eyes.

① that tears are stored
② when tears are stored
③ which tears are stored
④ where tears are stored
⑤ in which tears are stored

27 서술형

대화의 흐름이 자연스럽도록 괄호 안의 말을 바르게 배열하여 문장을 완성하시오. (단, what으로 시작할 것)

> A: May I help you?
> B: Yes. I bought this shirt here.
> ______________ (is, to, want, I, get a refund, what)
> A: Okay. Would you show me your receipt?
> B: Here it is.

→ ______________________________

신유형

28 밑줄 친 ⓐ~ⓔ에 대한 설명이 틀린 친구는 누구인가?

There are many ways that ⓐ add new words into languages. One interesting way is using brand names. One example is the word *Kleenex*, ⓑ which comes from the name of a product ⓒ which was made by a tissue company. The company produced a new facial tissue and named it *Kleenex*, ⓓ who became a common name ⓔ people use to refer to any common facial tissue now.

① 은지: ⓐ는 many ways와 수를 일치시킨 거야.
② 민영: ⓑ는 that으로도 쓸 수 있어.
③ 희진: ⓒ는 생략할 수 있어.
④ 민규: ⓓ는 선행사가 사물이니까 which로 써야 해.
⑤ 도현: ⓔ는 목적격 관계대명사가 생략된 거야.

29 밑줄 친 ⓐ~ⓔ중 어법상 어색한 것을 모두 고르면?

California is the state of America ⓐ which became an independent state in the shortest period of time. It became a popular place in ⓑ that people came to find gold in the late 1840s. After some gold was discovered in California in 1848, people ⓒ who was from all over the world came to California. And that's ⓓ why the population of California grew very fast, ⓔ which made California an independent state.

① ⓐ, ⓔ ② ⓑ, ⓒ ③ ⓑ, ⓓ
④ ⓒ, ⓔ ⑤ ⓑ, ⓔ

30 빈칸 ⓐ~ⓒ에 알맞은 말을 순서대로 바르게 나열한 것은?

We sweat ⓐ (whenever, whatever) we feel hot, and so do animals. The color of sweat is usually colorless, but a hippo's sweat is red. That's ⓑ (what, that) made people in the past think that hippos sweat blood! However, it actually protects hippo's skin from the sun and helps to heal injured skin. ⓒ (However, Whatever) strange it looks, it actually keeps hippos healthy!

① whatever, that, whatever
② whenever, what, however
③ whatever, what, however
④ whatever, that, however
⑤ whenever, that, whatever

실력 탄탄!
서술형 심화

1 표의 내용과 일치하도록 관계사를 활용하여 문장을 완성하시오.

Who	What	When
Yeongsil Jang	made a water clock	in 1398
Thomas Edison	invented a light bulb	in 1880

(1) Yeongsil Jang was the person ____________ ____________ a water clock in 1398.

(2) A light bulb is ____________ Thomas Edison ____________ in 1880.

2 다음 대화의 ⓐ~ⓑ에서 어법상 어색한 곳을 두 군데 찾아 바르게 고쳐 쓰시오.

A: May I help you?
B: Yes. ⓐ Can I try on the T-shirt what is hanging by the window?
A: Sure. ⓑ It is the most popular style which young people love to have. Hmm. It looks good on you.
B: Really? OK. I'll buy it.

ⓐ ____________ → ____________ ⓑ ____________ → ____________

3 다음을 읽고 물음에 답하시오.

Our family went to a beach ⓐ ____________ ____________ near Gangneung last summer. (a) 그 해변에는 내가 모래성을 쌓았던 아름다운 모래가 있었다. My father caught (b) 엄마가 맛있는 해물탕을 끓인 많은 물고기를. He also set up a tent ⓑ ____________ ____________ we were ready to sleep at night. Do you know (c) 내 남동생이 하루 종일 한 것? (d) 그가 한 유일한 것은 게를 쫓아다닌 것이었다.

* crab: 게 / * sea food pot stew: 해물탕

(1) 빈칸 ⓐ, ⓑ에 알맞은 말을 순서대로 쓰시오.

ⓐ ____________ ____________ ⓑ ____________ ____________

(2) 주어진 우리말과 뜻이 같도록 빈칸에 알맞은 말을 써서 문장을 완성하시오.

(a) The beach had beautiful sand ____________ a sand castle. (3단어)

(b) My father caught ____________ mom cooked a delicious seafood pot stew. (4단어)

(c) Do you know ____________ all day long? (4단어)

(d) ____________ chasing crabs. (7단어)

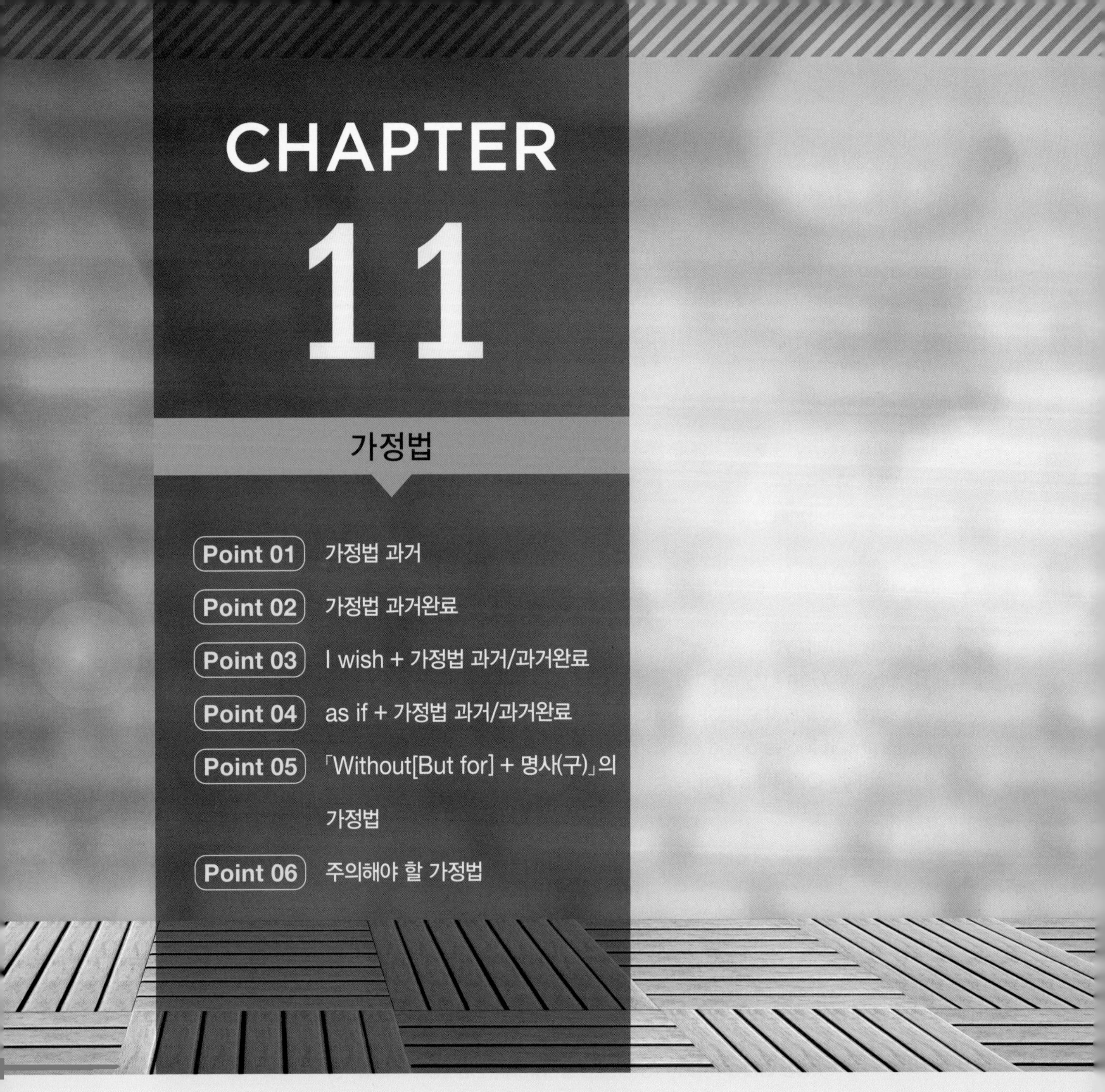

CHAPTER 11

가정법

가정법

실제 일어나지 않은 일에 대해 반대로 가정해서 자신의 의견이나 소망을 표현하는 방법이 가정법(假定法)이다. 즉, 거짓으로(假) 정하여(定) 표현하는 방법(法)을 뜻한다. 가정법에는 가정법 과거와 가정법 과거완료가 있으며, 대개 if, I wish, as if 등의 표현과 함께 쓴다.

• **가정법 과거와 가정법 과거완료**

가정법 과거	**If I had** time, **I could help** you. (가정법 과거) 내가 시간이 있다면 너를 도울 텐데. = As I don't have time, I can't help you. (직설법 현재) 나는 시간이 없어서 너를 도울 수가 없다.
가정법 과거완료	**If I had** had enough time, **I could have helped** him. (가정법 과거완료) 내가 충분한 시간이 있었더라면 그를 도울 수 있었을 텐데. = As I didn't have enough time, I couldn't help him. (직설법 과거) 나는 충분한 시간이 없었기 때문에 그를 도울 수가 없었다.

- 「I wish + 가정법」과 「as if + 가정법」

I wish +	가정법 과거	I wish I could pass the test. (가정법 과거) 내가 그 시험에 통과한다면 좋을 텐데. → I am sorry (that) I can't pass the test. (직설법 현재)
	가정법 과거완료	I wish I had passed the test. (가정법 과거완료) 내가 그 시험에 통과했더라면 좋았을 텐데. → I am sorry (that) I didn't pass the test. (직설법 과거)
as if +	가정법 과거	He kicks the ball as if he were a soccer player. (가정법 과거) 그는 마치 그가 축구 선수인 것처럼 공을 찬다. → In fact, he is not a soccer player. (직설법 현재)
	가정법 과거완료	He kicks the ball as if he had been a soccer player. (가정법 과거완료) 그는 마치 그가 축구선수였던 것처럼 공을 찬다. → In fact, he was not a soccer player. (직설법 과거)

Point 01 가정법 과거

- **가정법 과거**는 **현재 사실과 반대**되거나 **이루어질 가능성이 낮은 일**을 가정할 때 쓴다.

> **「If + 주어 + 동사의 과거형/were ~, 주어 + 조동사의 과거형 + 동사원형 …」** '만일 ~라면, …할 텐데'
> would/could/should/might

- **가정법 과거 → 직설법 현재 전환 방법**: 과거시제는 현재시제로 바꾸고, 긍정은 부정으로, 부정은 긍정으로 바꾼다. If는 접속사 as, so, because로 바꿔 쓴다.

  If we had wings, we could fly. 만약 우리에게 날개가 있다면, 우리는 날 수 있을 텐데. (가정법 과거)

  → As we don't have wings, we can't fly. 우리에게 날개가 없어서 날 수 없다. (직설법 현재)

- **가정법 과거에서 If절의 동사가 be동사일 경우**, 주어의 인칭이나 수에 상관없이 **were**를 쓴다.

  If I were you, I would buy that blouse. 만약 내가 너라면, 그 블라우스를 살 텐데.

A

괄호 안에서 알맞은 말을 고르시오.

1 If I (was, were) 10 years younger, I would study harder.

2 If the ring (were not, is not) so expensive, he would buy it.

3 If my dad were here, he (will allow, would allow) me to go out.

4 If the boy were 130cm tall, he (can, could) ride the roller coaster.

5 If she had enough money, she (would go, would have gone) on a trip to Europe.

B

두 문장의 뜻이 같도록 빈칸에 알맞은 말을 쓰시오.

1 As Tony doesn't know the problem, he can't solve it.

→ If ______________________________, he could solve it.

2 As I don't know the location of her house, I can't visit her.

→ If ______________________________, I could visit her.

3 As he doesn't have enough time, he can't finish the report.

→ If ______________________________, he could finish the report.

4 As I'm not in your shoes, I won't accept the offer.

→ If ______________________________, I would accept the offer.

C

우리말과 뜻이 같도록 괄호 안의 말을 바르게 배열하여 문장을 완성하시오.

1 만약 그가 약속이 없다면, 그는 좀 쉴 텐데. (didn't, if, have, he, he, would, an appointment)

→ ____ get some rest.

2 만약 그가 그곳에 있다면, 우리는 서로 만날 수 있을 텐데. (if, were, meet, he, there, could, we)

→ ____ each other.

3 만약 내가 운전을 할 수 있다면, 나는 바다에 갈 수 있을 텐데. (I, could, if, drive, I, a car, could, go, to)

→ ____ the sea.

4 만약 내가 다시 태어난다면, 나는 유명한 가수가 될 텐데. (born, if, were, I, would, I, become, again)

→ ____ a famous singer.

Point 02 가정법 과거완료

- 가정법 과거완료는 과거 사실과 반대되거나 이루어질 가능성이 낮은 일을 가정할 때 쓴다.

「If + 주어 + had p.p. ~, 주어 + 조동사의 과거형 + have p.p. …」 '만일 ~했다면, …했을 텐데'
would/could/should/might

- 가정법 과거완료 → 직설법 과거 전환 방법: 과거완료는 과거로 바꾸고, 긍정은 부정으로, 부정은 긍정으로 바꾼다. If는 접속사 as, so, because로 바꿔 쓴다.

If she had won the game, she would have been happy. (가정법 과거완료)
만약 그녀가 게임에서 이겼다면, 그녀는 행복했을 텐데.
→ As she didn't win the game, she wasn't happy. (직설법 과거)
그녀가 게임에서 이기지 않았기 때문에, 그녀는 행복하지 않았다.

If I had arrived on time, I wouldn't have missed the class. (가정법 과거완료)
만약 내가 제 시간에 도착했다면, 나는 수업에 빠지지 않았을 텐데.
→ As I didn't arrive on time, I missed the class. (직설법 과거)
내가 제 시간에 도착하지 않아서, 나는 수업에 빠졌다.

A 밑줄 친 동사의 시제를 어법에 맞게 고쳐 쓰시오.

1 If he had seen the movie, he would like it a lot. → ______
2 If a policeman saw her, he would have caught her. → ______
3 If she knew about the exhibition, she would have gone there. → ______
4 If the people had behaved well, there wouldn't be a big fight. → ______
5 If the girl hasn't had her hair permed, she would have looked prettier. → ______

B 두 문장의 뜻이 같도록 빈칸에 알맞은 말을 쓰시오.

1 If Henry had spoken English well, he would have gone abroad more often.
→ As ______ well, ______ more often.

2 If the weather had been warm, they would have swum in the sea.
→ As ______ warm, they ______ in the sea.

3 If I had studied hard, I could have gotten a good score.
→ As ______ hard, I ______ a good score.

C 우리말과 뜻이 같도록 괄호 안의 말을 바르게 배열하여 문장을 완성하시오.

1 만약 내가 아침밥을 먹었더라면, 나는 배고프지 않았을 텐데.
(if, breakfast, I, had, had, I, been, have, hungry, wouldn't)
→ ______

2 만약 그가 연습을 많이 했었다면, 그는 경기에서 이길 수 있었을 텐데.
(he, if, had, a lot, he, practiced, would, won, have, the game)
→ ______

Point 03 I wish + 가정법 과거/과거완료

■ 「**I wish + 가정법 과거**」는 현재나 미래의 실현될 수 없는 소망이나, 현재 사실에 대한 유감을 나타낸다.

> 「**I wish + 주어 + 동사의 과거형 ~.**」 '~이라면/하면 좋을 텐데'
> → 직설법: 「**I am sorry (that) + 주어+ 동사의 현재형**」
> ※ if절의 be동사는 주어의 수나 인칭에 상관없이 were를 쓴다.

I wish I had a new cell phone. 나는 새 핸드폰을 가지고 있다면 좋을 텐데. (가정법 과거)
→ I am sorry (that) I don't have a new cell phone. 나는 새 핸드폰이 없어 유감이다. (직설법 현재)

■ 「**I wish + 가정법 과거완료**」는 과거에 이루지 못한 일에 대한 아쉬움이나 소망을 나타낼 때 쓴다.

> 「**I wish + 주어 + had p.p. ~.**」 '~이었다면/했다면 ~좋았을 텐데'
> → 「**I'm sorry (that) + 주어 + 동사의 과거형**」

I wish I had studied English hard. 내가 영어를 열심히 공부했다면 좋을 텐데. (가정법 과거완료)
→ I am sorry (that) I didn't study English hard. (직설법 과거)
내가 영어를 열심히 공부하지 않아 유감이다.

A 밑줄 친 부분을 괄호 안의 지시대로 어법에 맞게 고쳐 쓰시오.

1 I wish I can fly like a bird. (I wish 가정법과거) → ____________
2 I wish it have not been raining so hard. (I wish 가정법과거완료) → ____________
3 I wish he was able to speak Chinese well. (I wish 가정법과거) → ____________
4 I wish you had solve the math problems. (I wish 가정법과거완료) → ____________

B 두 문장의 뜻이 같도록 빈칸에 알맞은 말을 쓰시오.

1 I am sorry that I don't have enough time.
→ I wish ______________________.
2 I am sorry that he didn't finish his homework on time.
→ I wish ______________________ on time.
3 I am sorry that I didn't practice hard for the presentation.
→ I wish ______________________ for the presentation.
4 I am sorry that Fred and Helen don't attend the meeting.
→ I wish ______________________ the meeting.

C 우리말과 뜻이 같도록 괄호 안의 말을 바르게 배열하여 문장을 완성하시오.

1 그가 그곳에 갈 수 있다면 좋을 텐데. (go, could, there)
→ I wish he ______________________.
2 어제 친구들과 영화를 봤다면 좋았을 텐데. (watched, had, a movie)
→ I wish I ______________________ with my friends yesterday.

Point 04 as if + 가정법 과거/과거완료

■ 「as if + 가정법 과거」: 주절의 동사가 현재형이면 현재 사실과 반대되는 일을, 주절의 동사가 과거형이면 과거 사실과 반대되는 일을 의미한다.

> **「동사의 과거형[또는 현재형] + as if + 주어 + 동사의 과거」** '마치 ~인 것처럼'
> ※ if절의 be동사는 주어의 수나 인칭에 상관없이 were를 쓴다.

(1) 주절 동사가 현재: 현재 사실과 반대되는 일

She **acts** as if she were a famous singer. (가정법 과거) 그녀는 마치 자신이 유명 가수인 것처럼 행동한다.

→ In fact, she is not a famous singer. (직설법 현재) 사실, 그녀는 유명 가수가 아니다.

(2) 주절 동사가 과거: 과거 사실과 반대되는 일

She **acted** as if she were a famous singer. (가정법 과거) 그녀는 마치 자신이 유명 가수인 것처럼 행동했다.

→ In fact, she was not a famous singer. (직설법 과거) 사실, 그녀는 유명 가수가 아니었다.

■ 「as if + 가정법 과거완료」: 주절의 동사가 현재형이면 과거 사실과 반대되는 일을, 주절의 동사가 과거형이면 주절의 시제인 과거보다 더 앞서 일어난 사실과 반대되는 일을 의미한다.

> **「동사의 현재형[또는 과거형] + as if + 주어 + had p.p.」** '마치 ~이었던/했던 것처럼'

(1) 주절 동사가 현재일 때: 과거 사실과 반대되는 일

He **sings** as if he had been a singer. (가정법 과거완료) 그는 마치 그가 가수였던 것처럼 노래한다.

→ In fact, he was not a singer. (직설법 과거) 사실, 그는 가수가 아니었다.

(2) 주절 동사가 과거일 때: 과거보다 더 앞서 일어난 사실과 반대되는 일

She **talked** as if she had been to New York. (가정법 과거완료)
그녀는 마치 그녀가 뉴욕에 갔었던 것처럼 말했다.

→ In fact, she had not been to New York. 사실, 그녀는 뉴욕에 가지 않았었다. (직설법 과거완료)

A 괄호 안에서 알맞은 말을 고르시오.

1 He talks as if he (knew, knows) the singer, but he doesn't.

2 She speaks English as if she (is, were) a native speaker, but she isn't.

3 We helped the poor as if they (were, had been) our family, but they were not.

B 우리말과 뜻이 같도록 괄호 안의 말을 활용하여 문장을 완성하시오.

1 James practices hard ______________________________.

→ In fact, he is not a main actor.

2 Kate acts ______________________________.

→ In fact, Kate doesn't know the answer to the question.

C 우리말과 뜻이 같도록 괄호 안의 말을 바르게 배열하여 문장을 완성하시오.

1 그는 마치 경기에서 이겼던 것처럼 말한다. (he, as, if, he, won, the game, talks, had)

→ ______________________________

2 그녀는 마치 건강을 회복했던 것처럼 보였다. (looked, she, as, had, if, she, well, gotten)

→ ______________________________

Point 05 「Without[But for] + 명사(구)」 구문의 가정법

■ 「**without[but for] + 명사(구)**」는 '**if it were not for**'나 '**if it had not been for**'와 바꿔 쓸 수 있다.

「**without[but for] + 명사(구)**」 '만약 ~가 아니라면(아니었다면), 만약 ~가 없다면(없었다면)'
→ 「**if it were not for ~**」 '만약 ~가 아니라면, 만약 ~가 없다면'
→ 「**if it had not been for ~**」 '만약 ~가 아니었다면, 만약 ~가 없었다면'

Without[But for] you, I could not win a gold medal.
→ If it were not for you, I could not win a gold medal.
만약 네가 없다면, 나는 금메달을 따지 못할 것이다.

Without[But for] a helping hand, the baby could not have received treatment.
→ If it had not been for a helping hand, the baby could not have received treatment.
도움의 손길이 없었더라면, 그 아기는 치료를 받지 못했을 것이다.

A
괄호 안에서 알맞은 말을 고르시오.

1 (With, Without) salt, no food could be tasty.
2 (And, But) for the sun, Earth would be dark.
3 But for his great effort, he (can, could) not have passed the test.
4 If it (had, have) not been for his advice, she couldn't have gotten a ticket to the concert.
5 Without an alarm clock, I couldn't (attended, have attended) the meeting on time.

B
두 문장의 뜻이 같도록 빈칸에 알맞은 말을 쓰시오.

1 Without this map, I could not find the place.
→ But ________________ this map, I could not find the place.

2 If it had not been for the song, she could not have become famous.
→ ________________ the song, she could not have become famous.

3 Without intense effort, you could not enter this university.
→ If ________________ intense effort, you could not enter this university.

4 But for the medicine, the sickness would last for a long time.
→ ________________ the medicine, the sickness would last for a long time.

C
우리말과 뜻이 같도록 괄호 안의 말을 바르게 배열하여 문장을 완성하시오.

1 만약 달이 없다면, 세상은 깜깜할 것이다. (without, the world, the moon, would, dark, be)
→ ____

2 만약 법이 없다면, 우리 사회는 위험할 것이다. (be, the laws, our society, but for, dangerous, would)
→ ____

3 만약 돈이 없다면, 나는 내가 원하는 것을 살 수 없을 것이다. (want, money, buy, without, I, could, not, what, I)
→ ____

Point 06 주의해야 할 가정법

- **가정법 과거/과거완료에서 if절에 'were, had, should'** 등이 오면, **접속사 if를 생략**하고 **주어와 동사를 도치**시킬 수 있다.
  If I were a magician, I would fly home. 만약 내가 마법사라면, 나는 집에 날아갈 텐데. (가정법 과거)
  → Were I a magician, I would fly home.
  If my dream had come true, I would have been happier. (가정법 과거완료)
  만약 내 꿈이 실현되었다면, 나는 더 행복했었을 텐데.
  → Had my dream come true, I would have been happier.

- **단순 조건문 *vs.* 가정법 과거**: '~라면'이라는 뜻의 접속사 if는 조건을 말할 때(단순 조건문)와 가정할 때(가정법) 둘 다 쓴다. 조건문과 가정법의 의미상 차이는 '실현 가능성'에 있다.
  (1) 단순 조건문(만약 ~한다면 ~할 것이다): 조건이 충족되면, 실현될 가능성이 있음.
  「If + 주어 + 동사의 현재형, 주어 + 조동사의 현재형 + 동사원형」으로 쓴다.
  If it is sunny, we will play outside. (날씨가 맑을 가능성이 충분히 있다고 생각함)
  만약 날씨가 맑으면, 우리는 밖에서 놀 수 있을 것이다.
  (2) 가정법(만약 ~한다면 ~할 텐데……): 실현 불가능한 일을 가정. 「If + 주어 + 동사의 과거형, 주어 + 조동사의 과거형 + 동사원형」으로 쓴다. 주절에 반드시 조동사의 과거형이 온다.
  If it were sunny, we could play outside. (날씨가 맑을 가능성이 희박함. 밖에서 놀 수 없음)
  만약 날씨가 맑으면, 우리는 밖에서 놀 텐데. (가정법 과거)

- **혼합가정법**: 과거의 일이 현재까지 영향을 끼칠 때 사용하며 '(과거에) ~했다면 (지금) ~할 텐데'라는 뜻으로, **if절에는 가정법 과거완료를, 주절에는 가정법 과거**를 쓴다.
  If I had studied harder yesterday, I could answer all these questions now.
  만약 내가 어제 더 열심히 공부했더라면, 지금 이 모든 문제에 답할 수 있을 텐데.

A 괄호 안에서 알맞은 말을 고르시오.

1 If you are busy, I (will, would) ask Tony to help me.
2 If I were you, I (will, would) finish the homework first.
3 If she (is, were) his mom, she could ask him to help the house chores.

B 두 문장의 뜻이 같도록 if를 생략하여 문장을 완성하시오.

1 If she were rich, she could buy the diamond necklace.
→ ______________________________, she could buy the diamond necklace.

2 If they had practiced harder, they could have been the winners.
→ ______________________________, they could have been the winners.

C 우리말과 뜻이 같도록 괄호 안의 말을 활용하여 문장을 완성하시오.

1 만약 내가 너라면, 나는 더 많이 공부할 텐데. (were, would, I, you, if, study)
→ ____________________, I ____________________ more.

2 만약 그가 다치지 않았더라면, 그는 훌륭한 축구 선수가 되었을 텐데.
(have, if, been, injured, he, not, would, had, been)
→ ____________________, he ____________________ a great soccer player.

일등 비법 노트

비법 ①

if절이 과거이면 주절은 「조동사 과거 + 동사원형」!
if절에 「had + p.p.」이면 주절은 「조동사 과거 + have p.p.」!

대표기출 1 빈칸 ⓐ, ⓑ에 알맞은 말이 순서대로 바르게 나열된 것은?

- If I ⓐ __________ him, I would call her.
- If she ⓑ __________ more careful, she wouldn't have lost her wallet.

① was, had been ② was, has been
③ were, had been ④ were, has been
⑤ were, have been

대표기출 2 어법상 옳은 문장을 모두 고르면? (2개)

① If I won the lottery, I would buy a new house.
② If she were honest, she would have been hired.
③ If it were not raining, we could going on a field trip.
④ If they had not have lunch at the restaurant, they would not see her.
⑤ If it had not snowed last night, the road would not be so slippery now.

비법 ②

I wish 뒤에 과거시제면 현재의 반대 소망, 과거완료시제면 과거의 반대 소망이다!

대표기출 1 두 문장의 뜻이 통하도록 주어진 말로 시작하여 문장을 완성하시오.

(1) I'm sorry I don't have a girlfriend.

→ I wish ______________________________.

(2) I'm sorry I couldn't help you.

→ I wish ______________________________.

비법 ③ 「as if + 가정법 과거」는 주절과 같은 시제! 「as if + 가정법 과거완료」는 주절보다 앞선 시제!

대표기출 1

어법상 옳지 않은 문장은?

① She talks as if she were my mom, but she isn't.
② He looked as if he had had a hard time, but he didn't.
③ Bob spends money as if he is a millionaire but he isn't.
④ Charles danced as if he had been a dancer, but he had never been one.
⑤ The man acted as if he had lived in New York, but he hadn't.

비법 ④ 「Without[But for] ~」 가정법은 「If it were not for ~」 혹은 「If it had not been for ~」로 바꿔 쓸 수 있다!

대표기출 1

다음 문장과 의미가 같은 것을 두 개 고르면?

Without my parents' support, I could not achieve my goals.

① But for my parents' support, I could achieve my goals.
② But for my parents' support, I could not achieve my goals.
③ If it were for my parents' support, I could not achieve my goals.
④ If it were not for my parents' support, I could achieve my goals.
⑤ If it were not for my parents' support, I could not achieve my goals.

비법 ⑤ 가정법 과거는 「if + 과거 시제, 주어 + 과거 시제」! 단순 조건문은 「if + 현재 시제, 주어 + 현재/미래 시제」이다!

대표기출 1

어법상 옳지 않은 문장은?

① If she arrives in time, I will go with her.
② If he saw a UFO, he would be delighted.
③ If I found out where she is, I will let you know.
④ If you were me, what would you do in this case?
⑤ If he had taken my advice, he wouldn't have been late for the meeting.

내신 만점! 실전 기출

[1~2] 빈칸 ⓐ, ⓑ에 알맞은 말이 순서대로 바르게 나열된 것을 고르시오.

01

만약 내가 외계인을 만난다면, 나는 도망갈 거야.
→ If I ⓐ __________ an alien, I ⓑ __________ away.

① meet, run ② meet, ran ③ met, run
④ met, will run ⑤ met, would run

02

If she ⓐ __________ her favorite actor last night, she ⓑ __________ very happy.

① sees, will be
② saw, would be
③ saw, would been
④ has seen, would have been
⑤ had seen, would have been

03 서술형

괄호 안의 단어를 활용하여 빈칸에 알맞은 말을 쓰시오.
(필요 시 단어의 형태 변화 가능)

(1) If he __________ rich, he could buy the sports car. (be)
(2) If I __________ a laptop computer, I would lend it to you. (have)
(3) If she had strawberries, she could __________ a strawberry cake. (make)

(1) __________, (2) __________, (3) __________

04 서술형

주어진 질문에 영어로 답하시오.

Q: If you saw a bear on a mountain, what would you do?

→ A: ______________________________

05 두 문장의 뜻이 같도록 빈칸 ⓐ, ⓑ에 알맞은 말이 차례대로 짝지어진 것은?

As I don't speak loudly, he can't hear me.
→ If I ⓐ __________ loudly, he ⓑ __________ me.

① speak, could hear
② spoke, could hear
③ spoke, couldn't hear
④ spoken, couldn't hear
⑤ had spoken, couldn't hear

[6~7] 두 문장의 뜻이 같도록 빈칸에 알맞은 말을 쓰시오.

06 서술형

If the brakes worked, the car could stop quickly in time.

→ __________ the brakes __________ __________, the car __________ stop quickly in time.

07 서술형

As I am so tired, I cannot go with them.

→ If __________ __________ __________ so tired, I __________ __________ with them.

08 빈칸에 알맞은 말은?

그는 마치 아무것도 모르는 것처럼 말하는데, 그것은 사실이 아니다.
→ He talks as if he __________ nothing, which is not true.

① know ② knew ③ knows
④ knowing ⑤ had known

09 빈칸 ⓐ, ⓑ에 알맞은 말이 차례대로 짝지어진 것은?

> 그것은 마치 그 영화가 신기록을 세웠었던 것처럼 들린다.
> → It sounds ⓐ __________ the movie ⓑ __________ a new record.

① as if, sets
② as if, set
③ even if, has set
④ as if, had set
⑤ even if, had set

10 서술형

세 문장이 같은 뜻이 되도록 빈칸에 알맞은 말을 쓰시오.

> Without the Internet, we could not get information so easily.

→ (1) __________ __________ the Internet, we __________ __________ __________ information so easily.

→ (2) If it __________ __________ __________ the internet, we __________ __________ __________ information so easily.

11 서술형

두 문장의 뜻이 같도록 if를 생략한 문장으로 바꿔 쓰시오.

> (A) If you were in the spacecraft, you could experience zero gravity.

→ ______________________________, you could experience zero gravity.

> (B) If I had had a bicycle, I would have ridden it to school then.

→ ______________________________, I would have ridden it to school then.

12 다음 밑줄 친 문장과 의미가 같은 것은?

> My friends and I were going to play baseball yesterday but we couldn't because it rained a lot. <u>I'm sorry that it rained cats and dogs.</u>

① I wish it will rain cats and dogs.
② I wish it was rained cats and dogs.
③ I wish it had rained cats and dogs.
④ I wish it hadn't rained cats and dogs.
⑤ I wish it haven't rained cats and dogs.

13 문맥에 맞도록 밑줄 친 우리말을 영어로 바르게 옮긴 것은?

> I made a rule to exercise every day at the beginning of this year, but I haven't kept the rule. These days, I get sick easily because I don't exercise. <u>만일 내가 규칙적으로 운동한다면 건강을 유지할 수 있을 텐데.</u>

① If I exercised regularly, I can stay healthy.
② If I exercised regularly, I can't stay healthy.
③ If I exercised regularly, I could stay healthy.
④ If I didn't exercised regularly, I could stay healthy.
⑤ If I don't exercise regularly, I couldn't stay healthy.

14 서술형

<보기>를 참고하여 빈칸에 알맞은 말을 쓰시오.

> 보기
> Sally는 마치 대학생인 것처럼 공부한다. (university student)
> → <u>Sally studies as if she were a university student.</u>

> 재민이는 마치 원어민인 것처럼 영어를 말한다. (native speaker)

→ Jaemin speaks English ______________________________.

최다빈출

[15~16] 짝지어진 두 문장의 의미가 다른 것을 고르시오.

15

① If he were free, he could join us.
→ As he wasn't free, he can't join us.
② If it were not cold, they could go hiking.
→ As it is cold, they can't go hiking.
③ If I had money, I could buy the ring.
→ As I don't have money, I can't buy the ring.
④ If I were hungry, I could finish all the food.
→ As I am not hungry, I can't finish all the food.
⑤ If she told me the truth, I could trust her.
→ As she doesn't tell me the truth, I can't trust her.

16

① If he were fine, he could go to the movies.
= As he isn't fine, he can't go to the movies.
② If I were not exhausted, I could play outside.
= I'm exhausted, so I can't play outside.
③ If there were no traffic, we could arrive on time.
= Because there is traffic, we can't arrive on time.
④ If she were from the U.S., she could speak English fluently.
= As she isn't from the U.S., she can speak English fluently.
⑤ If she knew Dr. Jackson's phone number, she would call and ask him.
= As she doesn't know Dr. Jackson's phone number, she can't call and ask him.

17 괄호 안에서 알맞은 단어를 차례대로 나열한 것은?

- I wish he ⓐ (has, had, have) not left me alone.
- I wish she ⓑ (can, could) sing well.

① have, could ② have, can ③ had, could
④ had, can ⑤ has, could

[18~19] 주어진 문장과 의미가 같은 것을 고르시오.

18

If she knew the password, she could open the door.

① She knew the password, so she could open the door.
② As she didn't know the password, she can't open the door.
③ She doesn't know the password, so she can open the door.
④ As she doesn't know the password, she can't open the door.
⑤ As she doesn't know the password, she couldn't open the door.

19

She acts like she is a high school student, but she isn't.

① She acts as if she is a high school student.
② She acts as if she isn't a high school student.
③ She acts as if she were a high school student.
④ She acts as if she weren't a high school student.
⑤ She acts as if she had not been a high school student.

20 서술형

두 문장의 뜻이 같도록 빈칸에 알맞은 말을 쓰시오.

(A) In fact, they do not know each other.

→ They look __________ __________ they __________ each other.

(B) In fact, they are the owners of this house.

→ My grandparents act __________ __________ they __________ __________ the owners of this house.

21 서술형

〈보기〉와 같이 괄호 안의 말을 활용하여 우리말을 완전한 영어 문장으로 바꿔 쓰시오.

> **보기**
>
> 세상의 모든 질병이 치료될 수 있다면 좋을 텐데.
> (all kinds of diseases, curable)
> → I wish all diseases in the world were curable.

> 내가 전과목 만점을 받으면 좋을 텐데.
> (get, straight A's)

→ ______________________________

____

22 어법상 옳은 문장은?

① If I had gotten up earlier, I would had not been late.
② If she has read the letter, she would have been glad.
③ If he had spoke Chinese well, she would have hired him.
④ If the rumor had been true, people would have criticized the actor.
⑤ If they had asked the boy his contact number yesterday, they could called him now.

최다빈출

23 어법상 옳지 않은 문장은?

① If he were here, I would ask him for help.
② If I sang well, I would join the singing club.
③ If you give him this letter, I will really appreciate it.
④ If I had enough money, I could have bought a house.
⑤ If she were not busy, she could play softball with her friends.

24 서술형

다음을 읽고 밑줄 친 ⓐ를 영작하시오.

> This winter vacation is going to be the best vacation of my life. I will go to Europe with my family. My dad's friends live in England and Germany, so we are going to visit them. I am very excited. ⓐ 내가 만약 교장선생님이라면 오늘 겨울방학을 시작할 수 있을 텐데.

→ ________ ________ ________ the school principal, I ________ ________ our winter vacation today.

25 서술형

주어진 우리말을 〈조건〉에 따라 영작하시오.

> **조건**
>
> 1. 다음 단어를 모두 사용할 것: finish, go, could
> 2. 필요하면 단어의 형태를 변형할 수 있음.

> 내가 아침에 숙제를 끝냈더라면, 지금 영화를 보러 갈 수 있을 텐데.

→ ________ ________ ________ ________ my homework in the morning, I ________ ________ to see a movie now.

신유형

26 대화의 흐름이 자연스럽도록 바르게 나열한 것은?

> ⓐ Did you try to talk to him about it?
> ⓑ Not yet. What would you tell him if you were me?
> ⓒ My roommate turns on the music so loud late at night.
> ⓓ If I were you, I would tell him to turn the volume down after midnight.

① ⓐ, ⓑ, ⓒ, ⓓ
② ⓒ, ⓐ, ⓑ, ⓓ
③ ⓒ, ⓑ, ⓐ, ⓓ
④ ⓒ, ⓓ, ⓐ, ⓑ
⑤ ⓑ, ⓓ, ⓒ, ⓐ

고난도

27 어법상 어색한 문장을 모두 고르면?

ⓐ If I am you, I would accept his apology.
ⓑ If we had no friends, we would feel lonely.
ⓒ If she had a cell phone now, she would have lent it to him.
ⓓ If you read a lot of books, you could become wiser.
ⓔ If I have no homework today, I could go to the party.

① ⓐ, ⓒ ② ⓒ, ⓔ ③ ⓑ, ⓒ, ⓔ
④ ⓐ, ⓓ, ⓔ ⑤ ⓐ, ⓒ, ⓔ

신유형 고난도

28 주어진 각 조건에 맞춰 우리말을 영어로 옮기시오.

조건
1. 'Practice makes perfect.'이 의미하는 바와 같게 쓸 것.
2. 단어 practice, make, hard, perfect를 사용할 것.
3. 10단어로 쓸 것.

(1) 만약 네가 열심히 연습한다면, 너는 네 일을 완벽하게 만들 것이다.

→ ______________________________
____

조건
1. busy와 go shopping을 사용할 것.
2. 11단어로 쓸 것.

(2) 만약 내가 바쁘지 않다면, 그녀와 함께 쇼핑하러 갈 수 있을 텐데.

→ ______________________________
____

신유형

29 서술형

대화를 읽고 밑줄 친 우리말 ⓐ와 같은 뜻이 되도록 빈칸에 알맞은 말을 쓰시오.

A: Do you know any famous sayings?
B: Yes, I do know one and it is my motto.
A: What is it?
B: It's what Steve Jobs said in his speech. He said, 'ⓐ <u>오늘을 인생의 마지막 날인 것처럼 살아라</u>'.

= Live today __________ __________ it __________ the last day of your life.

30 서술형

밑줄 친 ⓐ를 가정법 문장으로 바꿔 쓸 때, 조건에 맞춰 영작하시오.

조건
1. 과거 사실에 반대되는 가정법을 사용할 것.
2. 다음 단어를 활용하여, 총 14단어로 영작할 것: work hard, become, the Sales Queen
3. 부정어는 축약형을 사용하지 말 것.

Thanks to Belle's talent, she was very good at sales. As she was very polite and friendly, people bought new cars from her. She was even selected as the 'Salesperson of the Year' for 2015. ⓐ <u>As she worked so hard, she could become the Sales Queen.</u> So she decided to work much harder.

→ ______________________________
____

실력 탄탄!
서술형 심화

1 그림을 보고 괄호 안의 말을 활용하여 가정법 과거 문장을 완성하시오.
(필요하면 단어의 형태를 바꾸거나 추가)

(1) 

(2) 

(1) My mom and I were going to go to the zoo today, but now we can't. It is raining too much!
→ If it ______________________, ______________________.
(be, sunny, we, can, go, the zoo)

(2) It is my birthday today, but nobody seems to remember it. I am very sad.
→ I wish ______________________________ with my friends.
(have a birthday party, can)

2 Fill in the blanks using the words given. Change the form of the words if necessary.

> Sumi is taking a test now. She didn't prepare hard for the test yesterday, so there are a few questions that she doesn't know. "Oh, ⓐ ______________ (wish, go) back to this time yesterday. If I could, ⓑ ______________ (study) really hard! If only Minji ⓒ ______________ (visit) me yesterday, then ⓓ ______________ (have, study) much harder!" She knew that she ⓔ ______________ (get) a good grade ⓕ ______________ (without, work) hard, but she just didn't want to yesterday. Now, it's no use regretting it.

CHAPTER 12

일치와 화법

일치

단수 주어에는 단수 동사를, 복수 주어에는 복수 동사를 써서 **수를 일치**시킨다. 또한 주절 동사의 시제에 따라 종속절의 동사의 시제가 영향을 받는 **시제의 일치**도 있다.

수의 일치	• The boy **is** playing the guitar now. • The boys **are** playing musical instruments together.
시제의 일치	• He **says** that he **is** busy. • He **said** that he **was** busy.

화법

다른 사람의 말을 제3자에게 전달할 때 '말하는(話) 방식(法)'이다. 다른 사람이 한 말을 인용부호(" ")를 사용해 원래의 말 그대로 전달하는 **직접화법**과, 전달자의 입장에서 바꾸어 전달하는 **간접화법**이 있다.

직접화법	He said to me, "I love you."
간접화법	He told me that he loved me.

Point 01 수의 일치

- **수의 일치**: '주어의 수에 따라 동사의 수를 맞추는 것'을 수의 일치라고 한다.
- 다음 말이 주어로 오면, **단수 취급**한다.

each, every, -thing, -one, -body	Every dog has its day. 쥐구멍에도 볕들 날 있다.
병명, 학문명, 국가명, 과목명	Diabetes is a kind of an adult disease. (당뇨병: 병명) The United States has 50 states. (미국: 국가명)
집합적 의미의 시간, 거리, 금액, 무게 등	Fifty dollars was the price of the bag. (가격)
구와 절	Eating fast food too often is not healthy. (구) What he said was not clearly understood. (절)
「the number of + 복수명사」 (~의 수)	The number of people invited to the party was ten.
[most, all, some, part, half, percent, 분수] + 셀 수 없는 명사의 단수형	Some of the water in the bottle was gone.

- 다음 말이 주어로 오면, **복수 취급**한다.

both *A* and *B* (*A*와 *B* 둘 다)	Both Mike and Jack were late that day.
「the+형용사」 (~한 사람들)	The rich are not always happy. (the rich = rich people)
a number of ~ (많은 ~)	A number of people were present at the meeting.
[most, all, some, part, half, percent, 분수] + 셀 수 있는 명사의 복수형	Some of the books on the desk were gone.

A 괄호 안에서 알맞은 말을 고르시오.

1 Two hours (is, are) too long to wait in the rain.
2 One third of the lake water (has, have) dried up.
3 Every student (was, were) given his or her own locker.
4 The Philippines (is, are) a nation made up of many islands.
5 Someone (has, have) to be chosen to act on behalf of our group.
6 A number of fans of the singer (is, are) following him wherever he goes.
7 Both Jane and Jamie (was, were) watching a TV program on the 2014 Winter Olympic Games.

B 밑줄 친 부분이 어법에 맞으면 O표, 틀리면 바르게 고쳐 쓰시오.

1 Mathematics <u>are</u> the study of numbers. → ______
2 Some of the apples in the basket <u>are</u> rotten. → ______
3 The young <u>has</u> their own concerns about their future. → ______
4 What I couldn't understand <u>were</u> a symbol on the map. → ______
5 The number of Koreans <u>are</u> now over fifty million. → ______

Point 02 시제의 일치

- **시제의 일치**: 종속절의 시제는 주절의 시제에 영향을 받는다.
- **주절의 시제가 현재일 때**: 종속절에는 **모든 시제**가 올 수 있다.
  I think that she is satisfied with the result. (현재) 나는 그녀가 결과에 만족한다고 생각해.
  I think that she was satisfied with the result. (과거) 나는 그녀가 결과에 만족했다고 생각해.
  I think that she will be satisfied with the result. (미래) 나는 그녀가 결과에 만족할 것이라고 생각해.
- **주절의 시제가 과거일 때**: 종속절에 **과거** 또는 **과거완료**만 올 수 있다.
  I thought that she was satisfied with the result. (주절의 동작과 종속절 동작이 같은 시간에 일어남)
  나는 그녀가 결과에 만족했다고 생각했어.
  I thought that she had been satisfied with the result. (종속절의 동작이 주절의 동작보다 먼저 일어남)
  나는 그녀가 결과에 만족했었다고 생각했어.

A 주절의 시제를 과거로 바꿔서 문장을 다시 쓸 때, 빈칸에 알맞은 말을 쓰시오.

1 John thinks that his brother took his bike.
→ John thought that his brother ____________ his bike.

2 Sujin says that Minho spoke to a tourist in English.
→ Sujin said that Minho ____________ to a tourist in English.

3 He says that he visited Deoksugung two weeks ago.
→ He said that he ____________ Deoksugung two weeks before.

4 Mina tells me that she is going to go to Busan.
→ Mina told me that she ____________ going to go to Busan.

5 Emily says that we were supposed to finish our group project by today.
→ Emily said that we ____________ supposed to finish our group project by that day.

B 우리말과 뜻이 같도록 괄호 안의 말을 활용하여 빈칸에 알맞은 말을 쓰시오.

1 거기에서 그때까지 10년간 살아왔다고 2년 전에 그녀는 말했다. (live)
→ Two years ago, she said that she ____________ ____________ there for ten years.

2 그녀가 궁 안을 둘러보도록 안내해 주겠다고 했다. (show)
→ She told us that she ____________ ____________ us around the palace.

3 John은 어렸을 때 강에서 수영했었다고 말했다. (swim)
→ John said that he ____________ ____________ in the river when he was young.

4 그가 오는 길에 극심한 교통체증에 갇혀 있었다고 말했다. (be)
→ He said that he ____________ ____________ caught in heavy traffic on the way.

5 Tom은 우리가 오염으로부터 그 호수를 구하기 위해 뭔가 해야 한다고 생각했다. (have to)
→ Tom thought that we ____________ ____________ do something to save the lake from pollution.

Point 03 시제 일치의 예외

- 종속절에 **현재의 습관(반복적 행위), 불변의 진리, 속담, 격언, 과학적 사실** 등이 나오면 **항상 현재 시제**로 쓴다.
  She **said** that the library opens at 9 o'clock. (현재의 습관)
  그녀는 도서관이 9시에 문을 연다고 말했다.
  We **learned** that triangles have three sides. (불변의 진리)
  우리는 삼각형이 세 개의 변을 가진다고 배웠다.
  My mom **said** that it takes two to tango. (속담)
  어머니께서 손뼉도 마주 쳐야 소리가 난다고 말씀하셨다.
  He **told** me that habit is second nature. (격언)
  그는 나에게 습관은 제2의 천성이라고 말했다.
  She **taught** us that hot air goes up. (과학적 사실)
  그녀가 뜨거운 공기는 위로 올라간다고 가르쳐 주셨다.
- **종속절의 역사적 사실**: 주절의 시제와 상관 없이 **항상 과거**로 쓴다.
  The teacher said that the Korean War broke out in 1950.
  선생님께서 한국전쟁은 1950년에 발발했다고 말씀하셨다.

A 괄호 안에서 알맞은 말을 고르시오.

1 People in the past didn't believe that the Earth (is, was) round.
2 An old saying tells us that necessity (is, was) the mother of invention.
3 He said that Abraham Lincoln (was, had been) the 16th president of America.
4 Minjun explained to John that the school year in Korea usually (starts, started) in March.

B 주절의 시제를 과거로 바꿔서 문장을 다시 쓸 때, 빈칸에 알맞은 말을 쓰시오.

1 The science teacher says that the sun becomes farther from the northern hemisphere in winter.
→ The science teacher said that the sun ____________ farther from the northern hemisphere in winter.

2 Children learn that World War I broke out in 1914.
→ Children learned that World War I ____________ in 1914.

3 Sujin says that she is happy to see us again.
→ Sujin said that she ____________ happy to see us again.

C 우리말과 뜻이 같도록 괄호 안의 말을 활용하여 빈칸에 알맞은 말을 쓰시오.

1 지호는 비가 오든 날이 개든 언제나 걸어서 등교한다고 말했다. (walk)
→ Jiho said that he ____________ to school rain or shine.

2 너는 북극지방에서 여름에 백야가 6개월 정도 지속된다는 것을 알고 있었니? (last)
→ Did you know that White Night ____________ about 6 months during the Arctic summer?

Point 04 평서문의 화법 전환

- **직접화법 *vs.* 간접화법:**
  - 직접화법: 다른 사람이 한 말을 인용부호(" ")를 사용해 원래의 말 그대로 전달한다.
    Alice says, "I am thirsty." Alice가 말한다. "나는 목이 말라요."
  - 간접화법: 다른 사람이 한 말을 전달자의 입장에서 바꾸어 전달한다.
    Alice says that she is thirsty. Alice가 목이 마르다고 말한다.

- **직접화법을 간접화법으로 전환하는 방법**은 다음과 같다:

Dylan said to me, "I will give you five minutes now." Dylan이 내게, "네게 지금부터 5분을 줄게."라고 말했다.

① ②③ ④ ③ ⑤

Dylan told me (that) he would give me five minutes then. Dylan이 그때부터 5분을 주겠다고 나에게 말했다.

① 주절의 전달동사는 say to → tell, said to → told로 바꾼다. (단, say, said는 그대로 쓴다.)
② 쉼표(,)와 큰 따옴표(" ")를 없애고, 접속사 that을 쓴다.
단, 이 때의 that은 목적어절을 이끄는 접속사이므로 생략할 수 있다.
③ 전달되는 문장(= " "안의 문장)의 대명사를 알맞게 바꾼다.
(1인칭→ 주절의 주어와 일치, 2인칭→ 주절의 목적어와 일치, 3인칭은 그대로 쓴다.)
④ 전달되는 문장의 동사를 주절의 전달동사의 시제에 맞춰 바꾼다.
⑤ 전달되는 문장의 지시대명사, 부사구를 상황에 맞게 바꾼다.

※ 화법 전환 시 주요 어구의 변화

this(these) → that(those)	now → then	here → there
ago → before	tonight → that night	today → that day
yesterday → the previous day 또는 the day before	last month → the previous month	
tomorrow → the next day 또는 the following day	next week → the following week	

A 괄호 안에서 알맞은 말을 고르시오.

1 Minju (said, told) that she had watched a movie the previous day.
2 Yesterday at the library, the guard told us that we couldn't bring any food or drink in (here, there).
3 Jason (said, told) me that he would hand in his homework the following day.

B 다음 문장을 간접화법으로 바꿀 때 빈칸에 알맞은 말을 쓰시오.

1 He said, "I need to study English harder."
→ He ________ that ________ ________ to study English harder.

2 She said to me, "You are so nice to help Mira with her homework."
→ She told me that ________ ________ so nice to help Mira with her homework.

C 다음 문장을 직접화법으로 바꿀 때 빈칸에 알맞은 말을 쓰시오.

1 Minji said that she would visit the National Museum that day.
→ Minji said, "________ ________ visit the National Museum ________."

2 She told me that I would come to realize the importance of English someday.
→ She ________ ________ ________, "________ ________ come to realize the importance of English someday."

Point 05 의문문의 화법 전환

■ 전달하려는 말이 **의문사가 없는 의문문인 경우:**

She said to me, "Can I try on these pants?" 그녀는 나에게 "이 바지 입어 봐도 될까요?"라고 물었다.

① ② ③

She asked me if(whether) she could try on those pants. 그녀는 나에게 그 바지를 입어봐도 되는 지를 물었다.

① 전달동사 say(said) to를 상황에 맞게 ask, wonder등으로 바꾼다.
② 콤마(,)와 인용부호(" ")를 없애고, if(whether)을 쓴다.
③ if절을 「if(whether) + 주어 + 동사」의 어순으로 바꾸고, 지시대명사와 시제 및 부사구를 알맞게 바꾼다.

■ 전달하려는 말이 **의문사가 있는 의문문인 경우:**

She said to him, " What is your shoe size?" 그녀는 그에게 "너는 신발 사이즈가 몇이니?"라고 물었다.

① ② ③

She asked him what his shoe size was. 그녀는 그에게 신발 사이즈가 몇인지 물었다.

① 전달동사 say(said) to를 상황에 맞게 ask, wonder 등으로 바꾼다.
② 콤마(,)와 인용부호(" ")를 없앤다. 인용부호를 대신하여 접속사를 쓰지는 않는다.
③ 피전달문을 「의문사 + 주어 + 동사」의 어순으로 바꾸고, 지시대명사와 시제 및 부사구를 알맞게 바꾼다.

A 괄호 안에서 알맞은 말을 고르시오.

1 He said to me, "Can I ask you a favor?"
→ He (asked, said) me if he could ask me a favor.

2 She said to me, "Do you mind if I use your cell phone?"
→ She asked me (if, that) I minded if she used my cell phone.

3 Mike asked me what exams (I had, did I have) the following day.

4 I asked Bill if it was a Samsung cell phone he had bought (yesterday, the previous day).

B 다음 문장을 간접화법으로 바꿔 쓰시오.

1 My friend said to me, "Where did you park your bike?"
→ My friend asked me ______________________.

2 She said to him, "Are you hungry?"
→ She asked him ______________________.

C 다음 문장을 직접화법으로 바꿔 쓰시오.

1 She asked him when he had arrived at the airport.
→ She said to him, "______________________?"

2 He asked me how I had solved the puzzle so quickly.
→ He said to me, "______________________?"

Point 06 명령문의 화법 전환

■ **전달하려는 말이 명령문일 때** 화법전환: 명령문의 동사를 to부정사로 바꾼다.

The teacher said to us, "Finish cleaning by 3 o'clock." 선생님은 우리에게 "3시까지 청소를 끝내라"고 말씀하셨다.

① ② ③

The teacher told us to finish cleaning by 3 o'clock. 선생님은 우리에게 3시까지 청소를 끝내라고 말씀하셨다.

① 전달동사를 상황에 맞게 tell, ask, order, advise등으로 바꾼다.
② 콤마(,)와 인용부호(" ")를 없앤다.
③ 피전달문의 동사를 to부정사로 바꾼다. (부정 명령문의 경우 「not(never) + to부정사」로 쓴다.)

A 괄호 안에서 알맞은 말을 고르시오.

1 She told me (look, to look) at the blue sky.
2 Mom advised me (go, to go) to sleep early.
3 My friend advised me (try, to try) to speak to foreigners in English.
4 She advised me (to not keep, not to keep) the window open during the rainy season.

B 괄호 안의 말을 활용하여 〈보기〉와 같이 간접화법 문장으로 바꿔 쓰시오.

보기

Sumin said to Minsu, "Go to the School Uniform Bank to get a donated uniform." (advise)
→ Sumin advised Minsu to go to the School Uniform Bank to get a donated uniform.

1 She said to the children outside, "Be quiet!" (ask)
→ She ________ the children outside ________________.

2 Mom said to me, "Don't stay up too long." (tell)
→ Mom ________ me ________________.

3 Mom said to Jack, "Share your car with your younger brother." (advise)
→ Mom ________ Jack ________________.

C 직접화법은 간접화법으로, 간접화법은 직접화법으로 바꿀 때, 빈칸에 알맞은 말을 쓰시오.

1 My father told me to get up and go to bed regularly.
→ My father said to me, "________________ regularly."

2 The doctor said to my father, "Don't smoke anymore for your lung."
→ The doctor advised my father ________________.

일등 비법 노트

비법 1 every[each] + 단수명사 + 단수동사!

대표기출 1 빈칸 ⓐ, ⓑ에 알맞은 말이 순서대로 바르게 나열된 것은?

- Each finger on every hand ⓐ __________ a unique fingerprint.
- Every boy and girl ⓑ __________ supposed to do volunteer work.

① have, are ② has, is ③ have, is ④ has, are ⑤ had, were

비법 2 some/all/half/분수 + 단수명사 + 단수동사! some/all/half/분수 + 복수명사 + 복수동사!

대표기출 1 빈칸 ⓐ, ⓑ에 알맞은 말이 순서대로 바르게 나열된 것은?

A: I am hungry. Is there anything to eat at home?
B: Let's see. Oh! There are some apples in the fridge, but some of them ⓐ __________ rotten.
Ah! And there is also a pizza box on the table. Half of the pizza ⓑ __________ still left.

① is, is ② is, are ③ are, is ④ are, are ⑤ are, being

비법 3 'a number of'는 복수! 'the number of'는 단수!

대표기출 1 빈칸 ⓐ, ⓑ에 알맞은 말이 순서대로 바르게 나열된 것은?

A: How many students are there in your class?
B: The number of students in my class ⓐ __________ thirty-five.
A: Wow! We used to have more than 60 students in one class thirty years ago. There ⓑ __________ even a number of schools that had double-shift school systems.

* double-shift school system: 이부제 수업

① are, were ② is, was ③ are, was ④ is, were ⑤ is, had been

비법 4 주절이 과거일 때 종속절에 주절과 같은 시점 사건은 과거로, 앞서 일어난 사건은 과거완료로!

대표기출 1 다음 문장을 과거 시제로 바꿔 다시 쓸 때, 빈칸에 알맞은 말은?

I know that my friend Sally wants to go to the concert.
→ I knew that my friend Sally __________ to go to the concert.

① want ② wants ③ wanted ④ has wanted ⑤ had wanted

비법 5 불변의 진리, 과학적 사실, 속담, 격언은 항상 현재 시제로! 역사적 사실은 항상 과거로!

대표기출 1 각 문장에서 어법상 틀린 부분을 한 군데씩 찾아 바르게 고쳐 쓰시오.

ⓐ My little brother learned that the Earth went around the sun once a year.
ⓑ My teacher told us that America had become an independent country in 1783.

ⓐ ____________ → ____________ ⓑ ____________ → ____________

대표기출 2 밑줄 친 부분이 어법상 어색한 것은?

① She was shocked that her son had told her a lie.
② My little sister remembered an old saying that time flew like an arrow.
③ I told Matt and David that Hangeul was created by King Sejong.
④ Lisa said that her mom always gets up at 5 o'clock in the morning.
⑤ She didn't know that America was discovered by Columbus in 1492.

비법 6 화법 전환 시 〈전달자의 입장〉에서 대명사를 바꿔라! 1인칭은 주어와 일치! 2인칭은 목적어와 일치!

대표기출 1 다음 문장을 간접화법으로 바르게 바꾼 것은?

The man said to the girl, "I will not leave you alone."

① The man told the girl that I will not leave you alone.
② The man told the girl that I would not leave you alone.
③ The man told the girl that he would not leave you alone.
④ The man told the girl that he would not leave him alone.
⑤ The man told the girl that he would not leave her alone.

비법 7 의문문의 화법 전환 시 「의문사/if + 주어 + 동사」 어순을 기억하라!

대표기출 1 밑줄 친 ⓐ를 간접화법으로 바르게 고쳐 쓴 것은?

Today, when I was walking with Tom, we saw a sign that says "Valet Parking". I had no idea what it meant. So, ⓐ I said to Tom, "What does it mean?" He explained that it meant someone would park your car instead of you.

① I asked Tom what does it mean. ② I asked Tom what did it mean.
③ I asked Tom what it means. ④ I asked Tom what it meant.
⑤ I asked Tom what this had meant.

내신 만점! 실전 기출

01 빈칸에 알맞은 말은?

Amy thought that Mike ________ her what had happened.

① will tell ② would tell ③ told
④ tells ⑤ had told

[2~3] 빈칸에 알맞은 말을 고르시오.

02

Do you know who discovered that Halley's comet ____________ every sixty years?

① will return ② would return
③ returns ④ return
⑤ has returned

03

Mom told me that a stitch in time ________ nine.

① will save ② saves ③ saved
④ had saved ⑤ has saved

[4~6] 빈칸에 알맞은 말이 순서대로 바르게 나열된 것을 고르시오.

04

- Some of the students in the class ⓐ ________ bored of the lecture.
- All the money in the safe ⓑ ________ stolen by the thief last night.

① feel, was ② feels, were
③ feel, were ④ feels, was
⑤ felt, has been

05

- What he is very interested in now ⓐ ________ making a robot.
- The number of participants of the speech contest ⓑ ________ quite large.

① are, are ② is, is ③ are, is
④ is, are ⑤ was, were

06

- Politics ⓐ ________ the study of the management of a nation.
- Ten kilometers ⓑ ________ not an easy distance to walk for anybody.

① are, seem ② is, seem
③ are, seems ④ is, seems
⑤ has been, seem

[7~8] 다음 문장을 간접화법으로 바꿀 때, 어법상 틀린 부분을 고르시오.

07

John said to me, "Keep in touch with me."

→ John ① asked ② me ③ keep in touch ④ with ⑤ him.

08

I said to Mike, "Can I use your pen for a while?"

→ I ① asked Mike ② if ③ I ④ could use ⑤ your pen for a while.

09 빈칸에 알맞은 말이 나머지와 다른 하나는?

① He asked Sujin __________ she liked her food.
② She asked me __________ my favorite subject was.
③ Suho asked me __________ I had finished my homework.
④ Mina asked me __________ I would go shopping with her.
⑤ John asked me __________ we didn't have to hurry for the movie.

10 다음 중 화법 전환이 잘못된 것은?

① Kate said, "My hair was short three years ago."
→ Kate said that her hair was short three years ago.
② Rex said to me, "Will you join my study group?"
→ Rex asked me if I would join his study group.
③ Mom said to me, "Finish your homework before dinner."
→ Mom told me to finish my homework before dinner.
④ My sister said to me, "Can you help me with my homework now?"
→ My sister asked me if I could help her with her homework then.
⑤ Anne said, " I didn't study hard for my exam yesterday."
→ Anne said that she hadn't studied hard for her exam the previous day.

[11~12] 다음 문장을 간접화법으로 바꿔 쓰시오.

11 서술형

He said to me, "I will help you fix your bike."

→ ______________________________
____

12 서술형

She said to him, "Where were you two hours ago?"

→ ______________________________
____

13 다음 문장을 간접화법으로 바꿀 때, 빈칸에 알맞은 말은?

Minji said to me, "What movie do you want to watch?"
→ Minji asked me ____________________.

① what movie do you want to watch
② what movie do I want to watch
③ what movie I do want to watch
④ what movie I did want to watch
⑤ what movie I wanted to watch

[14~15] 다음을 읽고 물음에 답하시오.

Yesterday was our school festival. I invited my friend Amy to the festival. ⓐ 그녀는 우리 학교 축제가 굉장하다고 말했다. ⓑ I told her that we had prepared for it for a month.

14 서술형

괄호 안의 단어를 활용하여 ⓐ의 밑줄 친 우리말을 직접화법으로 영작하시오. (7단어)

→ ______________________________
______________________________ (say, great)

15 서술형

ⓑ를 직접화법으로 바꿀 때 빈칸에 알맞은 말을 써서 문장을 완성하시오.

→ I said to her, "______________________________
______________________________"

16 서술형

다음 표를 보고 〈보기〉와 같이 문장을 바꿔 쓰시오.

Doctor's Advice
(1) The doctor said to me, "Take the medicine right after each meal."
(2) The doctor also said to me, "Don't eat any dairy products or meat."

보기
→ (1) The doctor advised me to take the medicine right after each meal.

→ (2) The doctor also advised me ________
________________.

17 어법상 옳은 문장은?

① Somebody have broken into our house.
② Both Emily and Lily was worried about their test results.
③ Diabetes are growing common among children these days.
④ Listening to your friends carefully are the most important factor of being a good friend.
⑤ What you are interested in is the first thing to consider when you choose your future job.

18 어법상 어색한 문장은?

① My teacher said that success is not always what you see.
② Did you learn who had been the first queen of England?
③ Susan said that she was disappointed with the test result.
④ I taught my little brother yesterday that two and two equals four.
⑤ I thought that he had experienced a lot from his travels around the world.

[19~20] 대화의 빈칸 ⓐ, ⓑ에 알맞은 말이 순서대로 바르게 나열된 것을 고르시오.

19

A: I just saw on the news that an airplane made an emergency landing on Mt. Alps yesterday.
B: Oh, my! What did they say about it?
A: They said that two-thirds of the plane ⓐ ________ damaged and a number of people ⓑ ________ injured.

① are, are ② is, are ③ are, is
④ is, is ⑤ was, were

20

A: Wow, there is a singing contest next week in our town. Would you like to enter it?
B: I'd love to, but seven days ⓐ ________ not enough to prepare for the contest.
A: Come on! You said that you ⓑ ________ a chance to show your talent! Just give it a try!
B: I'll think about it.

① are, want ② are, wanted
③ is, want ④ is, wanted
⑤ are, had wanted

[21~22] 우리말과 뜻이 같도록 괄호 안의 말을 활용하여 문장을 완성하시오. (필요하면 형태를 바꾸시오.)

21 서술형

그는 모든 사람은 그(녀) 자신만의 특성을 가지고 있다고 말했다. (have)

→ He said that every person ________ his or her own characteristics.

22 서술형

그 젊은이들은 그들의 꿈을 이루기 위해 노력한다. (try)

→ The young ____________ to make their dreams come true.

23 어법상 옳은 문장을 모두 고르면?

ⓐ The librarian told us not chat in the library.
ⓑ She asked him what countries he had been to.
ⓒ Mike asked me that I knew the new math teacher.
ⓓ Jane asked Mike if he could help her move a heavy box.
ⓔ A man asked me how he could get to the subway station.

① ⓐ, ⓑ, ⓒ ② ⓐ, ⓒ, ⓓ ③ ⓑ, ⓒ, ⓓ
④ ⓑ, ⓓ, ⓔ ⑤ ⓒ, ⓓ, ⓔ

신유형

24 다음 문장 ⓐ~ⓔ에서 밑줄 친 부분은 어법에 맞지 않는다. 틀린 부분을 찾아 바르게 고친 학생을 두 명 고르면?

ⓐ I read that World War II had ended in 1945.
ⓑ She expected that I can go to Ulsan with her.
ⓒ Did you know how many states do the United States have?
ⓓ What Copernicus insisted were not accepted at first by scientists.
ⓔ My science teacher told us that the sun had eight planets going around it.

① Lisa: ⓐ에서 'had'를 'has'로 고쳐야 해.
② Mike: ⓑ에서 'can'을 'could'로 고쳐야 해.
③ Jack: ⓒ에서 'do'를 'did'로 고쳐야 해.
④ Jimmy: ⓓ에서 'were'를 'was'로 고쳐야 해.
⑤ Tim: ⓔ에서 'had'를 'have'로 고쳐야 해.

25 서술형

다음을 직접화법으로 바꿔 쓰시오.

She asked Jake if he had ever tried Vietnamese food.

→ She said to Jake, "____________________
____________________?"

26 서술형

우리말과 일치하도록 괄호 안의 말을 바르게 배열하여 문장을 완성하시오.

기자가 Mike에게 어떻게 성공했는지를 물었다.
(how, succeeded, had, he, asked, Mike)

→ A reporter ____________________
____________________.

[27~28] 다음을 읽고 물음에 답하시오.

I had an essay for homework. I didn't know what to write about, so ⓐ I said to Minji, "What are you going to write about?" ⓑ She said that she would search the Internet first. I thought that was a good idea.

27 서술형

다음은 윗글의 ⓐ를 간접화법으로 전환한 것이다. 어법상 틀린 곳을 찾아 바르게 고쳐 쓰시오.

I asked Minji what was she going to write about.

틀린 곳: ____________ → ____________

28 서술형

윗글의 ⓑ를 직접화법으로 전환할 때 빈칸에 알맞은 말을 쓰시오.

ⓑ She said that she would search the Internet first.

→ She said, "______________________________

______________________________."

29 다음 글의 ⓐ~ ⓒ에 알맞은 말이 순서대로 바르게 나열된 것은?

What do you do on New Year's Day? Many people set goals to achieve in the new year, but most of them ⓐ (give, gives) up the goals half way through the year. How can people successfully achieve their goals? A book taught me that setting impossible goals ⓑ (is, are) one problem. It also taught that I should ask myself ⓒ (if, that) I can reach my goal by going one step ahead at a time. Next time I set a goal, I will remember what this book said.

① gives, is, that ② gives, are, that
③ give, are, if ④ give, are, that
⑤ give, is, if

신유형

30 다음 글의 빈칸 ⓐ~ⓔ 어디에도 알맞지 않은 말은?

Yesterday my elder brother and I went to a park. A man and his dog were in the park. The man told us ⓐ __________ about his dog. He said that the dog ⓑ __________ anyone until ⓒ __________. That reminded me of an old saying that a barking dog ⓓ __________. My brother said that we ⓔ __________ not afraid of the dog.

① not to worry ② had never bitten
③ were ④ doesn't bite
⑤ now

실력 탄탄!
서술형 심화

1 다음 대화 내용을 한 문장으로 요약할 때, 빈칸에 알맞은 말을 쓰시오. (4단어)

Eunho: Do you see the sign "courtesy phone" over there? What does that mean?
Jane: That means that you can use the phone for free.
Eunho: Wow! That's nice.

→ Eunho asked Jane ____________________, and Jane explained it.

2 밑줄 친 ⓐ~ⓓ를 어법에 맞게 고쳐 쓰시오.

A: Look at all these people! This movie must be very successful!
B: Yeah. Every seat in this theater ⓐ <u>are taken</u>.
A: I heard that the number of people who have seen this movie ⓑ <u>are</u> over ten million.
B: I know. A number of people ⓒ <u>says</u> it's amazing.
A: Did Jim say that he also ⓓ <u>saw</u> it already?
B: Yes, he saw it last week.

ⓐ → ____________________ ⓑ → ____________________
ⓒ → ____________________ ⓓ → ____________________

3 Read the dialogue between Doctor and Amy. Complete the sentences.

Doctor: What made you come here?
Amy: I have a bad cold.
Doctor: Hmmm. Take this medicine three times a day and don't drink cold water.
Amy: What do I have to do if it doesn't help?
Doctor: Then, come again tomorrow.

Doctor asked Amy what had made her come there. Amy said that (1) ____________________ a bad cold. Doctor told Amy (2) ____________________ that medicine three times a day and (3) ____________________ cold water. Amy asked the doctor (4) ____________________ if it didn't help. Doctor told her (5) ____________________.

CHAPTER 13

특수 구문

특수 구문

영어에서 지금까지 배워온 정상적인 어순과는 다르게 쓰는 **특수한 구문**들이 있다. 즉, 어떤 내용을 특별히 **강조**하고 싶을 때 그 말 앞에 조동사를 추가하거나 어순을 바꾸어 **도치**하고, 어구의 반복을 피하기 위해 불필요하거나 반복되는 말을 생략해서 문장을 간결하게 만들기도 한다.

• **특수 구문**

강조 구문		I found this key <u>on the chair</u>. → **It was** on the chair **that** I found this key.
도치 구문	장소 부사구의 도치	This key was <u>on the chair</u>. → **On the chair was this key.**
	부정어(구)의 도치	He <u>rarely</u> gets up late in the morning. → **Rarely does he get up** late in the morning.
	동의할 때	• I'm hungry. — **So am I.** • I didn't like the movie. — **Neither did I.**

Point 01 강조 I – 조동사 do로 동사 강조

■ **조동사 do를 사용하여 동사를 강조**할 수 있다. 이 때, 주어나 시제에 따라 조동사 do를 변형시켜야 한다. 즉, 「do/does/did + 동사원형」의 형태로 쓰고, '정말, 꼭~'이라고 해석한다.

do + 동사원형	**현재 시제**에 주어가 **1, 2인칭이나 복수**인 경우 I do want to meet him in person. 나는 그를 꼭 직접 만나고 싶다.
does + 동사원형	**현재 시제**에 주어가 **3인칭이나 단수**인 경우 He does respect his parents. 그는 그의 부모님을 정말로 존경한다.
did + 동사원형	**과거 시제**인 경우 She did meet them again in the park. 그녀는 그들을 공원에서 정말로 다시 만났다.

A

괄호 안에서 알맞은 말을 고르시오.

1 I (do, does) want to know about it.

2 She (do, does) hate seafood, but I like it.

3 You (do, does) have to wake up early.

4 These cookies (do, does) taste great.

5 (Do, Does) practice harder before the contest.

6 Jake (do, did) think he was right about the matter.

B

밑줄 친 부분의 의미를 강조하고자 〈보기〉와 같이 문장을 다시 쓸 때, 빈칸에 알맞은 말을 쓰시오.

보기

Jimin exercised hard and lost a lot of weight.

→ Jimin exerciesed hard and did lose a lot of weight.

1 I hope he gets better soon.

→ I ____________ ____________ he gets better soon.

2 I finished all the work already.

→ I ____________ ____________ all the work already.

3 Jane knew it was his mistake.

→ Jane ____________ ____________ it was his mistake.

4 Peter believed what she told him.

→ Peter ____________ ____________ what she told him.

5 My older brother studied very hard, so he passed the exam.

→ My older brother studied very hard, so he ____________ ____________ the exam.

Point 02 강조 II - 「It ~ that …」 강조 구문

- It is[was]와 that 사이에 강조하고자 하는 주어, 목적어, 수식어구 등을 넣어 강조 구문을 만들 수 있고, '…한 것은 바로 ~이다'라고 해석한다.
  Ted bought a new cellphone yesterday. Ted는 어제 새로운 휴대폰을 샀다.
  (Ted: 주어 / a new cellphone: 목적어 / yesterday: 시간을 나타내는 부사)
  → It was Ted that[who] bought a new cellphone yesterday. (주어 강조)
  → It was a new cellphone that[which] Ted bought yesterday. (목적어 강조)
  → It was yesterday that[when] Ted bought a new cellphone. (시간 강조)

- 「It ~ that …」 강조 구문에서 강조 대상이 무엇인지에 따라 **that 대신 다른 관계사를 써줄 수 있다.** 즉, 강조하는 바가 **사람이면 who, 사물이면 which, 장소이면 where, 시간이면 when**이 that을 대신해서 올 수 있다.
  It was Jack that[who] made the report. 보고서를 작성한 것은 Jack이다.
  It was Christmas that[when] we met first. 우리가 처음 만난 것은 크리스마스이었다.

- 의문사를 강조할 때는 「의문사 + is[was] it that ~?」 표현을 사용한다.
  When was it that you had a long vacation? 네가 긴 휴가를 가진 것은 언제였니?
  cf. 「It ~ that …」이 강조 구문이 아닌 가주어, 진주어 구문으로 쓰일 때도 있다.
  It is unbelievable that Jenny broke up with Tim. Jenny가 Tim과 헤어진 것은 믿을 수 없다.
  (It: 가주어 / that Jenny broke up with Tim: 진주어)
  It is great that John joined our team. John이 우리 팀에 합류한 것은 좋다.
  (It: 가주어 / that John joined our team: 진주어)

PLUS Tip
※ 「It ~ that ...」 구문이 가주어 구문인지 강조 구문인지 구별하는 요령
(1) **that 이하에 생략된 문장요소가 있으면**, 강조구문이다.
It was Tom that Sally met yesterday at the park. (that 이하 절에서 목적어가 생략되었음)
(2) **that 이하에 생략된 문장요소가 없으면**, 가주어 구문이다.
It is said that Sally met Tom yesterday at the park. (that 이하 절에서 생략된 문장요소가 없음)

A 다음 주어진 문장의 각 요소를 「It ~ that …」 강조 구문을 이용하여 다시 쓰시오.

Jenny found the beautiful jewelry in the box yesterday.

1 Jenny 강조: ______
2 the beautiful jewelry 강조: ______
3 in the box 강조: ______
4 yesterday 강조: ______

B 우리말과 뜻이 같도록 괄호 안의 말을 바르게 배열하여 문장을 완성하시오.

1 나를 도와준 것은 바로 Jane이었다. (helped, that, me, Jane)
→ It was ______.
2 엄마가 나를 위해 요리한 것은 양파 수프였다. (cooked, me, for, that, my, mom, the onion soup)
→ It was ______.

Point 03 도치 I – 장소 부사(구)의 도치, 부정어의 도치

- **도치 구문**: 「주어 + 동사」의 어순이 「동사 + 주어」의 어순으로 바뀌는 것을 말한다. 주로 부사(구)나 부정어 등을 강조하기 위해 도치 구문을 쓴다.

- **장소 부사(구)의 도치**: 장소나 방향을 나타내는 부사구를 뒤에 오는 주어를 강조하기 위해 문장의 앞에 두면, **「부사(구) + (조)동사 + 주어」**의 어순으로 쓴다.

  The woman walks with her son down the street. 그 여자는 길을 따라 아들과 걷는다.
  → Down the street walks a woman with her son. 길을 따라 그 여자가 아들과 걷는다.

  ※ 단, 주어가 **대명사**인 경우: '주어 + 동사'의 도치가 일어나지 않고 「부사(구) + 주어 + 동사」 어순으로 쓴다.

  Jack comes here. → Here comes Jack. Jack이 여기 온다.
  cf. He comes here. → Here he comes. 그가 여기 온다.

- **부정어(구)의 강조**: 부정어 **never, no, nor, not only, little, few, hardly, rarely, seldom, not until, no sooner** 등이 문장의 맨 앞에 오면 **주어와 동사가 도치된다.**

  (1) be동사나 조동사가 쓰인 문장은 be동사(조동사)와 주어의 어순만 바뀐다.

  I am hardly pleased with anything these days. 나는 요즘 어떤 것에도 거의 기쁘지 않다.
  → Hardly am I pleased with anything these days. (be동사)
  I have never got such a high score. 나는 그렇게 높은 점수를 받은 적이 없다.
  → Never have I got such a high score. (조동사)

  (2) 일반동사가 쓰인 문장은 「do[does, did] + 주어 + 동사원형」의 형태로 쓴다.

  I never thought he would come. 나는 그가 올 거라고 결코 생각하지 않았다.
  → Never did I think he would come.
  cf. not until ~ 조동사 + 주어 + 동사: ~이 되어서야 비로소 ~했다
  Not until yesterday did I hear about the news. 나는 어제가 되어서야 비로소 그 소식을 들었다.

A 괄호 안에서 알맞은 말을 고르시오.

1 Here (they come, come they).
2 Down (came the rain, the rain came).
3 At the station (is, are) two girls standing.
4 On the second floor (a computer lab is, is a computer lab).
5 Little (she thought, did she think) that they would meet again.

B 밑줄 친 부분으로 시작하도록 〈보기〉와 같이 문장을 다시 쓰시오.

> 보기
> A grocery store is <u>around the corner</u>. → Around the corner is a grocery store.

1 Some books are <u>under the bed</u>.
→ ______________________________

2 We <u>rarely</u> eat dinner at home.
→ ______________________________

Point 04 도치 II – 동의할 때: 「So/Nor/Neither + 동사 + 주어」 구문

- 동의할 때 도치 구문을 쓸 수 있다. 즉, **so, neither, nor**가 앞문장의 내용을 받아 문장의 맨 앞에 오는 경우 도치가 일어난다.
- **「so + 동사 + 주어」** 구문: '~도 또한 …이다'라는 뜻으로 긍정문에 대한 동의를 나타낸다.
「so + be동사(do동사/조동사) + 주어」는 「주어 + be동사(do동사/조동사), too」로 바꿔 쓸 수 있다.
이때 앞 문장에 조동사나 be동사가 있으면 그대로, 일반동사이면 do나 does, 또는 did로 쓴다.
They are excited to go to the concert, and so am I. (= I am, too.)
그들은 콘서트에 가게 되어 신이 났고 나도 그렇다.
I liked the movie a lot, and so did Sally. (= Sally did, too.)
나는 영화를 무척 좋아했고 Sally 역시 그랬다.
- **「neither(nor) + be동사/do동사/조동사 + 주어」 구문**: '~도 또한 …가 아니다'의 뜻으로 부정문에 대한 동의를 나타낸다. 「neither(nor) + be동사/do동사/조동사 + 주어」는 「주어 + be동사/do동사/조동사, either.」로 바꿔 쓸 수 있다. 이때 앞 문장에 조동사나 be동사가 있으면 그대로, 일반동사이면 do/does/did로 쓴다.
They didn't enjoy the food in the restaurant, and neither[nor] did I. (=I didn't, either.)
그들은 그 레스토랑의 음식을 좋아하지 않았고, 나 역시 좋아하지 않았다.

A 대화의 흐름이 자연스럽도록 괄호 안에서 알맞은 말을 고르시오.

1 A: I don't want to eat pizza tonight. I am tired of it.
B: (So do I, Neither do I). Let's eat something else.

2 A: Jane is going to learn Chinese from next month.
B: (So am I, So do I). Actually, we are taking the same class.

3 A: I don't like that he always complains about everything.
B: (Neither am I, Neither do I). His complaining is so tiresome.

B 괄호 안의 말과 뜻이 같도록 so나 neither를 활용하여 문장을 완성하시오.

1 Chris doesn't like coffee, and ______________________. (= I don't, either.)

2 My mother is smart and pretty, and ______________________. (= I am, too.)

C 보기와 같이 B가 한 말을 완전한 영어 문장으로 풀어 쓰시오.

> 보기
> A: I don't have an umbrella now.
> B: Neither do I. (→ I don't have an umbrella, either.)

1 A: Tom did not pass the exam this time.
B: Neither did I. (→ ______________________)

2 A: They will go shopping tomorrow.
B: So will I. (→ ______________________)

일등 비법 노트

비법 1 강조의 do는 생략이 가능! 일반동사 do는 생략할 수 없다!

대표기출 1 밑줄 친 부분의 쓰임이 나머지와 다른 하나는?

① You did a great job.
② They did work hard this time.
③ They do love their parents.
④ I did wash the dishes already.
⑤ She does know his phone number.

비법 2 「It ~ that …」 강조 구문에서 강조할 부분을 It is[was]와 that 사이에 넣어라!

대표기출 1 밑줄 친 부분을 강조하여 다시 쓸 때 알맞은 것은?

I dropped my cellphone on the street.

① It is on the street that I dropped my cellphone.
② It was on the street that I dropped my cellphone.
③ It is on the street where I dropped my cellphone.
④ It was on the street when I dropped my cellphone.
⑤ I did drop my cellphone on the street.

대표기출 2 밑줄 친 부분을 강조하기 위해, it으로 시작하여 문장을 다시 쓰시오.

All clothes are 20% off in the department store today.

→ ______________________________
____

비법 3 부정어가 문장 앞으로 나가면, 일반동사의 경우에는 「do/does/did + 주어 + 동사」의 어순으로 쓴다!

대표기출 1 두 문장의 뜻이 통하도록 빈칸에 알맞은 말은?

I never ate such delicious food before.
→ ______________ such delicious food before.

① Never I ate ② Never did I ate
③ Never did I eat ④ Never I did eat
⑤ Never did eat I

대표기출 2 어법상 틀린 부분을 찾아 바르게 고쳐 쓰시오.

Hardly ever he came late for the class.

______________ → ______________

비법 4 so와 neither가 문장 앞에 오면 「(조)동사+주어」의 어순이다!

대표기출 1 밑줄 친 부분과 바꿔 쓸 수 있는 말은?

He didn't bring his umbrella. <u>I didn't bring my umbrella, either.</u>

① Neither didn't I. ② Neither I did.
③ Neither did I. ④ Either I didn't.
⑤ Either did I.

대표기출 2 빈칸에 알맞은 말은?

A: My brother plays the guitar very well.
B: ______________. People say I am like a professional guitarist.

① So I am. ② So am I.
③ Neither do I. ④ So do I.
⑤ Neither am I.

내신 만점! 실전 기출

[1~2] 빈칸에 알맞은 말을 고르시오.

01

A: I didn't finish my homework.
B: Neither ________ I.

① do ② does ③ did
④ have ⑤ had

02

Under the big tree ________ two children.

① stands ② stand ③ standing
④ to stand ⑤ be stood

03 밑줄 친 부분을 강조하여 문장을 다시 쓸 때 빈칸에 알맞은 말은?

We spent our summer vacation in Rome.
→ ________ in Rome ________ we spent our summer vacation.

① It so, that ② It is, that
③ It was, that ④ It does, that
⑤ It did, that

04 밑줄 친 부분 중 어법상 옳지 않은 것은?

Not only(①) came he(②) late(③), but also(④) he forgot(⑤) his bag.

① ② ③ ④ ⑤

05 밑줄 친 부분을 강조하는 문장으로 바꿔 쓸 때, 필요 없는 것을 모두 고르면?

I found his ID card on the floor.

① it ② that ③ did
④ when ⑤ on

06 도치된 다음 문장을 원래대로 바르게 바꾼 것은?

Never did I see such beautiful scenery.

① I see never such beautiful scenery.
② I don't see such beautiful scenery.
③ I never saw such beautiful scenery.
④ I saw never such beautiful scenery.
⑤ Never I did see such beautiful scenery.

07 우리말과 같도록 빈칸에 알맞은 말은?

어제 그에게 무슨 일이 있었는지 나는 Mary에게 결코 말하지 않았다.
→ Never ________ ________ ________ Mary what happened to him yesterday.

① I do tell ② I did tell
③ do I tell ④ did I tell
⑤ did I told

08 서술형

밑줄 친 부분을 강조하여 문장 전체를 다시 쓰시오.

They knew that their vacation was delayed.

→ ________________________________
____

09 서술형

밑줄 친 부분으로 시작하여 문장 전체를 다시 쓰시오.

> A huge tree was at the corner of the street.

→ ______________________________

____

10 밑줄 친 부분의 쓰임이 〈보기〉와 다른 하나는?

> 보기
> He did tell me a lie again.

① She does love her dog.
② We do believe it will come true.
③ He did forget our appointment.
④ Let's do our best on the exam.
⑤ I do trust her in any circumstance.

최다빈출

11 밑줄 친 부분의 쓰임이 나머지 넷과 다른 하나는?

① It was in the park that I saw Julie.
② It was last January that I started swimming.
③ It was amazing that we won the match.
④ It is Tom that I feel grateful to.
⑤ It was a wallet that I got from her.

12 빈칸에 공통으로 알맞은 말은?

> A: I think I don't look slim in this dress.
> B: Don't worry. You __________ look slim.
> A: You always tell me the truth, right?
> B: Yes, I always __________ tell you the truth.

① do　② does　③ did
④ don't　⑤ didn't

13 서술형

〈보기〉를 참고로 하여 주어진 문장을 다시 쓰시오.

> 보기
> She hardly ever shows her feelings to others.
> → Hardly ever does she show her feelings to others.

> He never forgot to call me when he got on the bus.

→ ______________________________

____

14 밑줄 친 부분의 쓰임이 올바른 것은?

① Terry really liked the movie, and so was I.
② My mom cooks well, and so do my sister.
③ I was excited, and so was everyone else.
④ Jimin has a camera, and so has Minho.
⑤ My sister likes Korean food, and so am I.

최다빈출

[14~15] 어법상 틀린 문장을 고르시오.

15

① He did eat everything on the table.
② Across the street is a man with black hair.
③ It was last weekend where I lost my wallet.
④ Never does Jack tell a lie.
⑤ Rarely did Edward smile in front of us.

16

① On every floor is a restroom.
② It was my mom that gave me this ring.
③ Not all of his friends agreed with his idea.
④ Never did he wake up early on weekends.
⑤ I did made a promise to her about that.

[17~18] 우리말과 같도록 빈칸에 알맞은 말을 고르시오.

17

그 문제를 해결해야 할 사람은 바로 너와 나다.
→ ____________ have to solve the problem.

① It is that you and I
② It is you and I
③ It is you and I that
④ It you and I is that
⑤ They are you and I that

18

우리는 건강을 잃고 나서야 비로소 그 중요성을 깨닫는다.
→ Not until we lose our health, ________ ________ its value.

① we realized
② did we realize
③ we realize
④ do we realize
⑤ we do realize

19 밑줄 친 부분을 강조하기 위해 다시 쓸 때, 바르게 고치지 않은 것은?

① Mr. Kim will make a speech.
→ It is Mr. Kim that will make a speech.
② We will go on a picnic tomorrow.
→ It is tomorrow that we will go on a picnic.
③ Terry met Susie on Christmas day.
→ It was Susie that Terry met her on Christmas day.
④ I found this key on the chair in your room.
→ It was on the chair in your room that I found this key.
⑤ She loves to eat apple pie not cookies.
→ It is apple pie not cookies that she loves to eat.

20 서술형

괄호 안의 말을 활용하여 우리말을 영어로 옮기시오.

(1) A: 난 Jack의 의견에 동의할 수 없었어.
B: 나도 그럴 수 없었어.
(2) A: 너 개 먹이를 또 안 줬구나!
B: 아니, 줬어요. 개가 다 먹어버렸을 뿐이에요.

→ (1) A: I couldn't agree with Jack's opinion.
B: ____________
____________ (neither, 3단어)

→ (2) A: You didn't feed the dog again!
B: No! I ____________.
He just ate all the food quickly.
(did, 4 words)

21 서술형

밑줄 친 부분을 강조하는 문장으로 바꿔 쓰시오.

Where did you see Kevin yesterday?

→ ____________
____

22 서술형

다음 문장을 주어진 조건에 맞춰 다시 쓰시오.

Jenny lost her wallet during her trip.

(1) 동사 lost를 강조하는 문장
→ Jenny ____________
____________. (7단어)

(2) during her trip을 강조하는 문장
→ It was ____________
____________. (8단어)

23 밑줄 친 부분을 강조하는 문장으로 바르게 고친 것은?

> Terry learned many English idioms from a lot of English novels.

① It was Terry that learned many English idioms from a lot of English novels.
② It was many English idioms that Terry learned from a lot of English novels.
③ It was a lot of English novels that Terry learned many English idioms.
④ It was from a lot of English novels that Terry learned many English idioms.
⑤ It was many English idioms from a lot of English novels that Terry learned.

24 밑줄 친 문장을 바르게 영작한 것을 모두 고르면?

> They didn't like the new product.
> 나 역시 좋아하지 않았다.

① So didn't I.　　② So did I.
③ Neither didn't I.　　④ Neither did I.
⑤ I didn't, either.

25 서술형

다음 문장에서 강조 부분을 괄호 안의 단어로 바꿔 문장을 다시 쓰시오.

> It was Gloria that I ran into in the elevator in the morning. (in the morning)

→ ______________________________

____

26 문장의 밑줄 친 부분과 바꿔 쓸 수 있는 것을 순서대로 바르게 나열한 것은?

> • It is this restaurant ⓐ that was in the magazine.
> • It was yesterday ⓑ that he gave us this homework.

① which, where　　② where, which
③ when, where　　④ which, when
⑤ when, when

고난도

27 어법상 옳은 것으로 짝지어진 것은?

> ⓐ Here he comes.
> ⓑ It was on New Year's day that I met them last.
> ⓒ Rarely ate our family out.
> ⓓ Next to the school is the library.
> ⓔ At the corner of the street was some children.

① ⓐ, ⓑ, ⓒ　　② ⓐ, ⓑ, ⓓ
③ ⓐ, ⓒ, ⓔ　　④ ⓑ, ⓒ, ⓓ
⑤ ⓑ, ⓒ, ⓔ

28 서술형

우리말과 뜻이 같도록 영작할 때, 어법상 어색한 곳을 찾아 바르게 고쳐 쓰시오.

> 쇼핑몰에 도착해서야 나는 그 곳이 문을 닫았다는 것을 알았다.
> → Not until I got to the shopping mall, I realized it was closed.

______________ → ______________

29 서술형

다음 문장을 밑줄 친 부분으로 시작하는 문장으로 바꿔 쓰시오.

ⓐ Her little brother was next to her.
ⓑ I little dreamed that I would see him again.
ⓒ He fell down.

ⓐ → ____________________

ⓑ → ____________________

ⓒ → ____________________

고난도

30 서술형

밑줄 친 부분 중 어법상 틀린 곳을 찾아 바르게 고쳐 쓰시오.

Last Saturday, I ran into Julie in the park near my house. It was a month ago ① that we last met. She told me that she had been to Paris to see her sister. She ② did talked a lot about how interesting her trip was. Rarely ③ had I seen her being so talkative. On the bench, ④ we chatted for two hours. She had fun talking with me. And, so ⑤ did I.

____________________ → ____________________

실력 탄탄!
서술형 심화

1 밑줄 친 부분이 어법에 맞으면 O표, 틀리면 바르게 고쳐 쓰시오.

(1) He did told me that he likes me.
(2) It was yesterday when I finished the science report.
(3) Never I have seen such a beautiful woman.
(4) I didn't like the movie at all, and so did Jenny.

(1) ________________ (2) ________________
(3) ________________ (4) ________________

2 주어진 조건에 맞춰 대화의 빈칸에 알맞은 말을 영작하시오.

A: I went to the library yesterday, and I saw Mike studying there.
B: What? Who was studying in the library?
A: (1) ________________
B: Really? I thought he would never go to the library to study.
A: I know, right? Who would expect to see Mike there ? I couldn't believe it at first, but (2) ________________

조건

※ (1)에 대한 조건
1. 'It ~ that' 강조 구문을 사용할 것
2. 과거 시제로 쓸 것
3. 9단어로 쓸 것

※ (2)에 대한 조건
1. 뜻: 나는 정말로 그곳에서 그를 보았다.
2. '강조의 do/did'를 사용할 것
3. I로 시작할 것
4. 5단어로 쓸 것

3 Read the chart, and complete the sentence.

Number of students who can speak each language	English	Chinese	French
Class A (Total: 27)	20	7	0
Class B (Total: 27)	15	10	2

(1) A: Which language is it that no student in *Class A* can speak?
B: ________ ________ ________ ________ no student in *Class A* can speak.

(2) A: How many students in *Class B* can speak Chinese?
B: ________ ________ ________ ________ ________ can speak French in *Class B*.

MEMO

부록

A. 불규칙동사 변화표

B. 자주 쓰이는 동명사 표현

C. by 이외의 전치사를 사용하는 수동태 표현

D. 자주 쓰이는 상관접속사 표현

A. 불규칙동사 변화표

원형	과거형	과거분사형	뜻
arise	arose	arisen	생겨나다
awake	awoke	awoken	깨어나다
bear	bore	born	참다, 낳다
become	became	become	~가 되다
begin	began	begun	시작하다
behold	beheld	beheld	주시하다
bend	bent	bent	구부리다
bite	bit	bitten	물다
blow	blew	blown	폭파하다
break	broke	broken	깨다
bring	brought	brought	가져오다
build	built	built	짓다
burn	burnt	burnt	태우다
buy	bought	bought	사다
catch	caught	caught	잡다
choose	chose	chosen	고르다
cost	cost	cost	(값이) ~들다
cut	cut	cut	자르다
deal	dealt	dealt	다루다
dig	dug	dug	파다
draw	drew	drawn	그리다, 당기다
drink	drank	drunk	마시다
drive	drove	driven	운전하다
fall	fell	fallen	떨어지다
feed	fed	fed	먹이다

원형	과거형	과거분사형	뜻
feel	felt	felt	느끼다
fight	fought	fought	싸우다
find	found	found	발견하다
flee	fled	fled	도망치다
fly	flew	flown	날다
forbid	forbade	forbidden	금지하다
forget	forgot	forgotten	잊다
forgive	forgave	forgiven	용서하다
found	founded	founded	설립하다
freeze	froze	frozen	얼리다
get	got	gotten/got	얻다
give	gave	given	주다
grow	grew	grown	자라다
hang	hung	hung	매달다
have	had	had	가지다, 먹다
hear	heard	heard	듣다
hide	hid	hidden	숨기다
hit	hit	hit	치다
hold	held	held	잡다, 개최하다
hurt	hurt	hurt	부상 입히다
keep	kept	kept	유지하다
know	knew	known	알다
lay	laid	laid	놓다
lead	led	led	이끌다
lean	leaned/leant	leaned/leant	기울다

원형	과거형	과거분사형	뜻
leave	left	left	떠나다
lend	lent	lent	빌려주다
let	let	let	놓다
lie	lied	lied	거짓말하다
lie	lay	lain	눕다
light	lit	lit	밝히다
lose	lost	lost	잃다
make	made	made	만들다
mean	meant	meant	의미하다
meet	met	met	만나다
mistake	mistook	mistaken	실수하다
outrun	outran	outrun	앞지르다
overcome	overcame	overcome	극복하다
pay	paid	paid	지불하다
prove	proved	proved/proven	증명하다
put	put	put	놓다
raise	raised	raised	~를 올리다
read	read	read	읽다
ride	rode	ridden	타다
ring	rang	rung	종을 울리다
rise	rose	risen	오르다
run	ran	run	뛰다
say	said	said	말하다
see	saw	seen	보다
sell	sold	sold	팔다

원형	과거형	과거분사형	뜻
send	sent	sent	보내다
set	set	set	정하다
shake	shook	shaken	흔들다
shut	shut	shut	닫다
sing	sang	sung	노래하다
sit	sat	sat	앉다
sleep	slept	slept	자다
slide	slid	slid	미끄러지다
spend	spent	spent	소비하다
spill	spilt	spilt	엎지르다
split	split	split	쪼개다
spoil	spoilt	spoilt	망치다
spread	spread	spread	퍼지다
stand	stood	stood	서다
steal	stole	stolen	훔치다
swear	swore	sworn	맹세하다
sweep	swept	swept	싹 쓸다
take	took	taken	가지고 가다
teach	taught	taught	가르치다
tear	tore	torn	찢다
tell	told	told	말하다
think	thought	thought	생각하다
wake	woke	woken	깨우다
wear	wore	worn	입다
write	wrote	written	쓰다

B. 자주 쓰이는 동명사 표현

look forward to -ing	~할 것을 고대하다	go -ing	~하러 가다
How[What] about -ing?	~하는 게 어때?	spend *A* (on) -ing	~하는 데 A를 쓰다
be used to -ing	~하는 데에 익숙하다	be busy -ing	~하느라 바쁘다
can't help -ing	~하지 않을 수 없다	have trouble -ing	~하는데 어려움을 겪다
keep[stop] *A* from -ing	*A*를 ~못하게 하다	feel like -ing	~하고 싶다
there is no -ing	~은 불가능하다	on -ing	~하자마자
It is no use -ing	~해도 소용없다	be worth -ing	~할 가치가 있다

C. by 이외의 전치사를 사용하는 수동태 표현

be ashamed of	~을 부끄러워하다	be known for	~로 유명하다
be based on	~에 근거를 두다	be known to	~에게 알려지다
be bored with	~에 지겨워지다	be made from	~로 만들어지다 (재료의 성질 변화)
be covered with	~으로 덮여 있다	be made of	~로 만들어지다 (재료의 모양 변화)
be composed of	~으로 구성되다	be pleased with	~에 기쁘다
be crowded with	~으로 혼잡하다	be satisfied with	~에 만족하다
be disappointed with	~하지 않을 수 없다	be shocked at	~에 충격을 받다
be filled with	~으로 가득 차다	be surprised by(at)	~에 놀라다
be interested in	~에 관심이 있다	be tired of	~에 싫증나다
be known as	~로서 알려지다	be worried about	~에 대해 걱정하다

D. 자주 쓰이는 상관접속사 표현

상관접속사 종류	의미	주어로 올 때 동사의 수 일치
both *A* and *B*	*A*와 *B* 둘 다	동사의 복수형을 취함
not *A* but *B*	*A*가 아닌 *B*	동사의 수는 *B*에 일치 (= 동사에 가까운 대상에 수 일치!)
either *A* or *B*	*A*나 *B* 둘 중 하나	
neither *A* nor *B*	*A*도 *B*도 아닌	
not only *A* but also *B*	*A*뿐만 아니라 *B*도	
B as well as *A*		

앞서가는 학생들의 일등 비법 봉인 해제!

비법 담은 중학

영문법

3 Level

Workbook

Point 01 현재 *vs.* 과거

A 괄호 안에서 알맞은 말을 고르시오.

1 Bowing to the elderly people on New Year's Day (is, was) a Korean tradition.

2 My family (lives, lived) in the countryside long time ago.

3 Buyeo (is, was) a place where we can learn about the history and culture of Baekje.

4 My mom (calls, called) my dad every day during her lunch break.

5 William Shakespeare (writes, wrote) many masterpieces in the 1590s.

6 The Earth (turns, turned) round the sun every 365 days.

7 Mark always (goes, went) hiking on weekends.

B 밑줄 친 부분이 어법에 맞으면 O표, 틀리면 바르게 고쳐 쓰시오.

1 Trees dropped their leaves before winter comes. → ________

2 Kenny usually rode his bike to school these days. → ________

3 The guide shows tourists around the Secret Garden of Changdeok Palace as a job. → ________

4 Judy comes back to London the day before yesterday. → ________

5 New York had the Statue of Liberty. → ________

6 My family traveled to Jeju Island last summer. → ________

7 Air pressure became lower when you go up. → ________

C 우리말과 뜻이 같도록 괄호 안의 말을 활용하여 문장을 완성하시오.

1 우리는 어제 한 농부의 집에서 잠을 잤다. (sleep)

→ We ________ at a local farmer's house last night.

2 할로윈데이는 10월 31일이다. (fall)

→ Halloween Day ________ on October 31st in the solar calendar.

3 제비들은 겨울에 남쪽으로 이동한다. (migrate)

→ Swallows ________ south in winter.

4 미국은 한 때 영국의 식민지였다. (be)

→ America once ________ a colony of England.

5 John은 여자아이들에게 말할 때는 매우 긴장한다. (get)

→ John ________ nervous when he talks to girls.

6 정직이 최선의 방책이다. (be)

→ Honesty ________ the best policy.

A 다음을 현재완료 문장으로 바꿀 때 괄호 안의 말을 빈칸에 알맞은 형태로 바꿔 쓰시오.

1 He went to school in the morning. He is back home now.
→ He ________ ________ back home from school. (come)

2 Janet lost her bike. She still doesn't have it.
→ Janet ________ ________ her bike. (lose)

3 Jisu went to Jeju Island last week. It was the second time for her.
→ Jisu ________ ________ ________ Jeju Island two times. (be)

4 Sumi borrowed my camera yesterday. She still has it.
→ Sumi ________ ________ my camera. (borrow)

5 Anna went to Europe. She is still there.
→ Anna ________ ________ ________ Europe. (go)

B 빈칸에 알맞은 말을 〈보기〉에서 골라 알맞은 시제로 고쳐 쓰시오. (단, 한 번씩만 사용할 것)

보기				
become	hear	read	sign	swim

1 Jinsu ________ up for the science camp yesterday.

2 This vase ________ recently ________ a National Treasure, so a lot of people want to see it.

3 I ________ already ________ the book.

4 Tim ________ never ________ in the sea before.

5 ________ you ever ________ about the flea market?

C 괄호 안의 동사를 활용하여 대화를 완성하시오. (단, 현재완료형 활용)

1 A: ________ you ever ________ (design) your own T-shirt?
B: No, I haven't. But I want to try some day.

2 A: Have you ever heard of the young boy who climbed Mt. Everest?
B: Yes I have. He is now 14 years old, and he ________ ________ (climb) mountains since he was 12.

3 A: You're supposed to return the books you checked out from the library.
B: Yeah, I know. I ________ ________ (not, forget) it.

4 A: I haven't tried *Kimchi* yet.
B: Really? I ________ ________ (love) it ever since I ________ (try) it two years ago.

Point 05~06 현재완료, 과거, 과거완료

A 괄호 안에서 알맞은 말을 고르시오.

1 Last week, the price was two times higher than he (paid, had paid) a week earlier.

2 I (got, has got) a text message from my classmate a few minutes ago.

3 Jack is visiting his grandma in the hospital. She (was, has been) sick for more than a week.

4 Mina (hasn't, hadn't) left for the camping trip yet. She's still packing.

5 By the time mom came back, my brother (has, had) watched TV for three hours.

6 There was little grass left because the deer (ate, had eaten) it all.

7 He (went, has gone) to the mainland to find a job last year.

B 밑줄 친 부분이 어법에 맞으면 O표, 틀리면 바르게 고쳐 쓰시오.

1 Did you ever find money on the street? → ____________

2 Sally has bought a pair of new shoes yesterday. → ____________

3 He had been a big fan of the band since he was an elementary school student. → ____________

4 When she became president, she worked for the company for 20 years. → ____________

5 Cindy plays flute for three years. → ____________

6 Mike broke his mom's favorite flower vase a few days ago. → ____________

7 Dana have read 'The Old Man and the Sea.' → ____________

C 우리말과 뜻이 같도록 괄호 안의 말을 활용하여 문장을 완성하시오.

1 그녀는 뉴욕에서 3년 간 무용을 배워 왔다. (learn)

→ She ____________ dance for three years in New York.

2 그는 아직 이번 주말에 무엇을 할지 결정하지 못했다. (decide)

→ He ____________ yet what to do this weekend.

3 그들은 어린 시절부터 친구였다. (be)

→ They ____________ friends since they were young.

4 나는 그 때 이전에 그를 만난 적이 없다. (never, meet)

→ I ____________ him before then.

5 그녀는 성경책을 5번 읽었다. (read)

→ She ____________ the Bible five times.

Point 07~08 현재진행, 과거진행, 미래진행, 완료진행

A **괄호 안에서 알맞은 말을 고르시오.**

1 Mr. Lee (is, has been) teaching science in middle school since last March.

2 The bus for Pohang (is, was) leaving in **10** minutes.

3 Father (is, was) reading a newspaper when the phone rang.

4 I (am, will be) cooking dinner when you come back.

5 She (has, had) been raising money for the poor until she went away on a volunteer trip.

6 What (have you been, are you) doing to protect the environment so far?

7 Mom doesn't like my habit of listening to music while I (studied, am studying).

B **밑줄 친 부분이 어법에 맞으면 O표, 틀리면 바르게 고쳐 쓰시오.**

1 I am thinking about riding my bike this weekend. → ____________

2 He is playing tennis when I saw him. → ____________

3 Jane has been recycling paper ever since she entered middle school. → ____________

4 I am thinking that health is more important than wealth. → ____________

5 She was having a hamburger at that time. → ____________

6 I am studying at school at this time tomorrow. → ____________

7 He was washing his father's car when the boy took the bike. → ____________

C **우리말과 뜻이 같도록 괄호 안의 말을 활용하여 문장을 완성하시오.**

1 우리가 파티에 도착했을 때, 많은 사람들이 재미있는 시간을 갖고 있었다. (have)

→ When we arrived at the party, many people ____________ fun.

2 내가 도서관에 갔을 때 그녀는 이미 거기서 세 시간째 공부하고 있었다. (been, study)

→ When I went to the library, she ____________ there for three hours.

3 그는 그 회사에서 20대 이후로 계속 일해 왔다. (been, work)

→ He ____________ for the company since his 20s.

4 나는 지금 음악을 듣고 있는 중이다. (listen)

→ I ____________ to music now.

5 Jake는 1시간 째 그의 자전거를 고치려고 애쓰고 있는 중이다. (been, try)

→ Jake ____________ to fix his bike for an hour.

Point 01~03 can, may, will

A

〈보기〉에서 빈칸에 알맞은 말을 골라 쓰시오. (단, 한번씩만 사용)

보기

can could can't couldn't be able to

1 I am afraid that I ______________ come to your party tonight.

2 ______________ you speak more quietly?

3 The class was too boring. I ______________ help falling asleep.

4 He is so strong that he ______________ carry the box alone.

5 If you read this, you will ______________ to understand it.

B

밑줄 친 조동사의 의미를 〈보기〉에서 찾아 그 기호를 쓰시오.

보기

ⓐ 가능 (~할 수 있다) ⓑ 허락 (~해도 된다) ⓒ 미래 (~일/할 것이다)
ⓓ 추측 (~일 지도 모른다) ⓔ 부정적 추측 (~일 리가 없다)

1 You may go home after you submit your assignment. → ______________

2 Do you think it will snow on Christmas? → ______________

3 What she told us cannot be true. → ______________

4 Jane may apologize to you first. → ______________

5 Chris can solve any math problems. → ______________

C

우리말과 뜻이 같도록 괄호 안의 말을 바르게 배열하여 문장을 완성하시오..

1 우리는 이번 여름에 유럽에 갈 것이다. (will, we, go, Europe, to)

→ ______________________________ this summer.

2 그는 1년 안에 중국어를 잘 할 수 있을 것이다. (be able to, will, he, speak, Chinese, well)

→ ______________________________ in a year.

3 이 문제 해결하는 것을 도와주겠어요? (you, could, help, solve, me)

→ ______________________________ this problem?

must, have to, should, ought to

A

괄호 안에서 알맞은 말을 고르시오.

1 He (has to, had to) think many times before he made that decision.

2 You (will must, will have to) switch trains at the next station.

3 He (must, has to) be tired after such a long journey.

4 The doctor suggested she (should, might) take vitamin pills.

5 We (ought, ought to) help the poor.

B

밑줄 친 조동사의 의미를 〈보기〉에서 찾아 그 기호를 쓰시오. (단, 중복 사용 가능)

보기		
ⓐ 가능 (~할 수 있다)	ⓑ 허락 (~해도 된다)	ⓒ 미래 (~일/할 것이다)
ⓓ 강한 추측 (~임이 틀림 없다)	ⓔ 의무 (~해야만 한다)	ⓕ 금지 (~해서는 안 된다)

1 It was my fault. I <u>must</u> apologize to him. → ____________

2 We <u>must not</u> violate the school rules. → ____________

3 He <u>should</u> be more polite to others. → ____________

4 The teacher suggested that we <u>should</u> memorize those words. → ____________

5 John <u>must</u> be disappointed to hear the news. → ____________

C

두 문장의 뜻이 통하도록 주어진 철자로 시작하는 표현을 넣어 문장을 완성하시오.

1 You should follow your teacher's directions.

→ You o____________ ____________ follow your teacher's directions.

2 He has to eat well to be healthy.

→ He m____________ eat well to be healthy.

3 You don't have to start the work today.

→ You n____________ ____________ start the work today.

4 You ought not to make fun of his accent.

→ You s____________ ____________ make fun of his accent.

Point 06~07 had better, would rather, used to, would

A 괄호 안에서 알맞은 말을 고르시오.

1 You had better (tell, to tell) me the truth.

2 I would rather (sleep, sleeping) than watch TV.

3 You (had better not, had not better) be late for class.

4 I (would rather not, would not rather) answer his question.

5 I used to (live, living) in London.

B 우리말과 뜻이 같도록 밑줄 친 부분을 어법에 맞게 고쳐 쓰시오.

1 우리 엄마는 매일 쿠키를 만들어 주곤 했다.
My mom used to <u>making</u> cookies every day. → ______________

2 나는 어릴 때 매일 일기를 쓰곤 했다.
I <u>was used</u> to keep a diary every day. → ______________

3 그는 집에서 혼자 시간을 보내는 데 익숙하다.
He is used <u>to spend</u> time at home alone. → ______________

4 그들은 방과 후 매일 만나곤 했다.
They would <u>to meet</u> every day after school. → ______________

C 다음 두 문장을 〈보기〉와 같이 한 문장으로 다시 만드시오.

보기
My mom made cookies every day. But she doesn't do it any more.
→ My mom used to make cookies every day.

1 I wrote in my diary every day. But I don't do it any more.
→ ______________________________

2 There was a restaurant in the building. But there isn't anymore.
→ ______________________________

3 My father smoked before. But he doesn't smoke anymore.
→ ______________________________

Point 08 조동사 + have + p.p.

A 괄호 안에서 알맞은 말을 고르시오.

1 I didn't pass the exam. I (might, should) have studied harder.

2 I can't find him. He (must, should) have left already.

3 He looks so pale. He (may, cannot) be sick.

4 She is an honest woman. She (may, cannot) have lied to us.

B 두 문장의 뜻이 같도록 〈보기〉에서 알맞은 표현을 골라 문장을 완성하시오. (단, 한 번씩만 쓰시오.)

보기

must have　　should have　　may have　　cannot have

1 I am sure that he broke his promise again.

→ He ______________________ his promise again.

2 She regrets that she didn't follow her teacher's advice.

→ She ______________________ her teacher's advice.

3 It is possible that he took a wrong train.

→ He ______________________ a wrong train.

4 It is impossible that he won the game.

→ He ______________________ the game.

C 우리말과 뜻이 같도록 괄호 안의 말을 바르게 배열하여 문장을 완성하시오.

1 우리는 전에 만난 적이 있음이 틀림 없다. (we, must, met, have, before)

→ ______________________

2 그녀는 서울을 이미 떠났을 지도 모른다. (she, have, left, may, Seoul, already)

→ ______________________

3 우리는 그 애를 도와줬어야만 했어. (should, we, have, helped, him)

→ ______________________

4 그녀가 그 약속을 잊었을 리가 없다. (she, have, forgotten, cannot, her, promise)

→ ______________________

Point 01~04 to부정사의 명사적 용법, 형용사적 용법

A 괄호 안에서 알맞은 말을 고르시오.

1 My dream is (be, to be) a robot scientist.

2 They planned (have, to have) a surprise party.

3 It is safer (to wear, wear) a seatbelt all the time.

4 I taught him (how to answer, to answer how) the question.

5 He found (it, that) difficult to book a concert ticket.

6 Children (are listen to, are to listen to) their parents well.

B 밑줄 친 부분을 어법에 맞게 고쳐 쓰시오.

1 It's midnight. It is time <u>go</u> to bed. → ____________

2 He needs some paper <u>to write</u>. → ____________

3 She wants <u>warm something</u> to wear. → ____________

4 Tina wants <u>eating</u> a hamburger. → ____________

5 They don't know <u>when have to</u> a party. → ____________

C 우리말과 뜻이 같도록 괄호 안의 말을 활용하여 문장을 완성하시오.

1 은행에 가는 방법을 알아냈니? (find, the way)

→ Did you ____________________ get to the bank?

2 도서관에는 읽을 책들이 많이 있다. (books, read, a lot of)

→ There are ____________________ in the library.

3 내가 쓸 펜 하나 빌려줄 수 있니? (a pen, write)

→ Can you lend me ____________________.

4 친구들과 축구를 하는 것은 흥미롭다. (soccer, play)

→ It is fun ____________________ with friends.

5 나는 휴일 동안 어디로 가야 할지 몰랐다. (go, where)

→ I didn't know ____________________ during the holidays.

Point 05~06 to부정사의 부사적 용법

A 밑줄 친 to부정사의 쓰임을 〈보기〉에서 골라 그 기호를 쓰시오.

보기
ⓐ 목적 ⓑ 감정의 원인 ⓒ 결과 ⓓ 판단의 근거

1 I am excited to see the movie. → ______
2 Grace was careless to do such a thing. → ______
3 I made a lot of effort to be a winner. → ______
4 He tried his best in the game only to lose. → ______
5 The visitors went to the information center to ask for directions. → ______

B 두 문장의 뜻이 같도록 괄호 안의 말을 사용하여 문장을 완성하시오.

1 She read a lot of books to build her knowledge. (so as to)
→ She read a lot of books ______________________.
2 He went to the dental clinic to see a doctor. (in order to)
→ He went to the dental clinic ______________________.
3 I went to a pharmacy to get my prescription. (in order to)
→ I went to a pharmacy ______________________.
4 Becky went to a bank to save some money. (so as to)
→ Becky went to a bank ______________________.
5 David always writes down his schedule not to forget it. (in order not to)
→ David writes down his schedule ______________________.

C 우리말과 뜻이 같도록 괄호 안의 말을 바르게 배열하여 문장을 완성하시오.

1 그 나무는 1000년을 살았다. (be, lived, years, 1000, to, old)
→ The tree ______________________.
2 Tom은 몇 권의 책을 빌리기 위해 도서관에 갔다. (some, to, books, borrow)
→ Tom went to the library ______________________.
3 그녀는 늦잠을 자지 않기 위해 자명종을 맞춰놨다. (not, to, in, order, late, get up)
→ She set an alarm clock ______________________.
4 그 작은 소년은 커서 대통령이 되었다. (to, grew up, the president, be)
→ The little boy ______________________.

Point 07~09 to부정사의 의미상의 주어, 부정, 시제, to부정사를 목적어, 목적격 보어로 쓰는 동사

A 괄호 안에서 알맞은 말을 고르시오.

1 It is kind (of, for) her to help sick people.

2 It is important (of, for) us to stay healthy.

3 Tim advised me (join, to join) the club with him.

4 I want you (make, to make) your room neat and clean.

5 It is very difficult (of, for) me to solve math problems.

B 두 문장의 뜻이 같도록 괄호 안의 말을 사용하여 문장을 완성하시오.

1 It seems that it is very serious. (seems to)

→ It ______________ very serious.

2 She seems to have lost 10kg last year. (seems that)

→ It ______________ 10kg last year.

3 He seems to be disappointed with his test score. (seems that)

→ It ______________ with his test score.

4 You seem to have missed the train this morning. (seems that)

→ It ______________ this morning.

5 It seems that this picture has been taken by a photographer. (seems to)

→ This picture ______________ by a photographer.

C 우리말과 뜻이 같도록 괄호 안의 말을 바르게 배열하여 문장을 완성하시오.

1 나는 주말에 일하지 않기를 소망한다. (wish, to, not, work)

→ I ______________ on the weekend.

2 그녀는 기말고사에서 좋은 점수 받기를 희망한다. (scores, hopes, to, good, get)

→ She ______________ on her final exams.

3 그는 영국에 가기를 희망한다. (to, would, go, like)

→ He ______________ to England.

4 예습과 복습은 필요하다. (for, necessary, to, you)

→ It is ______________ preview and review.

5 선생님께서는 학생들에게 책을 많이 읽으라고 충고했다. (read, the students, to, advised)

→ My teacher ______________ a lot of books.

Point 10~12 원형부정사를 목적격보어로 쓰는 동사, 자주 쓰이는 to부정사 구문

A 괄호 안에서 알맞은 말을 고르시오.

1 He sings well enough (being, to be) a professional singer.

2 I saw her (take, to take) pictures in the garden.

3 She had him (push, to push) the cart in the supermarket.

4 She watched the news (getting, to get) correct information about the government.

5 My parents let me (to go, go) to a movie after school.

B 두 문장의 뜻이 같도록 「so ~ that 주어 + can[can't]」 구문을 활용하여 문장을 완성하시오.

1 I was too tired to get up early.
→ I was ________ ________ ________ ________ ________ get up early.

2 The girl is too small to reach the bell.
→ The girl is ________ ________ ________ ________ ________ reach the bell.

3 The candy is small enough to put it in my mouth.
→ The candy is ________ ________ ________ ________ ________ put it in my mouth.

4 They are too young to drive.
→ They are ________ ________ ________ ________ ________ drive.

5 My dad is tall enough to reach the ceiling.
→ My dad is ________ ________ ________ ________ ________ reach the ceiling.

C 우리말과 뜻이 같도록 괄호 안의 말을 활용하여 문장을 완성하시오.

1 나는 언니가 바이올린 켜는 소리를 들었다. (hear, play)
→ I ________ ________ ________ ________ the violin.

2 그녀는 내가 그녀의 노트북을 쓸 수 있게 해주었다. (let)
→ She ________ ________ ________ her laptop computer.

3 그 소년은 그의 엄마가 쿠키 만드시는 것을 보았다. (watch)
→ The boy ________ ________ ________ ________ cookies.

4 그 의사는 환자가 약을 잘 먹도록 했다. (make, take medicine)
→ The doctor ________ ________ ________ ________ ________ well.

5 그는 그가 원하는 모든 것을 살 수 있을 정도로 부자이다. (enough to)
→ He is ________ ________ ________ ________ everything that he wants.

Point 01~02 동명사의 역할 – 주어, 보어, 목적어

A 밑줄 친 부분의 역할을 〈보기〉에서 골라 그 기호를 쓰시오.

보기
ⓐ 주어 ⓑ 보어 ⓒ 동사의 목적어 ⓓ 전치사의 목적어

1 Mark realized his dream by doing one small step at a time. → ______
2 Eating regularly will keep you healthy. → ______
3 We really enjoyed making delicious cookies with your mom. → ______
4 Kate is good at taking care of children. → ______
5 Susan's goal for this year is winning the taekwondo competition. → ______
6 Communicating through text messages is a part of modern culture. → ______
7 I practiced fixing the engine. → ______

B 괄호 안에서 알맞은 말을 고르시오.

1 She doesn't like (go, going) shopping.
2 Minji gave up (to enter, entering) the English speech contest.
3 (Eat, Eating) instant food too often is not healthy.
4 Taeho's hobby is (collect, collecting) coins from around the world.
5 She is afraid of (to lose, losing) the game.
6 Their plan is (visit, to visit) the famous museum in the city.
7 Reading fifty books (is, are) my goal for next year.

C 우리말과 뜻이 같도록 괄호 안의 말을 바르게 배열하여 문장을 완성하시오.

1 그 아기는 우는 것을 멈췄다. (crying, stopped)
→ The baby ______________________.

2 꿈을 이루기 위해서는 계속 열심히 공부해라. (hard, studying, keep)
→ To make your dreams come true, ______________________.

3 문 좀 열어 주시겠어요? (the door, opening, mind)
→ Would you ______________________ for me?

4 그녀는 그를 만나는 것을 피하려고 노력했다. (meeting, tried, avoid, to)
→ She ______________________ him.

5 빠른 음악을 트는 것은 사람들이 더 빠르게 먹고 더 빨리 떠나도록 합니다. (makes, fast music, playing)
→ ______________________ people eat faster and leave sooner.

6 칼로리가 높은 음식을 먹는 것은 살을 빼는 것에 도움이 되지 않아. (with, eating, high calories, food)
→ ______________________ doesn't help you lose weight.

A 괄호 안의 인칭대명사를 빈칸에 알맞은 형태로 쓰시오.

1 I don't mind ______________ sharing my table. (you)

2 We all really enjoyed ______________ singing and dancing. (she)

3 He was angry at ______________ coming late to school. (he)

4 Linda was afraid of ______________ making mistakes. (I)

5 They were all interested in ______________ building a robot dog. (Mike)

B 두 문장의 뜻이 같도록 빈칸에 알맞은 말을 쓰시오.

1 He was proud that he won first place.
→ He is proud of ___________ first place.

2 I am sorry that I didn't do my best at school.
→ I am sorry for ___________ ___________ ___________ my best at school.

3 Mom was worried that I wouldn't finish the competition.
→ Mom was worried about ___________ ___________ ___________ the competition.

4 She felt sorry that I was disappointed with the result.
→ She felt sorry for ___________ ___________ ___________ with the result.

5 All of us were surprised that he didn't come to school.
→ All of us were surprised at ___________ ___________ ___________ to school.

C 밑줄 친 부분이 어법에 맞으면 O표, 틀리면 바르게 고쳐 쓰시오.

1 Many people still enjoy <u>to swim</u> in this river. → ______________

2 He became famous for <u>use</u> vivid colors in his paintings. → ______________

3 He is considering <u>not to go</u> to the party. → ______________

4 He is afraid <u>of falling</u> out of the tree. → ______________

D 우리말과 뜻이 같도록 괄호 안의 말을 활용하여 완료형 동명사 구문으로 문장을 완성하시오.

1 그녀는 비웃음을 당한 것을 부끄러워하고 있다. (laugh)
→ She is ashamed of ___________ ___________ ___________ at.

2 그들은 트로피가 주어진 것을 매우 자랑스러워 했다. (give)
→ They were very proud of ___________ ___________ ___________ a trophy.

3 그는 그녀가 회의에 참석하지 않은 것에 대해 유감스러웠다. (attend)
→ He was sorry for ___________ ___________ ___________ ___________ the meeting.

Point 05~07 동명사 *vs.* to부정사 *vs.* 현재분사

A 괄호 안에서 알맞은 말을 고르시오.

1 He finally succeeded in (climb, climbing) to the top of the mountain.

2 Mina is used to (looking, look) after her pet dog.

3 We decided (eating, to eat) out tonight.

4 Bill promised not (being, to be) late again.

5 Mike is good at (doing, to do) crossword puzzles.

6 All of the audience enjoyed the band's (playing, to play).

7 Father plans (stopping, to stop) smoking next year.

B 밑줄 친 부분의 쓰임이 〈보기〉의 ⓐ와 ⓑ 중 어느 것과 같은지 그 기호를 쓰시오.

보기
ⓐ A rolling stone gathers no moss.
ⓑ People learn by doing.

1 Listening to music helps me relax. → ______

2 His plan for this summer is learning French cooking. → ______

3 The chef is putting butter into the pan. → ______

4 Would you tell me where the fitting room is? → ______

5 It's stupid to wake up a sleeping lion. → ______

6 The swimming pool was crowded with people. → ______

C 우리말과 뜻이 같도록 괄호 안의 말을 바르게 배열하여 문장을 완성하시오.

1 그녀는 그것을 할 수 있을 때까지 계속 연습했다. (practicing, kept)
→ She ______ until she could do it.

2 나의 아버지께서는 집에 오는 길에 나를 위한 책을 사오는 것을 기억하셨다. (buy, remembered, to)
→ My father ______ a book for me.

3 나는 나의 쓰기 실력을 향상시키기 위해 영어로 일기 쓰는 것을 생각 중이다. (keeping, of, thinking)
→ I am ______ a diary in English to improve my writing skills.

4 그 소년은 스스로 신발 끈을 묶으려고 노력하고 있었다. (tie, to, trying)
→ The boy was ______ his shoe laces for himself.

5 그는 어젯밤 공부를 더 열심히 하지 않은 것을 후회한다. (having, regrets, studied, not)
→ He ______ harder last night.

자주 쓰이는 동명사 표현

A 괄호 안에서 알맞은 말을 고르시오.

1 Janet is looking forward to (see, seeing) you soon.

2 There was no use (to try, trying) to block the flooding water.

3 She goes (to hike, hiking) on Saturdays.

4 He spent all his money (to buy, buying) a new bike.

5 Did you have trouble (to find, finding) my house?

6 He feels like (to have, having) spaghetti tonight.

7 They were busy (to do, doing) their team project.

B 밑줄 친 부분이 어법에 맞으면 O표, 틀리면 바르게 고쳐 쓰시오.

1 John is used to take care of his little brother. → ______

2 What about telling him the truth? → ______

3 The players couldn't help to stop the game because of heavy rain. → ______

4 You should not keep him to wait. → ______

5 Mom is busy to prepare dinner for our family. → ______

6 On arriving at Seoul, he called his friend to pick him up. → ______

7 This book is worth to read. → ______

C 우리말과 뜻이 같도록 괄호 안의 말을 활용하여 문장을 완성하시오.

1 너희 어머니께서는 네가 밤에 낚시 가는 것을 허락하셨니? (go)
→ Did your mom allow you to ______ ______ at night?

2 Peter는 다음 번 경기에 출전하는 것을 고대하고 있다. (play)
→ Peter is ______ ______ ______ ______ in the next game.

3 컴퓨터 게임 하는 데에 시간을 쓰지 않도록 해라. (play)
→ Try not to ______ ______ ______ computer games.

4 Amy는 아침에 일찍 일어나는 것에 익숙하다. (get)
→ Amy is ______ ______ ______ up early in the morning.

5 동물에 관한 다큐멘터리를 보는 게 어때? (watch)
→ How ______ ______ a documentary on animals?

6 궂은 날씨도 그가 꼭대기까지 오르는 것을 막지 못했다. (climb)
→ Bad weather couldn't ______ ______ ______ ______ to the top.

Point 01~03 분사의 종류 및 의미와 역할, 감정을 나타내는 분사

A 괄호 안에서 알맞은 말을 고르시오.

1 Next, you have to put the vegetables into (boiling, boiled) water.

2 Goods (producing, produced) in Korea are excellent.

3 I heard someone (shouting, shouted) outside.

4 Be careful not to wake up the (sleeping, slept) dog.

5 I got an e-mail (writing, written) in English.

B 밑줄 친 부분이 어법에 맞으면 O표, 틀리면 바르게 고쳐 쓰시오.

1 I think he has an amaze talent. → ____________

2 I met some people interesting in travelling. → ____________

3 He looked satisfied with the result he got. → ____________

4 The movie was more excited than I expected. → ____________

5 We were fascinated by his travel stories. → ____________

C 우리말과 뜻이 같도록 밑줄 친 부분을 어법에 맞게 고쳐 쓰시오.

1 눈으로 덮인 저 산을 보아라.
Look at the mountain cover with snow. → ____________

2 그들 모두는 그 이야기에 깊이 감동 받았다.
All of them were deeply moving by the story. → ____________

3 나는 블루베리로 채워진 요구르트를 좋아한다.
I like yogurt fill with blueberries. → ____________

4 나는 J.K. Rowling에 의해 쓰여진 소설을 읽고 있다.
I am reading a novel write by J.K. Rowling. → ____________

5 저기 서 있는 사람이 내 담임 선생님이다.
The guy stand over there is my homeroom teacher. → ____________

Point 04~05 분사구문을 만드는 법, 분사구문의 의미

A 두 문장의 뜻이 같도록 〈보기〉에서 알맞은 접속사를 골라 문장을 완성하시오.

보기		
because	if	while

1 Waiting for my friend, I saw my English teacher.

→ ______________________, I saw my English teacher.

2 Living far from their home, we can't visit our grandparents often.

→ ______________________, we can't visit our grandparents often.

3 Exercising every day, I will get stronger.

→ ______________________, I will get stronger.

B 두 문장의 뜻이 같도록 분사구문을 활용하여 문장을 다시 쓸 때, 빈칸에 알맞은 말을 쓰시오.

1 Because she got up late, she had to take a taxi.

→ ______________________, she had to take a taxi.

2 While we took a walk in the park, we chatted about this and that.

→ ______________________, we chatted about this and that.

3 When the kid saw the big bear, he couldn't move at all.

→ ______________________, he couldn't move at all.

4 If you join our club, you will have a lot of fun.

→ ______________________, you will have a lot of fun.

C 괄호 안의 말을 활용하여 다음 문장 전체를 다시 쓰시오.

1 Telling me his plan, he went to school. (after)

→ ______________________________

2 Feeling tired, I went to bed early. (as)

→ ______________________________

3 Hearing the news, we were all surprised. (when)

→ ______________________________

4 Wanting to sleep, he turned off the lights. (because)

→ ______________________________

Point 06~07 분사구문의 시제와 태, 분사구문의 부정, 독립분사구문

A 괄호 안에서 알맞은 말을 고르시오.

1 (Spent, Having spent) all my money, I can't buy the jeans now.

2 (Being, Having been) born and raised in the countryside, she knows a lot about plants.

3 (Not having, Having not) enough time, we had to hurry up.

4 (It, There) being a lot of visitors, the place was very crowded.

5 The road (is, being) so slippery, you should drive carefully.

B 우리말과 뜻이 같도록 밑줄 친 부분을 어법에 맞게 고쳐 쓰시오.

1 많은 비가 왔기 때문에 그 행사는 연기 되었다.

It rained heavily, the event was postponed. → ____________

2 전에 부상을 당했기 때문에 그는 스키를 타는 것이 두려웠다.

Being injured before, he was afraid of skiing. → ____________

3 Leonardo da Vinci에 의해 그려졌기 때문에 그 그림은 매우 귀중하다.

Having painted by Leonardo da Vinci, the painting is priceless. → ____________

4 잠을 충분히 자지 못했기 때문에 그녀는 지금 매우 피곤하다.

Not slept enough, she is very tired now. → ____________

C 두 문장의 뜻이 같도록 부사절을 분사구문으로 바꿔 쓰시오.

1 As she was given some money by her mom, she could buy the concert ticket.

→ ____________________, she could buy the concert ticket.

2 After he had finished his breakfast, Peter got dressed and went out.

→ ____________________, Peter got dressed and went out.

3 Because there is a lot of work to do, I can't go out for dinner tonight.

→ ____________________, I can't go out for dinner tonight.

4 As he was the first customer of the day, he got a free movie ticket.

→ ____________________, he got a free movie ticket.

Point 8 「with + 명사 + 분사」 구문, 비인칭 독립분사구문

A 우리말과 뜻이 같도록 괄호 안의 단어를 알맞은 형태로 빈칸에 쓰시오.

1 그는 눈을 감은 채 음악을 듣고 있었다. (close)

→ He was listening to music with his eyes ____________.

2 나는 그가 지켜보고 있어서 집중할 수 없었다. (watch)

→ I couldn't focus on with him ____________ me.

3 그녀는 선풍기를 켜둔 채로 방을 나갔다. (turn)

→ She left the room with the fan ____________ on.

4 그들은 팔짱을 낀 채로 벤치에 앉아 있었다. (fold)

→ They sat on the bench with their arms ____________.

B 주어진 문장을 〈보기〉와 같이 바꿔 쓸 때 빈칸에 알맞은 말을 쓰시오.

> 보기
> The man is walking and his dog is running beside him.
> → The man is walking with his dog running beside him.

1 The man got on the bus while he was waving his hand.

→ The man got on the bus ________________________.

2 Sally was sitting on the chair, and her legs were crossed.

→ Sally was sitting on the chair ________________________.

3 Tim was standing, and his back was leaning against the wall.

→ Tim was standing ________________________.

C 우리말과 뜻이 같도록 〈보기〉에서 알맞은 말을 골라 문장을 완성하시오.

> 보기
> compared with　　speaking of　　judging from　　generally speaking

1 일반적으로 말하자면, 지하철을 타는 것이 버스를 타는 것보다 빠르다.

→ ________________________, taking the subway is faster than taking the bus.

2 그녀와 비교한다면, 나는 그리 성실하지 않다.

→ ________________________ her, I am not that diligent.

3 Harry에 대해 말하자면, 그는 믿을만한 사람이다.

→ ________________________ Harry, he is a reliable person.

4 그의 외모로 판단하건대, 그는 인도인일 것이다.

→ ________________________ his appearance, he might be Indian.

Point 01~03 수동태의 의미와 형태, 조동사 수동태, 구동사 수동태

A 괄호 안에서 알맞은 말을 고르시오.

1 A famous architect (designed, was designed) our house.

2 A new idea (suggested, was suggested) by Tom at the meeting.

3 They (were planning, were planned) their trip to Europe.

4 The new magazine will (publish, be published) in March.

5 All the files (disappeared, were disappeared) from my laptop.

B 다음 문장을 수동태로 바꿀 때, 빈칸에 알맞은 말을 쓰시오.

1 Even some birds can eat them.

→ They ________ ________ ________ even by some birds.

2 The famous singer will perform a live concert.

→ A live concert ________ ________ ________ by the famous singer.

3 He delayed the meeting again.

→ The meeting ________ ________ by him again.

C 우리말과 뜻이 같도록 괄호 안의 말을 활용하여 문장을 완성하시오.

1 그 숙제의 마감일은 잊혀져서는 안 된다. (must, forget)

→ The deadline of the assignment ________ ________ ________ ________.

2 다른 사람들의 아이디어가 도용될 수 없다. (can't, copy)

→ Other people's ideas ________ ________ ________.

3 그는 그의 할머니에 의해 길러졌다. (bring up)

→ He ________ ________ ________ by his grandmother.

4 아이들은 그 선생님들에 의해 돌보아진다. (take care of)

→ The kids ________ ________ ________ ________ by the teachers.

Point 04~05 진행형, 완료형의 수동태

A 괄호 안에서 알맞은 말을 고르시오.

1 They were (selling, being sold) used items on the street.

2 The table is (cleaning, being cleaned) by David.

3 The car is (repairing, being repaired) in the garage.

4 The event is (preparing, being prepared) by Mr. Jones.

B 우리말과 뜻이 같도록 괄호 안의 말을 활용하여 문장을 완성하시오.

1 그 프로그램이 아직 방송되는 중이다. (air)

→ The program ______________ still ______________ ______________ now.

2 자연은 인간에 의해 파괴되고 있다. (destroy)

→ Nature ______________ ______________ ______________ by humans.

C 두 문장의 뜻이 같도록 빈칸에 알맞은 말을 쓰시오.

1 My parents have helped me to make good decisions.

→ I ______________ ______________ ______________ to make good decisions by my parents.

2 We have postponed the meeting a few times.

→ The meeting ______________ ______________ ______________ a few times by us.

3 The group of artists have made many interesting works.

→ Many interesting works ______________ ______________ ______________ by the group of artists.

D 주어진 문장을 수동태 문장으로 바꿔 쓰시오.

1 They have created many new ideas.

→ ____

2 The team has developed the robots for Mars exploration.

→ ____

3 The boys were laughing at his unusual accent.

→ ____

Point 06~08 4형식 문장, 5형식 문장의 수동태

A 우리말과 뜻이 같도록 괄호 안의 말을 활용하여 문장을 완성하시오.

1 그녀는 그들에 의해 좋은 사람으로 생각된다. (think, nice)

→ She is ____________ ____________ ____________ ____________ by them.

2 그는 엄마로부터 집에 있으라는 이야기를 들었다. (tell, stay home)

→ He was ____________ ____________ ____________ ____________ by his mom.

3 나는 매일 삼십 분씩 조깅하라는 조언을 들었다. (advise, jog)

→ I was ____________ ____________ ____________ thirty minutes a day.

4 그녀는 엄마에 의해 청소기를 돌리도록 시켜졌다. (make, vacuum)

→ She was ____________ ____________ ____________ the floor by her mom.

B 밑줄 친 부분을 어법에 맞게 고쳐 쓰시오.

1 Great gifts were <u>given for us</u> by them.

→ ____

2 The shirt was <u>bought to me</u> by Jack.

→ ____

3 Some questions were <u>asked for me</u> by the interviewer.

→ ____

4 He was <u>made learning</u> swimming.

→ ____

C 다음을 주어진 단어로 시작하는 수동태 문장으로 바꿔 쓰시오.

1 He showed me something in the box.

→ I ____.

2 Our parents let us sleep at Jenny's house.

→ We ____.

3 We saw them plant trees in the garden.

→ They ____.

4 My grandmother will cook me something nice.

→ Something nice ____.

5 My brother bought me a nice camera.

→ A nice camera ____.

Point 09~10 목적어로 쓰인 that절의 수동태, by 이외의 전치사를 쓰는 수동태

A 빈칸에 알맞은 말을 보기에서 골라 쓰시오. (단, 한 번씩만 쓰시오.)

보기

to　　of　　with　　about　　in

1 The bag is made ______________ leather.

2 The book is known ______________ many people around the world.

3 The team was pleased ______________ the result of the game.

4 I am worried ______________ his health.

5 Many people are interested ______________ travel.

B 우리말과 뜻이 같도록 괄호 안의 말을 활용하여 문장을 완성하시오.

1 나는 새로운 휴대폰에 만족한다. (satisfy)

→ I ____________ ____________ ____________ the new cellphone.

2 그 행사장은 많은 쇼핑객들로 붐빈다. (crowd)

→ The event hall ____________ ____________ ____________ a lot of shoppers.

3 흡연은 병을 일으킨다고들 말한다. (say, cause)

→ Smoking ____________ ____________ ____________ ____________ disease.

C 다음을 주어진 단어로 시작하는 수동태 문장으로 바꿔 쓰시오.

1 People believe that Mr. Kim is diligent.

→ It ____.

→ Mr. Kim. ____.

2 People say that eating breakfast is good for brain activity.

→ It ____.

→ Eating breakfast ____.

3 People say that the Internet has made our lives better than before.

→ It ____.

→ The Internet ____.

Point 01~02 재귀대명사, it의 여러 가지 쓰임

A 재귀대명사의 알맞은 용법을 괄호 안에서 고르시오.

1 Growing plants itself is very useful. (재귀 용법, 강조 용법)

2 He made the report himself. (재귀 용법, 강조 용법)

3 It is important to know ourselves. (재귀 용법, 강조 용법)

B 다음 밑줄 친 it의 용법을 보기에서 골라 그 기호를 쓰시오.

보기

ⓐ 지시대명사 ⓑ 비인칭주어 it ⓒ 가주어 it ⓓ 가목적어 it

1 It was a well-made movie. → ____________

2 I thought it dangerous travelling overseas alone. → ____________

3 It is hot and humid in summer. → ____________

4 It is important to finish this on time. → ____________

C 우리말과 뜻이 같도록 빈칸에 알맞은 말을 쓰시오.

1 그는 혼자 그 곳에 가기로 결정했다.

→ He decided to go there __________ __________.

2 그들은 스스로 그 수학 문제를 해결했다.

→ They solved the math problems __________ __________.

3 나는 때때로 혼잣말을 한다.

→ I sometimes talk to __________.

D 우리말과 뜻이 같도록 괄호 안의 말을 바르게 배열하여 문장을 완성하시오.

1 그 수업을 듣는 것은 꼭 필요하다. (necessary, it, to, take, the, is, class)

→ ____.

2 그녀는 소설을 읽는 것이 흥미롭다는 것을 알았다. (found, she, interesting, to, read, novels, it)

→ ____.

3 Hannah가 반에서 가장 똑똑한 것으로 보인다. (seems, it, Hannah, is, that, the, student, smartest)

→ ____ in the class.

A 우리말과 뜻이 같도록 빈칸에 알맞은 대명사를 써서 문장을 완성하시오.

1 그녀는 항상 다른 사람들에게 친절하다.

→ She is always nice to ______________.

2 또 다른 것을 제게 보여주시겠어요?

→ Would you show me ______________ one?

3 나는 가방을 잃어버렸다. 그래서 새 것을 사야 한다.

→ I lost my bag, so I need to buy a new ______________.

B 빈칸에 알맞은 말을 <보기>에서 골라 쓰시오. (단, 중복 사용 가능)

보기					
one	some	another	the other	the others	others

1 I learned two foreign languages this year. ______________ is Chinese, and ______________ is Japanese.

2 ______________ like pizza, but ______________ don't.

3 Three people are in the classroom. ______________ is reading a book, ______________ is taking a nap, and ______________ is sweeping the floor.

4 I have three shirts. ______________ is black, and ______________ are white.

5 I have two close friends. ______________ is Sangho, and ______________ is Yuna.

6 There are two different opinions among people in our club. ______________ want to go to a museum, and ______________ want to go to a gallery.

C 밑줄 친 문장에서 어법상 <u>어색한</u> 부분을 찾아 쓰고 바르게 고쳐 쓰시오.

1 She has two hobbies. <u>One is painting, and other is knitting.</u>

______________ → ______________

2 Three men came into the restaurant. <u>One ordered pizza, and others ordered burgers.</u>

______________ → ______________

3 In our school, <u>some like English, and other like mathematics.</u>

______________ → ______________

Point 05 something *vs.* anything

A 빈칸에 알맞은 말을 〈보기〉에서 골라 쓰시오. (단, 중복 사용 가능)

보기			
something	someone	anything	anyone

1 Wasn't there ______________ on the table?

2 Can ______________ tell me the answer?

3 I know ______________ who works at Success Company.

4 I didn't get ______________ from my sister.

5 I have ______________ to do now.

6 ______________ I don't know gave me this letter.

B 밑줄 친 부분을 어법에 맞게 고쳐 쓰시오.

1 Anybody helped me to find the way. → ______________

2 There isn't something serious about that matter. → ______________

3 Let me give you anything to eat. → ______________

4 Did someone call me when I was away? → ______________

C 우리말과 뜻이 같도록 빈칸에 알맞은 말을 쓰시오.

1 차가운 마실 것 좀 드릴까요?

→ Would you like ______________ cold to drink?

2 그는 생일에 아무 것도 받지 못했다.

→ He didn't get ______________ on his birthday.

3 물어볼 게 있다면 어떤 것이든 제게 메일을 보내주세요.

→ If you have ______________ to ask, please send me an e-mail.

4 누군가 교실 의자를 망가뜨렸다.

→ ______________ broke the chair in the classroom.

Point 06 전체부정 vs. 부분부정

A **우리말과 뜻이 같도록 빈칸에 알맞은 말을 쓰시오.**

1 아무도 그녀를 도와주려고 하지 않았다.

→ ______________ tried to help her.

2 나는 그 비밀에 대해 네게 아무것도 말하지 않을 것이다.

→ I will tell you ______________ about that secret.

3 모든 과일이 달콤한 것은 아니다. (단, every 사용)

→ ______________ ______________ fruit is sweet.

B **두 문장의 뜻이 같도록 빈칸에 알맞은 말을 쓰시오.**

1 There is nothing special we plan to do tonight.

→ There isn't ______________ special we plan to do tonight.

2 She has nothing to worry about.

→ She ______________ have ______________ to worry about.

3 He told no one why he quit his job.

→ He didn't tell ______________ why he quit his job.

4 She felt that she had no one to rely on.

→ She felt that she didn't have ______________ to rely on.

C **두 문장의 뜻이 같도록 〈보기〉와 같이 괄호 안의 말을 활용하여 빈칸에 알맞은 말을 쓰시오.**

> 보기
>
> Some students like Mr. Kim, but others don't.
>
> → Not every student likes Mr. Kim. (every)

1 Some of my friends are tall, but others aren't.

→ ______________________________ of my friends are tall. (all)

2 My dad is alive, but my mom isn't.

→ ______________________________ are alive. (both)

3 Watching movies is fun sometimes, but sometimes it's not.

→ Watching movies is ______________________________ fun. (always)

Point 01 원급 기본 표현

A 괄호 안에서 알맞은 말을 고르시오.

1 My car is as (big, bigger) as yours.

2 His test score is as (highest, high) as her score.

3 The final was as difficult (as, than) the midterm.

4 This one is not (so, more) delicious as that one.

5 My school is (not so far as, so not far as) the bank.

B 우리말과 뜻이 같도록 밑줄 친 부분을 어법에 맞게 고쳐 쓰시오.

1 Ben은 Cindy만큼 친구들에게 친절하지 않다

Ben is as not kind as Cindy to their friends. → __________

2 Adam은 Tommy만큼 영어 말하기를 유창하게 한다.

Adam speaks English as more fluently Tommy does. → __________

3 그 소년은 그 소녀만큼 행동이 바르지 않다.

The boy does not behave as better as the girl. → __________

C 우리말과 뜻이 같도록 괄호 안의 말을 활용하여 빈칸에 알맞은 말을 쓰시오.

1 그 상담사는 엄마만큼 친절하다. (nice)

→ The counselor is __________ my mom.

2 이 신발은 내가 생각했던 것만큼 편하다. (comfortable)

→ These shoes are __________ I thought they would be.

3 나는 하와이안 피자가 포테이토 피자 만큼 맛있지 않다고 생각한다. (delicious)

→ I think Hawaiian pizza is __________ potato pizza.

4 나는 작년만큼 PC방에 자주 가지 않는다. (often)

→ I don't go to a PC room __________ I did last year.

5 Bora는 원어민만큼 영어로 유창하게 말한다. (fluently)

→ Bora speaks English __________ a native speaker.

A 괄호 안에서 알맞은 말을 고르시오.

1 I like peanuts (more, the most) than almonds.

2 It is raining (harder even, even harder) than it was this morning.

3 This bed is (more comfortable, most comfortable) than that one.

4 My grandfather is (the older, the oldest) person in my family.

5 The Statue of Liberty is one of (the most popular, the more popular) statues.

B 밑줄 친 부분을 어법에 맞게 바르게 고쳐 쓰시오.

1 She finished the project very earlier than he did. → ____________

2 Playing baseball is more exciting to playing soccer. → ____________

3 *Friday the 13th* was the scariest movie that I've ever saw. → ____________

4 The Speech Contest was much most difficult than I thought it would be. → ____________

5 The teacher's voice is getting loud and loud as the students make more noise. → ____________

C 우리말과 뜻이 같도록 괄호 안의 단어를 활용하여 빈칸에 알맞은 말을 쓰시오.

1 이번 겨울은 작년 보다 더 추울 것이다. (cold)

→ This winter will be ____________ ____________ last winter.

2 8월은 일 년 중 가장 덥다. (hot)

→ August is ____________ ____________ month of the year.

3 Steve Jobs는 세계에서 가장 훌륭한 CEO들 중의 한 명이었다. (good)

→ Steve Jobs was ____________ ____________ ____________ ____________ ____________ in the world.

4 블루베리 케이크는 내가 먹어본 케이크들 중 가장 맛있다. (delicious)

→ This blueberry cake is ____________ ____________ ____________ ____________ I've ever eaten.

5 과학 과제는 내가 이제껏 한 과제들 중에서 가장 어려웠다. (hard)

→ The science assignment was ____________ ____________ ____________ I've ever done.

Point 04~05 여러 가지 비교 구문 I~II

A 우리말과 뜻이 같도록 밑줄 친 부분을 어법에 맞게 고쳐 쓰시오.

1 I feel more tired and more tired these days. (나는 요즘 점점 더 피곤함을 느낀다.)

→ ________________________________

2 Eric bought as much toy cars as possible. (Eric은 그가 살 수 있는 한 많은 장난감을 샀다.)

→ ________________________________

3 The girl plays the piano good and better. (그 소녀는 피아노를 점점 더 잘 친다.)

→ ________________________________

4 He ate as as he could much in the buffet restaurant.
(그는 뷔페 식당에서 그가 먹을 수 있는 한 많이 먹었다.)

→ ________________________________

5 The high you climb up the tree, the dizzy you feel.
(나무에 점점 더 높이 올라갈수록 너는 더 어지러움을 느낄 것이다.)

→ ________________________________

B 두 문장의 뜻이 같도록 as를 사용하여 비교급 문장을 완성하시오.

1 The fatter you get, the weaker you might get.

→ ________ you get ________, you might get ________.

2 I try to exercise as often as possible.

→ I try to exercise ________________.

3 An apple is five times cheaper than a watermelon.

→ An apple is ________________ a watermelon.

4 The goal keeper blocked the ball as hard as he could.

→ The goal keeper blocked the ball ________________ possible.

C 우리말과 뜻이 같도록 괄호 안의 말을 바르게 배열하여 문장을 완성하시오.

1 경제가 점점 더 나빠지고 있다. (worse, getting, and, worse)

→ The economy is ________________ globally.

2 선생님의 목소리는 학생들보다 두 배 더 크다. (as, twice, as, loud)

→ The teacher's voice is ________________ the students' voice.

3 그녀와 이야기를 나누면 나눌수록 나는 그녀를 더욱 존경하게 된다. (more, the, I, talk, with, her)

→ ________________, the more I respect her.

Point 06 여러 가지 비교 구문 III

A 주어진 문장과 의미가 같도록 빈칸에 알맞은 말을 쓰시오.

1 English is the most interesting subject.

→ ________ subject is as[so] ________ ________ English.

→ ________ subject is ________ interesting ________ English.

→ ________ is more interesting than ________ ________ subject.

→ English is more interesting than ________ ________ ________ ________.

2 Peter is the smartest student in my school.

→ No (other) student in my school is ________ ________ ________ Peter.

→ No (other) student in my school is ________ ________ Peter.

→ Peter is smarter than ________ ________ student in my school.

→ Peter is ________ ________ all the other students in my school.

B 우리말과 뜻이 같도록 괄호 안의 말을 바르게 배열하여 문장을 완성하시오.

1 나의 강아지만큼 예쁜 애완동물은 없다. (than, cuter)

→ No(other) pet is ________ ________ my dog.

2 수성은 태양계에서 모든 행성들 보다 더 작다. (other, than, the, all, smaller, planets)

→ Mercury is ________ ________ ________ ________ ________ ________ in the solar system.

3 우리 반에서 어떤 누구도 Robin만큼 키가 크지 않다. (Robin, taller, student, no, than)

→ ________ ________ in my class is ________ ________ ________.

4 독수리는 어떤 새보다도 높이 난다. (any, higher, than, other)

→ An eagle flies ________ ________ ________ ________ bird.

5 나는 미네랄 생수만큼 우유를 많이 마신다. (as, as, much)

→ I drink milk ________ ________ ________ mineral water.

6 어떤 과일도 내겐 사과만큼 맛있지 않다. (so, as, an, apple, delicious,)

→ To me, no other fruit is ________ ________ ________ ________ ________.

7 파란색 배낭은 다른 모든 배낭들보다도 더 저렴하다. (the, cheaper, all, than, other)

→ The blue backpack is ________ ________ ________ ________ ________ backpacks.

Point 01 부사절을 이끄는 접속사 – 시간, 이유

A 괄호 안에서 알맞은 말을 고르시오.

1 I have to be there (before, since) the meeting starts.

2 (Before, As) he had lost his bag, he went to the Lost and Found center.

3 (Since, Until) the traffic is terrible, you'd better take the subway.

4 The girl fell asleep (while, since) her mom was reading her a story.

5 (While, When) the boy came home, his younger sister was playing the piano.

B 밑줄 친 부분에 유의하여 다음 문장을 우리말로 해석하시오.

1 As it is foggy, I can't see anything.

→ ______________________________

2 I met my old friend accidentally as I was crossing the street.

→ ______________________________

3 You must brush your teeth within **3** minutes after you have meals.

→ ______________________________

4 Vicky listened to music while I was cleaning my room.

→ ______________________________

C 우리말과 뜻이 같도록 괄호 안의 말을 바르게 배열하여 문장을 완성하시오.

1 나의 가장 친한 친구를 만난 지 5년이 되었다. (since, met, I, my, friend, best)

→ It has been 5 years ______________________.

2 그녀는 말을 시작하면 어두워질 때까지 절대 멈추지 않는다. (until, gets, it, dark)

→ Once she starts talking, she never stops ______________________.

3 그는 그의 여동생을 돌봐야 해서 야구경기에 갈 수 없었다. (care, because, had, he, take, to ,of)

→ He couldn't go to the baseball game ______________________ his sister.

4 누군가 벨을 눌렀을 때 Wendy는 집에 없었다. (the doorbell, when, someone, rang)

→ ______________________, Wendy was not at home.

A 빈칸에 알맞은 말을 <보기>에서 찾아 쓰시오. (단, 중복 사용 가능)

보기			
if	unless	though	while

1 ______________ he meets her tomorrow, he will ask her out.

2 He had a nightmare ______________ he was sleeping last night.

3 ______________ you are really broke, you'd better donate some money.

4 She bought a new jacket ______________ she already has several in the closet.

5 Tony wants to be a pilot, ______________ his parents want him to be a doctor.

B 두 문장의 뜻이 같도록 빈칸에 알맞은 말을 쓰시오.

1 Unless it's too heavy, she can lift it by herself.

→ If it's ____________ ____________ ____________, she can lift it by herself.

2 He is so busy that he can't have meals regularly.

→ He is too ____________ ____________ ____________ ____________ regularly.

3 The athlete practiced hard so that he could win a gold medal.

→ The athlete practiced hard ____________ ____________ to win a gold medal.

4 The room was so dark that I couldn't see anything.

→ The room was ____________ ____________ to see anything.

5 I bought a cell phone so that I can talk to my friends.

→ I bought a cell phone ____________ ____________ to talk to my friends.

C 우리말과 뜻이 같도록 괄호 안의 말을 바르게 배열하여 문장을 완성하시오.

1 그 수프는 너무 뜨거워서 먹을 수가 없다. (so, eat, hot, I, that, can't, it)

→ The soup is ____.

2 시험이 쉬웠음에도 불구하고, 나는 몇몇 실수를 했다. (was, though, the test, easy)

→ Even ____, I made a few mistakes.

3 그녀는 교통표지판을 보았음에도 불구하고 속도위반을 했다. (she, although, the traffic signs, saw)

→ ____, she exceeded the speed limit.

Point 04~05 명사절을 이끄는 접속사, 간접의문문

A 괄호 안에서 알맞은 말을 고르시오.

1 (That, If) my best friend is friendly is true.

2 I doubt (that, whether) I can go skiing this winter or not.

3 It is important (that, if) you should eat a lot of vegetables.

4 The problem is (that, whether) I forgot to bring my wallet.

5 The main idea of the speech is (that, whether) people have to have big dreams.

B 주어진 두 문장을 〈보기〉와 같이 간접의문문이 포함된 한 문장으로 만드시오.

보기

I don't know. Where are you going?

→ I don't know where you are going.

1 I wonder. Can I go there?

→ ______________________________

2 Do you know? What is your dream?

→ ______________________________

3 Tell me. Why didn't you follow the rules?

→ ______________________________

4 I'm not sure. Do you want to go with me?

→ ______________________________

5 Do you think? Who will be your new homeroom teacher?

→ ______________________________

C 우리말과 뜻이 같도록 괄호 안의 말을 바르게 배열하여 문장을 완성하시오.

1 당신이 서비스에 만족하시는지 말씀해주세요. (If, with, are, you, satisfied)

→ Please let us know ______________________ our service.

2 사실은 그녀가 매일 아침 조식을 거른다는 것이다. (breakfast, she, that, skips)

→ The fact is ______________________ every morning.

3 너는 누가 그 대회 우승자가 될 거라고 생각하니? (who, you, do, think)

→ ______________________ will be the contest winner?

Point 06~08 상관접속사, 「명령문, and/or …」구문, 접속부사

A 괄호 안에서 알맞은 말을 고르시오.

1 (Both, Neither) Minhee and I like to go hiking.

2 Don't tell a lie, (and, or) people won't trust you.

3 The question is complicated (and, but) not difficult.

4 (Either, Not only) Eric or Helen wants to live in Jejudo.

5 The cell phone is mine. (In addition, However), you may use it for a while.

B 두 문장의 뜻이 같도록 주어진 문장을 if로 시작하는 문장으로 다시 쓰시오.

1 Buy a toy robot, and your nephew will be very happy.

→ ________________________________, your nephew will be very happy.

2 Drive slowly, or you will get a ticket.

→ ________________________________, you will get a ticket.

3 Make a daily schedule, and you can be more productive.

→ ________________________________, you can spend the time productively.

C 우리말과 뜻이 같도록 괄호 안의 말을 바르게 배열하여 문장을 완성하시오.

1 웃어라, 그러면 복이 올 것이다. (blessings, and, will, your way, come)

→ Smile, ________________________________.

2 나의 엄마와 나는 둘 다 피자를 먹고 싶어 한다. (and, my mom, both, I)

→ ________________________________ want to eat pizza.

3 따뜻한 계열의 색상은 마음을 안정시켜줄 뿐만 아니라 기분도 좋게 만든다.

(not, relaxed, only, but, better, also)

→ Warm colors make you feel ________________________________.

4 그는 3개 국어, 예를 들면 중국어, 일어, 그리고 영어를 잘 한다.

(Chinese, for example, Japanese, and, English)

→ He is good at 3 languages ________________________________.

5 Fred의 취미는 피아노를 치는 것뿐만 아니라 가구를 만드는 것이다.

(not, playing, only, the , but, piano, building, also, furniture)

→ Fred's hobby is ________________________________.

Point 01~03 관계대명사

A 괄호 안에서 알맞은 말을 고르시오.

1 This is the bag (who, which) I bought in this shop last Friday.

2 He ordered (what, that) he wanted to have for lunch.

3 (What, That) she said to us yesterday turned out to be true.

4 The boy (whom, that) made an amazing invention was an elementary-school dropout.

5 Do you know the girl (who, which) is picking up the garbage in the school yard?

B 밑줄 친 부분이 어법에 맞으면 O표, 틀리면 바르게 고쳐 쓰시오. (단, that은 쓰지 말 것)

1 People tend to believe which they see. → ____________

2 This book is about a journey whose a boy and his dog had. → ____________

3 The big house which roof is blue is the house for the president of Korea. → ____________

4 I am reading a newspaper article which are about friendship. → ____________

C 우리말과 뜻이 같도록 괄호 안의 말을 활용하여 문장을 완성하시오.

1 그녀의 그림에는 사람들을 감동시키는 무언가가 있다. (move)

→ Her paintings have something ________ ________ people.

2 사람들은 그들이 힘들 때 곁에 있어 주는 사람을 고마워한다. (stand)

→ People appreciate those ________ ________ by their side when they have a hard time.

3 너는 인터넷에서 너의 숙제에 도움이 되는 많은 정보를 찾을 수 있다. (help)

→ You can find a lot of information ________ ________ you do your homework on the Internet.

4 네가 말하는 것이 다른 사람들의 마음을 상하게 할 수도 있다. (say)

→ ________ ________ ________ to others might hurt their feelings.

5 벽에 걸려있는 그 사진들은 작년에 찍었다. (on, are, the wall)

→ The pictures ________ ________ ________ ________ ________ were taken last year.

A 다음 문장에서 생략할 수 있는 부분을 찾아 밑줄 치시오. (단, 없으면 X표시 하시오.)

1 A true friend doesn't always tell you things that you want to hear. → ____________

2. The girl who is cheering for our team is my friend Lisa. → ____________

3 The book which is written in old Korean is my teacher's. → ____________

4 I remember the day when I first met you. → ____________

5 Su-mi volunteered to guide foreign tourists who come to visit Seoul. → ____________

B 주어진 두 문장을 관계대명사를 이용하여 한 문장으로 만들 때, 빈칸에 알맞은 말을 쓰시오.

1 Do you know the boy? She is talking to him.

→ Do you know the boy ________ she is talking to?

→ Do you know the boy ________ ________ she is talking?

2 This is the picture of King Sejong, and he invented *Hangeul*.

→ This is the picture of King Sejong, ________ invented *Hangeul*.

C 밑줄 친 부분이 어법에 맞으면 O표, 틀리면 바르게 고쳐 쓰시오.

1 This is the skirt <u>for that</u> you were looking. → ____________

2 He is my friend who <u>encourage</u> and helps me when it's necessary. → ____________

3 Mom and I went shopping at a mall <u>in which</u> you can find various stores. → ____________

4 The teacher answered all the questions <u>I was wondering about</u>. → ____________

5 Science explains many things <u>what</u> happen in everyday life. → ____________

D 우리말과 뜻이 같도록 괄호 안의 말을 바르게 배열하여 문장을 완성하시오.

1 인생에서 너는 때때로 네가 원하지 않는 나쁜 일을 경험하게 된다. (to, don't, want, you)

→ You will experience bad things ____________________.

2 나는 전세계의 불쌍한 아이들을 돕는 UNICEF를 위해 일하고 싶다. (children, UNICEF, helps, poor, which)

→ I want to work for ____________________ around the world.

3 나에게는 내가 돌보아야 하는 어린 여동생이 있다. (should, of, I, take, whom)

→ I have a little sister ____________________ care.

4 벽에 걸려 있는 저 그림은 John에게서 받은 선물이다. (wall, on, hanging, was, the)

→ The picture ____________________ a present from John.

Point 07~08 관계부사

A 괄호 안에서 알맞은 말을 고르시오.

1 This is the tree house (which, where) Huck lived.

2 Tomorrow is the day (when, how) our school is going to hold a festival.

3 They didn't figure out the reason (how, why) their plan went wrong.

4 I will tell you the time (where, when) you stop pouring the water.

B 밑줄 친 부분이 어법에 맞으면 O표, 틀리면 바르게 고쳐 쓰시오.

1 He told me the way how he improved his English so quickly. → ______

2 The classroom where children studied was very small. → ______

3 I went to Seoul Station, which I took a train for Pusan. → ______

4 Do you remember the day which we first met? → ______

C 다음 두 문장을 관계대명사를 이용하여 한 문장으로 만들 때, 빈칸에 알맞은 말을 쓰시오.

1 Do you know the reason? She doesn't talk to me for the reason.

→ Do you know the reason ______ ______ she doesn't talk to me?

→ Do you know the reason ______ she doesn't talk to me?

2 Please tell me the way. You made a carrot cake in the way.

→ Please tell me the way ______ you made a carrot cake.

→ Please tell me ______ you made a carrot cake.

D 우리말과 뜻이 같도록 괄호 안의 말을 바르게 배열하여 문장을 완성하시오.

1 그는 유명한 작가가 될 수 있는 방법을 물었다. (become, he, the, could, way)

→ He asked ______ a famous writer.

2 너는 도서관이 문을 닫는 시간을 알고 있니? (library, when, the, closes)

→ Do you know ______?

3 그것이 그가 놀란 이유였다. (surprised, he, the, why, got, reason)

→ That's ______.

Point 09~10 복합관계사

A 괄호 안에서 알맞은 말을 고르시오.

1 You can buy (whoever, whatever) you want at a cheap price in the store.

2 (Whatever, Wherever) you go, don't forget that you are Korean.

3 (Whatever, However) hard it may be, I will never give up.

4 (Whenever, Whichever) I see her, she is always listening to music through earphones.

5 I will give you (however, whichever) you choose from these toys.

B 밑줄 친 부분에 유의하여 두 문장의 뜻이 같도록 빈칸에 알맞은 한 단어를 쓰시오.

1 Anyone who can speak English fluently will be hired.

→ ____________ can speak English well will be hired.

2 No matter what you make, you should finish it by tomorrow.

→ ____________ you make, you should finish it by tomorrow.

3 Anything that my mom makes is delicious.

→ ____________ my mom makes is delicious.

4 You will like it no matter which gift you choose.

→ You will like it, ____________ gift you choose.

C 우리말과 뜻이 같도록 괄호 안의 말을 바르게 배열하여 문장을 완성하시오.

1 질문이 있다면 언제든지 손을 들어라. (you, have, whenever, questions)

→ Raise your hands ______________________________.

2 네가 세계의 어디에 가든지 영어는 큰 도움이 될 것이다. (you, wherever, go)

→ English will be a great help ______________________________ around the world.

3 그가 만지는 것은 무엇이든지 금으로 변했다. (he, touched, whatever)

→ ______________________________ turned into gold.

4 그가 아무리 힘이 세도, 그 바위를 움직일 수는 없었다. (he, strong, was, however)

→ ______________________________, he couldn't move the rock.

5 역사에 관심 있는 사람은 누구나 이 책을 좋아할 것이다. (in, whoever, interested, is)

→ ______________________________ history will like this book.

Point 01 가정법 과거

A

〈보기〉에서 적절한 단어를 골라 빈칸에 알맞은 형태로 쓰시오. (단, 한 번씩만 사용 가능)

보기

try　　be　　live　　visit　　like　　have

1 If she ________ in Busan, she would call me.

2 If he ________ the food, he would finish it.

3 If he ________ harder, he could get better scores.

4 If I ________ a teacher, I would not give any homework.

5 If we ________ a senior center, we could do volunteer work there.

6 If they ________ time, they could play soccer in the playground.

B

〈보기〉와 같이 두 문장의 뜻이 통하도록 빈칸에 알맞은 말을 쓰시오.

보기

As he doesn't meet Helen, he can't apologize to her.

→ If he met Helen, he would apologize to her.

1 As I am not tall, I can't reach the book.

→ If I ________ tall, I ________ the book.

2 As she doesn't call me, I can't take a message.

→ If she ________ me, I ________ a message.

3 As he doesn't know the place, he can't come alone.

→ If he ________ the place, he ________ alone.

C

우리말과 뜻이 같도록 괄호 안의 말을 바르게 배열하여 문장을 완성하시오.

1 만약 내가 물고기라면, 나는 수영을 아주 잘 할 텐데.

(I, if, were, I could, a fish, swim, well, very)

→ ________

2 만약 네가 제 시간에 왔다면, 시험을 볼 수 있었을 텐데.

(had, you, have, could, come, on time, if, you, taken, the test)

→ ________

3 만약 그가 신분증을 가지고 있다면, 그곳에 들어갈 수 있을 텐데.

(he, if, had, there, could, he, enter, an ID card)

→ ________

Point 02 가정법 과거완료

A 괄호 안에서 알맞은 말을 고르시오.

1 If they had seen the game, they would have (enjoy, enjoyed) it.

2 If she had known his number, she would (call, have called) him.

3 If we had rented a car, we (can, could) have gone around easily.

4 If it were snowy, they (will, would) make a snowman.

5 If I (am, was, were) you, I would listen to your parents.

6 If you (was, are, were) free, you could go to a movie.

7 If he (has, had, have) had enough money, he would have gone on a round-the-world trip.

B 〈보기〉와 같이 두 문장의 뜻이 통하도록 빈칸에 알맞은 말을 쓰시오.

보기

As the skirt didn't fit, she couldn't wear it.

→ If the skirt had fit, she would have worn it.

1 As he didn't have money, he couldn't buy the jeans.

→ If he ______________ money, he __________________ the jeans.

2 As the alarm didn't work properly, I didn't wake up early.

→ If the alarm ______________ properly, I __________________ early.

3 As they didn't have a compass, they couldn't find the direction.

→ If they ______________ a compass, they __________________ the direction.

4 As the air conditioner wasn't out of order, we didn't feel so hot.

→ If the air conditioner ______________ out of order, we __________________ so hot.

C 우리말과 뜻이 같도록 괄호 안의 말을 활용하여 문장을 완성하시오.

1 만약 James가 서둘렀다면, 그는 수업에 지각을 하지 않았을 텐데. (be, late)

→ If James had been in a hurry, he ________________________________ for the class.

2 만약 내가 내기를 하지 않았었다면, 나는 돈을 잃지 않았었을 텐데. (lose)

→ If I hadn't bet, I ________________________________ money.

Point 03~04 I wish 가정법, as if 가정법

A 괄호 안에서 알맞은 말을 고르시오.

1 She talks as if she (is, were) my mom.

2 I wish I (can, could) write a letter in English well.

3 I wish he (is, were) able to solve math problems easily.

4 I wish my mom (had stayed, has stayed) at home today.

5 It looks as if it (was, were) the most expensive one in the shop.

6 They eat as if they (haven't eaten, hadn't eaten) for several days.

7 I wish she (has finished, had finished) the presentation successfully.

8 He behaves as if he (has been, had been) the owner of the company.

B 두 문장의 뜻이 통하도록 빈칸에 알맞은 말을 쓰시오.

1 In fact, he isn't close to the model.

→ He looks as if he ________________ the model.

2 In fact, she was not an expert driver.

→ She drove as if she ________________ an expert driver.

3 I'm sorry that she is not in our group.

→ I wish she ________________ in our group.

4 I'm sorry that he didn't ride The Viking with me at the amusement park.

→ I wish he ________________ The Viking with me at the amusement park.

C 우리말과 뜻이 같도록 괄호 안의 말을 바르게 배열하여 문장을 완성하시오.

1 범죄 없는 세상에서 살 수 있다면 좋을 텐데. (I, live, we, wish, could, in)

→ ________________________________ a world without any crime.

2 그 남자는 노숙자였던 것처럼 말했다. (as, had, if, been, he, homeless)

→ The man talked ________________________________.

3 그 소년은 본인이 어른인 것처럼 행동한다. (were, adult, if, as, an, he)

→ The boy acts ________________________________.

Point 05~06 주의해야 할 가정법

A 괄호 안에서 알맞은 말을 고르시오.

1 If I (was, were) a leopard, I could run very fast.

2 (It were not for, Were it not for) the coat, you would feel very cold.

3 But (by, for) his advice, she could not make it.

4 If I were not so tired, I (can, could) play soccer with them.

5 (But, Without) your help, I could not have finished this project.

6 Without an umbrella, he would (have gotten, not have gotten) wet.

B 두 문장의 뜻이 같도록 if으로 시작하여 문장을 다시 쓸 때 빈칸에 알맞은 말을 쓰시오.

1 Without this English dictionary, I could not have understood the book.

→ If ________________________, I could not have understood the book.

2 But for Social Network Service, we could not have made friends as easily.

→ If ________________________, we could not have made friends as easily.

C 접속사 if를 생략하고 도치 구문을 써서 문장을 다시 쓸 때 빈칸에 알맞은 말을 쓰시오.

1 If I were overweight, I would start working out immediately.

→ ________________________, I would start working out immediately.

2 If she had enough time, she could have finished her homework.

→ ________________________, she could have finished her homework.

D 우리말과 뜻이 같도록 괄호 안의 말을 바르게 배열하여 문장을 완성하시오.

1 만약 팀워크가 없었다면, 그 팀은 경기에서 이기지 못했을 텐데.

(without, could, the team, have won, not, the game, teamwork)

→ ____

2 만약 눈이 많이 온다면, 나는 친구들과 눈싸움을 할 것이다.

(if, friends, snows, it, a lot, have, I, a snowball fight, will, my, with)

→ ____

Point 01 수의 일치

A **괄호 안에서 알맞은 말을 고르시오.**

1 Both paper and cans (is, are) supposed to be recycled.

2 Each boy and girl (wear, wears) a uniform of the same style.

3 (Are, Is) there anyone here who read this book?

4 A number of houses (was, were) damaged by the hurricane.

5 Economics (is, are) about the money flow in a nation and the world.

6 Re-using donated uniforms (help, helps) you save money.

7 What I am looking for (is, are) a pair of shoes.

B **밑줄 친 부분이 어법에 맞으면 O표, 틀리면 바르게 고쳐 쓰시오.**

1 The number of babies born every year in our country is decreasing. → ______

2 The poor in Africa is suffering from famine. → ______

3 About 390 kilometers are the distance between Seoul and Busan. → ______

4 97 percent of the water in the world are salt water. → ______

5 The Netherlands is a country lower than sea level. → ______

C **우리말과 뜻이 같도록 괄호 안의 말을 빈칸에 알맞은 형태로 고쳐 쓰시오.**

1 그의 친구들의 대부분은 운동선수들이다. (be)

→ Most of his friends ______ athletes.

2 입장료는 모두 2000원씩 내야 한다.

→ Every person ______ to pay 2000 won for entrance. (have)

3 누구 이 문제에 대한 답을 말해 볼래?

→ ______ anybody want to answer this question? (do)

4 그가 가진 돈의 반 이상이 자선단체에 기부되었다. (have been)

→ More than half of his money ______ donated to charity.

5 부자가 항상 행복한 것은 아니다. (be)

→ The rich ______ not always happy.

6 10달러가 그의 일주일 동안의 용돈이다. (be)

→ Ten dollars ______ his allowance for a week.

시제의 일치, 시제 일치의 예외

A 괄호 안에서 알맞은 말을 고르시오.

1 Even little children knew that Korea (was, is) once a Japanese colony.

2 Lillian said that she (loses, had lost) her purse on the way.

3 I learned today that cold air (is, was) heavier than hot air.

4 They all knew that Edison (invented, had invented) the light bulb.

5 Jake said that he (goes, went) to a nursing home every Saturday for volunteer work.

B 우리말과 뜻이 같도록 밑줄 친 부분을 어법에 맞게 고쳐 쓰시오.

1 나의 코치께서는 우리에게 연습이 완벽을 만든다고 말씀하시곤 했었다.

My coach used to say <u>that practice make perfect</u>.

→ ______________________________

2 경찰은 그 남자가 전날 밤 무엇을 했는지 알아냈다.

The police found out <u>what the man has done the previous day</u>.

→ ______________________________

3 네가 토요일 아침마다 개를 데리고 산책을 간다고 들었다.

I heard <u>that you went for a walk with your dog every Saturday morning</u>.

→ ______________________________

4 그녀는 우리가 인도 영화를 통해 인도인들의 생활과 풍습을 배울 수 있다고 말했다.

She said <u>that we could learn Indian life and culture through Indian movies</u>.

→ ______________________________

C 다음과 같이 주절의 시제를 과거로 바꿔 문장을 다시 쓸 때 빈칸에 알맞은 말을 쓰시오.

1 Nobody realizes that he is gone.

→ Nobody realized that he ______________________.

2 I think that John will enter the science competition.

→ I thought that John ______________________ the science competition.

3 Mary reads that Peary reached the North Pole in 1909.

→ Mary read that Peary ______________________ the North Pole in 1909.

4 She asks me what I usually do on weekends.

→ She asked me what ______________________.

5 They teach children that water freezes at 0°C.

→ They taught children that ______________________.

Point 04 평서문의 화법 전환

A **괄호 안에서 알맞은 말을 고르시오.**

1 My mom (told, said) me that I would have to take care of my sister the next day.

2 Jim told me that he had forgotten to bring his book (today, that day).

3 Mom told me that she (would, will) buy me a new dress, and she did.

4 Jake told Lily that he (took, had taken) her bike for a while.

5 The doctor told me that I (will, would) get well soon.

B **다음 문장을 간접화법으로 바꿀 때, 빈칸에 알맞은 말을 쓰시오.**

1 She said, "I need to buy some flowers for my living room now."

→ She said that ______________________________.

2 My father said, "I am going fishing tonight."

→ My father said that ______________________________.

3 She said to me, "I saw Mary a few minutes ago."

→ She told me that ______________________________.

C **다음 문장을 직접화법으로 바꿀 때, 빈칸에 알맞은 말을 쓰시오.**

1 The doctor told me that my sister would get well soon.

→ The doctor said to me, "______________________________."

2 She said that she had a lot of things to do that day.

→ She said, "______________________________."

3 He told her that he could help her with her homework then.

→ He said to her, "______________________________."

D **우리말과 뜻이 같도록 괄호 안의 말을 활용하여 빈칸에 알맞은 말을 쓰시오.**

1 그는 그 때 노래수업을 듣고 있었다고 말했다. (take)

→ He said that he ______________ a singing lesson then.

2 그녀는 나에게 내가 시험에 통과할 것이라고 말했다. (pass)

→ She told me that ______________ the test.

3 사람들은 그 소년이 경찰이 그 사건을 해결하는 데 도와주었다고 믿었다. (help)

→ People believed that the boy ______________ the police to solve the case.

A 괄호 안에서 알맞은 말을 고르시오.

1 He told us (come, to come) to school early the next day.

2 The man asked me (if, that) I knew who he was.

3 She wonders how fast (he was, was he) at the competition.

4 Ms. Choi warned me (not to be, don't be) late for class again.

5 He asked her what (she was looking, was she looking) for.

6 She asked me what kind of movie (I wanted, did I want) to watch.

B 다음 문장을 간접화법으로 바꿀 때, 빈칸에 알맞은 말을 쓰시오.

1 He said to me, "Have you finished your homework?"

→ He asked me ______________________________.

2 He said to her, "How old are you?"

→ He asked her ______________________________.

3 He said to me, "Have you been to Canada?"

→ He asked me ______________________________.

4 Our teacher said to us, "Don't talk during the test."

→ Our teacher ordered us ______________________________.

5 He said to me, "Please call me back later."

→ He asked me ______________________________.

C 다음 문장을 직접화법으로 바꿀 때, 빈칸에 알맞은 말을 쓰시오.

1 John asked Mary if she would go to a movie with him.

→ John said to Mary, "______________________________?"

2 The teacher told her class to repeat after her.

→ The teacher said to her class, "______________________________."

3 She asked him when the bus had left.

→ She said to him, "______________________________?"

Point 01~02 강조 구문 – 조동사 do,「It ~ that ...」 강조 구문

A 괄호 안에서 알맞은 말을 고르시오.

1 They (do, does) respect their teachers.

2 I (do, did) call you last night.

3 She (do, does) love her pets.

4 These flowers (do, does) smell nice.

B 밑줄 친 부분을 강조하여 문장을 다시 쓰시오. (단, 조동사 do를 활용할 것)

1 I feel happy about the result.

→ ____________________

2 It takes a lot of time to write an essay.

→ ____________________

C 밑줄 친 부분을 강조하기 위해「It is ~ that ...」 강조구문을 이용하여 문장을 다시 쓰시오.

1 The man started wearing jewelry.

→ ____________________

2 They practiced soccer in the park.

→ ____________________

3 I lost one of my earrings yesterday.

→ ____________________

4 More than 500 people take part in the event every year.

→ ____________________

D 우리말과 뜻이 같도록 괄호 안의 말을 바르게 배열하여 문장을 완성하시오.

1 선생님이 학교에 오지 않은 것은 어제였다. (the, that, teacher, come, to, school, didn't)

→ It was yesterday ____________________.

2 내가 제일 좋아하는 것은 이 책이다. (that, most, I, like)

→ It is this book ____________________.

3 그녀가 일을 시작한 것은 3년 전 이었다. (ago, it, was, three, years, that)

→ ____________________ she started her job.

Point 03 장소 부사(구)의 도치

A **밑줄 친 부분으로 시작하도록 전체 문장을 다시 쓰시오.**

1 The rain came <u>down</u> when they were walking.

→ ______________________________

2 The boy stood <u>there</u> waiting for the girl.

→ ______________________________

3 He comes <u>here</u> with his friend.

→ ______________________________

4 The rocket heading for the moon went <u>up</u>.

→ ______________________________

B **밑줄 친 부분을 어법에 맞게 고쳐 쓰시오.**

1 Out <u>did the sun come</u>.

→ ______________________________

2 In the sky <u>many clouds are</u>.

→ ______________________________

3 Beyond the trees <u>are my grandfather's house</u>.

→ ______________________________

C **밑줄 친 부분이 강조되도록 괄호 안의 말을 바르게 배열하여 도치된 문장을 완성하시오.**

1 <u>언덕 위에</u> 그 건물이 서 있다. (the, building, stands, the, hill, on)

→ ______________________________

2 그들은 <u>내 머리 위를</u> 지나갔다. (passed, they, my, head, over)

→ ______________________________

3 <u>그들 주위에는</u> 많은 상자들이 있었다. (them, around, many, are, boxes)

→ ______________________________

4 <u>그 상자 안에는</u> 반지가 있었다. (box, the, inside, was, a, ring)

→ ______________________________

Point 03 부정어의 도치

A 괄호 안에서 알맞은 말을 고르시오.

1 Not until he told me the truth, (I believed, did I believe) what he said.

2 Not only (it was, was it) delicious, but also it was beautiful.

3 No sooner (the baby had seen me, had the baby seen me), he started to cry.

4 Little (I dreamed, did I dream) that I would win the game.

5 Rarely (Jane is, is Jane) late for class.

B 밑줄 친 부분을 강조하기 위해 도치하여 전체 문장을 다시 쓰시오.

1 She is <u>seldom</u> passionate about her work.

→ ______________________________

2 They could find the file <u>nowhere</u>.

→ ______________________________

3 He was <u>not only</u> tall but also handsome.

→ ______________________________

4 I have <u>never</u> seen a picture as beautiful as this.

→ ______________________________

C 밑줄 친 부분이 강조되도록 괄호 안의 말을 바르게 배열하여 도치된 문장을 완성하시오.

1 그가 올 것이라고 그녀는 <u>거의</u> 생각하지 <u>않았다</u>. (little, she, he, think, would, come, did, that)

→ ______________________________

2 나는 <u>어디서도</u> 그처럼 좋은 사람을 만나지 못했다. (nowhere else, could, meet, I, such, nice, a, guy)

→ ______________________________

3 나는 <u>어젯밤까지</u> 그 소식을 듣지 <u>못했다</u>. (until, night, last, not, I, did, the, hear, news)

→ ______________________________

4 그녀는 TV를 <u>거의</u> 보지 <u>않는다</u>. (rarely, she, watch, TV, does)

→ ______________________________

5 내가 너를 직접 만나기 <u>전까지는</u> 나는 너에 대해 별로 많이 생각하지 <u>않았다</u>.
(not, I, you, in person, I, think, did, met, much of you, until)

→ ______________________________

Point 04 동의할 때: 「So/Nor/Neither + 동사 + 주어」 구문

A 대화에서 A의 말에 동의하는 내용이 되도록 빈칸에 알맞은 말을 쓰시오.

1 A: I will go shopping tonight.

B: ______________________________. Why don't we go together?

2 A: My brother loves to eat meat.

B: ______________________________. I am a meat lover.

3 A: I didn't do well on the test.

B: ______________________________. I think the test was difficult.

4 A: I don't like the food in this restaurant.

B: ______________________________. Let's not come here anymore.

B 두 문장의 뜻이 같도록, so나 neither를 활용하여 문장을 완성하시오.

1 Susie didn't like the movie, and Tom didn't like it, either.

→ Susie didn't like the movie, and ______________________________.

2 I hope to travel to Europe, and my sister does, too.

→ I hope to travel to Europe, and ______________________________.

3 Jane is going to study dance, and I am going to, too.

→ Jane is going to study dance, and ______________________________.

4 They will eat pizza, and we will, too.

→ They will eat pizza, and ______________________________.

C 대화에서 A의 말에 동의하는 말을 빈칸에 쓰시오. (단, so나 neither로 시작할 것)

1 A: I don't like to go to crowded places.

B: ______________________________

2 A: I will be busy this weekend because of all this homework.

B: ______________________________

3 A: I can't play any musical instruments.

B: ______________________________

4 A: I haven't read the book.

B: ______________________________

MEMO

MEMO

MEMO

앞서가는 학생들의 일등 비법 봉인 해제!

woongjin compass

비법 다 담은 중학 영문법

Level 3

친절한 정답 및 해설

앞서가는 학생들의 일등 비법 봉인 해제!

비법 다은 중학

영문법

3 Level

친절한
정답 및 해설

Chapter 01 시제

Point 1 현재 *vs.* 과거

A	1. saves	2. is	3. did
	4. goes	5. is	6. leaves
	7. tried	8. was	
B	1. sets	2. gather	3. was
	4. leaves	5. go	6. walked
	7. puts		

A [해설]

1. 속담이나 격언은 항상 현재시제로 쓴다. (해석: 제 때의 바느질 한 번이 나중의 아홉 번의 바느질을 던다.)

2, 4~5. 현재의 상태(2번), 현재의 반복적인 일(4번), 과학적 사실(5번)은 현재시제로 쓴다.

3, 7~8. 과거의 사실임을 나타내는 시간부사(절)(각각 last night, yesterday, when I was young)가 있으므로 과거시제로 쓴다.

6. 왕래발착동사(come, go, leave, arrive)는 현재로 가까운 미래의 확정된 일을 나타낼 수 있다.

B [해설]

1. 일반적 사실은 현재시제로 쓴다.

2. 속담은 현재시제로 쓴다. (해석: 같은 깃털을 가진 새끼리 모인다. 유유상종)

3, 6. 'last weekend'와 'when he was alive'라는 과거를 뜻하는 시간 부사(구/절)가 있으므로 과거시제로 쓴다.

4. next week가 있으나 왕래발착동사(come, go, leave, arrive)는 현재형으로 미래를 나타낸다.

5, 7. 현재의 습관적인 사실임을 나타내므로 현재시제로 쓴다.

Point 2 현재완료의 쓰임과 형태

A	1. has, finished	2. has been
	3. has gone	4. have been
	5. has been	
B	1. hasn't stopped	2. have, had
	3. has stolen	

A [해설]

1. 과거에 시작된 동작이 지금 완료되었으므로 현재완료로 쓴다. (완료)

2, 4. 과거의 상태가 현재까지 계속 이어지고 있으므로 현재완료로 쓴다. (계속)

3. 과거의 동작이 현재까지 영향을 미치고 있으므로 현재완료로 쓴다. (결과)

5. 이제까지의 경험이므로 현재완료로 쓴다. (경험)

B [해설]

1. 과거에 시작된 일이 아직 완료되지 못한, '완료'의 부정을 의미한다. (완료)

2. 방금 먹는 동작을 완료했다는 의미이므로 현재완료로 쓴다. (완료)

3. 누군가 훔쳐 가서 지금 없다는 의미이므로 현재완료로 쓴다. (결과)

Point 3 현재완료의 용법 I – 경험, 계속

A	1. have seen	2. has learned
	3. have been	4. has studied
	5. have never left	6. Have, tried
	7. have lived	
B	1. has snowed	2. has lived
	3. have met	4. has liked
	5. have had	6. Have, wondered
	7. have, practiced	

A [해설]

1, 5, 6. 이제까지의 경험을 나타내므로 현재완료로 쓴다.

2, 3, 4, 7. 과거부터 지금까지 계속되는 상태 혹은 동작을 나타내므로 현재완료로 쓴다.

B [해설]

1~2, 4~5, 7. 과거부터 시작되어 현재까지 계속되는 동작을 나타낼 때는 현재완료로 쓴다.

3, 6. 이제까지의 경험을 나타낼 때는 현재완료로 쓴다.

Point 4 현재완료의 용법 II – 완료, 결과

A	1. has gone	2. has bought
	3. has left	4. has, finished
	5. has, arrived	
B	1. have had	2. has gone to
	3. Have, finished	4. have already found
	5. haven't received	

A [해설]

1~3. 과거의 동작이 현재까지 영향을 미치므로 현재완료로 쓴다. (결과)

4~5. 과거에 시작한 동작이 막 완료되었으므로 현재완료로 쓴다. (완료)

B [해설]

1~5. 과거의 동작으로 현재까지 영향을 미치고 있으므로 현재완료로 쓴다. 현재완료의 형태는 'have[has] + p.p.'이다.

Point 5 현재완료 *vs.* 과거

A	1. were you	2. did you find
	3. celebrated	4. O
	5. has taught	6. gained
	7. has been celebrated	
B	1. called	2. have lost
	3. haven't eaten	
C	1. went	2. has moved
	3. began	4. have you done

A [해설]

1, 3, 6. 분명한 과거를 나타내는 시간부사인 last night, last week, in 1921(과거년도)가 있으므로 과거시제로 써야 한다.

2. 정확한 때를 묻는 when(언제)으로 시작하는 질문은 완료형으로 쓰지 않는다.

4~5, 7. since와 for는 현재완료(계속)에 쓴다.

B [해설]

1. ago가 있으므로 과거시제로 쓴다.

2. 과거의 동작이 현재의 결과를 초래했으므로 현재완료를 쓴다.

3. 뒤에 'since + 과거시점'이 있으므로 주절의 시제는 현재완료를 쓴다.

C [해설]

1, 3. 분명한 과거를 나타내는 시간부사 (각각 last weekend, in 1999(과거년도))가 있으므로 과거시제로 써야 한다.

2. 과거의 동작이 현재의 결과를 초래했으므로 현재완료로 써야 한다.

4. so far(지금까지)가 있으므로 현재완료로 써야 한다.

Point 6 과거완료

A	1. had eaten	2. had left
	3. had ended	4. had never thought
B	1. had expected	2. had bought
	3. had done	4. had walked
C	1. had lost	2. had received
	3. had waited	4. had, gone

A [해설]

1~2. 과거보다 더 이전에 일어난 사건이 과거의 특정시점에 영향을 끼치므로 과거완료로 쓴다.

3. 특정 과거시점보다 더 이전에 시작된 어떤 일이 과거시점에 완료되었으므로 과거완료로 쓴다.

4. 특정 과거시점보다 더 이전부터 과거시점까지의 상태였으므로 과거완료로 쓴다.

B [해설]

1~3. 특정한 과거 시점보다 더 이전에 일어난 사건을 나타내므로 과거완료로 쓴다.

4. 특정 과거시점보다 더 이전에 시작된 동작이 과거시점까지 계속된 상태였으므로 과거완료로 쓴다.

C [해설]

1. 과거보다 더 이전에 일어난 사건이 과거의 특정시점에 영향을 끼치므로 과거완료로 쓴다.

2. 특정한 과거 시점보다 더 이전에 일어난 사건을 나타내므로 과거완료로 쓴다.

3. 과거보다 더 이전에 시작된 동작이 과거시점까지 계속되고 있으므로 과거완료로 쓴다.

4. 과거보다 더 이전에 일어난 사건이 과거의 특정시점에 영향을 끼치므로 과거완료로 쓴다.

Point 7 현재진행, 과거진행, 미래진행

A	1. were	2. feel	3. will be
	4. have	5. was	6. know
	7. are		
B	1. had	2. do you think	3. O
	4. will be having 또는 will have		5. O

A [해설]

1. 기준 시점이 과거(visited)로 되어 있으므로 과거진행으로 쓴다.
2. feel(~하게 느끼다)는 진행형으로 쓰지 않는다.
3. 미래에 일어날 사건이므로 미래진행형으로 쓴다.
4. have는 소유를 나타낼 때 진행형으로 쓰지 않는다.
5. 과거에 진행된 동작이므로 과거진행형으로 쓴다.
6. know는 인지동사이므로 진행형으로 쓰지 않는다.
7. 현재 진행되는 사실이므로 현재진행형으로 쓴다.

B [해설]

1. have는 소유를 뜻할 때 진행형으로 쓰지 않는다.
2. think은 인지동사이므로 진행형으로 쓰지 않는다. (단, 일시적 상태일 때는 가능)
3. 현재의 상태이므로 현재진행형으로 쓴다.
4. 미래에 진행될 일이므로 미래진행형으로 쓴다.
5. 왕래발착동사는 현재진행형으로 가까운 미래의 확정된 일을 나타낼 수 있다.

Point 8 완료진행

A	1. has been reading	2. has read
B	1. has been raining	2. have been studying
	3. has been staying	4. had been playing
C	1. has been swimming	
	2. had been eating	
	3. have you been watching	
	4. has been working	

A [해설]

1. David가 3시간 전에 책을 읽기 시작했고 지금도 계속 읽고 있으므로 현재완료 진행으로 쓴다.
2. 현재까지 100쪽을 읽은 상태이므로 (동작이 아니므로) 현재완료진행이 아닌 현재완료로 쓴다.

B [해설]

1~3. 과거 어느 시점에서부터 현재까지 어떤 동작이 계속 진행되고 있음을 강조하고 있으므로 현재완료진행으로 쓴다.

4. 과거 이전부터 시작된 동작이 기준시점이 되는 과거 시점까지 계속 진행되고 있었음을 강조하고 있으므로 과거완료 진행으로 쓴다.

일등 비법 노트

비법 1	1. Slow and steady wins the race. 2. ③, ⑤
비법 2	1. ② 2. ①, ③
비법 3	1. has taught
비법 4	1. ②
비법 5	1. ⓐ have been waiting ⓑ have been practicing 2. has been playing the piano for an hour

비법 1

1 [해설] 속담이므로 현재시제로 쓴다.

2 [해석]
ⓐ 당신은 지구에 왜 다른 계절이 있는지 궁금해 한 적이 있는가? ⓑ 그것은 지구가 기울어진 채로 태양을 주변을 돌기 때문이다. 그래서, 지구가 태양 주변을 돌 때는 ⓒ 우리는 다른 양의 햇빛을 받는다. 예를 들면, 여름에는, ⓓ 지구의 북쪽 부분이 태양 쪽으로 기울기 때문에 더 많은 햇빛을 받는다. 겨울에는, 반면에, ⓔ 이 부분이 태양에서 먼 쪽으로 기울게 된다. 그것은 이 부분이 더 적은 태양빛을 받게 될 것이라는 것을 의미한다. 우리는 지구가 일년 내내 움직이기 때문에 다른 계절을 가지고 있다.

[해설]

③ ⓒ 과학적 사실이므로 현재시제를 써야 한다. (got → get)

⑤ ⓔ 과학적 사실이므로 현재시제를 써야 한다. (became → becomes)

비법 2

1 [해석] 당신이 Abraham Lincoln에 대해서 들어 본 적이 있을 것이라고 확신한다. 그는 미국의 지도자였다. 비록 그가 1860년 대통령이 되기 전에 많은 실패를 거듭 겪었지만, 그는 그의 꿈을 이루는 것을 결코 포기하지 않았다. 당신도 어떤 실패를 경험했는가? 그것이 언제였는가? 당신이 낙담하게 될 때, 용감한 Lincoln을 생각하라.

[해설]

ⓐ 지금까지 들어본 적이 있는지 경험에 관한 문장이므로 현재완료(have heard)로 쓴다.

ⓑ 문장에 in 1860이라는 과거를 나타내는 시간부사구가 있으므로 과거시제(became)로 써야 한다.

ⓒ 실패한 적이 있는지 과거부터 지금까지의 경험을 묻는 질문 뒤에 when(언제)로 묻는 질문은 과거에 있었던 경험이므로 과거시제(was)로 써야 한다.

2 [해설]

① 일반적인 사실이므로 현재시제로 쓴다.

② when으로 시작하는 질문은 완료형으로 쓰지 못한다. (have you finished → did you finish)

③ 과거의 사실이므로 과거시제로 쓴다.

④ 과거(when he was young)에 행복했던 것이므로 과거시제로 써야 한다. (has been → was)

⑤ last Wednesday(지난 수요일)에 일어난 사건이므로 과거시제로 써야 한다. (have listened → listened)

비법 3

1 [해설] 문장에 'since + 과거 시점'이 있으므로 주절은 현재완료로 쓴다.

비법 4

1 [해설]

① ago는 현재완료와 함께 쓰지 못한다. (ago → before / 또는 has gone → went)

② 내가 도서관에 도착한 것이 과거이고, 그는 그때 이미 떠났으므로 과거완료로 써야 한다.

③ 엄마가 돌아온 것이 과거이고, John은 그때보다 몇 시간 이전부터 그 때까지 나가 있었으므로 과거완료로 써야 한다. (has → had)

④ 개를 본 것이 과거시제이고 개가 헤매고 있었던 것은 그 이전부터 계속된 것이므로 과거완료진행으로 써야 한다. (has → had)

⑤ 학교를 중퇴해야 했던 것이 과거시제이고, 학교를 다녔던 것은 그것보다 더 이전부터 계속되었던 일이므로 과거완료로 써야 한다. (went to → had been in, 혹은 had been going to)

비법 5

1 [해석]

기자: Julia, 당신 그룹이 새 앨범을 낸다고 들었는데요.

Julia: 네, 다음주가 될 것입니다.

기자: 그것 참 잘됐군요. 당신들의 팬이 오랫동안 새 앨범이 나올 것을 기다리고 있었는데요. 당신들은 또한 순회 공연을 계획하고 있지요, 그렇지요?

Julia: 네. 우리는 여러 달 동안 연습해 왔습니다. 우리는 팬들을 실망시키지 않을 겁니다.

[해설]

ⓐ 과거부터 지금까지 기다려 왔으므로 현재완료진행으로 쓴다.

ⓑ 과거부터 지금까지 연습해 왔으므로 현재완료진행으로 쓴다.

2 [해설] 과거에 시작해서 현재까지 계속되고 있는 동작임을 강조할 때 현재완료진행으로 쓴다.

내신 만점! 실전 기출

01. ⑤	**02.** ⑤	**03.** ①
04. ③	**05.** ③	**06.** ②
07. ⑤	**08.** ③	**09.** ③
10. ⓐ bought, ⓑ had wanted		**11.** ②
12. has been	**13.** has been learning	
14. ③	**15.** ②	**16.** ③
17. ①	**18.** ③	**19.** ④
20. had, left	**21.** Have, heard, sees	
22. has been snowing		**23.** ④

24. have finished → will have finished
25. has → had
26. is really resembling → really resembles
27. ④ 28. ② 29. ④
30. (2) had → have
(3) did you have → have you had

01 [해석] Emily는 경주에 두 번 가 봤다.
[해설] 이제까지의 경험을 나타내므로 현재완료로 나타내야 한다.

02 [해석] 내가 그를 만났을 때, 그는 서울에 5년 째 살고 있었다.
[해설] 기준이 되는 시점이 과거(when I met him)이고 그 이전부터 그때까지 살고 있었으므로 과거완료로 쓴다.

03 [해석] 나의 엄마는 항상 시간과 조류는 사람을 기다리지 않는다고 말씀하셨다.
[해설] 속담은 항상 현재시제로 쓴다.

04 [해석]
(1) Mike는 2011년 이래로 축구를 했다.
(2) Jake는 두 시간 째 컴퓨터 게임을 하고 있다.
[해설]
(1) 현재완료 문장에서 과거의 기준시점을 나타내기 위해서는 앞에 'since + 과거의 시점'을 쓴다.
(2) 숫자 개념의 기간을 나타낼 때는 for를 앞에 쓴다.

05 [해석]
A: 봐! 꽃 앞에서 날고 있는 매우 작은 새가 있어! 너는 저게 무엇인지 아니?
B: 응. TV의 동물의 왕국에서 한 번 본 적이 있어.
[해설] 지금까지의 경험을 나타내는 문장이므로 현재완료로 쓴다.

06 [해석]
A: 너는 언제 농구를 시작했니?
B: 나는 초등학생이었을 때 시작했어.
[해설] 농구를 시작한 과거의 시점을 물어보는 질문이므로 과거시제를 쓴다.

07 [해석]
A: 너는 어제 왜 화가 났었니?
B: 내가 집에 돌아 갔을 때, 나의 개가 나의 가장 좋아하는 신발을 물어 뜯고 있었어.

08 [해석]
A: 왜 한 시간 전에 전화를 받지 않았니?
B: 전화가 울릴 때 나는 샤워를 하고 있었어.
[해설] 과거 사건과 동시에 일어난 좀 더 긴 시간 동안 일어난 동작은 과거진행으로 쓴다.

09 [해석]
A: 영어를 공부하는 좋은 방법은 무엇이지?
B: 글쎄, 나는 중학생 때부터 계속 영어 음악을 들었어. 그게 한 가지 좋은 방법이야.
[해설] 과거 특정시점 이후로 계속 되어온 동작이므로 주절 시제는 현재완료로 쓰고, 부사구는 대개 'since + 과거시점' 으로 나타낸다.

10 [해석] 미아의 삼촌은 LA에 산다. 그는 작년 여름 한국을 방문하는 동안 그녀에게 멋진 가방을 사 주셨다. 미아는 그것이 매우 갖고 싶어하던 것이었기 때문에 매우 행복했다.
[해설]
ⓐ 뒤에 'last'라는 말이 있으므로 과거시제로 쓴다.
ⓑ 과거 이전부터 과거 특정 시점까지 계속된 일은 과거완료로 쓴다.

11 [해석]
A: 너 오늘 Sally를 본 적 있니?
B: 응. 너를 만나기 전에 나는 그녀와 함께 도서관에 있었어. 그녀는 쇼핑하러 갔어.
[해설]
ⓐ 과거 이전에 있었던 일은 대과거를 뜻하는 과거완료형으로 쓴다.
ⓑ 그녀가 지금 쇼핑에 가버리고 없으므로 현재완료 형태로 쓴다.

12 [해석] 미나는 작년에 미국에 갔다. 그녀는 아직도 거기에 있다.
→ 미나는 일년 동안 미국에 있다.
[해설] 과거부터 지금까지 계속되는 상태이므로 현재완료로 쓴다. 빈칸 뒤에 in이 있으므로 '~에 있다'의 의미로 be 동사를 활용해야 한다.

13 [해석] 유나는 3년 전에 중국어를 배우기 시작했다. 그녀는 지금까지 여전히 그것을 공부하고 있다.
→ 유나는 3년 동안 중국어를 배우고 있다.
[해설] 3년 전에 시작하여 지금까지 계속되고 있는 일이므로 현재완료진행으로 쓴다.

14 [해석]
① 나는 그를 전에 만난 적이 없다.
② 그는 베이징에 세 번 가 봤다.
③ 나는 3년 이상 영어 공부를 해 왔다.
④ 나의 할머니는 학교에서 교육을 받으신 적이 없다.
⑤ 너는 'panic'이라는 단어의 어원에 대해서 들어 본 적이 있니?
[해설] ①~②, ④~⑤은 현재완료의 경험 용법, ③은 현재완료의 계속 용법이다.

15 [해석]
① Susan은 이미 점심을 먹었다.
② 그 기차는 이미 가 버렸다.
③ 그들은 언제 시작해야 할 지 결정하지 않았다.
④ 그 젊은이는 그의 일을 끝마쳤다.
⑤ 내가 가장 좋아하는 TV 프로그램이 방금 끝났다.
[해설] ①, ③~⑤은 현재완료의 완료 용법이고, ②는 현재완료의 결과 용법이다.

16 [해석]
① A: 너는 얼마나 오랫동안 TV를 보고 있었니?
B: 대략 한 시간 정도요.
② A: 너는 보통 몇 시에 잠자리에 드니?
B: 나는 10시에 잠자리에 든다.
③ A: 당신은 어젯밤 어디에 있었나요?
B: 나는 책을 읽으면서 내 방에 있었어요.
④ A: 당신은 언제 요리수업을 듣기 시작했나요?
B: 지난 달이요. 난 그것이 정말 좋아요.
⑤ A: 우리 오늘 밤 영화 보러 갈까?
B: 나도 그러고 싶지만, 내가 숙제를 아직 끝내지 못했어.
[해설] ③ 과거에 대한 질문이므로 과거로 답해야 한다.
(have been → was)

17 [해석]
① 전화가 울렸다. 그러나 그녀는 듣지 못했다.
② Susie는 그 소식을 들었을 때, 충격을 받았다.
③ Mr. Park은 2000년에 영어를 가르쳤다.
④ 나는 서울로 이사 가기 전에 부산에서 살았다.
⑤ Jessie는 항상 6시에 일어나서 조깅을 간다.
[해설]
② 소식을 들은 것이 과거(heard)이므로 충격을 받은 것도 과거이어야 한다. (is → was)
③ in 2000(과거를 나타내는 시간 부사)가 있으므로 과거시제로 쓴다. (has been teaching → taught)
④ 과거 이전에 일어난 일은 과거완료로 쓴다.
(have lived → had lived)
⑤ 현재의 습관은 현재시제로 쓴다. (got → gets)

18 [해석]
① 당신은 아프리카에 가 본 적이 있습니까?
② 그는 번지점프를 해 본 적이 없다.
③ 어제 우리 팀이 경기에 이겼다.
④ 지난 번에 만난 이후로 오랜만이군요.
⑤ 너는 Mark가 글쓰기대회에서 우승한 것을 알고 있었니?
[해설] ③ yesterday가 있으므로 과거 시제로 쓴다.
(have won → won)

19 [해석]
① 나는 오늘 밤 대전으로 떠난다.
② 지나는 이번 주말에 집에 온다.
③ 이 비행기는 30분 후에 LA공항에 도착한다.
④ 우리는 지금 부엌에서 저녁을 준비하고 있다.
⑤ 그들은 내일 서울국립박물관에 방문한다.
[해설] ④는 현재 진행되고 있는 동작을 의미하고, ①, ②, ③, ⑤는 모두 확정된 가까운 미래를 나타낸다.

20 [해설] 과거인 기준시점 이전에 버스가 이미 떠나 없으므로 (결과) 과거완료로 쓴다.

21 [해설] 이제까지의 경험을 묻는 질문이므로 현재완료로 쓰고, 격언은 현재시제로 쓴다.

22 [해석] 뉴욕에는 3일 전에 눈이 오기 시작했는데, 아직도 눈이 오고 있다. → 뉴욕에는 3일동안 눈이 오고 있다.

[해설] 과거에 시작해서 지금까지 동작이 계속되고 있음을 강조하므로 현재완료진행형으로 쓴다.

23 [해석]

ⓐ 나는 어제 멋진 재킷을 샀다.

ⓑ 그녀는 업무상 파리를 여러 번 가 본 적이 있다.

ⓒ 네가 나에게 전화했을 때, 나는 다큐멘터리를 보고 있었다.

ⓓ 킬리만자로 산은 일년 내내 눈으로 덮여 있다.

ⓔ 수미는 두 시간 이상 테니스 연습을 하고 있다.

[해설]

ⓐ have bought → bought

ⓑ '다녀 온 적이 있다'의 의미로는 'has been to'를 쓴다. 'has gone to ~'는 '~에 가버리고 지금 여기에 없다'라는 뜻이다. (has gone to → has been to)

ⓓ was → is

24 [해설] 미래의 어느 시점을 기준으로 그 때까지 동작을 완료하는 것이므로 미래완료로 쓴다.

25 [해설] 기준이 되는 과거시제보다 더 이전에 시작하여 과거시점에 완료된 일이므로 과거완료로 쓴다.

26 [해설] resemble은 상태를 나타내는 동사로서 진행형으로 쓰지 않는다.

27 [해석]

진수: 너 괜찮니?

민지: (A) 나는 일주일 동안 아팠어, 그래서 아직 조금 기운이 없어.

진수: 저런! 어디가 아팠는데?

민지: 지난 주말에 내가 비를 맞았거든. 그래서 (B) 그때 이후로 심한 감기에 걸렸어.

진수: (C) 약은 먹고 있니?

민지: 응. (D) 의사 선생님이 처방을 해 주었어. 그 약이 정말 많은 도움이 돼.

진수: 일찍 집에 가서 쉬어야겠다.

민지: (E) 조사를 할 게 좀 있긴 하지만, 그게 좋은 생각인 것 같아.

[해설] 현재완료진행인 질문(C)에 대하여 민지가 'Yes, I have.' 라고 대답했으므로, 지금도 먹고 있는 중이다.

28 [해설] (B) 'since + 과거시점'이 있는 문장의 주절에는 현재완료가 와야 한다. (had had → have had)

29 [해석]

A: 안녕, Bill. 라스베이거스로의 여행은 어땠어?

B: 멋졌어. 내 친구와 나는 사막을 관통해서 후버댐으로 운전했지.

A: 우와! 시간이 얼마나 걸렸어?

B: 보통 약 7시간 정도 걸려. 그렇지만 우리는 가는 길에 여러 곳을 들렀어. 그래서 그것보다 더 걸렸어.

A: 음... 거기에 몇 번이나 가 봤니?

B: 그게 첫 번째였어. 전에는 그곳에 가 본 적이 없었지.

[해설]

ⓐ 과거에 있었던 일이므로 과거시제로 쓴다.

ⓑ 이제까지의 경험을 물어보는 것이므로 현재완료로 쓴다.

ⓒ 특정 과거시점보다 더 이전부터 그때까지의 경험을 나타내므로 과거완료로 쓴다.

30 [해석]

A: 어떻게 오셨나요?

B: 목이 아파서요.

A: 얼마나 오래 되었나요?

B: 3일 되었어요. 지난 월요일부터요.

A: 감기가 걸린 것 같군요. 약을 처방해 드리지요.

[해설]

(2) 현재의 상태이므로 현재시제로 쓴다.

(3) 얼마나 오래 되었는지 기간을 물어보는 것이므로 현재완료로 쓴다.

실력 탄탄! 서술형 심화

1 (1) feels
(2) has had

2 (1) has got
(2) has been reading
(3) for five hours

3 (1) read
(2) has used
(3) trying
(4) is

1 [해석] 〈문제〉 대화를 읽고, 빈칸을 채워 요약문을 완성하시오.

미나: 얼굴에 뭐가 묻었네.

Judy: 뭐라고? 오! 김 조각이네! 점심때부터 계속 얼굴에 붙이고 있었어.

미나: 저런!

Judy: 다른 사람들이 내가 지저분하다고 생각하겠어!

미나: 걱정하지마. 사람들은 그저 자기 자신들에게만 관심이 있거든.

[해설] (1) 현재 느끼는 감정이므로 현재시제(feels)가 오고, (2) 한동안(for a while) 계속된 상태이므로 현재완료로 나타낸다.

2 [해석] 〈문제〉 다음 두 그림을 비교하시오. 주어진 단어를 사용하여 문장을 완성하시오.

Susie는 3시에 책 읽기를 시작했다. 지금은 8시이고 (1) 어두워졌다. 그녀는 (3) 5시간 동안 (2) 책을 읽고 있다.

[해설]

(1) 이미 어두워졌으므로 현재완료의 '완료' 용법이다. (get dark: 어두워지다)

(2) 과거에 시작하여 현재까지 계속되는 동작이고, 세 단어로 써야 하므로 현재완료진행으로 써야 한다.

(3) '다섯 시간 동안'이라는 뜻으로 'for + 기간'을 쓴다.

3 [해석] 〈문제〉 밑줄 친 부분은 어법에 맞지 않으니 고치시오.

지나는 한 달 전에 지구의 환경 문제에 관한 책을 읽은 후 그녀는 환경을 위해 무언가를 하겠다고 결심했다. 그때 이후로 그녀는 엘리베이터 보다는 계단을 이용하고 있다. 그녀는 또한 종이컵은 사용하지 않으려고 노력하고 있다. 그녀는 환경에 나쁜 우리의 습관을 바꾸기 위한 캠페인을 다음 주에 열 것을 계획하고 있다.

[해설]

(1) ago가 있으므로 과거시제로 써야 한다.

(2) since가 있으므로 주절은 현재완료나 현재완료 진행이 올 수 있다.

(3) 주어가 동작을 하는 '능동'의 현재완료진행이어야 하므로 'have been + -ing'를 쓴다.

(4) 지금 계획을 하고 있으므로 현재진행으로 쓴다.

Chapter 02 조동사

Point 1 can, be able to

A 1. win 2. stand 3. to answer
4. falling 5. be able to

B 1. may 2. is able to 3. was able to

C 1. 그것에 대한 정보를 얻을 수 있을까요?
2. 그 소문은 사실일 리가 없다.
3. 나는 슬픈 결말 때문에 울지 않을 수 없었다.
4. 이 짐을 좀 도와주실 수 있나요?

A [해석]
1. 그는 마침내 경주를 이길 수 있었다.
2. 나는 그의 예의 없는 태도를 더 이상 견딜 수가 없다.
3. 그는 그 질문에 답할 수 없었다.
4. 나는 너무 졸렸기 때문에 잠들지 않을 수 없었다.
5. 그녀는 일년 안에 중국어를 유창하게 구사할 수 있을 것이다.
[해설]
1~2. 조동사 다음엔 동사원형이 온다.
3. be able to + 동사원형 = 가능의 can
4. cannot help + -ing: ~하지 않을 수 없다
5. can의 미래형은 will be able to를 쓴다.

B [해석]
1. 시험을 끝내면 집에 가도 좋습니다.
2. 그는 다섯 개의 다른 언어를 말할 수 있다.
3. 그녀는 그녀의 학교에서 가장 빨리 달릴 수 있었다.
[해설]
1. 허락의 can이므로 may로 바꿔 쓸 수 있다.
2~3. 가능의 can/could이므로 be able to로 바꿔 쓸 수 있다.

C [해설]
1. 요청의 can이다.
2. 강한 부정의 추측을 나타내는 cannot이다.
3. cannot help + -ing:~하지 않을 수 없다.
4. 요청의 could이다.

Point 2 may

A 1. might 2. may
3. may not 4. may as well

B 1. be never → never be 2. may is → may be
3. changed → change 4. telling → tell

C 1. May I have your attention?
2. What she said might be true.
3. You may visit any time after twelve.

A [해설]
1~2. 추측을 나타내는 may/might를 쓴다.
3. 허락을 나타내는 may의 부정은 may not을 쓴다.
4. may as well + 동사원형: ~하는 것이 낫다.

B [해설]
1. may의 부정: may 뒤에 부정어를 붙인다.
2. 조동사 may 다음에 동사원형이 와야 한다.
3. 조동사(might) 다음에는 동사원형이 온다.

Point 3 will

A 1. will 2. take 3. will
4. Would 5. may

B 1. It will take about three hours
2. I would like to book a table for two at 7
3. Will you open the door for me

C 1. would like to eat[have] 2. would like

A [해설]
1. '~할 것이다'의 의미이므로 will을 쓴다.
2. will 다음에는 동사원형이 온다.
3. '~일 것이다'의 의미이므로 will을 쓴다.
4. 요청을 나타내므로 Would를 쓴다.
5. '~일지도 모른다'는 may를 쓴다.

C [해설]
1. would like to('d like to) + 동사원형: '~을 하고 싶다'라는 뜻의 정중한 표현이다.
2. would like('d like) 명사: '~을 원한다'는 표현이다.

Point 4 must, have to

A 1. must 2. have 3. must

B 1. You must not enter this area
2. I don't have to wake up early tomorrow

C 1. He must not lie to his mom
2. He didn't have to hide his feelings

A [해석]
1. 그는 우리에게 진실을 말해야만 한다.
2. 그들은 그 곳에 도착하기 위해 몇 시간을 걸어야 한다.
3. 그에 대한 소문은 사실임이 틀림없다.
[해설]
1. 뒤에 동사원형이 왔으므로 must가 온다
2. 뒤에 to가 왔으므로 have가 온다.
3. 강한 추측을 나타내는 must이다.

B [해설]
1. '~해서는 안 된다'라는 뜻이므로 금지의 must를 써야 한다.
2. '~할 필요가 없다'는 뜻이므로 don't have to가 와야 한다.

Point 5 should, ought to

A 1. wear 2. to follow 3. should do

B 1. He suggested that we join the team
2. It is essential that students study hard

C 1. ought to think twice 2. ought not to fight
3. should not believe

A [해설]
1. should 다음엔 동사원형이 온다.
2. ought 다음엔 'to + 동사원형'이 온다.
3. 'should + 동사원형'이 올바른 어순이다.

B [해설] 주장, 명령, 충고, 제안, 요구, 필요 등을 나타내는 동사나 형용사가 주절에 쓰였을 때, 종속절에 should를 사용한다. 이 때의 should는 생략 가능하다.

C [해석]
1. 너는 돈을 쓰기 전에 두 번 생각해야 한다.
2. 너는 학급 친구들과 싸워서는 안 된다.
3. 너는 인터넷에서 읽은 모든 것을 믿어서는 안 된다.

Point 6 had better, would rather

A 1. rather 2. had
3. replace 4. had better not
5. would rather not

B 1. He had better hurry up
2. You'd better not be late again
3. I would rather not eat anything
4. I would rather take a walk than stay at home

C 1. had better exercise 2. had better not be
3. had better not give up

A [해석]
1. 나는 차라리 그에게 나를 도와달라고 이야기하겠다.
2. 그 아이는 늦게 자지 않는 편이 좋겠다.
3. 깨진 유리창을 당장 교체하는 게 좋겠다.
4. 당신은 아침을 건너뛰지 않는 편이 좋겠다.
5. 우리는 차라리 내일 등산을 가지 않겠다.
[해설]
1. would rather: 차라리 ~하겠다
2~3. had better + 동사원형: ~하는 편이 좋겠다
4~5. had better의 부정은 had better not이고, would rather의 부정은 would rather not이다.

B [해설]
2. had better not('d better not): ~하지 않는 편이 좋겠다
3. would rather not: 차라리 ~하지 않겠다
4. would rather A than B: B하느니 차라리 A하겠다

C [해석]
1. 너는 더 건강해지기 위해서 규칙적으로 운동하는 편이 좋겠다.
2. 너는 학교에 다시 늦지 않는 편이 좋겠다.
3. 우리는 이 좋은 기회를 포기하지 않는 게 좋겠다.
[해설]
1. had better 동사원형: ~하는 편이 좋겠다
2~3. had better not 동사원형: ~하지 않는 편이 좋겠다

Point 7 used to, would

A 1. used to 2. would
3. bite 4. be

B	1. There used to be a big tree		
	2. We used to spend a lot of time outside		
	3. He would give us some presents		
C	1. live	2. measure	3. cooking

A [해설]

1. 과거의 상태를 나타내므로 used to가 온다.

2. 과거의 습관을 나타내므로 would가 온다.

3~4. used to 다음에는 동사원형이 온다.

C [해석]

1. 나는 어릴 때 부산에 살았다.

2. 저울은 물건의 무게를 재는데 사용된다.

3. 그녀는 가족들을 위해 요리하는데 익숙하다.

[해설]

1. used to + 동사원형: ~하곤 했다

2. be used to + 동사원형: ~하는 데에 사용되다

3. be used to + 동명사: ~하는 데에 익숙하다

Point 8 조동사 + have + p.p.

A	1. should have come	2. may have been
	3. must have fought	4. can't have said
B	1. We may have met before	
	2. He must have forgotten the appointment	
	3. You should have told him the truth	
	4. He cannot have made such a big mistake	
C	1 shouldn't have yelled	
	2. may have forgotten	

A [해설]

1. ~했어야만 했다: should have p.p.

2. ~이었을지도 모른다: may have p.p.

3. ~했음이 틀림없다: must have p.p.

4. ~했을 리 없다: cannot have p.p.

일등 비법 노트

비법 1	1. ③	
비법 2	1. ③	
비법 3	1. You will have to finish the work.	
	2. will can → will be able to	
비법 4	1. You had better not eat fast food.	
	2. ③	
비법 5	1. ③	2. ④

비법 1

1 [해석] 손기정은 올림픽 경기에서 한국의 첫 번째 마라톤 우승자였다. 그는 1936년 베를린 올림픽에서 태극기를 달 수 없었는데, 왜냐하면 한국이 그 당시 일본의 식민지였기 때문이다. 대신 그는 일장기를 달아야만 했다. 그 후에, 그는 많은 한국 선수들을 훈련시켰다. 손기정이 훈련시킨 선수 중 한 사람인 서윤복은 1947년 보스톤 마라톤 대회에서 우승할 수 있었다. 그가 성취했던 것은 우리의 역사에서 잊혀져서는 안 된다.

[해설]

ⓐ 조동사 뒤에는 동사원형이 와야 하므로 어법상 맞다.

ⓑ 역사적 사실이고, 'in 과거년도'가 있으므로 과거시제로 쓴 것이 맞다.

ⓒ 조동사 뒤에는 동사원형이 와야 하므로 wearing → wear

ⓓ be able to + 동사원형

ⓔ 조동사 should의 부정은 'should not 동사원형'이다. be not → not be

비법 2

1 [해설] 의미상 '~할 필요가 없다'라는 뜻의 'don't have to'나 'don't need to'로 바꿔 쓸 수 있다.

비법 3

1 [해석] 당신은 그 일을 끝내야만 해요.
[해설] must의 미래는 will have to를 쓴다.

2 [해석] 나는 내년에 새로운 핸드폰을 살 수 있도록 용돈을 모으고 있다.
[해설] can의 미래는 will be able to를 쓴다.

비법 4

1 [해설] had better의 부정은 had better not이다.

2 [해설] would rather의 부정은 would rather not이다.

비법 5

1 [해석]

A: 시험을 망쳤어.

B: 정말? 열심히 공부하지 않았어?

A: 아니, 안 했어. 난 더 열심히 공부했어야만 했어.

[해설] '~했어야만 했다'는 과거에 대한 후회는 should have p.p.를 쓴다.

2 [해석] 그녀는 어제 아팠던 것이 틀림없다.

[해설] 과거에 대한 강한 추측은 must have p.p.를 쓴다.

내신 만점! 실전 기출

01. ②	02. ⑤	03. ③, ⑤
04. ④	05. ③	
06. shouldn't have stayed up		
07. He could speak Japanese.		08. ④
09. ⑤	10. ④	11. ⑤
12. ④	13. ④	14. ②
15. should have finished		
16. may have told	17. ④	18. ④
19. will can → will be able to		
20. you had better not eat with your left hand		
21. ⑤	22. ④	23. ④
24. cannot have gotten(혹은 got) broken		
25. ③	26. ③	
27. She suggested that Mike visit a nursing home on Saturdays.		
28. Minho used to be the fastest student.		
29. must read → must have read		
30. ①		

01 [해석] 당신은 이 일을 마치고 떠날 수 있다.

[해설] 허락의 can은 may로 바꿔 쓸 수 있다.

02 [해설] would like to + 동사원형: ~하고 싶다 (= want to + 동사원형)

03 [해설] '~할 필요가 없다'는 don't have to 또는 need not을 써서 나타낸다.

04 [해석]

① 책 한 권이 당신의 인생을 바꿀 수도 있다.

② 저는 10분 정도 늦을 수도 있어요.

③ 어떤 사람들은 그것이 쉬운 일이라고 말할 수도 있다.

④ 당신은 당신이 원할 때마다 제 것을 써도 좋습니다.

⑤ 그 버스는 교통체증 때문에 연착될 수도 있다.

[해설]

④는 허락의 may, 나머지는 추측을 나타내는 may이다.

05 [해석]

① 그는 내가 하는 말을 어떤 것도 믿지 않을 것이다.

② 나는 같은 실수를 또 하지 않을 것이다.

③ 그녀는 오늘 일찍 일어날 필요가 없다.

④ 그들은 가까운 미래에 결정을 내려야 한다.

⑤ 그 고객들은 다음 달 그 상품을 살 수 있을 것이다.

[해설] ③ 주어가 3인칭 단수 she이므로, 'don't have to'가 아니라 'doesn't have to'가 와야 맞다.

06 [해석]

A: 나는 늦게 일어나서 학교에 또 늦었어.

B: 너는 밤 늦게까지 깨어있지 말았어야 했어.

[해설] '과거에 ~하지 말았어야 했다'의 의미로는 'should not have p.p.'의 형태로 쓴다.

07 [해석] 그는 일본어를 말할 수 있었다.

[해설] was able to는 can의 과거 could로 바꿀 수 있다.

08 [해석] 이 곳에 학교가 있었는데 지금은 더 이상 존재하지 않는다.

[해설] 과거의 상태를 나타내는 경우에는 'used to 동사원형'을 쓴다.

09 [해석] 당신은 그것에 대해 내게 물어봤어야 했다.

= 나는 당신이 그것에 대해 내게 물어보지 않아서 유감이다.

[해설] '~했어야만 했다'는 'should have p.p.'를 써서 나타낸다.

10 [해설] '~했음이 틀림없다'는 'must have p.p.'를 쓴다.

11 [해설] '차라리~하겠다'는 'would rather 동사원형'을 쓴다.

12 [해석] 〈보기〉 이 의자를 사용해도 되나요?
① 그는 5살 때 책을 읽을 수 있었다.
② 저에게 소금을 건네주시겠어요?
③ Gloria는 4개의 언어를 구사할 수 있다.
④ 당신 것이 없으면 내 것을 사용해도 좋아요.
⑤ 그는 그 소식을 듣고 미소 짓지 않을 수 없다.
[해설] 〈보기〉는 허락의 can
①, ③, ⑤는 가능의 can, ②는 요청의 can이고 〈보기〉와 같은 허락의 can은 ④이다.

13 [해석]
① 우리는 돈을 돌려줘야만 한다.
② 그는 시험을 통과하기 위해 열심히 공부해야만 한다
③ 학생들은 시험 때 부정 행위를 해서는 안 된다.
④ 그는 오랜 시간을 걸어서 피곤할 것이 틀림없다.
⑤ 당신은 박물관에서 어떤 작품도 만져서는 안 된다.
[해설] ①, ②, ③, ⑤ 의무를 나타내는 must ④ 강한 추측을 나타내는 must이다.

14 [해설] '~했을 리 없다'는 'cannot have p.p.'를 쓴다.

15 [해설] '~했어야만 했다'는 'should have p.p.'를 쓴다.

16 [해설] '~했을지도 모른다'는 'may have p.p.'를 쓴다.

17 [해석]
A: 숙제 다 했니?
B: 아니요. 하지만 이 프로그램을 보고 나중에 해도 될까요?
A: 안돼. 당장 그 것을 끄는 편이 좋겠다.
[해설] 문맥상 TV를 끄라고 말하는 내용이 어울린다.
had better 동사원형:~하는 편이 낫겠다

18 [해석]
A: 무슨 문제 있어?
B: 난 너무 졸려. 너무 늦게 자지 않았어야 했어.
A: 몇 시에 잠자리에 들었는데?
B: 대략 새벽 세시쯤.
[해설] '~하지 말았어야 했다'는 과거에 대한 후회는 'should not have p.p.'를 쓴다.

19 [해석] 나는 최근에 중국어를 배우기 시작했다. 수업 후, 나는 가능한 여러 번 단어를 적으려고 노력한다. 그렇게 하면 나는 그것들을 더 잘 기억할 수 있을 것이라고 생각한다.
[해설] 조동사는 두 개가 나란히 올 수 없으므로 will can은 will be able to로 쓴다.

20 [해석]
A: Roy, 전에 인도에 가봤다고 들었어. 내게 그들의 문화에 대해서 약간의 정보를 줄 수 있겠니?
B: 응. 알겠어. 먹을 때 왼손을 쓰지 않는 게 좋아. 거기서 그렇게 하는 건 예절에 어긋나.
A: 오, 나는 모르고 있었어. 조언 고마워.
[해설] '~하지 않는 게 좋겠다'는 'had better 동사원형'을 쓴다.

21 [해석]
① 그는 일찍 일어났어야 했다.
② 나는 지금 떠나야만 한다. 그렇지 않으면 늦을 것이다.
③ 그들은 그것에 대해 잊었을 리가 없다.
④ 그녀는 기차에서 잠들었을 수도 있다.
⑤ 그는 교통 체증에 걸려있다. 그는 전철을 탔어야만 했었다.
[해설] should have + p.p.: ~해야만 했는데 그렇게 하지 못했다.

22 [해석] · 그가 그렇게 말하다니 화가 많이 났음이 틀림없다. / · 당신은 그들에게 존경심을 보여야 한다. / · John은 기차를 놓쳤음이 틀림 없다. 그렇지 않으면 그는 이 시간에 여기에 와 있어야 해.
[해설] must는 '~임이 틀림없다' 또는 '~해야 한다'라는 뜻을 나타낸다. 또한, 'must have p.p.'형태로 과거에 대한 강한 추측을 나타낸다.

23 [해석]
① A: 우리는 지금 떠나야만 하나요?
B: 아니요. 그럴 필요 없어요.
② A: 저기 이층 집이 있지 않았나요?
B: 있었지만 더 이상 거기에 없어요.
③ A: 나는 오늘 아침 수업에 늦었어.
B: 넌 더 일찍 일어났어야만 했어.
④ A: 이것을 좀 도와줄 수 있나요?
B: 미안하지만 도와줬을 리 없어요.
⑤ A: 냉장고에 샌드위치가 있어. 그것을 먹는 게 어때?
B: 그걸 먹느니 아무것도 먹지 않겠어.
[해설] ④ 'cannot have p.p.'는 '~이었을리 없다'는 과거에 대한 강한 의심을 나타낸다. 여기서는 지금 도와 줄 수 없다는 내용이므로 'I can't help you.'로 표현해야 맞다.

24 [해석] 그녀의 컴퓨터가 또 망가졌다는 것은 불가능하다.
→ 그녀의 컴퓨터는 또 망가졌을 리 없다.
[해설] '~했을 리 없다'는 과거에 대한 강한 의심은 'cannot have p.p.'를 쓴다.

25 [해석] 요즘 많은 여행객들이 한국에 온다. 당신은 특히 서울에서 아무 때나 그들을 만날 수 있다. 그들 중 많은 사람들이 중국인들이다. 그들은 많은 관광지를 방문하고, 한국 상품들을 사고 한국 음식들을 먹는다. 그들은 돈을 많이 씀으로써 우리 경제에 기여한다. 우리는 그들에게 좋은 인상을 줘야 한다. 그래야 그들이 미래에 다시 방문할 수 있다. 나는 우리가 항상 관광객들에게 잘 해야 한다고 제안한다.
[해설]
ⓒ 내용상 '~했어야만 했다'가 아닌 '~해야 한다'의 should가 와야 한다.
ⓔ 당위를 나타내는 suggest는 종속절에 '주어+(should)+동사원형'으로 써야 하므로 맞다.

26~27 [해설]
주장, 명령, 충고, 제안, 요구, 필요 등을 나타내는 동사나 형용사가 주절에 쓰였을 때, 종속절에는 'should + 동사원형'이 오는데, 이 때의 should는 생략할 수 있다.

26 [해석] 그가 그들의 도움을 요청한 것은 필수적이었다.

27 [해설] visit 앞에 조동사 should가 생략되어 있다.

28 [해석]
A: 너희 학교에서 누가 제일 빠른 학생이니?
B: (예전에는) 민호가 제일 빠른 학생이었지. 하지만 지금은 상호가 가장 빠른 학생이야.
[해설] 과거의 상태는 'used to 동사원형'을 쓴다.

29 [해석] 내 생각에 창수는 이미 그 책을 읽었음이 틀림없어. 그는 그 책의 전체 이야기를 알고 있거든.
[해설] 전체 이야기를 알고 있으므로 그 책을 읽었음이 틀림없다는 내용이 어울리고, 'must have p.p.'를 써야 한다.

30 [해설] 의미상 ⓐ shouldn't → couldn't, ⓑ can't → couldn't, ⓔ can → might[may]가 와야 맞다.

실력 탄탄! 서술형 심화

1 (1) should have listened
(2) cannot have been
(3) must have studied hard

2 (1) should have learned to play the piano
(2) should have made more friends
(3) should have been nicer to her sisters
(4) [예시 답안]
should have exercised more
should have eaten less
should have studied harder

1 [해석]
(1) A: 엄마, 타월을 좀 가져다 주세요. 저는 완전히 젖었어요.
B: 오, Tom. 우산을 가져가지 않았니? 가져가라고 이야기 했잖니.
A: 아니요. 엄마 말을 들었어야만 했어요.
(2) A: Jack은 왜 어제 파티에 오지 않았니?
B: 나는 Jack이 어제 아팠다고 들었어.
A: 그는 아팠을 리 없어. 나는 어제 그를 영화관에서 봤어.
(3) A: Paul이 수학 시험에서 만점을 받은 소식을 들었니?
B: 정말? 그는 열심히 공부했음이 틀림없어. 내가 알기론 그는 수학을 그렇게 잘하지 못하거든.
A: 네 이야기가 맞다고 생각해. 그가 지난 번에 좋은 점수를 받지 못한 것을 기억하거든.
[해설]
(1) ~했어야만 했다: should have p.p.
(2) ~했을 리 없다: cannot have p.p.
(3) ~했음이 틀림 없다: must have p.p.

2 [해석] 〈보기〉 Jenny는 그녀가 책을 더 많은 책을 읽었어야 했다고 생각한다.
(1) Tom은 그가 피아노 연주를 배워야 했다고 생각한다.
(2) Harry는 그가 더 많은 친구를 사귀었어야 했다고 생각한다.
(3) Julie는 그녀가 여동생들에게 더 잘했어야 한다고 생각한다.
[해설] ~했어야만 했다: should have p.p.

Chapter 03 to부정사

Point 1 to부정사의 명사적 용법 I

A 1. 보어　　2. 목적어
3. 주어　　4. 보어

B 1. what　　2. when
3. where　　4. how

C 1. to make comic books
2. To learn a foreign language
3. to become a world-famous singer

A [해설]

1~4. to부정사는 문장에서 명사처럼 주어, 목적어, 보어 역할을 할 수 있다.

1. to become: ~가 되는 것이다 (주격 보어)

2. to watch: ~보는 것을

3. To take care of: 돌보는 것은

4. to study: 공부하라고 (목적격 보어)

B [해설]

1~4. '의문사 + to부정사'는 명사(주로 동사의 목적어) 역할을 한다.

1. what to eat: 무엇을 먹어야 할지

2. when to call: 언제 전화 할지

3. where to go: 어디를 가야 할지

4. how to solve: 어떻게 풀지

Point 2 to부정사의 명사적 용법 II

A 1. It　　2. to drive
3. to tell　　4. it

B 1. is necessary to find your talent
2. is important to have a true friend
3. is fantastic to go to Paris during the vacation

C 1. to go backpacking around the world
2. it is important to read many books
3. how to solve the math problems

A [해설]

1. 진주어인 to make kimchi가 뒤에 있으므로 앞에는 가주어 it이 있어야 한다.

2~3. 앞에 가주어 it이 있으므로 뒤에 진주어인 to부정사가 있음을 알 수 있다.

4. 진목적어인 to부정사가 뒤에 있으므로 동사 바로 뒤에 가목적어 it이 있어야 한다.

C [해설]

1. 문장의 보어로 쓰인 to부정사이다.

2. 종속절(목적어절)의 주어로 쓰인 to부정사이다.

3. how to + 동사원형: 어떻게 ~해야 할지

Point 3 to부정사의 형용사적 용법 I

A 1. to play with　　2. to sit on
3. to do　　4. something to give

B 1. to wash　　2. to talk with
3. to ask　　4. to take care of

C 1. It is time to study　　2. secrets to tell
3. a pencil to write with

A [해설]

1~2. to부정사가 수식하는 명사가 전치사의 목적어로 사용된 경우 to부정사 뒤에 반드시 전치사를 써야 한다.

3. to부정사의 수식을 받는 homework가 전치사의 목적어가 아니므로 전치사를 넣지 않는다.

4. -thing으로 끝나는 대명사를 to부정사가 수식할 때 '-thing + to부정사'의 어순으로 쓴다.

B [해설]

1, 3. to부정사는 바로 앞에 나온 명사(time, a question)를 형용사처럼 꾸며준다.

2, 4. 부정사가 수식하는 명사가 전치사의 목적어로 사용된 경우이므로 to부정사 뒤에 반드시 전치사를 써야 한다.

C [해설]

1~2. to부정사는 바로 앞에 나온 명사를 형용사처럼 꾸며준다.

3. 부정사가 수식하는 명사가 전치사의 목적어로 사용된 경우이므로 to부정사 뒤에 반드시 전치사를 써야 한다.

Point 4 to부정사의 형용사적 용법 II

A 1. ⓑ 의무 2. ⓒ 가능 3. ⓔ 운명
4. ⓐ 예정 5. ⓓ 의도

B 1. am to ride 2. were to fall
3. are to submit

C 1. is to be held 2. are to come back

A [해설]
1. are to clean: 깨끗이해야 한다 (의무)
2. was to be seen: 보였다 (가능)
3. was to be: 될 운명이었다 (운명)
4. is to arrive: 도착할 예정이다 (예정)
5. are to enter: 입학할 작정이다 (의도)

B [해설]
1. am to ride: 자전거를 탈 것이다 (예정)
2. were to fall: 빠질 운명이었다 (운명)
3. are to submit: 제출해야 한다 (의무)

Point 5 to부정사의 부사적 용법 I

A 1. to stay 2. to see
3. not to be 4. to buy
5. so as to learn

B 1. order not to fail the exam, as not to fail the exam
2. order to make a reservation, as to make a reservation

C 1. to buy some fruits
2. not to fail
3. in order not to forget

A [해설]
1. to stay healthy: 건강을 유지하기 위해
2. to see a movie: 영화를 보기 위해
3. not to be late: 늦지 않기 위해
4. to buy: 구입하기 위해
5. so as to learn: 배우기 위해

B [해설]
1~2. to부정사가 목적(~하기 위해)으로 쓰이면, 'in order to + 동사원형' 또는 'so as to + 동사원형'으로 바꿔 쓸 수 있다. to부정사의 부정형은 to 앞에 not을 붙인다.

Point 6 to부정사의 부사적 용법 II

A 1. 판단의 근거 2. 감정의 원인 3. 결과

B 1. to tell the truth
2. to help the poor children there

C 1. very happy to win 2. grew up to be

A [해설]
1. 판단의 근거: '~하다니'라는 뜻이다.
2. 감정의 원인: 감정을 나타내는 형용사뒤에 to부정사가 오면, '~해서, ~하니'라고 해석한다.

B [해설]
1. must be honest to tell the truth: 진실을 말하다니 정직함에 틀림없다 (판단의 근거)
2. to help: 돕기 위해서 (목적)

C [해설]
1. happy to win: ~(상)을 타서 기쁜 (감정의 원인)
2. grew up to be: 자라서 ~가 되다 (결과)

Point 7 to부정사의 의미상의 주어, to부정사의 부정

A 1. for 2. for 3. of
4. for 5. of

B 1. not to miss the train
2. decided not to attend the meeting
3. impossible for me

C 1. for us to tell a lie
2. to swim in the deep sea

A [해석]
1. 이 버스가 우리가 탈 버스다.
2. 신선한 바람이 들어오도록 하기위해 창문을 열었다.
3. 노인이 자리에 앉도록 도와주는 그녀는 친절하다.

4. 인터뷰를 하는 것은 그에게 중요하다.

5. 그들의 선생님을 위해 깜짝 파티를 계획하는 그들은 매우 사려깊다.

[해설]

1~2, 4. 대부분의 to부정사의 의미상의 주어로 'for + 목적격'을 쓴다.

3, 5. 'of + 목적격'은 to부정사 앞에 사람의 성격을 나타내는 형용사(kind, thoughtful 등)가 있을 때 쓴다.

B [해설]

1~2. to 부정사의 부정은 to부정사 앞에 not을 붙인다.

Point 8 to부정사의 시제

A 1. be 2. had been 3. they know
4. she saw something in the kitchen

B 1. seems to have had fun
2. seems to have enjoyed
3. seemed to like spicy food

A [해설]

1. 주절의 시제와 종속절의 시제가 같으므로 'seem to 동사원형'으로 바꿀 수 있다.

2, 4. 완료부정사(to have p.p.)는 본동사보다 한 시제 앞선 것이므로 복문으로 고칠 때 주절의 시제보다 한 시제 앞서게 한다.

3. 단순부정사(to + 동사원형)는 본동사와 같은 시제이므로 복문으로 고칠 때 종속절의 동사의 시제를 주절의 동사와 같게 한다.

Point 9 목적어, 목적격 보어로 쓰이는 to부정사

A 1. to study 2. to take 3. to meet
4. to win 5. to play

B 1. to study 2. to buy 3. to visit
4. to take 5. to ride

C 1. want to live
2. allowed his son to play
3. expects me to come home

A [해설]

1. wish(소망하다), would like(하고 싶어하다), expect(기대하다)는 미래상관동사들로 목적어로 to부정사가 오는 동사들이다.

2~5. 5형식에서 목적어와 목적격 보어가 '주 + 동'관계일 때는 목적격 보어로 to부정사가 온다.

B [해설]

1~4. advise, want, decide, ask 등의 동사 + 목적어 + to부정사: ~가 …하도록 조언하다/원하다/결정하다/부탁하다

C [해설]

1. want + to부정사: ~하기를 원하다

2. allow + 목적어 + to부정사: ~가 …하도록 허락하다

3. expect + 목적어 + to부정사: ~가 …하기를 기대하다

Point 10 사역동사 + 목적어 + 원형부정사

A 1. helping → help 2. to cry → cry
3. to dance → dance 4. pick → to pick
5. fixing → fixed 6. moving → (to) move
7. to go → go

B 1. have Ron call me back
2. had the waiter bring
3. got my sister to clean
4. made us think about
5. helped her little son put on

A [해설]

1~3, 5, 7. 사역동사 make, have, let은 목적격 보어로 원형부정사를 쓴다.

4. get은 사역동사의 의미를 갖지만 목적격 보어로 to부정사가 온다.

5. 목적어와 목적격 보어가 수동 관계일 때 사역동사라도 목적격 보어로 과거분사를 쓴다.

6. help는 목적격 보어로 to부정사와 원형부정사 둘 다 올 수 있다.

B [해설]

1~2, 4. 사역동사 make, have, let은 목적격 보어로 원형부정사를 쓴다.

3. get은 사역동사의 의미를 갖지만 목적격 보어로 to부정사가 온다.

5. help는 목적격 보어로 to부정사와 원형부정사를 쓴다.

Point 11 지각동사 + 목적어 + 원형부정사

A	1. dance	2. run	3. shouting
	4. make	5. touching	6. repairing
	7. sing	8. be	9. playing
	10. to finish		
B	1. burn[burning]	2. stare[staring]	
	3. cry[crying]	4. leave[leaving]	

A [해설]

1~7, 9. 지각동사(see, look at, watch, listen to, hear, feel, smell, notice 등)는 목적어와 목적격 보어의 관계가 능동일 때, 목적격 보어로 원형부정사나 현재분사를 쓴다.

8. 사역동사 make는 목적격 보어로 원형부정사를 쓴다.

10. help는 목적격 보어로 to부정사와 원형부정사를 쓴다.

Point 12 자주 쓰이는 to부정사 구문

A
1. too hot to drink
2. long enough to measure
3. too busy to answer
4. too cold to wear

B
1. smart that she could
2. strong that he can
3. shy that she[he] can't
4. small that it can't hold all my textbooks

C
1. too cold to go　　2. fast enough to win
3. too expensive to buy

A [해설]

1. too hot to drink: 너무 뜨거워서 마실 수 없는

2. long enough to measure: 측정하기에 충분히 긴

3. too busy to answer: 너무 바빠서 바로 (전화를) 받을 수 없는

4. too cold to wear: 너무 추워서 입을 수 없는

B [해설]

1~2. 형용사/부사 + enough + to부정사 = so ~ that + 주어 + can: 할 수 있을 정도로 충분히 ~한

3~4. too + 형용사/부사 + to부정사 = so ~ that + 주어 + can't

일등 비법 노트

비법 1	1. ③
비법 2	1. ①
비법 3	1. pretend not to see them 2. The teacher told us not to use cell phones in class.
비법 4	1. I want to refund it. 2. [예시 답안] (1) I am planning to watch a movie this weekend. (2) I am planning to go shopping this weekend.
비법 5	1. friend to play with
비법 6	1. ④　　2. how to use

비법 1

1 [해설]

①, ③, ⑤ kind, silly, careless는 사람의 성품을 나타내는 형용사이므로 to부정사의 의미상 주어는 'of + 목적격'으로 써야 한다. (for → of)

②, ④ hard, difficult는 사람의 성품을 나타내는 말이 아니므로 to부정사의 의미상 주어는 'for + 목적격'으로 써야 한다. (② of him → for him, ④ of me → for me)

비법 2

1 [해설]

① 지각동사 + 목적어 + 원형부정사 = felt the floor shake: 바닥이 흔들리는 것을 느꼈다.

②~⑤ wish, expect, want, get은 뒤에 to부정사를 쓴다.

② wants me to visit: 내가 집을 방문하기를 원한다

③ expect him to make: 그가 만드는 것을 기대한다

④ wish to study: 공부하기를 소망한다

⑤ got her students to clean: 그녀의 학생들이 청소하게 했다

비법 3

1 [해석] 한국사람들은 때때로 서양인들이 서로 키스를 할 때 불편함을 느낀다. 그들이(서양인들이) 키스를 할 때, 한국 사람들은 때때로 다른 곳을 보거나 (그들을 보지 않는 척 한다.)
[해설] pretend는 부정사를 목적어로 취하는 동사이고, 부정사의 부정은 'not + to + 동사원형'이다.

2 [해설] tell은 to부정사를 목적격 보어로 취하는 동사이고, '휴대폰을 사용하지 말라'고 하셨으므로 부정사의 부정인 not to use를 써야 한다.

비법 4

1 [해설] want + to부정사: ~하기를 원하다

2 [해설] plan은 to부정사를 목적어로 취하는 동사이므로 'I am planning' 뒤에 'to + 동사원형'의 형태로 쓴다.

비법 5

1 [해설] 부정사의 수식을 받는 명사 a friend를 play 뒤에 놓아보면 play with a friend가 되어야 한다. 그러므로 부정사 to play 뒤에도 with를 넣어야 한다.

비법 6

1 [해설]
ⓐ 부정사 'to take care'의 수식을 받는 명사 children을 부정사 뒤에 넣어보면 'to take care of children'이 되어야 하므로 부정사 뒤에 of를 써야 한다.
ⓑ 'only to 동사원형' → '결국 ~했다'
ⓒ 5형식에서 긴 to부정사구가 목적어이면, 가목적어 it을 쓰고 to부정사구는 뒤로 보낸다.
ⓓ '의문사 how + to부정사' → ~하는 방법
ⓔ '의문사 to부정사' = '의문사 주어 should 동사원형'

2 [해설] '의문사 to부정사' = '의문사 주어 should 동사원형'

내신 만점! 실전 기출

01. ④ **02.** ①, ⑤ **03.** to become
04. ③ **05.** how to play the flute
06. ③
07. to hate her children's bad habits
08. ①
09. (1) be proud of himself[herself]
(2) he[she] is proud of himself[herself]
10. ③ **11.** ③ **12.** ⑤
13. (1) felt someone grab
(2) see my mom get angry
14. Her parents are so poor that they can't pay her school tuition.
15. ①
16. when to meet[see] my older sister[her]
17. ④ **18.** ③, ④
19. She asked him to eat together.
20. ② **21.** ⑤ **22.** ②
23. ④ **24.** ③
25. (1) had me feed the dog
(2) asked me to take care of my brother
26. ④
27. (1) She was so busy that she couldn't attend the meeting.
(2) He is so diligent that he can get up early every morning.
28. (It) is important for him to practice as much as possible
29. (1) for you → of you (2) of him → for him
(3) O (4) of her → for her (5) O (6) O
30. ②

01 [해석] 그녀는 그가 방과 후에 영어를 공부하도록 했다.
[해설] ④ tell은 목적격 보어 자리에 to부정사를 쓴다.
①, ③, ⑤ 사역동사(make, have, let)은 목적격 보어로 원형부정사를 쓴다.
② 지각동사(see)는 목적격 보어로 원형부정사를 쓴다.

02 [해석] 나는 그가 영어 말하기 대회에서 금메달 따는 것을 보았다.
[해설] 지각동사(see)는 목적격 보어로 원형부정사를 쓰고, 진행의 의미를 강조할 때는 목적격 보어로 현재분사를 쓰기도 한다.

03 [해설] to부정사가 '감정의 원인'의 의미를 나타내면 부사적용법이라 하며 '~하니', '~해서'의 의미로 쓰인다. (happy to become ~: ~가 되어 기쁜)

04 [해석] 종이 한 장은 나의 소원들을 적기에는 충분하지 않다.
[해설] 「형용사/부사 + enough + to부정사」는 '~할 수 있을 정도로 충분히 ~한'이라는 뜻이다.

05 [해석] 나는 플루트 연주하는 법을 배우기를 희망한다.
[해설] '의문사 + to부정사'는 명사구의 역할을 하며 '의문사 + 주어 + should + 동사원형'으로 바꾸어 쓸 수 있다.

06 [해석]
· 그녀는 겨울방학 동안 파리 여행하기를 원한다.
· Tony의 엄마는 그가 컴퓨터 게임 하는 것을 허락하셨다.
[해설]
· want + to부정사 + 동사원형: ~을 원하다
· allow + 목적어 + to부정사: ~가 ~할 것을 허락하다

07 [해석] Mrs. Wilson은 그녀 아이들의 나쁜 습관을 몹시 싫어하는 듯 하다.
[해설] 단순부정사는 본동사와 시제가 같음을 의미한다. 복문으로 고칠 때는 종속절의 시제를 주절과 같게 하여 '주어 + seem(s) + to부정사 ~ = It seems that + 주어 + 동사 ~'로 고친다.

08 [해석]
① 나는 빨리 운전하는 것이 위험하다는 것을 알았다.
② 꿈을 가지는 것은 중요하다.
③ 컴퓨터를 고치는 것은 쉽지 않다.
④ 질문에 답하는 것은 어렵다.
⑤ 내가 그것을 정오까지 끝내는 것은 불가능하다.
[해설] ① 동사 뒤에 가목적어 it이 있으므로 뒤에 진짜 목적어인 to부정사가 와야 한다. drive → to drive

09 [해설] 주어 + seem(s) + to 동사원형 = It seems that + 주어 + 주절과 같은 시제의 동사 ~.

10 [해석] 그는 내 이웃들 중의 한 명인 것 같다.
[해설] 주어 + seem(s) + to부정사 ~. = It seems that + 주어 + 동사 ~.

11 [해석] 1960년대에는 많은 한국 간호사들과 광부들이 일을 하기 위해 독일로 갔다.
① 그녀는 항상 배드민턴 치는 것을 원한다.
② 내게 배드민턴을 칠 라켓을 주어라.
③ 그녀는 그녀가 배드민턴을 즐기기 위해 친다고 말했다.
④ 배드민턴 경기를 이기는 것은 쉽지 않다.
⑤ 슈퍼마켓에서 살 것들이 많이 있다.
[해설] ⓐ to work: 일을 하기 위해 (부사적 용법: 목적)
① want to play badminton: 배드민턴 치는 것을 원하다 (명사적 용법: 목적어 역할)
② a racket to play badminton with: 배드민턴을 칠 라켓 (형용사적 용법)
③ to have fun: 즐기기 위해서 (부사적 용법: 목적)
④ to win: 이기는 것은 (명사적 용법: 주어 역할)
⑤ to buy: 사야 할 (형용사적 용법)

12 [해석]
① 그녀는 어디로 가야 할지 몰랐다.
② 언제 보고서를 제출해야 하는지 내게 말해주세요.
③ 나는 Tom에게 그가 파티에 무엇을 준비해야 할지 말했다.
④ 이 기계를 어떻게 사용하는지 내게 알려 줄래?
⑤ 그는 내게 수학 문제를 어떻게 푸는지 가르쳐 주었다.
[해설]
①~④ 의문사 뒤에 오는 to부정사의 의미상 주어가 문장의 주어와 같으므로, '의문사 + 주어 + should + 동사원형'에서의 주어는 문장 주어와 일치시킨다.
⑤ 'He told me how to solve the math problem.'에서 'to solve'의 의미상 주어는 me이므로 복문으로 고칠 때 종속절의 주어는 I가 되어야 한다. 'He told me how I should solve the math problem.'이 된다.

13 [해석]
(1) A: 무슨 일이니?
B: 조용히 해. 나는 누군가 내 가방을 잡는 것이 느껴져.
(2) A: 너는 언제 슬프니?
B: 나는 엄마가 나에게 화난 것을 볼 때 슬퍼.
[해설] 지각동사(feel, see)뒤에는 목적어 + 원형부정사의 형태로 쓴다.

14 [해석]
A: Sally에게 무슨 일이 있는 거니?
B: 그녀의 부모님은 너무 가난해서 학비를 낼 수가 없어.
[해설] 'too + 형용사/부사 + to부정사(너무 ~해서 ~할 수 없는)'는 'so ~ that + 주어 + can't'로 바꾸어 쓸 수 있다.

15 [해석]

① 그렇게 말하다니 그는 관대하다.
② 시험에서 떨어지다니 나는 어리석었다.
③ 다른 사람들을 돕다니 그녀는 착하다.
④ 아침 일찍 일어나는 것은 내게는 어렵다.
⑤ 밤 늦게 나가는 것은 그들에게 위험하다.

[해설] ①~③ to부정사 앞에 사람의 성격이나 주관적 평가를 나타내는 형용사(generous, silly, nice)가 있으면 'of + 형용사'를 쓴다.

② for me → of me
③ for her → of her
④ of me → for me
⑤ of them → for them

16 [해설] '언제 만날 지(를)' → when to meet. '의문사 + to부정사'는 명사구의 역할을 한다.

17 [해석]

〈보기〉 그의 질문은 내가 대답하기엔 너무 어렵다.
① 나에게 수학을 가르쳐주다니 그녀는 착하다.
② 음식을 요리하는 것은 그에겐 쉽지 않다.
③ 영어로 말하는 것은 내겐 어렵다.
④ 이 닭고기 스프는 내가 먹기엔 너무 뜨겁다.
⑤ 선생님에게 말대꾸를 하다니 그들은 무례하다.

[해설] 〈보기〉, ⓑ, ⓒ, ⓓ: to부정사의 의미상 주어로 'for + 목적격'을 취한다.
ⓐ, ⓔ 앞에 사람의 성품을 나타내는 형용사가 있으므로 to부정사의 의미상 주어로 'of + 목적격'을 취한다.

18 [해석]

① 그는 유명해지기를 원한다.
② 나는 더 열심히 공부하기로 결심했다.
③ 그녀는 점심식사 후에 시작하는 것에 동의했다.
④ 나는 네가 네 미래의 꿈에 대해 생각했으면 한다.
⑤ 그들은 언젠가 그 연사를 다시 보기를 기대한다.

[해설]

③ agree는 to부정사를 목적어로 취한다. agreed starting를 agreed to start로 바꾸어야 한다.
④ would like는 5형식에서 목적어와 목적격 보어가 능동의 '주 + 동'관계일 때, 목적격 보어로 to부정사를 취한다. think → to think

19 [해설] 5형식에서 목적어와 목적격 보어가 능동의 '주 + 동' 관계일 때, 목적격 보어로 to부정사를 취한다.

20 [해석]

① 강에서 수영하기엔 날씨가 너무 추웠다.
② 날씨가 너무 추워서 나는 강에서 수영할 수 있었다.
③ 날씨가 너무 추워서 나는 강에서 수영할 수 없었다.
④ 날씨가 매우 추웠다. 그래서 나는 강에서 수영할 수 없었다.
⑤ 날씨가 너무 추웠기 때문에 나는 강에서 수영할 수 없었다.

[해설]

①, ③~⑤: 너무 추워서 강에서 수영할 수 없었다는 의미이다.
② 너무 추워서(too cold) 강에서 수영할 수 있었다로 그 의미가 나머지 넷과 같지 않다.

21 [해석]

(1) 그녀는 내가 스파게티를 어떻게 만드는 지 물어보기 위해 전화했다.
(2) 끝났어요. 학교에서 언제 떠날 지 말해주세요.
(3) 그 나쁜 소식을 들어서 유감이다. 네게 뭐라 말할 지 모르겠다.
(4) 나 좀 도와줄래? 나는 정말로 이 문제를 어떻게 푸는지 모르겠어.

[해설]

(1) ③ how to make: 어떻게 만드는지
(2) ④ when to leave: 언제 떠날지
(3) ① what to say to: 뭐라 말할지
(4) ② how to solve: 어떻게 푸는지
⑤ where to meet: 어디서 만날지

22 [해석] 너 자신을 잘 알기 위한 가장 좋은 방법은 네가 무엇을 잘하는지 알아내는 것이다. 그것은 네 자신을 더 잘 이해할 수 있고 너를 위한 적절한 직업을 찾는 데에도 도움을 줄 수 있다.

① 나는 마실 무엇인가가 필요하다.
② 그의 취미는 책을 읽는 것이다.
③ 그녀는 시험에 통과하기 위해서 공부했다.
④ 그는 에펠탑을 보기 위해서 프랑스에 갔다.
⑤ 너는 맞는 직업을 찾기 위해 너 자신을 잘 알아야 한다.

[해설] ⓐ to find out: ~찾는 것(이다) (명사적 용법: 보어 역할)

① to drink: 마실 (형용사적 용법)
② to take: 찍는 것 (명사적 용법: 보어 역할)
③ to pass: 통과하기 위해서(부사적 용법: 목적)
④ to see: 보기 위해서 (부사적 용법: 목적)
⑤ to find: 찾기 위해서 (부사적 용법: 목적)

23 [해석] 나의 가족은 언니를 제외하고는 캠핑에 갔다. 그녀는 그룹 프로젝트를 준비해야 해서 우리와 합류 할 시간이 없었다. 나는 그녀가 다음 번에는 우리와 함께 가기를 희망한다.
① 그들은 햄버거 먹기를 원한다.
② 너를 다시 만나서 기쁘다.
③ 컴퓨터 게임을 하는 것은 흥미진진하다.
④ 나는 비행기에서 읽을 잡지가 필요하다.
⑤ 그는 만리장성을 보기 위해 중국에 갔다.
[해설] ⓐ to join: 합류할 (형용사적 용법)
① to have: 먹기를 (명사적 용법: 목적어)
② glad to meet: 만나서 반가운 (부사적 용법: 감정의 원인)
③ to play computer games: 컴퓨터 게임을 하는 것은 (명사적 용법: 주어)
④ a magazine to read: 읽을 잡지 (형용사적 용법)
⑤ to see: 보기 위해서 (부사적 용법: 목적)

24 [해석] 그 풍차는 바람을 이용하여 전기를 만들었다. 그녀는 풍차가 잘 작동하는 것을 보고 놀랐다. 그녀는 기뻐서 박수를 쳤다.
① 나는 그가 일찍 올 것을 기대한다.
② 그녀는 나에게 입을 재킷을 주었다.
③ 그는 학교에 돌아와서 기뻤다.
④ 나의 꿈은 영어 선생님이 되는 것이다.
⑤ 외국어를 배우는 것은 어렵다.
[해설] ⓐ amazed to see: 보아서 놀란 (부사적 용법: 감정의 원인)
① expect + 목적어 + to부정사: ~가 …하기를 기대하다
② a jacket to wear: 입을 재킷 (형용사적 용법)
③ glad to be back: 돌아와서 기쁜 (부사적 용법: 감정의 원인)
④ 명사적 용법: 보어 역할
⑤ to learn: 배우는 것은 (명사적 용법: 주어 역할) (가주어 it, 진짜 주어는 to learn a foreign language)

25 [해석]
Q1: 엄마는 네게 아침에 무엇을 하게 하셨니?
A1: 엄마는 내게 강아지 밥을 주게 하셨다.
Q2: 엄마는 네게 오후에 무엇을 하게 하셨니?
A2: 엄마는 내게 나의 남동생을 돌보라고 하셨다.
[해설]
Q1: 사역동사(have)는 목적격 보어로 원형부정사가 온다.
Q2: ask + 목적어 + to부정사: ~에게 ~하라고 부탁하다

26 [해석] 너는 여름방학 동안 어디에 갈 건지 특별한 계획이 있니? 만일 없다면, 영국을 방문하는 건 어때? 너는 타워브리지, 버킹엄 궁전, 그리고 런던아이를 볼 수 있어.
① A: 나는 이 기계를 어떻게 사용하는지 모르겠다.
B: 사용서를 읽자.
② A: 엄마는 화가 났다. 나는 그녀에게 뭐라 말할지 모르겠다.
B: 그녀에게 죄송하다고 해라.
③ A: 나는 오늘 오후에 James를 만날 것이다. 나와 함께 가자.
B: 좋아. 어디에서 언제 만날지 말해 줘.
④ A: 네 재킷이 예쁘다. 어디에서 살 수 있는지 말해줄래?
B: 나는 Lily's Closet에서 샀어.
⑤ A: 나는 두 명의 학생에게 설문조사를 해야 해.
B: 정말? 너는 누구에게 설문 질문을 물어볼지 결정했니?
[해설]
ⓐ where to go: 어디로 갈지
① how to use: 어떻게 사용하는지
② what to tell: 무어라 말할지
③ where and when to meet: 어디에서 언제 만날지
④ where to buy: 어디에서 살 수 있는지
⑤ whom to ask: 누구에게 물어볼지

27 [해석]
(1) 그녀는 너무 바빠서 회의에 참석할 수 없었다.
(2) 그는 매일 아침 일찍 일어날 수 있을 만큼 근면하다.
[해설]
(1) 'too + 형용사/부사 + to부정사'는 '너무 ~해서 ~할 수 없다'라는 뜻이며' 'so ~ that + 주어 + can't로 바꿔 쓸 수 있다.
(2) '형용사/부사 + enough + to부정사'는 '~할 수 있을 정도로 충분히 ~한'이라는 뜻이며, 'so ~ that + 주어 + can'으로 바꿔 쓸 수 있다.

28 [해석]
W: Kevin은 훌륭한 가수가 되기 위해 무엇을 해야 하니?
M: 연습을 가능한 한 많이 하는 것은 그에게 중요해.
[해설] to부정사의 의미상의 주어는 대개 'for + 목적격'를 쓴다.

29 [해석]
(1) 나를 돕다니 너는 매우 착하다.
(2) 가난한 사람들을 돕는 것은 그에게 자연스럽다.
(3) 지갑을 잃어버리다니 너는 부주의 하다.
(4) 그녀가 학급 회장이 되는 것은 가능하다.
(5) 이 기회를 우리에게 주다니 너는 매우 관대하다.
(6) 나의 선생님은 우리들에게 수업시간에 소란을 피우지 말라고 말씀하셨다.
[해설]
(1) to부정사 앞에 사람의 성품을 나타내는 형용사(nice)가 있으므로 'of + 목적격'으로 써야 한다. (for you → of you)
(2) to부정사의 의미상 주어는 대개 'for + 목적격'을 써야 한다. 따라서, 'of him'을 'for him'으로 바꾼다.
(4) to부정사 앞에 사람의 성품을 나타내는 형용사가 오면 의미상의 주어로 'of + 목적격'을 쓴다. possible은 사람의 성격을 나타내는 형용사가 아니므로 'for + 목적격'을 써야 한다.

30 [해석] Wright 형제는 최초의 비행기를 발명했다. 그들은 그것이 하늘을 나는 것을 보고 매우 흥분했다. 사람들은 그들의 첫 번째 비행기를 보기 위해 왔다. 그것은 단지 12초만 날았다. 대부분의 사람들은 그들을 비웃었지만 그들은 더 열심히 연구하고 더 나은 것을 만들 것이라 결심했다. 그들은 성공을 하기 위해 기계 조작 기술을 익히고 많은 책들을 읽었다.
[해설]
ⓐ excited to see it: 그것을 보고 신이 난 (부사적 용법: 감정의 원인)
ⓑ to see ~: ~을 보기 위해 (부사적 용법: 목적)
ⓒ decided to study: 연구할 것을 결심했다. (명사적 용법: 목적어)
ⓓ to succeed: 성공하기 위해서 (부사적 용법: 목적)

실력 탄탄! 서술형 심화

1 (1) asked him to wash the dishes
(2) how to get to the bank
(3) difficult for me to answer

2 ⓐ inconsiderate of her to make
ⓑ foolish of her to keep
ⓒ easy for her to be quiet

1 [해석]
(A) A: Nick의 엄마가 그에게 무엇을 부탁했니?
B: 그의 엄마가 설거지를 부탁하셨어.
(B) B: 이곳에서 은행에 어떻게 가는지 말씀해 주시겠어요?
G: 물론이죠. 752번 버스를 타세요.
(C) B: 영어시험 어땠니?
G: 질문들에 답하기가 어려웠어.
[해설]
(A) ask는 목적격 보어로 to부정사가 오는 동사로 목적어 + to부정사로 쓰며, '~가 …하도록 부탁하다'는 뜻이다.
(B) how to + 동사원형: 어떻게 ~할지/ ~하는 방법
(C) to부정사의 의미상 주어는 to부정사 앞에 'for + 목적격'으로 쓴다.

2 [해석]
G: 나는 이사를 생각 중이야. 내 룸메이트는 밤 늦게 너무 소란스러워. ⓐ 그녀가 소음을 만드는 것은 정말 사려 깊지 못한 거야.
B: 안됐구나. 그녀와 그 문제에 대해 이야기 해 봤니?
G: 물론 했지만 변한 건 없어.
B: ⓑ 계속 시끄럽게 하다니 그녀는 어리석구나.
G: 그러게 말이야. ⓒ 아마도, 밤 늦게 조용히 하는 것이 그녀에게는 쉽지 않은가 봐.
B: 네가 더 좋은 장소를 찾기 바랄게.
[해설] ⓐ~ⓑ 사람의 성격이나 주관적 평가를 나타내는 형용사(inconsiderate, foolish)의 to부정사의 보어로 쓰이면 'of + 목적격 + to부정사'를 쓴다.
ⓒ to부정사의 의미상 주어는 to부정사 앞에 'for + 목적격'으로 쓴다.

Chapter 04 동명사

Point 1 동명사의 역할 I – 주어, 보어

A	1. is	2. Drawing	3. Being
	4. is	5. correcting	
B	1. winning	2. Keeping	3. watching
C	1. Watching	2. solving	3. climbing
	4. Living	5. getting	

A [해설]

1, 4. 주어로 쓰인 동명사는 단수로 취급한다.

2, 3. 문장의 주어자리에 오는 동사는 동명사나 to부정사의 형태로 온다.

5. 문장의 보어자리에 오는 동사는 동명사나 to부정사의 형태로 온다.

B [해설]

1, 3. 문장의 보어로 쓰인 명사적 용법의 to부정사로 동명사와 바꾸어 쓸 수 있다.

2. 문장의 주어로 쓰인 명사적 용법의 to부정사로 동명사와 바꾸어 쓸 수 있다.

C [해설]

1, 4. 문장의 주어 역할을 하는 동명사 형태로 와야 한다.

2~3, 5. 문장의 보어 역할을 하는 동명사 형태로 와야 한다.

Point 2 동명사의 역할 II – 목적어

A	1. opening	2. working	
	3. inviting	4. going	
B	1. O	2. meeting	3. making
C	1. being late	2. learning	3. doing

A [해설]

1~2, 4. mind, enjoy, give up은 동명사를 목적어로 취하는 동사들이다.

3. 전치사의 목적어로는 to부정사는 오지 못하고, 동명사만 올 수 있다.

B [해설]

1, 3. 전치사의 목적어로는 동명사가 온다.

2. avoid, practice, finish는 동명사를 목적어로 취하는 동사들이다.

Point 3 동명사의 의미상의 주어, 동명사의 부정

A	1. my[me]	2. their[them]
	3. her	4. his[him]
B	1. not coming	2. my[me] turning
	3. his[him] not cleaning	
C	1. her being	2. not missing

A [해설] 문장의 주어와 동명사의 의미상 주어가 다르므로 동명사 앞에 소유격 혹은 목적격으로 써 준다.

B [해설]

1. 동명사의 의미상 주어가 문장의 주어와 같으므로 따로 쓰지 않는다.

2~3. 동명사의 의미상 주어가 문장의 주어, 목적어와 같지 않으므로 동명사 앞에 소유격, 목적격으로 나타낸다.

C [해설]

1. 앞에 전치사가 있으므로 동명사를 써야 하고, 동명사의 의미상 주어가 문장의 주어와 다르므로 동명사 앞에 소유격/목적격으로 쓴다.

2. 앞에 전치사가 있으므로 동명사를 써야 한다. 동명사의 의미상 주어가 문장의 주어와 같으므로 따로 쓰지 않는다.

Point 4 동명사의 시제와 태

A	1. being	2. having lost
	3. being accepted	4. having been treated
	5. not having been known	
B	1. her being	
	2. me losing confidence	
	3. my having given up the competition	

A [해설]

1. 주절의 시제와 종속절의 시제가 같으므로 '동사원형-ing'의 형태로 쓴다.

2. 종속절의 시제가 주절의 시제보다 한 시제 앞서므로 'having + p.p.'의 형태로 쓴다.

4. 종속절의 시제가 주절의 시제보다 한 시제 앞서는 〈수동태〉 문장이므로 'having + been + p.p.'의 형태로 쓴다.

5. 종속절의 시제가 주절의 시제보다 한 시제 앞서는 〈수동태〉 문장이므로 'having + been + p.p.'의 형태로 쓰고, 부정의 not을 동명사 앞에 쓴다.

Point 5 동명사 *vs.* to부정사 I

A 1. to stop 2. to save 3. waiting
4. to go 5. playing 6. talking

B 1. O 2. to visit
3. O 4. listening

C 1. to accept 2. running
3. to start 4. to finish

A [해설]

1~2, 4. promise, decide, plan은 to부정사를 목적어로 취한다.

3, 5~6. mind, practice, stop은 동명사를 목적어로 취한다.

B [해설]

1, 3~4. give up, consider, enjoy는 동명사를 목적어로 취한다.

2. hope는 to부정사를 목적어로 취한다.

C [해설]

1, 3~4. refuse, want, expect는 to부정사를 목적어로 취한다.

2. practice는 동명사를 목적어로 취한다.

Point 6 동명사 *vs.* to부정사 II

A 1. (a) not keeping (b) to say
2. (a) to open (b) adding
3. (a) to buy (b) telling
4. (a) to pick (b) drinking
5. (a) to bring (b) leaving

B 1. loves climbing
2. continued playing soccer

A [해석]

1. (a) 그는 자신이 약속을 지키지 않은 것을 후회한다.
(b) 당신이 우리 팀 멤버로 선택되지 못한 것을 말하게 되어 유감입니다.

2. (a) 그녀는 병 뚜껑을 열려고 애썼으나, 열지 못했다.
(b) 그녀는 김치찌개에 시험 삼아 설탕을 넣어 보았다.

3. (a) 집에 오는 길에 아이스크림 사오는 거 기억해 주세요.
(b) 그는 나에게 동물원에 데려가 주겠다고 말한 것을 기억하지 못했다.

4. (a) 상호는 복도에 있는 휴지를 줍기 위해 멈췄다.
(b) 그녀는 밤에 잠을 잘 자기 위해 늦은 오후에 커피를 마시는 것을 그만 두었다.

5. (a) 나는 과학 책을 가져오는 것을 잊었다. 그래서 친구와 함께 책을 보았다.
(b) 엄마는 그녀의 지갑을 차에 둔 것을 잊어버리고 집 안에서 그것을 찾아 다녔다.

[해설]

1. (a) 문맥상 '과거에 약속을 지키지 않은 것을 후회'하는 것이고, 과거의 사실에 대한 후회는 'regret + -ing'로 쓴다.
(b) 좋지 않은 소식을 알리게 되었으므로 '~하게 되어 유감이다'의 뜻이 필요하고, 그 형태로는 'regret + to동사원형'을 쓴다.

2. (a) 문맥상 '열려고 애썼으나 열지 못했다'의 의미이고, '~하려고 애쓰다'의 의미가 필요하므로 'try + to 동사원형'
(b) '시험 삼아 김치찌개에 설탕을 넣어 본 것이므로 'try + -ing'가 필요하다.

3. (a) '미래에 ~할 것을 기억하라'는 의미이므로 'remember + to 동사원형'
(b) '과거에 한 약속을 기억하지 못하는 것이므로 '이미 ~한 것을 기억하다'의 의미로 'remember + -ing'이 필요하다.

4. (a) 복도에 있던 휴지를 줍기 위해 멈췄을 것이므로 '~하기 위해 멈추다'의 의미로 'stop + to 동사원형'으로 쓴다.
(b) 밤에 잠을 잘 자기 위해 커피 마시는 것을 멈춘 상황이므로 '~하는 것을 멈추다'의 의미로 'stop + -ing'이 필요하다.

5. (a) 친구와 책을 함께 봤다고 했으므로 '책을 가져오는 것을 잊어버렸다'의 의미이므로 'forget to bring'이 들어간다.
(b) 엄마가 집안에서 지갑을 찾고 있다고 했으므로 '차 안에 지갑을 두고 내린 것을 잊어버린' 것이므로 'forget + -ing'라 필요하다.

B [해설]

1~2. '동사 + 목적어' 어순으로 쓴다.

Point 7 동명사 *vs.* 현재분사

A 1. 현재분사 2. 동명사 3. 현재분사
4. 동명사 5. 동명사 6. 동명사
7. 동명사

B 1. 그는 걸어 다니는 사전으로 불린다.
2. 그 노인은 지팡이를 짚고 있다.
3. 나는 당신의 쇼의 음악을 듣는 것을 매우 즐겨 했습니다.
4. 그는 마침내 산 꼭대기에 오르는 것에 성공했다.
5. 사진 속에서 헤드폰을 끼고 있는 소년이 내 남동생이다.
6. 뭔가가 타고 있어! 방에서 연기가 나오는 것이 보여!

A [해설]

1. '사람들이 카메라를 보고 웃고 있는'의 의미로 보어로 쓰인 현재분사이다.

2. '공원을 청소하는 것'의 의미로 보어로 쓰인 동명사이다.

3. '미나는 그녀의 방에서 지금 책을 읽고 있는 중'이므로 보어로 쓰인 현재분사이다.

4. '흡연실'의 의미로 명사의 용도를 보여주므로 동명사이다.

5. '그녀는 꽃병에 꽃을 꽂는 것을 매우 잘한다.'이므로 전치사의 목적어로 쓰인 동명사이다.

6. '복사하는 기계'의 의미로 명사의 용도를 나타내므로 동명사이다.

7. '화성에 사는 것'의 의미로 문장의 주어로 쓰인 동명사이다.

B [해설]

1. 명사를 수식하면서 상태를 나타내므로 현재분사이다.

2. 명사의 용도를 나타내므로 동명사이다.

3. 동사 enjoy의 목적어로 쓰였으므로 동명사이다.

4. 전치사의 목적어로 쓰였으므로 동명사이다.

5. 명사를 뒤에서 수식하면서 상태를 나타내므로 현재분사이다.

6. burning: be동사 뒤에 보어로 쓰인 현재분사이다.
coming: smoke를 뒤에서 수식하면서 상태를 나타내므로 현재분사이다.

Point 8 자주 쓰이는 동명사 표현

A 1. going 2. shopping
3. doing 4. helping

B 1. O 2. studying
3. laughing 4. finding

C 1. is no use crying
2. looking forward to going

A [해설]

1. feel like ~ing: ~하고 싶다

2. go ~ing: ~하러 가다

3. be busy ~ing: ~하느라 바쁘다

4. spend *A* ~ing: ~하는 데 A를 쓰다

B [해설]

1. be worth ~ing: ~할 가치가 있다

2. How about ~ing: ~하는 게 어때?

3. can't help ~ing: ~하지 않을 수 없다

4. have trouble ~ing: ~하는 데 어려움을 겪다

C [해설]

1. ~하는 것은 소용없다: It is no use ~ing

2. ~을 고대하다: look forward to ~ing

일등 비법 노트

비법 1 1. ③
2. ⓐ → playing, ⓒ → practicing, ⓓ → preparing

비법 2 1. looking forward to visiting his uncle in America this summer

비법 3 1. ③
2. forgetting how to spell words in the contest

비법 4 1. ①, ③
2. Going shopping makes me tired.

비법 1

1 [해석]

기자: 당신은 당신만의 상표를 어떻게 시작했나요?

Tina: 나는 액세서리나 머리핀과 같은 것들을 만드는 것을 좋아합니다. 그래서 나는 자주 그것들을 만들어서 친구들에게 줍니다. 어느 날 내 친구 중 한 명이 나에게 그것들 더 만들어서 팔라고 했습니다. 나는 내가 물건을 만드는 것을 매우 즐기므로 그것이 좋은 생각이라고 생각했습니다. 그렇게 시작되었지요.

기자: 그래서, 그 때 사업은 어땠나요?

Tina: 상표를 만드는 것은 쉽지 않았고, 매우 힘든 시기가 있었지요. 하지만 나는 내가 나의 사업을 시작하는 것을 포기하지 않아서 기뻐요.

[해설]

ⓒ enjoy는 동명사를 목적어로 취한다.
to make → making

ⓔ give up은 동명사를 목적어로 취한다.
to start→ starting

2 [해석]

지나: 엄마, 나 피아노 치는 것을 포기하고 싶어요.

엄마: 오! 왜? 난 네가 그것을 매우 좋아한다고 생각했는데?

지나: 네, 그러나 저는 그다지 재능이 없는 것 같아요. 저보다 더 잘 치는 아이들이 많아요.

엄마: 연습하는 것을 멈추지 않으면 너도 점점 더 나아질 거야.

지나: 잘 모르겠어요.

엄마: 저녁 준비하는 것을 끝낸 후에 네가 연주하는 것을 들어볼까?

지나: 그러실래요? 그러면, 저에게 무엇을 결정해야 할지 솔직히 말해 주세요.

[해설]

ⓐ give up은 뒤에 동명사를 목적어로 취하는 동사이다.

ⓒ stop은 뒤에 동명사를 목적어로 취하는 동사이다.

ⓓ finish는 뒤에 동명사를 목적어로 취하는 동사이다.

비법 2

1 [해석]

호진: 나는 이번 여름에 미국에 계시는 삼촌을 방문할 거야. 너무 기다려 져.

민지: 와! 그것 참 멋지다! 네가 매우 신이 난 걸 알겠어.

[해설] 'look forward to'의 'to'는 to부정사의 to와는 달리 전치사이기 때문에 뒤에 동명사가 나와야 한다.

비법 3

1 [해석] Sally는 물건을 잘 만든다. 그녀는 Mandy를 위해 쿠션을 만들었는데, 그녀는 그것을 매우 좋아했다. 그래서, 그녀는 Sally에게 쿠션 만드는 법을 배우고 싶다고 말했다. Sally는 자신이 가르쳐 주겠다고 했다. 지금 그들은 금요일에 한 시간씩 쿠션을 함께 만든다.

[해설]

ⓐ 전치사 at 뒤에는 동명사가 온다.

ⓑ want는 to부정사를 목적어로 취한다.

ⓒ spend + *A* (+ in) ~ing: ~하는 데에 A를 쓰다

2 [해석]

엄마: 네 철자법 맞추기 대회가 내일이지, 그렇지?

Tom: 네. 저는 너무 긴장이 되요.

엄마: 왜? 너는 매일 많은 단어를 외우잖아.

Tom: 대회에서 어떻게 철자를 쓰는 지 잊어버릴까 봐 걱정이에요.

엄마: 걱정하지마! 너는 잘 할거야.

[해설] 전치사 of 뒤에는 동명사가 온다.

비법 4

1 [해설] 〈보기〉의 밑줄은 문장의 주어 역할을 하는 동명사이다.
①은 '음악을 들으면서'라는 의미로, 보어 역할을 하는 현재분사이다.
②, ④~⑤는 문장의 주어 역할을 하는 동명사이다.
③은 '눈이 오고 있는 중인'의 의미로, 보어 역할을 하는 현재분사이다.

2 [해설] 주어가 '쇼핑하러 가는 것'이므로 동명사로 주어를 삼는다.

내신 만점! 실전 기출

01. ③	**02.** ②	**03.** ③
04. ①	**05.** ④	**06.** ④
07. ④	**08.** ④	**09.** using
10. looking forward to taking		**11.** ②
12. ②	**13.** ①	**14.** ⑤
15. not finding	**16.** having missed	
17. having been stolen		**18.** ④
19. ⑤	**20.** ③	**21.** ②, ③
22. in → from	**23.** to fish → fishing	

24. ⑤	**25.** getting tired of wearing	
26. ④	**27.** ⑤	**28.** ③
29. Caring about how they look		
30. ⓐ O ⓑ watching ⓒ O ⓓ seeing ⓔ trying		

01 [해석] 규칙적으로 먹는 것은 건강한 습관이다.
[해설] 문장의 주어로 쓰이는 동사는 동명사나 to부정사로 온다.

02 [해석] 그녀는 영어로 일기를 쓰는 것을 즐긴다.
[해설] enjoy는 동명사를 목적어로 취한다.

03 [해석] 미나는 이탈리아 요리를 배우는 것에 관심이 있었다.
[해설] 전치사 in 뒤에는 동명사가 온다.

04 [해석] 우리는 모두 ________가 대회를 포기해서 놀랐다.
[해설] 동명사의 의미상 주어가 문장의 주어나 목적어가 아닐 때는 동명사 앞에 소유격이나 목적격으로 따로 명시한다.

05 [해석] 그녀는 인터넷에서 정보를 찾는 것을 ________.
[해설] 동사 decide는 to부정사를 목적어로 취한다.

06 [해설] forget + to부정사: ~할 것을 잊다

07 [해설] '~할 것을 기억하다'는 'remember + to부정사'를 쓴다.

08 [해설] '~하려고 노력하다'는 'try + to부정사'를 쓴다.

09 [해설] consider는 동명사를 목적어로 취하는 동사이다.

10 [해설] '~할 것을 고대하고 있다'는 'look forward to ~ing'이다.

11 [해석]
① 너와 함께 제주도를 방문한 것은 매우 재미있었다.
② 오염 때문에 많은 물고기가 죽어가고 있다.
③ 그는 환경을 구하는 것에 관심이 있다.
④ 그의 목표는 한 번에 한 발자국 앞으로 가는 것이다.
⑤ 그녀는 Jenny에게 어제 자신의 비밀을 말한 것을 후회했다.
[해설] ①, ③, ④, ⑤ 는 동명사, ②는 현재분사

12 [해석]
① 저 요람에서 잠자고 있는 아기가 너무 귀엽다!
② 대기실에 몇몇 사람이 있었다.
③ 그의 그림에 있는 춤추는 소녀들은 모두 아름다워 보인다.
④ 늪은 많은 살아있는 생물들에게 살기 좋은 곳이다.
⑤ 피사의 사탑(기울고 있는 탑)은 이탈리아에 있는 유명한 관광명소이다.
[해설]
① baby의 상태를 설명해 주고 있으므로 현재분사이다.
② room의 용도를 설명해 주고 있으므로 동명사이다.
③ girls의 상태를 설명해 주고 있으므로 현재분사이다.
④ creatures의 상태를 설명해 주고 있으므로 현재분사이다.
⑤ tower의 상태를 설명해 주고 있으므로 현재분사이다.

13 [해석]
① 어머니들은 결코 자식을 사랑하기를 멈추지 않는다.
② 그들은 새 차를 사기 위해 돈을 모으기로 결심했다.
③ 좋은 습관을 만드는 것은 많은 시간과 노력이 필요하다.
④ 그녀는 가방을 대기실에 두고 가는 것을 싫어하지 않았다.
⑤ 돌아올 때 아이스크림 사오는 것을 잊지 마세요.
[해설]
② decide는 to부정사는 목적어로 취한다.
saving → to save
③ 문장의 주어로 쓰이는 동사는 동명사나 to부정사의 형태로 온다.
(Develop → Developing 또는 To develop)
④ mind는 동명사를 목적어로 취한다.
to leave → leaving
⑤ '~할 것을 잊다'는 'forget + to부정사'
(buying → to buy)

14 [해석]
① 잠시 쉬는 것이 어때?
② 지구 온난화는 이산화탄소의 증가의 결과이다.
③ 어떤 사람들은 그들 자신의 사진을 찍기를 원했다.
④ 퀴즈 쇼 진행자가 참가자들에게 질문을 하기 시작했다.
⑤ 내일 아침에 일어나자마자 나에게 전화하는 것 기억해.
[해설] ⑤ '~할 것을 기억하다'는 'remember to부정사'의 형태로 써야 하므로 calling → to call

15 [해석] 책 선장은 그가 보물을 찾지 못할지도 모른다고 걱정하고 있다.

[해설] 종속절의 사건은 동명사나 to부정사로 바꿀 수 있다. 이 때, 주절과 종속절의 시제가 같고, 전치사 뒤에 오므로 단순동명사(동사원형-ing)로 하고, 부정어 not은 동명사 앞에 온다.

16 [해석] 나는 내가 영화의 앞 부분을 놓친 것이 유감스럽다.
[해설] 종속절의 사건은 동명사나 to부정사로 바꿀 수 있다. 이 때, 주절보다 종속절의 사건이 한 시제 앞서고, 전치사(at) 뒤에 오므로 완료 동명사(having p.p.)로 쓴다.

17 [해석] 그는 그의 자전거가 도둑 맞은 것에 대해 놀랐다.
[해설] 종속절의 사건은 동명사나 to부정사로 바꿀 수 있다. 이 때, 주절보다 종속절의 사건이 한 시제 앞서고, 전치사(at) 뒤에 오며, 수동태이므로 수동태 완료 동명사(having been p.p.)로 쓴다.

18 [해석]
· 집에 돌아오자마자, Peter는 Sally에게서 온 이 메일을 확인하기 위하여 컴퓨터를 켰다.
· 우리 엄마는 아침에 일찍 일어나는 것에 익숙하시다.
[해설] '~하자마자'는 'on ~ing', '~하는 데 익숙하다'는 'be used to ~ing'

19 [해석] 내 이름은 Mike야. 나는 컴퓨터 게임을 매우 좋아해. 나는 또한 그것을 잘하기도 해. 그래서, 나는 장래에 프로게이머가 되기를 소망해. 오늘 나는 게임 대회에 참가해서, 2등을 했어. 나는 너무나 기뻐서 울지 않을 수 없었어.
[해설]
ⓐ 전치사 at 뒤에는 동명사가 목적어로 와야 한다.
ⓑ want는 to부정사를 목적어로 취한다.
ⓒ 'can't help(~하지 않을 수 없다)' 뒤에는 동명사가 온다.

20 [해석]
A: 아빠, 난 이제 아빠가 나에게 인형 사주시는 게 달갑지 않아요.
B: 오! 왜 달갑지 않은데?
A: 저는 십대에요. 나는 더 이상 어린 아이처럼 취급 받는 것이 싫어요.
[해설] 동사 like는 to부정사와 동명사를 모두 목적어로 취할 수 있다. 그러나 문맥상 수동태가 되어야 하므로 ①~②는 해당되지 않는다. 동명사의 수동태는 'being + p.p.'이다.

21 [해석]
A: 이메일로 독후감 제출했니? 내가 아직 그것을 못 받았거든.
B: 죄송해요. __________.
① 제가 이메일을 (이미) 보냈다는 사실을 잊어버렸어요.
② 이메일 보내는 걸 잊어버렸어요.
③ 이메일을 보내는 데에 어려움이 있었어요.
[해설] 의미상 이메일을 보내지 않은 ②, ③이 들어가야 자연스럽다.

22 [해설] '*A*가 ~못하게 하다'는 'keep *A* from ~ing'

23 go –ing: ~하러 가다.

24 [해석]
Jenny는 내일 환경에 관하여 발표를 한다. 그녀는 환경을 돕는 방법에 대해서 이야기 할 계획이다. 그녀는 지구를 구하는 것에 대해 관심이 있다. 그녀는 요전에 사람들의 기름 유출로 죽어가는 바다 동물들에 관한 다큐멘터리를 본 것을 기억한다. 그녀는 발표에 그 비디오를 보여 주는 것이 매우 도움이 될 것이라고 생각한다.
[해설]
ⓐ plan은 to부정사를 목적어로 취하는 동사이므로 어법상 옳다.
ⓑ 전치사 of 뒤에는 동명사가 온다.
ⓒ 전치사 in 뒤에는 동명사가 온다.
ⓓ 과거에 이미 일어난 사건을 기억하는 것은 'remember + ~ing'
ⓔ 문장의 주어로 쓰이는 동사는 동명사나 to부정사 형태로 모두 쓰인다.

25 [해석]
A: 너는 속상해 보이는구나. 무슨 문제가 있니?
B: 나는 매일 똑 같은 교복을 입는 것이 싫증이 나.
[해설] 전치사 of 뒤에는 동명사로 쓴다.

26 [해석]
지수: 이 콘서트에 초대해 주어서 고마워. 나는 이것을 아주 오랫동안 고대해 왔어.
민호: 정말? 그 말을 들으니 나도 좋네.
지수: 나는 표를 사려고 한 시간 정도를 보냈는데 하나도 못 샀어.
민호: 나도 알아. 나도 처음에 표를 구하는 데 애먹었어. 이 사람들은 정말 인기가 많아.

지수: 정말 그래! 무대로 좀 더 가까이 갈 수 있을까? 우리 앞에 있는 키가 큰 남자들이 내 시야를 가려.

민호: 사람들이 너무 많아서 무대로 더 가까이 가는 것은 불가능한 것 같은데.

지수: 오, 이를 어쩌나!

[해설] 앞에 키가 큰 사람들이 지수의 시야를 가린다고 했으므로 무대가 잘 보이지 않음.

27 [해설]

ⓑ look forward to ~ing 이므로 to see → seeing

ⓒ spend *A* ~ing 이므로 to buy → buying

ⓔ keep은 동명사를 목적어로 취한다. block → blocking

28 [해석]

ⓐ John은 로봇을 만드는 것을 곧 끝낼 것이다.

ⓑ 그는 그의 잃어버린 개를 찾는 것을 절대로 포기하지 않았다.

ⓒ 그가 규칙을 따르지 않는 것이 그를 곤경에 처하게 할 수 있다.

ⓓ 이제 영화가 시작되니 이야기를 그만 하세요.

ⓔ 그들은 한 달 이상 노래연습을 해 왔다.

ⓕ Jerry는 대회에서 실수한 것을 부끄러워한다.

[해설] ⓐ, ⓑ, ⓓ, ⓔ finish, give up, stop, practice는 동명사를 목적어로 취하므로, ⓑ to look → looking, ⓓ to talk → talking으로 고친다.

ⓒ 동사를 주어 자리에 놓을 때는 to부정사나 동명사의 형태로 온다. 이 때 부정의 동명사는 동명사 앞에 not을 쓰고 의미상 주어는 그 앞에 소유격(혹은 목적격)으로 써야 하므로 맞다.

ⓕ 동명사의 의미상 주어는 동명사 앞에 소유격이나 목적격을 쓴다. he → his(him)

29 [해설] 문장의 주어로 쓰이는 동사는 동명사나 to부정사로 쓴다. 하지만 여기는 빈칸의 수에 맞추기 위해 동명사로 써야 한다.

30 [해석] 너는 영화를 보는 것을 좋아하니? 그렇다면, 영화평론가가 되는 것이 어때? 너는 많은 영화를 보는 것을 즐길 수 있고, 그러면서 생활을 할 돈도 벌 수 있어! 그들의 일은 영화를 보고 그것들에 대해 감상을 쓰는 거야. 그러면 그 영화를 보고 싶은 사람들이 그들의 감상을 읽고 그것을 볼 지 어떨 지를 결정하지. 그것은 많은 노력이 필요하지만 해 볼 만한 가치가 있지 않니?

[해설]

ⓑ enjoy는 동명사를 목적어로 취한다.

ⓓ '~하고 싶다'는 'feel like ~ing'이다.

ⓔ '~할 가치가 있다'는 'be worth ~ing'이다.

실력 탄탄! 서술형 심화

1 (1) to arrange (2) helping (3) from playing

2 1. to raise your hand 2. Using a cell phone 3. talking with your friends

3 ⓐ taking ⓑ feed ⓒ crying ⓓ helping ⓔ to help

1 [해석]

(1) 수진이는 책장에 있는 책을 정리할 것을 잊어버렸다.

(2) 수진이는 동생의 숙제를 도와주느라 얼마간의 시간을 보냈다.

(3) 추운 날씨 때문에 수진이는 친구와 배드민턴을 치지 못했다.

[해설]

(1) forget + to부정사: ~할 것을 잊어버리다

(2) spend + 시간 + (in) + -ing: ~하면서 시간을 보내다

(3) keep[stop] ~ from + -ing: ~가 …하지 못하게 하다

2 [해설]

1. remember + to부정사: ~할 것을 기억하다
2. 문장의 주어로 오는 동사는 동명사나 to부정사로 쓴다.
3. avoid는 동명사를 목적어로 취한다.

3 [해석] Jane은 그녀의 가족의 다섯 명의 아이 중 첫째이다. 그래서 그녀는 아이들을 돌보는 데 익숙하다. 그녀의 동생들이 매우 어렸을 때, 그들이 계속 울 때는 우유를 주곤 했다. 또한, 그녀는 집안일에 대해 엄마를 도와 드리는 것을 절대로 피하지 않는다. 그녀는 엄마가 바쁠 때는 항상 도와드리려고 노력한다.

[해설]

ⓐ be used to ~ing (~하는 데 익숙하다)

ⓑ used to 동사원형 (~하곤 했다)

ⓒ keep ~ing (계속해서 ~하다)

ⓓ 동사 avoid는 동명사를 목적어로 취한다.

ⓔ try + to부정사: (노력) ~하려고 애쓰다

Chapter 05 분사

Point 1 분사의 종류: 현재분사 *vs.* 과거분사

A	1. rising	2. filled	3. made
	4. used	5. playing	6. published
	7. sentenced	8. written	9. sleeping
	10. surrounded	11. waiting	12. shocked
B	1. stolen	2. O	3. pleased
	4. writing	5. written	6. O

A [해석]

1. 금 값은 요즘 오르고 있다.
2. 우리의 삶은 해야 할 많은 일로 가득 차 있다.
3. 스위스에서 만들어진 시계는 인기 있다.
4. 이 프로그램은 많은 사업체에서 사용되고 있다.
5. 그들은 두 시간 동안 게임을 하고 있다.
6. 그 잡지는 15개국에서 발간된다.
7. 그녀는 오늘 법원에서 형을 선고 받을 것이다.
8. 그 아이들은 영어로 쓰여 있는 이메일을 받았다.
9. 잠자고 있는 개를 깨우지 않도록 조심해라.
10. 우리 집은 아름다운 산들에 둘러싸여 있다.
11. 우리는 거의 한 시간 동안 여기에서 기다리고 있었다.
12. 그 노부인은 그녀의 눈 앞의 광경에 놀랐다.

B [해석]

1. 내 생각에 내 지갑은 도둑맞은 것 같다.
2. 그 접시들은 Tom에 의해 깨졌다.
3. 그녀의 부모님은 그 결과에 기뻤다.
4. 편지를 쓰고 있는 저 아름다운 소녀를 보아라.
5. 나는 영어로 쓰여진 만화책을 읽고 있다.
6. 나는 저기 벤치에 앉아 있는 소녀를 알고 있다.

[해설]

1. 지갑은 도난을 당하는(stolen) 것이므로 수동의 의미인 과거분사로 써야 한다.
2. 그릇은 깨어지는 것이므로 수동의 의미인 과거분사로 써야 한다.
3. 그 결과에 의해 기뻐지는 감정이므로 수동의 의미인 과거분사로 써야 한다.
4. 소녀가 편지를 쓰고 있는(writing) 것이므로 능동의 의미인 현재분사(writing)이 와야 한다.
5. 영어로 쓰여진 것이므로 수동의 의미인 과거분사(written)가 와야 한다.

Point 2 분사의 역할

A	1. looking	2. used	3. knitting
	4. taken	5. produced	6. speaking
	7. sold		

B
1. novels written by this author
2. the shocking news from our teacher
3. always crowded with many visitors

A [해설]

1, 3. 목적어와 목적격 보어의 관계가 능동이므로 현재분사가 와야 한다.
2. 차는 사용되는 것으로 수동의 의미이므로 과거분사가 와야 한다.
4. 사진은 찍히는 것이므로 과거분사가 와야 한다.
5, 7. 시계가 생산되었고, 제품들은 팔리는 것이므로, 과거분사를 쓴다.
6. 사람이 주체적으로 말하는 것이므로 능동의 현재분사를 쓴다.

B [해설]

1. 작가에 의해 씌어진 것으로 수동의 의미 (written)
2. 소식이 놀라운 감정을 불러일으키므로 능동의 의미 (shocking)
3. 식당이 붐비는 것이므로 수동의 의미 (crowded)

Point 3 감정을 나타내는 분사

A	1. moving, moved	2. confusing, confused
	3. excited, exciting	
B	1. fascinating	2. confused
	3. touched	4. bored
	5. disappointing	6. frightened

A [해석] 〈보기〉 그 결과는 많은 사람들을 실망시켰다.
그 결과는 실망스러웠다.
많은 사람들은 실망했다.

1. 노인에 대한 이야기는 우리들 모두를 감동시켰다.
→ 노인에 대한 이야기는 감동스러웠다.
→ 우리 모두는 노인에 대한 이야기에 감동했다.

2. 그 선생님의 지침은 나를 혼란스럽게 했다.
→ 그 선생님의 지침은 혼란스럽게 했다.
→ 나는 선생님의 지침 때문에 혼란스러워졌다.
3. 그 축구 경기는 모든 관객들을 흥분시켰다.
→ 그 관객들은 그 축구 경기에 대해서 흥분했다.
→ 그 축구 경기는 모든 관객들에게 흥미진진했다.
[해설] **1~3.** 감정을 일으키는 대상이 주어일 때는 현재분사, 감정을 느끼는 대상이 주어일 때는 과거분사를 쓴다.

B [해석]
1. 나는 그녀가 매혹적인 목소리를 가졌다고 생각한다.
2. 그녀는 혼란스러워 무엇을 해야 할 지 몰랐다.
3. 사람들은 아름다운 이야기에 감동했다.
4. 대부분의 관객들은 그 연극에 지루해 했다.
5. 나는 네게 실망스러운 소식을 말해야 한다.
6. 방에 있는 모든 사람들은 그 큰 소리에 놀랐다.
[해설]
1. voice가 매혹시키는 것이므로 현재분사가 온다.
2. she가 혼란스러워진 것이므로 과거분사가 온다.
3. people이 감동 받은 것이므로 과거분사가 온다.
4. audience가 지루해진 것이므로 과거분사가 온다.
5. 실망을 느끼게 하는 news이므로 현재분사가 온다.

Point 4 분사구문을 만드는 법

A 1. spending money
2. Studying hard
3. Feeling so tired,
4. Not (being) written clearly
5. Waiting for the bus

B 1. Because 2. After

A [해석]
1. 돈을 쓸 때는 두 번 생각해야 한다.
2. 열심히 공부했기 때문에, Sally는 장학금을 받았다.
3. 나는 매우 피곤했기 때문에, 수영하러 안 갔다.
4. 분명하게 쓰여 있지 않기 때문에 그 설명서는 이해하기 힘들다.
5. 버스를 기다리는 동안 Tim은 그의 친구와 우연히 마주쳤다.

B [해석]
1. 먹을 게 없기 때문에 그는 스스로 요리하기로 결심했다.
2. 그 학교를 졸업한 후에 나는 이 회사에서 일자리를 얻었다.

Point 5 분사구문의 의미

A 1. Visiting France 2. Being sad
3. Washing the dishes

B 1. Crossing the street, she noticed the post office.
2. Having many things to do, he couldn't
3. Hearing the news, he grew pale.

A [해석]
1. 프랑스를 방문했을 때 나는 내 친구 Hannah를 만났다.
2. 그녀는 슬펐기 때문에 아무도 만나고 싶지 않았다.
3. 설거지를 하는 동안 나는 항상 영어 라디오를 듣는다.
[해설] 분사구문을 만들 때는 ① 접속사를 생략하고(단, 강조를 위해 남겨둘 수 있음), ② 부사절의 주어가 주절과 일치하면 부사절 주어를 생략하고, ③ 부사절 시제가 주절과 일치하는 경우 동사를 동사원형-ing로 바꾼다.

B [해설]
1. cross the street: 길을 건너다
2. take a break: 휴식을 취하다
3. grow pale: 창백해지다

Point 6 분사구문의 시제와 태

A 1. Having spent all her money
2. (Having been) Impressed by her music
3. Having got a good score on the test
4. Having finished his work

B 1. Being 2. Having been 3. Being

A [해석]
1. 돈을 다 썼기 때문에 그녀는 새 옷을 살 수 없었다.
2. 그녀의 음악에 깊게 감동 받아서 그는 그녀의 팬이 되었다.
3. 시험에서 좋은 점수를 받아서 Tim은 좋은 대학에 들어갈 수 있었다.
4. 일을 마친 후에 John은 그의 친구들을 만나러 나갔다.

[해설] **1~4.** 분사구문을 만들 때, 접속사를 포함한 절의 시제가 주절의 시제보다 앞 설 경우, 'having + 과거분사'의 형태로 분사구문을 만든다.

Point 7 주의해야 할 분사구문 I

A 1. being → were
2. wanted → didn't want
3. had → hadn't
4. don't → didn't

B 1. Not feeling hungry
2. There being no bus so late at night
3. Not having finished the project

A [해석]

1. 많은 사람들이 있었기 때문에 우리는 한 시간을 기다렸다.

2. 그의 기분을 나쁘게 하고 싶지 않아서 그녀는 그에게 진실을 말하지 않았다.

3. 몇 달 동안 만나지 못했기 때문에 그들은 서로를 그리워했다.

4. 그 문제를 해결할 방법을 몰라서 나는 Mr. Kim에게 질문을 했다.

[해설]

1. 분사구문에 동사 + ing가 쓰였으므로 부사절에는 주절과 같은 시제의 동사가 와야 한다.

2. 분사구문에 not이 붙어 부정의 의미이므로 wanted가 아닌 didn't want가 와야 한다.

3. 분사구문에 not이 붙어 부정의 의미이므로 had seen이 아닌 hadn't seen이 와야 한다.

4. 분사구문에 동사 + ing가 쓰였으므로 부사절에는 주절과 같은 시제의 동사가 와야 한다.

B [해석]

1. 나는 배가 고프지 않았기 때문에 점심을 건너 뛰었다.

2. 그렇게 밤늦게는 버스가 없었기 때문에 그는 택시를 타야만 했다.

3. 프로젝트를 끝내지 않아서 Jake는 영화를 보러 갈 수 없었다.

[해설]

1, 3. 분사구문의 부정은 분사 앞에 not을 붙인다.

3. 접속사를 포함한 절의 시제가 주절의 시제보다 앞 설 경우, 'having + 과거분사'의 형태로 분사구문을 만든다.

Point 8 주의해야 할 분사구문 II

A 1. with the TV turned on
2. with his eyes closed
3. with his arms folded
4. with his dog following him
5. with her finger pointing to the chart

B 1. Judging from 2. Frankly speaking
3. Compared with 4. Generally speaking

A [해석]

1. 그녀는 TV를 켜 둔 채로 잠에 들었다.

2. 그 남자는 그의 눈을 감은 채로 노래를 들었다.

3. 그 남자는 팔짱을 낀 채로 깊은 생각을 하고 있다.

4. 그는 그의 개가 그를 따라오도록 한 채로 공원을 걸었다.

5. Jenny는 손가락으로 도표를 가리키면서 그 상황을 설명했다.

[해설] 1~**5.** 'with + 명사 + 분사'는 '~을 한 채로'라는 의미를 나타낸다. 명사와 분사가 능동 관계이면 현재분사, 수동 관계이면 과거분사를 쓴다.

일등 비법 노트

비법 1 1. ⑤ 2. ⑤

비법 2 1. (1) Entering the room
(2) Not remembering her password
2. ③

비법 3 1. (1) Since I had read the book many times
(2) Since she has finished her dinner
2. Seeing → Having seen

비법 4 1. (1) with his dog following him
(2) with his eyes closed
2. ②

비법 1

1 [해석]

· 그 강의는 지루해서 많은 사람들이 잠들었다.

· 나는 재미난 할 일이 없어서 지루했다.

[해설] 강의는 지루함을 일으키는 것이므로 boring, 나는 지루함을 느끼므로 bored가 맞다.

2 [해석]

① 달리는 저 소년을 보아라.

② 나는 그의 똑똑한 대답에 놀랐다.

③ 그녀의 책장은 지루한 책들로 채워져 있다.

④ 그 결과는 우리에게 꽤 실망스러웠다.

⑤ 나는 장마철에는 다소 우울하다.

[해설] ⑤ 감정을 느끼는 사람이 주어이므로 depressing → depressed으로 고쳐야 한다.

비법 2

1 [해석]

(1) 방에 들어갔을 때, 나는 내 책상 위에 선물이 놓여 있는 것을 발견했다.

(2) 그녀는 암호를 기억하지 못해서, 그녀의 컴퓨터에 로그인할 수 없었다.

[해설] 분사구문을 만들 때, 부사절의 시제가 주절과 일치하는 경우 동사를 '동사원형 + ing'로 바꾼다. 분사구문의 부정은 분사 앞에 Not을 붙인다는 사실에 유의한다.

2 [해석] 그 소식을 듣고 놀래서 우리는 모두 기쁨의 비명을 질렀다.

[해설] Being surprised나 Surprised가 와야 한다.

비법 3

1 [해석]

(1) 그 책을 여러 번 읽었기 때문에 나는 몇몇 문장을 외우기까지 했다.

(2) 저녁 식사를 마쳤기 때문에 Molly는 후식을 주문할 것이다.

[해설] 'Having p.p.'가 쓰인 분사구문을 부사구로 바꿀 때 종속절의 시제는 주절의 시제보다 앞선다.

2 [해석]

A: 왜 영화를 보러 가지 않았니?

B: 그 영화를 이미 보았기 때문에 다시 보고 싶지 않았어.

[해설] 부사절의 시제가 주절보다 앞 서 있기 때문에 'Having p.p.'의 형태를 써 줘야 한다.

비법 4

1 [해설]

(1) 명사(his dog)와 분사의 관계가 능동이므로 following을 쓴다.

(2) 'His eyes were closed.'라는 문장을 연관 지어 생각해 보면 이해하기 쉽다. 눈은 감긴(closed) 것이므로, 수동의 의미를 나타내는 과거분사를 써서 'with his eyes closed'가 되어야 맞다.

2 [해설] 명사(his arms)와 분사의 관계가 수동이므로 과거분사 folded를 써야 한다.

내신 만점! 실전 기출

01. ③ 02. ③

03. The man riding a wheelchair

04. made 05. ② 06. ④

07. ③

08. blocking the narrow road to my house

09. I was very disappointed with the news.

10. ② 11. ③ 12. ③

13. ④ 14. ②, ④ 15. ②

16. (While) Walking along the street

17. (Because) Not having brought my wallet

18. ④

19. Because she has many friends

20. Not knowing how to solve the problem

21. Since she was sick 22. ④

23. ③ 24. ②, ④ 25. ③

26. ④ 27. ②

28. ⓑ → There being no one around me, I couldn't ask for help.

29. ⑤

30. with her eyes fixed on the board

01 [해석]

· 바닥에 깨진 유리를 조심해라.

· Linda 옆에 앉아 있는 소년을 아니?

[해설] 유리는 깨어짐을 당하는 것이므로 수동의 의미로 과거분사, 소년이 주체가 되어 앉아 있으므로 능동의 의미로 현재분사를 써야 한다.

02 [해석]

· Mr. Johnson은 학생들에 둘러싸여 앉아 이야기를 했다.

· 나는 두 마리의 소가 풀밭에서 누워 있는 것을 보았다.

[해설] Mr. Johnson은 아이들에게 둘러싸여 있으므로 수동(과거분사), 소는 풀밭에 스스로 누워 있는 것이므로 능동(현재분사)이다.

03 [해석]

A: 네 삼촌은 어디 계시니?

B: 그는 저기에 계셔. 휠체어를 타고 있는 남자가 내 삼촌이셔.

[해설] 명사를 수식하는 분사구가 길면 명사 뒤에서 수식한다. The man과 ride의 관계는 능동 관계이므로 현재분사를 쓴다.

04 [해석]

A: 왼손잡이 사람들을 위해 만들어진 가위가 있다는 것을 아니?

B: 오, 정말? 난 한번도 보지 못했어. 그것들은 어떻게 달라?

[해설] 가위는 만들어 지는 것으로 수동의 의미이므로 과거분사를 써야 한다.

05 [해석]

① 무대 위에서 노래하는 소녀를 보아라.

② 운동장에서 놀고 있는 소년은 John이다.

③ Sue에 의해 쓰여진 시는 매우 감동적이었다.

④ 파티에 초대된 사람들은 나타나지 않았다.

⑤ Christopher Nolan에 의해 만들어진 영화는 놀랍다.

[해설] ② The boy와 play의 관계는 능동 관계이므로 played → playing가 되어야 한다.

06 [해석] 내 잘못이라는 것을 알았기에 나는 정중히 사과했다.

[해설] 분사구문을 만들 때, ① 접속사를 생략하고 ② 주어가 같으면 주어를 생략하고 ③ 부사절 시제가 주절과 일치할 경우 부사절의 동사를 '동사원형 + ing'로 고친다. (시제에 유의)

07 [해석] 인생은 매우 짧기 때문에 우리는 우리가 하고 싶은 일을 해야 한다.

[해설] 분사구문을 만들 때, 부사절의 주어가 주절의 주어와 다를 때에는 부사절의 주어를 남겨 두어야 한다.

08 [해석] 나는 큰 트레일러를 보았다. 그것은 우리 집으로 향하는 좁은 길을 막고 있었다.

→ 나는 우리 집으로 향하는 좁은 길을 막고 있는 큰 트레일러를 보았다.

[해설] 긴 분사구는 명사를 뒤에서 수식한다. trailer와 block은 능동 관계이므로 현재분사로 쓴다.

09 [해설] be disappointed with: ~에 실망하다

10 [해석] 음악을 들으면서 그녀는 그녀에게 스트레스를 불러일으키는 것들을 잊어버렸다.

[해설] 분사구문을 만들 때 부사절의 시제와 주절의 시제가 같으면 부사절의 동사를 '동사원형-ing'로 쓴다.

11 [해석] 그의 할머니에 의해 길러졌기 때문에 그는 그녀와 매우 가깝다.

[해설] 분사구문을 만들 때, 종속절의 시제가 주절보다 앞 서 있는 경우 'Having p.p.'를 쓴다.

12 [해석]

① 우리 아빠는 얼린 요구르트 먹는 것을 좋아하신다.

② 어젯밤에 연주된 노래는 정말 좋았다.

③ 상자를 나르는 소년은 우리 반 회장이다.

④ 눈으로 덮인 그 산은 정말 아름다웠다.

⑤ 나는 집에 오는 길에 큰 개를 보고 겁먹었다.

[해설] ③ 소년이 상자를 나르는 것은 능동이므로 carried → carrying이 되어야 한다.

13 [해석]

① 몸이 좋지 않아서 그는 곧장 집으로 돌아갔다.

② 기진맥진해서 그녀는 집에 오자마자 잠이 들었다.

③ 부유하지 않기 때문에, 그녀는 그 시계를 살 수 없었다.

④ 그가 한 일이 잘못된 것임을 인정하면서 그는 미안하다고 말했다.

⑤ 내 차례를 기다리면서 나는 다른 사람들과 이야기를 나눴다.

[해설] ④ 분사구문의 주어가 생략되었으므로 주절의 주어와 같았음을 알 수 있는데, 주절 주어 he와 admit의 관계는 능동 관계이므로 현재분사가 와야 한다.

Admitted → Admitting

14 [해석] 추운 도시에서 태어나고 자랐기 때문에 나는 추위에 익숙하다.

[해설] 분사구문을 만들 때, 종속절의 시제가 주어보다 앞서면 동사를 'having p.p.'로 쓴다. 분사구문이 Having been으로 시작할 경우, 이를 생략할 수 있다.

15 [해설] 딸이 따르는 것은 능동이므로 following, 아빠가 가방을 들고 있는 것도 능동이므로 carrying을 쓴다.

16 [해석] 길을 따라 걸으면서 나는 친구를 우연히 만났다.
[해설] 분사구문을 만들 때는 ① 접속사를 생략하고, ② 주어가 주절과 일치하는 경우 생략하고, ③ 시제가 주절과 일치하는 경우 동사를 동사원형+ing로 바꾼다.

17 [해석] 지갑을 안 가져왔기 때문에 점심을 살 돈이 없었다.
[해설] 부사절의 시제가 주절의 시제보다 앞서 있으므로 분사구문으로 'Having p.p.'를 써야 한다. 분사구문의 부정은 분사 앞에 not을 붙인다.

18 [해석]
· 그는 근처에 그의 고양이가 자고 있는 채로 나무 아래 앉아있었다.
· 나는 음악이 틀어진 채로 공부하는 것은 좋지 않다고 생각한다.
· 그 소년은 그의 등을 벽에 기댄 채로 서 있었다.
[해설] 'with + 명사 + 분사'는 '명사가 ~한 채로'의 의미이다.

19 [해석] 친구가 많기 때문에 그녀의 학교 생활은 더 이상 외롭지 않다.
[해설] '~때문에'로 해석되는 이유를 나타내는 분사구문이므로 Because를 쓰고, 분사구문에 주어가 있으므로 그대로 써 주고, 동사 + ing가 쓰였으므로 종속절의 시제가 주어와 일치함에 유의한다.

20 [해석] 문제를 어떻게 해결할지 몰랐기 때문에 나는 언니에게 도움을 요청했다.
[해설] 분사구문의 부정은 not을 분사 앞에 붙인다.

21 [해석] 아팠기 때문에 그녀는 집에 하루 종일 있어야만 했다.
[해설] 분사구문에 동사 + ing가 왔으므로 부사절의 시제는 주절의 시제와 일치한다.

22 [해석] 준수가 그의 지갑을 잃어버렸기 때문에 우리는 그에게 점심을 사야 했다.
[해설] 분사구문을 만들 때, 종속절의 시제가 주절보다 앞선 경우 동사는 Having p.p를 쓴다. 따라서, ⓒ having lost가 와야 한다. 분사구문에서 강조의 의미로 접속사를 남겨둘 수도 있으니 무조건 생략할 필요는 없고, 종속절과 주절의 주어가 다른 경우에는 주어는 생략하지 않으므로 ⓐⓑⓓ는 맞다.

23 [해석]
A: Jenny, 쉬기 위해 뭘 하는 걸 좋아해?
B: 음, 나는 눈을 감고 음악을 듣는 것을 좋아해. 그것은 정말 날 편안하게 해. 너는?
A: 나는 목욕을 하는 것이 좋아. 스트레스를 푸는데 도움을 줘.
[해설]
· 'with + 명사+ 분사'는 '명사가~한 채로'의 의미이다. 이 때, 명사와 분사의 관계가 수동이면 과거분사를 쓴다.
· 음악을 듣는 것이 편안한 감정을 일으키므로 현재분사가 와야 한다.

24 [해석] 영어를 말하는 것을 잘하기 때문에 그는 외국 친구들을 쉽게 사귈 수 있었다.
[해설] '~때문에'의 의미로 해석되므로 because나 since가 쓰여야 한다.

25 [해석]
A: 야, 뭐가 문제야?
B: 영어로 쓰인 이메일을 읽고 있는데 완벽하게 이해를 못하겠어. 몇몇 단어들이 너무 헷갈려.
A: 내가 좀 볼게. 내가 도움이 될 수 있을 것 같아.
[해설]
ⓐ 영어로 쓰여진 메일이므로 수동의 의미로 과거분사 written이 와야 한다.
ⓑ 단어들이 혼란을 일으키므로 현재분사인 confusing이 와야 한다.

26 [해석] 오랫동안 만나지 못했기 때문에 우리는 이야기할 게 많았다.
[해설] Having p.p.가 쓰였으므로 부사절로 고칠 때 부사절의 시제가 주절의 시제보다 앞서야 한다.

27 [해석]
① 그는 라디오를 켜둔 채 방을 떠났다.
② 나는 무릎을 구부린 채 누워 있었다.
③ 그 남자는 다리를 꼬고 앉아 있다.
④ 그녀는 뺨에 눈물이 흐르는 채 그 이야기를 했다.
⑤ kevin은 신문을 읽고 그의 부인은 스웨터를 뜨고 있었다.

[해설] ② 명사(my knees)와 분사(bending)의 관계가 수동이므로 bent가 와야 한다.

28 [해석]

ⓐ 바다에 둘러 싸여 있어서 내 고향은 많은 아름다운 해변이 있다.

ⓑ 내 주위에 아무도 없어서 도움을 청할 수 없었다.

[해설] ⓑ 접속사 없이 ',(쉼표)'로 연결된 것으로 보아 분사구문으로 바꿔 쓰거나 또는 알맞은 접속사로 연결해야 어법에 맞는다. 분사구문을 활용한다면, 부사절에 '동사원형 + ing'가 와야 하므로 was를 being으로 고쳐야 한다. there은 주절의 주어와 같은 주어가 아니라서 생략되지 않았다. (= There was no one around me, so I couldn't ask for help.)

29 [해석] 지난 주말 내 친구들과 나는 자원 봉사를 하기 위해 지역 병원에 방문했다. 병원에서 나는 환자들을 도우며 모두에게 아름답게 웃는 어린 소녀를 보았다. 그녀는 우리와 같은 자원봉사자 중 한 명처럼 보였다. 곧 우리는 친해졌고 그녀에 대한 놀라운 소식을 들었다. 그녀는 암으로 고통 받았고 다 나은 후 규칙적으로 환자들을 돕도록 결심했다고 했다. 나는 그녀의 이야기에 깊은 감명을 받았다.

[해설] ⓐ 의미상 주어인 a little girl과 분사화 된 동사 smile의 관계가 능동, 진행의 의미이므로 현재분사, ⓑ news는 감정을 일으키는 주체이므로 현재분사, ⓒ I가 감정을 받으므로 과거분사를 쓴다.

30 [해설] 'with + 명사 + 분사' 구문에서 명사(eyes)와 분사(fix)의 관계가 수동이므로 과거분사를 쓴다.

실력 탄탄! 서술형 심화

1 (1) Getting first prize in the contest
(2) waving his hand to his friends
(3) Holding her baby in her arms

2 (1) Having lost my luggage, I have no clothes to wear.
(2) Having spent all my money, I can't buy anything.

3 (B) Being a fine day → It being a fine day
(D) Not seen → Not having seen

1 [해설] 〈보기〉

ⓐ 그는 친구에게 손을 흔들었다.

ⓑ 나는 대회에서 일등상을 받았다.

ⓒ 그녀는 그녀의 아이를 팔로 안고 있다.

2 [해설] 〈보기〉

Tim: 영어 보고서를 마쳤기 때문에 나는 그것을 제출할 수 있다.

(1) 짐을 잃어버렸기 때문에 나는 입을 옷이 없다.

(2) 돈을 다 썼기 때문에 아무 것도 살 수 없다.

[해설] 부사절의 시제가 주절의 시제보다 앞 서 있는 경우 분사구문으로 고칠 때 having p.p.를 쓴다.

3 [해석] 4월 5일

숙제를 마치고 나는 지루했다. 나는 안에서 공부하는 데에 지쳤다. 날씨가 좋아서 공원에 가기로 결정했다. 공원에서 걷는 동안 Jane을 우연히 마주쳤다. 그녀는 유럽을 여행 중이었었다. 이 주 가량 서로 만나지 못했었기 때문에, 우리는 벤치에 앉아 오랫동안 이야기를 했다. 그녀는 그녀의 여행에 대해 몇 가지 이야기를 해주었다. 정말 재미있었다. 이제는 나 역시 그곳에 몹시 가 보고 싶다.

[해설]

(B) 부사절의 주어가 주절의 주어와 다를 경우, 분사구문으로 고칠 때 부사절의 주어를 생략하지 않는다.

(D) 부사절의 시제가 주절의 시제보다 앞서 있는 경우, 분사구문은 'Having p.p.'가 와야 한다.

Chapter 06 수동태

Point 1 수동태의 의미와 형태

A 1. released 2. resembles
3. happened 4. prepare
5. built 6. were injured
7. preparing 8. are loved

B 1. was criticized 2. was delayed
3. was painted by 4. was developed by
5. is attracted by

A [해석]

1. 그의 새 영화는 어제 개봉되었다.
2. 사람들은 Jenny가 그녀의 아빠를 닮았다고 말한다.
3. 여기서 무슨 일이 일어났는지 아시나요?
4. 누가 그 이벤트를 준비할 것인가요?
5. 그 아이들은 해변에서 모래성을 지었다.
6. 100여 명의 사람들이 그 사고로 부상을 입었다.
7. 그녀는 그녀의 엄마를 위해 깜짝 파티를 준비하고 있었다.
8. 그의 소설은 전세계 많은 사람들에 의해 사랑 받는다.

[해설]

1, 6, 8. 주어가 행위를 당하는 수동태이므로 'be + p.p.'를 쓴다.
2. resemble은 수동태로 나타낼 수 없다.
3. happen은 수동태로 나타낼 수 없다.
4~5, 7. 주어가 행위를 하는 능동태이다.

B [해석]

1. 사람들은 그의 나쁜 태도를 비난했다.
→ 그는 그의 나쁜 태도 때문에 사람들에게 비난 받았다.
2. 나쁜 날씨는 비행 스케줄을 연기시켰다.
→ 비행 스케줄은 나쁜 날씨에 의해 연기 되었다.
3. 유명한 화가가 그의 초상화를 그렸다.
→ 그의 초상화는 유명한 화가에 의해 그려졌다.
4. Mr. Jones의 팀은 새로운 사업을 개발했다.
→ 새로운 사업은 Mr. Jones에 의해 개발되었다.
5. 그녀의 아름다운 목소리는 반의 모든 사람들을 매료시킨다.
→ 반의 모든 사람들은 그녀의 아름다운 목소리에 매료 당한다.

[해설] 수동태 문장은 '주어 + be동사 + 과거분사(+ by + 목적격(행위자))'의 형태로 나타낸다.

Point 2 조동사가 있는 문장의 수동태

A 1. can be solved 2. will be shown
3. must be returned 4. should be eaten
5. must be kept 6. have to be taught

B 1. The work can be finished (by us)
2. A ticket should be shown (by everyone)
3. Consumers will love these products
4. The city government will provide free lunch

A [해설]

1~5. 조동사가 있는 문장의 수동태는 '조동사 + be + p.p.'를 쓴다.

B [해석]

1. 우리는 이번 달 말까지 그 일을 마칠 수 있다.
2. 모든 사람들은 문 앞에서 티켓을 보여야 한다.
3. 이 제품들은 소비자들에 의해 사랑 받을 것이다.
4. 무료 점심은 시 정부에 의해 제공될 것이다.

[해설]

1~2. 능동태를 수동태로 바꿀 때는 목적어를 주어로 보내고, 동사를 'be + p.p.'의 형태로 바꾸고, 주어를 by + 행위자의 형태로 바꿔 뒤로 보낸다.
3~4. 수동태를 능동태로 바꿀 때는 주어를 목적어로 'by + 행위자'를 주어로 바꾸고 be동사를 없애고 동사를 시제에 맞도록 쓴다.

Point 3 구동사가 있는 문장의 수동태

A 1. The school trip was called off by the teacher
2. Their baby is taken care of by them
3. The good opportunity was given up by Sally
4. He is looked up to by many people in his country
5. The weak should not be looked down on by them

B 1. The problem was dealt with by her.
2. Kids should be looked after by their parents.

A [해설]

1~5. 구동사가 쓰인 능동태 문장을 수동태로 바꿀 경우, 구동사를 한 단어처럼 취급한다. 수동태는 '주어 + be 동사 + 과거분사 (+ by + 행위자)'의 형태로 나타낸다.

B [해설]

1. deal with (~를 다루다)
→ be dealt with by (~에 의해 다뤄지다)

2. look after (~를 돌보다)
→ be looked after by (~에 의해 보살핌을 받다)

Point 4 진행형의 수동태

A 1. are being cut　2. is not being　3. cleaning　4. was being painted　5. being destroyed

B 1. is being prepared　2. is being played　3. was being painted

C 1. The bread was being baked (by her)
2. Plants are being used (by them)
3. The plant in the garden was being watered by her

A [해석]

1. 그 나무들은 지금 잘려지고 있다.
2. 그 차는 아빠에 의해 고쳐지지 않고 있다.
3. 그 일꾼은 창문을 청소하고 있다.
4. 그 벽은 아이들에 의해 칠해지고 있다.
5. 그 건물은 일꾼들에 의해 부서지고 있다.

[해설]

1~2, 4~5. 주어가 행위를 당하는 진행형의 수동태이다. 진행형의 수동태는 'be + being + p.p. + (by + 목적격(행위자))'로 나타낸다.

3. 주어가 행위를 하는 능동태이다.

B~C [해설]

1~3. 진행형의 수동태는 'be + being + p.p. + (by + 목적격(행위자))'로 나타낸다.

Point 5 완료형의 수동태

A 1. been held　2. been helped　3. been cleaned　4. been　5. carried　6. has been used　7. has not been　8. exposed

B 1. have been organized
2. has been taught
3. has developed
4. have been provided
5. have been composed

A [해설]

1. 주어가 행위를 당하는 수동태의 현재완료형이므로 been held가 온다.
2~3. 뒤에 'by + 목적격(행위자)'가 왔으므로 수동태이다.
4. 주어가 행위를 당하는 수동태의 현재완료형이므로 been이 온다.
5. 주어가 행위를 당하는 수동태의 현재완료형이므로 carried가 온다.
6. 'for five years'가 왔으므로 현재완료이어야 하고, 수동태이다.
7. 현재완료 수동태의 부정은 have/has 뒤에 not을 쓴다.
8. 주어가 행위를 당하는 수동태의 현재완료형이므로 exposed 가 온다.

B [해석]

1. Jane은 서랍 속의 파일들을 정리했다.
→ 서랍 속 파일들은 Jane에 의해 정리 되었다.

2. Mr. White는 2년 동안 우리에게 영어를 가르쳤다.
→ 영어는 2년 동안 Mr. White에 의해 우리에게 가르쳐졌다.

3. 새로운 소프트웨어는 그의 팀에 의해 개발 되었다.
→ 그의 팀은 새로운 소프트웨어를 개발했다.

4. 그 자원봉사자들은 노숙자들에게 무료 식사를 제공해 주었다.
→ 노숙자들을 위한 무료 식사가 자원 봉사자들에 의해 제공되었다.

5. 그 작곡가는 여러 해 동안 많은 인기 곡을 작곡했다.
→ 많은 인기 곡들이 여러 해 동안 그 작곡가에 의해 작곡 되었다.

[해설]

1~2, 4~5. 현재완료 문장을 수동태로 바꿀 때 'have[has] been + (by + 목적격)'를 쓴다.

3. 현재완료 수동태를 능동태로 바꿀 때에는 동사에서 been(p.p.)을 빼면 된다.

Point 6 4형식 문장의 수동태

A 1. to 2. for 3. for
4. to 5. made for me

B 1. was told to me by my sister, was told a funny story by my sister
2. was given to us by our mom, were given great responsibility by our mom
3. was asked of the teacher by a student, was asked a very difficult question by a student

A [해설] 4형식 문장을 수동태로 전환할 때, 직접목적어를 주어로 하는 수동태는 간접 목적어 앞에 적절한 전치사를 쓴다. give, offer, show에는 to를 쓰고, find, buy, make에는 for를 쓴다.

B [해설] **1~3.** 4형식 문장은 직접목적어와 간접목적어를 주어로 하는 두 개의 수동태를 만들 수 있다. 직접목적어를 주어로 하는 수동태는 간접 목적어 앞에 적절한 전치사를 쓰는데, tell, give에는 to를 쓰고, ask에는 of를 쓴다.

Point 7 5형식 문장의 수동태 I

A 1. come → to come
2. named to Nabi → named Nabi
3. starting → start
4. buying → to buy

B 1. was called an angel 2. was painted white
3. was told to eat 4. was advised to learn
5. was told to hand in

A [해설]

1~4. 5형식문장을 수동태로 바꿀 때, 목적격 보어는 'be동사 + 과거분사(p.p.)' 다음에 원래 있던 목적격 보어를 그대로 이어서 쓴다.

B [해설]

1~5. 5형식 문장의 수동태는 주어 + be동사 + 과거분사 + 목적격보어로 이루어진다. 이 때 목적격보어로 쓰인 형용사, 분사, 명사, 부정사는 그대로 쓴다.

Point 8 5형식 문장의 수동태 II

A 1. to sing 2. to help
3. allowed 4. were seen

B 1. were seen to break 2. were made to do
3. were allowed to ask 4. was heard to make

A [해석]

1. 새들이 숲 속에서 노래 부르는 것이 들렸다.

2. 우리는 그의 차를 세차해야 했다.

3. 나는 그녀의 옷을 빌리도록 허락 받았다.

4. 몇몇 사람들이 그의 집에 들어가는 것이 목격 되었다.

[해설]

1~2. 5형식 문장에서 지각동사나 사역동사가 쓰여 목적격 보어로 동사원형을 취할 때, 이를 수동태로 전환하는 경우 동사원형을 to부정사로 바꾼다.

3. let은 수동태로 전환할 때, 'be allowed to 동사원형'을 쓴다.

B [해설]

1~4. 5형식 문장에서 지각동사나 사역동사가 쓰여 목적격 보어로 동사원형을 취할 때, 이를 수동태로 전환하는 경우 동사원형을 to부정사로 바꾼다.

Point 9 주의해야 할 수동태 I

A 1. are said to be 2. is thought to be

B 1. It is supposed that his new movie is great. / His new movie is supposed to be great.
2. It is said that eating an apple a day keeps the doctor away. / Eating an apple a day is said to keep the doctor away.

A [해설]

1~2. 목적어가 that절일 때 수동태의 형태는 It + be동사 + 과거분사 + that절 또는 that절의 주어 + be동사 + 과거분사 + to동사원형(that절 내의 동사)로 바꿀 수 있다.

B [해석] 〈보기〉 사람들은 그가 말한 것이 사실이었다고 믿었다.

1. 우리는 그의 새 영화가 훌륭할 것이라고 생각한다.

2. 사람들은 하루에 사과를 하나씩 먹는 것이 의사를 멀리 하게 한다고 말한다.

[해설]

1~2. 목적어가 that절일 때 수동태의 형태는 'It + be동사 + 과거분사(p.p.) + that절' 또는 'that절의 주어 + be동사 + 과거분사(p.p.) + to동사원형(that절 내의 동사)'로 바꿀 수 있다.

Point 10 주의해야 할 수동태 II

A	1. at	2. about	3. of
	4. in	5. with	
B	1. known to	2. based on	
	3. covered with	4. were pleased with	

A [해설]

1. be surprised at ~: ~에 놀라다
2. be worried about ~: ~를 걱정하다
3. be ashamed of ~: ~을 부끄러워하다
4. be interested in ~: ~에 관심을 갖다
5. be crowded with ~:~으로 혼잡하다

B [해설]

1. be known to ~: ~에게 알려지다
2. be based on ~: ~에 근거를 두다
3. be covered with ~: ~로 덮여있다
4. be pleased with: ~에 기뻐하다

일등 비법 노트

비법 1	1. ②
	2. (1) were given (2) was given to us
비법 2	1. ④ 2. ③, ④
비법 3	1. ⑤
	2. is thought to be a global language
비법 4	1. ② 2. ②

비법 1

1 [해석]

① 영어는 Mr. Kim에 의해 내게 가르쳐졌다.

② 맛있는 식사가 그녀에 의해 나를 위해 요리되었다.

③ 중요한 질문이 그 남자에게 물어졌다.

④ 많은 수업료가 내 부모님에 의해서 학교에 지불되었다.

⑤ 몇몇 흥미로운 일이 내 선생님에 의해서 내게 주어졌다.

[해설] ② to → for, cook이 쓰인 4형식 문장을 직접 목적어가 주어인 수동태로 전환할 때 전치사는 for를 쓴다.

2 [해석] 아빠가 우리에게 귀여운 작은 강아지를 주셨다.

[해설] 동사 give는 직접 목적어가 주어인 수동태 문장으로 전환할 때 전치사 to를 수반한다.

비법 2

1 [해석] 그는 수업을 마치고 강당을 청소하도록 시켜졌다.

[해설] ④ 수동태 'be p.p.'뒤에 오는 동사는 'to부정사'로 온다.

2 [해설] 지각동사의 수동태는 'be p.p.'뒤에 'to + 동사'나 '-ing'가 올 수 있다.

비법 3

1 [해석] 사람들은 비타민제를 먹는 것이 도움이 된다고 생각한다.

→ 비타민제를 먹는 것이 도움이 된다고 여겨진다.

2 [해석]

사람들은 그가 말한 것이 사실이라 믿는다.

→ 그가 말한 것이 사실이라 믿어진다.

사람들은 영어가 세계 공용어라고 여긴다.

→ 영어는 세계 공용어로 여겨진다.

비법 4

1 [해석]

① 그것은 우리에 의해 결정될 것이다.

② 그 의자는 나무와 금속으로 만들어진다.

③ 그 아기는 그녀의 할머니에 의해 길러졌다.
④ 그 벽은 아이들에 의해 칠해지고 있다.
⑤ 이 소설은 같은 작가에 의해 쓰여졌다.
[해설] ②는 of 또는 with가 오고 나머지는 by가 온다.
(be made with/of: (물리적 변화) ~으로 만들어지다)

2 [해석]
① 나는 그녀의 칭찬에 기뻤다.
② 나는 중국어를 배우는 것에 관심이 있다.
③ 그 땅은 잔디로 덮여있었다.
④ 내 부모님은 그 일에 대해 만족했다.
⑤ 그 방은 아이들로 붐볐다.
[해설] ②는 in, 나머지는 with가 와야 한다. (be interested in: ~에 관심이 있다)

내신 만점! 실전 기출

01. ④ 02. ④ 03. ③
04. ④ 05. ① 06. ②
07. is being prepared
08. should change → should be changed
09. will be cleaned up 10. ⑤
11. ③ 12. ② 13. ⑤
14. ④
15. was called captain by everyone in his class
16. was offered a great opportunity by his teacher, was offered to him by his teacher
17. ④ 18. was shown to
19. ⑤ 20. ③
21. (1) is said to be one of the best soccer players
(2) is said that Ji-sung Park is one of the best soccer players
22. ② 23. ②, ③ 24. be
25. is building → is being built 26. ④
27. ⑤ 28. ①
29. is looked up to by many people
30. ⑤

01 [해석] 이 기계는 John이 능숙하기 때문에 그에 의해 고쳐질 수 있다.
[해설] 조동사의 수동태는 '조동사 + be + p.p.'의 형태로 쓴다.

02 [해석] 새로운 학교 건물은 지금 건설되고 있다.
[해설] 진행형의 수동태는 'be + being + p.p.'의 형태로 쓴다.

03 [해석] 당신은 우유를 냉장고에 보관해야만 한다.
→ 그 우유는 냉장고에 보관되어야 한다.
[해설] 조동사의 수동태는 '조동사 + be + p.p.'의 형태로 쓴다.

04 [해석] 그는 수 년 동안 많은 훌륭한 노래들을 작곡하였다.
→ 많은 훌륭한 노래들이 수 년 동안 그에 의해 작곡되었다.
[해설] 수 년 동안의 의미인 for years가 왔으므로 현재완료를 쓴다. 현재완료형의 수동태는 'have/has + been + p.p.'를 쓴다.

05 [해석]
ⓐ 우리는 모두 교장선생님의 끝없는 연설에 지루해졌다.
ⓑ 그 소식을 들었을 때 내 마음은 기쁨으로 가득 찼다.
[해설]
ⓐ be bored with ~: ~에 질리다, 지루해지다
ⓑ be filled with ~: ~로 가득 차다

06 [해석]
ⓐ 몇 가지 규칙들이 칠판에 적혀지고 있다.
ⓑ 그 방은 두 사람에 의해 칠해지고 있었다.
[해설] ② be동사 다음에 빈칸과 과거분사(p.p.)가 왔으므로 진행형의 수동태임을 알 수 있다. 진행형의 수동태는 'be + being + p.p.'를 쓴다.

07 [해석] 그들은 지금 사업 보고서를 준비하고 있다.
→ 그 사업 보고서는 그들에 의해 지금 준비되고 있다.
[해설] 진행형의 수동태는 'be being p.p.'를 쓴다.

08 [해설] 조동사가 있는 문장의 수동태는 '조동사 + be + p.p.'의 형태로 쓴다.

09 [해석] 〈보기〉
A: 누가 쿠키를 만들었나요?
B: 그 쿠키들은 Jane에 의해 만들어졌어요.
〈문제〉
A: 누가 강당을 치울 건가요?
B: 강당은 우리에 의해 치워질 거에요.

[해설] 조동사가 있는 문장의 수동태는 '조동사 + be + p.p.'의 형태로 쓴다.

10 [해석]

① 비밀스런 비결이 그들에게 주어졌다.

② 종이 몇 장이 우리에게 건네졌다.

③ 그 메일은 어제 내게 보내졌다.

④ 몇몇 물건들은 그들에 의해 우리에게 팔렸다.

⑤ 새로운 여행가방이 아빠에 의해 나를 위해 구매되었다.

[해설]

⑤ 4형식 문장을 직접목적어를 주어로 하는 수동태로 바꿀 때, buy의 경우엔 뒤에 남은 간접목적어 앞에 전치사 for를 쓴다.

①~④ 4형식 문장을 직접목적어를 주어로 하는 수동태로 바꿀 때, give, pass, send, sell의 경우엔 뒤에 남은 간접목적어 앞에 to를 쓴다.

11 [해석]

· 그 감독은 그 부상 이후 그가 출전하는 것을 그만두게 했다.

→ 그는 부상 이후 감독에 의해 출전을 그만두게 되었다.

· 내 언니는 내가 그녀의 노트북을 쓰는 것을 허락했다.

→ 나는 언니에 의해 그녀의 노트북을 쓰도록 허락 받았다.

[해설]

· 5형식의 사역동사 make의 목적격 보어로 쓰인 동사원형은 수동태로 전환할 때 to부정사'로 쓴다.

· let의 수동태는 'be allowed to + 동사원형'으로 쓴다.

12 [해석] 그 면접관은 내게 많은 어려운 질문을 했다.

→ 많은 어려운 질문들이 그 면접관에 의해 내게 물어졌다.

[해설] ② 4형식 문장을 직접 목적어를 주어로 하는 수동태로 전환할 때 ask의 경우는 뒤에 남은 간접목적어 앞에 of를 쓴다.

13 [해석]

① 나는 내 틀에 박힌 일상에 질렸다.

② 우리는 역사에 관심이 없다.

③ 그 남자는 그의 실수에 부끄러웠다.

④ Sally는 그녀의 좋은 성격으로 알려져 있다.

⑤ 그 관광객은 아름다운 경치에 놀랐다.

[해설] ⑤ to를 at으로 고쳐야 한다. (be amazed at ~: ~에 놀라다, 경탄하다)

14 [해석] 한국 사람들은 열심히 일하고 근면하다고 믿어진다.

[해설] ④ that절이 포함된 문장의 수동태는 'It is p.p. that S + V'나 '주어 + be p.p. to V'를 쓴다.

15 [해석] 그의 반의 모두가 Jack을 대장이라고 불렀다.

→ Jack은 그의 반 모두에 의해 대장이라고 불렸다.

[해설] 5형식 문장을 수동태로 바꿀 때, 동사를 'be p.p.'로 바꾸고 그 뒤에 목적격 보어를 그대로 써준다.

16 [해석] 그의 선생님은 그에게 멋진 기회를 제공했다.

[해설] 4형식 문장을 수동태로 바꿀 때는 간접목적어, 직접목적어를 각각 주어로 하는 두 가지 형태로 바꿀 수 있다. 직접목적어를 주어로 하는 수동태로 바꿀 때 offer의 경우엔 뒤에 남은 간접목적어 앞에 전치사 to를 쓴다.

17 [해석]

① 그들은 그 약속을 취소했다.

→ 그 약속은 그들에 의해 취소되었다.

② 그는 내게 그와 함께 영화관에 가자고 요청했다.

→ 나는 그와 함께 영화관에 가는 것을 요청 받았다.

③ 아빠는 내게 이 안경을 사주셨다.

→ 이 안경은 아빠에 의해 나를 위해 구매되었다.

④ 그들은 지난 주에 그를 회장으로 선출했다.

→ 그는 지난 주에 회장으로 선출되었다.

⑤ 의사는 그 환자를 약물로 치료해야 한다.

→ 그 환자는 의사에 의해 약물로 치료되어야 한다.

[해설] ④ 5형식의 보어는 수동태의 주어로 쓰일 수 없다. 올바른 수동태 문장은 'He was elected president by them last week.'이 되어야 한다.

18 [해설] 수동태 문장은 'be + p.p.'를 쓴다. 4형식 문장을 직접목적어를 주어로 하는 수동태로 바꿀 경우 동사 show는 뒤에 남은 간접목적어 앞에 전치사 to를 쓴다.

19 [해석]

① 우리는 그 결과에 기뻤다.

② 그의 얼굴은 행복으로 가득 찼다.

③ 그는 그의 직업에 만족한 듯 보인다.

④ 그들은 내 행동에 실망했음이 틀림없다.

⑤ 우리는 매일 같은 음식에 질렸다.

[해설] ⑤는 of, 나머지는 with를 써야 한다. (be tired of ~: ~에 질리다)

20 [해석]
① 그는 내게 오래된 책을 보여주었다.
② 우리는 그가 바이올린을 연주하는 것을 들었다.
③ 모든 사람들이 그를 천재라고 생각한다.
④ 그는 내게 방정식을 어떻게 푸는지 가르쳐 주었다.
⑤ 그녀의 아름다운 미소는 모든 이들을 행복하게 만든다.
[해설] ③ 5형식의 목적격 보어를 주어로 수동태를 만들 수는 없다.
① → The old book was shown to me by him.
② → He was heard to play the violin by us.
④ → I was taught how to solve the equation by him.
⑤ → Everyone is made happy by her beautiful smile.

21 [해석] 사람들은 박지성이 최고의 축구선수들 중 한 명이라고 말한다. → 박지성은 최고의 축구 선수들 중 한 명이라고 말하여진다.
[해설] that절이 포함된 문장의 수동태는 'It is p.p. that S + V'나 '주어 + be p.p. to V'를 쓴다.

22 [해석]
① 나를 위한 새로운 가방이 그녀에 의해 구입되었다.
② 새로운 학생에 의해 Jane에게 한 가지 질문이 질문되었다.
③ 러브레터가 John에 의해 그녀에게 보내졌다.
④ 장학금이 대학교에 의해 그에게 제공되었다.
⑤ 약간의 맛있는 쿠키가 엄마에 의해 아이들에게 구어졌다.
[해설] 4형식 문장을 직접목적어가 주어로 오는 수동태로 전환할 때, 뒤에 남는 간접목적어 앞에 ① buy는 for, ② ask는 of, ③ give는 to, ④ offer는 to, ⑤ cook은 for를 쓴다.

23 [해석]
① 우리는 모두 그 장면에 놀랐다.
② 그의 이름은 많은 사람들에게 잘 알려졌다.
③ 그 책상은 많은 서류들로 덮여 있었다.
④ 실내는 식물과 나무들로 가득 차 있었다.
⑤ 그들 모두는 그들의 시험 결과에 대해 걱정했다.
[해설] ② as → to, ③ of → with
(② be well-known to ~: ~에게 잘 알려지다. / ③ be covered with ~: ~로 덮이다)

24 [해설] 'The books had better be returned as soon as possible.'의 5번째 단어는 be이다.

25 [해석] 시 정부는 그 지역의 북쪽 지역에 댐을 짓고 있다.
→ 그 댐은 그 지역 북쪽 지역에 시 정부에 의해 지어지고 있다.
[해설] 댐이 스스로 짓는 것이 아니라 지어지는 것이므로 수동태를 써야 하는데 진행시제 이므로 'be + being + p.p.'를 쓴다.

26 [해석]
ⓐ 음식은 그녀에 의해 만들어지고 있나요?
ⓑ 내 머리카락은 너무 짧게 잘렸다.
ⓒ 그는 그들에 의해 회장으로 선출되었다.
ⓓ 그들이 무언가에 대해 싸우고 있는 소리가 들려왔다.
ⓔ 그 소년들은 그들의 엄마에 의해 조용하도록 시켜졌다.
[해설]
ⓒ 5형식을 수동태로 전환할 때 목적격 보어는 동사 뒤에 그대로 쓴다.
ⓔ 수동태 뒤에 오는 동사는 to부정사 형태로 온다. (단, 지각사의 수동태인 경우는 뒤에 -ing 형태로 올 수 있다.)

27 [해석]
① 그는 지금 그의 자전거를 고치고 있다.
→ 그의 자전거는 지금 그에 의해 고쳐지고 있다.
② 우리 엄마는 작은 빵집을 운영하신다.
→ 작은 빵집이 우리 엄마에 의해 운영된다.
③ 사람들은 그가 열심히 일한다고 생각한다.
→ 그는 열심히 일한다고 여겨진다.
④ 우리는 요즘 대부분의 쓰레기를 재활용할 수 있다.
→ 대부분의 쓰레기는 요즘 재활용 될 수 있다.
⑤ Tiffany가 내년에 우리에게 영어를 가르칠 것이다.
→ 내년에 Tiffany에 의해 우리에게 영어가 가르쳐질 것이다.
[해설] ⑤ 4형식 문장을 수동태로 전환할 때 간접목적어를 주어로 하는 경우에는 직접목적어 앞에 전치사를 쓰지 않는다. (to 삭제)

28 [해석]
A: 그 뉴스 들었어?
B: 무슨 뉴스?
A: 좋은 뉴스는 아니야 사실. 우리 마을 근처 쇼핑몰에서 불이 났어.

B: 정말? 누가 죽었어?

A: 누구도 죽었다고 보도되진 않았어. 라디오 뉴스에 따르면 소방관들이 불을 끄려고 하고 있는데 아직 연기들이 보이고 있대.

[해설] ① break out은 그 자체로 '일어나다, 발생하다'라는 뜻이고, 수동태로 쓰일 수 없다.

29 [해설] 구동사는 한 단어로 취급해서 수동태를 만든다. (look up to ~: ~를 존경하다)

30 [해석] 전 시대적으로 가장 위대한 발명품은 무엇인가? 많은 사람들이 컴퓨터라고 대답할 것이다. 컴퓨터는 자동으로 논리적인 작동이 수행되도록 ⓐ 설계될 수 있는 기기이다. 일련의 운영이 바뀔 수 있으므로 컴퓨터는 한 가지 이상의 문제를 ⓑ 해결할 수 있다. 그러면 누가 컴퓨터를 처음 발명했는가? Charles Babbage라는 영국 엔지니어가 컴퓨터의 개념을 처음 만들었다고 알려진다. 그는 컴퓨터의 아버지라고 ⓒ 여겨진다.

[해설] ⓐ는 주어(a device)가 동작(program)을 당하므로 수동태(be + p.p.)로 'programmed'를 써야 한다. / ⓑ 문장의 목적어인 one kind of problem이 있으므로 능동태이다. 조동사 can뒤에는 동사 원형 'solve'를 써야 한다. / ⓒ는 주어(He)가 동작(consider)를 당하므로 수동태(be + p.p.)로 considered를 써야 한다.

실력 탄탄! 서술형 심화

1 (1) ate → eaten (4) turn → turned

2 ⓐ Jeju island is said to be famous for its beautiful beaches.
ⓑ I was asked to book a hotel by my mom

3 useful information about good hotels in Jeju island will be given

1 [해석]

(1) 음식은 교실에서 먹어져서는 안 된다.

(2) 숙제는 수업 전에 되어야 한다.

(3) 교실에서는 영어만 사용되어야 한다.

(4) 핸드폰은 수업 중에는 꺼져야 한다.

2~3 [해석]

A: Chris, 이번 여름 방학 계획이 뭐야?

B: 응, 나는 제주도에 갈 거야.

A: 와, 그거 멋지다. ⓐ 제주도는 그 곳의 아름다운 해변들로 유명하다고 하잖아.

B: 맞아. 기다릴 수 없을 만큼 기대 돼. 음식과 해변 둘 다 멋지다고 들었어.

A: 어디 묵을지는 정했어?

B: 아직. ⓑ 엄마가 내게 호텔을 예약하라고 부탁하셔서, 이번 주에 할 거야.

A: 네가 원하면 제주도에 있는 좋은 호텔에 대한 유용한 몇 가지 정보들을 줄 수 있어. 우리 언니가 그거에 대해 잘 아는데, 내가 언니에게 물어보고 네게 알려줄게.

B: 와, Jenny야. 넌 참 친절하구나. 그거 좋겠어. 고마워.

2 [해설]

· ⓐ that절이 포함된 문장의 수동태는 'It is p.p. that S + V' 또는 '주어 + be p.p. to V'를 쓴다.

· ⓑ be asked to + 동사원형: ~하는 것을 요청 받다.

3 [해설] Jenny가 'I can give you some useful information about good hotels in Jeju island.' 라고 말했고 Chris가 그렇게 해주면 좋겠다고 응답했다.

Chapter 07 대명사

Point 1 재귀대명사

A 1. 강조 2. 재귀 3. 강조

B 1. yourself 2. me 3. himself

C 1. for themselves 2. by himself
3. herself

A [해석]

1. 그의 연기 자체는 훌륭했다.
2. 나는 스스로 생각했다. "나는 할 수 있어."
3. Jack은 집 전체를 청소했다.

[해설]

1,3. 생략 가능하므로 강조용법이다. 주어의 행위를 강조하기 위해 강조하고자 하는 명사의 뒤에, 또는 문장 맨 끝에 재귀대명사를 써 준다. 직접, 스스로라고 해석한다.

2. 문장의 주어와 목적어의 대상이 같을 때, 재귀대명사가 목적어로 쓰이고 생략 불가능하다.

B [해설]

1. 생략된 명령문의 주어(You)와 같은 대상이고 know의 목적어이므로 재귀대명사를 써야 한다.
2. 문장의 주어와 전치사 to의 목적어가 가리키는 대상이 일치하지 않으므로 me를 쓴다.

Point 2 it의 여러 가지 쓰임

A 1. 그것은 쉬운 결정이 아니었다.
2. 함께 자전거를 타는 것은 재미있다.
3. 숙제를 마치는데 2시간이 걸렸다.
4. 나는 애완동물을 돌보는 것이 어렵다는 것을 알았다.

B 1. It is interesting to learn foreign languages
2. It rains a lot in the summer
3. I found it necessary to exercise regularly

A [해설]

1. '그것'이라고 해석되므로 지시대명사이다.
2. 진주어(to ride ~)를 대신해서 쓰인 가주어이다.
3. 시간을 나타내는 비인칭 주어이다.
4. 진목적어(to take ~)를 대신해서 쓰인 가목적어이다.

B [해설]

2. 날씨를 나타내는 비인칭 주어 it
3. 가목적어 it, 진목적어 to exercise regularly

Point 3 부정대명사 one vs. it / others vs. the other(s)

A 1. others 2. another
3. one 4. the other

B 1. another 2. others 3. the others

A [해석]

1. 그녀는 항상 다른 사람들에게 친절하다.
2. 죄송하지만 또 다른 것을 가져다 주세요.
3. 나는 오늘 펜을 안 가져왔어. 하나 빌릴 수 있을까?
4. 나는 고양이 두 마리를 가지고 있다. 하나는 검은색이고 다른 하나는 하얀색이다.

[해설]

1. 불특정한 사람들을 가리키므로 others를 쓴다.
2. '또 다른 것'을 의미하므로 another을 쓴다.
3. 동일한 종류의 정해지지 않은 사물을 가리키므로 one을 쓴다.
4. 둘 중의 나머지 하나를 가리키므로 the other를 쓴다.

Point 4 짝을 이루어 쓰는 표현

A 1. One, the others 2. Some, others
3. the others 4. the other

B 1. another → the other
2. the other → the others

A [해석]

1. 나는 모자 세 개가 있다. 하나는 검은색, 나머지 것들은 파란색이다.
2. 몇몇은 바다에 가는 것을 좋아하고 다른 몇몇은 산에 가는 것을 좋아한다.
3. 나는 그에게 두 종류의 꽃을 받았다. 몇몇은 장미꽃이고 나머지는 백합이다.
4. 선생님은 두 권의 책을 내게 추천해 주셨다. 하나는 소설이고 다른 하나는 수필이다.

B [해설]

1. 둘일 때는 'one..., the other ~'을 쓴다.

2. 세 명일 때는 하나는 one, 나머지 모두는 the others

Point 5 something *vs.* anything

A	1. anyone	2. anyone	3. someone
	4. anything	5. something	6. Someone

B 1. I don't know anyone in the city
2. There isn't anything left to eat
3. You should not worry about anything
4. Someone in my neighborhood stole my bike last night

A [해설]

1~2. 권유가 아닌 일반 의문문이므로 anyone을 쓴다.

4. 부정문이므로 anything을 쓴다.

5. 긍정문이며 사물이므로 something을 쓴다.

B [해석]

1. 나는 도시에 어떤 누구도 알지 못한다.

2. 먹을 것이 아무것도 남지 않았다.

3. 어떤 것도 걱정하지 않아도 된다.

4. 어젯밤 내 이웃의 누군가가 내 자전거를 훔쳐갔다.

[해설]

1~3. 부정문이므로 anyone, anything을 써야 한다.

4. 긍정문에는 대개 someone을 쓴다.

Point 6 전체부정 *vs.* 부분부정

A 1. Nobody 2. nothing

B 1. don't, anything
2. isn't anyone[anybody]

C 1. Not all my friends
2. Not both of my sisters
3. not always fun
4. Not every movie

A [해설]

1. '아무도'는 전체부정이므로 nobody를 써야 한다.

2. '아무것도'는 전체부정이므로 nothing을 써야 한다.

B [해석]

1. 네게 말해줄 것이 아무것도 없다.

2. 죄송하지만 여기에는 그런 이름의 사람이 없습니다.

[해설]

1. nothing = not + anything

2. no one = not + anyone[anybody]

C [해석]

1. 몇몇 친구들은 파티에 왔지만 나머지는 오지 않았다.
= 모든 친구들이 파티에 온 것은 아니다.

2. 큰 언니는 수다스럽지만 내 여동생은 아니다.
= 내 여자형제들이 둘 다 수다스러운 것은 아니다.

3. 게임을 하는 것은 때때로 재미있다. 하지만 때로는 그렇지 않다.
= 게임을 하는 것이 항상 재미있는 것은 아니다.

4. 몇몇 영화는 재미있지만 다른 것들은 재미 없다.
= 모든 영화가 재미있는 것은 아니다.

[해설]

1. not all ~: 모두 ~는 아니다

2. not both ~: 둘 다 ~는 아니다

3. not always ~: 항상 ~은 아니다

4. not every ~: 모두 ~은 아니다

일등 비법 노트

비법 1	1. ②	2. ③
비법 2	1. ⑤	
비법 3	1. ②	2. ②
비법 4	1. ③	

비법 1

1 [해석]

① 내가 직접 자전거를 수리했다.
② 마음껏 드세요.
③ 그 소년은 스스로 방을 청소했다.
④ 당신은 영화 자체에 감동을 받을 것이다.
⑤ 내 여자형제들은 유럽을 여행할 것이다.

[해설] ②는 생략이 불가능한 재귀용법이고, 나머지는 모두 생략이 가능하므로 강조를 위해 쓴 강조용법이다.

2 [해석]

① 그녀는 스스로를 자랑스러워하는 것처럼 보인다.

② 집처럼 편안하게 계세요.

③ 내 선생님은 직접 이 책을 썼다.

④ 나는 혼자 모든 일을 해야 했다.

⑤ 그 남자는 혼자 생각했다. “시도해 보자.”

[해설] ③은 생략할 수 있는 강조용법이다.

비법 2

1 [해석] 외국어를 배우는 것은 실용적이다.

① 그때는 밖이 어두웠다.

② 차로 세 시간 걸릴 것이다.

③ 그것은 정말로 훌륭한 연설이었다.

④ 나는 어딘가에서 지갑을 잃어버린 것 같다.

⑤ 함께 자주 시간을 보내는 것은 좋다.

[해설] ①~②는 비인칭 주어 , ③은 지시대명사, ④는 it seems의 it이다. 보기와 ⑤는 가주어 it이다.

비법 3

1 [해석] 나는 집에 가방이 세 개 있다. ⓐ 하나는 학교, ⓑ 또 다른 하나는 학원, 그리고 ⓒ 나머지 하나는 여행을 위한 것이다.

[해설] 셋일 때 ‘하나는…, 다른 하나는…, 나머지 하나는…’의 표현은 ‘One… , another…., the other…’을 쓴다.

2 [해석] 공원에 두 명의 아이들이 있다. ⓐ 한 명은 벤치에 앉아있고, ⓑ 나머지 다른 한 명은 공을 가지고 뛰고 있다.

[해설] 둘일 때, ‘one…, the other ~’를 쓴다.

비법 4

1 [해석]

① 모든 사람들이 야구팀에 합류하지는 않았다.

② 내가 항상 그의 말을 듣는 것은 아니다.

③ Sally는 그들 중 아무도 초대하지 않았다.

④ 그녀는 그 학생들 둘 다 아는 것은 아니다. (한 명은 모른다.)

⑤ 모든 지원자들이 인터뷰할 기회를 갖지는 않았다.

[해설] ①②④⑤: 전체(every, always, both)를 부정하면 부분부정이 된다.

③: any(부분)를 부정하면 전체를 부정하는 의미(아무도 ~ 하지 않다)가 된다.

내신 만점! 실전 기출

01. ③	02. ③	03. ③
04. ①	05. ④	06. ⑤
07. It seems	08. himself	09. ①
10. ⑤	11. It is	12. ②
13. yourself	14. ②	15. ⑤
16. ④	17. ②	
18. ⓐ another, ⓑ the other		
19. by themselves	20. Not, Some, the others	
21. ④	22. ④	23. some, others
24. Some, the others		25. ④
26. ④	27. ②	
28. the other is listening to music		
29. the others → others		
30. (1) the others (2) others		

01 [해석]

A: 방금 이 사과들을 샀어요. 그런데 신선해 보이지 않네요.

B: 아, 죄송합니다. 신선한 것으로 드릴께요.

[해설] ③ 앞서 나온 명사와 종류는 같지만 대상이 다르므로 one을 쓰는데 앞에 a가 없으므로 복수형 ones가 와야 한다.

02 [해석] 몇몇 사람들은 커피를 좋아하고 다른 사람들은 차를 좋아한다.

[해설] ③ ‘어떤 사람들은…, 또 어떤 사람들은 ~’이라는 뜻으로 ‘Some…, others ~’를 쓴다.

03 [해석]

① 그런 말을 하다니 당신은 친절하군요.

② 그가 경기를 이긴 것은 놀랍다.

③ 어젯밤에 폭우가 내렸다.

④ 엎질러진 우유를 놓고 우는 것은 소용없다.

⑤ 그녀의 억양을 이해하는 것은 어렵다.

[해설] ③은 날씨를 나타내는 비인칭 주어 it, 나머지는 가주어 it이다.

04 [해석]

① 바로 내가 그 문제를 해결했다.

② 그녀는 그녀의 가족에게 자신을 헌신했다.

③ 그녀는 저녁을 하면서 (스스로) 데었다.

④ 그는 스스로에게 "너는 다시 해낼 수 있어" 라고 말했다.

⑤ 마음껏 드세요. 당신이 음식을 맘에 들어 하길 바래요.

[해설]

①은 강조용법으로 생략할 수 있다.

②~⑤ 재귀대명사가 목적어로 쓰인 재귀용법이다. 생략할 수 없다.

05 [해석] 다른 모든 친구들은 집에 일찍 가야만 했다. 그래서 나는 교실을 오로지 혼자서 청소해야만 했다.

[해설] by oneself: 혼자서

06 [해석] 〈보기〉 그렇게 말을 하다니 그녀는 무례하구나.

① 그것은 당장 되어야만 한다.

② 요즘 날씨가 따뜻해지고 있다.

③ 드럼을 연주한 것은 Tom이다.

④ 그것은 우리 누나(언니)의 드럼이다. 내 것이 아니다.

⑤ 이 곳에서 너희 모두를 보게 되어 좋다.

[해설] 〈보기〉는 가주어로 쓰인 it이므로 ⑤와 같다. ①은 지시대명사 ②날씨를 나타내는 비인칭 주어 ③ it ~ that(who) 강조구문 ④ 지시대명사 ⑤ 가주어로 쓰인 it이다.

07 [해석] James와 민호는 매우 가까운 듯 보인다.

[해설] 'It seems that 주어 + 동사.' 구문은 '주어 seems to 동사원형'으로 바꿔 쓸 수 있다.

08 [해설]

· be proud of oneself: 스스로를 자랑스러워하다

· love oneself: 스스로를 사랑하다

09 [해석]

① 나는 때때로 혼잣말을 한다.

② 그 영화 자체는 훌륭했다.

③ 내 할아버지께서 그 집을 지었다.

④ 당신은 그 책 자체에 감동받을 것이다.

⑤ 학생들조차 그 아이디어를 좋아하지 않는다.

[해설] ①은 생략이 불가능하므로 강조용법이 아니다. ②~⑤ 주어의 행위를 강조하기 위해 강조하고자 하는 명사의 뒤에, 또는 문장 맨 끝에 쓰인 강조용법으로 생략이 가능하며, '직접' 또는 '스스로'라고 해석한다.

10 [해석]

① 나는 아침을 먹는 것이 중요하다는 것을 알았다.

② 더 덥고 습해지고 있었다.

③ 그녀가 비밀을 아는 것처럼 보인다.

④ 차로 부산까지 얼마나 걸리나요?

⑤ 나는 그녀가 의사가 될 것이라고 생각했다.

[해설] ① 가주어 ② 비인칭 주어 ③ It seems that 구문, ④ 비인칭 주어인 it이다. ⑤는 it이 아니라 that이 들어간다.

11 [해석] 도움이 필요한 남을 돕는 것은 보람되다.

[해설] 동명사 주어를 뒤로 보내고 가주어 it을 앞에 쓸 수 있다.

12 [해석]

· 이 외투는 너무 작아요. 또 다른 것을 보여주시겠어요?

· 우리 집에는 카메라가 세 대가 있다. 하나는 내 것이고 나머지 것들은 남동생의 것이다.

[해설] 종류는 같지만 대상이 다른 것은 one, 여러 개 중의 처음 하나는 one을 써서 나타낸다.

13 [해석]

· 내가 너를 위해 이 쿠키들을 만들었어. 마음껏 먹어.

· 당신은 다른 사람들 보다 스스로를 먼저 돌봐야 한다.

· 당신 집에서처럼 편안하게 계세요.

[해설]

· Help yourself: 마음껏 드세요

· Make yourself at home: 집에서처럼 편하게 있으세요.

14 [해석]

M: Sally, 방학 전에 더 바쁠 것 같다는 게 무슨 말이었니?

W: 음, 그게 … 방학이 시작하기 전에 해야만 하는 일이 두 개가 있어. 하나는 과제를 마치는 것이고 다른 하나는 중국 여행을 계획하는 것이야.

15 [해석] 우리는 강아지 세 마리를 키운다. 하나는 말티즈이고, 나머지는 포메라니안이다. 당신은 그들이 얼마나 귀여운지 상상조차 할 수 없다.

16 [해석]

· 축구 경기를 보는 것은 재미있다.

· 비가 온 후에 추워질 것이다.

· 우리가 그것을 함께 하면 한 시간이 채 걸리지 않을 것이다.

[해설] ⓐ 가주어 it, ⓑ 비인칭 주어 it, ⓒ 시간을 나타내는 it이다.

17 [해석]

① 누군가 이 메시지를 내게 남겼다.

② 나는 이것에 대해 아무에게도 말하지 않을 것이다.

③ 그녀는 누구와도 방을 함께 쓰는 것을 원치 않는다.

④ 나는 이 반에서 그녀 말고는 아무도 모른다.

⑤ 나는 누군가 나를 도와줄 사람이 있을 거라고 확신한다.

[해설] ② 부정문에서는 someone이 아닌 anyone을 써야 한다.

18 [해석]

A: Jenny, 난 네가 언어에 능숙하다고 들었어. 몇 개의 언어를 구사할 수 있니?

B: 나는 세 개의 언어를 구사할 수 있어. 하나는 한국어, 또 다른 하나는 영어, 나머지는 중국어야.

[해설] 셋일 때 '하나는… 또 다른 하나는…나머지 하나는…'의 뜻으로는 'One…, another…, the other…'를 쓴다.

19 [해석] 최근 조사에 따르면, 서울에 혼자 사는 사람들의 수가 증가했다.

[해설] by oneself: 혼자

20 [해설] 몇몇은 some, 나머지 모두는 the others를 쓴다.

21 [해석] 제주도는 멋진 관광명소라고 말해진다. 그 곳은 많은 아름다운 해변을 가지고 있다. 어느 계절에 방문해도 좋지만 봄은 최고의 계절이 될 수 있다. 봄에는 날씨가 따뜻하고 우리는 많은 아름다운 꽃들을 볼 수 있다. 제주도를 방문하라. 그것은 잊지 못할 경험이 될 것이다.

[해설] ⓐ는 가주어 it, ⓑ는 지시대명사, ⓒ는 가주어, ⓓ는 날씨를 나타내는 비인칭주어 it, ⓔ는 지시대명사이다.

22 [해석]

· 지난 주말 나는 세 편의 영화를 보았다. 하나는 흥미로웠고 나머지 둘은 지루했다.

· 나는 세 명의 사촌이 있다. 한 명은 나와 나이가 같고 다른 한 명은 한 살 어리고 나머지 한 명은 나보다 한 살 더 많다.

[해설]

· '정해진 범위(영화 세 편) 안에서, 하나는…, 나머지 전부는…'이라는 뜻으로 'One…, the others…'를 쓴다.

· 셋일 때, '하나는…, 다른 하나는…, 나머지 하나는…'이라는 뜻으로 'One…, another…, the other…'를 쓴다.

23 [해석] '몇몇은…, 또 다른 몇몇은 ~'의 뜻으로는 'Some…, others ~'를 쓴다.

24 [해석] '몇몇은…, 나머지 모두는…'의 뜻으로는 'Some…, the others…'를 쓴다.

25 [해석] 〈보기〉 바로 내가 내 가족을 위해 전체 저녁을 전부 준비했다.

① 그녀는 거울 속의 자신을 보는 것을 좋아한다.

② 당신은 스스로를 자랑스럽게 여겨야 한다.

③ 나는 내게 선물을 사줄 것이다.

④ James 그 자신이 그 어려운 문제를 해결했다.

⑤ 나는 혼자 있을 때, 때때로 혼잣말을 한다.

[해설] 〈보기〉와 ④는 생략할 수 있으므로 강조용법이다. ①②③⑤는 목적어로 쓰인 재귀용법이다.

26 [해석]

① 모든 사람이 이 아이디어를 좋아한 것은 아니다.

② 영화를 보는 것이 항상 재미있는 것은 아니다.

③ 내 오빠들이 둘 다 고등학생인 것은 아니다.

④ 그 반의 아무도 그 수학 문제를 풀 수 없었다.

⑤ 그 반의 모든 아이들이 활발하고 시끄러운 것은 아니다.

[해설] ④는 '아무도 ~할 수 없었다'는 뜻의 전체부정이다. 나머지는 '모두가[둘 다] ~한 것은 아니다'는 뜻의 부분부정이다.

27 [해석]

A: 제 구매에 대한 할인을 받을 수 있나요?

B: 물론입니다. 저희는 두 가지의 쿠폰을 제공해 드릴 수 있습니다. 하나는 5%할인, 다른 하나는 10달러 할인 쿠폰입니다. 어느 것을 선호하시나요?

A: 첫 번째 것을 받겠습니다. 감사합니다.

[해설] 둘일 때, '하나(one)는… 나머지 하나(the other)는 ~'으로 쓴다.

28 [해석]

A: 네 취미는 무엇이니, Julie?

B: 나는 취미가 두 개 있어. 하나는 영화를 보는 것이고 나머지 하나는 음악을 듣는 것이야. 둘 다 내 스트레스를 줄이는 것을 도와줘.

[해설] '둘 중 하나는…, 나머지 하나는…'의 뜻으로는 'One…, the other…'를 쓴다.

29 [해석] 많은 사람들이 요즘 들어 스포츠 클럽에 가입한다. 몇몇은 야구 팀에 가입하고 다른 몇몇은 축구 팀에 가입한다.
[해설] 야구팀에 가입하는 사람들을 뺀 세상의 사람들 모두가 축구 팀에 가입하는 것이 아니므로 the others가 아닌 others가 와야 한다.

30 [해석]
(1) 우리 학교에서 Jane은 금메달을 받았지만 나머지는 아무것도 받지 못했다.
(2) 우리 학교에서 30%의 학생들은 체육 수업을 좋아하지만 50%는 음악 수업을 더 좋아한다.

[해설]
(1) 학교라는 정해진 범위에서 Jane을 빼고 남은 사람들 전부를 가리키는 표현은 the others이다.
(2) 50%가 나머지 전부는 아니므로 the others가 아닌 others가 와야 한다.

실력 탄탄! 서술형 심화

1 (1) some, the others
(2) some, others, the others

2 (1) ⓐ another ⓑ the others
(2) ① yourself → you
② One → It

1 [해석]
(1) 민호의 반에서는 여름방학 동안 몇몇은 등산을 가고 나머지는 수영하러 갈 것이다.
(2) 지민의 반에서는 여름방학 동안 몇몇은 등산을 가고 몇몇은 수영하러 가고, 그리고 나머지는 스키 타러 갈 것이다.

2 [해석]
A: 이 모자는 제게 좀 작아요. ⓐ 또 다른 것을 보여주실 수 있나요?
B: 물론입니다. 이걸 한 번 써 보세요.
A: 오, 좋아 보이네요. 저는 이 흰색 셔츠, 이 넥타이, 그리고 이 모자를 사겠습니다.
B: 물론입니다. ① 당신을 위해 포장을 해드릴까요?
A: ② 모자만요. 그것은 선물이에요. ⓑ 나머지들은 쇼핑백에 넣어 주시겠어요?
B: 물론입니다. 문제 없습니다.

[해설]
(1) ⓐ 또 다른 불특정한 것을 의미하므로 another을 써야 한다. ⓑ 문맥상 모자를 제외한 나머지 물건들(흰색 셔츠와 넥타이) 모두를 의미하므로 the others를 써야 한다.
(2) ① 주어와 목적어가 일치하지 않으므로 재귀대명사를 쓰면 안 된다. ② cap을 가리키므로 one이 아닌 지시대명사 it을 써야 한다.

Chapter 08 비교

Point 1 원급을 이용한 비교

A 1. fast 2. pretty 3. high
4. thin 5. as 6. diligent
7. well 8. poor 9. near
10. difficult

B 1. as rich as 2. as difficult as
3. not as[so] big as 4. as well as

C 1. as tall as 2. not as[so] warm as

A [해설]

1~3, 5, 7, 8. 'as + 형용사/부사의 원급 + as'는 비교하는 대상의 정도가 같을 때 쓰이며, '~만큼 ~한/하게'라는 뜻이다.

4, 6, 9~10. 원급 비교의 부정은 비교하는 두 대상의 정도가 같지 않을 때 'not + as(so) + 형용사/부사의 원급 + as'의 형태로 쓰며, '~만큼 ~하지 않은/않게' 라는 뜻이다.

1. as fast as: ~만큼 빠른
2. as pretty as: ~만큼 예쁜
3. as high as: ~만큼 높이
4. not so thin as: ~만큼 날씬하지 않은
5. as expensive as: ~만큼 비싼
6. not as diligent as: ~만큼 부지런하지 않은
7. as well as: ~만큼 잘
8. as poor as a church mouse: 찢어지게 가난한
9. not so near as: ~만큼 가깝지 않은
10. not as difficult as: ~만큼 어렵지 않은

B [해설]

1~2. 'as + 형용사/부사의 원급 + as'는 비교하는 대상의 정도가 같을 때 쓰이며, '~만큼 ~한/하게'라는 뜻이다.

3~4. 원급 비교의 부정은 비교하는 두 대상의 정도가 같지 않을 때 'not + as(so) + 형용사/부사의 원급 + as'의 형태로 쓰며, '~만큼 ~하지 않은/않게' 라는 뜻이다. as ~ as 사이에 들어가는 원급이 문장의 동사를 수식하므로 부사인 well이 들어가야 한다.

Point 2 비교급을 이용한 비교

A 1. cuter 2. taller 3. than
4. louder 5. much 6. large
7. as 8. earlier 9. farther

B 1. much warmer than
2. newer than
3. more expensive than
4. much more money than
5. earlier than our neighbors did

A [해설]

1, 3~4, 8~9. 두 가지의 대상을 비교할 때 '비교급 + than'을 쓰며, '~보다 더 ~한/하게'이라는 의미이다.

2, 5. 비교급을 강조할 때에는 비교급 앞에 much, a lot 등을 붙이며, '훨씬 더 ~한/하게'이라는 의미이다. 'very'는 원급에서만 강조가 가능하며 비교급 앞에 쓸 수 없다.

6. 원급 비교의 부정은 비교하는 두 대상의 정도가 같지 않을 때 'not + as[so] + 형용사/부사의 원급 + as'의 형태로 쓰며, '~만큼 ~하지 않은/않게' 라는 뜻이다.

7. 'as + 형용사/부사의 원급 + as'는 비교하는 대상의 정도가 같을 때 쓰이며, '~만큼 ~한/하게' 라는 뜻이다.

Point 3 최상급을 이용한 비교

A 1. largest 2. best
3. players 4. newest
5. most 6. have ever met
7. the greatest 8. have ever heard
9. the most delicious

B 1. the highest mountain
2. the nearest planet
3. one of the most handsome students
4. the busiest city that I've ever visited
5. one of the oldest schools

A [해설]

1~2, 4~5. 'the + 최상급'은 최상급을 이용한 비교의 표현이다. 최상급 뒤에 'in'을 써서 비교하는 대상의 범위를 나타낼 수 있으며, '가장 ~한/하게' 라는 의미이다.

3, 7. 'one of the 최상급 + 복수명사'는 '가장 ~한 것들 중의 하나'라는 뜻이다.

6, 8~9. 'the + 최상급 + 명사(+ that) + 주어 + have/has (ever) + p.p.'는 과거의 한 시점부터 지금까지의 경험을 통틀어 '~가 가장 ~하다' 는 뜻이다.

1. the largest: 가장 큰
2. the best: 최고의
3. one of the best players: 최고의 선수들 중 한 명
4. the newest: 가장 새 것의
5. the most difficult: 가장 어려운
6. the smartest student I have ever met: 내가 만난 학생들 중 가장 똑똑한 학생
7. one of the greatest natural treasures: 가장 훌륭한 천연기념물들 중 하나
8. the most beautiful voice that I have ever heard: 내가 들었던 목소리 중 가장 아름다운 목소리
9. the most delicious: 가장 맛있는

Point 4 여러 가지 비교 구문 I

A 1. as 2. fast 3. possible

B 1. seven times longer than
2. five times thicker than
3. twice more expensive than

C 1. as quickly as I can
2. three times as large as

A [해석]
1. as often as she can: 그녀가 할 수 있는 한 가장 자주
2. as fast as he could: 그가 할 수 있는 한 가장 빠르게
3. as hard as possible: 할 수 있는 한 열심히

B [해석] 〈보기〉 three times heavier than: 3배 더 무거운
1. seven times longer than: 7배 더 긴
2. five times thicker than: 5배 더 두꺼운
3. twice more expensive than: 두 배 더 비싼

C [해설]
1. as quickly as I can: 내가 할 수 있는 한(가능한) 빠르게
2. three times as large as: 세 배가 더 큰

Point 5 여러 가지 비교 구문 II

A 1. colder 2. fatter and fatter
3. The more 4. worse and worse
5. higher and higher

B 1. The longer, the harder
2. The sooner, the better
3. The more fast food, the fatter
4. higher and higher

C 1. the more knowledge you'll get
2. the weaker your body will become

A [해설]
1. 'as + 주어 + 동사 + 비교급, 주어 + 동사 + 비교급'은 '~하면 할수록 더 ~한/하게' 라는 뜻이다.
2, 4~5. '비교급 + and + 비교급'은 '점점 더 ~한/하게' 라는 뜻이다.
2. fatter and fatter: 점점 더 살이 찌는
3. The more, the better ~: 더 많이 ~할수록, 더 좋은
4. worse and worse: 점점 더 나쁜
5. higher and higher: 점점 더 높은

B [해설]
1. The longer, the harder: 더 길게 ~할수록 더 힘든
2. The sooner, the better: 빠르면 빠를수록 더 좋은
3. The more, the fatter: 더 많이 ~할수록 더 뚱뚱한
4. higher and higher: 점점 더 높이

C [해설] 'As + 주어 + 동사 + 비교급, 주어 + 동사 + 비교급'는 '~하면 할수록 더 ~한/하게' 라는 뜻이다. 의미상 'the + 비교급 + 주어 + 동사, the + 비교급 + 주어 + 동사'로 바꾸어 쓸 수 있다.

Point 6 여러 가지 비교 구문 III

A 1. (1) memorable (2) than
(3) any other (4) all the other

2. (1) as lucky as (2) luckier than
(3) person
(4) luckier, all the other persons

B 1. (1) No (other), as[so] high as
(2) No (other), higher than
(3) higher than any other
(4) higher than all the other

A [해설] 1~2. 최상급 + 형용사/부사: 가장 ~한
= No (other) ~ as[so] + 원급 + as …: 어떤 ~도 …만큼 ~하지 않은(않게)
= No (other) ~비교급 + than: 어떤 ~도 …보다 ~하지 않은(않게)
= 비교급 + than + any other + 단수명사: 다른 어떤 ~보다도 더 ~한/하게
= 비교급 + than + all the other + 복수명사: 다른 모든 …보다도 더 ~한/하게

B [해설] 최상급 + 형용사/부사: 가장 ~한
= No(other) ~ as[so] + 원급 + as ~ : 어떤 ~도 ~만큼 ~하지 않은(않게)
= No(other) ~비교급 + than: 어떤 ~도 ~보다 ~하지 않은(않게)
= 비교급 + than + any other + 단수명사: 다른 어떤 ~보다도 더 ~한/하게
= 비교급 + than + all the other + 복수명사: 다른 모든 ~보다도 더 ~한/하게

일등 비법 노트

비법 1	1. ③	2. ③
비법 2	1. ②	
비법 3	1. ①	
비법 4	1. the most beautiful dress (that) I have ever seen	
비법 5	1. ②	

비법 1

1 [해석] 나의 엄마는 우리가 기대했던 것보다 훨씬 더 고급스럽게 식탁을 꾸몄다.
[해설] very는 원급에서만 강조가 가능하며 비교급 앞에 쓸 수 없다.

2 [해석]
① Mark는 Walter보다 훨씬 더 어리다.
② Tom은 Brandon보다 훨씬 더 키가 크다.
③ Brandon은 Patrick보다 훨씬 더 말랐다.
④ Charlie는 Patrick보다 훨씬 더 똑똑하다.
⑤ Abraham은 Adam보다 훨씬 더 힘이 세다.
[해설] very는 원급에서만 강조가 가능하며 비교급 앞에 쓸 수 없다. 비교급을 강조할 때에는 비교급 강조 부사를 써야 한다. (very → even, much, still, far, a lot 등)

비법 2

1 [해석] Sarah는 나의 학급의 그 어떤 다른 학생보다도 더 부지런하다.

비법 3

1 [해석]
② 그는 그의 여동생/누나만큼 똑똑하다.
③ 그녀는 그녀의 가장 친한 친구만큼 키가 크다.
④ 그의 집은 그녀의 집만큼 크다.
⑤ 이 전화는 저것만큼 비싸다.
[해설] ① 'as + 형용사/부사의 원급 + as'는 비교하는 대상의 정도가 같을 때 쓰이며, '~만큼 ~한/하게' 라는 뜻이다. 따라서 비교급 faster가 아닌 원급 fast가 와야 한다.

비법 4

1 [해설] 'the + 최상급 + 명사 (+ that) + 주어 + have/has (ever) + p.p.'는 과거의 한 시점부터 지금까지의 경험을 통틀어 '~가 지금껏 ~한 것 중에 가장 ~하다'는 뜻이다.

비법 5

1 [해설] '점점 더 ~한/하게'라는 뜻으로는 '비교급 + and + 비교급'으로 나타낸다. (bad and bad → worse and worse)

내신 만점! 실전 기출

01. ①　　**02.** ③
03. She is as famous as Jack.　　**04.** ④
05. The less, the more　　**06.** ②
07. ④
08. no (other) person cooks better than my mom
09. ①, ④　　**10.** ②, ⑤
11. (1) more books than any other
(2) No, many books as
12. ②　　**13.** ④　　**14.** ④
15. (1) is as tall as Eric　　(2) is heavier than Eric

16. ③ 17. the fastest animal
18. ③, ⑤ 19. ① 20. ③
21. better than any other pitcher 22. ①
23. ① 24. ⑤
25. I want to know what Nicole likes to do more than dancing.
26. The nearer the test date comes, the more nervous
27. ④
28. ⓐ kinder → kind ⓔ good → better
ⓕ harder → hard
ⓖ very → a lot, even, far, much 중의 하나를 쓰거나 very를 삭제한다.
29. I think that you are the best person in the world.
30. four times faster than

01 [해석] 그녀는 그녀가 가진 시간보다 더 많이 필요하다.
[해설] ① 뒤에 than이 있으므로 빈칸에는 비교급이 와야 하므로, much를 more로 바꿔야 한다.

02 [해석]
① 그는 Tom만큼 힘이 세다.
② 그녀는 너만큼 빨리 달릴 수 있다.
③ 이 의자는 저것만큼 무겁다.
④ 어제는 오늘만큼 춥지 않았다.
⑤ 나는 그 배우보다 더 유명해지고 싶다.
[해설]
① as ~ as 사이에는 원급이 와야 한다.
stronger → strong
② as + 형용사/부사의 원급 +as 이다.
as run fast as → run as fast as
④ so not cold as → not so cold as
⑤ popular의 비교급은 more popular이다.

03 [해설] 'as + 형용사/부사의 원급 + as'는 비교하는 대상의 정도가 같을 때 쓰이며, '~만큼 ~한/하게' 라는 의미이다.
as famous as: ~만큼 유명한

04 [해설] The warmer ~, the better ~: 더 따뜻할수록, 더 좋은

05 [해석]
A: 나는 살을 빼기 원한다. 무엇을 해야 할까?
B: 네가 적게 먹으면 먹을수록 너는 더 살이 빠질 것이다.
[해설] 'the + 비교급 + 주어 + 동사, the + 비교급 + 주어 + 동사'는 '~하면 할수록 더 ~한/하게' 라는 뜻이다. The less ~, the more ~: 더 적게 ~할수록, 더 많이 ~한

06 [해석]
① 그는 오늘 기분이 훨씬 더 좋다.
② 나의 새 가방은 내 오래된 가방보다 훨씬 더 싸다.
③ 이 일기는 금보다 훨씬 더 의미가 있다.
④ 그 시험은 내가 기대했던 것보다 훨씬 더 어려웠다.
⑤ 나의 엄마는 아빠보다 훨씬 더 조심스럽게 운전한다.
[해설] very는 비교급 앞에 올 수 없다.

07 [해석]
① 어떤 것도 진정한 사랑만큼 아름답지 않다.
② 진정한 사랑은 가장 아름다운 것이다.
③ 어떤 것도 진정한 사랑보다 아름답지 않다.
④ 진정한 사랑은 가장 아름다운 것들 중 하나이다.
⑤ 진정한 사랑은 다른 어떤 것 보다 더 아름답다.
[해설]
①~③, ⑤는 '어떤 것도 ~보다 더 ~하지 않은'의 뜻이다.
④ 'one of the 최상급 복수명사'는 '가장 ~한 것들 중 하나'라는 뜻이다.

08 [해석]
A: 너희 엄마는 요리를 잘 하시는 분이니?
B: 응, ⓐ 나는 나의 엄마보다 더 맛있는 요리를 하는 사람은 없다고 생각해.
[해설] No (other) ~ 비교급 + than: '어떤 ~도 ~보다 ~하지 않은(않게)'라는 의미이다.

09 [해석]
① 그녀는 경주에서 점점 더 빨리 달렸다.
② 환상적일수록 나는 그것을 더 즐기게 된다.
③ 그는 자라면서 점점 더 키가 크고 있다.
④ 위험할수록 너는 더 조심해야 한다.
⑤ 날씨가 더워질수록 우리는 차가운 차를 더 많이 마신다.
[해설]
① '점점 더 ~한/하게'라는 뜻으로는 '비교급 + and + 비교급'이므로, fast and fast를 faster and faster로 바꾸어야 한다.

② the 비교급 ~, the 비교급 ~: '~하면 할 수록 더욱 더 ~한'

③ get 비교급 and 비교급: 점점 더 ~해지다

④ 'the + 비교급 + 주어 + 동사, the + 비교급 + 주어 + 동사'는 '~하면 할수록 더 ~한/하게' 라는 뜻이다. (the most → the more)

⑤ 'the + 비교급 + 주어 + 동사, the + 비교급 + 주어 + 동사'는 '~하면 할수록 더 ~한/하게' 라는 뜻이다.

10 [해석]

① Yuna는 가장 지적인 소녀이다.

② 내가 어제 본 영화는 최악의 영화였다.

③ 우리 학교 교복은 가장 편안한 교복이다.

④ 경복궁은 서울에서 가장 유명한 궁이다.

⑤ 인터넷 용어들은 표준어보다 더 규칙적이지 않다.

[해설]

② the 뒤에는 최상급이 와야 한다. (worse → worst)

⑤ as ~ as 사이에 들어가는 원급은 문장의 보어로 쓰인 것이다. 보어로는 형용사가 들어가야 하므로 regularly를 regular로 써야 한다.

11 [해석] Michael은 학교에서 책을 가장 많이 읽었다.

[해설]

(1) '비교급 + than + any other + 단수명사'는 '다른 어떤 ~보다도 더 ~한/하게'라는 의미이다.

(2) 'No(other) ~ as[so] + 원급 + as …'는 '어떤 ~도 ~만큼 ~하지 않은/않게'라는 의미이다.

12 [해석] 그녀는 경주에서 그녀가 달릴 수 있는 한 가장 빠르게 달렸다.

[해설] 'as + 형용사/부사의 원급 + as + 주어 + can[could]'는 'as + 형용사/부사의 원급 + as possible'로 바꾸어 쓸 수 있고 '~할 수 있는 한 (가능한) ~하게'라는 의미이다.

13 [해석] 뉴욕은 미국에서 가장 붐비는 도시이다.

① 미국의 모든 도시는 뉴욕만큼 붐빈다.

② 뉴욕은 미국의 다른 도시들만큼 붐빈다.

③ 미국의 모든 도시는 뉴욕보다 더 붐빈다.

④ 뉴욕은 미국에서 다른 어떤 도시보다 더 붐비는 도시이다.

⑤ 뉴욕은 미국의 다른 도시들만큼 붐비지 않는다.

[해설] The + 최상급

= 비교급 + than + any other + 단수명사: 다른 어떤 ~보다도 더 ~한/하게

= 비교급 + than + all the other + 복수명사: 다른 모든 ~보다도 더 ~한/하게

14 [해설]

② one of the + 최상급 복수명사: 가장 ~한 것 중의 하나

③ the 뒤에는 최상급이 와야 한다.

④ 'the + 최상급 + 명사(+ that) + 주어 + have/has (ever) + p.p.'는 과거의 한 시점부터 지금까지의 경험을 통틀어 '~가 가장 ~하다' 는 뜻이다.

⑤ less ~ than any other animal: 다른 어떤 동물보다 덜 ~한

15 [해석]

이름	Adam	Eric
키	172cm	172cm
몸무게	67kg	62kg

[해설]

(1) 'as + 형용사/부사의 원급 + as'는 비교하는 대상의 정도가 같을 때 쓰이며, '~만큼 ~한/하게' 라는 의미이다. Adam과 Eric의 키가 같으므로 as ~ as를 쓴다.

(2) Adam이 Eric보다 무거우므로 '비교급 + than'을 써서 나타낸다.

16 [해설] '배수사 + 비교급 + than'은 '보다 ~배 ~하다'라는 뜻이다.

~보다 다섯 배 더 긴: five times longer than ~

17 [해설] 'the + 최상급'은 뒤에 'in'을 써서 비교하는 대상의 범위를 나타낼 수 있으며, '가장 ~한/하게' 라는 의미이다.

18 [해석] 그와 나는 매일 같은 양의 우유를 마신다.

① 그는 나만큼 우유를 많이 마신다.

② 그는 나의 우유만큼 많이 마신다.

③ 그는 나만큼 많은 우유를 마신다.

④ 그는 나만큼 우유를 많이 마신다.

⑤ 그는 나만큼 우유를 많이 마신다.

[해설] ① 우유는 셀 수 없으므로 many를 much로 바꾼다.

④ 우유는 셀 수 없으므로 many milk를 much milk로 바꾼다.

19 [해석]

A: 너는 너의 인생에서 가장 중요한 것이 무엇이라고 생각하니?

B: 나는 __________(라)고 생각해.

① 사랑이 가장 중요하다.

② 정직은 사랑만큼 중요하다.

③ 건강은 부보다 더 중요하다.

④ 우정은 내 인생에서 매우 중요하다.

⑤ 현명함은 어리석음보다 훨씬 더 낫다.

[해설] 질문이 '가장 ~한 것'에 관한 것이므로 대답도 '가장 ~한 것'으로 한다.

20 [해설] '가장 쉬운'이라는 뜻의 최상급: the easiest

21 [해석] 〈보기〉 러시아는 세계에서 가장 큰 나라이다.

→ 러시아는 세계의 다른 어떤 나라들보다 더 크다.

ⓐ Michael은 미국에서 가장 훌륭한 투수이다.

[해설] '비교급 + than'은 두 가지의 대상을 비교할 때 쓰이며 '~보다 더 ~한/하게'이라는 의미이다. 'the + 최상급'은 '비교급 + than + any other + 단수명사'와 바꾸어 쓸 수 있다.

22 [해석] 나는 5살 천재소년 Jacob에 대한 보고서를 읽었다. 보고서에 따르면, 그의 IQ는 157이다. (A) <u>그는 수학 문제를 수학선생님만큼 잘 푼다.</u> 그는 멘사 회원이 되기에 충분하게 똑똑하다. 그가 만일 가입한다면, 그는 그곳의 회원들 중 최연소가 될 것이다.

[해설] 'as + 형용사/부사의 원급 + as'는 비교하는 대상의 정도가 같을 때 쓰이며, '~만큼 ~한/하게' 라는 의미이다.

23 [해석]

ⓐ 더 많이 읽을수록 너는 더 똑똑해질 것이다.

ⓑ 날씨가 더 추워질수록, 너는 더 쉽게 감기에 걸릴 것이다.

ⓒ 운동을 더 많이 할수록, 너는 더 건강해 질 것이다.

ⓓ 더 일찍 구입할수록, 너는 더 많은 할인을 받을 수 있을 것이다.

ⓔ 밖에서 더 오래 놀수록 너는 더 쉽게 피곤해 질 것이다.

[해설] ⓐ the + 비교급 + 주어 + 동사, the + 비교급 + 주어 + 동사'는 '~하면 할수록 더 ~한/하게' 라는 뜻이다. smartest를 smarter로 바꾼다. ⓒ healthyer → healthier, ⓓ the early → the earlier

24 [해석] Kakao Talk은 스마트폰에서 사용하는 무료 모바일 메신저이다. 그것은 현재 13개 언어로 제공되고 있고, 많은 해외 가입자들이 있다. 사용자들은 예전보다 훨씬 더 쉽게 서로 이야기할 수 있다.

[해설] 비교급을 강조할 때에는 비교급 앞에 even, much, still, far, a lot등을 붙이며, '훨씬 더 ~한/하게'이라는 의미이다.

25 [해설] '비교급 + than'은 두 가지의 대상을 비교할 때 쓰이며 '~보다 더 ~한/하게'이라는 의미이다.

26 [해설] 'the + 비교급 + 주어 + 동사, the + 비교급 + 주어 + 동사'는 '~하면 할수록 더 ~한/하게' 라는 뜻이다. 의미상 'As + 주어 + 동사 + 비교급, 주어 + 동사 + 비교급'으로 바꾸어 쓸 수 있다.

27 [해석]

A: 너 그 뉴스 들었니?

B: 무슨 뉴스?

A: Jordan이 세계 복싱 챔피언이 되었대.

B: 정말? 기분 좋다.

A: 나도 그래. ⓐ <u>그는 내가 아는 다른 어떤 복서보다 더 열심히 연습했어.</u>

[해설] '다른 어떤 ~보다도 더 ~한/하게'라는 의미로는 '비교급 + than + any other + 단수명사'를 쓴다.

28 [해석]

ⓐ Tony는 Sumin만큼 친절하다.

ⓑ Bell은 여기에 Tim만큼 일찍 오지 않았다.

ⓒ 나는 나의 여동생/언니보다 돈을 더 적게 가지고 있다.

ⓓ 그녀는 과거에 나만큼 마르지는 않았었다.

ⓔ 나는 내가 그보다 어떻게 더 노래를 잘할 수 있는지 궁금하다.

ⓕ 그는 그의 형/남동생만큼 열심히 일하지 않는다.

ⓖ 우리 학교의 선생님들께서는 다른 학교 선생님들보다 더 잘 가르치신다.

[해설] ⓐ kinder → kind, ⓔ good → better, ⓕ harder → hard ⓖ very → a lot, even, far, much 중의 하나로 바꾸거나 삭제한다.

29 [해석] 아빠께,

저는 감사하다는 말씀을 드리고 싶어 이메일을 써요. 저는 아빠를 많이 사랑해요. 저는 아빠가 세상에서 최고의 사람이라고 생각해요. 아빠는 항상 자상하시고 친절하세요. 저에게 해주신 모든 것에 감사 드립니다.

사랑을 담아,

Joe 드림

[해설] good의 최상급을 써서 'the best person'이라고 표현하면 된다.

30 [해석] 〈보기〉 내 배낭은 10달러이다.

· 내 남동생/오빠의 배낭은 30달러이다.

→ 내 남동생/오빠의 배낭은 내 것보다 세 배 더 비싸다.

· 학교보호구역의 속도 제한은 시속 30이다.

· 고속도로의 속도 제한은 시속 120이다.

→ 고속도로의 속도 제한은 학교보호구역의 속도 제한보다 네 배 더 빠르다.

[해설] 「배수사 + as + 형용사/부사의 원급 + as」는 「배수사 + 비교급 + than」으로 바꾸어 쓸 수 있고 '~보다 ~배 ~한'이라는 의미이다.

실력 탄탄! 서술형 심화

1 The more books you read, the wiser you will become.

2 (1) more books than all the other students
(2) No student, as well as

3 not as[so] high as, study as hard as

1 [해설] 'the + 비교급 + 주어 + 동사, the + 비교급 + 주어 + 동사'는 '~하면 할수록 더 ~한/하게' 라는 뜻이다.

2 [해석]

(1) James는 다른 모든 학생들보다도 더 많은 책을 읽는다.

(2) 어떤 학생도 Ricky만큼 영어 단어를 잘 외우지 못한다.

3 [해설] 「as + 형용사/부사의 원급 + as」는 비교하는 대상의 정도가 같을 때 쓰이며, '~만큼 ~한/하게' 라는 의미이다.

Chapter 09 접속사

Point 1 부사절을 이끄는 종속접속사 I

A 1. When 2. Since 3. While
4. As 5. As

B 1. 우리가 외출해 있는 동안에 너의 남동생을 잘 돌봐주렴.
2. (출퇴근) 혼잡 시간대(러시아워)여서 교통체증이 정말 심했다.

C 1. after 2. because/since

A [해설]
1. 학교에 갔을 때 아무도 없었으므로, '~할 때'를 나타내는 'when'을 쓴다.
2. 날씨가 맑아서 소풍을 가는 것이므로, '~하니까(이유)'를 나타내는 'since'를 쓴다.
3. 그가 나가있는 동안 친구가 전화한 것이므로, '~동안(시간)'을 나타내는 'while'을 쓴다.
4. 영화가 재미있어서 원작 소설을 산 것이므로, '~하므로(이유)'를 나타내는 'as'를 쓴다.
5. 전화 통화를 하면서 지하철을 탔으므로, '~하면서(시간)'를 나타내는 'as'를 쓴다.

B [해설]
1. while: ~하는 동안(시간을 나타내는 종속접속사)
2. since: ~하니까(이유를 나타내는 종속접속사)

C [해설]
1. after: ~이후(시간을 나타내는 종속접속사)
2. because/since: ~때문에, ~하니까(이유를 나타내는 종속접속사)

Point 2 부사절을 이끄는 종속접속사 II

A 1. If 2. Although
3. while 4. Unless

B 1. 만일 내가 스쿨버스를 놓친다면, 나는 학교에 자전거를 타고 갈 것이다.
2. 그녀가 실수만하지 않는다면 그녀는 승자가 될 것이다.
3. 나의 부모님께서는 내가 선생님이 되기를 원하시는 반면에 나는 요리사가 되기를 원한다.
4. 그는 겨우 4살임에도 불구하고 그의 이름을 깔끔하게 쓸 수 있다.

C 1. Even though it is spring
2. while others like soccer

A [해설]
1. If(만일 ~한다면): 조건을 나타내는 종속접속사
2. Although(비록 ~이지만): 양보를 나타내는 종속접속사
3. while(~하는 반면에): 대조를 나타내는 종속접속사
4. Unless(만일 ~하지 않는다면): 조건을 나타내는 종속접속사

B [해설]
1. If(만일 ~한다면): 조건을 나타내는 종속접속사
2. unless(만일 ~하지 않는다면): 조건을 나타내는 종속접속사
3. while(~하는 반면에): 대조를 나타내는 종속접속사)
4. even though(비록 ~이지만): 양보를 나타내는 종속접속사

C [해설]
1. even though: (~임에도 불구하고): 양보를 나타내는 종속접속사
2. while(~하는 반면에): 대조를 나타내는 종속접속사

Point 3 부사절을 이끄는 종속접속사 III

A 1. to 2. that
3. to score 4. so that
5. in order to

B 1. soft to
2. tired to
3. order to communicate with people around the world

C 1. enough to buy
2. so fast that I couldn't

A [해설]
1. too big to wear: 너무 커서 입을 수 없다
2. so delicious that: 너무 맛있어서 ~하다
3. excellent enough to: ~하기에 충분히 훌륭한
4. so that she can: 그녀가 가능하도록
5. in order to: ~을 하기 위해

Point 4 명사절을 이끄는 종속접속사

A	1. Whether	2. whether	3. That
	4. that	5. that	

B 1. that the rumor is true
2. if my mom is at home
3. Whether the food is good
4. that their parents will understand them

A [해석]

1. 그가 부자이든 아니든 중요하지 않다.
2. 나는 그가 약간의 간식을 가져올지 아닐 지 모르겠다.
3. 소년이 그의 부모님과 닮은 것은 당연하다.
4. 가장 안 좋은 점은 모든 표가 팔렸다는 것이다.
5. 그 기사는 우리가 약 2주간 휴식을 가질 거라 한다.

B [해설]

1, 4. 명사절을 이끄는 종속접속사 that: 'that + 주어 + 동사'로 보어로 쓰였다.
2. 명사절을 이끄는 종속접속사 if: if + 주어 + 동사'로 '~인지 아닌지'라는 의미로, 목적어로 쓰였다.
3. 명사절을 이끄는 종속접속사 whether: whether + 주어 + 동사'로'~인지 아닌지'라는 의미로, 목적어로 쓰였다. 뒤에 'or not'이 있으므로 if는 오지 못한다.

Point 5 명사절 – 간접의문문

A 1. when the party is
2. if[whether] the people were safe
3. When do you think

B 1. Can you tell me where the post office is?
2. She wonders if he loves her.
3. He asked when the bus would arrive.

A [해설]

1, 3. 의문사가 있는 경우: '의문사 + 주어 + 동사'의 어순으로 쓴다.
2. 의문사가 없는 경우: 'if/whether + 주어 + 동사 + ~(or not): ~인지 아닌지'의 어순으로 쓴다.

Point 6 상관접속사

A	1. nor	2. and	3. but
	4. or	5. but	
B	1. have	2. like	3. is
C	1. neither, nor	2. either, or	

A [해설]

1. Neither Jason nor Becky: Jason도 Becky도 ~아닌
2. Both Mr. Jackson and Mrs. Jackson: Mr. Jackson과 Mrs. Jackson은 둘 다
3. Not Ben but Sarah: Ben이 아닌 Sarah는
4. Either my mom or my dad: 엄마나 아빠
5. not only a horror movie but also a comedy movie: 공포 영화 뿐만 아니라 코미디 영화도

B [해설]

1. both *A* and *B*: '*A*와 *B* 둘 다'라는 뜻으로 동사의 복수형을 취한다.
2. neither *A* nor *B*: '*A*도 *B*도 ~아닌'이라는 뜻으로 동사의 수는 B에 일치시킨다.
3. not *A* but *B*: '*A*가 아닌 *B*'라는 뜻으로 동사의 수는 *B*에 일치시킨다.

Point 7 「명령문, and/or …」

A 1. If you take public transportation
2. If you don't submit the report on time, Unless you submit the report on time
3. If you don't run (또는 Unless you run)
4. If you read the directions carefully

B 1. and people will like you
2. and your dreams will come true
3. or the sleeping baby will wake up

A [해설]

1, 4. '명령문 + and' 구문: '~해라, 그러면 ~할 것이다'라는 뜻으로, 'if you ~로 바꿔 쓸 수 있다.
2~3. '명령문 + or' 구문: '~해라, 그렇지 않으면 ~할 것이다'라는 뜻으로, 'if you don't ~' 또는 'Unless you ~'로 바꿔 쓸 수 있다.

Point 8 접속부사

A	1. Besides	2. Therefore	3. For example
	4. However	5. As a result	
B	1. Therefore	2. However	3. Moreover
	4. Therefore	5. However	
C	1. In addition, she is smart.		
	2. Therefore, I didn't do well on the test.		

A [해설]

1. 외식하고 싶지 않고, 게다가 돈도 없다는 내용이므로 besides가 맞다.
2. toothache(치통)와 can't eat well(잘 먹을 수 없다)를 자연스럽게 연결해주는 접속부사는 therefore (그러므로)이다.
3. like fruits(과일을 좋아한다)와 apples, and cherries를 자연스럽게 연결해주는 접속부사는 for example (예를 들면)이다.
4. fought with(싸웠다)와 good friends now(지금은 좋은 친구)를 자연스럽게 연결해주는 접속부사는 However (그렇지만)이다.
5. didn't follow traffic rule(교통법규를 지키지 않았다)과 pay the fine(벌금을 내다)를 자연스럽게 연결해주는 접속부사는 as a result(그 결과)이다.

B [해설]

1. high fever(고열)와 took a medicine(약을 먹었다)을 자연스럽게 연결해주는 접속부사는 therefore (그러므로)이다.
2. mine(내 것)과 may use it (그것을 사용해도 된다)를 자연스럽게 연결해주는 접속부사는 However (그렇지만)이다.
3. cold(추운)와 raining(비가 오는)을 자연스럽게 연결해주는 접속부사는 Moreover (게다가)이다.
4. got up late (늦게 일어났다)와 late for school (학교에 늦은)를 자연스럽게 연결해주는 접속부사는 Therefore (그렇기 때문에)이다. Terra는 오늘 아침에 늦게 일어났다. 그렇기 때문에 학교에 지각했다.
5. likes to teach her friends(친구들을 가르치는 것을 좋아하는 것)와 doesn't want to be a teacher (선생님이 되기 원하지 않는다)를 자연스럽게 연결해주는 접속부사는 However(그러나)이다.

C [해설]

1. In addition: 게다가
2. Therefore: 그렇기 때문에

일등 비법 노트

비법 1	1. ②, ③
비법 2	1. ⑤
비법 3	1. ②
비법 4	1. ⑤ 2. (1) goes (2) like 3. (1) smartness → smart (2) going → go (3) to listen to the radio → listening to the radio

비법 1

1 [해설] because 뒤에는 '주어 + 동사', because of 뒤에는 명사(구)가 온다.

비법 2

1 [해설] ⑤ 조건을 나타내는 부사절에서는 현재시제로 미래를 나타내므로 will rain을 rains로 바꿔야 한다.

비법 3

1 [해설]

① 'That she is very smart(그녀가 매우똑똑하다는 것은)'가 전체 문장의 주어 역할을 한다. that 다음에 완전한 문장(She is very smart.)가 왔으므로 that은 명사절을 이끄는 종속접속사 that이다.

② 관계대명사절(that you bought for me)가 that 앞의 명사 a present를 꾸며주는 형용사절이다. that 다음에 온 'you bought for me'에서 무엇을 샀는지 목적어가 빠져있으므로 that은 관계대명사 that이다.

③~④ 접속사 that이 이끄는 절이 전체 문장의 목적어 역할을 하는 명사절이다.

⑤ 접속사 that이 이끄는 절(that she can't afford to buy the watch)이 전체 문장의 보어 역할을 하는 명사절이다.

비법 4

1 [해석]

① Tom은 나에게 김치가 매운지 물어봤다.

② 그는 회의가 3시 혹은 4시인지 확신하지 못했다.

③ 그가 도서관에 오는지 안 오는지 내게 알려줘.

④ 그 소년은 그의 아빠가 그에게 프리스비를 샀는지 궁금했다.

⑤ 만일 네가 일찍 집에 온다면, 너는 나와 배드민턴을 칠 수 있다.

[해설]

①~④ if가 '~인지 아닌지'라는 뜻의 명사절로 쓰였다.

⑤ if가 '만일 ~라면'이라는 뜻의 부사절로 쓰였다.

비법 5

1 [해설]

(1) '*B* as well as *A*'는 '*A*뿐만 아니라 *B*도'라는 뜻으로, 동사의 수는 *B*(Jisu)에 일치시켜야 하므로 goes이다.

(2) 'not only *A* but also *B*'는 '*A*뿐만 아니라 *B*도'라는 뜻으로, 동사의 수는 *B*(I)에 일치시켜야 하므로 like이다.

비법 6

1 [해석]

(1) 태호는 잘생겼을 뿐만 아니라 똑똑하다.

(2) 그는 네팔을 방문하거나 유럽에 갈 수 있다.

(3) 우리는 TV를 보거나 라디오를 듣기로 했다.

[해설]

(1) not only *A* but also *B*: '*A*뿐만 아니라 *B*도'라는 뜻으로 *A* 와 *B*는 병렬 관계를 이루어야 하는데, *A*가 handsome(형용사)가 이므로, 뒤에도 smartness(명사)가 아닌 smart(형용사)가 와야 한다.

(2) either *A* or *B*: '*A*나 *B* 둘 중 하나'라는 뜻으로, *A*와 *B*는 병렬관계를 이루어야 하는데, *A*가 visit(동사원형)이므로 뒤에도 going(분사)가 아닌 go(동사원형)이 와야 한다.

내신 만점! 실전 기출

01. ②	**02.** ①	**03.** ③
04. ③	**05.** ③	**06.** ②
07. As	**08.** ⑤	**09.** ⑤
10. ③	**11.** ②, ⑤	**12.** ④
13. that	**14.** ④	
15. whether they will do well		**16.** ③
17. order not to	**18.** if	

19. ⓐ until ⓑ although ⓒ before ⓓ Since

20. Although happiness may seem far away

21. ⑤ **22.** ④

23. Though[Although]

24. not only, but also **25.** ④

26. She stopped eating junk food so that she could stay healthy.

27. ⑤

28. so that I can give them to the poor

29. because/since/as she helped the poor

30. ③

01 [해석]

① 내가 멀리 있는 동안 내 강아지를 돌봐줘.

② 나는 아닌 반면에 나의 언니(여동생)은 영어를 매우 잘한다.

③ 나는 집 청소를 하는 동안 대개 음악을 듣는다.

④ 그는 대개 TV를 보는 동안 감자칩을 먹는다.

⑤ 운전을 하는 동안 전화 통화를 하는 것은 안전하지 않다.

[해설] ② '반면에'라는 의미, ①, ③~⑤ '~하는 동안'이라는 의미이다.

02 [해석]

② 그는 네가 원한다면 당연히 도와 줄 것이다.

③ 너는 그들이 수업 시간을 엄수했는지 아니?

④ Julie는 내게 그녀의 집에 올 수 있는 지 물어봤다.

⑤ 나는 우주에 다른 생명체가 있는지 매우 궁금하다.

[해설]

① 나의 도움이 필요한지 아닌지가 궁금하므로 that을 명사절을 이끄는 종속접속사 if나 whether로 바꾸어야 한다.

② 조건을 나타내는 종속접속사 if: '만일 ~한다면'이라는 의미이다.

③~⑤ 명사절을 이끄는 종속접속사 if: if + 주어 + 동사'로 '~인지 아닌지'라는 의미이다.

03 [해석] 〈보기〉 우리는 하이킹을 하는 동안 아름다운 산의 경치를 즐겼다.

① 그녀는 잠시 동안 휴식을 취하고 있는 중이다.

② Sue는 영어를 좋아하는 반면에 Tom은 과학을 좋아한다.

③ 너는 공부를 하는 동안 음악을 듣지 말아라.

④ 그가 병에서 회복하는 데 한참이 걸렸다.

⑤ 그는 만드는 것을 매우 잘하는 반면에 그의 동생은 가망이 없다.

[해설] 〈보기〉 ③ while: ~하는 동안
① for a while: 잠시 동안
②, ⑤ while: 반면에
④ quite a while: 한참, 꽤 오랫동안

04 [해석]
· 어떤 사람들은 주스를 좋아하는 반면, 다른 사람들은 안 좋아한다.
· 비행기에 탄 동안에는 전자기기를 꺼두어라.
[해설] while: ~ 반면에, ~하는 동안

05 [해석]
① 그녀는 춤도 추고 노래도 한다.
② 그들은 피곤하고 졸리다.
③ 그녀와 그녀의 언니는 둘 다 샌프란시스코에 산다.
④ Sue와 Frank는 둘 다 중국어를 매우 잘한다.
⑤ 비둘기는 평화와 자유의 상징이다.
[해설] ③ Both *A* and *B*는 둘 다의 의미이므로 복수형 동사를 써야 하므로 lives를 live로 바꿔야 한다.

06 [해석]
① 테이블은 너무 무거워서 내가 옮길 수가 없다.
② 그는 일찍 일어날 수 있을 정도로 너무 피곤했다.
③ 경기는 너무 재미있어서 멈출 수가 없었다.
④ 그녀는 너무 바빠서 제 시간에 올 수 없었다.
⑤ 영화가 너무 재미있어서 모든 표가 다 팔렸다.
[해설] ② 'so + 형용사 + that + 주어 + can't ~' 구문은 '너무 ~ 해서 …할 수 없다'는 뜻이다. 문맥상 so tired that(너무 피곤해서) 일찍 일어나지 못했다가 더 어울리므로 could를 couldn't로 바꿔야 한다.

07 [해석]
ⓐ 너도 알다시피, Julia는 우리 반에서 가장 똑똑하다.
ⓑ 과학이 발전함에 따라, 로봇들은 우리 삶의 더 큰 부분이 될 것이다.
[해설] ⓐ 너도 알다시피, ⓑ 과학이 발전함에 따라

08 [해석]
① 나는 그가 무죄라는 것을 믿는다.
② 그녀는 그가 정직하다고 생각한다.
③ 진실은 그것이 그저 소문에 불과하다는 것이다.
④ 달콤한 것을 먹는 것을 멈출 수 없다는 것이 문제이다.
⑤ 나는 우리에게 유용한 기계를 발명하고 싶다.
[해설] ⑤ 앞에 명사가 있고 that 뒤의 절이 불완전하므로 관계대명사 that, ①~④ 앞에 동사가 있고 that 뒤의 절이 완전하므로 접속사 that

09 [해석]
① 그녀는 내게 충고했다. ______ 나는 그것을 따르지 않았다.
② 나는 열이 있는 것 같다. ______ 나는 약 먹는 것을 원하지 않는다.
③ 흰색 바지는 매우 깔끔하고 깨끗해 보인다. ______ 그것은 쉽게 더러워진다.
④ 나는 해야 할 숙제가 많았다. ______ 나는 내 친구들과 함께 쇼핑하러 갔다.
⑤ 우리는 우리의 그룹 프로젝트를 막 끝냈다. ______ 우리는 가서 축구를 할 수 있다.
[해설] ⑤ finished our group project (그룹 과제)를 끝낸 결과로 go out and play soccer(나가서 축구)를 할 수 있었으므로, 결과를 나타내는 접속부사(therefore, as a result)를 써야 한다. 대조를 나타내는 접속부사 however은 자연스럽지 않다.

10 [해석] 그녀는 책을 읽기에는 너무 졸리다.
[해설] 'so ~ that … can't' 구문은 '너무 ~해서 …할 수 없다'라는 의미로 'too ~ to' 와 바꾸어 쓸 수 있다.

11 [해석]
① 나는 너뿐만 아니라 그도 좋아한다.
② Jisu는 얼굴이 예쁠 뿐만 아니라, 마음도 따뜻하다.
③ Eric 뿐만 아니라 나도 회의에 참석할 예정이다.
④ 그들은 영어로 말하는 것뿐만 아니라 쓰는 것도 배우고 있다.
⑤ Tim은 축구를 잘 할뿐만 아니라 야구도 잘한다.
[해설]
① not only *A* but also *B*의 구조에서 *A*와 *B*는 같은 형태로 와야 한다. 여기서는 문장의 목적어가 필요하므로 *A*와 *B*는 각각 you와 him이 들어간다.
② not only *A* but also *B*의 구조에서 *A*와 *B*는 같은 형태로 와야 한다. 여기서는 문장의 보어가 필요하므로 *A*와 *B*는 둘 다 형용사(또는 분사)가 들어가야 하므로 어법상 맞다.

③ not only *A* but also *B*는 동사를 *B*에 일치시켜야 한다. 따라서, I에 동사를 일치시켜 am으로 고쳐야 한다.

④ not only *A* but also *B*의 구조에서 *A*와 *B*는 같은 형태로 와야 한다. 여기서는 전치사 at의 목적어가 필요하므로 *A*와 *B*는 각각 명사 상당어구가 들어가야 하는데 앞에 speaking이 있으므로 *B*에 이와 같은 형태인, writing이 들어간다.

⑤ not only *A* but also *B*의 구조에서 *A*와 *B*는 같은 형태로 와야 한다. 여기서는 전치사 at의 목적어가 필요하므로 *A*와 *B*는 각각 명사 상당어구가 들어가야 하므로 틀린 곳이 없다.

12 [해석] 〈보기〉 우리는 날이 어두워지면서 하늘에서 많은 별들을 볼 수 있었다.

① 사과는 설탕만큼 달콤했다.

② 그녀는 이 곳이 처음이기 때문에 그녀는 도움이 필요할 것이다.

③ 그 소년은 그의 엄마가 말한 대로 그의 우산을 잃어버렸다.

④ 그녀는 나이가 들면서 많은 사람들에게 알려졌다.

⑤ 너도 알다시피, 그 과제에 많은 노력을 기울이는 것이 낫다.

13 [해석]

ⓐ 그는 너무 어려서 혼자 집에 있을 수 없다.

ⓑ 그녀는 너무 똑똑해서 수학문제를 쉽게 풀 수 있다.

[해설] 부사절을 이끄는 접속사 'so ~ that …'은 결과를 나타내며, '너무 ~해서 …하다' 라는 의미다. 'too ~ to' 와 바꾸어 쓸 수 있으며 'so ~ that … can't/couldn't', '너무 ~해서 …하지 못하다' 라는 의미다.

14 [해석] 소년은 닭이 날 수 있는지 궁금했다.

① 너는 그가 여자친구가 있는지 아니?

② 제가 올바른 방향으로 가고 있는지 아닌지 제게 말해 주시겠어요?

③ Mrs. Audrey는 내가 과제를 제출했는지 내게 물어보셨다.

④ 엄마는 만일 내가 약속을 어긴다면 화를 내실 것이다.

⑤ 그는 새 핸드폰을 사야 하는지 고민한다.

[해설] ①~③, ⑤, 명사절을 이끄는 접속사 if는 'if + 주어 + 동사'의 형태로 쓰여 주어, 목적어, 보어의 역할을 하며 '~인지 아닌지'라는 의미이다.

④ 접속사 if가 조건(만약 ~라면)을 나타내는 접속사로 쓰였다.

15 [해설] 명사절을 이끄는 접속사 whether은 'whether + 주어 + 동사'의 형태로 쓰여 주어, 목적어, 보어의 역할을 하며 '~인지 아닌지'라는 의미이다.

④의 'so that ~'은 '~하기 위해'의 뜻이므로 '강의를 잘 이해하기 위해 열심히 집중했다.'의 의미가 된다.

16 [해석] 〈보기〉 나는 열심히 강의에 집중해서 그것을 잘 이해할 수 있었다.

③ 나는 잘 이해할 수 있을 만큼 매우 열심히 강의에 집중했다.

④ 강의를 잘 이해하기 위해 열심히 집중했다.

[해설]

③ 'so + 형용사 + that + 주어 + 동사' 구문은 '너무 ~해서 ~하다'는 뜻으로, '~하기에 충분하다'라는 뜻의 '형용사 + enough to + 동사원형' 구문으로 바꿔 쓸 수 있다.

17 [해석] 그는 벌금을 내지 않기 위해서 책을 반납하기 위해 도서관에 갔다.

[해설] 부사절을 이끄는 접속사 'so that + 주어 + 동사'은 목적을 나타내며, '~하기 위해, ~하도록'이라는 의미다. 'in order to'와 바꾸어 쓸 수 있다.

18 [해설] ⓐ 조건을 나타내는 종속접속사 if: '만일 ~한다면'이라는 의미이다.

ⓑ~ⓓ 명사절을 이끄는 종속접속사 if: 'if + 주어 + 동사'로 '~인지 아닌지'라는 의미이다.

19 [해석]

ⓐ 그 회의는 2시까지 계속되었다.

ⓑ 비가 왔음에도 불구하고 그녀는 버스정거장에서 그를 기다렸다.

ⓒ 학생들은 선생님이 교실에 들어오시기 전까지 자리에 앉아야 한다.

ⓓ 네가 늦게 일어났으므로, 너는 비행기에 늦지 않기 위해 서두르는 것이 낫다.

[해설] until: ~까지, before: ~전에, since: ~이래로, 이후로, although: 비록 ~일지라도, unless: 만일 ~하지 않는다면

20 [해설] although: ~임에도 불구하고

21 [해석] 나의 할머니께서는 내게 오래된 사진을 보여주셨다. 사진 속에는 조부모님, 아빠, 그리고 삼촌들이 집 앞에 서 있었다. 집이 꽤 낡았지만 그들은 모두 매우 행복해 보였다.
[해설] ⑤ Although: '비록 ~이지만', ~임에도 불구하고' 의 양보를 나타내는 접속사이다.

22 [해석]
Kevin: Sarah야, 너의 좌우명은 뭐니?
Sarah: '열심히 일해라. _______ 너는 어떤 것도 달성할 수 없다.'야. 너는?
Kevin: '일찍 일어나는 새가 되어라. _______ 너는 먹이를 잡을 수 있다.'
Sarah: 멋지네.
[해설] '명령문 + and'는 '~해라, 그러면 ~할 것이다'라는 의미이며, '명령문 + or'은 '~해라, 그렇지 않으면 ~할 것이다'라는 의미이다.

23 [해석]
ⓐ 날씨가 너무 추웠음에도 불구하고, 그는 양말을 신지 않았다.
ⓑ 소문이 거짓인 것이 드러났음에도 불구하고, 사람들은 여전히 그것을 믿었다.
[해설] 양보를 나타내는 접속사 although: '비록 ~이지만', '~임에도 불구하고'라는 뜻이다.

24 [해설] 'not only *A* but also *B* (= B as well as *A*)'는 '*A*뿐만 아니라 *B*도'라는 의미로, 동사의 수는 *B*에 일치시킨다.

25 [해석]
Adams: 너는 지구의 온도가 매년 올라간다는 것을 아니?
Becky: 응. 지구가 빠르게 따뜻해지기 때문에 심각한 문제야.
Adams: 맞아. 그래서 농부들이 채소와 과일을 재배하는데 어려움을 겪고 있어.
① 그녀가 그를 만난 지 10년이다.
② 나는 5살 이후로 피아노를 쳤다.
③ 오늘은 지난 달 이후로 가장 춥다.
④ 그가 한가해서 나는 그와 함께 콘서트를 보러 갈 수 있다.
⑤ 가게가 이 지역에 오픈 한지 3개월이 되었다.
[해설] ④ '~하기 때문에'의 뜻으로 이유를 나타내는 접속사이다. ①, ②~③, ⑤ '~이래로'의 뜻으로 시간을 나타낸다.

26 [해석] 그녀는 건강을 유지하기 위해 햄버거와 피자 같은 정크푸드 먹는 것을 멈췄다.
[해설] 'in order to'는 목적을 나타내며, '~하기 위해, ~하도록'이라는 의미다. 'so that + 주어 + 동사'와 바꾸어 쓸 수 있다.

27 [해석] 나는 무엇일까요? 나는 빨강, 노랑, 그리고 분홍 같은 많은 다른 색을 가지고 있어요. 사람들은 생일이나 밸런타인 데이 같은 특별한 날에 나를 구입해요. 또한, 미혼 남성들은 그들의 여자친구들에게 프로포즈를 하기 위해 나를 반지와 함께 구입하죠. 몇몇 사람들은 차를 만들 때뿐만 아니라 아로마테라피 오일을 만들 때에 나를 사용해요. 내가 무엇인지 아직 모르겠나요? 나는 장미입니다.
[해설] 'not only *A* but also *B* (= B as well as *A*)'는 '*A*뿐만 아니라 *B*도'라는 의미로, 동사의 수는 *B*에 일치시킨다.

28 [해석]
Q: 너는 왜 이 입던 옷들을 싸고 있니?
A: 나는 아프리카의 가난한 사람들에게 보내기 위해 그것들을 싸고 있어.
[해설] 'so that + 주어 + 동사'는 목적을 나타내며, '~하기 위해, ~하도록'이라는 의미다. 'in order to'와 바꾸어 쓸 수 있다.

29 [해석]
A: 너는 테레사 수녀님이 누구인지 아니?
B: 물론이지. 그녀는 '가난한 이들의 천사'로 알려져 있어.
[해설] because/since/as: 이유를 나타내는 접속사로 '~때문에'라는 뜻이다.

30 [해석] 〈보기〉 나는 내가 입학시험에 통과할 수 있을 지 모르겠다.
ⓐ 네가 만일 그것을 좋아한다면, 그것을 구매하는데 망설이지 말아라.
ⓑ 만일 눈이 많이 온다면, 눈사람을 만들자.
ⓒ 네가 내게 선물을 주었는지 아닌지 말해줘.
ⓓ 그들은 그 식당이 여전히 열려있다면 저녁을 먹을 것이다.

ⓔ 그는 그의 엄마가 그가 Jack의 집에서 잠자는 것을 허락하실 지 궁금하다.

[해설]

ⓒⓔ 명사절을 이끄는 접속사 if/whether은 'if/whether + 주어 + 동사'의 형태로 쓰여 주어, 목적어, 보어의 역할을 하며 '~인지 아닌지'라는 의미이다.

ⓐⓑⓓ 접속사 if가 조건(만약 ~라면)을 나타내는 접속사로 쓰였다.

실력 탄탄! 서술형 심화

1 (1) I don't know whether[if] I am tall enough to ride this roller coaster.

(2) I'm not sure whether[if] I passed the test or not. / I'm not sure whether or not I passed the test.

2 (1) If you want to, prepare and review lessons

(2) Unless you save, you won't have enough money to buy / Unless you save money, you won't have enough to buy

(3) If you don't eat, get sick easily

1 [해설] 'if/whether + 주어 + 동사'의 형태로 쓰여 '~인지 아닌지'라는 의미이다. (단, 'I am not sure if or not I can pass the test.'라고는 쓸 수 없다는 사실에 유의하자. or not은 if 뒤에 바로 붙여 올 수 없다.)

2 [해석]

(1) 미나: 나는 영어시험에서 A를 받고 싶어.

→ 만일 네가 영어시험에서 A를 받고 싶다면, 매일 예습과 복습을 해.

(2) 미나: 나는 새 노트북 컴퓨터를 사고 싶은데 돈이 충분하지 않아.

→ 네가 저축하지 않으면, 너는 새 노트북 컴퓨터를 살 수 없을 것이다.

(3) 미나: 나는 패스트푸드 먹는 것을 즐겨.

→ 만일 네가 건강한 음식을 먹지 않으면, 너는 쉽게 병에 걸릴 거야.

[해설]

(1), (3) if: 조건을 나타내는 종속접속사로 '만일 ~한다면'이라는 뜻이다.

(2) unless: 조건을 나타내는 종속접속사로 '만일 ~하지 않는다면'이라는 뜻이다.

Chapter 10 관계사

Point 1 관계대명사의 역할, 종류

A 1. which 2. whom 3. whose

B 1. which was titled *Using Energy*
2. who(m) she met at the park
3. whose hair is grey

A [해설]

1. 선행사가 사물(the history test)이므로 which를 쓴다.
2. 선행사가 사람(the Korean soccer player)이므로 whom을 쓴다.
3. 선행사가 사물(the building)이고 선행사와 관계사절의 주어가 소유의 관계이므로 소유격 관계대명사 whose를 써야 한다.

B [해설]

1. 선행사가 사물(a book)이고, 선행사와 같은 대상이 뒤 문장의 주어이므로 주격 관계대명사 which로 쓴다.
2. 선행사가 사람(a new friend)이고, 선행사와 같은 대상이 뒤 문장의 목적어이므로 목적격 관계대명사 who(m)으로 쓴다.
3. 선행사가 사람(my grandmother)이고, 선행사와 같은 대상이 뒤 문장의 소유격이므로 소유격 관계대명사 whose로 쓴다.

Point 2 관계대명사 that

A 1. that 2. that
3. that 4. O

B 1. Everything that he had told us
2. The only chore that Tom does
3. He's the tallest boy that I have ever seen
4. Tell me anything that you saw

A [해설]

1~4. 선행사가 all, the very, the first, '사람 + 동물'일 때는 관계대명사 that을 쓴다.

B [해설]

1. '모든 것(everything)'이 '우리에게 말했던(he had told us)'의 수식을 받는 구조이다. 선행사가 everything이므로 관계대명사 that을 쓰고 그 뒤에 수식하는 절을 쓴다.
2. '유일한 집안 일(the only chore)'이 'Tom이 하는(Tom does)'의 수식을 받고 있는 구조이다. 선행사에 the only가 포함되어 있으므로 관계대명사 that을 쓰고 그 뒤에 수식하는 절을 쓴다.
3. '내가 본'이 '가장 키가 큰 소년'을 수식하는 구조이므로 선행사 'the tallest boy' 뒤에 관계사절 'that I have ever seen'를 쓴다.
4. '네가 본'이 '아무거나'를 수식하는 구조이므로 선행사 anything 뒤에 관계사절 'that you saw'를 쓴다.

Point 3 관계대명사 what

A 1. what 2. what
3. that 4. What

B 1. what we should do
2. what you are looking for
3. What I want to do
4. what I saw
5. What I did all day long
6. what you have done for us

A [해설]

1. 앞에 선행사가 없으므로 선행사를 포함한 관계대명사 what이 필요하다.
2. be동사 뒤에 오는 것이므로 명사의 역할을 하는 관계대명사 what이 필요하다.
3. 앞에 선행사(the thing)가 있으므로 선행사를 포함하는 관계대명사 what은 올 수 없다.
4. '~것'의 의미를 가져야 하므로 관계대명사 what이 필요하다.

Point 4 관계대명사의 생략

A 1. that 2. which 3. whom
4. X 5. who was

B 1. ② which[that] 2. ② which[that] were
3. ① which[that] was 4. ① which[that] is

C 1. holding flowers is
2. written in English
3. I saw there is this boy
4. I had borrowed

A [해설]
1~3. 목적격 관계대명사 that / which / whom은 생략할 수 있다.
5. '주격관계대명사 + be동사'는 생략할 수 있다.

B [해설]
1. 목적격 관계대명사가 생략되었다.
2~4. '주격관계대명사 + be동사'가 생략되었다.

C [해설]
1~2. '주격관계대명사 + be동사'가 생략되었다.
3. 관계대명사절 '그곳에서 본'이 The person을 수식하고 있으므로, 'The person + 관계대명사 + 주어 + 동사'로 써야 한다. 이 때 목적격 관계대명사가 생략되었다.
4. 관계대명사절 '내가 도서관에서 빌린'이 the books를 수식하고 있으므로, 'the books + 관계대명사 + 주어 + 동사'로 써야 한다. 이 때 목적격 관계대명사가 생략되었다.

Point 5 「전치사 + 관계대명사」

A 1. whom 2. which
3. which 4. X, which, that
5. who, that 6. in which
7. X, who, whom, that

B 1. which[that], about which
2. which[that], at, at which
3. which[that], to, to which
4. which[that], in which
5. which[that], on, on which

A [해설]
1~3. 앞에 전치사가 있으므로 목적격 관계대명사이지만 생략 불가이고, that도 올 수 없다. 전치사 뒤에는 whom을 대신하여 who가 올 수 없다.
4. 목적격 관계대명사는 생략 가능하고, 선행사가 사물일 때 which나 that으로도 쓸 수 있다.
5. 뒤에 is가 왔으므로 주격 관계대명사 who나 that이 와야 한다.
6. 관계대명사절에 전치사가 생략되었으므로 앞에 '전치사 + 관계대명사'가 와야 한다.
7. 목적격 관계대명사는 생략 가능하고, 선행사가 사람일 때 who나 that으로 쓸 수 있다.

B [해설]
1~5. 관계대명사절에서 선행사와 같은 대상이 전치사의 목적어로 쓰였을 때는 선행사와 같은 대상인 목적어만 생략하고 전치사는 뒤에 남겨 두거나, 전치사를 관계대명사 앞으로 보낼 수 있다.
전치사를 관계대명사 앞으로 보내서 「전치사 + 관계대명사」로 쓸 때에는 관계대명사로 that은 쓸 수 없다.

Point 6 관계대명사의 제한적 용법, 계속적 용법

A 1. which
2. Seoul, which is
3. his friend Jane, who was
4. which is in Paris

B 1. 그녀는 군인이 된 두 아들이 있었다. (→ 해설: 아들이 모두 몇 명인지는 알수 없음)
2. 그녀는 아들이 (딱) 두 명 있는데, (그들은) 군인이 되었다.
3. 템즈강은 런던을 관통하여 흐르는 강이다.
4. 이것은 런던아이인데, 이것은 영국의 수도의 중심에 있다.
5. 'narcissism(자아도취)'이라는 단어는 그리스 신화에서 비롯되었는데, '너 자신을 너무 사랑하는 것'을 의미한다.

A [해설]
1. 앞에 그녀의 전화번호는 이미 지시하는 바가 명확하므로, 관계대명사절이 계속적 용법이 되어야 한다.
2~4. 선행사인 Seoul, 'his friend, Jane', the Eiffel Tower는 정해져 있는 대상이므로 관계대명사절이 계속적 용법이 되어야 한다.

B [해설]
1, 3. 쉼표(,)가 없으므로 제한적 용법이다.

2, 4~5. 쉼표(,)가 있으므로 계속적 용법이다.

Point 7 관계부사

A	1. how	2. which	3. which
	4. when	5. where	6. which
	7. where		
B	1. for which, why	2. on which, when	

A [해설]

1. 의미상 '쿠키를 어떻게 만들었는지'라는 말이 와야 하므로 방법의 관계부사가 와야 한다. 선행사는 생략되었다.

2~3, 6. 관계사절에 목적어의 전치사가 남아 있으므로 관계대명사가 필요하다.

4. 선행사가 시간이고 관계사절이 완전하므로 관계부사 when이 와야 한다.

5. 선행사가 장소이고 관계사절에 목적어의 전치사 in이 생략되었으므로 관계부사 where이 와야 한다.

7. 선행사는 장소이다. 뒤에 오는 절에서 'in the parking lot'이라는 부사구 혹은 there이 생략된 것이지, 문장의 주어나 목적어가 생략된 것이 아니므로 관계대명사가 아니라 관계부사가 와야 한다.

B [해설]

1. 선행사가 이유(the reason)이므로 관계부사 why를 쓴다. 이유를 나타내는 전치사 for와 함께 관계대명사가 올 수도 있다.

2. 선행사가 시간(the day)이므로 관계부사 when을 쓴다. 시간을 나타내는 전치사 on을 쓰고 뒤에 관계대명사를 써서 표현할 수도 있다.

Point 8 관계부사/선행사의 생략, 관계부사의 계속적 용법

A	1. how, that	2. there	3. then
B	1. the reason	2. how	
	3. when	4. where	

A [해설]

1. 방법의 관계부사 how는 선행사 the way를 생략하고 단독으로 쓴다. which는 선행사가 없으므로 올 수 없다. 선행사 the way가 있을 때는 how를 대신하여 that이 올 수 있다.

2~3. 계속적 용법으로 쓰인 관계부사는 「접속사 + 부사」로 바꿀 수 있다.

B [해설]

1. 관계부사 why를 생략한 경우이다.

2. 선행사 the way를 생략하고 관계부사 how를 쓰는 경우이다.

3. 선행사 the date를 생략하고 관계부사 when만 쓰는 경우이다.

4. 선행사 the place를 생략하고 관계부사 where만 쓰는 경우이다.

Point 9 복합관계대명사

A	1. Whichever 2. who(m)ever 3. Whoever	
B	1. whatever you know	2. Whatever happens
	3. whoever knocks	4. whichever you like

A [해설]

1. No matter which = whichever

2~3. anyone who(m) = who(m)ever

B [해설]

1. '무엇이든지'의 의미이므로 whatever를 쓴다.

2. '무슨 일이든지'의 의미이므로 whatever를 쓴다.

3. '누구든지'의 의미이므로 whoever를 쓴다.

4. '메뉴에 있는 것 중에서'로 범위가 제한되어 있으므로 whichever를 쓴다.

Point 10 복합관계부사

A	1. whatever	2. wherever	
	3. whenever	4. However	
B	1. Whenever	2. However	3. Wherever
C	1. however rich they are		
	2. Whatever his mother said		

A [해석]

1. 그는 그가 가진 질문은 무엇이든지 물어 본다.

2. 파파라치는 유명인들이 어디로 가든 따라간다.

3. 그 어린 소녀는 그녀가 두려움을 느낄 때마다 엄마 뒤에 숨는다.

4. 아무리 문제가 어렵더라도, 그것을 푸는 방법이 있게 마련이다.

B [해석]

1. 그는 조깅을 갈 때마다 그의 개를 데리고 간다.

2. 네가 아무리 화가 날 지라도, 아이들에게 소리지르면 안 된다.

3. 네가 어디로 가든지, 너는 그 지방의 문화를 존중해야 한다.

C [해석]

1~2. 「복합관계사 + 주어 + 동사」 어순으로 쓴다.

일등 비법 노트

비법 1	1. ④	2. What
비법 2	1. ②, ③	
비법 3	1. ②	
비법 4	1. ①	
비법 5	1. ④	
비법 6	1. ②	

비법 1

1 [해석]

① 네가 산 것을 나에게 보여 줄래?

② 그녀가 저녁식사로 원했던 것은 스파게티였다.

③ 나는 파티에서 네가 입었던 옷이 마음에 들어.

④ 이것이 어제 내가 그에게서 빌린 책이야.

⑤ 너는 요전 날에 잃어버린 네 휴대폰을 찾았니?

[해설]

① 앞에 선행사가 없으므로 관계대명사 what을 쓰는 것이 맞다.

② 앞에 선행사가 없으므로 관계대명사 what을 쓰는 것이 맞다.

③ 앞에 선행사가 있고 선행사가 사물이므로 관계대명사 that을 쓴 것이 맞다.

④ 앞에 선행사가 있고 선행사가 사물이므로 관계대명사 that[which]을 써야 한다. what→ that[which]

⑤ 앞에 선행사가 있고 선행사가 사물이므로 관계대명사 that(which)를 쓴 것이 맞다.

2 [해석]

A: 저 사진들은 당신이 찍은 것인가요?

B: 네, 그리고 이것들은 제가 그린 것입니다.

[해설] 앞에 선행사가 없으므로 관계대명사 what을 써야 한다.

비법 2

1 [해석]

① 나의 사촌은 자전거를 하나 샀는데, 그것은 매우 비쌌다.

② Mr. Park는 그가 항상 산책할 때 데리고 오는 개가 한 마리 있다.

③ 여기에 아이들이 올라가기 좋아했던 커다란 나무가 있었다.

④ 그녀가 가장 좋아하는 가게는 *All that Sweets*인데, 그것은 그녀의 집 가까이에 있다.

⑤ 나는 스위스에 사는 친구에게서 받은 멋진 시계가 하나 있다.

[해설]

② 관계대명사 that 앞에는 전치사가 오지 못한다.

③ 관계대명사 that 앞에는 쉼표(,)가 오지 못한다.

비법 3

1 [해석]

① 그가 좋아하는 것은 그저 스포츠를 하는 것이다.

② 그녀는 사람들을 감동시키는 멋진 목소리를 가지고 있다.

③ 그녀가 원하는 모든 것은 한마디의 충고이다.

④ 네 손에 있는 것을 나에게 다오.

⑤ 그녀는 덤불에 숨어 있는 몇몇의 소년들을 보았다.

[해설]

① 관계대명사 what이 이끄는 절이 문장의 주어로 쓰였으므로 동사는 단수형태로 와야 한다.

②④⑤ 관계대명사절에 주어가 생략되었으므로 선행사와 같은 대상이 주어였음을 알 수 있다. 그러므로 선행사에 관계대명사절의 동사의 수를 일치시킨다.

③ 선행사가 all이고, 이것을 수식하는 절인 '그녀가 원하는 것'은 추상적인 개념이므로, 여기서 all은 단수로 취급해야 한다. 그러므로 동사를 단수 형태로 쓴다.

비법 4

1 [해석] David는 딸이 두 명 있는데, 그들은 가수가 되었다.

[해설]

① 관계대명사의 계속적 용법에서는 선행사가 이미 정해진 대상이다. 즉, 딸이 두 명뿐이다.

③ 관계대명사 that은 계속적 용법으로 쓸 수 없다. 즉, that 앞에 쉼표(,)가 오지 못한다.

④ 계속적 용법인 경우에는 관계사절이 앞에 있는 선행사를 수식한다기 보다는, 부가적인 보충 설명을 해 주는 기능을 한다.

⑤ two daughters는 사람이므로 관계대명사 who가 온다.

비법 5

1 [해설]

①⑤ 목적격 관계대명사이므로 생략할 수 있다.

②③ '주격 관계대명사 + be동사'가 뒤에 형용사(분사)가 따라오므로 생략할 수 있다.'

④ '주격 관계대명사 + be동사'의 구조에서 주격 관계대명사만 생략할 수는 없다.

비법 6

1 [해석]

① 저것이 그녀가 앉았던 의자이다.

② 너는 내가 가지고 쓰던 펜을 찾을 수 있니?

③ 너는 그가 듣고 있는 음악을 좋아하니?

④ 여기가 그가 많은 책을 쓴 집이다.

⑤ 5월 15일이 세종대왕께서 태어나신 날이다.

[해설]

① 관계대명사절에 전치사 on의 목적어가 생략되었으므로 선행사가 사물(the chair)일 때 쓰는 관계대명사 which가 오는 것이 맞다.

② 관계대명사절에서 'with the pens'가 생략되었는데 관계대명사 which가 왔으므로 틀렸다. 앞에 with which가 오거나 wrote 뒤에 with를 써야 한다.

③ 관계대명사절에 전치사 to의 목적어가 생략되었으므로 선행사가 사물(the music)일 때 쓰는 관계대명사 which가 오는 것이 맞다.

④ 관계대명사절에서 'in the house'가 생략되었는데 앞에 '전치사 + 관계대명사(in which)'가 왔으므로 어법에 맞다.

⑤ 관계대명사절에서 'on the day'가 생략되었는데 앞에 '전치사 + 관계대명사(on which)'가 왔으므로 어법에 맞다.

내신 만점! 실전 기출

01. ① **02.** ② **03.** ⑤

04. ③ **05.** ③ **06.** ②

07. Imagine all the fossils that we will see

08. Whatever **09.** ① **10.** ②

11. where **12.** ①

13. sent by my uncle was very interesting

14. ③ **15.** the Greek myth, which

16. the way **17.** ③

18. This is my father, who teaches science.

19. ③ **20.** ② **21.** ③

22. ③ **23.** ④

24. Tell me the reason for which you came to class very late.

25. when leaves change color **26.** ④, ⑤

27. What I want is to get a refund.

28. ② **29.** ② **30.** ②

01 [해석] 그 우주비행사는 우주에 가고 싶어하는 사람들에게 약간의 충고를 해 주었다.

[해설] 선행사가 사람(people)이고 빈칸 뒤에 주어가 없이 동사가 바로 오므로 주격 관계대명사 who나 that이 필요하다.

02 [해석] 그는 나에게, '다리나 부러져라.'라고 말했는데, 그것은 '행운을 빌어.'라는 뜻이다.

[해설] 앞에 쉼표(,)가 있고 선행사가 사람이 아니므로 which가 와야 한다. 관계대명사 that은 계속적 용법으로는 쓸 수 없다.

03 [해석] 사람들의 이름이 기원이 된 많은 단어들이 있다.

[해설] 선행사 many words와 origins가 소유의 관계이므로 소유대명사가 와야 한다.

04 [해석] 아무리 어려울지라도 나는 포기하지 않겠다.

[해설] 'however + 형/부 + 주 + 동'는 '아무리 ~할지라도'라는 뜻이다.

05 [해석]

(1) 너는 'doggie bag'이 무엇을 의미하는지 아니?

(2) 그녀는 그 경찰관에게 그녀가 본 것을 말했다.

[해설]
(1) '무엇'이라는 뜻의 의문대명사 what이 필요하다.
(2) '~것'이라는 뜻의 관계대명사 what이 필요하다.

06 [해석]
(1) 런던동물원에 아이들에게 매우 인기 있었던 거대한 코끼리가 있었다.
(2) 그는 그가 나를 다시 만났을 때 매우 기뻤다고 말했다.
[해설]
(1) 선행사(a giant elephant)를 수식하는 절을 이끄는 관계대명사 which나 that이 필요하다.
(2) 'he felt very pleased when he saw me again'를 문장의 목적어 역할을 하는 명사절로 만들어 줄 접속사 that이 필요하다.

07 [해설] '우리가 볼'이라는 문구가 '모든 화석'을 수식하는 구조이므로 선행사를 fossils로 앞에 두고 관계대명사절 (that we will see)를 그 뒤에 놓는다.

08 [해설] '무엇을 하든지'라는 뜻은 복합관계대명사 whatever로 표현할 수 있다.

09 [해석]
(1) 네가 좋아하는 색이면 어떤 것이든 골라라.
(2) 네가 언제 오든지 우리는 너를 환영할 것이다.
[해설]
(1) 색깔 중에 범위가 한정되어 고르는 것이므로 whichever를 쓴다.
(2) 때를 나타내는 것이므로 whenever을 쓴다.

10 [해석]
① 그녀는 할인 중인 가방을 보여 주었다.
② 그녀는 핫도그보다 와플을 더 좋아한다고 말했다.
③ 너를 최신 유행을 따르는 사람으로 보이도록 만들어 줄 이 티셔츠를 입어라.
④ 제가 기차 안에서 읽을 만한 책을 추천해 주시겠어요?
⑤ 이것이 젊은이들 사이에 매우 인기 있는 새로운 모델입니다.
[해설]
①③⑤ that 뒤에 오는 절에 주어가 없으므로 that은 주격 관계대명사이다.
② that 뒤에 주어나 목적어가 생략되지 않은 완전한 절이 오므로 접속사이다.
④ that 뒤에 오는 절에 목적어가 없으므로 that은 목적격 관계대명사이다.

11 [해석]
(1) 이 곳이 그가 그 개를 발견한 곳이다.
(2) 어디서 나의 컴퓨터를 고칠 수 있나요?
[해설]
(1) 선행사가 the place이고 뒤에 오는 문장에 주어나 목적어가 생략되지 않은 완전한 절이므로 관계부사 where이 들어가야 한다.
(2) '어디서'라는 의미의 의문사 where이 들어갈 수 있다.

12 [해석] 공을 던지고 있는 그 소년이 내 남동생이다.
[해설] 생략된 주격관계대명사와 be동사는 현재분사 앞에 온다.

13 [해설] 앞에 선행사 The book 이 있으므로 주격관계대명사 that이나 which가 와야 한다. 그런데 주어진 단어에 which와 that이 없으므로 생략된 것으로 본다. '주격관계대명사 + be동사 + 분사/형용사' 구문에서 '주격관계대명사 + be 동사'는 생략할 수 있다.

14 [해석] 〈보기〉 나는 내가 할 수 있는 것을 하겠다고 약속한다.
① 그녀는 'panic'이 무슨 뜻인지 물었다.
② 너는 어떤 종류의 직업을 갖길 원하니?
③ 내가 가장 하고 싶은 것은 영화를 보는 것이다.
④ 그는 그 때 무슨 말을 해야 할 지 몰랐다.
⑤ 나는 그 퍼즐을 풀기 위해 다음에 무엇을 해야 할지 몰랐다.
[해설] 〈보기〉 '~것'의 의미를 가지므로 관계대명사 what 이다.
①, ④~⑤ '무엇'의 의미를 가지므로 의문대명사 what이다.
② '어떤'의 의미를 가지므로 의문형용사 what이다.
③ '~것'의 의미를 가지므로 관계대명사 what이다.

15 [해석] '판도라의 상자'라는 표현은 그리스의 신화에서 유래했는데, 그것은 신들과 여신들에 대해 이야기하고 있다.
[해설] 선행사가 'the Greek myth'인데 이것은 이미 한정되어 있고, 이어지는 관계대명사절은 부연설명을 해 주고 있으므로 계속적 용법으로 which 앞에 쉼표(,)를 써 준다.

16 [해석] 너는 그가 어떻게 풍차를 만들었는지 아니?
[해설] how와 같은 뜻으로 사용할 수 있는 두 단어의 표현은 'the way'이다.

17 [해석]
· 저것이 우리가 오늘 밤 머물게 될 호텔인가요?
· 그것이 그녀가 일찍 오지 않은 이유이다.
· 우리는 모두 우리가 결승에서 처음으로 이긴 날을 기억한다.
· 이곳이 사람들이 마을로 가기 위해 통과하는 숲이다.
[해설]
· 앞에 선행사가 장소(the hotel)이고, 뒤에 주어나 목적어가 생략되지 않은 완전한 절이 왔으므로 관계부사 where이 들어가야 한다.
· 앞에 선행사가 이유(the reason)이고, 뒤에 주어나 목적어가 생략되지 않은 완전한 절이 왔으므로 관계부사 why가 들어가야 한다.
· 뒤에 주어나 목적어가 생략되지 않은 완전한 절이 오고, 앞에 선행사가 생략되어 있으므로, 관계부사가 와야 하는데, 의미상 가능한 관계부사는 when이다.
· 앞에 선행사 the forest가 있고, 관계대명사 앞에 전치사 through가 있으며, 뒤 문장에서 passed의 목적어가 생략되어 있으므로 관계대명사 which가 와야 한다. that은 앞에 전치사가 있으므로 올 수 없다.

18 [해설] 선행사가 이미 구체적으로 정해진 대상이므로 부가적인 설명을 하는 기능인 계속적 용법의 관계대명사절을 써야 한다.

19 [해석]
① 저것이 은행이 있는 건물이다.
② 이것이 내가 학교 교과서를 넣는 물품 보관함이다.
③ 그는 전기 자동차를 만든 열정을 가지고 있었다.
④ 독일은 햄버거가 유래한 나라이다.
⑤ 나는 나의 남동생에게 2천원을 주고 산 장난감을 주었다.
[해설]
① 은행은 건물 안에 있는 것이므로 'in which'이다.
② 보관함 안에 넣는 것이므로 'in(to) which'이다.
③ '열정을 가지고'의 의미로는 'with a passion'이므로 'with which'이다.
④ 독일로부터 유래한 것이므로 'from which'이다.
⑤ pay는 목적어를 취할 때 전치사 for를 동반하므로 'for which'를 써야 한다.

20 [해석]
① 그것이 그녀가 시간 안에 오지 못한 이유였다.
② 이것이 그가 수수께끼를 매우 쉽게 푼 방법이다.
③ 나는 내 배낭을 어디에 놓았는지 잊어버렸다.
④ 한국이 일본의 식민지였던 때가 있었다.
⑤ 피라미드는 많은 관광객이 가기를 원하는 곳이다.
[해설] ② the way와 how는 함께 쓰지 않는다. 둘 중 하나를 삭제하거나 how 대신 that을 쓸 수 있다.

21 [해석]
① 나는 그녀를 처음 만났던 때를 기억한다.
② 너는 John이 지금 이야기하고 있는 소년을 아니?
③ 당신이 가장 좋아하는 식당을 추천해 주실 수 있나요?
④ 영화 'Avengers'는 아이들이 보기를 몹시 좋아했던 영화인데, 매우 재미있었다.
⑤ 'paparazzi'라는 단어는 유명 연예인들을 따라다니는 골치 아픈 사진기자들을 의미한다.
[해설]
① 선행사가 이미 생략되었으므로 관계부사 when은 생략 불가능하다.
② 앞에 전치사가 있는 목적격 관계대명사는 생략 불가능하다.
③ 목적격 관계대명사이므로 생략 가능하다.
④ 계속적 용법으로 쓰인 관계대명사는 생략 불가능하다.
⑤ 주격 관계대명사이므로 생략 불가능하다.

22 [해석]
① 사람들은 그들이 필요로 했던 것을 받을 수 있었다.
② 그가 어둠 속에서 본 것은 커다란 들개였다.
③ 이것은 Mandy가 나에게서 빌리기를 원하던 책이다.
④ 초콜릿 아이스크림이 그녀가 디저트로 원하는 것이다.
⑤ Bill은 돈이 없었는데, 그것 때문에 그는 이번에 우리와 함께 여행을 오지 못했다.
[해설] ①②④ that → what
③ 선행사(the book)이 있고, 관계대명사절에 borrow의 목적어가 생략되었으므로 관계대명사 that으로 쓴 게 맞다.
⑤ that은 계속적 용법으로 쓰지 못한다. (that → which)

23 [해설] ④ 관계대명사 that 앞에는 전치사가 올 수 없다.

24 [해석] 나에게 이유를 말해다오. 너는 그 이유로 학교에 매우 늦게 왔다. → 네가 학교에 매우 늦게 온 이유를 내게 말해 다오.

[해설] 앞, 뒷절의 공통 부분은 the reason이므로 뒤 문장에서 the reason을 없애고, 관계대명사 which를 뒷문장 앞에 넣고, '전치사 + 관계대명사'의 형태로 넣어야 하므로 전치사 for를 관계대명사 앞으로 옮긴다. (= Tell me the reason why you came to class very late.)

25 [해설] '~한 때'는 관계부사 when을 사용한다.

26 [해석] 당신은 우리가 하품을 할 때 왜 눈물이 나오는 지 아는가? 그것은 우리가 하품할 때 입을 크게 벌리기 때문이다. 그것은 눈물이 있는 곳을 자극하게 되고, 눈에서 눈물이 나온다.

[해설] 관계사절에 '전치사 + 명사(in the place)'가 생략되었으므로 앞에 관계부사 where, 또는 in which가 와야 한다.

27 [해석]

A: 뭘 도와드릴까요?

B: 네. 저는 이 셔츠를 여기서 샀어요. (내가 원하는 것은 환불을 받는 것입니다).

A: 알겠습니다. 제게 영수증을 보여 주시겠어요?

B: 여기 있습니다.

[해설] 앞에 관계대명사 What이 있으므로 그 뒤로 '주어 + 동사'를 쓴다. 관계대명사 what이 이끄는 절이 문장의 주어가 되므로 관계대명사절 뒤에 본동사가 와야 한다.

28 [해석] 언어에 새로운 단어들은 더하는 많은 다양한 방법이 있다. 하나의 흥미로운 방법은 브랜드 이름을 사용하는 것이다. 한가지 예는 Kleenex라는 단어인데, 그것은 휴지를 만드는 회사에 의해 만들어 진 상품의 이름에서 왔다. 그 회사는 새로운 얼굴용 화장지를 만들어서 Kleenex라고 이름을 붙였는데, 그것이 지금 사람들이 일반적인 얼굴용 화장지를 지칭할 때 쓰는 일반적인 이름이 되었다.

[해설]

ⓑ that은 계속적 용법으로는 쓰이지 않으므로 which로 써야 한다.

ⓒ '주격 관계대명사 + be동사'는 생략할 수 있다.

29 [해석] 캘리포니아는 가장 짧은 기간 동안 독립된 주가 된 미국의 주이다. 그것은 1840년대 후반에 사람들이 금을 캐러 왔던 인기 있는 장소가 되었다. 1848년에 캘리포니아에서 약간의 금이 채굴된 후, 전 세계로부터 사람들이 캘리포니아로 왔다. 그리고 그것이 바로 캘리포니아의 인구가 매우 빠르게 성장한 이유이고, 그것이 캘리포니아를 독립된 주로 만들었다.

[해설]

ⓐ 선행사가 the state(사물)이고, 관계사절에서 주어가 생략되었으므로 주격관계대명사 which[that]이 필요하므로 어법상 맞다.

ⓑ 관계대명사 that 앞에는 전치사가 오지 못한다.

ⓒ 관계대명사 뒤에 주어가 생략되어 있으면 동사는 선행사와 수를 일치시킨다. 선행사가 people(복수)이므로 동사는 were가 와야 한다.

ⓓ why 뒤에 문장이 생략된 주어나 목적어가 없는 완전한 절이므로 관계부사가 필요한데, 앞에 생략된 선행사는 'the reason'이므로 관계부사 why가 오는 것이 맞다.

ⓔ 앞 문장 전체를 받는 계속적 관계대명사 which를 쓰는 게 맞다.

30 [해석] 덥다고 느낄 때마다 우리는 땀을 흘리고, 동물들도 또한 그러하다. 땀은 보통 색깔이 없지만, 하마의 땀은 빨간색이다. 그것이 옛날 사람들로 하여금 하마는 피를 땀으로 흘린다고 생각하게 했다. 그러나, 그것은 사실 하마의 피부를 태양으로부터 보호해 주고, 하마의 상처 난 피부를 치료해 준다. 아무리 이상하게 보일지라도, 그것은 실제로 하마를 건강하게 지켜 준다!

[해설]

ⓐ 때를 나타내는 문장이므로 whenever를 쓴다.

ⓑ 선행사가 없으므로 what을 쓴다

ⓒ '아무리 ~할지라도'라는 뜻이므로 however를 쓴다.

실력 탄탄! 서술형 심화

1 (1) who[that] made (2) what, invented

2 (1) what → that[which] (2) which → that

3 (1) ⓐ which[that] was ⓑ in which

(2) (a) where I built

(b) many fish with which

(c) what my brother did

(d) The only thing that he did was

1 [해석]

(1) 장영실은 1398년에 물시계를 만든 사람이다.

(2) 전구는 1880년에 Thomas Edison이 발명한 것이다.

[해설]

(1) 선행사가 사람이므로 관계대명사 who[that]을 쓴다.

(2) '~것'이라는 선행사를 포함하고 있는 관계대명사(the thing which)가 필요하므로 관계대명사 what을 쓴다.

2 [해석]

A: 도와드릴까요?

B: 네. 창문 옆에 달려 있는 티셔츠를 입어봐도 될까요?

A: 그럼요. 그것이 젊은이들이라면 꼭 하나씩은 갖고 싶어하는 가장 인기 있는 스타일입니다. 흠, 잘 어울리시네요.

B: 그래요? 좋아요. 그것을 사겠어요.

[해설]

(1) the T-shirt가 선행사이므로 which[that]을 써야 한다.

(2) 선행사가 최상급의 수식을 받으므로 that으로 써야 한다.

3 [해석] 우리 가족은 지난 여름에 강릉 근처에 있는 해변에 갔다. (a) 그 해변에는 내가 모래성을 쌓았던 아름다운 모래가 있었다. 나의 아빠는 (b) 엄마가 맛있는 해물탕을 끓인 많은 물고기를 잡아 오셨다. 그는 또한 우리가 밤에 잠잘 준비를 했던 텐트도 세우셨다. 너는 (c) 내 남동생이 하루 종일 한 것을 알고 있니? (d) 그가 한 유일한 것은 게를 쫓아 다닌 것이었다.

[해설]

(1) ⓐ 선행사가 a beach이고 뒤에 주어와 동사가 다 없으므로 '주격관계대명사 + 동사'를 써야 한다.

ⓑ 관계사절에 주어나 목적어가 생략되지 않았으므로 관계부사가 들어가야 한다. 그런데 빈칸이 두 개이므로 '전치사 + 관계대명사' 형태로 써야 한다. 전치사는, '텐트 안에서' 자는 것이므로 'in the tent'가 생략되었음을 알 수 있으므로 'in which'로 쓴다. 앞에 전치사가 오니까 관계대명사 that은 쓸 수 없다.

(2) (a) 선행사가 sand이고 관계사절에 주어나 목적어가 생략되지 않았으므로 관계부사가 들어가야 한다. 생략된 어구는 'on the sand'이고, 전치사가 함께 생략되었으므로 장소의 관계부사 where을 쓴다.

(b) 관계사절에 주어나 목적어가 생략되지 않았으므로 관계부사가 들어가야 한다. 그런데 선행사가 fish이므로 알맞은 관계부사가 없다. 그러므로 '전치사 + 관계대명사' 형태로 써야 한다. '물고기를 가지고' 매운탕을 끓이는 것이므로 'with the fish'가 생략되었음을 알 수 있으므로 'with which'로 쓴다. 앞에 전치사가 오면 관계대명사 that은 쓸 수 없다.

(c) 선행사가 없고, '~것'이라는 의미의 말이 필요하므로 관계대명사 what을 써야 한다.

(d) 선행사에 the only가 포함되어 있으므로 관계대명사 that을 써야 한다.

Chapter 11 가정법

Point 1 가정법 과거

A 1. were 2. were not
3. would allow 4. could
5. would go

B 1. Tony knew the problem
2. I knew the location of her house
3. he had enough time
4. I were in your shoes

C 1. If he didn't have an appointment, he would
2. If he were there, we could meet
3. If I could drive a car, I could go to
4. If I were born again, I would become

A [해설]

1~2. 가정법 과거에서 if절의 be동사는 주어에 상관없이 were/weren't를 쓴다.

3. If절이 과거시제이므로, 주절에 '조동사의 과거형(would) + 동사원형(allow)'를 쓴다. (가정법 과거)

4. If절이 과거시제이므로, 주절에 '조동사의 과거형(could) +동사원형'이 온다.(가정법 과거)

5. If절이 과거시제이므로, 주절에 '조동사의 과거형 would + 동사원형 go'를 쓴다. (가정법 과거)

B [해설]

1~4. 〈직설법에서 가정법으로 전환하는 방법〉
① 긍정은 부정으로
② 부정은 긍정으로
③ 현재 시제는 과거 시제로
④ 접속사 As는 If로 바꿔 준다.

C [해설]

1~4. 현재 사실을 반대로 가정할 때는 'If + 주어 + 동사의 과거형, 주어 + 조동사의 과거형 + 동사원형'의 형태로 쓴다.

Point 2 가정법 과거완료

A 1. have liked 2. had seen
3. had known 4. wouldn't have been
5. hadn't had

B 1. Henry didn't speak English, he didn't go abroad
2. the weather wasn't, didn't swim
3. I didn't study, couldn't get

C 1. If I had had breakfast, I wouldn't have been hungry.
2. If he had practiced a lot, he would have won the game.

A [해설]

1~5. 과거의 사실과 반대되는 상황을 가정할 때 쓰는 가정법 과거완료는 'If + 주어 + had p.p. ~, 주어 + 조동사의 과거형(would, could, might) + have p.p.'로 쓴다.

B [해설]

1~3. 가정법 과거완료 → 직설법 전환 방법: 과거완료는 과거로 바꾸고, 긍정은 부정으로, 부정은 긍정으로 바꿔준다. If는 접속사 as로 바꿔 쓴다.

C [해설]

1~2. 가정법 과거완료: 'if + 주어 + had p.p. ~, 주어 + 조동사의 과거형(would, could, might) + have p.p.'로, '만일 ~였다면, ~했을 텐데….'라는 뜻이다.

Point 3 I wish + 가정법 과거/과거완료

A 1. could 2. had not been
3. were able to 4. had solved

B 1. I had enough time
2. he had finished his homework
3. I had practiced hard
4. Fred and Helen attended

C 1. could go there 2. had watched a movie

A [해설]

1, 3. I wish + 가정법과거는 'I wish + 주어 + 동사의 과거형 ~.'의 형태로 쓰며, '~이라면/하면 좋을 텐데' 라는 뜻이다.

1. I wish 뒤에 과거 시제가 와야 하므로, can의 과거형인 could를 쓴다.

2. I wish 뒤에 과거 시제가 와야 하므로, have를 had로 바꾼다.
3. I wish 가정법과거는 'I wish 주어 + 동사의 과거' 형태로 써야 하고, be동사는 주어에 관계없이 were를 쓰므로, was를 were로 바꾼다.
4. I wish 뒤에 과거완료가 와야 하므로, had solve를 had solved로 바꾼다.

B [해설]

1, 4. 직설법은 'I am sorry (that) + 주어 + 동사의 현재형'은 현재의 사실에 대한 반대되는 소망을 나타낼 때 'I wish + 주어 + 동사의 과거형 ~.'으로 쓴다.
1. don't have → had
4. don't attend → attended

2~3. 직설법은 'I am sorry (that) + 주어 + 동사의 과거형'은 과거의 사실에 대한 반대되는 소망을 나타낼 때 'I wish + 주어 + had p.p. ~.'로 쓴다.
2. didn't finish → had finished
3. didn't practice → had practiced

C [해설]

1. 현재의 사실을 반대로 소망하는 표현으로는 '~이라면/하면 좋을 텐데'라는 뜻으로 'I wish + 주어 + 동사의 과거형 ~'으로 쓴다.
2. 과거의 사실을 반대로 소망하는 표현으로는 '~이었다면/했다면 좋을 텐데'라는 뜻으로, 'I wish + 주어 + had p.p. ~.'로 쓴다.

Point 4 as if + 가정법 과거/과거완료

A 1. knew 2. were 3. were

B 1. as if he were a main actor
2. as if she knew the answer to the question

C 1. He talks as if he had won the game.
2. She looked as if she had gotten well.

A [해설] 1~3. 주절과 같은 때의 사실의 반대일 경우 'as if + 가정법 과거'로 쓴다.

B [해설]

1. 직설법 현재 is not이므로 가정법 과거로는 were로 바꾼다.
2. 직설법 현재 doesn't know이므로 가정법 과거는 knew로 바꾼다.

C [해설] 1~2. 주절보다 한 시제 앞선 사실에 반대되는 내용일 때는 'as if 과거완료'로 쓴다.

Point 5 「Without[But for] + 명사(구)」 구문의 가정법

A 1. Without 2. But 3. could
4. had 5. have attended

B 1. for
2. Without[But for]
3. it were not for
4. Without [If it were not for]

C 1. Without the moon, the world would be dark.
2. But for the laws, our society would be dangerous.
3. Without money, I could not buy what I want.

A [해설]

1. Without salt: 소금이 없다면
2. But for the sun: 태양이 없다면
3. 가정법 과거완료는 '조동사의 과거형 + have p.p.'이다.
4. 뒤에 '조동사의 과거형 + have p.p.'가 있으므로, if 절에는 과거완료로 쓴다.
5. 조동사 couldn't 뒤에는 동사원형이 와야 하므로, have attended를 쓴다.

B [해설]

1. Without은 But for로 바꾸어 쓸 수 있다.
 · Without[But for] a map: 지도가 없다면
2. 'if it had not been for ~'는 'Without(But for)'로 바꾸어 쓸 수 있다. If it had not been for the song: 그 노래가 없었다면
3. 'Without[But for] + 명사(구) + 가정법 과거'는 'if it were not for ~'로 바꾸어 쓸 수 있다.
4. But for는 Without이나 If it were not for로 바꾸어 쓸 수 있다.

C [해설]

1~3. 'without[but for] + 명사(구), 주어 + 과거시제'는 '만약 ~가 없다면, ~할 것이다'이라는 뜻이다.

Point 6 주의해야 할 가정법

A	1. will 2. would 3 were
B	1. Were she rich 2. Had they practiced harder
C	1. If I were you, would study 2 If he had not been injured, would have been

A [해설]

1. if절에 현재시제이므로 단순 조건문이다. 주절에 조동사의 현재형이 와야 한다.

2. if절에 과거시제이므로 가정법 과거이다. 주절에 조동사의 과거형이 와야 한다.

3. 주절에 조동사의 과거형이 왔으므로 가정법 과거다. if절에 과거시제를 써야 한다. if절의 be동사는 주어의 수나 인칭에 상관없이 were를 쓴다.

B [해설]

1~2. 가정법 과거에서 if절에 'were', 'had'가 오면, 접속사 if를 생략하고 주어와 동사를 도치시킬 수 있다.

C [해설]

1. 가정법 과거(만약 ~한다면, ~할 텐데): 주절에 반드시 조동사의 과거형이 온다.

2. 가정법 과거완료(만약 ~했다면, ~할 텐데): 주절에 반드시 '조동사의 과거형 + have p.p.'가 온다.

일등 비법 노트

비법 1	1. ③ 2. ①, ⑤
비법 2	1. I had a girlfriend. 2. I could have helped you.
비법 3	1. ③
비법 4	1. ②, ⑤
비법 5	1. ③

비법 1

1 [해석]

· 만약 내가 그라면, 나는 그녀에게 전화할 텐데.

· 만약 그녀가 더 조심했었더라면, 그녀는 지갑을 잃어버리지 않았을 텐데.

[해설]

ⓐ 주절에 조동사의 과거형(would)가 있으므로 가정법 과거임을 알 수 있다. 'If + 주어 + 동사의 과거형/were~, 주어 + 조동사의 과거형 + 동사원형'의 순으로 쓰고, '만일 ~라면, ~할 텐데….'라는 뜻이다. 또한, if절의 be동사는 주어의 수나 인칭에 상관없이 were를 쓴다.

ⓑ 주절에 '조동사의 과거형(would) + have p.p.'가 있으므로 가정법 과거완료임을 알 수 있다. 'If + 주어 + had p.p., 주어 + 조동사의 과거형 + have p.p.'의 순으로 쓰고, '만일 ~였다면, ~했을 텐데….'라는 뜻이다.

2 [해석]

① 만약 내가 복권에 당첨된다면, 나는 새 집을 살 텐데.

② 만약 그녀가 정직하다면, 그녀는 고용될 텐데.

③ 만약 비가 오지 않는다면, 우리는 소풍을 갈 수 있을 텐데.

④ 만약 그들이 그 식당에서 점심을 먹지 않았더라면, 그들은 그녀를 보지 않았을 텐데.

⑤ 만약 어젯밤 눈이 오지 않았더라면, 지금 길이 이렇게 미끄럽지 않을 텐데.

[해설]

① 가정법 과거: 현재 사실과 반대되거나 이루어질 수 없는 것을 가정하여 말하는 표현이며, 'If + 주어 + 동사의 과거형. ~, 주어 + 조동사의 과거형 + 동사원형'의 형태로 쓴다. 따라서, 'If I won ~, I would buy ~'는 맞는 표현이다.

②③ 현재의 사실을 반대로 가정하는 표현이므로 가정법 과거(If + 주어 + 동사의 과거형/were ~, 주어 + 조동사의 과거형 + 동사원형)의 형태로 쓴다. 따라서, ②번의 would have been을 would be로, ③번의 could going은 could go로 고쳐야 한다.

④ 가정법 과거완료: 과거의 사실을 반대로 가정하는 표현이며, 'If + 주어 + had p.p. ~, 주어 + 조동사의 과거형 + have p.p.'의 형태로 쓴다. 따라서 had not have → had not had로, would not see → would not have seen으로 고쳐야 한다.

⑤ 혼합가정법: 과거의 일이 현재까지 영향을 끼칠 때 사용하며 '(과거에) ~했다면 (지금) ~할 텐데'라는 뜻으로, if절에는 가정법과거완료를, 주절에는 가정법 과거를 쓴다. 따라서, 'If it had not snowed ~, the road would not be ~.'는 맞는 표현이다.

비법 2

1 [해석]

(1) 나는 여자친구가 없어 유감이다. → 내게 여자친구가 있다면 좋을 텐데.

(2) 내가 너를 도와줄 수 없었어서 유감이다. → 내가 너에게 도움을 줄 수 있었더라면 좋았을 텐데.

비법 3

1 [해석]

① 그녀는 그녀가 마치 나의 엄마인 것처럼 말하지만, 사실 그녀는 그렇지 않다.

② 그는 마치 그가 힘든 시간을 보냈던 것처럼 보였지만, 사실 그는 그러지 않았다.

③ Bob은 마치 그가 백만장자인 것처럼 돈을 쓰지만, 사실 그는 그렇지 않다.

④ Charles 마치 그가 댄서였었던 것처럼 춤을 추었지만, 사실 그는 그렇지 않았다.

⑤ 그 남자는 마치 그가 뉴욕에 살았었던 것처럼 행동했지만, 사실 그는 그러지 않았다.

[해설]

③ Bob은 현재 백만장자가 아닌데 현재의 사실과 반대로 행동하고 있으므로, as if he is a millionaire → as if he were a millionaire.

비법 4

1 [해석] 나의 부모님의 지원이 없다면, 나는 내 목표를 이룰 수 없을텐데.

[해설] without = but for = if it were not for

비법 5

1 [해석]

① 만약 그녀가 정시에 온다면, 나는 그녀와 함께 갈 것이다.

② 만약 그가 UFO를 본다면, 그는 기뻐할텐데.

③ 만약 내가 그녀가 어디에 있는 지 알아낸다면, 나는 네게 알려줄 것이다.

④ 만약 네가 나라면, 이런 경우 너는 어떻게 하겠니?

⑤ 만약 그가 내 충고를 받아들였다면 그는 회의에 늦지 않았을 텐데.

[해설]

① 단순 조건문은 실제로 발생할 가능성이 있는 '조건'을 나타낼 때 쓰며, 주절에 조동사의 현재형이 와야한다. 따라서, will go가 왔으므로 맞는 문장이다.

②④ 가정법 과거는 현재 사실과 반대되거나 이루어질 가능성이 없는 것을 '가정'할 때 쓰고, 주절에 반드시 조동사의 과거형이 온다. 따라서, would가 왔으므로 맞는 문장이다.

③ 단순 조건문은 실제로 발생할 가능성이 있는 '조건'을 나타낼 때 쓰며, 주절에 조동사의 현재형이 와야 한다. 따라서, will let은 맞으나, If절의 found를 find로 바꾸어야 한다.

⑤ 가정법 과거완료는 과거의 사실과 반대되는 상황을 가정할 때 쓴다. If절이 과거완료(가정법 과거완료)가 왔으므로 주절에도 '조동사의 과거형 + have. p.p.'가 오는 것이 맞다.

내신 만점! 실전 기출

01. ⑤ **02.** ⑤

03. (1) were (2) had (3) make

04. 예) I would yell/ run away/ climb up a tree/ hold my breath/ lie with my face down on the ground. 등

05. ② **06.** As, don't work, can't

07. I were not, could go

08. ② **09.** ④

10. (1) But for, could not get

(2) were not for, could not get

11. (A) Were you in the spacecraft

(B) Had I had a bicycle

12. ④ **13.** ③

14. as if he were a native speaker

15. ① **16.** ④ **17.** ③

18. ④ **19.** ③

20. (A) as if, knew, (B) as if, were not

21. I wish I got straight A's. **22.** ④

23. ④ **24.** If I were, could start

25. If I had finished, could go

26. ② **27.** ⑤

28. (1) If you practice hard, you will make your work perfect.

(2) If I were not busy, I could go shopping with her.

29. as if, were

30. If she had not worked so hard, she could not have become the Sales Queen.

01 [해설] 가정법 과거: 현재 사실과 반대되거나 이루어질 수 없는 것을 가정하여 말하는 표현이며, 'If + 주어 + 동사의 과거형. ~ 주어 + 조동사의 과거형 + 동사원형'의 형태로 쓴다. 따라서, If절에는 met, 주절에는 would run을 쓴다.

02 [해석] 만약 지난 밤에 그녀가 좋아하는 배우를 만났더라면, 그녀는 매우 행복했었을 텐데.

[해설] ⑤ 가정법 과거완료는 과거 사실과 반대되는 거나 이루어질 가능성이 없는 것을 가정해서 말한다. 'If + 주어 + had + p.p. ~, 주어 + would + have + p.p.'의 순서로 쓰고 '만약 ~였다면 ~했을 텐데'라고 해석한다. 따라서, ⓐ는 had seen으로, ⓑ는 would have been으로 쓴다.

03 [해석]

(1) 만약 그가 부자라면, 그는 스포츠카를 살 텐데.

(2) 만약 내가 노트북을 가지고 있다면, 나는 네게 그것을 빌려 줄 텐데.

(3) 만약 그녀가 딸기를 가지고 있다면, 그녀는 딸기 케이크를 만들 수 있을텐데.

[해설]

(1), (2) 주절의 시제가 과거이므로 If절도 가정법 과거형(주어 + 조동사의 과거형 + 동사원형)으로 써야 한다. 가정법 과거의 if절의 be동사는 주어의 수나 인칭에 상관없이 were를 쓴다.

(3) If절에 과거가 왔으므로 가정법 과거임을 알 수 있다. 주절에 '조동사의 과거형 + 동사원형'을 쓴다.

04 [해석]

Q: 만약 네가 산에서 곰을 본다면, 너는 어떻게 할 거니?

A: 나는 소리지를 거야/ 도망갈 거야/ 나무위로 올라 갈 거야/ 숨을 참을 거야/ 땅에 엎드릴 거야. 등

[해설] 가정법 과거: 현재 사실과 반대되거나 이루어질 수 없는 것을 가정하여 말하는 표현이며, 'If + 주어 + 동사의 과거형, 주어 + 조동사의 과거형 + 동사원형'의 형태로 쓰며, '만일 ~라면, ~할 텐데...' 라는 뜻이다. 곰을 봤을 때 어떻게 할 것인지를 물었으므로, 그에 해당하는 본인의 의견을 가정법 과거로 쓰면 된다.

05 [해석] 내가 크게 말하지 않아서, 그는 내 말이 들리지 않는다.
= 만약 내가 크게 말한다면, 그는 내 말이 들릴 텐데.

[해설] ② 현재의 사실을 반대로 가정할 때는 가정법 과거 'If + 주어 + 동사의 과거형 ~, 주어 + 조동사의 과거형 + 동사원형'의 형태로 쓰고 '만약 ~라면 ~할 텐데'라고 해석한다. 따라서 ⓐ에는 speak의 과거형인 spoke로 쓰고, ⓑ에는 could + 동사원형(hear)를 쓴다.

06 [해석] 만약 그 차의 브레이크가 작동한다면, 차를 제때에 멈출 수 있을 텐데. → 그 차의 브레이크가 작동하지 않아서 차를 제때에 멈출 수가 없다.

[해설] 가정법 과거 → 직설법 현재 전환: 과거 시제는 현재 시제로 바꾸고, 긍정은 부정, 부정은 긍정으로 바꾼다.

07 [해석] 나는 너무 피곤해서, 그들과 함께 갈 수 없다.
→ 만약 내가 너무 피곤하지 않다면, 나는 그들과 함께 갈 수 있을 텐데.

[해설] 직설법 → 가정법 과거 전환 방법: 현재시제는 과거시제로 바꾸고, 긍정은 부정으로, 부정은 긍정으로 바꿔준다. As는 접속사 If로 바꿔 쓴다.

08 [해설] ② 현재의 사실과 반대의 내용일 때는 'as if + 주어 + 동사의 과거'로 써야 하므로, know의 과거형인 knew로 써야 한다.

09 as if + 가정법 과거완료: 'as if + 주어 + had p.p.'의 형태로 쓰고, 주절의 동사가 나타내는 때보다 한 시제 앞선 때를 나타낸다. '마치 ~였던 것처럼'이라는 뜻이다. 따라서, ⓐ에는 as if, ⓑ에는 had set를 쓴다.

10 [해석] 만약 인터넷이 없다면, 나는 쉽게 정보를 얻지 못할 텐데.

[해설] without = but for = if it were not for

11 [해석]

(A) 만약 네가 우주선에 있다면, 너는 무중력을 경험할 수 있을 텐데.

(B) 만약 그 때 내게 자전거가 있었다면, 나는 학교에 자전거를 타고 갔을 텐데.

[해설] 가정법 과거에서 if절에 'were, had 등'이 오면, 접속사 if를 생략하고 주어와 동사를 도치시킬 수 있다.

(A) If you were ~ → Were you ~

(B) If I had ~ → Had I ~

12 [해석] 나의 친구들과 나는 어제 야구를 할 예정이었지만 우리는 비가 많이 와서 할 수 없었다. 비가 억수같이 내렸기에 유감이다.
[해설] ④ 비가 억수같이 안 왔다면 좋을 텐데. 'I wish + 가정법 과거완료'는 'I wish + 주어 + had p.p.'로 쓰고, 'I am sorry (that) + 주어 + 동사의 과거형' 형태의 직설법으로 전환(긍정 · 부정)이 가능하다. '~이었다면/했다면 좋을 텐데'라는 뜻이다.

13 [해석] 나는 올해 초에 매일 운동을 하기로 정했지만 그 규칙을 지키지 못해왔다. 요즘 나는 운동을 하지 않아서 쉽게 아프다. 만일 내가 규칙적으로 운동한다면 건강을 유지할 수 있을 텐데.
[해설] ③ 현재의 사실을 반대로 가정할 때 쓰는 가정법 과거는 'If + 주어 + 동사의 과거형~, 주어 + could + 동사원형'으로 쓰며, '만일 ~라면, ~할 텐데…'라는 뜻이다.

14 [해설] 'as if + 가정법 과거'는 현재 사실에 반대되는 가정을 나타내며, 'as if + 주어 + 동사의 과거형'의 형태로 쓰고, '마치 ~인 것처럼'이라는 뜻을 가진다. If절의 be동사는 주어의 수나 인칭에 상관없이 were를 쓴다.

15 [해석]
① 만약 그가 자유롭다면, 그는 우리와 함께 할 수 있을 텐데.
→ 그가 자유롭지 않아서, 그는 우리와 함께 할 수 없다.
② 만약 날씨가 춥지 않다면, 그들은 등산을 갈 수 있을 텐데.
→ 날씨가 추워서, 그들 등산을 갈 수 없다.
③ 만약 내가 돈이 있다면, 나는 그 반지를 살 수 있을 텐데.
→ 나는 돈이 없어서, 나는 그 반지를 살 수 없다.
④ 만약 내가 배가 고프다면, 나는 그 모든 음식을 다 먹을 수 있을 텐데.
→ 내가 배가 고프지 않아서, 나는 그 모든 음식을 다 먹을 수 없다.
⑤ 만약 그녀가 내게 진실을 말한다면, 나는 그녀를 믿을 수 있을 텐데.
→ 그녀가 내게 진실을 말하지 않아서, 나는 그녀를 믿을 수 없다.
[해설] ① 직설법 현재로는 'As he isn't free, he can't join us.'라고 써야 맞다.

16 [해설] ④ 직설법 현재로 바꿀 때, 주절은 'she can't speak'로 바꾸어야 한다.

17 [해석]
· 그가 나를 혼자 집에 남겨 두지 않았다면 좋을 텐데.
그녀가 노래를 정말 잘 하면 좋을 텐데.
[해설] ③
ⓐ 'I wish + 가정법 과거 완료'는 과거의 사실에 대한 아쉬움이나 이루지 못한 소망을 나타낼 때 쓰인다.
ⓑ 'I wish + 가정법 과거'는 현재 상황에 대한 아쉬움이나 이루지 못한 소망을 나타낼 때 쓰인다.

18 [해석] 만약 그녀가 비밀번호를 안다면, 그녀는 문을 열 텐데.
[해설] ④ 가정법 과거인 'If + 주어 + 동사의 과거형~, 주어 + could + 동사원형'은 직설법 문장인 'As + 주어 + 동사의 현재형(긍정 ↔ 부정), 주어 + can/can't(긍정 ↔ 부정) + 동사원형'으로 바꿔 쓸 수 있다. 따라서, knew는 doesn't know로, could는 can't로 바꾼다.

19 [해석] 그녀는 고등학생처럼 행동하지만 사실은 아니다.
[해설] 'as if + 동사의 과거형' 은 주절 시제와 같은 시제의 사실과 반대인 내용을 나타내는 표현으로, '마치 ~인 것처럼'이라는 뜻이다. 직설법을 가정법으로 고칠 때는 긍정은 부정으로, 부정은 긍정으로 바꾼다.

20 [해석]
(A) 그들은 그들이 서로 아는 것처럼 보인다.
→ 사실 그들은 서로를 모른다.
(B) 나의 조부모님은 그들이 이 집의 주인이 아닌 것처럼 행동하신다.
→ 사실 나의 조부모님은 이 집의 주인이다.
[해설] (A)의 knew를 didn't know로, (B)의 were를 are not으로 바꾼다. (긍정 ↔ 부정)

21 [해설] 'I wish + 가정법 과거'는 'I wish + 주어 + 동사의 과거형 ~.'의 형태로 쓴다. 따라서, get(받다)를 got(동사의 과거형)으로 쓴다.

22 [해석]
① 만약 내가 좀 더 일찍 일어났더라면, 나는 늦지 않았을 텐데.
② 만약 그녀가 편지를 읽었다면, 그녀는 기뻐했을 텐데.
③ 만약 그가 중국어를 잘했다면, 그녀는 그를 고용했을 텐데.
④ 만약 소문이 사실이었다면, 그 배우는 사람들로부터 비난을 받았을 텐데.

⑤ 만약 그들이 어제 그 소년에게 연락처를 물어보았더라면, 그들은 그에게 지금 전화를 할 수 있을 텐데.

[해설] ①~④ 가정법 과거완료는 과거 사실과 반대되는 거나 이루어질 가능성이 없는 것을 가정해서 말한다. 'If + 주어 + had + p.p.~, 주어 + would + have + p.p.'의 형태로 쓰고 '만약 ~였다면 ~했을 텐데'라고 해석한다.

⑤ 혼합가정법은 과거의 일이 현재까지 영향을 끼칠 때 사용하며 '~했다면 ~할 텐데'라는 뜻으로, if절에는 가정법과거완료를, 주절에는 가정법 과거를 쓴다.

① would had not → would have not

② has read → had read

③ had spoke → had spoken

⑤ could called → could call

23 [해석]

① 만약 그가 여기에 있다면, 나는 그에게 도움을 요청할 텐데.

② 만약 내가 노래를 잘한다면, 나는 노래 동아리에 들어갈 텐데.

③ 만약 네가 이 편지를 그에게 준다면, 나는 정말 고마워할 텐데.

④ 만약 내가 충분한 돈을 가지고 있다면, 나는 집을 구입할 수 있을 텐데.

⑤ 만약 그녀가 바쁘지 않다면, 그녀는 그녀의 친구들과 함께 소프트볼을 할 텐데.

[해설] ①~②, ④~⑤ 가정법 과거: 'If + 주어 + 동사의 과거형/were~, 주어 + 조동사의 과거형 +동사원형'으로, 만약 ~한다면, ~할 텐데'라는 뜻이다. 현재 사실과 반대되거나 이루어질 가능성이 없는 것을 '가정'할 때 쓴다. 따라서, ④번의 could have bought를 could buy로 바꾸어야 한다.

③ 단순 조건문: '만약 ~한다면, ~할 것이다'라는 뜻으로, 실제로 발생 가능한 것에 대한 '조건'을 나타낼 때 쓴다.

24 [해석] 이번 겨울 방학은 내 인생에게 최고의 방학이 될 것이다. 나는 가족과 함께 유럽에 갈 것이다. 아빠의 친구분들이 영국과 독일에 사셔서 우리는 그들을 방문할 것이다. 나는 매우 신이 난다. ⓐ 만약 내가 교장선생님이라면, 오늘 겨울 방학을 시작할 수 있을 텐데.

[해설] 현재 사실과 반대되는 가정은 가정법 과거로 나타낸다. 'If + 주어 + 동사의 과거형~, 주어 + could + 동사원형'의 형태로 쓰고 '만약 ~라면 ~할 텐데'라고 해석한다. If절의 동사가 be동사일 경우, 주어에 상관없이 were를 쓴다.

25 [해설] 혼합가정법은 과거의 일이 현재까지 영향을 끼칠 때 사용하며 '~했다면 ~할 텐데'라는 뜻으로, if절에는 가정법과거완료(had p.p.)를, 주절에는 가정법 과거(주어 + would + 동사원형)를 쓴다.

26 [해석]

ⓒ 내 룸메이트는 밤 늦게까지 음악을 너무 크게 틀어.

ⓐ 그에게 그것에 대해 이야기 해보려 노력했니?

ⓑ 아니 아직. 네가 만약 나라면 뭐라 할 거야?

ⓓ 만약 내가 너라면, 나는 자정 이후에는 볼륨을 낮추라고 말할 거야.

[해설] 해석참조. 'If + 주어 + 동사의 과거형~, 주어 + would + 동사원형'의 형태로 쓰고 '만약 ~라면 ~할 텐데' 라고 해석한다.

27 [해석]

ⓐ 만약 내가 너라면, 나는 그의 사과를 받아 줄 텐데.

ⓑ 만약 우리에게 친구가 없다면, 우리는 외로울 텐데.

ⓒ 만약 그녀가 핸드폰을 가지고 있다면, 그녀는 그에게 그것을 빌려줄 텐데.

ⓓ 만약 네가 많은 책을 읽는다면, 너는 더 현명해 질 수 있을 텐데.

ⓔ 만약 내가 오늘 숙제가 없다면, 나는 파티에 갈 수 있을 텐데.

[해설] ⓐ, ⓔ 주절에 '조동사의 과거형 + 동사원형'이 왔으므로 가정법 과거임을 알 수 있다. if절에 과거시제로 와야 한다.

ⓐ am → were, ⓔ have → had

ⓒ if절에 now가 있고, 과거시제로 썼으므로 가정법 과거임을 알 수 있다. 주절에 '조동사의 과거형 + 동사원형'으로 써야 한다. would have lent → would lend

28 [해설]

(1) 단순 조건문은 실제로 발생 가능한 것에 대한 '조건'을 나타낼 때 쓰며, 주절에 조동사의 현재형이 와야 한다. 따라서, 주절에 will make를 쓴다. Practice makes perfect.: 노력(훈련)이 완벽을 만든다. practice hard: 열심히 연습하다, perfect: 완벽한

(2) 현재의 사실을 반대로 가정할 때는 가정법 과거 'If + 주어 + 동사의 과거형, 주어 + 조동사의 과거형 + 동사원형'로 쓴다.

29 [해석]

A: 너는 명언을 알고 있니?

B: 응. 하나 아는데 내 좌우명이야.

A: 그게 뭔데?

B: Steve Jobs가 그의 연설에서 한 말이야. 그는 'ⓐ 오늘을 인생의 마지막 날인 것처럼 살아라'라고 말했어.

[해설] 'as if + 가정법 과거'는 'as if + 주어 + 동사의 과거형'으로 쓰며, '마치 ~인 것처럼'이라는 뜻이다.

30 [해석] Belle의 재능 덕분에, 그녀는 판매에 매우 능했다. 그녀는 매우 친절하고 사교적이어서 사람들은 그녀에게서 새 차를 샀다. 그녀는 심지어 2015년에 '올해의 판매왕'으로 선정됐다. ⓐ 만약 그녀가 열심히 일하지 않았더라면, 그녀는 판매 왕이 될 수 없었을 텐데. 그래서 그녀는 더 열심히 일하기로 다짐했다.

[해설] 과거의 사실을 반대로 가정할 때는 가정법 과거 완료 'If + 주어 + had p.p. ~, 주어 + 조동사의 과거형 + have + p.p.'로 쓴다.

실력 탄탄! 서술형 심화

1 (1) were sunny, we could go to the zoo
(2) I could have a birthday party

2 ⓐ I wish I could go ⓑ I would study
ⓒ hadn't visited ⓓ I would have studied
ⓔ wouldn't get ⓕ without working

1 [해석] 문제 해석:

(1) 엄마와 나는 동물원에 갈 예정이었지만 그러지 못한다. 폭우 때문이다.

(2) 오늘은 나의 생일이지만, 아무도 그것을 기억하지 못하는 것 같다. 나는 매우 슬프다.

정답 해석:

(1) 만약 날씨가 맑다면, 우리는 동물원에 갈 수 있을텐데.

(2) 나는 친구들과 생일 파티를 할 수 있다면 좋을텐데.

[해설]

(1) 현재의 사실을 반대로 가정하는 가정법 과거는 'If + 주어 + 동사의 과거형~, 주어 + 조동사의 과거형 + 동사원형'의 형태로 쓰고 '만약 ~라면 ~할 텐데'라고 해석한다.

(2) 현재의 사실을 반대로 소망하는 표현은 'I wish + 주어 + 동사의 과거형'의 형태로 쓴다.

2 [해석] Sumi는 지금 시험을 보고 있다. 그녀는 어제 시험에 열심히 대비하지 않아서, 그녀가 모르는 문제들이 몇 개 있다. '아, 어제 이맘때로 ⓐ 돌아가면 좋을 텐데.' 만일 가능하다면, 나는 정말 열심히 ⓑ 공부할 텐데! 만일 어제 Minji가 나를 ⓒ 방문하지 않았더라면, 훨씬 더 열심히 ⓓ 공부했을 텐데. 그녀는 그녀가 열심히 ⓔ 공부하지 않으면 좋은 점수를 ⓕ 받지 못할 것이라는 것을 알았지만, 그녀는 어제는 (열심히 공부)하고 싶지 않았다. 이제 와서 그것을 후회해도 소용없다.

[해설]

ⓐ 현재의 사실을 반대로 소망하는 것이므로 'I wish 주어 + 동사의 과거'로 쓴다.

ⓑ 현재사실을 반대로 가정할 때는 'If + 주어 +동사의 과거형, 주어 + 조동사의 과거형 + 동사원형'의 형태로 쓴다(가정법 과거).

ⓒ~ⓓ 'if + 주어 + had p.p. ~, 주어 + 조동사의 과거형 (would, could, might) + have p.p.'로 쓴다.

ⓔ 주절의 시제가 과거이므로 종속절의 현재형(여기서는 조동사 will)을 과거형(would)로 쓴다.

ⓕ without + 명사(구)는 '만약 ~가 없다면, ~할 것이다'이라는 뜻이다.

Chapter 12 일치와 화법

Point 1 수의 일치

A	1. is	2. has	3. was
	4. is	5. has	6. are
	7. were		
B	1. is	2. O	3. have
	4. was	5. is	

A [해설]

1. 집단적 의미의 시간은 단수로 취급한다.
2. 분수는 뒤에 단수명사가 오면 단수로 취급한다.
3. 'every + 단수명사'는 단수로 취급한다.
4. 나라명(The Philippines)는 단수로 취급한다.
5. 주어가 단수이므로 단수동사가 와야 한다.
6. 'A number of'는 복수로 취급한다.
7. 'Both A and B'는 복수로 취급한다.

B [해설]

1. 과목명(mathematics)는 단수로 취급한다.
2. some은 뒤에 복수명사가 오면 복수로 취급한다.
3. 'the 형용사'는 복수보통명사로 복수 취급한다.
4. 절이 주어로 오면 단수로 취급한다.
5. 'the number of'는 '~의 수'라는 뜻으로 단수로 취급한다.

Point 2 시제의 일치

A	1. had taken	2. had spoken
	3. had visited	4. was
	5. had been	
B	1. had lived	2. would show
	3. had swum	4. had been
	5. had to	

A [해설]

1~3, 5. 주절의 현재시제가 과거시제로 바뀌면 종속절의 과거시제는 과거완료로 바꾼다.
4. 주절의 현재시제가 과거시제로 바뀌면 종속절의 현재시제도 과거로 바꾼다.

B [해설]

1. 주절이 과거시제일 때 종속절의 사건이 주절보다 이전에 시작되어 기준이 되는 과거까지 지속된 일이므로 과거완료로 쓴다.
2. 주절이 과거시제일 때 종속절의 조동사 will을 과거형(would)으로 바꾼다.
3~4. 주절이 과거시제일 때 종속절의 사건이 주절보다 이전에 일어났을 때 종속절의 시제를 과거완료로 쓴다.
5. 주절의 시제가 과거이고 종속절의 시제가 주어와 일치하므로 과거 시제를 쓴다.

Point 3 시제 일치의 예외

A	1. is	2. is
	3. was	4. starts
B	1. becomes	2. broke out
	3. was	
C	1. walks	2. lasts

A [해설]

1. 일반적 진리이므로 현재시제로 쓴다.
2. 속담이므로 현재시제로 쓴다.
3. 역사적 사실은 주절의 시제와 상관없이 항상 과거로 쓴다.
4. 현재의 사실(상태)는 현재시제로 쓴다.

B [해설]

1. 주절의 현재시제가 과거시제로 바뀌면 종속절의 현재시제도 과거시제로 바꾸어 준다. 그러나 과학적 사실이므로 현재시제로 그냥 둔다.
2. 종속절에 역사적 사실이 오면 주절의 시제와 상관없이 항상 과거시제로 쓴다.
3. 주절의 현재시제가 과거시제로 바뀌면 종속절의 현재시제도 과거시제로 바꾸어 준다.

C [해설]

1. 현재의 습관적인 동작은 현재시제로 쓴다.
2. 과학적 사실은 현재시제로 쓴다.

Point 4 평서문의 화법 전환

A	1. said	2. there	3. told
B	1. said, he needed	2. I was	
C	1. I will, today	2. said to me, You will	

A [해설]

1. 문장이 3형식으로서 뒤에 직접목적어가 오면 동사는 say를 쓴다.
2. 주절의 시제가 과거일 때 종속절의 시간부사 here는 there로 바꾼다.
3. 문장이 4형식으로 뒤에 간접목적어가 오면 동사는 tell로 쓴다.

B [해설]

1. 주절의 시제가 과거일 때, 직접화법의 현재시제는 간접화법으로 고칠 때 과거시제로 바꾼다. 이 때 now는 then으로 바꾼다. 인칭대명사 I는 주절의 주어와 일치시킨다.
2. 주절의 시제가 과거일 때, 직접화법의 현재시제는 간접화법으로 고칠 때 과거시제로 바꾼다. 인칭대명사 you는 주절의 목적어와 일치시키고, 3인칭은 그대로 쓴다.

C [해설]

1. 간접화법의 종속절의 시제가 주절과 같으면 직접화법으로 고칠 때 피전달문의 시제를 현재시제로 바꾼다. 인칭대명사는 주절의 주어와 같으면 I로 바꾸고, that day는 today로 바꾼다.
2. 간접화법의 종속절의 시제가 주절과 같으면 직접화법으로 고칠 때 피전달문의 시제를 현재시제로 바꾼다. 인칭대명사는 주절의 목적어와 같으면 you로 바꾼다.

Point 5 의문문의 화법 전환

A	1. asked	2. if
	3. I had	4. the previous day
B	1. where I had parked my bike	
	2. if[whether] he was hungry	
C	1. When did you arrive at the airport	
	2. How did you solve the puzzle so quickly	

A [해설]

1. 피전달문(종속절)이 의문문이면 간접화법으로 고칠 때 주절의 동사를 ask로 쓴다.
2. 피전달문(종속절)이 의문사가 없는 의문문이면 간접화법으로 고칠 때 콤마(,)와 인용부호(" ")를 없애고, if[whether]를 쓴다.
3. 의문문이 있는 의문문이 종속절(명사절)이 되면 '의문사 + 주어 + 동사' 어순이 된다.
4. 종속절의 시제가 과거완료일 때 어울리는 시간부사는 the previous day이다. yesterday는 과거시제와 함께 온다.

B [해설]

1. 직접화법의 피전달문이 의문사가 있는 의문문이면 간접화법으로 바꿀 때 '의문사 + 주어 + 동사' 어순으로 쓴다.
2. 직접화법의 피전달문이 의문사가 없는 의문문이면 간접화법으로 바꿀 때 콤마(,)와 인용부호(" ")를 없애고, if[whether]를 쓰고 이어서 '주어 + 동사' 어순으로 쓴다.

C [해설]

1. 간접화법의 피전달문(종속절)이 '의문사 + 주어 + 동사'이면 직접화법으로 전환할 때 피전달문을 '의문사 + 동사 + 주어'의 어순으로 고치고, 인칭대명사가 목적어와 같으면 you로 바꾸고, 간접화법의 시제가 과거완료이면 직접화법에서는 과거시제로 바꾼다.
2. 간접화법의 피전달문(종속절)이 '의문사 + 주어 + 동사'이면 직접화법으로 전환할 때 피전달문을 '의문사 + 동사 + 주어'의 어순으로 고치고, 인칭대명사가 목적어와 같으면 you로 바꾸고 간접화법의 시제가 과거완료이면 직접화법에서는 과거시제로 바꾼다.

Point 6 명령문의 화법 전환

A	1. to look	2. to go
	3. to try	4. not to keep
B	1. asked, to be quiet	
	2. told, not to stay up too long	
	3. advised, to share his car with his younger brother	

C 1. Get up and go to bed
2. not to smoke anymore for his lung

A [해설]

1~3. 직접화법의 명령문을 간접화법으로 전환할 때는 피전달문의 동사원형을 to부정사로 바꾼다.

4. 직접화법의 명령문을 간접화법으로 전환할 때는 피전달문의 동사원형을 to부정사로 바꾼다. 이 때 부정명령문이므로 to부정사 앞에 not(never)을 붙인다.

B [해설]

1~3. 피전달문이 명령문일 때 전달동사(주절) say to를 상황에 맞게 tell, ask, order, advise 등으로 바꾸고, 피전달문의 동사원형을 to부정사로 바꾼다.

2. 피전달문이 명령문일 때 주절의 전달동사 say to를 상황에 맞게 tell, ask, order, advise등으로 바꾸고, 피전달문의 동사원형을 to부정사로 바꾼다. 이 때 부정명령문이므로 to부정사 앞에 not을 붙인다. 주절의 시제가 과거로 바뀌면 피전달문의 현재시제도 과거로 바꾼다.

C [해설]

1. 간접화법의 to부정사로 쓰인 목적보어는 직접화법으로 고칠 때 피전달문에 명령문으로 쓴다.

2. 직접화법의 피전달문이 명령문이면 간접화법으로 고칠 때 피전달문의 동사원형을 to부정사로 바꾼다. 이 때 부정명령문이므로 to부정사 앞에 not을 붙인다. 피전달문의 인칭대명사 your은 주절의 목적어에 일치시킨다.

일등 비법 노트

비법 1	1. ②
비법 2	1. ③
비법 3	1. ④
비법 4	1. ③
비법 5	1. ⓐ went → goes ⓑ had become → became 2. ②
비법 6	1. ⑤
비법 7	1. ④

비법 1

1 [해석]

ⓐ 사람들의 각각의 손가락은 독특한 지문을 가지고 있다.

ⓑ 모든 소년 소녀는 봉사활동을 하게 되어 있다.

[해설] every와 each는 단수로 취급한다.

비법 2

1 [해석]

A: 배고프다. 집에 먹을 것이 있을까?

B: 어디 보자. 아! 냉장고에 사과가 좀 있네. 하지만 그것들 중 몇 개는 썩었어. 아! 그리고 탁자 위에 피자 상자가 있어. 피자의 반은 남아 있어.

비법 3

1 [해석]

A: 너희 반에는 학생이 몇 명이니?

B: 우리 반 학생 수는 35명이에요.

A: 와우! 30년 전 우리는 한 반에 60명 이상의 학생이 있었는데. 이부제 수업을 하는 학교도 많이 있었지.

[해설]

ⓐ the number of는 '~의 수'의 의미로 단수로 취급한다.

ⓑ a number of는 '많은'의 의미로 복수로 취급한다. 'There is/are ~'구문에서는 주어가 be동사 뒤에 오는 것이므로 뒤의 a number of schools가 주어이다. 그러므로 동사는 were가 된다.

비법 4

1 [해석] 나는 내 친구 Sally가 콘서트에 가고 싶어한다는 것을 알고 있다.

→ 나는 내 친구 Sally가 콘서트에 가고 싶어했다는 것을 알고 있었다.

[해설] 주절의 시제가 과거시제로 바뀌면 종속절의 현재시제도 과거로 바꾼다.

비법 5

1 [해석]

ⓐ 나의 남동생은 지구가 일년에 한 번 태양 주위를 돈다고 배웠다.

ⓑ 나의 선생님은 우리에게 미국이 1783년에 독립국가가 되었다고 말씀하셨다.

[해설]

ⓐ 종속절에 쓰인 과학적 사실은 주절의 시제와 상관없이 항상 현재시제로 쓴다.

ⓑ 종속절에 쓰인 역사적 사건은 주절의 시제와 상관없이 항상 과거시제로 쓴다.

2 [해설]

① 주절의 시제가 과거일 때 종속절의 사건이 주절보다 더 이전에 일어난 사건이면 종속절의 시제는 과거완료 형태로 쓴다.

② 종속절에 온 속담은 주절의 시제와 상관없이 항상 현재시제로 쓴다. flew → flies

③ 역사적인 사건은 주절의 시제와 상관없이 항상 과거로 쓴다.

④ 현재의 습관적인 사실은 주절의 시제와 상관없이 항상 현재시제로 쓴다.

⑤ 역사적인 사건은 주절의 시제와 상관없이 항상 과거로 쓴다.

비법 6

1 [해설] 직접화법을 간접화법으로 고칠 때, 피전달문의 I(1인칭)는 주절의 주어 the man과 일치하게, you(2인칭)는 목적어와 일치하도록 바꾸어 주고, 주절의 시제가 과거이면 종속절의 미래시제(will)를 과거(would)로 바꾸어 준다.

비법 7

1 [해석] 오늘, 내가 Tom과 함께 걷고 있을 때, 우리는 "Valet Parking" 이라고 쓰인 표지판을 보았다. 나는 그것이 무슨 뜻인지 전혀 몰랐다. 그래서, 나는 Tom에게, "저것이 무슨 뜻이니?" 라고 말했다. 그는 그것이 누군가 너를 대신해서 주차를 해 주는 것이라고 설명해 주었다.

[해설] 의문문을 간접화법으로 전환할 때에는 '의문사 + 주어 + 동사' 어순으로 바꾸어 준다.

내신 만점! 실전 기출

01. ②	**02.** ③	**03.** ②
04. ①	**05.** ②	**06.** ④
07. ③	**08.** ⑤	**09.** ②
10. ①		

11. He told me that he would help me fix my bike.

12. She asked him where he had been two hours before.

13. ⑤

14. She said, "Your school festival is great."

15. We have prepared for it for a month

16. not to eat any dairy products or meat

17. ⑤	**18.** ②	**19.** ⑤
20. ④	**21.** has	**22.** try
23. ④	**24.** ②, ④	

25. Have you ever tried Vietnamese food

26. asked Mike how he had succeeded

27. was she → she was

28. I will search the Internet first

29. ⑤ **30.** ⑤

01 [해석] Amy는 Mike가 그녀에게 무슨 일이 있었는지 설명해 줄 거라고 생각했다.

[해설] 주절이 과거이므로 종속절도 과거로 써야 하는데 의미상 이야기해 줄 것으로 기대하고 있으므로 would tell이 와야 한다.

02 [해석] 너는 핼리 혜성이 60년마다 돌아온다는 것을 발견한 것이 누구였는지 아니?

[해설] 과학적 사실은 항상 현재로 쓴다.

03 [해석] 엄마는 나에게 '제 때의 한 땀이 아홉 땀을 구한다'는 속담을 말씀해 주셨다.

[해설] 속담은 주절과 상관없이 항상 현재 시제로 쓴다.

04 [해석]

· 그 반의 몇몇 학생은 지루함을 느낀다.

· 금고에 있던 모든 돈이 어젯밤에 도둑에게 도난당했다.

[해설] ⓐ 'some of + 복수명사'는 복수로 취급한다.

ⓑ 'all + 단수명사'는 단수로 취급한다.

05 [해석]

· 그가 지금 매우 흥미 있어 하는 것은 로봇을 만드는 것이다.

· 웅변대회에 참가한 사람들의 수는 꽤 크다.

[해설]

ⓐ 관계대명사 what이 이끄는 절은 단수 취급한다.

ⓑ 'The number of ~'는 단수로 취급한다.

06 [해석]

· 정치학은 나라를 관리하는 것에 관한 학문이다.

· 10킬로미터는 누구에게도 걷기엔 쉬운 거리가 아닌 것 같다.

[해설]

ⓐ 학문명(politics)은 단수로 취급한다.

ⓑ 집합적 의미 단위로서의 거리는 전체를 하나의 묶음으로 보기 때문에 단수로 취급한다.

07 [해석] John은 나에게, "나와 계속 연락하자."라고 말했다.

→ John은 그와 계속 연락하자고 요청했다.

[해설] 명령문의 직접화법을 간접화법으로 고칠 때는 명령문 앞에 to를 붙인다. ③ keep → to keep

08 [해석] 나는 Mike에게, "네 펜을 잠시 사용해도 될까?"라고 말했다.

→ 나는 Mike에게 그의 펜을 잠시 사용해도 될 지를 물었다.

[해설] 피전달문의 2인칭 대명사는 주절의 목적어와 일치시킨다. (⑤ your → his)

09 [해석]

① 그는 수진이에게 그녀의 음식이 좋았는지 물었다.

② 그녀는 나에게 내가 가장 좋아하는 과목이 무엇인지 물었다.

③ 수호는 내가 숙제를 다 끝냈는지 물었다.

④ 미나는 나에게 내가 그녀와 함께 쇼핑을 갈 것인지 물었다.

⑤ John은 우리가 영화를 위해 서둘러야 하지 않는지 물었다.

[해설]

② 은 '무엇'의 의미가 필요하므로 what이 들어간다.

①③④⑤는 '~인지 아닌지'의 의미가 필요하므로 if 또는 whether가 들어간다.

10 [해석]

① Kate는 "내 머리는 3년 전에 짧았어." 라고 말했다.

→ Kate는 그녀의 머리가 3년 전에 짧았다고 말했다.

② Rex는 나에게, "너 우리 스터디 그룹에 들어올래?"라고 말했다.

→ Rex는 나에게 그의 스터디 그룹에 들어 올지 물었다.

③ 엄마는 나에게, "저녁식사 전까지 숙제를 끝내라."라고 말씀하셨다.

→ 엄마는 나에게 내 숙제를 저녁식사 전까지 끝내라고 말씀하셨다.

④ 나의 여동생은 나에게, "지금 내 숙제를 좀 도와줄 수 있어?"라고 말했다.

→ 나의 여동생은 나에게 그녀의 숙제를 그 때 도와줄 수 있는지를 물었다.

⑤ Anne은 "나는 어제 시험을 위해서 열심히 공부하지 않았어."라고 말했다.

→ Anne은 그녀가 그 전날 시험을 위해서 열심히 공부하지 않았다고 말했다.

[해설] 주절의 시제가 과거일 때 간접화법으로 전환 시 피전달문의 과거시제는 과거완료로 고쳐야 하고, 시간부사 ago는 before로 고쳐야 한다. was → had been, ago → before

11 [해석] 그는 나에게, "내가 네 자전거 고치는 것을 도와줄게."라고 말했다.

[해설] 주절의 전달동사인 said to는 told로 바꾸고, 주절이 과거시제일 때 직접화법의 피전달문의 미래 시제는 과거형(would)로 바꾸고, I는 주절의 주어에 일치하게, you는 목적어에 일치하도록 바꾼다.

12 [해석] 그녀는 나에게, "두 시간 전에 너는 어디에 있었니?"라고 말했다.

[해설] 주절이 과거시제일 때 직접화법의 피전달문의 과거시제는 과거완료로 바꾸고, '의문사 + 주어 + 동사'의 어순으로 쓴다. 그리고 ago는 before로 바꾼다.

13 [해석] 민지는 나에게, "너는 어떤 영화를 보기를 원하니?"

→ 민지는 나에게 어떤 영화를 보기를 원하는지 물었다.

[해설] 의문사가 있는 의문문을 간접화법으로 바꿀 때는 '의문사 + 주어 + 동사' 어순으로 고치고, 주절의 시제가 과거일 때 종속절의 현재시제는 과거시제로 바꾼다.

14~15 [해석] 어제는 우리학교 축제였다. 나는 내 친구 Amy를 축제에 초대했다. ⓐ 그녀는 우리 학교 축제는 굉장하다고 말했다. ⓑ나는 우리가 그것을 위해 한 달 동안 준비해 왔다고 그녀에게 말했다.

14 [해설] 간접화법에서 주절이 과거 시제일 때 종속절의 시제가 주절과 같으면 직접화법으로 바꿀 때는 피전달문의 시제를 현재로 쓴다.

15 [해설] 간접화법에서 주절의 시제가 과거일 때 종속절의 과거완료는 동작이 한 달 전부터 그 때까지 계속되었던 것을 나타내므로 직접화법으로 고칠 때는 현재완료로 바꾼다.

16 [해석] 의사의 권고

(1) 의사는 나에게, "이 약을 매 식사 직후에 복용하시오." 라고 말했다.

(2) 의사는 또한 나에게, "어떤 유제품이나 고기를 먹지 마시오."

[해설] 명령문을 간접화법으로 고칠 때는 전달되는 문장의 명령문을 to부정사로 고친다.

17 [해석]

① 누군가 우리 집에 침입했었다.

② Emily와 Lily는 모두 그들의 시험에 대해 걱정하고 있었다.

③ 당뇨병은 요즘 아이들 사이에서 흔해지고 있다.

④ 너의 친구들의 말에 귀를 기울이는 것은 좋은 친구가 되는 가장 중요한 요소이다.

⑤ 네가 흥미가 있는 것이 너의 미래 직업을 고를 때 첫째로 고려해야 하는 것이다.

[해설]

① -body로 끝나는 단어는 단수로 취급한다. (have → has)

② both A and B는 복수로 취급한다. (was → were)

③ 병명(Diabetes)은 단수로 취급한다. (are → is)

④ 동명사가 주어일 때는 단수로 취급한다. (are → is)

⑤ 절이 주어일 때는 단수로 취급하므로 동사 is를 쓴 것이 적절하다.

18 [해석]

① 내 선생님께서 성공이란 항상 보이는 것만이 아니라고 말씀하셨다.

② 너는 영국의 최초의 여왕이 누구였는지 배웠니?

③ Susan은 그녀가 시험 결과에 실망했다고 말했다.

④ 나는 내 남동생에게 어제 2 더하기 2는 4라고 가르쳐 주었다.

⑤ 나는 그가 세계를 여행한 것에서 많은 경험을 쌓았을 거라고 생각했다.

[해설]

① 격언은 항상 현재시제로 쓴다.

② 역사적 사실은 항상 과거로 쓴다. (had been → was)

③ 종속절의 사건이 주절과 같은 시점에 일어난 일이므로 같은 시제인 과거로 쓴다.

④ 일반적인 진리는 항상 현재 시제로 쓴다.

⑤ 주절의 시제가 과거인데 종속절의 사건이 더 이전부터 그 때까지의 경험을 나타내므로 과거완료로 써야 한다.

19 [해석]

A: 나는 어제 비행기 한 대가 알프스 산에 비상착륙을 했다는 TV 뉴스를 보았어.

B: 오, 저런! 그것에 대해 뭐라고 했니?

A: 그들이 그러는데 비행기의 일부가 손상되었고, 많은 사람들이 다쳤다고 했어.

[해설]

ⓐ '분수 + 단수명사'는 단수로 취급하고, 주절의 시제가 과거이므로 종속절도 과거시제로 쓴다.

ⓑ 'a number of ~'는 복수로 취급한다. 주절의 시제가 과거이므로 종속절도 과거시제로 쓴다.

20 [해석]

A: 와우! 다음 주에 노래 경연대회가 우리 동네에서 열린대. 너 참가하지 않을래?

B: 그러고 싶지만, 7일은 대회를 준비하기엔 충분하지 않아.

A: 왜 이래! 너는 너의 재능을 보여줄 수 있는 기회를 원한다고 했잖아. 그냥 한 번 해 봐!

B: 생각해 볼게.

[해설]

ⓐ 집합적 의미 단위의 시간을 나타낼 때는 단수로 취급한다.

ⓑ 주절의 시제가 과거일 때는 종속절의 시제는 과거나 과거완료로 쓴다. 여기서는 주절의 사건과 종속절의 사건이 같은 시점에 일어났을 것이므로 주절의 시제(과거)와 같이 종속절의 시제도 과거시제로 쓴다.

21 [해설] every는 단수로 취급하므로 단수동사가 와야 한다.

22 [해설] 'the + 형용사'(~한 사람들)는 복수로 취급하므로 복수동사가 와야 한다.

23 [해석]

ⓐ 사서는 우리에게 도서관에서 잡담하지 말라고 말했다.

ⓑ 그녀는 그에게 어느 나라들을 가 봤는지 물었다.

ⓒ Mike는 나에게 내가 새로운 수학 선생님을 알고 있는지 물었다.

ⓓ Jane은 Mike에게 그가 무거운 상자를 나르는 것을 도와줄 수 있는지 물었다.

ⓔ 한 남자가 나에게 전철역에 어떻게 가는지 물었다.

[해설]

ⓐ 명령문의 간접화법은 명령문 앞에 to를 써야 한다. not chat → not to chat

ⓑ 주절의 사건보다 종속절의 사건이 더 먼저 일어난 사건이고 주절의 시제가 과거이므로 종속절의 시제는 과거완료로 쓴다.

ⓒ '~인지 아닌지'의 의미인 의문문이 없는 의문문을 간접화법으로 전환한 것이므로 that을 if로 고쳐야 한다.

ⓓ 의문문이 없는 의문문을 간접화법으로 고칠 때는 'if(whether) + 주어 + 동사'로 쓴다.

ⓔ 의문사가 있는 의문문을 간접화법으로 고치면 종속절의 어순이 '의문사 + 주어 + 동사'가 된다.

24 [해석]

ⓐ 나는 2차 세계대전이 1945년에 끝났다고 읽었다.

ⓑ 그녀는 내가 그녀와 함께 울산에 갈 수 있을 거라고 기대했다.

ⓒ 너는 미국에 몇 개의 주가 있는지 알고 있었니?

ⓓ Copernicus가 주장한 것은 과학자들에 의해 처음에 받아들여지지 않았다.

ⓔ 나의 과학 선생님은 태양이 주위에 8개의 행성이 있다고 말씀하셨다.

[해설]

ⓐ 역사적 사실은 주절의 시제와 관계없이 항상 과거로 쓴다. had ended → ended

ⓑ 주절의 시제가 과거일 때는 종속절의 시제는 과거나 과거완료가 온다. can → could

ⓒ the United States는 국가명이므로 단수로 취급해야 하고, 현재 사실이므로 현재시제로 쓴다. 그런데 의문문이 있는 의문문을 간접화법으로 고칠 때는 '의문사 + 주어 + 동사'의 어순을 취하므로, 여기서는 do를 없애고 have를 has로 고쳐야 한다.

ⓓ 절이 주어로 올 때는 단수로 취급한다. were → was

ⓔ 과학적 사실은 항상 현재 시제로 쓴다. had → has

25 [해석] 그녀는 Jake에게 그가 베트남 음식을 먹어 본 적이 있는 지 물었다.

→ 그녀는 Jake에게, "너는 베트남 음식을 먹어 본 적이 있니?"라고 말했다.

[해설] 간접화법의 주절이 과거시제이고, 피전달문의 내용이 그 때까지의 경험을 나타내는 과거완료이므로, 직접화법으로 고칠 때는 질문하는 그 당시 현재까지의 경험이므로 현재완료로 쓴다.

26 [해설] 의문문을 간접 화법으로 전환할 때, '의문사 + 주어 + 동사'의 어순에 유의한다.

27~28 [해석] 나는 에세이 숙제가 있었다. 나는 무엇에 관해 써야 할 지 몰랐다. 그래서 나는 민지에게, "너는 무엇에 관해 쓸 거니?"라고 말했다. 그녀는 먼저 인터넷으로 조사를 할 거라고 말했다. 나는 그것이 좋은 생각이라고 생각했다.

27 [해설] 의문사가 있는 의문문을 간접화법으로 전환할 때는, 종속절의 어순을 '의문사 + 주어 + 동사'의 어순으로 바꾸어야 한다.

28 [해설] 간접화법에서 주절의 시제가 과거일 때 종속절의 시제가 과거이면 직접화법에서 현재시제 (혹은 미래시제)로 바꾸고, 주절의 주어와 종속절의 주어가 같으므로 직접화법의 피전달문의 주어는 I로 바꾼다.

29 [해석] 당신은 새해 첫날에 무엇을 하는가? 많은 사람들이 새해에 성취할 목표를 정하지만, 그들 중 대부분은 중도에 포기한다. 그렇다면, 사람들은 어떻게 성공적으로 목표를 성취할 수 있을까? 한 권의 책이 나에게 불가능한 목표를 정하는 것이 하나의 문제라고 가르쳐 주었다. 그것은 또한 내가 한 번에 한 단계씩 나아가고 있는 지 스스로에게 물어볼 것을 가르쳤다. 다음에 목표를 세울 때는 나는 이 책이 말한 것을 꼭 기억할 것이다.

[해설]

ⓐ 'most of + 복수명사'는 복수로 취급하므로 동사는 give를 쓴다.

ⓑ 동명사(setting) 주어는 단수로 취급하므로 동사는 is를 쓴다.

ⓒ '~인지 아닌지'의 뜻을 가지고, 의문문이 없는 의문문인 직접화법을 간접화법으로 고칠 때는 피전달문 앞에 접속사 if를 쓴다.

30 [해석] 어제 나는 형과 함께 공원에 갔다. 공원에는 한 남자와 그의 개가 있었다. 그 남자는 우리에게 개에 대해서 걱정하지 말라고 말했다. 그는 그 개는 그때까지 어떤 사람도 문 적이 없다고 말했다. 그 말이 나에게 '짖는 개는 물지 않는다'는 옛 속담을 떠올렸다. 나의 형이 우리는 그 개를 두려워하지 않는다고 말했다.

[해설] ⓐ not to worry, ⓑ had never bitten, ⓒ then (화법 전환 시, 주절이 과거일 때 종속절에 온 now는 then이 되어야 한다), ⓓ doesn't bite, ⓔ were

실력 탄탄! 서술형 심화

1 what 'courtesy phone' meant

2 ⓐ are taken → is taken
ⓑ are → is
ⓒ says → say
ⓓ saw → had seen

3 (1) she had
(2) to take
(3) not to drink
(4) what she had to do
(5) to come again the next[following] day

1 [해석] 너는 저기에 "courtesy phone"이라는 표지판이 보이니? 저게 무슨 뜻이야?
Jane: 그것은 네가 공짜로 쓸 수 있는 전화라는 뜻이야.
은호: 와우! 그것 좋구나.
[해설] 의문문이 있는 의문문의 직접화법을 간접화법으로 전환할 때는 종속절에 '의문사 + 주어 + 동사' 어순으로 바꾼다. 또한 주절의 시제가 과거일 때 피전달문의 현재시제는 과거시제로 바꾼다.

2 [해석]
A: 이 사람들 좀 봐! 이 영화는 틀림없이 매우 성공적일 거야.
B: 응. 이 극장의 모든 좌석이 찼어.
A: 나는 이 영화를 본 사람의 수가 천만 명이 넘었다는 것을 들었어.
B: 나도 알아. 많은 사람들이 이 영화가 멋지다고 말한대.
A: Jim은 이 영화를 벌써 보았다고 했어?
B: 응. 그는 지난 주에 봤어.
[해설]
ⓐ every는 단수로 취급한다.
ⓑ the number of는 단수로 취급한다.
ⓒ a number of는 복수로 취급한다.
ⓓ 주절의 시제가 과거일 때는 종속절의 사건이 주절보다 앞서서 일어난 사건이면 종속절에 과거완료 시제로 쓴다.

3 [해석]
의사: 어떻게 오셨나요?
Amy: 심한 감기가 걸렸어요.
의사: 흠... 이 약을 하루에 세 번 드세요. 그리고 찬 물은 드시지 마세요.
Amy: 그것이 도움이 안되면 어떻게 해야 하나요?
의사: 그러면, 내일 다시 오세요.
[해설]
(1) 직접화법을 간접화법으로 고칠 때, 간접화법의 주절이 과거이면 피전달문의 현재 시제를 과거로 고친다.
(2) 피전달문이 명령문인 직접화법은 간접화법으로 고칠 때 명령문을 to부정사 형태로 고친다.
(3) 피전달문이 부정명령문인 직접화법은 간접화법으로 고칠 때 부정명령문을 'not + to부정사' 형태로 고친다.
(4) 의문문이 있는 의문문의 직접화법을 간접화법으로 전환할 때는 종속절에 '의문사 + 주어 + 동사' 어순으로 바꾼다. 또한 주절의 시제가 과거일 때 피전달문의 현재시제는 과거시제로 바꾼다.
(5) 피전달문이 명령문인 직접화법은 간접화법으로 고칠 때 명령문을 to부정사 형태로 고친다. 또한 tomorrow는 the following(next) day로 바꾼다.

Chapter 13 특수 구문

Point 1 강조 I – 조동사 do로 동사 강조

A 1. do. 2. does 3. do
4. do 5. Do 6. did

B 1. do hope 2. did finish
3. did know 4. did believe
5. did pass

A [해석]
1. 나는 그것에 대해 정말로 알고 싶다.
2. 그녀는 나와는 달리 정말로 해산물을 싫어한다.
3. 너는 꼭 일찍 일어나야만 한다.
4. 이 쿠키들은 정말로 맛이 좋다.
5. 대회 전에 정말로 더 열심히 연습해라.
6. Jake는 정말로 그가 그 사실에 대해 옳다고 생각했다.
[해설]
1, 3, 4. 주어가 1인칭, 2인칭, 복수인 경우에는 강조를 위해 do를 쓴다.
2. 주어가 3인칭인 경우에는 강조를 위해 does를 쓴다.
5. 명령문 앞에 강조의 의미로 do를 쓸 수 있다.
6. 주어가 3인칭 이므로 does가 오거나 과거를 의미하는 did가 올 수 있다.

B [해석] 〈보기〉 우리 오빠는 공부를 (매우) 열심히 해서 시험에 통과했다.
1. 나는 그가 호전되기를 정말로 바란다.
2. 나는 모든 일을 이미 정말로 마쳤다.
3. Jane은 그것이 그의 실수임을 정말로 알고 있었다.
4. Peter는 그녀가 그에게 말한 것을 정말로 믿었다.
[해설]
1. 주어가 1인칭이고 현재시제이므로 강조를 위해 do를 쓴다.
2~5. 과거 시제이므로 강조를 위해 did를 쓴다.

Point 2 강조 II – 「It ~ that ...」 강조 구문

A 1. It was Jenny that[who] found the beautiful jewelry in the box yesterday.
2. It was the beautiful jewelry that[which] Jenny found in the box yesterday.
3. It was in the box that[where] Jenny found the beautiful jewelry yesterday.
4. It was yesterday that[when] Jenny found the beautiful jewelry in the box.

B 1. Jane that helped me
2. the onion soup that my mom cooked for me

A [해석]
1. 어제 상자 안에서 예쁜 보석을 발견한 것은 Jenny였다.
2. Jenny가 어제 상자 안에서 발견한 것은 예쁜 보석이었다.
3. Jenny가 어제 예쁜 보석을 발견한 곳은 상자 안이었다.
4. Jenny가 상자 안에서 예쁜 보석을 발견한 것은 어제였다.
[해설]
1~4. 과거 시제이므로 'It was ~ that'사이에 강조하고 싶은 내용을 넣고 나머지는 that 이후에 써준다.
1. 강조하는 바가 사람(Jenny)이므로 that 대신에 who를 쓰는 것도 가능하다.
2. 강조하는 바가 사물(the beautiful jewelry)이므로 that 대신에 which를 쓰는 것도 가능하다.
3. 강조하는 바가 장소(in the box)이므로 that 대신에 where를 쓰는 것도 가능하다.
4. 강조하는 바가 시간(yesterday)이므로 that 대신에 when을 쓰는 것도 가능하다

B [해설]
1~2. 'It is/was ~ that' 사이에 강조하고자 하는 내용을 넣어 강조구문을 만든다. 강조하는 바가 사람이면 who, 사물이면 which가 that을 대신하여 올 수 있다.

Point 3 도치 I – 장소 부사(구)의 도치, 부정어의 도치

A 1. they come 2. came the rain
3. are 4. is a computer lab
5. did she think

B 1. Under the bed are some books.
2. Rarely do we eat dinner at home.

A [해석]
1. 여기 그들이 온다.
2. 비가 내렸다.
3. 정류장에 두 명의 소녀들이 서 있다.
4. 2층에 컴퓨터 랩이 있다.
5. 그들이 다시 만나리라곤 그녀는 거의 생각 안 했다.

[해설]

1. 도치구문에서 주어가 대명사일 경우, '주어+동사'의 도치가 일어나지 않고 '부사(구) + 주어 + 동사' 어순으로 쓴다.

2, 4. 장소나 방향을 나타내는 부사구를 문장의 앞에 두면, '부사(구) + (조)동사 + 주어'의 어순으로 쓴다.

3. At the station이 문장의 앞으로 나가면서 도치가 일어난 구문이므로 실제 주어는 two girls이고, 따라서 동사는 are을 써야 한다.

5. 부정어 도치에서 일반동사가 쓰인 문장은 'do(does/did)+주어+동사원형'의 형태로 쓴다.

B [해석] 〈보기〉 식료품점은 길 모퉁이에 있다.

1. 침대 밑에 책 몇 권이 있다.
2. 우리는 집에서 저녁을 거의 먹지 않는다.

[해설]

1. 장소나 방향을 나타내는 부사구를 문장의 앞에 두면, '부사(구) + (조)동사 + 주어'의 어순으로 쓴다.
2. 부정어 도치에서 일반동사가 쓰인 문장은 'do(does/did) + 주어 + 동사원형'의 형태로 쓴다.

Point 4 도치 II – 동의할 때: 「So/Nor/Neither + 동사 + 주어」 구문

A 1. Neither do I 2. So am I
3. Neither do I

B 1. neither do I 2. so am I

C 1. I didn't pass the exam this time, either.
2. I will go shopping tomorrow, too.

A [해석]

1. A: 나는 오늘밤 피자를 먹고 싶지 않아. 그것에 질렸어.
B: 나도야. 다른 걸 먹자.
2. A: Jane은 다음 달부터 중국어를 배울 거래.
B: 나도야. 사실 우리는 같은 반을 들을 거야.
3. A: 나는 그가 매사 불만을 늘여놓는 것을 좋아하지 않아.
B: 나도야. 그는 주변 사람들을 피곤하게 만들어.

[해설]

1, 3. 부정문에 대한 동의이고 일반동사가 쓰였으므로 'Neitehr do I.'를 쓴다.

2. 긍정문에 대한 동의이고 be동사가 쓰였으므로 'So am I.'를 쓴다.

B [해석]

1. Chris는 커피를 좋아하지 않고 나 역시 좋아하지 않는다.
2. 우리 엄마는 똑똑하고 예쁘고 나 역시 그렇다.

[해설]

1. I don't, either. = Neither do I.
2. I am, too. = So am I.

C [해석] 〈보기〉

A: 나는 지금 우산이 없어.
B: 나 역시 없어. → 나 또한 우산이 없어.

1. A: Tom은 이번에 시험을 통과하지 못했어.
B: 나도야.
2. A: 그들은 내일 쇼핑을 갈 거야.
B: 나도야.

[해설]

1. 「neither(nor) + 동사 + 주어」는 「주어 + be동사(do동사/조동사), either.」로 바꿀 수 있다.
2. 「So + be동사(do동사/조동사) + 주어」는 「주어 + be동사(do동사/조동사), too」로 바꿀 수 있다.

일등 비법 노트

비법 1	1. ①	
비법 2	1. ②	
	2. It is in the department store that all clothes are 20% off today.	
비법 3	1. ③	2. he came → did he come
비법 4	1. ③	2. ④

비법 1

1 [해석]

① 너 참 잘했어.
② 그들은 이번에 (정말로) 열심히 일했다.
③ 그들은 부모님을 사랑한다.
④ 나는 이미 설거지를 했다.
⑤ 그녀는 그의 전화 번호를 안다.

[해설] ①은 일반동사 do의 과거형으로 문장의 본동사의 역할을 하므로 생략이 불가하지만 나머지는 강조를 위한 do/did이다. ②~⑤는 강조의 do로서 생략이 가능하다.

비법 2

1 [해석] 나는 내 핸드폰을 거리에서 떨어뜨렸다.
[해설] 강조하고 싶은 구를 It is와 that 사이에 넣으면 되는데 전체 시제가 과거이므로 It was ~ that이 맞다. 장소를 강조하므로 that을 대신하여 where을 쓰는 것도 가능하다.

2 [해석] 옷이 오늘 백화점에서 20% 할인된 가격으로 팔린다.
[해설] 강조하고 싶은 부분을 It is ~ that 사이에 넣으면 된다.

비법 3

1 [해석] 나는 이와 같이 맛있는 음식을 먹지 못했다.
[해설] 부정어가 문장 앞으로 도치되면 일반동사의 경우 'do/does/did + 주어 + 동사원형'의 어순으로 쓴다!

2 [해석] 그는 수업에 좀처럼 늦지 않는다.

비법 4

1 [해석] 그는 그의 우산을 가져오지 않았다. 나도 내 우산을 가져오지 않았다.
[해설] 부정내용을 동의할 때는 'Neither + 동사 + 주어'로 쓴다. 과거 시제 일반동사이므로 'Neither did I.'가 온다.

2 [해석]
A: 내 남동생은 기타를 정말 잘 쳐.
B: 나도 그래. 사람들은 내가 기타리스트 같다고 해.
[해설] 긍정문에 대한 동의이고, 동사가 일반동사이므로 So do I 가 와야 한다.

내신 만점! 실전 기출

01. ③ 02. ② 03. ③
04. ② 05. ③, ④ 06. ③
07. ④
08. They did know that their vacation was delayed.
09. At the corner of the street was a huge tree.
10. ④ 11. ③ 12. ①
13. Never did he forget to call me when he got on the bus.
14. ③ 15. ③ 16. ⑤
17. ③ 18. ④ 19. ③
20. (1) Neither could I. (2) did feed the dog
21. Where was it that you saw Kevin yesterday?
22. (1) did lose her wallet during her trip
(2) during her trip that(when) Jenny lost her wallet
23. ④ 24. ④, ⑤
25. It was in the morning that I ran into Gloria in the elevator.
26. ④ 27. ②
28. I realized → did I realize
29. ⓐ Next to her was her little brother.
ⓑ Little did I dream that I would see him again.
ⓒ Down he fell.
30. ② did talked → did talk

01 [해석]
A: 나는 아직 숙제를 못 끝냈어.
B: 나도야.
[해설] 부정문에 대한 동의이고, 일반동사과거이므로 neither과 did를 써야 한다.

02 [해석] 큰 나무 아래 두 명의 아이들이 서있다.
[해설] 장소 부사구가 문장의 앞에 오면 뒤에 '동사 + 주어' 순서가 된다. 이 때 동사의 수는 뒤에 오는 주어에 일치시킨다.

03 [해석] 우리가 여름 휴가를 보낸 곳은 바로 로마에서였다.
[해설] 「It is ~ that」 강조구문을 쓸 때 문장의 시제가 과거이면 「It was ~ that」을 쓴다.

04 [해석] 그는 늦게 왔을 뿐 아니라 그의 가방 또한 잊었다.

[해설] 부정어가 문장의 앞에 오면 도치가 일어나는데 일반동사는 'do/does/did + 주어 + 동사원형'의 어순이 된다. came he → did he come

05 [해석] 나는 그의 학생증을 바닥에서 찾았다.

[해설] on the floor를 강조하는 문장은 'It was on the floor that(where) I found his ID card.'가 된다.

06 [해석] 나는 결코 그렇게나 아름다운 경치를 보지 못했다.

[해설] did가 쓰였으므로 시제는 과거이고, never이 빈도부사이므로 일반동사 앞에 위치해야 한다.

07 [해설] 부정어 도치에서 일반동사가 있는 문장의 경우에는 '부정어 + 조동사[do동사] + 주어 + 동사'의 어순이다. 도치되기 전의 원래 문장은, 'I never told Mary what happened to him yesterday.'이다.

08 [해석] 그들은 그들의 휴가가 연기되었다는 것을 알았다.

[해설] 동사를 강조할 때는 do를 쓰는데 시제가 과거이므로 did를 써준다.

09 [해석] 큰 나무가 그 길 모퉁이에 있었다.

[해설] 장소 부사구가 문장 앞으로 오면(도치) 뒤에 '동사 + 주어'의 순으로 쓴다.

10 [해석] 〈보기〉 그는 나에게 또 거짓말을 했다.

① 그녀는 그녀의 개를 정말로 사랑한다.
② 우리는 그것이 이루어질 것이라고 정말로 믿는다.
③ 그는 우리의 약속을 정말로 잊었다.
④ 시험에서 최선을 다하자.
⑤ 나는 어떤 상황에서도 그녀를 정말로 믿는다.

[해설]

④ do one's best: 최선을 다하다
①, ②, ③, ⑤는 강조를 위한 do/does/did이다.

11 [해석]

① 내가 Julie를 본 것은 그 공원에서였다.
② 내가 수영을 시작했던 것은 지난 1월이었다.
③ 우리가 경기를 이긴 것은 정말 멋졌다.
④ 내가 감사함을 느끼는 것은 Tom이다.
⑤ 내가 그녀에게 받은 것은 지갑이다.

[해설] ③은 가주어 it이고 나머지는 It is ~ that 강조구문의 it이다.

12 [해석]

A: 난 이 드레스를 입으니 날씬해 보이지 않는 거 같아요.
B: 걱정 하지 말아요. 당신은 정말로 날씬해 보여요.
A: 당신은 나한테 항상 진실을 말하지요. 그렇죠?
B: 그럼요. 저는 당신에게 정말로 항상 진실을 말하지요.

13 [해설] 부정어 도치에서 부정어 다음에 '동사 + 주어' 순으로 쓴다.

14 [해석]

① Terry는 그 영화를 매우 좋아했고 나도 그랬다.
② 우리 엄마는 요리를 잘하고 우리 언니도 그렇다.
③ 나는 흥분했고 다른 사람들도 모두 마찬가지였다.
④ 지민은 카메라를 가지고 있고 민호도 그렇다.
⑤ 내 여동생은 한국 음식을 좋아하고 나도 그렇다.

[해설] ① 앞에 동사가 일반동사이고 과거이므로 so was I → so did I

② 앞에 동사가 일반동사이고, 뒤에 주어가 3인칭 단수(my sister)이므로 so do my sister → so does my sister
③ 앞에 동사가 be동사이고 과거이며, 뒤에 주어가 everyone이므로 was를 쓴 것이 맞다.
④ 앞에 동사가 일반동사이고 현재시제이므로 so has Minho → so does Minho
⑤ 앞에 동사가 일반동사이고 현재시제이므로 so am I → so do I

15 [해석]

① 그는 탁자 위에 있는 모든 것을 먹었다.
② 길 건너에 검은 머리 남자가 있다.
③ 내가 지갑을 잃어버린 것은 지난 주말이다.
④ Jack은 결코 거짓말을 하지 않는다.
⑤ 좀처럼 Edward는 우리 앞에서 웃지 않았다.

[해설] ③ 지갑을 잃어버린 때(시간)를 강조하므로 where이 아닌 when 혹은 that이 와야 한다.

16 [해석]

① 매 층마다 화장실이 있다.
② 내게 이 반지를 준 사람은 엄마다.

③ 그의 친구들 모두가 그의 아이디어에 동의한 것은 아니다.
④ 그는 주말에 절대 일찍 일어나지 않았다.
⑤ 나는 그것에 대해 그녀에게 약속을 했다.
[해설] 강조의 did를 쓸 때 뒤에는 동사 원형을 써야 한다. did made → did make

17 [해설] 'It is ~ that' 강조구문에서는 강조하려는 대상을 It is와 that 사이에 넣는다.

18 [해설] 부정어가 문장의 앞에 오고, 일반동사가 쓰인 경우에는 'do/does/did + 주어 + 동사원형'의 형태로 도치된다. 주어가 복수(we)이고, 동사가 현재시제(realize)이므로, do we realize가 옳은 답이다.
· not until ~ 조동사 + 주어 + 동사: ~이 되어서야 비로소 ~했다

19 [해석]
① Mr. Kim이 연설을 할 것이다.
→ 연설을 하는 것은 Mr. Kim이다.
② 우리는 내일 소풍을 갈 것이다.
→ 우리가 소풍을 가는 것은 내일이다.
③ Terry는 크리스마스에 Susie를 만났다.
→ Terry가 크리스마스에 만난 사람은 Susie이다.
④ 나는 이 열쇠를 네 방 안의 의자 위에서 찾았다.
→ 내가 이 열쇠를 찾은 것은 네 방 안의 의자 위에서이다.
⑤ 그녀는 사과 쿠키가 아닌 사과 파이를 먹는 것을 좋아한다.
→ 그녀가 먹기를 좋아하는 것은 사과 쿠키가 아닌 사과 파이이다.
[해설] 'It is ~ that …' 강조구문으로 강조할 때: 문장에서 강조할 부분을 It is와 that 사이에 넣는다. 강조하기 위해 끌어 온 표현을 대신한 다른 단어를 넣지 않는다. that이후에 her가 불필요하게 들어가 있다.

20 [해설]
(1) 'neither(nor) + 동사 + 주어' 구문: '~도 또한 …가 아니다'의 뜻으로 부정문에 대한 동의를 나타낸다. couldn't가 쓰였으므로 neither 다음에는 could를 쓴다.
(2) 조동사 do를 써서 동사를 강조할 때, 'do/does/did + 동사원형'의 형태로 쓴다. 과거 시제이므로 made는 did make로 변형된다.

21 [해설] 의문사를 강조하려고 할 때는 '의문사 + is[was] + it that ~'의 어순으로 쓴다.

22 [해설]
(1) 조동사 do를 써서 동사를 강조할 때, 'do/does/did + 동사원형'의 형태로 쓰인다. 과거 시제이므로 lost는 did lose로 변형된다.
(2) 'It is/was ~ that' 사이에 강조하고 싶은 부분을 넣어 강조의 의미를 전달할 수 있다. 과거 시제이므로 강조하려는 during the trip을 It was ~ that 사이에 넣고, 나머지는 that 다음에 써준다. 또한, 강조하는 내용이 때를 나타낼 때는 that을 대신하여 when으로 쓸 수 있다.

24 [해석] 그들은 새로운 상품을 좋아하지 않았다. 나 역시 좋아하지 않았다.
[해설] neither(nor) + 동사 + 주어 「~도 또한 …가 아니다」의 뜻으로 부정문에 대한 동의를 나타낸다. 「neither(nor) + 동사 + 주어」는 「주어 + be동사(do 동사/조동사, either.」로 바꿀 수 있다.

25 [해석] 내가 아침에 엘리베이터에서 마주친 것은 Gloria였다.
[해설] 강조하고자 하는 말을 It is[was] ~ that 사이에 넣어 쓴다.

26 [해석]
ⓐ 잡지에 나온 것은 그 음식점이다.
ⓑ 그가 우리에게 이 숙제를 준 것은 어제였다.
[해설] that을 대신해서 ⓐ which, ⓑ when으로 바꾸어 쓸 수 있다.

27 [해석]
ⓐ 여기 그가 온다.
ⓑ 내가 그들을 마지막으로 만난 것은 설날이었다.
ⓒ 우리 가족은 거의 외식하지 않았다.
ⓓ 학교 옆에는 도서관이 있다.
ⓔ 거리의 모퉁이에 아이들 몇 명이 있었다.
[해설]
ⓒ ate our family → did our family eat: 부정어가 문장 앞에 나오면, 일반동사는 'do/does + 주어 + 동사원형'의 어순이 된다.

ⓔ was → were 장소 부사구 도치가 일어날 때 동사는 뒤에 있는 주어에 일치시킨다.

28 [해설] 부정어가 문장 앞에 나가면(도치), 일반동사는 'do 동사 + 주어 + 동사'의 순으로 써야 한다. 과거 시제이므로 'did I realize'가 와야 한다.

29 [해설]

ⓐ 장소나 방향을 나타내는 부사구를 강조하기 위해 문장의 앞에 두면, '부사(구) + (조)동사 + 주어'의 어순으로 쓴다.

ⓑ 부정어 도치에서 일반동사가 쓰인 문장은 'do(does/did) + 주어 + 동사원형'의 형태로 쓴다.

ⓒ 장소 부사구 도치에서 주어가 대명사인 경우에는 주어와 동사를 도치시키지 않는다.

30 [해석] 지난 토요일 나는 집 근처 공원에서 Julie를 우연히 만났다. 우리가 마지막으로 만난 것은 한달 전이었다. 그녀는 그녀의 언니를 만나러 파리에 갔다고 이야기 했다. 그녀는 여행이 얼마나 흥미진진했는지 한껏 이야기했다. 나는 그녀가 그렇게 수다스러운 것을 거의 본 적이 없다. 벤치에서 우리는 두 시간 동안 잡담을 나눴다. 그녀는 나와 이야기하는 것이 재미있다고 했고, 나 또한 그랬다.

[해설] 강조를 위해 do/did를 쓰는 경우, 뒤에는 동사원형이 와야 한다.

실력 탄탄! 서술형 심화

1 (1) did tell
(2) O
(3) Never have I seen
(4) and neither did Jenny

2 (1) It was Mike that was studying in the library.
(2) I did see him there.

3 (1) It is French that (2) It is ten students that

1 [해석]

(1) 그는 나를 좋아한다고 정말로 말했다.

(2) 내가 과학 보고서를 마친 것은 어제였다.

(3) 나는 그토록 아름다운 여자를 결코 본 적이 없다.

(4) 나는 그 영화를 전혀 좋아하지 않았고, Jenny 역시 그랬다.

[해설]

(1) 강조의 do/does/did 뒤에는 동사원형이 와야 한다.

(2) It is ~ that 강조구문에서 "때"를 강조할 때는 that 대신 when을 쓸 수 있다.

(3) 부정어 도치에서 조동사가 쓰인 문장은 부정어 + 조동사 + 주어 순으로 도치가 된다.

(4) 부정적 내용을 동의할 때는 Neither + 동사 + 주어를 쓴다.

2 [해석]

A: 나 어제 도서관 갔는데 Mike가 공부하고 있는 것을 봤어.

B: 누가 도서관에서 공부하고 있었다고?

A: (1) ____________________.

B: 정말? 난 그는 공부하러 도서관엔 절대 안 갈거라고 생각했어.

A: 누가 아니래? 누가 Mike를 거기서 볼 것을 기대했겠니? 난 처음에는 내가 본 것을 믿을 수 없었는데, (2) ____________________.

[해설]

(1) 목적어를 강조할 때 It is/was와 that 사이에 목적어를 넣는다.

(2) 동사를 강조할 때 do/does/did + 동사원형을 쓸 수 있다.

3 [해설] 'It is/was ~ that' 사이에 강조하고 싶은 부분을 넣어 강조의 의미를 전달할 수 있다. 현재 시제이므로 'It is'를 쓰고 도표에 확인하는 바대로 (1)은 French, (2)는 ten students를 It is ~ that 사이에 넣는다.

비법 담은 중학 영문법

Workbook 정답

3
Level

CHAPTER 01

시제

p. 02

Point 1 현재 *vs.* 과거

A 1. is 2. lived 3. is 4. calls 5. wrote 6. turns 7. goes

B 1. drop 2. rides 3. O 4. came 5. has 6. O 7. becomes

C 1. slept 2. falls 3. migrate 4.was 5. gets 6. is

Point 2~4 현재완료

A 1. has come 2. has lost 3. has been to 4. has borrowed 5. has gone to

B 1. signed 2. has, become 3. have read 4. has, swum 5. Have, heard

C 1. Have, designed 2. has climbed 3. haven't forgotten 4. have loved, tried

Point 5~6 현재완료, 과거, 과거완료

A 1. had paid 2. got 3. has been 4. hasn't 5. had 6. had eaten 7. went

B 1. Have you ever found 2. bought 3. has been 4. had worked 5. has played 6. O 7. has read

C 1. has learned 2. hasn't decided 3. have been 4. had never met 5. has read

Point 7~8 현재진행, 과거진행, 미래진행, 완료진행

A 1. has been 2. is 3. was 4. will be 5. had 6. have you been 7. am studying

B 1. O 2. was playing 3. O 4. think 5. O 6. will be studying 7. O

C 1. were having 2. had been studying 3. has been working 4. am listening 5. has been trying

CHAPTER 02

조동사

p. 06

Point 1~3 can, may, will

A 1. can't 2. Could 3. couldn't 4. can 5. be able to

B 1. ⓑ 2. ⓒ 3. ⓔ 4. ⓓ 5. ⓐ

C 1. We will go to Europe 2. He will be able to speak Chinese well 3. Could you help me solve

Point 4~5 must, have to, should, ought to

A 1. had to 2. will have to 3. must 4. should 5. ought to

B 1. ⓔ 2. ⓕ 3. ⓔ 4. ⓔ 5. ⓓ

C 1. (o)ught to 2. (m)ust 3. (n)eed not 4. (s)hould not

Point 6~7 had better, would rather, used to, would

A 1. tell 2. sleep
3. had better not 4. would rather not
5. live

B 1. make 2. used
3. to spending 4. meet

C 1. I used to[would] write in my diary.
2. There used to be a restaurant in the building.
3. My father used to smoke.

Point 8 조동사 + have + p.p.

A 1. should 2. must
3. may 4. cannot

B 1. must have broken 2. should have followed
3. may have taken 4. cannot have won

C 1. We must have met before.
2. She may already have left Seoul.
(또는 She may have left Seoul already.
또는 She may have already left Seoul.)
3. We should have helped him.
4. She cannot have forgotten her promise.

CHAPTER 03
to부정사

p. 10

Point 1~4 to부정사의 명사적 용법, 형용사적 용법

A 1. to be 2. to have
3. to wear 4. how to answer
5. it 6. are to listen to

B 1. to go 2. to write on
3. something warm 4. to eat
5. when to have

C 1. find the way to 2. a lot of books to read
3. a pen to write with 4. to play soccer
5. where to go

Point 5~6 to부정사의 부사적 용법

A 1. ⓑ 2. ⓓ 3. ⓐ 4. ⓒ 5. ⓐ

B 1. so as to build her knowledge
2. in order to see a doctor
3. in order to get my prescription
4. so as to save some money
5. in order not to forget it

C 1. lived to be 1000 years old
2. to borrow some books
3. in order not to get up late
4. grew up to be the president

Point 7~9 to부정사의 의미상의 주어, 부정, 시제, to부정사를 목적어, 목적격 보어로 쓰는 동사

A 1. of 2. for 3. to join
4. to make 5. for

B 1. seems to be
2. seems that she lost
3. seems that he is disappointed
4. seems that you missed the train
5. seems to have been taken

C 1. wish not to work
2. hopes to get good scores
3. would like to go
4. necessary for you to
5. advised the students to read

Point 10~12 원형부정사를 목적격 보어로 쓰는 동사, 자주 쓰이는 to부정사 구문

A 1. to be 2. take 3. push
4. getting 5. go

B 1. so tired that I couldn't
2. so small that she can't
3. so small that I can
4. so young that they can't
5. so tall that he can

C 1. heard my sister play
2. let me use
3. watched his mom make
4. made the patient take medicine
5. rich enough to buy

CHAPTER 04
동명사

p. 14

Point 1~2 동명사의 역할 – 주어, 보어, 목적어

A 1. ⓓ 2. ⓐ 3. ⓒ 4. ⓓ
5. ⓑ 6. ⓐ 7. ⓒ

B 1. going 2. entering 3. Eating
4. collecting 5. losing 6. to visit
7. is

C 1. stopped crying
2. keep studying hard
3. mind opening the door
4. tried to avoid meeting
5. Playing fast music makes
6. Eating food with high calories

Point 3~4 동명사의 의미상 주어, 동명사의 부정, 시제와 태

A 1. your[you] 2. her 3. his[him]
4. my[me] 5. Mike[Mike's]

B 1. winning
2. not having done
3. my[me] not finishing
4. my[me] being disappointed
5. his not coming

C 1. swimming 2. using
3. not going 4. O

D 1. having been laughed
2. having been given
3. her not having attended

Point 5~7 동명사 *vs.* to부정사 *vs.* 현재분사

A 1. climbing 2. looking 3. to eat
4. to be 5. doing 6. playing
7. to stop

B 1. ⓑ 2. ⓑ 3. ⓐ
4. ⓑ 5. ⓐ 6. ⓑ

C 1. kept practicing 2. remembered to buy
3. thinking of keeping 4. trying to tie
5. regrets not having studied

Point 8 자주 쓰이는 동명사 표현

A 1. seeing 2. trying 3. hiking
4. buying 5. finding 6. having
7. doing

B 1. taking 2. O 3. stopping
4. waiting 5. preparing 6. O
7. reading

C 1. go fishing
2. looking forward to playing
3. spend time playing
4. used to getting
5. about watching
6. stop[keep] him from climbing

CHAPTER 05
분사

p. 18

Point 1~3 분사의 종류 및 의미와 역할, 감정을 나타내는 분사

A 1. boiling 2. produced 3. shouting
4. sleeping 5. written

B 1. amazing 2. interested 3. O
4. exciting 5. O

C 1. covered 2. moved 3. filled
4. written 5. standing

Point 4~5 분사구문을 만드는 법, 분사구문의 의미

A 1. While I waited for my friend
2. Because we live far from their home
3. If I exercise every day

B 1. Getting up late
2. Taking a walk in the park
3. Seeing the big bear
4. Joining our club

C 1. After he told me his plan, he went to school.
2. As I felt tired, I went to bed early.
3. When we heard the news, we were all surprised.
4. Because he wanted to sleep, he turned off the lights.

Point 6~7 분사구문의 시제와 태, 분사구문의 부정, 독립분사구문

A 1. Having spent 2. Having been
3. Not having 4. There
5. being

B 1. raining
2. Having been injured (또는 Injured)
3. Having been painted (또는 Painted)
4. Not having slept

C 1. (Being) Given some money by her mom
2. Having finished his breakfast
3. There being a lot of work to do
4. Being the first customer of the day

Point 8 「with + 명사 + 분사」 구문, 비인칭 독립분사구문

A 1. closed 2. watching
3. turned 4. folded

B 1. with his hand waving
2. with her legs crossed
3. with his back leaning against the wall

C 1. Generally speaking 2. Compared with
3. Speaking of 4. Judging from

CHAPTER 06
수동태

p. 22

Point 1~3 수동태의 의미와 형태, 조동사 수동태, 구동사 수동태

A 1. designed 2. was suggested
3. were planning 4. be published
5. disappeared

B 1. can be eaten 2. will be performed
3. was delayed

C 1. must not be forgotten
2. can't be copied
3. was brought up
4. are taken care of

Point 4~5 진행형, 완료형 수동태

A 1. selling 2. being cleaned
3. being repaired 4. being prepared

B 1. is, being aired 2. is being destroyed

C 1. have been helped 2. has been postponed
3. have been made

D 1. Many new ideas have been created by them.
2. The robots for Mars exploration have been developed by the team.
3. His unusual accent was being laughed at by the boys.

Point 6~8 4형식 문장, 5형식 문장의 수동태

A 1. thought to be nice 2. told to stay home
3. advised to jog 4. made to vacuum

B 1. given to us 2. bought for me
3. asked of me 4. made to learn

C 1. was shown something in the box by him
2. were[are] allowed to sleep at Jenny's house by our parents
3. were seen to plant trees in the garden by us.
4. will be cooked for me by my grandmother
5. was bought for me by my brother

Point 9~10 목적어로 쓰인 that절의 수동태, by 이외의 전치사를 쓰는 수동태

A 1. of 2. to 3. with
4. about 5. in

B 1. am satisfied with 2. is crowded with
3. is said to cause

C 1. is believed that Mr. Kim is diligent / is believed to be diligent
2. is said that eating breakfast is good for brain activity / is said to be good for brain activity
3. is said that the Internet has made our lives better than before / is said to have made our lives better than before

CHAPTER 07

대명사

p. 26

Point 1~2 재귀대명사, it의 여러 가지 쓰임

A 1. 강조 용법 2. 강조 용법 3. 재귀 용법

B 1. ⓐ 2. ⓓ 3. ⓑ 4. ⓒ

C 1. by himself 2. for themselves
3. myself

D 1. It is necessary to take the class
2. She found it interesting to read novels
3. It seems that Hannah is the smartest student

Point 3~4 부정대명사, 짝을 이루어 쓰는 표현

A 1. others 2. another 3. one

B 1. One, the other 2. Some, others
3. One, another, the other 4. One, the others
5. One, the other 6. Some, the others

C 1. other → the other 2. others → the others
3. other → others

Point 5 something *vs.* anything

A 1. anything 2. anyone 3. someone
4. anything 5. something 6. Someone

B 1. Somebody 2. anything
3. something 4. anyone

C 1. something 2. anything
3. anything 4. Someone

Point 6 전체부정 *vs.* 부분부정

A 1. Nobody[No one] 2. nothing
3. Not every

B 1. anything 2. doesn't, anything
3. anyone 4. anyone

C 1. Not all
2. Not both of my parents
3. not always

CHAPTER 08

비교

p. 30

Point 1 원급 기본 표현

A 1. big 2. high 3. as
4. so 5. not so far as

B 1. not as kind as 2. fluently as
3. well

C 1. as nice as 2. as comfortable as
3. not as delicious as 4. as often as
5. as fluently as

Point 2~3 비교급, 최상급 기본 표현

A 1. more 2. even harder
3. more comfortable 4. the oldest
5. the most popular

B 1. a lot[far, much, even, still]
2. than 3. I've ever seen
4. more 5. louder and louder

C 1. colder than 2. the hottest
3. one of the best CEOs
4. the most delicious cake
5. the hardest assignment

Point 4~5 여러 가지 비교 구문 I~II

A 1. more and more tired
2. as many toy cars as possible / as many toy cars as he could
3. better and better
4. as much as he could
5. The higher, the dizzier

B 1. As, fatter, weaker 2. as often as I can
3. five times as cheap as
4. as hard as

C 1. getting worse and worse
2. twice as loud as
3. The more I talk with her

Point 6 여러 가지 비교 구문 III

A 1. → No (other), interesting as
→ No (other), more, than
→ English, any other
→ all the other subjects
2. → as smart as
→ smarter than
→ any other
→ smarter than

B 1. cuter than
2. smaller than all the other planets
3. No student, taller than Robin
4. higher than any other
5. as much as
6. so delicious as an apple
7. cheaper than all the other

CHAPTER 09
접속사

p. 34

Point 1 부사절을 이끄는 접속사 – 시간, 이유

A 1. before 2. As 3. Since
4. while 5. When

B 1. 안개 때문에 나는 아무것도 볼 수 없다.
2. 나는 길을 건너면서 우연히 옛 친구를 만났다.
3. 너는 밥을 먹은 후 3분 이내에 양치질을 해야 한다.
4. Vicky는 내가 방 청소를 하고 있는 동안 음악을 들었다.

C 1. since I met my best friend
2. until it gets dark
3. because he had to take care of
4. When someone rang the doorbell

Point 2~3 부사절을 이끄는 접속사 – 조건, 양보, 대조, 결과, 목적

A 1. If 2. while 3. Unless
4. though 5. while

B 1. not too heavy 2. busy to have meals
3. in order 4. too dark
5. in order[so as]

C 1. so hot that I can't eat it
2. though the test was easy
3. Although she saw the traffic signs

Point 4~5 명사절을 이끄는 접속사, 간접의문문

A 1. That 2. whether 3. that
4. that 5. that

B 1. I wonder if[whether] I can go there.
2. Do you know what your dream is?
3. Tell me why you didn't follow the rules.
4. I'm not sure if[whether] you want to go with me.
5. Who do you think will be your new homeroom teacher?

C 1. if you are satisfied with
2. that she skips breakfast
3. Who do you think

Point 6~8 상관접속사, 「명령문, and/or …」 구문, 접속부사

A 1. Both 2. or 3. but
4. Either 5. However

B 1. If you buy a toy robot
2. If you don't drive slowly
3. If you make a daily schedule

C 1. and blessings will come your way
2. Both my mom and I
3. not only relaxed but also better
4. for example Chinese, Japanese, and English
5. not only playing the piano but also building furniture

CHAPTER 10
관계사

p. 38

Point 1~3 관계대명사

A 1. which 2. what 3. What
4. that 5. who

B 1. what 2. which
3. whose 4. is

C 1. that moves 2. who stand
3. which[that] helps 4. What you say
5. which[that] are on the wall

Point 4~6 관계대명사의 생략, 계속적 용법, 「전치사 + 관계대명사」

A 1. that 2. who is 3. which is
4. when 또는 the day 5. X

B 1. who[whom, that], to whom
2. who

C 1. for which 2. encourages
3. O 4. O
5. which[that]

D 1. you don't want to
2. UNICEF which helps poor children
3. of whom I should take
4. hanging on the wall was

Point 7~8 관계부사

A 1. where 2. when
3. why 4. when

B 1. the way를 삭제해야 함. 2. O
3. where 4. when[that]

C 1. for which, why 2. that, how

D 1. the way he could become
2. when the library closes
3. the reason why he got surprised

Point 9~10 복합관계사

A 1. whatever 2. Wherever 3. However
4. Whenever 5. whichever

B 1. Whoever 2. Whatever
3. Whatever 4. whichever

C 1. whenever you have questions
2. wherever you go
3. Whatever he touched
4. However strong he was
5. Whoever is interested in

CHAPTER 11
가정법

p. 42

Point 1 가정법 과거

A 1. lived 2. liked 3. tried
4. were 5. visited 6. had

B 1. were, could reach 2. called, would take
3. knew, could come

C 1. If I were a fish, I could swim very well.
2. If you had come on time, you could have taken the test.
3. If he had an ID card, he could enter there.

Point 2 가정법 과거완료

A 1. enjoyed 2. have called
3. could 4. would
5. were 6. were
7. had

B 1. had had, would have bought
2. had worked, would have woken up
3. had had, could have found
4. had been, would have felt

C 1. would not have been late
2. wouldn't have lost

Point 3~4 I wish 가정법, as if 가정법

A 1. were 2. could
3. were 4. had stayed
5. were 6. hadn't eaten
7. had finished 8. had been

B 1. were close to 2. were
3. were 4. had ridden

C 1. I wish we could live in
2. as if he had been homeless
3. as if he were an adult

Point 5~6 주의해야 할 가정법

A 1. were 2. Were it not for
3. for 4. could
5. Without 6. have gotten

B 1. it had not been for this English dictionary
2. it had not been for Social Network Service

C 1. Were I overweight
2. Had she enough time

D 1. Without teamwork, the team could not have won the game.
2. If it snows a lot, I will have a snowball fight with my friends.

CHAPTER 12
일치와 화법

p. 46

Point 1 수의 일치

A 1. are 2. wears 3. Is
4. were 5. is 6. helps
7. is

B 1. O 2. are 3. is
4. is 5. O

C 1. are 2. has 3. Does
4. has been 5. are 6. is

Point 2~3 시제의 일치, 시제 일치의 예외

A 1. was 2. had lost 3. is
4. invented 5. goes

B 1. that practice makes perfect
2. what the man had done the previous day
3. that you go for a walk with your dog every Saturday morning
4. that we can learn about Indian life and culture through Indian movies

C 1. was gone 2. would enter
3. reached 4. I usually do on weekends
5. water freezes at 0°C

Point 4 평서문의 화법 전환

A 1. told 2. that day 3. would
4. had taken 5. would

B 1.she needed to buy some flowers for her living room then
2. he was going fishing that night
3. she had seen Mary a few minutes before

C 1. Your sister will get well soon
2. I have a lot of things to do today
3. I can help you with your homework now

D 1. was taking 2. I would pass
3. had helped

Point 5~6 의문문과 명령문의 화법 전환

A 1. to come 2. if
3. he was 4. not to be
5. she was looking 6. I wanted

B 1. if I had finished my homework
2. how old she was
3. if I had been to Canada
4. not to talk during the test
5. to call him back later

C 1. Will you go to a movie with me
2. Repeat after me
3. When did the bus leave

CHAPTER 13
특수구문

p. 50

Point 1~2 강조 구문

A 1. do 2. did
3. does 4. do

B 1. I do feel happy about the result.
2. It does take a lot of time to write an essay.

C 1. It was the man that started wearing jewelry.
2. It was in the park that they practiced soccer.
3. It was one of my earrings that I lost yesterday.
4. It is every year that more than 500 people take part in the event.

D 1. that the teacher didn't come to school
2. that I like most
3. It was three years ago that

Point 3 장소 부사(구)의 도치

A 1. Down came the rain when they were walking.
2. There stood the boy waiting for the girl.
3. Here he comes with his friend.
4. Up went the rocket heading for the moon.

B 1. came the sun
2. are many clouds
3. is my grandfather's house

C 1. On the hill stands the building.
2. Over my head they passed.
3. Around them are many boxes.
4. Inside the box was a ring.

Point 3 부정어의 도치

A 1. did I believe 2. was it
3. had the baby seen me 4. did I dream
5. is Jane

B 1. Seldom is she passionate about her work.
2. Nowhere could they find the file.
3. Not only was he tall but also he was handsome.
4. Never have I seen a picture as beautiful as this.

C 1. Little did she think that he would come.
2. Nowhere else could I meet such a nice guy.
3. Not until last night did I hear the news.
4. Rarely does she watch TV.
5. Not until I met you in person did I think much of you.

Point 4 동의할 때 「So/Nor/Neither + 동사 + 주어」 구문

A 1. So will I 2. So do I
3. Neither did I 4. Neither do I

B 1. neither did Tom 2. so does my sister
3. so am I 4. so will we

C 1. Neither do I. 2. So will I.
3. Neither can I. 4. Neither have I.

MEMO

MEMO

MEMO

MEMO